Back to
THE
TRUTH

5000 Years of ADVAITA

Winchester, UK
Washington, USA)

First published by O Books, 2007
O Books is an imprint of John Hunt Publishing Ltd.,
The Bothy, Deershot Lodge, Park Lane, Ropley, Hants, SO24 0BE, UK
office1@o-books.net
www.o-books.net

Distribution in:

UK and Europe
Orca Book Services
orders@orcabookservices.co.uk
Tel: 01202 665432 Fax: 01202 666219 Int. code (44)

USA and Canada
NBN
custserv@nbnbooks.com
Tel: 1 800 462 6420 Fax: 1 800 338 4550

Australia and New Zealand
Brumby Books
sales@brumbybooks.com.au
Tel: 61 3 9761 5535 Fax: 61 3 9761 7095

Far East (offices in Singapore, Thailand, Hong Kong, Taiwan)
Pansing Distribution Pte Ltd
kemal@pansing.com
Tel: 65 6319 9939 Fax: 65 6462 5761

South Africa
Alternative Books
altbook@peterhyde.co.za
Tel: 021 447 5300 Fax: 021 447 1430

Text copyright Dennis Waite 2007

Design: Stuart Davies

ISBN-13: 978 1 905047 61 1
ISBN-10: 1 905047 61 4

A CIP catalogue record for this book is available from the British Library.

Printed in the US by Maple Vail

Back to
THE
TRUTH

5000 Years of ADVAITA

DENNIS WAITE

BOOKS

Winchester, UK
Washington, USA

A wonderful book. Encyclopedic in nature, and destined to become a classic. James Braha, author

It will surely prove to be a most helpful guide to the contemporary reader. Alan Jacobs, President of the Ramana Maharshi Foundation UK, and author

This excellent and long awaited book is essential reading for anyone at all interested in the subject. It is a clear and refreshing overview of the whole genre that is Advaita - not just one aspect of it - offering the facts, from the historical past right up until today, when non-dualistic teachings abound but often emphasise different aspects of the historical teachings. Roy Whenary, author

A beautiful, articulate and extensive, yet compact anthology of pointers adverting to Truth. This compilation in itself is all that is needed for true understanding. Justus Kramer Schippers, teacher and author

Well written and meticulously researched. It forms a valuable and much needed basis for an in depth investigation into the ancient Advaita Vedanta teachings. It is a major achievement and should appeal to a wide audience of serious seekers and other students of life. Möller de la Rouvière, author

This is definitely one of the most complete and exhaustive books on advaita ever, and yet remains eminently readable. It is the first book that I have seen that not only deals with advaita but also expands upon the various different types and styles of teachings including contemporary ones, analyses and compares them and helps the seeker in selecting the one that matches his temperament the most. A rare book, of great practical value to any sincere spiritual seeker, and a "must". Dr. Nitin Trasi, author

The text is lucid, the references relevant and wide ranging, and the overall effect expansive and clarifying. This book is recommended to experienced Advaitins, as well as to those whose initial interest has led to a desire for a

*comprehensive review of the principles underlying this remarkable philoso-
phy.* John Lehmann, Principal, School of Advaita, Philosophy Foundation,
Waltham, Massachusetts, USA

*Dennis has poured his love of Truth and humanity into this precise and lumi-
nous work. Highly recommended.* Isaac Shapiro, teacher and author

*I had that delicious feeling you get once in a while when you're reading a
book where you know you're a party to something truly profound... I have
no doubt that this book will become the standard reference work for the
advaita movement, both past and present.*
Paula Marvelly, author

*Brilliantly succeeds in challenging the validity of the beliefs we use to pro-
tect our non-existent ego from total annihilation.*
Chuck Hillig, author

*A detailed, clear and balanced study of what this ancient wisdom means to
us modern seekers, particularly with respect to the differences between the
traditional school based on the scriptures and the more direct approach
which finds favour with many spiritual seekers today.* The Mountain Path
(Journal of Sri Ramanasramam)

*Excellent for "beginners" and newcomers to Advaita simply because he
covers all the bases with scrupulous honesty. But his writing is also excellent for long time seekers and those who have already "gotten it,"* Philip T.
Mistlberger, teacher and author

*This is the most comprehensive, academic book on the so called "tradition"
of non-duality we have seen.* Brian Lake and Naama Livni, teachers

*A profoundly astute and masterful guide to the field of Self-discovery. An
authoritative scholar, Dennis writes with supreme clarity as he skillfully*

expounds, logically analyzes and insightfully integrates the wisdom of classical and contemporary teachers with the principles of Advaita. Katie Davis, teacher and author

Dennis Waite is the West's pre-eminent explicator of Advaita Vedanta. He brings to light many of Advaita's "hidden" teachings, which have never been circulated outside of specialist schools. Fascinating! Dr. Gregory Goode, PhD (Philosophy), Philosophical Counselor and non-dual teacher.

Rigorous and exhaustive; a grand tour of the advaita world, both ancient and neo. Robin Dale, author

Dennis Waite has rendered the complex concepts of Advaita in terms that can be easily absorbed and appreciated by the western mind. The presentation is logical and educational, simple yet profound.
Dr. Kuntimaddi Sadananda, disciple of Swami Chinmayananda and a principal teacher at the Washington Chinmaya Mission.

A book that will be invaluable to the many students of Advaita, and more importantly, to many of the teachers as well. Aja Thomas, director of the Atma Institute in Oregon, teacher of Advaita and Sanskrit, author

This book is essential reading for all who are walking the path where every step is destination. Karl Renz, teacher and author

Scholarly, accurate and precise, Dennis' books are a tremendous contribution to the field of Advaita,. David Carse, author

Dennis Waite explains Advaita with delight and rigor. Jerry Katz, author and owner of Non-Duality Salon (http://nonduality.com/)

A wonderful book – which truly provides everything that one wants to know about the philosophy of non-duality. Ram Chandran, owner of the Advaitin Egroup

CONTENTS

FOREWORD

Is it really possible to formulate into words something which is ultimately indefinable, indescribable and utterly beyond all human comprehension? It is an interesting dilemma. And yet, the teaching of Advaita ("not two") is essentially the philosophical framework that attempts to do just that – to make some sort of sense of the mysterious universe in which we live.

Advaita is no New Age set of platitudes, however; it is the timeless and eternal message that has been revealed to us ever since the beginning of recorded history through scripture, poetry and the voices of the great philosophers and mystics. And what is that message? It is the revelation that everything – you, me, the world around us and beyond – is a manifestation of the Self, God, the All and the One.

There has of late, somewhat ironically, been a great deal of confusion regarding the interpretation of Advaita. Indeed, the spectrum of delineations is becoming more and more dissipated, ranging from the purist theories of Traditional Advaita right through to the more radical approach of Neo-Advaita, with a number of other "schools" in between. Traditional Advaita essentially takes its authority from the Upanishads, as well as the great Indian teacher Shankara. It postulates that there is a "path" that we must follow, albeit an apparent one, which helps us come to know the essence of our true selves, to realize the Self within us. Practices are undertaken to aid this discovery, which may include study of the scriptures, meditation, surrender and self enquiry.

Neo-Advaita (of which Tony Parsons is its greatest exponent) says there is no path. You are already that which you seek. You are THAT.

So which is correct? The answer is it depends. Traditional Advaita is right in that it addresses the seeker, still caught up in the illusion of his or her own ego. Nevertheless, it can become bogged down with complicated Hindu theory, enmeshed in an antiquated guru hierarchy. Neo-Advaita is right in that it bypasses all of that by simply addressing the Self. However, no concession is made for the seeker, staggering through phenomenality, still believing that he or she is the doer.

A much more amenable approach, called the Direct Path, has been gaining ground recently. Distilled by the great teachers Ramana Maharshi, Nisargadatta and Atmananda Krishna Menon, it takes the recognition that we are already the Self as its point of departure and yet suggests simple "techniques", such as the use of rigorous logic, to help deconstruct the ignorance that obscures our innate divinity. In modern times, it finds expression through teachers such as Greg Goode and Francis Lucille. For many, the Direct Path has also become the most accessible means to self remembering and forms a midway balance between the Traditional and Neo-Advaita extremes.

Dennis's landmark book investigates all of these different approaches – Traditional and Neo Advaita, the Direct Path, as well as other nuances of interpretation – so that it is possible to dispel much of the current bewilderment and finally get to grips with the true Advaita teaching once and for all. More importantly, however, his extensive work addresses ideas that go far beyond issues pertaining to which school is technically correct or not. Through meticulous research of the world's profoundest spiritual and philosophical texts, as well as personal correspondence with many contemporary Advaita teachers, Dennis has effectively compiled the source of reference in this field.

I have no doubt that "Back to the Truth" will become a classic of its kind. Moreover, it is written by someone who makes no claims for himself by proselytizing or promoting himself as to whether he is "self realized" or not. What Dennis has done is to present, diligently and humbly, a model of the ultimate reality based on ancient and contemporary teachings, tempered by personal observation and authentic experience. After all the confusion and competition between many of the teaching "camps" in recent years, his erudite insight into the non-dual philosophy is a welcome and much needed relief. His exemplary work will most certainly become the authoritative interpretation of modern-day Advaita.

Paula Marvelly, March, 2006

PREFACE

The literal meaning of the word "religion" is "to bind back" (from the Latin re-ligare); i.e. to return to the reality of our true nature. All religions have the same objective and, though most will deny this, the same truth. Reality itself cannot be spoken of, however (that would necessitate that we, doing the speaking, would have to stand outside of reality), and herein lies the ultimate problem and the root of all contention between the different teachings. The ways in which this difficulty is tackled vary. For the majority of Christians, Muslims and Hindus, the provisional and relative truth of a separate God (or Gods) is accepted as final. Taoism makes the valid but unhelpful claim that 'the Tao which can be spoken of is not the true Tao'. Zen Buddhism utilizes the tool of the koan to try to trick the mind into acknowledging the impossibility of thinking about reality and thereby trigger an intuitive understanding but, again, this approach is only suited for a very few.

Philosophy is the secular approach that uses reason and logic to look for meaning in our lives and to explore the nature of reality. It does this without reliance upon faith in something that initially lies outside of reason. Nevertheless, the aim of both religion and philosophy is one, as Swami Nikhilananda has pointed out: *"The goal of philosophy may be Truth, and the goal of religion, God; but in the final experience God and Truth are one and the same Reality."* (Ref. 193)

Advaita is both a philosophy and a religion in the original meaning of the word. It is one of the few teachings that provide what is effectively a graded approach that is suitable for practically everyone, excluding only those who will not listen. There is a path for those who wish to use only the clearest reasoning to approach an understanding of the nature of reality and there is one for those who merely want to surrender all of their day to day worries to a personal God. Whatever the nature or circumstances of the individual, there is a strategy to suit.

This is achieved through the utilization of a number of models or metaphors representing what might be regarded as "levels" of reality. The novice spiritual aspirant is initially taught that the grossest level or approach represents the true situation. As his understanding grows, however, this provisional story is shown to be untrue and a new picture, which is more subtle, is given. Ultimately, each new view of reality has to be rescinded since none could ever be true in any objective sense but the giving up of the grosser standpoint entails the sublation of false ideas and ignorance – and it is this very ignorance that is preventing the intuitive realization of the truth.

This book will describe these various techniques and illustrate, using extracts from the very best of traditional scriptures and the writings of modern teachers, how they are used to take us to the brink of understanding. It can then be but a short intuitive step to realization rather than the impossible leap across a gulf of ignorance that may be left for seekers following other, less clear paths, where dogma or lack of understanding may have obscured the route.

Advaita, being the non-dual reality, necessarily points to the essential truth in all religions. Paula Marvelly points out that: *"All religions and faiths contain an esoteric heart, a mystical belief that I AM is in fact synonymous with God."* (Ref. 353) As Gandhi said: *"If the same divinity constitutes the core of all individuals, they cannot but be equal. Further, divinity in one person cannot in any way be unjust to the same divinity in another person."* (Ref. 215) Sayings from the bible such as those of God to Moses (*"I am that I am"*) or of Christ (*"The kingdom of heaven is within you"*) express the fundamental truth of Advaita, the non-dual reality of Brahman.

Contrary to the claims of a recent television series, the Truth is not out there. For those wishing to discover God, it is not a question of looking forever outwards, making new discoveries about the universe or speculating about the nature of heaven. It is rather a matter of turning back and looking within. As the Kena Upanishad says (II.1.1): *"Now and again a daring soul, desiring immortality, has looked back and found himself."* (Ref. 74) It is an inward search that is needed; a return to the background reality of our very existence back to the Truth.

INTRODUCTION

It is a puzzling thing. The truth knocks on the door and you say, "Go away, I'm looking for the truth"... and so it goes away. Puzzling. **Robert Pirsig**

The subject of this book, as the title implies, is "Truth" – the truth about who we are, the nature of the world and reality – and the ways in which the teachers of the philosophy of Advaita attempt to lead us to that truth. But it should be made clear at the outset that this truth is not ultimately describable. An intellectual appreciation may be gained but that is not It. Indeed some modern teachers are at pains to demolish all attempts to rationalize or explain. Instead they encourage a direct intuitive "seeing" of what is already the case.

The **Kena Upanishad** talks about this and explains that the Self cannot be known by the intellect; that it must be understood to be beyond the duality of knower and known. Only the ignorant think that they "know" Brahman. In fact, it is beyond thought, perception and speech – it is that which *enables* us to think, perceive and speak. It is only by understanding this that it can be "known" in any sense.

Swami Chinmayananda, one of the great traditional teachers of recent times explains it thus:

> The moment we comprehended a thing, it is always through the instruments of our comprehension and understanding. They being limited, they cannot but fail in grasping the whole. Whatever words can express must necessarily be something grasped earlier by our understanding. Thus, as we have already noted, Truth expressed can be but the conditioned or the limited Truth. [†] (Ref. 75)

Accordingly, a more honest title for this book might be "Pointers to Truth."

[†] Kenopanishad, Swami Chinmayananda, © Central Chinmaya Mission Trust, Mumbai.

It aims to highlight the ways in which the various teachers and writings on Advaita have attempted to help us to realize that truth which is ultimately beyond the mind.

In the past, if you had what might be termed "spiritual" problems, as opposed to practical or abstract ones, there were traditional sources that might supply an answer. The most likely was probably your parents and the older members of your family. Problems of this type are never new and past solutions would probably be as acceptable to you as they had been to them. Systems of belief tend to continue down through the ages, changing little until some radical new discovery forces a paradigm shift.

If your nature meant that you were unable to accept the authority of your family, you might have turned to a teacher or a senior member of the community, someone with more knowledge and/or experience. The ultimate recourse, however, if no satisfaction was found there, would have been the local representative of the church, mosque, temple or equivalent.

It was assumed that religious teachers knew all about these things. The church made this knowledge available to its followers. The knowledge itself originated with God, having been divinely communicated at some distant time in the past. This is then passed on by authorized guardians of the faith, updated as necessary via revelation. All of this was taken more or less for granted by most people. They were "believers" because there was no alternative source for this sort of guidance and therefore few dissenters to challenge the foundations of that belief. Though people might sometimes suffer without obvious reason, most simply accepted that this was how things were.

The successive advances of science eroded this tendency. The church might state categorically that the earth was at the centre of the universe and the sun and moon rotate around it. But once telescopes and mathematics had demonstrated that this simply could not be true, then something had to give. The claimed literal truths had, at best, to be transposed into metaphor, at worst discarded completely. Today, the number of people who fully accept a religious doctrine and turn to it in times of stress and uncertainty, is much reduced from earlier centuries.

As the knowledge discovered by science grew, the confidence in the guidance of the church waned. The so-called truths passed on for generations were found to be nothing more than myth and superstition. Man expanded his vision with the aid of artificial devices, enabling him to see out into the vastness of space and inward to atoms and beyond. Nowhere did he find gods or heavens. But, while science proved to be marvelous at investigating objects – indeed its methods became synonymous with "being objective" – it was found to be useless regarding our subjective lives. It has been entirely unable to tell us who we are, why we are here or what we ought to do. Though there are many books written on the subject of consciousness for example, which is fundamental to our perception of ourselves, there is little in the way of consensus about what it actually is. Most scientists believe that consciousness is somehow generated or imagined when a certain level of complexity of life is attained.

Modern western society inculcates the idea of the supremacy of the individual in an ethos that is materially, rather than spiritually motivated. When the important problems of life arise – What is the purpose of (my) life? How can I be happy? Who am I? – we are expected to look for the answer ourselves. We are unique and only *I* can say what is important for me. Unfortunately, this is so far away from the truth that it is hardly surprising that the approach fails completely. Hence it is that there is increasing dissatisfaction with life, increasing moral turpitude, lack of concern for others and so on.

What is needed is some spiritual authority that does not contradict either science or our own experience and which does not require faith, in so far as that is understood in connection with traditional religions. These sources do exist and some discover them. Zen Buddhism, for example, has been popular in the west for the past few decades. Taoism and Sufism are two others, with which readers may be familiar. One which is less well known, but is even more logical and scientific in its approach, is Advaita.

Access to the Vedas is the greatest privilege this century may claim over all previous centuries... In the whole world there is no study so beneficial and so elevating as that of the Upanishads. It has been the solace of my life and it will be the solace of my death.

Schopenhauer (quoted in Ref. 140)

Advaita Vedanta is a philosophy that was systematized in India around the eighth century AD by someone named Adi Shankara. In fact, the essence of the teaching had been around for very much longer than this, being based upon the material contained in the Upanishads. The Upanishads are a part of the sacred Indian texts called the Vedas, written around 1500BC, though they are said to have existed in spoken form long before this. (Some evidence suggests this may have been prior to 6,000 BC, with the written Sanskrit alphabet – Devanagari - in use in 3000 BC in western India.) The Vedas consist primarily of hymns and rituals relating to the various Gods of what came to be the Hindu religion. The Upanishads are mostly found in the final sections of the Vedas, which are also called Vedanta (i.e. end or culmination – Sanskrit *anta* - of the *veda*-s). They summarize the philosophy underlying these practices and it is from them that Advaita derives.

It is a non-dual philosophy, which means that in reality there are not two. This is the literal meaning of the word "Advaita" – *a* meaning "not," and *dvaita* "two." This is an alien and apparently meaningless concept to most people at first hearing and I will not attempt to elaborate further at this point. Suffice to say that, if you have not met it before, you will hopefully be persuaded that it is literally true by the end of this book.

A very brief description of Hindu philosophies

[Note that Sanskrit terms will be used throughout this book where relevant. The actual Devanagari script will not be used, however, except in the Glossary, since few readers are likely to be familiar with it. Instead, they will be shown in ITRANS format, which is explained in Appendix A, along with a presentation of the alphabet and a guide to pronunciation. The glossary provides a definition of all of the Sanskrit words used in the book. Sanskrit words will always be shown in *italics*. The names of Indian teachers and characters from the scriptures will usually be given in their English or "Romanized" version, since this is the form that is most often encountered. Thus Shankara will usually be written as shown rather than the correct form – *shaMkara* - and Gaudapada rather than *gauDapAda*. In the case of the titles of scriptural texts, both forms will be encountered. E.g. the Vivekachudamani is usually written as that, though it is actually *vivekachUDAmaNi* in ITRANS format. The names of Upanishads, however, will usually be shown in their correct ITRANS format, e.g. the Brihadaranyaka Upanishad will usually be written *bRRihadAraNyaka upaniShad.*]

This section is included so that the terms will be understandable when encountered later in the book. But it is also of interest to know where Advaita fits into the complex of systems that comprise Hinduism. There are six philosophies, which can be separated into three groups as shown below, representing the three divisions of orthodox Hindu philosophy.

1. *nyAya*
2. *vaisheShika*

3. *sAMkhya*
4. *yoga*

5. *pUrva mImAMsA*
6. *uttara mImAMsA*

nyAya literally means "that into which a thing goes back," a "standard" or "rule." Its traditional originator was Gautama in the 3rd Century BC. It was so called because the system "goes into" all physical and metaphysical subjects in a very logical manner.

vaisheShika was a later development of *nyAya* by the theologian, Kanada and was named after the nine "essentially different substances" believed to constitute matter.

sAMkhya was founded by Kapila. The word literally means "relating to number" and refers to the "reckoning up or enumerating" of the 25 *tattva-s* or "true principles." It is a dualistic system concerned with the liberation of the spirit (*puruSha*) from the bonds of creation (*prakRRiti*).

yoga refers to the system of Patanjali, which aims to unite the individual spirit with *Ishvara*, the manifest form of the Absolute. It is closely related to *sAMkhya* and its practices bear some relation to Buddhism.

mImAMsA literally means "profound thought, reflection or consideration" and "examination of the Vedic text."

pUrva mImAMsA is principally concerned with the earlier parts of the Vedas, i.e. those sections which talk about the rituals and behaviour - the *karma kANDa* (*kANDa* just means "part or section of a book"). It is associated with the philosopher Jaimini, supposedly a pupil of *vyAsa* (regarded as the original compiler of the Vedas). *pUrva* means "prior, preceding, first."

uttara mImAMsA is concerned chiefly with the latter parts of the Vedas, the more philosophical *j~nAna kANDa*, i.e. the Upanishads, and is commonly known as Vedanta. Its founder was *bAdarAyaNa*, who authored the *brahmasUtra*-s. There are three main schools:

* *dvaita*, the dualistic philosophy associated with the philosopher *madhva*;
* *advaita*, non-dualism associated with *shaMkara*;
* *vishiShTAdvaita*, qualified non-dualism, associated with *rAmAnuja*.

(*uttara* means "later, following, subsequent" and also "superior, chief, excellent.")

Sources of the Teaching

The sources of this teaching, then, began with the Upanishads. Over the centuries which followed the writing down of those scriptures, other important works, which interpreted or attempted to summarize them, followed. Amongst these, perhaps the most famous is the Bhagavad Gita, the "Song of the Lord." This is a book whose importance to the Hindu religion is on a par with that of the Bible for Christians. It forms the central part of a much larger, epic poem called the Mahabharata. At the level of the story, it speaks about the crisis of confidence, facing the prince Arjuna, as he faces his old teachers and members of his family at the start of a great battle in which most of them will be killed. His charioteer is the lord Krishna and the Bhagavad Gita tells of the conversation in which Krishna persuades Arjuna that it is his duty and destiny to fight. It is, of course, very much more than this, effectively using the essence of the Upanishadic philosophy to provide guidance to the ordinary person as to how to live his or her life.

Aldous Huxley refers to the "Perennial Philosophy" and summarizes his understanding in his introduction to the Bhagavad Gita:

At the core of the Perennial Philosophy we find four fundamental doctrines.

First: the phenomenal world of matter and of individualized conscious-ness - the world of things and animals and men and even gods - is the manifestation of a Divine Ground within which all partial realities have their being, and apart from which they would be non-existent.

Second: human beings are capable not merely of knowing *about* the Divine Ground by inference; they can also realize its existence by a direct intuition, superior to discursive reasoning. This immediate knowledge unites the knower with that which is known.

Third: man possesses a double nature, a phenomenal ego and an eternal Self, which is the inner man, the spirit, the spark of divinity within the soul. It is possible for a man, if he so desires, to identify himself with the spirit and therefore with the Divine Ground, which is of the same or like nature with the spirit.

Fourth: man's life on earth has only one end and purpose: to identify himself with his eternal Self and so to come to unitive knowledge of the Divine Ground. (Ref. 273)

The principal book that attempts to explicate the actual philosophy of the Upanishads is called the Brahmasutra. Commentaries have been made by various scholars and their interpretations have not always coincided. In addition to Advaita, two other main branches resulted, one of them dualistic (*dvaita*, associated with the philosopher Madhva) and the other "qualified" non-dualism (*vishiShTAdvaita*, associated with the philosopher Ramanuja) but Shankara, in his own commentary (*bhAShya*), brilliantly challenges and demolishes all interpretations other than that of Advaita.

Further to these three sources, there have been other classics that have become frequent reference works for students of Advaita. Examples are the Astavakra Gita, the Panchadasi and the Yoga Vasishta. A number of others are very well known, many of them being attributed to Shankara, though the authorship is sometimes disputed. Examples are the Vivekachudamani, Atma Bodha, Tattwa Bodha and Upadesha Sahasri. That the authorship is uncertain is understandable since loss of ego accompanies the gaining of understanding at this level and there would be no interest on the part of such a person in attaching their name to what was believed to be a pointer to absolute truth.

In the past hundred years, there has been a resurgence of interest in Advaita in the west. (Note that there is a timeline illustrating the key events/people/writings in Appendix B, along with lineage charts for the principal teachers in Appendix C.) This has been associated with a number of specific Sages (a Sage is someone who has had direct realization of the truth regarding the nature of reality). Ramakrishna (1836 – 1886) is possibly the teacher most responsible for increasing the popularity of Advaita in recent times, with missions now operating throughout the world. His principal disciple was Swami Vivekananda (1863 – 1902), who toured the world with the aim of uniting all religions, the underlying truth of all of them being realized in Advaita. Amongst seekers in the west, however, Ramana Maharshi (1880 – 1950) is perhaps the most famous of all latter-day sages, having influenced so many modern teachers, as well as writers such as Paul Brunton and Somerset Maugham. Nisargadatta Maharaj (~1897 – 1981), the uneducated servant and tobacconist in Bombay, is currently one of the most popular, owing perhaps to the fact that his radical and uncompromising approach appeals to the modern mind. And Atmananda Krishna Menon (1883 - 1959), not so well known as yet, was one of the most logical. (He was well educated and held a high position in the police force.)

Today, it is principally the disciples of these sages who tour the world giving satsangs and seminars. A satsang is a gathering of teacher and students in which the teacher usually gives a short   presentation, which is then followed by questions and answers. The word comes from the Sanskrit *satsa~Nga*, meaning "association with the good" (*sat* is "real, true, good" and *sa~Nga* means "association or intercourse with"). Traditionally, the knowledge that gives rise to enlightenment is passed down from teacher (*guru*) to disciple through the ages. Of course, it is possible for this knowledge to arise spontaneously, or in response to some ordinary or life-threatening event, but habit and our attachment to conventional modes of thinking make this very unlikely.

Nevertheless, there is a relatively new class of teacher, growing in popularity, which denigrates this traditional approach. They insist that there is nothing that can be done to attain this knowledge; that in truth there is no seeker, nothing to be sought. There is no "realization" of a person because there is no person. Reality is now – "this is it." This method of teaching has become known as "Neo-Advaita," from the Greek *neos*, meaning "new." In fact, the essence of what these adherents say is extremely old, not differing from classical Advaita. The differences lie in their descriptions of the world-appearance and in their style of teaching.

[Note: It must be noted that there is another approach that is recognized, especially in India, called Neo-Vedanta, which is particularly associated with the disciples of Swami Vivekananda. Although there are differences between it and Traditional Advaita, I have ignored these for most of the book, which is aimed primarily at a western audience. More is mentioned about this in the final chapter, on Teaching Methods, by which time the subtleties of the differences will be better appreciated. Therefore, whenever the term 'neo-Advaita' is used, I refer to the new western method epitomized by Tony Parsons and not to neo-Vedanta. Other sources, especially any of Indian origin, may use these terms interchangeably to refer to the Vivekananda teaching.]

The expansion of the Internet and its rapid integration into the modern world as the principal reference source has meant that a wealth of information on Advaita is now readily available to everyone. Teachers advertise their services and make available extracts from their books and satsangs. Organizations such as those of Sri Ramakrishna and Swami Chinmayananda provide schedules of their meetings. Even Indian temples describe their facilities and give historical details of their development. Many scriptures are now directly downloadable in both original Sanskrit and transliterated form with many different translations and commentaries. Finally, the most basic and the most abstruse questions that challenge spiritual seekers are discussed on Email groups by students from beginner level to the most advanced.

Examples from all of these sources will be given to illustrate the various approaches to explaining some of the typical problems of our lives and in answering life's fundamental questions. *NB. The reader should note that any given section may quote extracts from several different teaching methods. Although the essential truth is always the same, care must be taken to note the source so as not to confuse them!*

There are two major problems with the explanations from some of the sources. The first of these is that the original documents, i.e. the Vedas, were written in Sanskrit. Few westerners understand Sanskrit. Accordingly, not only does the text have to be understood and explained, it first has to be translated. If it is being translated into English, the writer has to understand both languages well. But it is even worse than this. There are many concepts in the traditional philosophy that have no direct equivalent in English and, of course, the words were originally directed at a society that differed drastically from our own. Thus it is that the only person really able to communicate the wisdom of the Vedas is someone who can read Sanskrit and speak English fluently, is as familiar with the ancient Hindu concepts and way of life as he is with those of western society and ideally is already enlightened. Needless to say there are not many such people around!

That this can cause very serious problems is highlighted by **Stanley Sobottka** (Ref. 205). The Bhagavad Gita is a practical manual for *karma yoga*, describing how we should act in our lives. Chapter II, Verse 47 tells us that we should only concern ourselves with the action itself and not worry about the outcome. We should not do something because we want a particular result, nor should we be attached to inaction. But, says Sobottka, Ramesh Balsekar interprets this to mean that *"there is no free-will and work merely happens spontaneously."* A quite contrary interpretation is provided by Maharishi Mahesh Yogi, who says that *"you have control over action alone, never over its fruits."* As Sobottka points out: *"Any translation will inevitably convey the message that the translator wishes to convey."*

The second major problem is that, intrinsically, it is not possible to describe reality in any sense. As will become clear later in the book, who we truly are is the "ultimate subject," that which is effectively "dreaming" the universe. Obviously, this "subject" can never be treated objectively – otherwise it would not be the ultimate subject. Thus it is that teachers have to approach the truth obliquely, using stories and metaphor, even resorting to half-truths as a step along the way to understanding. What is "half-truth" and helpful to one student may be nonsense and distinctly unhelpful to another. It is the perennial problem of the teacher to be able to judge where the student currently is in his or her understanding and lead them onwards from there. This is why a living "guru" is really needed, so that questions may be asked and answered face to face.

When we read a book, or even listen to a tape recording of a lecture or dialogue, we are receiving only a particular viewpoint, aimed at a student of a particular level. It may resonate or it may not. Even the method of expression is crucial. Whilst one person may appreciate logic and intellectual analysis, another may need sympathetic reassurance and practical guidance. Some benefit from the crutch-like support of a personal God, others from the karate-chop of a Zen koan. Ultimately, the truth is one and everything else that might be said is only at the level of appearance, using a language that is necessarily objective and dualistic. What is needed is a teacher whose words and style "click" with our particular mental conditioning. This book aims to present excerpts from traditional and modern teaching in a wide variety of styles, in the hope that something will click.

It is also apparent that many modern teachers are diverging from or even shunning the traditional scriptural sources. This is in keeping with the tendency of individuals in modern western society to want results *now*, to want to hear the bottom line and avoid preparatory material, especially when it may be admitted that this is only provisional anyway. Many students are no longer interested in studying the Upanishads, which are often alien to the western mind, and most of them certainly do not wish to learn Sanskrit. Thus it is that many of the teachers themselves are also in this position.

What this means, unfortunately, is that a background understanding of the ultimate claims of Advaita is often lacking completely and there is a grave danger that students will "have the experience but miss the meaning" as T. S. Eliot puts it in his Four Quartets (Ref. 196). Many teachers today seem almost to be providing more of a psychotherapy session through their meetings than a spiritual unfolding of the truth and, unfortunately, this seems to be effectively what many of their students are looking for. But that is not Advaita.

These differences in approach are compared and contrasted and the intention is to provide a balanced view of the best of the teachings that are available from all of these sources, which include:

1. "Original scriptures"- *prasthAna traya: shruti* - Aitareya, Amritabindu, Atma, Brihadaranyaka, Chandogya, Isha, Katha, Kaushitaki, Kena, Maitri, Mandukya, Muktika, Mundaka, Narada-Parivrajaka, Prashna, Sarva-sara, Shvetashvatara, Taittiriya Upanishads; *smRRiti* - Bhagavad Gita; *nyAya prasthAna* – Shankara's Brahmasutra *bhAShya.*

2. Later Commentaries and works - *prakaraNa grantha* Aparokshanubhuti, Astavakra Gita, Atmabodha, Bhaja Govindam, *dRRig-dRRishya-viveka, pa~nchadashI,* Sadananda's Vedantasara, *sarva-vedAnta-siddhAnta-sArasaMgrahaH,* Tattva Bodha, *yoga vasiShTha, upadesha sAhasrI, vivekachUDAmaNi,* Yoga Sutras of Patanjali.

3. Historical Sages/writers – Gaudapada, Patanjali, Sadananda,

Shankara, Vidyaranya, Vyasa. **4. Recent Sages/Teachers** – Robert Adams, Sri Aurobindo, Swami Chinmayananda, Jean Klein, Sri Atmananda Krishna Menon, Jiddu Krishnamurti, Swami Krishnananda, Nisargadatta Maharaj, Swami Nikhilananda, Osho, H. W. L. Poonja, Ramana Maharshi, Ramakrishna Paramahamsa, Ranjit Maharaj, Swami Satchidananda, Swami Satchidanandendra Saraswati (Holenarasipur, Karnataka, India), HH Sri Shantanand Saraswati, Swami Sivananda, Swami Vivekananda, Wei Wu Wei. **5. Modern Satsang Teachers** – Bob Adamson, Adyashanti, Ramesh S. Balsekar, Sundance Burke, David Carse, Cee, Katie Davis, Gangaji, Nathan Gill, Burt Harding, Leo Hartong, Chuck Hillig, Unmani Liza Hyde, Catherine Ingram, Wolter Keers, Jan Kersschot, Jan Koehoorn, Brian Lake & Naama Livni, Gina Lake, Hans Laurentius, Roger Linden, Wayne Liquorman, Francis Lucille, P. T. Mistlberger, Nirmala, Tony Parsons, Robert Powell, Karl Renz, Justus Kramer Schippers, Isaac Shapiro, Alexander Smit, Aja Thomas, Madhukar Thompson, Eckhart Tolle, Joan Tollifson, John Wheeler. **6. Other Teachers and writers** - Monica Alderton, A. J. Alston, Amber, Danielle Arin, Atagrasin, Pujya Swami Atmananda, Sri Atmananda Saraswati, Ramakrishnan Balasubramanium, Dr. Hubert Benoit, Bhaskar, Chandrashekhara Bharati, James Braha, Swami Budhananda, Thomas Byrom, Chandi, Ram Chandran, Swami Chidbhavananda, Tanya Davis, Swami Dayananda, Anthony De Mello, Eliot Deutsch, Eknath Easwaran, Swami Gambhirananda, D. B. Gangolli, David Godman, Dr. Gregory Goode, Bina Gupta, Steven Harrison, Hans Heimer, Chuck Hillig, Anand Hudli, Aldous Huxley, Alan Jacobs, Swami Jagadananda, Jagmohan, David Jennings, Sri Karapatra Swami, Dr. A. G. Krishna Warrier, Prof. V. Krishnamurthy, U. G. Krishnamurti, Balakrishna Kumthekar, Stig Lundgren, Dr. Harsh K. Luthar, Swami Madhavananda, Sachindra K. Majumdar, Paula Marvelly, Juan Mascaro, A. R. Natarajan, Jay Mazo, Mark McCloskey, K. Padmanabha Menon, Jock Millensen, A. Devaraja Mudaliar, Bithika

Mukerji, Govindagopal Mukhopadhyaya, Gummuluru Murthy, Muruganar, Suri Nagamma, Chittaranjan Naik, Madathil Nair, Shawn Nevins, Swami Nityaswarupananda, Wendy Doniger O'Flaherty, Arthur Osborne, Swami Paramananda, A. Parthasarathy, Dr. Ramanand Prasad, Swami Muni Narayana Prasad, Chris Quilkey, S. Radhakrishnan, Anantanand Rambachan, Prof. A. A. Ramanathan, Sri Ramanananda Saraswathi, Swami Ranganathananda, Raphael, Michael Reidy, John Richards, Dr. E. Röer, Richard Rose, Möller de la Rouvière, Dr. K. Sadananda, Ranjeet Sankar, S. N. Sastri, Alladi Mahadeva Sastry, Swami Satprakashananda, Fernando Savater, Arthur Schopenhauer, Arvind Sharma, Swami Sharvananda, Vamadeva Shastri, Stanley Sobottka, K. N. Subramanian, V. Subrahmanian, Vidyasankar Sundaresan, Swami Swahananda, James Swartz, Ramananda Swarnagiri, Swami Tapasyananda, Swami Tattwananda, Paul Tillich, Nitin Trasi, Swami Tyagisananda, Swami Venkatesananda, T. N. Venkataraman, Andrew Vernon, Swami Viditatmananda Saraswati, Swami Vimuktananda, Alan W. Watts, Roy Whenary, "Who," Charles Wikner, Ken Wilber, Stephen Wingate, Ananda Wood.

Advaita is about discovering who we essentially are. It is not about establishing the well being of who we think we are. Therefore the reader will find nothing in these pages about self-improvement (the Self is already perfect and complete), or about becoming healthier or wealthier (such things relate only to the body or person and we are not those). The world and our seeming place in it have little relevance to any of these discussions, as will be explained.

The overall format of the book will be such as to present a logical development of the philosophy of Advaita, beginning with who we seem to be and the problems that we appear to have, and proceeding to an explanation of our true nature and that of the world and reality. Extracts from the above sources will be used to help explain all of these aspects and the final chapter will specifically look at the assumptions and styles of the three main teaching approaches – Traditional Advaita, Direct Path and

Neo-Advaita.

Summary

At the end of each chapter, there will be a short summary, in which I will attempt to provide bullet points of the key topics that have been covered.

- Science may have relegated religion to the status of superstition but it has failed to answer the fundamental questions of life.
- Advaita provides answers which contradict neither science nor our own experience.
- It derives from the Upanishads in the Vedic scriptures and means "not two."
- Teaching Advaita is difficult because of the need to interpret scriptures for a modern western audience and because Truth cannot be "known," only pointed to.
- Different natures require different methods and teachers.
- Language is necessarily dualistic.

1. DISCOVERING WHO WE ARE NOT

We are completely unaware of our true nature because we identify ourselves with our body, our emotions and our thoughts, thus losing sight of our unchanging centre, which is pure consciousness. When we return to our true nature, our thoughts and perceptions no longer appear as modifications of a single substance, they come into being and subside like waves of the ocean.

Jean Klein (Ref. 64)

Advaita is a supremely logical philosophy. There are a number of systematic procedures or methods, called *prakriyA*-s in Sanskrit. Each of these begins with our actual experience here and now, not asking for us to believe in anything that contradicts that experience or to put our faith in Gods that are entirely beyond it. Thus there is a *sRRiShTi prakriyA* to discuss the nature of creation and an analysis of the relationship between cause and effect, the *kAraNa-kArya-prakriyA* – these will be looked at in detail in Chapter 7. There is the *avasthA-traya-prakriyA* to analyze the three states of consciousness – see Chapter 6. The function of these methods is not to learn about the topic of the method but to see that the topic is misconceived. Thus, in examining creation, we discover that there has never been a creation. The net outcome of all these investigations is the realization that there is nothing other than Brahman.

In this chapter, we look at the most fundamental of these methods – the discrimination between the seer and the seen, the *dRRig-dRRishya–prakriyA*, in order to discover who we are not. There appears to be me here while you and the table are over there – clearly the appearance of separation. We can appreciate that we are not the objects that we see – we go out of the room and can no longer see them but we continue to exist. Likewise, we are not the other people that we see. But the same argument extends to our own bodies and senses – we can each lose bits of our bodies and even go blind or deaf, yet "we" remain. Similarly, we are not the thoughts or emotions, which come and go. We are not the mind – we continue to exist even when its operation ceases during deep sleep or under anesthetic. Even the I-thought is just that - another idea. The only constant aspect in all of this is Consciousness, so that is what I must be - not an object but the ultimate subject. But I can never describe it because everything that I might use in such a description is itself an object of Consciousness and has therefore already been negated.

There is thus a process of negating all of those aspects that we think we are, until what remains and cannot be negated must be the real Self. A special phrase is used to describe that process. It is called the "seer-seen discrimination" (*dRRigdRRishya-viveka*). This is the title of a short book (*prakaraNa grantha*) attributed to **Shankara**, which opens with the following statement:

The form is perceived and the eye is its perceiver. It (eye) is perceived and the mind is its perceiver. The mind with its modifications is perceived and the Witness (the Self) is verily the perceiver. But It (the Witness) is not perceived (by any other). (Ref. 73)

The exercise that is usually associated with it is to exclaim "not this, not this" with respect to anything that we perceive or think we might be – "*neti, neti*" in Sanskrit.

Probably the oldest known occurrence of this expression is in the Brihadaranyaka Upanishad. It acknowledges that no direct description of truth, of who we really are, is possible. The four "great sayings" or *mahAvAkya*-s of the Upanishads are: "Consciousness is Brahman," "That thou art," "this Self is Brahman" and "I am Brahman." These *mahAvAkya*-s together contain the ultimate purport of the entire Upanishads. All other sentences are called *avAntara vAkya*-s – intermediate statements, which may only be true in an empirical sense.

Brahman is what we truly are but is beyond description. II.3.6 of the

Brihadaranyaka Upanishad states:

> Now therefore the description (of Brahman): "Not this, not this."
> Because there is no other and more appropriate description than this
> "Not this." Now Its name: "the Truth of truth." The vital force is truth,
> and It is the Truth of that. (Ref. 1)

and in III.9.26:

> This self is That which has been described as "Not this, not this." It is
> imperceptible, for it is never perceived; undecaying, for It never decays;
> unattached, for It is never attached; unfettered – It never feels pain, and
> never suffers injury. (Ref. 1)

[Note that scriptural references will be given in the above form so that
III.9.26 refers to Book III, chapter 9, verse 26.]

Direct translations of the Upanishads are frequently difficult to
appreciate without further explanation. **Swami Krishnananda** provides
helpful commentary on the last verse:

> You can only say, "what it is not." You cannot say, "what it is." It is not
> the body; it is not the senses; it is not any one of the *prANa*-s; it is not
> even the mind; it is not the intellect. What else it is? You do not know.
> If anyone asks you, what is this essential Self in you, you can only say;
> "it is not this;" "it is not this." But you cannot say, "what it is," because
> to characterize it in any manner would be to define it in terms of
> qualities that are obtainable in the world of objects. The world of objects
> can be defined by characters perceivable to the eyes or sensible to the
> touch etc. But the Atman is the presupposition and the precondition of
> every kind of perception. It is the proof of all proofs. Everything
> requires a proof, but the Atman does not require a proof because it is the
> source of all proofs. And therefore, no one can define it; no one can say,
> "what it is." It can only be inferred, because if it were not to be, nothing

else could be. So, it can be said to be capable of definition only in a negative manner as "not this, not this, *neti neti Atma*." This Atman is defined as "not this, not this, or not that, not that, not in this manner, nothing that is known, nothing that is sensed, nothing that is capable of being expressed by words, nothing that is definable, nothing of this sort" etc. What it is, no one can say! It is impossible to grasp it through either the power of speech, or the power of the senses, or the power of the mind. (Ref. 2)

Not the Body

The notion that "I am the body" is the most basic identification. This is quite understandable when "I am ill," since pain and discomfort have a tendency to disrupt clear thinking. But spending vast amounts of money on the latest fashions so that "I look beautiful" or even more money on injections or surgery to try to counteract the aging process, ought to make us wonder whether something has gone wrong with our thinking. The body, after all, is nothing more than the food that we have eaten, reprocessed and reconstructed into a new form. And the scriptures are quick to point this out in no uncertain terms, as in the **Narada-Parivrajaka Upanishad**:

III-45-47. ...(This body) pillared by bones, bound together by tendons, plastered with flesh and blood, covered by skin, foul smelling, filled with urine and feces, subject to old age and affliction, an abode of diseases, liable to injury, full of passion, impermanent and the abode of the elements (i.e. the body) one may abandon (without regret).

III-48. If one were to take delight in the body, which is a conglomerate of flesh, blood, pus, feces, urine, tendons, marrow and bones, that fool will be (delighted) in hell as well.

III-49. The attitude "I am the body" is (the same as) the path leading to the hell... (Ref. 3)

It is through the body and senses that we enjoy the apparent objects in the material world and this is the grossest level of identification to which we are prone. **Shankara** describes it as follows, in the Vivekachudamani:

> 88. This material body, which arises from past action out of material elements formed by the combination of subtle elements, is the vehicle of sensation for the individual. This is the state of a waking person perceiving material objects.
>
> 89. The life force creates for itself, out of itself, material object of enjoyment by means of the external senses - such colorful things as flowers, perfumes, women, etc. That is why this has its fullest enjoyment in the waking state. (Ref. 4)

Even for a moment do not think that you are the body. Give yourself no name, no shape. In the darkness and the silence reality is found. **Nisargadatta Maharaj** (Ref. 5)

Thinking that we are the body, we are dependent upon its comfort and health. If it is hungry, "we" are hungry and if it is damaged or ill, we feel incomplete and suffer accordingly. Worst of all, we believe that who-we-actually-are is doomed to grow old and die. More often than not, if someone asks "How are you?," they are inquiring into the state of your physical welfare. We choose our partner according to the attractiveness of their body and bemoan the failing faculties as the body ages. **Swami Chinmayananda** comments as follows on the verse from the Bhaja Govindam, another of the works attributed to **Shankara**:

> As long as there dwells breath (life) in the body, so long they inquire of your welfare at home. Once the breath (life) leaves, the body decays, even the wife fears that very same body.
> (Seek Govind, Seek Govind . . .) (Verse 6)

In short, to spend one's entire lifetime in sheer body-worship, in earning more so that this futile worship may be made more elaborate, is one of the abominable intellectual stupidities into which humanity readily sinks. For, if the body be the altar of worship, it may not remain permanently there as the days of decay and old age are not far away even for today's young bodies. To sweat and toil, to fight and procure, to feed and breed, to clothe and shelter the body — are all in themselves necessary, but to spend the whole lifetime in these alone is a criminal waste of human abilities. For, erelong it is to grow old, tottering, infirm and, in the end, die away.[†] (Ref. 6)

Nisargadatta Maharaj explains to an inquirer how we cannot be these bodies, which are nothing more than the food that we have eaten, having grown as a result from the moment of conception. He asks an enquirer to remember himself as a young man, then as a boy and as an infant. He continues:

And before the baby acquired its body and was delivered what were you? Think. What happened in your mother's womb? What was developing into a body with bones, blood, marrow, muscles etc., over a period of nine months? Was it not a male sperm cell that combined with ovum in the female womb thus beginning a new life and, in the process, going through numerous hazards? Who guarded this new life during this period of hazards? Is it not that very infinitesimally tiny sperm cell which is now so proud of his achievements? And who asked particularly for you? Your mother? Your father? Did they particularly want you for a son? Did you have anything to do with being born to these particular parents?

If you go deeper into the matter, you will realize that the source of the body — the male sperm and the female ovum— is in itself the essence of food consumed by the parents; that the physical form is made of, and fed by, the five elements constituting the food; and also that

---

[†] Bhaja Govindam, Swami Chinmayananda, © Central Chinmaya Mission Trust, Mumbai.

quite often the body of one creature does become the food for another creature.

Find out what it is that gives sentience to a sentient being, that without which you would not even know that you exist, let alone the world outside. And finally, go deeper yet and examine if this beingness, this consciousness itself is not time-bound. (Ref. 7)

Strictly speaking, it should be noted that we do not normally think "I am the body." What we actually identify with is an attribute of the body such as "I am ugly" or "I am fat." We are in fact mistakenly associating the characteristics of the body, which is not my real self with the real "I." This can be appreciated in the case of those who have lost a limb or become blind etc. The body may be significantly changed but they do not believe that who they really are is any different.

Modern scientists, philosophers and psychologists have written very many books in recent years on the subject of consciousness. There is no universally accepted theory but there is a prevailing trend to believe that consciousness somehow originates in the mind, once a certain level of complexity has been reached by an organism. The expression that is often used is that consciousness is an *epiphenomenon* of the mind, i.e. a side-effect, almost to the extent that it is something with which we could quite happily do without. Thus it is that it is firmly believed by almost everyone that consciousness is something (whatever it might be!) that is *in* the mind, which in turn is *in* the body. The view of Advaita is that everything, including the body and the mind is an apparent arising within Consciousness (with a capital "C" since this does not refer to an individual's consciousness). This viewpoint is expressed simply by **Francis Lucille**, a modern teacher influenced by Atmananda Krishna Menon and Jean Klein:

> You were never in your body, so the question of coming back into it doesn't come up. Your body is in you. You are not in it. Your body appears to you as a series of sensory perceptions and concepts. It is in this way that you know you have a body, when you feel it or when you

think of it. These perceptions and these thoughts appear in you, pure conscious attention. You do not appear in them, contrary to what your parents, your teachers and nearly the whole of the society you live in has taught you. In flagrant contradiction to your actual experience, they have taught you that you are in your body as consciousness, that consciousness is a function emerging from the brain, an organ of your body. I suggest that you do not give undue credence to this second-hand knowledge and that you inquire into the raw data of your own experience. Remember the recipes for happiness that were given to you by these same people when you were a child, study hard, get a good job, marry the right man, etc.? These recipes don't work, otherwise you wouldn't be here asking these questions. They don't work because they are based on a false perspective of reality, a perspective that I am suggesting that you put into question. (Ref. 8)

Not the Mind

I can find little solace in the profound "I think, therefore I am" solution. In the first place Descartes never proved that it was he doing the thinking.
Richard Rose (Ref 209)

It is not so difficult to accept that we are not the body when we are presented with arguments such as these. We can see the body in just the same way that we can see external objects, albeit that the body seems somewhat more intimate. When it comes to the mind, the situation is much less clear. Whilst we may say 'there is a pain in my leg," thus to some extent dissociating myself from the body, we are unlikely to say 'there is an idea in my mind." We always say "I have an idea," although if we are pressed to explain exactly what we did in order to bring this about, we might have a problem. And, of course, we are quite unable to actually point to this "idea"!

The "I" in "I think" and "I do" is as real as the "it" in "it rains" and "it is cold." **Leo Hartong** (Ref. 238)

The fact is that we do not "think" thoughts. They arise and we witness them. Later, if the memory of an earlier thought arises (as a new thought) we claim that we originated it and say "I thought that..." but this is simply not true. The mind is always passive in this respect; it is only in subsequent processing of a thought that it becomes active.

David Carse expresses it thus:

> Everything, including the body/mind organism you call yourself, does not exist as something separate in itself, but only as an apparent functioning in Consciousness. There is no separate self or mind, only dream characters in Self or Consciousness. There is only thinking happening in this apparent organism, in these dream characters. We experience this. We experience thoughts happening; but the assumption that they originate inside these heads in something we call a mind is an unwarranted leap. It's the basic misperception from which everything else, all of dualism, all of the illusion of separation, all *saMsAra* [the cycle of death and birth] [†], follows. (Ref. 313)

The mind is like the moon, deriving its light of consciousness from the Self, which thus resembles the Sun. Hence when the Self begins to shine, the mind, like the moon, becomes useless. **Ramana Maharshi**. (Ref. 39)

In respect of thoughts, the mind acts like a processor of data. Information is transmitted from the senses. This is compared to data already stored in the memory; decisions are taken accordingly and instructions passed down to the body as appropriate. All this takes place automatically, powered by consciousness but there is no "I," in the form of the mind, "doing" anything. A modern teacher, **"Sailor" Bob Adamson**, a disciple of Nisargadatta Maharaj, uses the classic metaphor of red-hot iron to explain this:

> The mind is just really a translator, a translator of what is coming up. I use the analogy of putting a piece of iron in the fire. It'll get red like fire. It'll get hot like fire. Pick it up, and it'll burn you like fire. So, it has

taken on the qualities of the fire. If it was like our minds, it would say 'look at me! Look what I can do; I'm red; I'm hot; I can burn!" But take it out of the fire, and what can it do? It can't do any of those things. It is the same with thinking. Thinking is so closely aligned to that pure intelligence that it has come to believe that it is the intelligence itself. It thinks, "I choose" or "I have got will" or "I can do this" or "I'm not good enough" or "I am an evil person" or whatever. But all thought really does, when you look at it closely, is translate. When you question it and look at it, you can see that of itself it hasn't got any power. It hasn't got any substance or independent nature. In seeing that and realizing that, then what does the mind do? It just aligns itself with that intelligence. It just translates from that, instead of taking the belief that it has some power or some sense of entity and separateness of itself. (Ref. 9)

Abiding in the midst of ignorance, but thinking themselves wise and learned, fools aimlessly go hither and thither, like blind led by the blind. **Mundaka Upanishad** I.2.8 (Ref. 21)

Traditional Advaita does not really differentiate emotions from thoughts/perceptions and volitions. All arise in the mind (*manas*) and then identification takes place, causing all of the problems with which we are familiar. Cognition is the basic mode of the mind, which can occur without the other two but both emotion and volition can only occur if thinking/ perception is also present. All of the various functions of mind – feeling, willing, thinking, imagining, remembering and ego – are illuminated by the light of Consciousness, which is the essence of the Self and the only reality. Therefore, all the states are effectively just (apparent) objects of Consciousness. All of this will be explained later.

One Sanskrit word for emotion is *bhAva*, which means: "any state of

---

† Note that, throughout the book, text in square brackets [ ] within quoted extracts have been inserted by myself to provide translations of Sanskrit terms that may not have been encountered previously.

mind or body, way of thinking or feeling, sentiment, opinion, disposition, intention, love, affection, attachment; the seat of the feelings or affections, heart, soul, mind" but this word is used in the Bhagavad Gita in the more general sense of "being, existence" or "becoming." Another word is *rasa* and Atmananda Krishna Menon uses it as "general emotion."

It is more usual to find specific emotions referred to, such as anger (*krodha*), desire (*kAma*), passionate love (*rAga*), hatred (*dveSha*). Strong emotions of any kind prevent discrimination and lead to delusion and death (as the Gita puts it), since they lead to impulsive, rather than discriminatory action.

Since the mind is the effective obstacle to realising our true nature, becoming detached from emotions is part of the preparation for spiritual enquiry. This is presented as becoming "dispassionate" (*vairAgya* - meaning absence of *rAga*).

Krishna Menon has the following to say on the subject of feelings and emotions:

Every feeling is said to be a wave in the ocean of Peace. The analogy is not strictly correct. Here we must understand that there is wave only in the ocean and that there is no wave in Peace. In Peace, there is neither ocean nor wave, as there is neither ocean nor wave in water. Similarly, there are no thoughts or feelings in me, the real "I"- principle. Understanding feelings in this manner, we can enjoy even the feeling of misery, by emphasizing the real content of that misery and dismissing the illusory name and form.

Thus every emotion is a clear pointer to that permanent background Peace. So you can very well lose your apparent self at the upsurge of any emotion; not in the emotion itself, but in its permanent background.

We have all had the occasion of witnessing tragic dramas brimming over with pathos and cold cruelty towards the righteous, at which we have wept from start to finish. But the next day again we are prepared to pay in order to witness the same drama, so that we may continue to weep. What is the secret of this? Is this not the enjoyment of misery?

This shows you that there is something inherent in the so-called misery that tempts you to court it again. It is nothing but the background, Peace, which is behind all emotions.

Therefore, see through every emotion and perceive that Peace alone is there. This is what every *j~nAnin* does. So he enjoys every feeling which you so carefully separate from Peace and thereby suffer. (Ref. 13 Note 776, [Ref. 13 is divided up into "Notes"])

As long as we remain identified with the mind with its thoughts and emotions we are bound to suffer the consequences of its mistaken view of reality. **Möller de la Rouvière** explains:

Through the process of identifying ourselves with the activities of thought, it no longer serves human life, but has become human life. Identification with thought means that no separation exists between the human mind (as thought) and human life. What we know, we are. In this way I am my religion. I am my nationality. I am my war. I am the image I have made of myself and others. I am my political party. I am the way I interpret my field of experience. I am my morality, social order and social conditioning. I am both that which thought presumes to be me and not-me. In fact, I am the entire fragmentary, destiny creating and uninspected projections of my own thinking. All these are creations of thought, and while I am identified with thought, this thought-world is me. In this, there is no other. And it is this projected reality we suffer and enjoy for as long as we are identified with it. (Ref. 91)

We have to let go of the thoughts and emotions, recognizing that they are only temporary arisings within Consciousness and that they will soon disappear, leaving our essential Self totally unaffected. Here is **"Sailor" Bob Adamson** again:

As long as you have a body, you'll have thoughts, and you'll still think in the same way. The nature of thinking is in the pairs of opposites, which is dualism. You can't think in another way. Past/future, painful/happy, hot/cold, and so on. In understanding it, you're no longer bound by it. Let the mind do what it likes. It's not you. It's an appearance that comes and goes. (Ref. 346)

And:

> Being thought-free means *just let the thought be free*. Let it do what it likes. Let it float around and then leave. No thought has ever lasted. Where are yesterday's thoughts? (Ref. 346)

Not the Ego

Nevertheless, most people believe that they **are** the mind. The sense of self is referred to as "ego" in the west and when Advaita speaks about obstacles to realizing the truth, the mind and ego are used almost interchangeably. We would probably admit on reflection that all of our ideas, opinions and beliefs stem from conditioning by parents, teachers and the society into which we happened to be born. These become an indelible part of our memories and it is the identification with these that effectively forms what we might call our ego.

It is only when the chattering of the mind ceases and all of these whirling thoughts momentarily disappear that we can acknowledge that there remains something else, that is unrelated to all of these acquired ideas and that those ideas are *not* who we are.

A simple example would be our nationality or religion. Where we happen to be born is purely accidental (though this will be questioned later when we look at the theory of *karma*). We may have been brought up to be a Christian in a materialistic, western society so that all of our initial reactions to questions of morality for example are likely to be governed by those standards. Had we been born in China or in a Moslem country, our reactions might well have been different.

What we must try to do is to be in the present, aware of what is here and now, to transcend rather than be conditioned by all of this mental baggage.

As long as we are identified in this way, believing ourselves to be a separate body-mind, it is this fictional ego that is involved. This is why modern teachers especially repeatedly emphasise that the seeker will never find any truth or realisation, the seeker is that which is sought, the ego cannot commit suicide etc. **Atmananda Krishna Menon** puts it very succinctly:

> However much you may try to kill the ego, it will only become stronger. So you have to approach it from the other end. Everybody understands in spite of the ego. The truth is that the ego automatically dies when you understand anything. You will never succeed in bringing in light, if you insist upon removing all the darkness from your room before you do so. Therefore simply ignore the ego and try to understand, and the understanding itself will remove the ego. (Note 847 – Ref 13)

> The moment you begin to do that, you unknowingly take your stand in the Awareness beyond the ego or the mind. Then the ego sheds all its accretions and stands revealed as that Awareness itself. Looking from that position, the baffling world problem disappears like mist before the sun, never to appear again. (Note 1354 - Ref. 13)

Thus, **Ramana Maharshi** advocates Self-Enquiry as the "method" for discovering our true Self. The investigation is conducted by the ego and its efforts are, of course, doomed to failure. What happens however is that, in the process of discovering that the "I" cannot be found, because it does not exist, the investigation collapses, the ego disappears and the Self remains. The illusion dissolves and the reality stands revealed:

> Hold the ego first and then ask how it is to be destroyed. Who asks the question? It is the ego. This question is a sure way to cherish the ego and not to kill it. If you seek the ego you will find that it does not exist. That is the way to destroy it. (Ref. 17)

Behind the mind, ever-changing because of the changing thoughts, feelings and desires, lies the unchanging Consciousness, the Self of all. **Swami Satchidananda**, in his commentary on the Yoga Sutras of Patanjali, says:

But behind all these differences, in the Self, we never differ. That means behind all these ever-changing phenomena is a never-changing One. That One appears to change due to our mental modifications. So, by changing your mind you change everything. If only we could understand this point, we would see that there is nothing wrong outside; it is all in the mind. By correcting our vision we correct things outside. If we can cure our jaundiced eye, nothing will look yellow. But without correcting the jaundice, however much we scrub the outside things, we are not going to make them white or blue or green; they will always be yellow. (Ref. 11)

Attachment

It is not the world but attachment to it which is the root of all misery. **Swami Nityaswarupananda** (Ref. 12)

This attachment is called *ahaMkAra* in Sanskrit, which literally means the 'making" of the utterance "I am." It is that element of the mind that tends to identify with ideas such as "I am a man," or a teacher or a father etc. Even though all of these may be true at the relative level, none relate to my essential nature, as will become clear later. Such associations are only being made at the level of the mind and do not affect in the slightest who I really am.

If we really were attached to an idea or a state, then it would stay with us all of the time. Yet, even during the waking state, happiness is succeeded by misery, often in a very short time and tiredness will vanish in an instant if an emergency arises. And when we go to sleep, all of the worries, joys and pains disappear completely.

Yet this identification extends to the deepest level. We believe that we think, that we act and that we enjoy (or not). It will become apparent that none of these are true. That we have no free will, as ordinarily understood, will be discussed in the next chapter, and the third will show how we are already happiness itself, irrespective of whether we are currently enjoying life or in pain. As for thinking, thoughts certainly arise but do we actually do anything to originate them? Thoughts occur in the mind and "we" see them. Action may result and "we" witness this, just as we witness the pleasure or pain that may ensue. But we are none of these things, not even this "witness." We are that which is the unchanging background to all of these transient phenomena.

The metaphor of an actor, playing a role on the stage is often used to speak of the way we should conduct ourselves in the world. We should remember all the time that we are not the body, mind or intellect:

> Does a man who is acting on the stage in a female part forget that he is a man? Similarly, we too must play our parts on the stage of life, but we must not identify ourselves with those parts. **Ramana Maharshi** (Ref. 17)

Neither are we a "person." In fact, the very meaning of the word - deriving from the Latin *persona* - being the mask worn by actors in the Greco-Roman theatre, tells us that we cannot be such a thing. At the very least we must be whatever it is that is wearing the mask. **Nisargadatta Maharaj** again:

> The person is merely the result of a misunderstanding. In reality, there is no such thing. Feelings, thoughts and actions race before the watcher in endless succession, leaving traces in the brain and creating an illusion of continuity. A reflection of the watcher in the mind creates the sense of I and the person acquires an apparently independent existence. In reality there is no person, only the watcher identifying himself with the I and the "mine." The teacher tells the watcher: you are not this, there is nothing of yours in this, except the little point of "I am," which is the bridge between the watcher and his dream. "I am this, I am that" is dream, while pure "I am" has the stamp of reality on it. You have tasted

> so many things — all came to naught. Only the sense "I am" persisted — unchanged. Stay with the changeless among the changeful, until you are able to go beyond. (Ref. 5)

All that we need to know about the truth may be found in the Upanishads but there is a problem in knowing where to look and in understanding what is found. An informed commentary is essential. The Kena Upanishad, for example, is quite short and imparts the knowledge of our true nature in four different ways, according to the spiritual readiness of the listener. The first section is the most direct and succinct but consequently apparently the most difficult. Verse two tells us that we are that which enables or empowers the mind etc., not the mind itself. A beautifully clear explanation is provided by **Swami Paramananda**:

> *It is the ear of the ear, the mind of the mind, the speech of the speech, the life of the life, the eye of the eye. The wise, freed (from the senses and from mortal desires), after leaving this world, become immortal.* **(Kena Upanishad I.2)**
>
> An ordinary man hears, sees, thinks, but he is satisfied to know only as much as can be known through the senses; he does not analyze and try to find that which stands behind the ear or eye or mind. He is completely identified with his external nature. His conception does not go beyond the little circle of his bodily life, which concerns the outer man only. He has no consciousness of that which enables his senses and organs to perform their tasks.
>
> There is a vast difference between the manifested form and That which is manifested through the form. When we know That, we shall not die with the body. One who clings to the senses and to things that are ephemeral, must die many deaths; but that man who knows the eye of the eye, the ear of the ear, having severed himself from his physical nature, becomes immortal. Immortality is attained when man transcends his apparent nature and finds that subtle, eternal and inexhaustible essence which is within him. (Ref. 14)

The "Sheaths" that surround our true essence

Traditional Advaita uses a model to illustrate the successive levels of identification that take place and thus obscure our real nature. This supposes that our true essence is effectively covered over by "sheaths," in the same way that a scabbard encloses the blade of a sword. In fact, the Sanskrit word *kosha* is even more evocative since one of its meanings is a "treasury" where something of great value is stored. The model is called the *pa~ncha kosha prakriyA* – the method of the five sheaths and it is explained in detail in the Taittiriya Upanishad.

This is how I described it in my earlier book, "The Book of One":

The first of these layers – the grossest and the one with which we first tend to identify - is the body. This is referred to as the sheath made of food, *annamayakosha*. The body is born, grows old, dies and decays back into the food from which it originally came (well, food for worms anyway) but this has nothing to do with the real Self, which is much closer than hand or skin.

The second layer is called the "vital sheath" or sheath made of breath, *prANamayakosha*. Hindu mythology refers to the "air" as breathing life into the body. We might call it the vital force by means of which the body is animated and actions are performed. Although this force derives from the Self, as indeed everything does, it is *not* the Self. We each of us tend to believe that we are somehow immortal. Although we acknowledge that the body must eventually die we feel that there is this animating force which will survive that death. This is the identification with the vital sheath.

The next layer is the mental sheath consisting of the thinking mind and the organs of perception, *manomayakosha*. This is the part of the mental makeup responsible for transmitting information from the outside world but which usually gets up to mischief that is really none of its business, i.e. thinking and trying to understand everything. The Sanskrit word for this "organ" of mind is *manas*. This is probably the sheath with which most of us identify.

Beyond this, however, there is the higher faculty of mind, responsible for discrimination, recognizing truth or falsehood, real or unreal, without recourse to mundane things like thought and memory. In silence, it *knows* without needing to think. We might call this the intellect; Sanskrit calls it *buddhi*. It is responsible for such judgments as Solomon's in respect of the two mothers claiming the same child. He suggested sawing the baby in two and giving half to each woman. Supposedly the false mother agreed to this while the real mother said that the other woman could have the child. This is the intellectual sheath, *vij~nAnamayakosha*.

Some readers who meditate may have been fortunate enough to experience moments of the most profound peace and silence, when the mind is completely absent and a feeling of deep contentment can be felt. It might be thought that this is the state of realization for which we are aiming, if only it could be maintained. Instead it lasts mere minutes or, very rarely hours for a few dedicated ascetics. But no, this is just another state, albeit perhaps a desirable and blissful one. We are still observing it and therefore cannot be it. It is the final sheath, called appropriately enough the Bliss sheath, *Anandamayakosha*. Because of its supremely blissful nature, it is reputedly the most difficult of the sheaths to transcend. (Ref. 84)

What we truly are, then, is the "Real Self" or simply "Self" with a capital "S" as it will be called in this book. The Sanskrit terms are *Atman*, when referring to the apparent individual, or *brahman*, when referring to the apparent universe – though these are discovered to be identical. But, through identification with these various layers or sheaths, this Self is obscured. It is like water contained in a colored glass bottle. The water itself seems to take on the color of the glass, though it is itself colorless.

[In fact, the sheaths do not "cover" up anything. It is rather the case that they are levels at which we experience the world and with which we identify. There is nothing other than *Atman-brahman* so that each of the sheaths is itself Atman and this is realized once we stop the identification.

Once the sheaths have been negated, what remains is that which cannot be negated - the eternal witness. The model is presented as an aid to understanding and later shown to be false as our understanding increases. This methodology is fundamental to the teaching of Advaita. All of this will be revisited and made clearer in later chapters.]

Another, similar model is worth mentioning in passing, since it illustrates again the classic Advaitic method of claiming that X is true but then later retracting it, as the knowledge of the student improves and his ability intellectually to accept unintuitive concepts increases. This method is similar to the popular Zen metaphor of the "finger pointing to the moon" and is, in fact, called the "rule of the moon on a bough" – *shAkhA-chandra-nyAya*. In the *AtmopaniShad*, we are told that who we are is first the "outer-*Atman*" of skin, nails, hair etc. and then the "inner-*Atman*," who is the hearer, thinker, doer etc. Then, in the third and final verse, we are told about the *paramAtman* who cannot be perceived, conceived of; who does not die and is beyond qualities etc. **Swami Madhavananda** explains:

Just as the moon, though immensely distant from the bough of the tree, is pointed out to a child as the moon *on* the bough, because she appears to be contiguous to it, even so the *paramAtman* - though He has really no relation with the body and the mind, still for the sake of ease to the learner - is first pointed out through the body and the mind, which are called here the Outer and the Inner Atman respectively, because of His appearing very much akin to them to a child-mind. Thus by leading the seeker after Truth step by step, the real nature of the Atman is disclosed. (Ref. 85)

Negation of all that we think we are

You are neither earth, nor water, nor fire, nor air, nor space. In order to attain liberation, know the Self as the witness of all these and as Consciousness itself. **Astavakra Gita** I.3 (Ref. 12)

One way in which it is described by many teachers is that we are not the body, thoughts, feelings etc. but the "background" on which these arise. Thus we have the metaphor of a cinema screen. We are not the images, which have no real existence, but the screen itself. Atmananda Krishna Menon used the metaphor of a rock, with faces carved into it. Looking at it, we tend to see the faces without realizing that they are only rock. When we look at a book, we see the words written there and not the paper that is the true substratum. Always we are lured away by the form and miss the essence.

In respect of the identification with the mind, **Sri Poonja** speaks of needing rather to look at the interval between thoughts:

In that interval is Consciousness. Between two clouds, there is an interval and that interval is the blue sky! Slow down the thoughts and look into the intervals. Yes! Look into the intervals and pay more attention to the interval than the cloud!

First thought has left, other is not arisen, That is Consciousness. That is Freedom. That is your own place, your own abode. You are always there, you see.

Shift the attention, change the gestalt. Don't look at the figure, look at the background! If I put a big blackboard the size of the wall here and mark it with a white point and ask you, "What do you see?" Ninety-nine percent of you will not see the blackboard! (laughs) You will say, "I see a little white spot." Such a big blackboard and it is not seen, and only a little white spot, which is almost invisible, is seen!! Why? Because this is the fixed pattern of the mind: To look at the figure, not the blackboard; to look at the cloud, not at the sky; to look at the thought, not at Consciousness.

That's all the teaching is. Always look to Consciousness. Always look to Consciousness and know this is what you are! This is your own place, your own abode. Stay Here. No one can touch you. Who can enter Here where you are? Even your mind cannot enter. (Ref. 15)

Another metaphor is that of a mirror. The mirror represents our true Self and is the only reality; the rest is mere reflection. **Swami Chinmayananda** expands on this metaphor in his commentary on the Astavakra Gita:

Just as a mirror exists inside and outside the image reflected in it, so the Supreme Self exists inside and outside this body. (**Astavakra Gita I.19**)

With reference to a room, or a pot, we can qualify space as space-within and space-without. But when the pot is broken or the walls are pulled down, there can be only one all-pervading space. Similarly, the seeker, so long as he is within his conditionings, he meditates upon his Self, as the Pure-Subject within himself. But on apprehending the Self, he experiences Its All-pervading Infinite Nature.

In order to communicate this idea, Astavakra uses here a very original example. The reflection is in the mirror and the mirror pervades within and without the reflection caught in it. The reflection has no existence apart from the mirror. Even when the reflection is not there, the mirror continues to be. Similarly, reflected in the three bodies — the gross, the subtle and the causal — the Consciousness appears to dance to the rhythm of the bodies and this reflection, caught in our bosom, is the ego.

The very existence of the three-bodies is brought about by one's own illusions. They are superimposed upon the Self by "ignorance." As the post is within the ghost-vision, the Self is within the body.

But the Infinite Self, the Consciousness, is within and without the individualized-ego and its matter-wrappings. Just as the reflection cannot in any way disturb the reflecting medium, so too the Self is not affected by the superimposition of the equipments, or the reflection of the ego. [†] (Ref. 18)

The process outlined above, then, is one of negation – *neti, neti* – rejecting all of the things that we are not in order to discover what we truly are. It is

---

[†] Astavakra Gita, Swami Chinmayananda, © Central Chinmaya Mission Trust, Mumbai.

an apparent paradox, then, to be told later that everything is Brahman, or Consciousness, including all of the aspects that we have just supposedly rejected. **Swami Parthasarathy** addresses this confusion in his commentary on the Atmabodha:

> *Whatever is seen or heard cannot be anything other than Brahman and on realization of Truth one (recognizes) that Brahman as existence-knowledge-bliss and non-dual.* (**Atmabodha Verse 64**)

The previous verse states that the universe is something other than Brahman while this verse declares that the universe (whatever is seen or heard) is nothing other than Brahman. These two statements present an apparent contradiction. It is because of the two angles from which the universe is viewed. To one who has not realized Brahman the universe appears real. He gets involved in the transitory objects and beings of the universe that he perceives. In order to release him from his entanglements the infinite, imperishable Reality is pointed out to him as different from the finite, perishable universe. But a Self-realized one in the homogeneous experience of pure Consciousness sees the universe itself as nothing other than Brahman. (Ref. 16)

He goes on to explain that our normal states of consciousness – waking, dream and deep sleep – are at the level of appearance. Reality is the non-dual background to these states. Just as our dreams seem real to the dreamer, so this world-appearance seem real to the waker. But, on waking, it is realized that those dreams are nothing but an illusion generated by the mind.

Similarly only on awakening to god-consciousness will you appreciate and realize the staggering truth that there exists nothing other than Brahman everywhere. Until that supreme state is reached, the universe will appear real. Living in your present state of ignorance you will have to accept the world that you experience. But at the same time try to contemplate and realize the truth proclaimed by Self-realized souls that Brahman alone exists. (Ref. 16)

Who am I?

Ultimately, the question "Who am I" cannot be answered. Who I am is the ultimate subject. Only the objective can be thought about or spoken of. Language is of the nature of duality so that, if reality is non-dual as claimed by Advaita, then neither book nor teacher can describe it. Conversely, if we are able to talk about it in any way, then we can be certain that we are *not* that. **Jean Klein** talks about precisely this problem in his book "I Am":

In his life a man can ask himself many questions but they all revolve around one question: "Who am I?" All questions stem from this one. So that the answer to "Who am I?" is the answer to all questions, the ultimate answer. But we must be quite clear about certain things, so that we don't appropriate this question as just another idea among many.

A man always speaks of himself as an I and gives this I many roles: I run, I eat, I'm hungry, I'm sitting, sleeping. All these activities refer to the body he firmly believes himself to be. He also says: I remember, I think, I'm surprised, worried, etc., etc. Thus he also takes himself to be his thoughts. Here the I-image identifies with the body and the mind. But if we observe things more closely, we soon come to realize that it is the body that is doing the acting and the mind the thinking. These are the tools of consciousness which function without any I-image…

The question "Who am I?" springs from the "I am." The reply is already present before we even ask the question, the question in fact originates in the answer.

The question itself, on the level on which it is asked, the level of conflict, cannot give rise to a reply, for when we look at it more closely, we cannot possibly put the answer into words, even less think of it. However, the driving force pushing us on to find an answer by means of thought finally dies away, and is reabsorbed into the eternal, all-answering presence, I am. (Ref. 19)

The Self will always be a mystery because there can never be anything apart from it to comprehend it, analyse it or understand it. **Sri Poonja**

Ranjit Maharaj, a disciple of Shri Siddharameshwar Maharaj, along with the better known Nisargadatta Maharaj, said: *"What is true? Self without self. (2.11)"* and his commentator, **Andrew Vernon** explains:

The word "self," like the word "I," points back to the one who is uttering it. It is a "reflexive" word, one that indicates the eternal subject, rather than one of Its objects. The real owner of the word Self is the One who is always present, the very essence of reality, reality Itself. It is a very sacred word and receives an upper case letter "s." On the other hand, the small ego-self receives a lower-case letter "s" to indicate its insignificance. It is rebuffed, dismissed as the impostor it is. This fraudulent self robs you of your birthright, which is to know yourself as you truly are, the universal and ever-free Self of all.

and *"Reality is myself. (2.19),"* with the commentary:

To find a cup in the dark, you need eyes and a lamp, but to find a lamp in the dark, you only need eyes, you don't need a lamp. Reality is self-evident, self-illuminating. You don't need anything external to find it, because it is already what you are. When Self-knowledge occurs, it becomes very clear to you that you and reality are one and the same, and that your nature is bright and pure like a flame that is always burning. (Ref. 20)

Some of the modern, Neo-Advaitin writers and teachers also have some very useful things to say. **Leo Hartong** is one of the clearest of these and his book "Awakening to the Dream" is recommended very highly. Here is what he has to say in answer to the question "Who am I?":

Ramana Maharshi recommended that one investigates by asking the question "Who am I?" When asked who you are, there might be a hesitation as to what to answer; but when asked if you exist, there is no such doubt. The answer is a resounding, "Yes, of course I exist." When the answer to the first question is as clear as the answer to the second question, there is understanding.

The realization is that both questions have in fact the same answer. That which is sure of its existence – the innermost certainty of I Am – is what you essentially are. In other words: I Am this knowing that knows that I Am. The Hindus say "*tat tvam asi*" (Thou Art That). In the Old Testament, God says, "I Am that I Am." This undeniable "I Am" is not you in the personal sense, but the universal Self. Ramana Maharshi called the fundamental oneness of "I Am" and the universal Self "I-I."

Watching from this understanding, I see how thoughts appear in "my" awareness like clouds in a clear sky and then, without a trace, dissolve back in to it. There's even no need to proclaim that thoughts appear in my awareness. In Awareness suffices. Thoughts and everything else simply happen. Everything is, without a "me" orchestrating it from behind the scenes. The ego is as non-essential to thinking or to the general functioning of the body-mind organism as Atlas is to supporting the heavens. Just as the ancient Greeks at some point realized that, in fact, there never was a titan named Atlas supporting the firmament, you can realize there never was an actual ego supporting the absolute certainty of "I Am." (Ref. 22)

Summary

- Advaita uses various methods (*prakriyA*-s) to analyze topics about which we have mistaken beliefs in order to reveal our errors and to demonstrate that there is only Brahman.
- The method of discriminating between who we are (the seer) and what we are not (the seen – body, mind etc.) is called *dRRig-dRRiSya-viveka*.

- Who we really are – Brahman – is beyond description and immaculate.
- The body is nothing more than the food we have eaten, yet we worry about its comfort, aging and death.
- Consciousness is not an epiphenomenon of the mind. Everything "appears" in Consciousness.
- We do not "think" thoughts – they arise and we witness them.
- The mind assumes the power of Consciousness in the way that an iron ball in the fire becomes hot.
- Attachment to emotions occurs similarly and we must cultivate dispassion (*vairAgya*). Peace is beyond all emotions.
- The ego is a construction of concepts and its power is destroyed once the truth is understood. This is the basis of "Self-enquiry."
- *ahaMkAra* is the process by which we identify with ideas, emotions, roles etc. All disappear in sleep so we cannot be them.
- Neither are we the mask of a "person." We are the changeless "I am," the essence of the changing forms.
- The sheath model (*pa~ncha-kosha-prakriyA*) is used to illustrate the various levels of identification.
- The true Self has nothing to do with the body and mind etc, just as the moon has nothing to do with the bough of the tree on which it appears to rest.
- We are constantly lured by the form and miss the essence.
- Everything transient is first rejected (*neti, neti*) in order to discover who we truly are, the eternal unchanging. It is then realized that the changing, too, is none other than the non-dual Self.
- Just as dreams are seen to have been nothing but the mind itself on awakening, so the world is seen to be the Self on enlightenment.
- If it can be spoken of, I am not that. Truth is beyond language, which is necessarily in duality. I am the eternal subject. Reality is self-evident.

2. ACTION, KARMA AND FREE WILL

This chapter will look at the belief that we are a doer, thinker, feeler, chooser etc. These beliefs arise from identification with the intellectual sheath in the model of the five *kosha*-s. In fact, there is no active principle involved. In traditional Advaita, it is simply movement of the "qualities" (*guNa*) of nature.

The theory of *karma* states that actions have consequences either in this or later lives through the medium of *saMskAra*. While we believe ourselves to be individuals, such beliefs remain valid. In reality, since we are not the body or mind, we cannot be born or reincarnate. *karma* can be better thought of as the creative urge by which reality takes on new forms.

The apparent conflict between fate and free will is discussed. At the phenomenal level, we have acquired tendencies - *vAsanA*-s - as a result of past actions and conditioning. These act as the "river current" against which we must strive using the "motor" of self-effort. Again, the concept of free will is valid in the phenomenal realm. In reality, the Self is free but there is no one to act.

As ever, in the philosophy of Advaita, the teaching is graded to suit the level of understanding of the student - and it is no use trying to "jump levels" if we have not yet grasped the lower level principles. To do so is liable to result in confusion, a sense of failure or worse. This particularly applies to the exclusive concentration by some teachers on the concept of "non-doership." All levels of identification must be transcended and this should be done in a controlled and stepwise manner that has been validated through millennia of teaching. Attractive though it might seem, it is not possible to jump straight to the end.

Belief that we are a "doer"

In the first chapter, we started to look at who we are not. It was argued that we are not the body, mind or ego. The *prakriyA* of the five *kosha*-s or sheaths illustrated the various levels of misidentification that take place and effectively cover over who we really are. Thus, we think we are the body by identifying with the sheath made of food, the *annamayakosha*. We think we are the vital essence in the body by identifying with the sheath made of breath, the *prANamayakosha*. And we think we are the mind by identifying with the mental sheath consisting of the thinking mind and the organs of perception, the *manomayakosha*.

If we identify with the next sheath, the intellectual sheath or *vij~nAnamayakosha*, we think we are able to judge and discriminate or, more generally, we believe we are a "doer." The Sanskrit word for this is *kartRRi*, meaning "one who makes or does or acts or effects; the agent of an action." This "doing" also includes all of the other actions, such as knowing, seeing, hearing etc. The senses and mind are simply instruments for all of these.

Being able to "do" is something that we ordinarily take for granted and most people would undoubtedly regard the very questioning of this as absurd. **Jock Millensen** is someone who wondered why it was that he called his body-mind organism "I" or "me" but the chair on the other side of the room "not me." He writes:

Gradually the answer to my question began to emerge. As I sit here and write this, a hand moves and words are appearing on the page. I have the definite sense that "I" am writing them. And yet, in truth, they are simply being written and being watched in the same way that, as I look out my window, cars are passing by. The words get written through the complex machinery of an immensely complicated psychophysical computer, and in fact that same machinery could also stand up and go across the room and move the chair. Why, therefore, is the chair any less me than this arm that moved it? The mediation of the movements is different in details, but not in principle. It was only when I supposed that there was an "I" who had the will to move things and do things independently of the conditioning and genetic hardware of this psychophysical instrument that I was inclined to call one "me" and the other, "other." (Ref. 115)

If we return briefly to the identification with the mind, in the *manomayakosha*, we believe we are a "thinker" but, as **Robert Powell** points out, this notion only comes in *after* the thought:

> Most of us think there is a thinker who produces his thoughts; that is the conventional wisdom. But if you examine it more closely, you will find it is the other way around. There is the thought and immediately thereafter another phenomenon takes place. A "thinker" comes in who reacts with the original thought. Now the interesting thing is that that "thinker" is only another thought, or, more accurately, is made up of thoughts and memories and is therefore not truly "personal." In other words, the thinker as such does not actually exist but is a concept that has been accepted through lack of examination; it is the image one has of oneself. (Ref. 116)

And so it is in respect of our belief that we are a doer. Actions no doubt take place - after all it would be ridiculous to deny that we witness them – but what actually happens is that we (i.e. the ego) simply claim responsibility for them. **Atmananda Krishna Menon** says that:

> When you look at it minutely, you will find he was not there. The doer was not there; the thinker was not there; the perceiver was not there; the enjoyer was not there; the sufferer was not there; but it is all the Background itself. (Ref. 117)

And **Jean Klein**:

> When you act, you are one with the action, it is only afterwards that the ego appropriates the act from which it was absent and says "I have done this." At the moment of acting there is only acting, without an actor. (Ref. 19)

Much more will be said about this "background" later! Meanwhile, if we are convinced by what was said in the last chapter, then we have already accepted that we are not the body. This being the case, then it surely follows that we are not the doer. Who we really are does not "run" – it is the body, specifically the legs, that runs, powered by the heart and lungs etc. We do not "speak" – this is performed by the pharynx and the mouth, triggered by the relevant part of the brain. And all of the other innumerable activities are clearly being carried out by various parts of the body, while we merely observe. **Catherine Ingram** made the following observations in response to questions from **Paula Marvelly**:

Catherine: When people say that there's no doing, it's because there's not a "you" there to do it. It's like watching these trees blowing here outside the window in the wind. The wind is moving for some conditioned causes, the leaves are blowing for the conditioned cause of the wind passing through them. There's nothing personal about it. And yet, it happens!

Paula: I can see that in the external world, particularly in nature. I can even see that with events in my life - you can never know what's round the corner. But with the mental plane, because it's so close to you, it's right inside…

Catherine: Right. You take it much more personally. But it's as impersonal as, well, I often say, "You're not growing your hair. You're not growing your bones." And in the same way, you are not thinking your thoughts. For the simple reason that the one, the "you" who's the controller, the boss, the manifester, is just an idea - just another idea. So, there's this flow of phenomena, this flow of thoughts. Digestion is going on, hair is growing, wind is blowing through the trees, thoughts are flowing. And there's an interest arising in something called the spiritual life. It's very impersonal and at some point even the idea of the spiritual life falls away and there is only *this*. And everything, as I've been saying this week, just becomes normalized in its own extraordinary ordinariness. (Ref. 78)

The aim is to realize that who we really are is Consciousness, witnessing the activities and that in fact "we" do nothing, as **Hans Laurentius** explains:

The nice thing is that to the extent that you identify with Consciousness, you just see things happening while prior to that you had the feeling that they overcame you and that you did something. And so you can arrive to the point of saying what many Realized ones have said: "I do nothing," even to what seems to ordinary people an absurd level. Nisargadatta, one of my favorite gurus smoked like a chimney, and if someone called him on it, he looked surprised and said: "I don't have the impression that I smoke."

And naturally not, the smoking is something that is witnessed, and I am the observing. Thus, how can there be the capacity to observe smoking? Impossible. Only a thing can smoke and that is just what you are not. There is no doer. Things happen. Nisargadatta makes it here clear that he does not experience himself as a thing, as a person, but as consciousness. And that is also what I always try to propound. You are not a thing. I am not a thing. Thus, whatever you see this thing doing, I am not that. We identify with the behavior of the apparatus. But that behavior is nothing but movement in consciousness. You witness it. (Ref. 128)

These ideas can often seem somewhat bizarre at first sight so that the best thing to do is simply to see for yourself the truth of them in your own supposed activities. The example that I often use is one of making a cup of coffee (or tea if you prefer):

Have you ever watched yourself doing something, for example making a cup of coffee? If not, get up and do it now – I know you'd like one! Don't interfere; just watch it happening. Legs walking, arm raising, hand moving etc. Incredible complexity even at this level but below that impulses moving along nerves, blood vessels contracting muscles and below that synapses triggering in the brain and below that enzymes and proteins interacting etc. Are "you" *doing* any of this? Would you indeed have the slightest idea of where to begin?

You are the observer of all of this (well, some of it anyway!), which, in a very real sense, just "happens." You, the Self, *do* nothing. Without the petrol, the car can do nothing but in no sense could the petrol be said to be acting. In an analogous manner, no-*body* can act without the support of the Self – it is after all just a lump of food - but the Self does not act. The Self will support the actions of a murderer just as much as those of a doctor in the same way as the petrol will enable both tank and ambulance to perform their respective functions. You are simply the equivalent of the petrol in the car - without it the car cannot move but the petrol is in no real sense responsible for how the car behaves. This is determined by the nature of the car - whether it is a tuned racing car or a rusty heap. (Ref. 84)

Nature of Action

If we are not the mind, then it follows that we cannot be the "thinker" or the "perceiver." All of these actions apparently occur but I am merely, somehow, the witness of them and do not in any sense "do" them. I am the awareness in which these activities take place but do not actually participate in them. In fact, I am the still center around which the world forever whirls, as T. S. Eliot has put it. And this is the meaning of one of the more obscure verses from the Bhagavad Gita:

> *He who sees inaction in action, and action in inaction, he is wise among men, he is a yogi and accomplisher of everything.* **IV.18**

Swami Chidbhavananda explains Shankara's understanding of this verse: Action is innate in *prakRRiti* and inaction in *Atman*. The former is kinetic and the latter static; one is the becoming and the other the Being;

one is the perishable and the other the Imperishable. The ignorant are confused being unable to distinguish between the two. A passenger in a running train mistakes the nearby trees as running in the opposite direction. Here motion is attributed wrongly to the motionless. Action is seen in inaction due to ignorance. A man on the shore mistakes a sailing ship at a distance in the sea as one that stands still. Here inaction is seen in action.

Thus it is seen that actions and inactions in nature do not always present themselves in their true perspective. The characteristics of the one are often imposed on the other due to ignorance. The ignorant man thinks of himself as the body. "Now I work; now I rest" - thus does he transpose the function of *prakRRiti* on *Atman*. Mistaking the non-Self for Self is egoism. There is agency in the egoistic man. The agency-laden egoistic man may be sitting quiet abandoning all his duties. Even in that inert state he is verily a doer of *karma*. This ignorant condition is designated as action in inaction.

In contrast with this, there is no trace of egoism in the man of Self-realization. While his body works incessantly, the Self remains as a witness. *Atman* is in nowise entangled in *karma*. The sense of overwork, under-work or neglect of duty is not in the knower of the Self. This supreme position is recognized as inaction in action. Only they who have attained Self-knowledge and they who are on the right path to Self-knowledge can be in this benign State. (Ref. 118)

prakRRiti and the guNa

There are several Sanskrit terms that require further explanation here: *prakRRiti, guNa* and *karma. prakRRiti* is usually translated as "nature." In *sAMkhya* philosophy, it refers to the entire material world and is contrasted with *puruSha*, the "spirit" but the word is also used in Advaita. Here, it means much the same, though strictly within the realm of the phenomenal appearance, i.e. inherent in *mAyA*. (Advaita is a non-dual philosophy whereas *sAMkhya* is not.) *prakRRiti* is said to consist of three "qualities" or *guNa*.

A significant part of the Bhagavad Gita is concerned with this topic and an understanding of the *guNa*-s can be very useful for explaining aspects of everyday life such as the state of one's own being or that of a crowd or nation. There are no equivalent concepts in western philosophy so this is another example where the use of the Sanskrit terms is essential. **Swami Muni Narayana Prasad** explains:

> Each form emerging from the one Self has within it the creative urge, *karma*, that caused its emergence. It is the functioning of the three *guNa*-s (*triguNa*-s), the modalities inherent in *prakRRiti* (Nature), which brings about the distinct qualities and characteristics differentiating one entity from another... The *guNa*-s are *sattva, rajas,* and *tamas...*
>
> These qualities of Nature (*guNa*-s) condition both the physical and mental aspects of everything in the world. *sattva* characterizes the pure, bright aspects of manifest existence. It can, however, exert a binding influence by causing an attachment to feelings of well-being and pleasurable aspects of life. *rajas*, the activating force in Nature, creates strong and intense desires in living beings, binding them to their actions. *tamas* is the dark and inert modality. It shrouds wisdom, causes delusion and lassitude, and creates bonds of illusion. The *guNa*-s are reflected in and give shape to life at every moment. They dictate one's character, values, interests and even preferences for food. (Ref. 101)

Thus, it is another aspect of the identification that takes us away from the realization of our true nature. In modern western society, *rajas* dominates and we are forever "doing"; wanting this and that and working all hours to earn money to buy them. *tamas* rules the lives of the depressed, the alcoholic or the simply lazy, unable to summon the energy to drag themselves out of their inertia. The artist or musician may be attached to beauty through sight or sound and even the monk may be effectively bound through his life of stillness and peace. Here the dominant *guNa* is *sattva*.

Sri Ramakrishna had a story that illustrates how the *guNa*-s function:

Under the spell of God's *mAyA* man forgets his true nature. He forgets that he is heir to the infinite glories of his Father. This divine *mAyA* is made up of three *guNa*-s. And all three are robbers; for they rob man of all his treasures and make him forget his true nature. The three *guNa*-s are *sattva*, *rajas*, and *tamas*. Of these, *sattva* alone points the way to God. But even *sattva* cannot take a man to God.

Let me tell you a story. Once a rich man was passing through a forest, when three robbers surrounded him and robbed him of everything he had. Then one of the robbers said: "What's the good of keeping the man alive? Kill him." He was about to strike their victim with his sword, when the second robber intervened and said: "There's no use in killing him. Let us bind him fast and leave him here. Then he won't be able to tell the police." Accordingly the robbers tied him with a rope and went away.

After a while the third robber returned to the rich man and said: "Ah! You're badly hurt, aren't you? Come, I'm going to release you." The robber set the man free and led him out of the forest. When they came near the highway, the robber said, "Follow this road and you will reach home easily."

"But you must come with me too," said the man. "You have done so much for me. All my people will be happy to see you."

"No," said the robber, "it is not possible for me to go there. The police will arrest me." So saying, he left the rich man after pointing out his way.

Now, the first robber, who said: "What's the good of keeping the man alive? Kill him," is *tamas*. It destroys. The second robber is *rajas*, which binds a man to the world and entangles him in a variety of activities. *rajas* makes him forget God. *sattva* alone shows the way to God. It produces virtues like compassion, righteousness, and devotion. Again, *sattva* is like the last step of the stairs. Next to it is the roof. The Supreme Brahman is man's own abode. One cannot attain the Knowledge of Brahman unless one transcends the three *guNa*-s. (Ref. 120)

Karma

The principle of *karma* is key to all of the subjects of this chapter. The basic noun *karman* can mean variously: act, action, rite, work, result. **Swami Nikhilananda** has a good summary definition in a footnote in one of his books:

> The word *karma* is used in Vedanta in more senses than one. *karma* primarily means "action." It also signifies the destiny forged by one in one's past incarnation or present: the store of tendencies, impulses, characteristics and habits, which determine one's future embodiment and environment. Another meaning of *karma,* often used in reference to one's caste or position in life, is ritual, the course of conduct, which one ought to follow in pursuance of the tendencies acquired in the past, with a view to work them out. (Ref. 35)

In his book "Advaita Vedanta - A Philosophical Reconstruction" (Ref. 82), **Eliot Deutsch** argues that the existence of *karma* cannot be demonstrated by any of the traditional means of knowledge (*pramANa-s* – see chapter 4 on Knowledge and Ignorance). He says that its use in the teaching of Advaita is really just a "convenient fiction." In the summary to this chapter, I will be agreeing with Swami Muni Narayana Prasad that *karma* does not really apply at the level of the individual at all but only at the universal level. For the time being, however, in order to understand the other topics in this chapter, it will be necessary to go along with it provisionally!

The basic idea is that when one performs any action with a particular result in mind, there is an unavoidable consequence for that person's subtle being. It is summed up by this interpretation from IV.4.v of the *bRRihadAraNyaka upaniShad* from **Alan Jacobs**:

> Now as a man or woman
> Is like this or like that,
> As he or she acts and behaves,
> So will he or she be.

A man or woman of good deeds
Becomes good,
A man or woman of bad deeds
Becomes bad.
He or she becomes pure
By pure acts,
Impure by impure acts.
A person consists of desires
And as his or her desire so is
His or her Will,
And as his or her Will, so his or her deed.
What deed he or she does
So he or she shall reap. (Ref. 121)

This ego-originated sense of being the doer of actions is the cause of so many of our problems because of its corollary of wanting to benefit from the results of those actions. A large part of the **Gita** is concerned with discussing all aspects of this process. It explains that it is the "qualities" in Nature that act – the *guNa* – and not man himself:

> *Action is the product of the Qualities inherent in Nature. It is only the ignorant man who, misled by personal egotism, says: "I am the doer."*
> **III.27** (Ref. 119)

A number of other terms are used in connection with the idea of *karma* and there is often confusion amongst them. Karma itself really refers to the theory or principle, which states that our actions have consequences for us in the future unless they are performed in a completely dispassionate manner. We tend to act in habitual ways according to our upbringing, education etc. or, more particularly, depending upon how we have behaved in the past. These "tendencies" to behave in certain ways are called *vAsanA*-s in Sanskrit. In more detail, these tendencies are brought about by actual impressions in the mind. These "impressions" are called *saMskAra* and there are three types, as will be discussed below. Thus, pedantically, *saMskAra* bring about particular *vAsanA*-s, which in turn influence us to act. Karma is the theory to explain all of this. Unfortunately, you can find explanations that mix up these three terms and use any one in place of any other.

vAsanA-s

Swami Chinmayananda explains the mechanism of *vAsanA*-s:

> We had explained earlier how spiritual ignorance expresses itself at the intellectual level as desires, which again, in the mental zone, manifests as thoughts, and the very thoughts, coloured by our mental tendencies, manifest themselves, in their fulfilment in the outer world-of-objects, as our actions. Thus, the tendencies of the mind (*vAsanA*-s) express in the outer world as actions. Where there are noble-thoughts, there, noble-actions manifest. When the thoughts are agitated, the actions also are uncertain, faltering, and confused. And where the thoughts are dull and animalistic, the actions generated from them are also correspondingly base, vicious, and cruel. Thus, the mind's projections in the outer-world are in fact a kind of crystallisation of the mental *vAsanA* among the objects of the world and these constitute the "actions."
>
> Where there is a mind, there actions also must be performed. These actions are therefore *generated* by the mind, *strengthened* in the mind and ultimately *performed* with the mind. But the individual, due to his wrong identification with his own mind, gets the false notion that he himself is the "actor" - the "doer." This action-arrogating-ego naturally starts feeling an anxiety for its success and a burning attachment for the result of its actions. [†] (Ref. 122)

We are not always aware of the motivating factors behind our actions. The

---

[†] The Holy Geeta, Swami Chinmayananda, © Central Chinmaya Mission Trust, Mumbai.

theory of *karma* tells us that actions and ways of behaving in the past will generate habitual ways of reacting to new events – and the key word here is "re-acting." If we have, for some reason, developed a phobia in respect of spiders, we will jump and find our heart racing as soon as we encounter one, without any conscious input to the situation.

The root of the word *vAsanA* is *vAs*, meaning "to perfume or make fragrant." **Swami Parthasarathy** suggests in Ref. 123 that the Hindu ritual of burning camphor in a temple is symbolic of cleansing the mind of its *vAsanA*-s. He explains that the idol of the God is worshipped in an inner room, surrounded by three outer ones through which the devotee must first pass, representing the *Atman* "covered over" by body, mind and intellect. The *Atman* is initially not known to us, just as the idol is kept in the dark. A priest then ignites a piece of camphor so as to illuminate the scene. The camphor represents the *vAsanA*-s. It burns completely, leaving no residue, simply a fragrance. The light created enables one to see the idol just as the teacher provides the knowledge to burn up the *vAsanA*-s and enable us to realize the Self.

> *Our actions are always re-actions to what happened in the past and therefore there is no freedom.* **Robert Powell** (Ref. 116)

Modern scientific investigations into what goes on in the brain when actions take place suggest that there are two neural pathways involved. One of these – the faster of the two – is the one that actually causes muscles to act, limbs to move and so on. The other is the one that connects to the part of the brain responsible for awareness of what is taking place. This second pathway does not need to be so fast, evolutionarily speaking. It is clearly important for the organism to react to dangerous situations as quickly as possible. If it doesn't, natural selection will soon see to it that the species does not survive.

It can be understood that some such mechanism must be involved in, for example, returning a fast serve in tennis. There is simply insufficient time to see the serve coming, decide how to return it and then instruct the appropriate muscles. By the time that all this processing had taken place, the point would have been lost.

So what is actually happening in all cases is that a reaction takes place according to previous conditioning and learnt responses, i.e. mechanical neural pathways in the brain. After the event, the other pathway completes and we become perceptually aware of what has happened. The ego then claims that it initiated the action. The "previous conditioning and learnt responses" are the *vAsanA*-s. These actions are simply movements of the *guNa* in *prakRRiti* and all that we actually "do" is witness what is happening. It is the attachment to the results and the assumption of the existence of an actual responsible individual that cause the problems.

It is Consciousness, the Self or Atman that "enables" all of the actions to take place – the innate response of the organism, the awareness of the event and the identification with the idea of agency. But the distinction must be carefully made between Consciousness and "being conscious of." The latter is merely synonymous with the second action above – becoming aware of the event. In a dangerous situation, such as coming round a corner and encountering a poisonous snake, Consciousness gets the body out of danger long before it enables us to become conscious of that danger. And in none of these situations are we ever a "doer."

Ramana Maharshi used the example of someone journeying to the ashram:

> Why do you think you are active? Take the case of your coming here. You left home in a cart, took your seat in a train, alighted at the (Tiruvannamalai) station, again got into a cart and found yourself here. When asked, you say that *you* came here from your town. Is it true? As a matter of fact you remained as you were; only the conveyances moved; just as these movements are taken as yours, so also are the other activities. They are not yours; they are God's activities. (Ref. 39)

When I say that "I" travelled, the "I" is the ego claiming itself to be the instigator of the actions but this is a mistake. The body itself is inert and it is just the movement of the *guNa* that is taking place. I do nothing.

Atmananda Krishna Menon explains:

> Examine any activity. There seem to be two "I"s, functioning simultaneously: the ego or apparent "I" as the doer, and the "I" -principle or real "I" as the knower. The former is ever-changing and the latter is never-changing. Therefore I am always the knower and never the doer. Thus there is no doer or subject, and there is only action without an actor.
>
> The real "I"-principle is present in all action. You believe that an actor or subject is indispensable for every action; therefore you conclude that the "I"-principle is acting. Really, the "I"-principle is not concerned with the acting at all. Thus you are no doer, enjoyer or perceiver, but only the knower. (Note 1187 Ref. 13)

Karmaphala – the fruit of action

The idea behind *karma* is simply one of cause and effect. If we throw a pebble into a still pond, the ripples will spread out inexorably from the point of impact. Once we have pulled the trigger of a gun, the bullet will follow the laws of motion to its destination and there is nothing we can do to prevent it. The mechanism of *karma* is that as a consequence of action, in the case where there is a desire for a particular result, the person acquires merit or demerit. If the action is unselfish, wishing to bring about a favourable result for another, then it accrues what is called *puNya*, meaning "auspicious, meritorious, virtuous." Conversely, if the action was performed with a selfish result in mind or wishing ill to another, it accrues *pApa*, meaning "bad, evil, misfortune or sin." These results are called *karmaphala* – the "fruit of action."

The doctrine is that, if you carry out an evil act, you will incur bad *karma*, which will rebound upon you at some time in the future, in a straightforward cause-effect manner. It need not necessarily happen in this lifetime either, since it is part of the belief that the effects carry over across future embodiments until such time as they are worked out or nullified. Reincarnation is an integral part of the creed so as to ensure that the consequential reward or punishment will be received.

saMskAra

Swami Vivekananda explains the traditional understanding:

Each work we do, each thought we think, produces an impression, called in Sanskrit *saMskAra*, upon the mind, and the sum total of these impressions becomes the tremendous force which is called "character." The character of a man is what he has created for himself; it is the result of the mental and physical actions that he has done in his life. The sum total of the *saMskAra*-s is the force which gives a man the next direction after death. A man dies; the body falls away and goes back to the elements; but the *saMskAra*-s remain, adhering to the mind which, being made of fine material, does not dissolve, because the finer the material, the more persistent it is. But the mind also dissolves in the long run, and that is what we are struggling for.

In this connection, the best illustration that comes to my mind is that of the whirlwind. Different currents of air coming from different directions meet and at the meeting-point become united and go on rotating; as they rotate, they form a body of dust, drawing in bits of paper, straw, etc., at one place, only to drop them and go on to another, and so go on rotating, raising and forming bodies out of the materials which are before them. Even so the forces, called *prANa* in Sanskrit, come together and form the body and the mind out of matter, and move on until the body falls down, when they raise other materials, to make another body, and when this falls, another rises, and thus the process goes on. Force cannot travel without matter. So when the body falls down, the mind-stuff remains, *prANa* in the form of *saMskAra*-s acting on it; and then it goes on to another point, raises up another whirl from fresh materials, and begins another motion; and so it travels from place to place until the force is all spent; and then it falls down, ended. So when the mind will end, be broken to pieces entirely, without leaving any *saMskAra*, we shall be entirely free, and until that time we are in bondage... (Ref. 124)

The word *saMskAra* means "the impression on the mind of acts done in a former state of existence" and would appear at first sight to be synonymous with *karma*. The two words are used interchangeably by many writers, though the latter is more common. The word *saMskAra* also has the meaning "making perfect, purifying, cleansing" and has more positive connotations than the somewhat doom-laden overtones of *karma*.

There are actually three types of *saMskAra*. *saMchita saMskAra* is the sum total of *saMskAra* accumulated from all of the actions performed in the past (including past lives). The literal meaning of *saMchita* is "collected or piled up." Some of that *saMskAra* is maturing now in this body – this is called *prArabdha saMskAra*, meaning "begun or undertaken." This manifests in the form of new experiences. In fact, the traditional belief is that we are given this specific body in this particular time and place in order that this *saMskAra* may be fulfilled. If they are met in the right way, the *saMskAra*-s are nullified. (This will be dealt with when *karma yoga* is discussed in chapter 5 on spiritual paths but briefly, it means acting without any desire for a particular result.) Whenever we act inappropriately in the present, whether selfishly or not, the third type of *saMskAra* results - *AgAmin*, which is *saMskAra* destined to mature at some time in the future.

Upon Self-realization, with the total understanding that one is not the doer, all of the *saMchita saMskAra* is destroyed and future actions incur no more *AgAmin saMskAra*. The *prArabdha saMskAra*, however, is said (by some teachers) to continue because they are associated with the body, which is an objective part of creation. I.e. it belongs to *Ishvara* and not to the *jIva* (*Ishvara* will be discussed in chapter 7 on Reality in connection with creation). This is why the realized man still appears to continue as before with the same idiosyncrasies, likes and dislikes (though there is no longer attachment to any of these).

In fact, there are three varieties of *prArabdha saMskAra* and two of these could be said to still apply to the realized man according to **Ramana Maharshi**:

prArabdha karma [i.e. *saMskAra*] is of three categories, *ichChA*, *anichChA* and *parechChA* [personally desired, without desire and due to others' desire]. For the one who has realized the Self, there is no *ichChA prArabdha* but the two others, *anichChA* and *parechChA*, remain. Whatever a *j~nAnI* [Self-realized man] does is for others only. If there are things to be done by him for others, he does them but the results do not affect him. Whatever be the actions that such people do, there is no *puNya* and no *pApa* attached to them. But they do only what is proper according to the accepted standard of the world – nothing else. (Ref. 173)

It should be noted, however, that elsewhere he does state that there is no further *saMskAra*, once realized:

But the truth is the *j~nAnI* has transcended all *karma*-s, including the *prArabdha karma* and he is not bound by the body or its *karma*-s. (Ref. 174)

D. B. Gangolli, in Ref. 292, points out that the realized man no longer believes himself to be a doer or an enjoyer. He suggests that both are essential in order for the *saMskAra* to "germinate," since they are effectively the water and fertilizer. There is therefore neither fruit of past action nor seeds being sown for future *karma*. There can also be no attachment to results when one knows that there is only the Self.

This illustrates that the truth of reality cannot be expressed at all. The way that things appear at the level of the phenomenal world is related to the state of the mind that perceives them and the sage aims to address the listener according to his level of understanding.

Death and reincarnation

Every body dies; nobody dies. **Swami Chinmayananda**

First find your true nature in the present moment. Then see how much you still care about what happens after the physical body expires. **Philip T. Mistlberger** (Ref. 134)

It is the idea of death, more than anything else, which motivates the apparent person in their ignorance. Identified with body and mind, we cannot conceive how death can mean anything other than the extinction of who we are. Thus it is that so many people journey through life attempting the impossible – trying to establish some spurious immortality. If they do not have the skill or knowledge to produce a work of art, an invention or book, they may strive to ensure that they somehow "live on" through their children. They may even commit an act of murder or terrorism to achieve posthumous notoriety. This is a grave error (pun partially intended), as **Gangaji** explains:

> The way that death and fear of death are usually seen in our culture is a clear indication of deep misalignment with truth. Because of our conditioning, physical death is seen as the problem. In actuality, facing the reality of the death of personal identity is an immense opportunity to directly encounter eternal, undying presence.
>
> There is a strong, conditioned belief that you are a psychological entity located in a body. In truth, there is no real psychological entity except as an image or a thought coupled with physical sensation.
>
> When fear of death is directly investigated, it is discovered that only form is born and dies. Consciousness is free of formation, free of birth, free of death. (Ref. 131, extract quoted in Ref. 78)

This view is echoed by **Jean Klein**:

> What you understand by death is really nothing other than a pointer to silence, to life itself. Death has no reality. But if you don't see it in this way, it remains a stagnant idea in which you are trapped. As long as you take yourself for an independent entity you are submitted to *karma*. Let us put it another way: before speaking of death, ask yourself "What is

life?" All perception is, only because you are eternal present beingness. This is the background to waking, dreams, and deep sleep. In living knowledge, in this presentness, the problem of death has no meaning. (Ref. 132, extract quoted in Ref. 63)

Nevertheless, most of us are identified with the body-mind and it is for them that the notion of *karma* and reincarnation is valid. The process is governed by the law of *karma* and this depends upon the desires that motivate us. Basically, any action that is carried out with a specific desire or intention generates *saMskAra*-s and, if unresolved in this lifetime, the traditional belief is that they will cause rebirth, as **Swami Krishnananda** explains:

Any thought which is connected with an object other than yourself, with a motive behind it, or an intention behind it, will produce a reaction. I am looking at the wall. I am thinking of the wall. It won't produce any reaction, because I'm not looking at it with any motive or intention. It is just there, visible. There are two ways of seeing things. One is the general perception of things, like when you walk, you see a tree, or a building; you are not concerned with it. Another is a thought which is connected with objects with a purpose, intention, or motive, with a like or dislike - to get something from it, or to avoid it. Such thoughts will produce a reaction. That reaction is called *karma*... That kind of *karma* is what causes rebirth. (Ref. 126)

In answer to a question as to how the soul is caused to reincarnate if *karma* only affects the body-mind-intellect (BMI), **Professor V. Krishnamurthy** replied as follows:

This is the subtlest point in Hindu philosophy. You said that the *karma* affects the BMI. But do you know that body, mind and intellect - all three of them - are inert? You will certainly accept that body is inert. The body cannot act by itself. There is a life-force within to make it act. But that is also true of the mind and intellect. They cannot act without the life-force behind it. This life-force is the spiritual spark said to be "within," but actually pervading the entire body, mind and intellect.

When this spiritual spark is thus pervading the BMI, we call it the *jIva*. The English usage is the word "soul" which is only an apology for a translation. Now we have to consider the body as distinct from the mind and intellect. For the purpose of this discussion we may safely put the mind and intellect together and talk only of the mind. When the body meets with its death, the mind does not die. It clings to the *jIva* which leaves the body.

In due time, the *jIva* goes to another body. The mind of the earlier birth also goes along, but not as the same mind with all its memories. The memories die with the brain. But the imprints of all the memories and of the actions remain in the mind as *vAsanA*-s [pedantically *saMskAra*-s] and they go along with the *jIva* to the other body. So in the new incarnation the *jIva* has a new body, but the mind in it now has the same stamp as was brought about by the tendencies that it had developed when it left the previous body.

Therefore all *karma* that was done in the previous birth by that BMI has a consequence in the next birth also because the mind, in the above sense, is the same. A *jIva* cannot express itself without a mind or body. And a mind cannot express itself because it is inert. It is the mind that does everything (in the presence of the life-force which the *jIva* gives it) and it is the mind that gets the consequences of what it does - either in the same birth or in future births. But the mind has to act and react only through a body and it is the *jIva* that carries the mind from body to body. This is the process of reincarnation. (Ref. 135)

The law of *karma* is unaffected by the death of the physical body. It impacts on what is called the subtle body, the *sUkShma sharIra* or *li~Nga sharIra*, as opposed to the gross or physical body, *sthUla sharIra*. (The causal body, *kAraNa sharIra*, is *mAyA*, where the three *guNa*-s are in their unmanifest state.) Obviously the physical body which, as we saw earlier is only food, returns to the earth on death and could not itself be reincarnated by any stretch of the imagination. The subtle body, however, accumulates *puNya* and *papa*, which are held in the form of *saMchita saMskAra* for a future embodiment. The word *li~Nga* also means a "mark, sign, badge or evidence." If it is present, it is evidence that the physical body is alive. It is the subtle body that forms the *upAdhi*, or limiting adjunct for *Atman*. It is also through the subtle body that we experience the dream state, in which we are unaware of our physical body.

[The word *upAdhi* derives from *upa* (as in *upaniShad*), meaning "near to or by the side of," and *AdhadAti*, meaning "imparts." The idea is that something external appears to limit us, from the standpoint of an observer, but doesn't really affect us at all. (Ref. 335)]

Death is an occurrence by which all the specific attributes of an individual disappear. It is not a process of becoming nothing. What really exists cannot become non-existent. **Swami Muni Narayana Prasad** (Ref. 130)

It is said then, that the *sUkShma sharIra* leaves the physical body on death and eventually is reborn in a suitable new one in which the *saMchita saMskAra* can be activated. The new body is provided by god (*Ishvara*) in accordance with the merit and demerit gained from action in the previous lives. Such things as country of birth, parents, genetic defects etc, are all chosen so as to be optimally conducive to fulfilling the *saMchita saMskAra*.

A reviewer commented on this by suggesting that it did not seem very just that "my" bad *karma* should be inflicted upon a new (innocent) body-mind. This is confusing several factors. The *karma* is associated with the subtle body (mind) of the *jIva* and it is this that reincarnates (in the context of the theory). The gross physical body is an inert lump of food unless it has the power of Consciousness to enliven it. Finally, who we actually are is not the body in any form, gross, subtle or causal. We are That in which all of these bodies seem to arise. Answers to other questions that may arise in relation to this must await the discussion of *Ishvara* in chapter 7.

Those whose conduct during the previous life has been good presently obtain good birth, such as the birth of a brAhmaNa, a kShatriya, or a vaishya; those whose conduct has been bad presently obtain some evil birth such as that of a dog or a Pig. **Chandogya Upanishad** V 107.

Most modern teachers do not follow such traditional views regarding the carrying over of one's *karmaphala* into a future life. To the extent that reincarnation has any meaning at all, they prefer a much freer interpretation. **Wayne Liquorman** (Ref. 133) has a helpful metaphor to explain how this works. He imagines the non-dual Consciousness as a vast lump of clay. If small bits of this are extruded from the surface, whilst remaining joined on to and still part of the whole, each bit can be imagined to be an "individual." Being born is to begin this extrusion process and dying is to have the material squashed back into the lump. They are never really separate from Consciousness or from each other - it is only their name and form that distinguishes them – but we do not see the link of Brahman in the same way that we see the link of clay in the clay model.

After their reabsorption into the lump, another form may be born with parts that previously "belonged" to others. This could include memories, for example, so that someone might have thoughts that are apparently from prior to their own life. But the point is that, if I have such a thought, it is not "my" thought but simply an impersonal arising in Consciousness, to which "I" am erroneously laying claim.

There is also a significant psychological element that is worth noting in passing. **Philip Mistlberger** points out that, in the west at least since the notion of reincarnation became popular, it is surprising how many people who claim to remember their previous life, believe that it was as someone now historically famous. This does rather make one wonder if their egos find more meaning in such a past life than they do in the present one. He goes on to provide an excellent summary of the truth and fiction regarding reincarnation:

Most new age teachings about reincarnation have been gross oversimplifications of a complex, profound, and subtle teaching. In reality, reincarnation is a paradoxical process that is both true and not true. True because due to the workings of identification and projection we are indeed capable of identifying with one, or more than one, body-minds (lifetimes). Not true because our *real nature* is, and always will be, unidentified and unattached to *any* body-mind. Our real nature has the miraculous ability to experience itself via the limitations of one body-mind, but recognizes that ultimately it is *not* the body-mind.

Another way of putting this is that our true nature does not take birth, and does not die. But through the functions of identification and projection, we are capable of "visiting" a given lifetime. We are only capable of *fully experiencing* this physical lifetime because of our spiritual amnesia, the forgetting of the natural state - pure consciousness that is beyond space, time, or bodies. (Ref. 134)

Swami Nikhilananda clarifies this distinction between the "real" and the "relative" levels of existence, the noumenal and the phenomenal as western philosophy describes it, the way things really are as opposed the way things seem to be. (The Sanskrit terms for these are *paramArtha*, the non-dual reality, and *vyavahAra*, the apparent, dualistic world. These will be discussed in detail in chapter 7.) Who we really are is the *Atman* – the "real soul" as he describes it in the following extract – while who we appear to be is the *jIva* or "apparent soul":

The *RRiShi*-s speak of two souls: the real soul and the apparent soul. The real soul is birth less, death less, immortal, and infinite. The same real soul, under the spell of ignorance, appears as the apparent man identified with the body, mind and senses. This apparent man becomes, on account of his attachment to the body, a victim of birth and death, virtue and vice, and the other pairs of opposites. The apparent man is bound to the world, and it is he, again, who strives for liberation. The enjoyment of material pleasures, and the subsequent satiation and weariness; the consciousness of bondage, and the struggle for freedom;

the injunctions of the scriptures, and the practice of moral and spiritual disciplines - all this refers to the apparent man. Again, it is the apparent man who performs virtuous or sinful deeds, goes, after death, to heaven or hell, and assumes different bodies. But it must never be forgotten that rewards and punishments are spoken of only with reference to the reflected or apparent soul. The real soul is... always free, illumined, and perfect. The real sun, non-dual and resplendent, shines brilliantly in the sky, though millions of its reflections are seen to move with the movement of the waves. (Ref. 136)

The process of *saMsAra*, then (the cycle of birth, death and transmigration which continues forever, or at least until the end of the present creation, unless we gain enlightenment) is a logical chain of cause and effect. Who we really are, the *Atman*, becomes identified with the body, mind etc. and we believe ourselves to be doers (*kartRRi*). Consequently, we become experiencers and enjoyers (*bhoktRRi*). As a result of this, we accumulate good and bad *karma* (*puNya* and *pApa*). These form the *saMskAra*-s that are carried within the subtle body and necessitate rebirth in order that they may be exhausted. Unfortunately, rather than doing this, we tend to accumulate more and the whole process continues inexorably.

Free Will

All the activities that the body performs are predetermined. The only freedom you have is to choose not to identify with the body that is performing the actions. **Sri Poonja**

From a western point of view, possibly the most important of all actions is that of choice. In order to be able to choose between alternative courses of action, we must have free will. I emphasised the "western" aspect because it is very interesting to note that there is no obvious, well-known Sanskrit term for this concept nor, therefore, any noteworthy references to it in the scriptures. The most likely contender would be *svechChA* from *sva*, meaning "ones own" and *ichChA*, meaning "desire, wish, inclination." The other contender is *svAtantrya*. *sva* again refers to oneself and *atantra* means "unrestrained" so that a literal meaning would be "independence, following ones own will."

Some definition of terms is first needed:

Free will is the presumed power possessed by an individual to act other than in the way that he/she actually does. It is the idea that we are able to choose according to our desires and moral beliefs.

Determinism states that everything that happens has prior causes. One of these causes may be our own will, so that it does not preclude the existence of free will. This is the stance that most of us actually take. We believe that actions have an effect (otherwise, the world would be anarchic) but we feel, nevertheless, that we have choice in whether we, for example, follow the dictates of our conscience.

Fatalism, on the other hand, says that what happens does so irrespective of our own will. Things happen neither because we want them nor because of any cause-effect relationship but because some power (i.e. usually God) has decreed that they should happen in that way.

Pre-destination is slightly different in that it does accept causality but believes that the cause-effect chain has been established by a supernatural power.

Our natural inclination is to claim that, of course, we do have free will. Unless we are being actively coerced by someone or circumstances do not reasonably allow for an alternative course of action, we feel that we can freely choose between all available options. But if we analyse what exactly happens when such choices are made, we may begin to have doubts. Ultimately, the data upon which we base our decisions arise from thoughts (or memories, which can be regarded as thoughts in this context). And the question that must be asked is this: can you will a particular thought? Or is it rather the case that thoughts simply arise in our minds without any sort of conscious control? And, once particular thoughts have come, is it not the sum of all of our upbringing, education and conditioning that arbitrates between the various thoughts in a mechanistic manner?

Arthur Schopenhauer expressed such a view in his prize winning essay on the freedom of will:

It is six o'clock in the evening, the working day is over. Now I can go for a walk, or I can go to the club; I can also climb up the tower to see the sun set; I can go to the theater; I can visit this friend or that one; indeed, I also can run out of the gate, into the wide world, and never return. All of this is strictly up to me, in this I have complete freedom. But still I shall do none of these things now, but with just as free a will I shall go home to my wife. Now this is exactly as if water spoke to itself: I can make high waves (during a storm), I can rush down hill (in the river bed), I can plunge down foaming and gushing (in the waterfall), I can rise freely as a stream of water into the air (in the fountain), I can, finally, boil away and disappear (if its hot enough); but I am doing none of these things now, and am voluntarily remaining quiet and clear water in the reflecting pond. As the water can do all those things only when the determining causes operate for the one or the other, so too man can do what he imagines himself able to do only on the same condition. In the case of each motive, the man thinks that he can will it and so can fix the weathervane of his will at this point, but this is sheer delusion. For this "I can will this" is in reality hypothetical - and carries with it the additional clause, if I did not prefer the other. But this addition annuls that ability to will! (Ref. 142)

It is certainly the case that it appears to the mind that choice is available and it makes sense from an evolutionary point of view for this to be the case. But clearly if we do not initiate actions voluntarily, we do not "choose" either. The illusion of choice is then simply a part of the mental reflection of the mechanics of action. **Steve Harrison** states that:

Thought always appears to have a choice. Thought's essential function is to measure and predict, to present the best possibilities for our survival. In this respect, we live in a world of choosing. But this choosing, this free will, has a mechanical quality to it, and while it may appear to be free, it is free only to roam the confines of its conceptual interpretation. (Ref. 210)

Traditional Advaita is effectively deterministic, as defined above. The law of *karma* states that our lives are as they are as a result of past action, in this life or former ones. Thus, it also acknowledges that we are able to contribute our own will to actions in the present. It claims, as noted above, that we are born with *prArabdha saMskAra*, which on the one hand accounts for the particular circumstances of our birth and, on the other, represents the impressions from the *karmaphala* of previous lives that now have to be "worked out" in this lifetime. And Advaita states that we also have *puruShArtha*, the "self-effort" that enables us to (try to) overcome the fruit of our past actions.

To this extent, we are the instrument of our own destiny. There is no God ordaining our future. We have sown and so shall we reap! It is Consciousness or God that enables all that takes place and the *guNa* that actually act but all this is in accordance with the imprint of our *saMskAra*. How we act now is determined partly by this *prArabdha saMskAra* and partly by our *puruShArtha* and how we eventually act will determine the *AgAmin saMskAra* that is subsequently added to the store for future lives. The extent to which we are limited now is determined by our behaviour in the past. We are both bound and free. **Swami Parthasarathy** (Ref. 123) uses the metaphor of a train – it is free to go anywhere... but only on the railway tracks that happen to be present.

Thus, our actions are an effective combination of our limitations due to the past – call this "destiny" – and our self-effort in the present – call this "free will." **Swami Chinmayananda** used the metaphor of a motor boat in a river. With the engine working at a given rate, the actual speed of the boat will depend upon the current in the river and the direction of the boat. It will obviously travel much more quickly downstream, with the force of the current behind it, than it will trying to battle its way upstream against a powerful flow. The basic engine speed can be compared to *puruShArtha* and the current of the river to *prArabdha* or destiny. Both operate independently but the net effect is determined by their relative strengths.

Swami Parthasarathy also has another metaphor:

A wall is painted with yellow color. There is a tin of blue paint. Take a little of blue paint and apply it on the wall. Blue mixes with yellow to form green. Those who look at the wall directly do not see blue at all. They believe you are applying green paint. But in fact you are applying only blue. Keep painting blue over and over again. Yellow gets neutralized and blue appears on the wall. Now compare blue paint to your free-will or *puruShArtha*, yellow background to your destiny or *prArabdha*. Just as blue is independent of yellow your free-will is independent of your destiny. But when you apply your free-will in the background of your destiny its effect is changed. The only way to assert your free-will is to keep on applying it. Sooner or later it neutralizes your destiny and establishes itself. (Ref. 123)

There is a dialogue impressively entitled "The Riddle of Fate and Free-Will Solved" that is often quoted in Advaita discussion groups on the Internet. This takes place between His Holiness **Shri Chandrashekhara Bharati Mahaswami**, one of the *shaMkarAchArya*-s of Sringeri Math (one of the four teaching centres traditionally established by Shankara – a *maTha* is a religious college or temple) and a disciple. The master explains:

Fate is past *karma*; free-will is present *karma*. Both are really one, that is, *karma*, though they may differ in the matter of time. There can be no conflict when they are really one.

By exercising your free-will in the past, you brought on the resultant fate. By exercising your free-will in the present, I want you to wipe out your past record if it hurts you, or to add to it if you find it enjoyable. In any case, whether for acquiring more happiness or for reducing misery, you have to exercise your free-will in the present. (Ref. 143)

He goes on to illustrate this with a useful metaphor. Suppose that there is a nail embedded in a thick wooden post. We do not know how long the nail is or the hardness of the wood so that we have no idea how much effort will be required to remove the nail. The depth of penetration will depend upon the wood and the effort that was uses to hammer it in. All of those factors occurred in the past and are now unknown to us. They correspond to our accumulated *saMskAra*-s. The effort now to remove the nail is analogous to the *puruShArtha* that must now be applied to overcome our past *karma*. But the implication is that we will eventually succeed if we keep trying.

Earlier, he talks about how *vAsanA*-s accumulate by considering how easily someone might become a thief. Initially finding it difficult to steal, perhaps knowing it to be wrong, he soon finds that such concerns no longer arise and may end up stealing even if it is not actually necessary. But, to my mind, the nail metaphor would correspond with the example of an habitual thief who is trying to reform. The implication is that the thieving tendencies are now inbuilt and that the wish to change is something that the thief suddenly wants to do. And it is further implied that he can exert self-effort freely to (try to) act contrary to his natural tendencies.

But from where would such an idea come? And wouldn't the extent to which he was able to exert this effort depend also upon his nature, i.e. upon his *vAsanA*-s? Free will implies doing something that we *want* to do as opposed to something that our conditioning forces us to do but surely what we want is *also* the result of conditioning.

There is a problem here in the implication that the *prArabdha* element is caused (by past actions) but that the *puruShArtha* is not. Although slightly out of the Advaita tradition, this is pointed out succinctly by **Alan Watts**:

It should be apparent, however, that the concept of individual free will is meaningless, since unmotivated, uncaused, spontaneous action would be something possible only for First Cause. If, then, the gift of free will to creatures means anything, it means - as every metaphysical doctrine insists - that God gives HIMSELF to creatures, so that free will is not the property of any creature in so far as he is an individual, but only in so far as the actual reality of his being, his true Self, IS God, and acts like

God. (Ref. 137)

The conflict between fate and free will seems an insoluble paradox but it must be remembered that paradoxes are by their very nature for the mind only, which is attempting to apply reason and logic. It is the mind itself that is the real problem, not the paradox. **Swami Venkatesananda** explains how the sage *vAsiShTha* attempts to resolve it:

Although the wonderful sage Vasishtha insists upon self-effort, there is always the question of freedom of choice: self-effort versus predestination, destiny, *karma*. How does Vasishtha solve this, how does he reconcile it? If you study the scripture carefully, you will be puzzled. A few chapters are devoted entirely to self-effort. Vasishtha says: "What is called God and what is called destiny is nonsense. There is nothing called destiny, self-effort is the most important thing." Then let us roll up our sleeves and fight the battle of life - Vasishtha says: "No, that is not it. What can you, a puny little human being, do? Everything is pre-determined, everything is destiny." Then you are tempted to turn around to the sage and say: "Please, make up your mind—am I free to act or am I destined to act?" And Vasishtha says: "You are destined to feel you are free, and what is called destiny is a choice which you exercised earlier on! You are free, but not free to change your color, change your shape, change your sex, change your genes. You have already exercised that choice. And so, what you call destiny is nothing but the fruition of your own free will exercised earlier on. All right, now start a new chain-reaction. Plant a seed now which will germinate in its own time, which will bring up its shoot in its own good time." Thus, these two are reconciled... (Ref. 144)

It seems that the extent to which we are able to act freely is being slowly eroded. In the context of the boat in the river metaphor discussed earlier, the current is becoming increasingly strong. With many modern teachers, that current becomes irresistible!

Destiny is usually thought of as something that is going to happen in the future. Destiny is all here-now. The script has already been written. I am playing all the characters in the movie; and I am witnessing the movie which is already done. **Nisargadatta Maharaj**

The most extreme form of this doctrine of predestination is represented by the Navnath *sampradAya* (lineage) of Nisargadatta and **Ramesh Balsekar** is one of its most forthright representatives. Here is part of an interview with him published in the magazine "What is Enlightenment?":

RB: An action happens if it is God's will for that action to happen. If it is not God's will, the action does not happen...

The only difference, as I said, is that the ordinary man thinks, "It's *my* action," whereas the sage knows it is *nobody's* action. The sage knows that "Deeds are done, events happen, but there is no individual doer." That is the *only* difference as far as I'm concerned, as far as my concept goes. The only difference between a sage and an ordinary person is that the ordinary person thinks each individual *does* what happens through that body/mind organism. So since the sage knows that there is no action which *he* does, if an action happens to hurt someone, then he will do all he can to help that person - but there will be no feelings of guilt.

WIE: *My point is that saying that everything is preprogrammed, that it's all destiny and that there's no choice seems like a very extreme form of reductionism. According to this view, human beings are like computers; everything about us is completely set.*

RB: That's precisely it, yes.

WIE: *But that seems to me to be a view that lacks a human heart. Then we're just like machines - everything's happening to us. There's nothing we can do, nothing we can change.*

RB: Yes, exactly! (Ref. 145)

And he emphasises that doing God's will is what he means by freedom:

Whatever you decide to do at any moment cannot be against God's will, you see? So your decision is God's will, what happens to the decision as an action is God's will. The results and consequences of that action are God's will, whoever may be affected by those results or consequences. That is why I say you'll never ever have to ask for God's forgiveness for any action, for it is not your action. What more freedom can you want? (Ref. 146)

Burt Harding supports this view:

When Buddha left his father's palace, it wasn't his personal choice but his destiny. When Ramana Maharshi retired to the mountain Arunachala at 17 it wasn't his personal choice but his destiny. When men achieve their cherished goals it is their destiny. Mother Theresa did not decide to help the poor in India, it was her destiny. When people asked her about her sacrifices and her constant energy in working around the clock and showing no stress. She replied, "This is all a play of God and I obey!" Destiny is something that takes over and there is no struggle in it. It is something that is natural for you to do. Destiny is the play.

Some people ask, "What is my destiny?" This is a redundant and unaware statement. Destiny is the natural way for you to be. When you suffer it is because your ego is defying it. (Ref. 147)

Resolution

So, do I have free will, even if limited by my *prArabdha saMskAra*, or is my life entirely predestined? **Francis Lucille** explains how a change of viewpoint, from that of the ego that appears to suffer in its predestined life to that of the Self that orchestrates the entire play, resolves the apparent conflict:

We are entirely conditioned; therefore, there is no free will. It appears as though we exercise free choice, but in fact we are only reacting like automatons, running through the same patterns of our bio-sociological heritage without respite, leading invariably to the same old reactions, like a vending machine dispensing soft drinks in a train station. As individuals, our freedom is illusory, with the exception of the freedom which is ours at each moment to stop taking ourselves for separate individuals and thus putting an end to our ignorance and our suffering.

On the other hand, at the level of our deepest being, everything flows out of our freedom. Every thought, every perception takes birth because we want it to. We cannot understand this at the level of thought, but we can experience it. When we are totally open to the unknown, the personal entity is absent; then we realize that the tangible and intelligible universe arises out of this openness in the eternal present. We want, create and are at every moment everything in the unity of awareness. (Ref. 8)

In reality, the Self is ever free. It is only in the world of appearance that, seemingly limited by the ignorance associated with the body-mind, the *jiva* believes itself to be bound. The problem will be seen in a sense to be a pseudo-problem, arising as a result of coming to believe in the reality of our existence as separate beings in a real world. If who we believe ourselves to be is itself an illusion, then it becomes genuinely meaningless to ask whether we have free will. **Jan Kersschot** explains:

But what is it like from the standpoint of the mirage itself? How can that little lake examine itself? Can an illusion discover that it is an illusion? And does it make any sense to assign properties to that "I"? In other words, asking ourselves if we have free will or not is just like a mirage asking itself if the water in "her" little lake is blue or orange. As long as we have no insight into the mirage being an illusion it makes little sense to examine it further. How can an illusory I go in search of its illusory properties? And what do we hope to reach that way? And who is so eager to know all that? Thus, if we want to be honest with this material, we have to admit that every investigation and every possible proof takes place in the very illusion where the mirage finds itself. (Ref. 148)

Nitin Trasi puts the point very clearly without metaphors:

> The idea of free will in religion is fundamentally based upon the belief in the existence of a separate, autonomous entity. But we have already shown that such an entity does not exist. However, what usually happens is that the average hearer misses the main implication of the statement, namely that there *is* no entity to have free will, and takes the statement to mean that *the entity* has no free will. Actually, belief in the separate entity (the self) and belief in free will go together (and they disappear together). You can have both or neither, but you cannot have one without the other. The average man believes in both, while the Enlightened One sees both to be illusions. So long as the belief in a separate self remains, the person will perforce believe in free will.
> (Ref. 149)

Things simply (appear to) happen. There is no doer and therefore no one to choose. **Jan Koehoorn**:

> When the illusion of the doer is seen through, you immediately see that everything always happens spontaneously. The NOW is the only possibility. There are no alternatives for it. So there is actually nothing about which you could make a choice. Sometimes you can see that choices are made, but all that happens in the film of which I am the audience. Thinking that I could make a choice means that I identify myself with one of the actors in the film, or with the choosing itself.
> (Ref. 151)

We are neither the doer nor the chooser. It is simply the case that sometimes things happen in the manner that we expect and coincide with our wishes. **Stanley Sobottka** explains:

> Since we are not free to choose our thoughts, emotions, or actions, why do things sometimes go our way? Because sometimes our decisions are

in agreement with what happens. This reinforces our mistaken sense that we decided what we were going to do. At other times, no matter how determined we are to do something or not to do something, our actions are just the opposite. This merely causes guilt and frustration at our incompetence, lack of discipline, or lack of character. The truth in both cases is that neither our decisions nor our actions are ever in our hands, but are entirely spontaneous. An action will take place either with our sense of volition or without it, but the sense of volition will not affect the action. It will, however, affect our reaction. We will feel pride at what we perceive as our success, or guilt at what we perceive as our failure. (Ref. 205)

Karl Renz uses the metaphor of a merry-go-round. He says that it is as if we sit in one of the vehicles on a merry-go-round and delude ourselves into thinking that we are actually driving it:

During all this steering your ego ripens tremendously. And if by chance you were aiming in the same direction as the merry-go-round, then you can triumph: "Wow, I did that really well! Now, I think I've got it!" Now you've discovered how all this works. "I have complete control. Look here!" You are in harmony with the cosmos, in harmony with creation. An ego which is so coherent, steers in the same direction as the merry-go-round is moving. "Look, how I can steer! The entire merry-go-round moves because I am steering this way! Here, look at me!"...

Until one day, you accidentally let go of the steering wheel. Ooops! Now you are surprised. It also works on its own! This thing drives by itself! Exactly, the Self is driving. You don't have to strain yourself. You can lean back and enjoy your Self. It always drives directly to happiness. (Ref. 157)

Ultimately, the difficulty with the concept of free-will is only at the level of appearance. There is no problem in reality. If you accept that the reality is non-dual Consciousness, then who or what is there to have free will? The concept has no meaning. Indeed there could be no concepts either. There are no objects, no thoughts, no separate entities gross or subtle, no doing. There is nothing to want anything to be different because there is only what is and that is already infinite and complete: infinitely free, including free from the burden of free will. Unfortunately, these statements have to be made at this point in order to rationalize the differing views on the topic but it must be noted that they do presuppose later discussions.

The mechanism of choice cannot be understood unless you understand the entity that exercises choice. **Robert Powell** (Ref. 116)

So, the consensus seems to be that, at the level of the individual living a life in the apparent world, the concept of free will seems to be a necessary belief for most. Yes, it is ultimately illusory but, within the context of spiritual progress toward realization of the truth, the entire theory of *karma*, with its entailed beliefs in reincarnation and free will has its place. In reality, since there are no individuals and no free will, there is no problem. As **Dr. K. Sadananda** puts it:

One has free-will until the freedom from free-will is recognized.
If one knows that the world is an illusion not as a thought but as a fact, the problem is already solved. *vyavahAra* is as real as the process of overcoming it. Until one recognizes *paramArtha*, the illusion appears to be real. When one recognizes *paramArtha*, there will not be any further discussion of free will, whether it exists or not! Existence and non-existence of free-will will both be illusory.

Free will is the basis for *sAdhana* [seeking] until all the duality, including both *sAdhana* and *sAdhaka* [seeker], merges into one. It is the recognition of the fact of advaita or non-duality in spite of duality. Only then do all concepts, including free will or lack of it, dissolve into one.

Krishna says (BG 3.5) – "No one can remain without performing an action even for a second." Later he says (B.G. 13.29) – "All actions are being done by *prakRRiti* and the *Atman* is actionless." One who knows this alone knows the truth. (Ref. 153)

Until such time as the truth is fully realized, traditional Advaita teaches that we *are* able to exercise a degree of free will, restricted by our accumulated *saMskAra*. This is quite deliberate. If there remains the belief that we are a separate person, yet to become enlightened, it is expedient also to believe that we can choose (to continue to follow a teacher, for example, or to read books such as this one). Without this "loop hole," there is a significant danger that a student may become nihilistic and never reach the final understanding. Of course, teachers who advocate "non-doership" to the exclusion of all else will maintain that it is precisely such beliefs that *prevent* us from reaching it. But the reasoning is quite logical – you cannot, for example, expect to understand quantum mechanics without a thorough grounding in mathematics and physics.

The resolution of all of these apparently problematical areas of action, karma, reincarnation and free will can be seen once it is realized that we are confusing the apparent world of individuals, objects and actions with the non-dual reality in which no-thing exists. This will become clearer once we consider these topics in detail in chapter 7. For example, **Dr. K. Sadananda** says this about the question of reincarnation:

[Nisargadatta said: "Reincarnation implies a reincarnating self. There is no such thing." Ref. 5]

The discussion of reincarnation is only from the perspective of the *jIva*, who identifies himself with the equipments and not from the perspective of the all pervading Self from which viewpoint the statement of Nisargadatta Maharaj is made. Hence both statements are correct within their references. As long as we do not confuse from which reference these statements are made, there is no problem.

It is like the ring which thinks: "I am a ring now; I was a bangle in my last life and I may reincarnate as a bracelet in my next life." But from the point of view of the Gold, I am gold all the time - never a ring, a bangle nor a necklace - they are in me and I am not in them. Who reincarnates? From the point of view of the gold – no one. From the point of view of the egotistical ring, I reincarnate all the time. (Ref. 154)

No personal karma or free will

In reality, there is no *karma*, no *saMskAra*, no *puruShArtha* because there is no person who could have them. They are all teaching devices used to bring the student to a realization of the truth by means of carefully gauged, progressive levels of understanding. **Robert Adams** explains how it is necessary to utilise this teaching initially because this is the level at which the student is functioning – the "useful fiction" referred to by Eliot Deutsch. It is pointless to introduce the sublating truths of no doer etc. until the mind has been prepared to appreciate it.

You have to do whatever you have to do. But for those who can understand what I'm talking about, and realize that you're dealing with no mind, no body, no world, no universe, no God, the awakening comes immediately because there is no one who is sleeping. Do you follow this? If you think you've got something to overcome, if you believe that you've got to work on yourself, you've got to make some kind of effort, it will be hard. After all, who makes the effort? The ego. Who is telling you all these things you have to overcome? The mind. You think you have to overcome your bad habits, you have to overcome past karma, you have to overcome *saMskAra*-s. That's all a lie.

I realize that I talk about these things sometimes. It sounds like a contradiction, but I am sharing with you the highest truth. There are no *saMskAra*-s to overcome, because they never existed. There is no *karma* to overcome because it doesn't exist. But it does for the immature students. They have to work on something. So I explain to them there's *karma*, there are *saMskAra*-s, there are latent tendencies that have got hold of you, and you have to transcend them. Yet I'm telling them a lie. But they really need to hear that at this time of their evolution, otherwise they cannot work on anything else. (Ref. 155)

And you have the freedom to choose what to see – that's the only freedom you have. Everything else is preordained...

In other words, to the extent that you see the truth about yourself - that you are really Brahman, GOD, that you are that which is, and can never change - to that extent you are free. (Ref. 42)

The *jIva* functions at the level of *vyavahAra* and is apparently bound by the rules of the world, including those of *karma*, and **Robert Adams** repeatedly emphasized this, saying that: "This [highest teaching] does not give one license to go out and do whatever you want, or to hurt other people." As will be seen in the chapter on Spiritual Practices, such traits as *ahimsa* (not injuring others in any way) are intrinsic to the mental preparation needed to assimilate this knowledge.

Swami Muni Narayana Prasad believes that this is the picture that the *shruti* presents also, if we read it correctly. Although the Upanishads and Bhagavad Gita allude to reincarnation of the *jIva*, for example, this is a "lower level" teaching for those still firmly mired in the illusory world of separate bodies and minds. Where these subjects are discussed, later verses always clarify what has been said and make further statements that deny the existence of personal *karma*.

For example, as has been stated earlier, only the *guNa*-s act:

A person deluded by egoism thinks he is the actor when all actions are performed by the *guNa*-s of *prakRRiti* (constituents of nature). **Bhagavad Gita III.27** (Ref. 158)

The idea that there is such a thing as individual *karma* is the product of ignorance brought about by believing that I am the doer, when in fact the human being (body-mind-intellect) is simply a part of nature and the "doing" is nothing other than the movement of the *guNa* within nature – the mechanical movement of the car on the merry-go-round. To the extent that *karma* has any meaning, then, it belongs to nature itself.

Swami Prasad refers to the Bhagavad Gita II.22 as the verse most often quoted in justification of reincarnation:

As a man discards his threadbare robes and puts on new, so the Spirit throws off Its worn-out bodies and takes fresh ones. (Ref. 119)

He points out that the word "Spirit" is in the singular (*dehI*) while "bodies" is in the plural (*sharIrANi*). He goes on to interpret the passage using the metaphor of gold and ornaments that was used by Dr. Sadananda above (and which comes from the Chandogya Upanishad) and deduces that reincarnation is not part of the essential teaching of the *gIta* at all:

Gold assumes the body of an ornament. This body or form of the ornament is not eternal, while the gold in it is eternal. This gold has always existed in one form or another and will exist forever. The gold before us in the form of an ornament must have assumed countless forms before appearing before us in the present form. It will likewise assume countless forms in the future also. The same gold exists eternally as its form gets changed. When one form is changed into another it could be treated as the death of the former form and the birth of the new one. Gold here is in the place of the Self, and ornaments getting formed one after another are in the place of bodies. The gold gives up an old form even as a man casts off his old garments. It takes a new form just as a man receives new garments. The same man continues to exist while the garments are being changed. Likewise the same Reality continues to exist forever while its visible forms are constantly changing. The context of the *gIta* in which the stanza appears is also not of thinking about the life after death, but of discriminating between the eternal and the transient aspects of existence and their value. (Ref. 130)

He concludes:

There is only one Reality. It is imperishable. It transforms itself creatively. The creative urge in the Reality which causes the constant emergence of new forms is called *karma*. Thus *karma* does not belong to any individual. Manifested forms emerge and re-emerge incessantly as a result of this creative urge. The emergence of a new form in effect is the disappearance of an old form. We call the former birth and the latter death. But the imperishable Reality continues to exist in and through all these transformations, just as gold continues to exist in and through the various forms of ornaments into which it is shaped. (Ref. 130)

The problem of free will or not is dissolved in the understanding that there is no one there who could make a choice. Thoughts arise and apparent decisions are triggered according to the particular conditioning of that body-mind. All of these things take place but there is no one doing anything. It is all simply movement of name and form under the deterministic law of cause and effect. One effect is the thought (after the event) of "I chose to do that" – but it is only a thought arising in Consciousness.

The non-dual reality manifests as all of this - people, things etc. - and it is continually changing, evolving, dying, being reborn etc., only at the level of appearance. In fact it is only ever Consciousness, just as if the gold is continually being melted and reformed into new ornaments but however many "separate" forms there might be they are all always the one gold. This continual movement all "belongs" to *brahman*. In our ignorance, we (a particular ornament) think that we are somehow in charge of our local form and destiny but this is all delusion. Acknowledging this is the true surrender.

Summary

Identification
* We identify with the *vij~nAnamayakosha* and then believe we are a "doer."
* The sense of "I" arises from identification with the idea of will. In fact, actions take place and the claiming of responsibility arises later.

Only the guNa act
* The body acts and "we" simply observe. There is no doer.
* We confuse the constantly changing *prakRRiti* with the unchanging

Atman.

- Nature has three *guNa*-s (qualities) – *sattva, rajas* and *tamas*. We have to transcend all three to attain knowledge of *brahman.*

Theory of karma

- *karma* literally means "action." It refers to accumulated characteristics and habits and to the course of our lives in the exhausting of these tendencies.
- Habitual tendencies of the mind are called *vAsanA*-s.
- Acting with a particular result in mind generates *karmaphala* (fruit of action). Good action causes *puNya* (merit) and bad causes *pApa* (sin).
- The *karmaphala* is held as *saMskAra* in the subtle body until it matures.
- There are 3 types of *saMskAra*: *saMchita* is the total of all *saMskAra* resulting from past action; *prArabdha* is that maturing now in this body; *AgAmin* is that from current action destined to mature in the future.
- There are 3 types of *prArabdha*: *ichChA* resulting from personal desire; *anichChA* unrelated to desire; *parechChA* resulting from other's desire. *ichChA* disappears for the realized man.

Reincarnation

- Only bodies die. Death is a motivator whilst we believe we are the body. The Self cannot die because it was never born.
- Traditionally, unresolved *saMskAra* causes rebirth. It is held in the subtle body (*sUkShma sharIra*) which survives death of the physical body.
- The subtle body (mind) is the *upAdhi*, limiting adjunct, for the *Atman.*
- It is reborn in a new body in accord with its *saMchita saMskAra* so that the *jIva* may exhaust them. A bad life may give rebirth as a lower life form.
- Modern teachers do not usually teach *karma*, especially reincarnation.
- In reality we are not the physical or subtle bodies so that birth, death and reincarnation do not apply.
- Until we realize our true Self, the apparent process (*saMsAra*) will continue.

Free Will

* Free will is the idea that we can act in ways other than the way that we do.
* In fact, thoughts arise (beyond our control) and action follows mechanistically based on conditioning. The illusion of choice is part of this.
* Advaita is effectively deterministic. Accumulated *saMskAra* determines our birth. We are able to exercise self-effort to try to annul this in the present, like the motor boat moving against the current.
* Free will is present *karma*; fate is past *karma*.
* There is an apparent contradiction in the implication that *saMskAra* comes from conditioning (past action) but *puruShArtha* (what we want) doesn't.
* We can say that destiny is the result of the past exercising of free will.
* The *jIva* appears to be bound in the phenomenal realm but the Self is always free in reality. Who we thought we were is an illusion.
* The concept of free will is valid in the phenomenal realm and goes along with the theory of *karma* within the context of a spiritual path. In reality, there are no individuals and free will has no meaning.
* The teaching is graded to suit the knowledge of the student. Since "doing" belongs to *prakRRiti* and not to the *jIva*, so does *karma*.
* It is the non-dual reality that takes on the form of new bodies in the same way that gold takes on the form of new ornaments. *karma* can therefore be understood as the creative urge by which reality takes on a new form.
* The resolution is in the recognition that there is no doer and therefore no "chooser." Whatever is done is "God's will". Reality is always perfectly free.

3. MEANING, PURPOSE AND HAPPINESS

In the first chapter, we looked at how we mistakenly identify with the body (which is actually only food – the *annamayakosha*), with the "life- force" that animates the body (the vital-air sheath or *prANamayakosha*) and with the mind and organs of perception (the mental sheath or *manomayakosha*). Then, in the second chapter, we considered how the idea of being a "doer" and having free will originates from the mistaken identification with the intellectual sheath (*vij~nAnamayakosha*). The final level of attachment in this model is with the "innermost" sheath of bliss – the *Anandamayakosha*. This results in our believing that we are an "enjoyer" of the results of action, a *bhoktRRi*. This word also means "experiencer" and "feeler" and so relates to negative aspects as well as positive – suffering as well as pleasure.

This chapter will first look at the various ways in which we try to find meaning in our lives and thereby some motivation for acting in one way rather than another. We fear death and therefore pursue all means for avoiding this. Good and evil are relative terms but evil is the result of ignorance. The pursuit of pleasure in the world is especially significant but the (spiritual) "good" is more likely to bring happiness. Beauty, love, wealth, satisfying desires and achieving enlightenment are all examined as being significant factors.

Ideas about what makes us happy are many and varied but they are just ideas and we have no control over them. We look for happiness to fulfill a perceived lack but it is not to be found in transient things; it is an aspect of our true Self. Language is part of the problem but desires take us away from the Self and the present moment. The key to happiness is in the renunciation of desire. To the extent that any purpose is meaningful, the most valid is to seek knowledge of the Self. All others are limited and ultimately unsatisfactory.

Finally, the model of the five sheaths is reviewed in depth since it is a fundamental *prakriyA* in Advaita.

Motivation and Meaning

For many people, the sense of meaning in their lives relates solely to a constant striving to maximize pleasure and minimize pain. Any sense of purpose is often confused with this and may frequently be summed up simply as a desire "to be happy." **Ramesh Balsekar** explains:

When one talks of what one would want most in daily living - being anchored in peace and harmony - what precisely do we mean by daily living? A little reflection would show us clearly that the very basis of life is the concept of "time": the concept and experience of a beginning, a middle and an end - a journey beginning with a wanting or desire, proceeding with effort towards the realization (or the failure) of the goal. This process happens to be applied by the individual to everything in his life: one has to do something, to achieve something, and to become something. In other words, the concept of "time" and the flow of time brought with it the concept of purpose, the investment of effort and the expectation of the result of the effort. And surely this is the very basis of one's daily living, beginning with going to school, then the university and the end of education; then falling in love and marriage, to be followed by the happy family; in the meantime, one's career, again a beginning, middle and end, with the purpose of eventual "success."

Thus daily living gets based essentially on time: purpose - effort - expectation. Success means happiness; failure means frustration, unhappiness. (Ref. 164)

Time is related to the mind. It is a concept that we use in order to make sense of the apparent world. As we saw earlier, whatever we really are, it is not the mind so that, on these grounds alone, it seems inevitable that all efforts to achieve perceived purposes are going to be in vain, when it comes to realizing our true nature.

Osho (Ref. 166) tells the story of an apparent madman who is heard walking about on the roof of the king's palace. When caught by the guards, he claims he was looking for his camel. Later that night the king cannot sleep, thinking that there must have been some hidden meaning in the words and that the man must be a great mystic.

Later the next day, a beggar arrives at the door to the palace saying that he wishes to spend a few days at this inn. He will not listen to explanations that it is the king's palace and not an inn at all. The king overhears the arguments and sends for the beggar who explains that he came once before and someone else was on the throne. When he comes again next time, there will be yet another king. Clearly this is no one's residence and, since people are coming and going, it must be an inn for travellers.

The king suddenly realizes that this was the man from the previous night and accuses him of being a madman. The beggar admits this and tells the king that he, too, is a madman; that looking for meaning in material possessions is like looking for a camel on the roof.

We can appreciate the confusion by asking what it is that enjoys or suffers. There is still a level of mistaken identification here and, once this has been seen through, the seeming problems of life dissolve. It will be known that happiness is, in a transcendent sense, our true nature whilst the concepts of meaning and purpose lose their significance.

Definition of terms

Firstly it will be useful to clarify the distinction between these two words, *meaning* and *purpose*:

A useful metaphor for differentiating these would be a map. If you understand how to use a map, how contour lines represent height above sea level and how other symbols show lakes, forests and so on, then you appreciate the *meaning* of a map and can make use of one when the need arises.

If you are going for a walk in strange territory and have to navigate across hills and find your way through woods, then it is extremely valuable to have a map of the area and a compass. In such a situation, having a map serves a clear *purpose*, for helping you to get from A to B. If you did not understand how to use it, you might appreciate this purpose but the map would be without meaning. If you were familiar with map reading, then you would appreciate the meaning of a map of Borneo but it would serve no purpose in helping you to find your way out of the New Forest.

To put this into context in the actual topic, we might say that our purpose is to find everlasting happiness and we believe that the philosophy of Advaita provides a map of this territory. The metaphor is a good one because it reminds us that the concepts of Advaita are merely symbols in the same way as are the shapes on the map. The metaphor is a bad one in that, strictly speaking, we do not have to go anywhere in order to find happiness – we are already there. What Advaita can do, if we "follow" the notional paths of the map, is to help us clear the mind of all the ignorance that prevents us from recognising this. (Ref. 160)

Sources of Meaning

Apart from the obvious search for happiness, which is addressed in detail below, there are many other values and pursuits that may provide sources of meaning in people's lives. At its most basic, a sense of meaning derives from a style of living that brings satisfaction and a feeling that continued living is worthwhile irrespective of whether there is any ultimate purpose – an ongoing rationale for one's day to day life. Purpose is rather having some final aim in mind for what one wants to achieve before one dies or a belief that humanity itself has an ultimate purpose in which one is playing a part. Purpose will be covered in the final section of this chapter.

Neither aspect is specifically addressed by traditional Advaita in the way that western philosophy and psychology do (and produce libraries of books on the subject). The key belief – that there is only Atman-brahman – makes all such considerations pointless. There is nothing to do and nowhere to go.

There is, of course, much in the *karmakANDa* portion of the Upanishads on the subject of *dharma* (discussed below) and rituals to be followed in worship of the Gods, and so on. Traditional Hindus will aim to use such instruction as guidance in the devotion of *bhakti yoga* and this will almost certainly be seen by them in the sense of both meaning and purpose. But, as far as *j~nAna yoga* is concerned (the *yoga* of knowledge), they are no longer relevant. (I use the phrase "no longer," since preparation of the mind is first required, to enable it to receive that knowledge, as will be described in chapter 5.)

And it must always be remembered that:

...meaning is something that *we* impose upon the changing world in order to make it more acceptable. It is not something intrinsic in the universe itself. Ultimately, it is only a concept through which we see and interpret what is happening. If the concept is stable, we can delude ourselves into thinking that the external situation too is stable and therefore under our control. (Ref. 77)

Death

Death is seen by practically all westerners as the key motivator in life, both from the point of avoidance and as a "deadline" by which all one's ambitions should be achieved. This passage from **Fernando Savater** clearly indicates the way in which the fear of death may colour our entire life:

Human beings know that they are mortal, and their awareness of their fate is what leads them to think. Their first reaction to the certainty of death - provided they have not opted for denying it, and do not take refuge in the illusion of some kind of existence beyond it - is anguished despair, for the reasons that Kant so clearly outlined. What attitude will they adopt in the face of such despair? They will no doubt be afraid of all that threatens to hasten their end (poverty, hostility, illness); they will also try to acquire as many as possible of those things that appear to offer a safeguard against death (wealth, security, social standing, fame); and will hate those who might prevent them from acquiring them or force them to share them. Whoever fears nothingness needs everything.) Fear, greed and hate characterize a life lived in despair. Of course this attitude to life will not prevent anybody from dying, but it does succeed in darkening every moment of life, even the most joyful, with the uneasy shadow of death. (Ref. 183)

For the believer in Advaita, death is of the body only and is of no ultimate importance at all. It is only at the level of the apparent world that it has any meaning. **Schopenhauer**, who was very much influenced by the Upanishads, said this is in a dialogue about death:

> Transcendental knowledge is that which, going beyond the boundary of possible experience, endeavors to determine the nature of things as they are in themselves; while immanent knowledge keeps itself within the boundary of possible experience, therefore it can only apply to phenomena. As an individual, with your death there will be an end of you. But your individuality is not your true and final being, indeed it is rather the mere expression of it; it is not the thing-in-itself, but only the phenomenon presented in the form of time, and accordingly has both a beginning and an end. Your being in itself, on the contrary, knows neither time, nor beginning, nor end, nor the limits of a given individuality; hence no individuality can be without it, but it is there in each and all. So that, in the first sense, after death you become nothing; in the second, you are and remain everything. That is why I said that after death you would be all and nothing. (Ref. 184)

No one really dies and even suffering of body-minds in this life is simply according to *saMskAra*-s accrued during previous lives, all as a result of mistaking who we really are for these transient forms. **Ramesh Balsekar** explains, using the emotive example of Hitler:

> A body-mind organism called Hitler came into being. Who produced Hitler? The same God who produced Jesus Christ also produced Hitler.

Why did God create a Hitler? Because in the functioning of Totality, millions of Jews had to be slaughtered — that was according to the destiny of the Jews. So, because it was the destiny of millions of Jews to be annihilated, God created the body-mind organism called Hitler and programmed it in such a way that only those actions could happen. And the result of those actions also affected the body-mind organism called Hitler. That organism committed suicide.

So, a body-mind is created, and certain actions happen through it according to its destiny, and then the body-mind organism is dead. So, who is concerned? Who dies? No one dies. Only the body-mind organism which is created by God dies at that moment, and in that manner, in which God wants it to die. The body is created and the body dies. There is no "who" to die.

As a matter of fact, everybody dies every night. But that doesn't mean you are afraid of sleep. You actually desire sleep. And you can't resist sleep, either. If you are sleepy, you can't stay awake. So, the wise man knows that death means merely rest for the body-mind organism. The sage is not afraid of sleep. And he is not afraid of death, because he knows "he" doesn't die. (Ref. 185)

Good and Evil

Chittaranjan Naik took up the question of Hitler in the context of good and evil in the world - another key topic in respect of meaning in our lives:

Q: *Was Hitler not responsible for anything he did? If Consciousness was responsible, how can this be termed an expression of Love?*

A: Hitler is not consciousness pure - he derives his name "Hitler" due to the specific persona-complex superimposed on consciousness.

Your use of the word "responsible" in the question already tends to situate the problem in the context of "good and evil." But that is not the way Advaita Vedanta looks at it. According to Advaita, the cause of evil lies in ignorance. Nobody does an evil deed in the full light of knowledge - he/she simply can't. The thief, the murderer, the worst of the diabolic, are all impelled by the same motive - to fulfill a need created due to the seeming privation of their innate being.

What is this privation? It is the loss of fullness or plenitude. It is also the loss of the native bliss of plenitude. The Self is infinite and *pUrNa* - full. There is nothing lacking in It. It is only *avidyA* (ignorance) that generates the false notion of limitedness, and it is because of the thralldom of this notion that it tries to gain something which it thinks it is lacking. It has lost its innate bliss, and thus arises the desire for happiness and pleasure (*kAma*). It thinks it is a limited thing bound in the body, and therefore it tries to make up for its limitation through the acquisition of objects, wealth, name and position (*artha*). Thus arise the two *puruShArtha*-s (basic aims of life) of an embodied being - *kAma* and *artha*. (Ref. 188) – [Note – the *puruShArtha*-s are discussed below.]

Good and evil are terms relating to the particular moral standards of a given society and to the ideas that individuals have about these, i.e. this is all in the realm of appearances and does not relate to the non-dual reality behind names and forms. The following was forwarded to the Advaitin Email list in September 2001, written by someone called **Chandi**:

The question, "Why does God permit evil?" is, in fact, most misleading. It is as absurd as if one were to ask, "Why does God permit good?" Nobody today would ask why rain *permitted* a catastrophic flood; nobody would blame or praise fire because it burns one man's house and cooks another man's dinner. Nor can it be properly said that Brahman is *good* in any personal sense of the word. Brahman is not *good* in the sense that Christ was *good* - for Christ's goodness was within *mAyA*; his life expressed the light of Reality reflected upon the relative world. The Reality itself is beyond all phenomena; even the noblest. It is beyond purity, beauty, happiness, glory, or success. It can be described as *good* only if we mean that absolute consciousness is absolute knowledge, and that absolute knowledge is absolute joy. (Ref. 125)

The Pleasant and the Good

There are only three references to the distinction between *shreyas* (the good) and *preyas* (the pleasant) in the Upanishads according to Ref. 189 and two of these occur in consecutive verses of the kaThopaniShad (I.2.1 – 2). **Alan Jacobs'** free translation is as follows:

The Good is one thing,
Pleasure another.
These two have different aims,
They bind a man or woman
In cords of attachment.
It goes well with him or her
Who clings to the Good,
But he who chooses Pleasure
Is like an arrow which
Misses the mark.

The Good and the Pleasurable
Both woo men and women, continuously.
The wise circumnavigate
Them and distinguish one from
The other very clearly.
The wise prefer the Good
To the Pleasurable, the fool
Chooses what is Pleasurable,
Driven by greed, lust and indulgence. (Ref. 121)

The implication is that we are continually faced with situations in which we must choose between alternative course of action, one of which we may desire and which provides temporary satisfaction and the other which follows unselfish and moral principles. Even though this latter path may bring us suffering of some sort in the short term, it is claimed that following this path will ultimately lead us to some auspicious goal. And, of course, it assumes that we have the freedom to make such a choice. This is the attitude that is advocated by most religions.

The Hindu culture that forms the background to Advaita utilizes the concept of *dharma* to determine what is "right" or "wrong" in a given situation and this would equate to the western doctrine of moral relativism, where attitudes become part of tradition, advocating those courses of action that have been found to work best within the society, for the general good. That might seem to imply also an element of pragmatism and utilitarianism, i.e. actions that seem to result in satisfactory outcomes and for the benefit of the majority. But that would miss the point. Whilst *dharma* is certainly relative, *shreyas* is absolute. Although each of us pursues different aims and objects at the level of day to day life, what everyone wants ultimately is the same – eternal and absolute happiness, without limit, i.e. *ananta Ananda*.

(It may be noted that the Upanishad says that pursuing *either* path will bind a man. This statement may cause some confusion and should be understood as relating to the *attitude* one has to the pursuit. As was indicated in the last chapter, "bad" actions, i.e. selfishly seeking worldly pleasures, incur *pApa* or sin and this could ultimately lead to rebirth as a lower life form. But even "good" actions, for the sake of others according to established moral laws, incur *karma* in the form of *puNya* (merit) if they are carried out with any sort of selfish intent. Supposedly, this may lead to a prolonged stay in heaven but, eventually, the *jIva* must be reborn in order to attain realization. Thus it is that our actions should follow the guidelines of *karma yoga*, responding to the need rather than because we want a result. This topic is addressed in Chapter 5.)

The metaphors of light and darkness are often used, with the pleasant leading to darkness and the good taking us into light. The dark symbolizes the ignorance that prevents us from seeing the truth, while the light is the light of knowledge that disperses the ignorance. It is ignorance of our true nature that causes us to seek illusory fulfillment through the acquisition of desired objects or ultimately fleeting pleasures. Once the knowledge of our identity with Brahman has been absorbed, the pleasant ceases to have any attraction. That which is limited in time or space can have no relevance to that which is unlimited. **Swami Atmananda** comments:

> Everything thing which is perceptible is in the realm of time, and is therefore changing and ephemeral. This is an extremely evident fact and really speaking requires no logical validation. Thus when we keep an extraneous goal then we simultaneously affirm our presumptions that I am a limited & lacking person and the world outside is permanent and capable of giving me that which I lack. When our life will be based on these untruths then how can we ever expect to awake to a state of cherished fulfilment & contentment? (Ref. 190)

It is only when this is fully accepted that we are able to reject the short-term, but ultimately meaningless pleasures of life and pursue whole-heartedly the knowledge and understanding that will liberate us from the confusion and ignorance that obscures our already-existing fulfillment. **Swami Chinmayananda** comments on these verses from the Katha Upanishad as follows:

> Having thus tested the disciple and found him worthy of the great Knowledge, Lord Death said, "*good is one thing and pleasant is another.*" Every action of all the living beings is motivated by an irresistible instinct to be happy. Happiness seems to be the goal of every struggle and strife in life. Even a worm crawling in fecal matter wanders about motivated by a hope that it would reach a point where a greater joy than it is enjoying at the moment, would be its lot. In full and Absolute Contentment all desires and hopes end, and this Supreme State of Desirelessness or Hopelessness is the Goal of life. This is called Godhood, or the State of Kaivalya. [†] (Ref. 156)

The **Bhagavad Gita**, probably the scripture most relevant to describing how

---

[†] Kathopanishad, Swami Chinmayananda, © Central Chinmaya Mission Trust, Mumbai.

we ought to live, differentiates between the good and pleasant as follows, relating them to the *guNa*:

And now hear from Me, O Arjuna, about the threefold pleasure. The pleasure one enjoys from (spiritual) practice results in cessation of sorrow. This pleasure appears as poison in the beginning but is like nectar in the end, comes by the grace of Self-knowledge; is good or *sAttvika*. Sensual pleasures appear as nectar in the beginning, but become poison in the end; such pleasures are called *rAjasika* pleasures. Pleasure that deludes a person in the beginning and in the end; which comes from sleep, laziness, and confusion; such pleasure is called *tAmasika* (pleasure). (XVII 36 – 39) (Ref. 192)

Those pleasures that derive from such things as drugs do not allow for any discrimination or proper functioning of the mind and lead only to delusion and death. This is apparent from the outset and only becomes worse. They are dominated by *tamas*. More *rAjasika* pursuits involve much mental activity and bring short-term gains in apparent happiness. But anything that is grounded in worldly activities and therefore body-based is doomed ultimately to bring pain and misery because we are not the body, which must eventually die. So the initial "nectar" must soon become "poison," too. Only so-called "spiritual" pursuits, which may initially seem unattractive or even something we would wish to avoid altogether, nevertheless bring at least consolation as the body grows old and at best total liberation from the apparent bondage. **Swami Chidbhavananda** comments on verse 36 as follows:

To a beginner swimming seems as dreadful as death; but the same becomes delightful to him after he picks it up… The *jIvAtman* has been used to the life in the body and the senses in his previous births. His switching on now to the control of the senses, detachment from the body and meditation on the glory of Atman – all these practices seem to him strange and painful. But as he perseveres in them he comes to know that his plenitude is in the Self and not in the mundane. (Ref. 118)

Who we really are is unlimited so that we can never find satisfaction in the limited world. Thus we are never going to be happy pursuing any of the traditional worldly values, even if we are lucky enough to get them all in the end. Only by realizing our true nature can we attain the eternal happiness that we are forever vainly seeking, ignorant of the fact that we are already That. **Swami Dayananda** expresses this as follows:

A person is *svayaM-pUrNa*, full by nature [*svayam* means "of or by oneself"]; that is why he cannot accept anything less. While in the physical body occasionally he has the experience of fullness which is his very nature. Looking at the stars, he is full. Listening to music he experiences happiness. At these moments of happiness one has the experience of being full. *saMsAra* teases you with these moments of happiness. Once you have experienced this fullness, you cannot settle for anything less. Therefore you always seek for this fullness, this fulfillment. That is the cause for wandering. (Ref. 58)

Beauty

Beauty is the harmonious relation between something in our nature and the quality of the object which delights us. **Blaise Pascal**

Beauty is akin to *Ananda*. It is the recognition of our true nature in what is believed to be an external object. **Gina Lake:**

Beauty is the visual doorway into the now, where we find the Self. We can enter the now through the sense of sight, and the easiest way of doing this is by becoming absorbed in something beautiful. It is possible, however, to enter the now by looking - really looking - at anything. Everything is part of the Self, and becoming fully engaged with it brings us to the Self. Beauty may be the easiest visual doorway because we are generally more willing to become fully engaged with something beautiful than with something that is not. We say yes to beauty, and that yes takes us into the now. However, anything we see that we do not reject can bring us into the now.

Beauty connects us instantly with joy. Think of some of your happiest moments. The beauty of nature was probably part of many of them. Spending time in a beautiful, natural setting is one of the easiest ways to get in touch with the Real, with the Self. Natural beauty brings us into the moment because it captures our attention so completely. (Ref. 203)

and **Catherine Ingram** has the following to say about it:

In awakened intelligence the experience of beauty is not about how a person, place, or thing looks; it is about how the one who is looking *feels*. We are able to see beauty even in what our instincts or cultural conditioning define as horrid. This is not in a Pollyanna sense of seeing a silver lining in every cloud or telling stories that deny the horrid. The horrid is also seen and noted in awakened intelligence but is accepted as part of the whole. As a human animal we may move away from an unpleasant smell, but we need not experience the smell as an alien force, separate from totality. Rumi said, "Imagine the delight of walking on a noisy street and *being* the noise." In awakened awareness we are not mentally carving up the world into what should be included or not. We sense the world as a vast extension of ourselves. We belong to it and it belongs to us. Imagine the delight.

The beauty that we experience in outward manifestation is a direct reflection of the beauty of our internal reality. Have you ever noticed how someone you love or one who has simply been kind to you may suddenly look beautiful even though you might have once considered that same face to be plain? What was it that changed? In awakened intelligence we are not solely dependent on visual stimulation to experience beauty because we recognize that the greatest conduit for the experience of beauty is love. When we love, we see beauty; we speak in beauty; we walk in beauty. In love, we are beauty itself. (Ref. 312)

Atmananda Krishna Menon puts it thus:

Beauty is something by which you are attracted without a cause. You are most attracted to your own self. Or in other words, your own nature is the only thing that can attract you.

So beauty is only an experience of one's own nature, at the instance of an external object. It is then that you find beauty in that object. **Note 527** (Ref.13)

Love

Love, as the word is trivially used in the sense of attraction to and possessive feeling for a particular member of the opposite sex, is almost certainly genetic in origin. It makes evolutionary sense that a couple who are bringing up a child together should feel mutual attachment and protectiveness etc. so as maintain a stable environment and thereby maximize the chances of that child's reaching maturity. In so far as the feeling presents itself at the level of the individual, it is often simply another manifestation of the ego:

Usually, what passes for love tends to be ego-related, as with most other aspects of life. We need to feel that our existence has some meaning. Recognition by another, being perceived as worthy by someone else, who freely chooses to spend the rest of his or her life with us, provides that sense of meaning. Being loved and valued makes our lives seem worthwhile. And in passionate love we can lose our sense of ego in just the same way that we can through involvement or dangerous sports...

Ultimately, love ceases to be an emotion in the usually accepted sense of the word and transcends the physical altogether. The ego in this context loses all meaning. The word 'Philosophy' is used in this sense, being 'love of wisdom'. There can be no higher aim in life than to discover the truth... (Ref. 77)

The distinction is brought out by use of different words in Sanskrit. The selfish love of one individual for another, usually based upon lust and delusion is termed *moha*, while the unselfish and undirected love is *prema*. **His Holiness Sri Shantanand Saraswati** clarifies:

Expression of love depends on the measure and truth of knowledge. Due to the widespread ignorance, love does not manifest in its purity and becomes *moha* (attachment, infatuation or bondage). To differentiate between pure love, *prema*, and *moha*, one can see that in love there is no injustice, no compulsion or pressure, no darkness and no partiality or preferentiality towards anyone. Law considers everyone as equal. In a positive manner, Love is just, light, ready in response and equality, through the whole *samaShTi* [totality]. This impulse of Love in creation goes on for a very long time before it comes to rest. In *moha* there is an absence of knowledge, injustice, pressure, compulsion, darkness and inequality. Ignorance reduces *samaShTi* into small limits. The power of Love is the same as that which works through *moha*, but it is directed in the interest of individuals. The *vyaShTi* [individual] takes it entirely for himself or herself. (Ref. 217)

When love transcends its narrow egotistical sense, it is yet another facet of truth, happiness and beauty. Love of another person is then the recognition of our Self in the presumed "other." As **Andrew Vernon** says:

In fact when we love anyone or anything, it is really the Self that is loving and the Self that is being loved. In the Brihadaranyaka Upanishad, it says:
"It is not for the sake of itself, my beloved, that anything whatever is esteemed, but for the sake of the Self." (**5.26** Ref. 20)

This is not usually realized, of course, and the ego imagines that the "other" is really the source of the happiness that is found in the relationship, as **Philip Mistlberger** explains:

Spiritually, the search for a present-time love is a distortion of our longing to rediscover the natural state, our true nature. Seen through the filters of the ego, this longing becomes the longing to experience being loved by an ultimate Source of love - and a Source that is *outside* of us. This longing at its root is the impulse to be united with our Source again, a longing that is even dimly recognized in those who profess a rejection of spiritual realities. However, because the ego projects this vague notion of Source *externally,* we simply end up turning our primary partner (or other key relationships) into this Source. We literally fashion our partner into the god or goddess of our deep unconscious spiritual longing. We make them *special.* This is why, when they disappoint us, leave us, betray us, etc., it is experienced as so devastating. (Ref. 134)

The true situation - that there is no other – means fully accepting that there is no "me" either and this is resisted by the ego as long as possible, as **Adyashanti** explains:

Inherent in the revelation of perfect unity is the realization that there is no personal me, no personal other, and therefore no personal relationships. Coming to terms with the challenging implications of this stunning realization is something that few people are willing to do. Because realizing the true impersonality of all that seems so personal, challenges every aspect of the illusion of a separate, personal self. It challenges the entire structure of personal relationships which are born of needs, wants, and expectations. It is in the arena of personal relationships that the illusion of a separate self clings most tenaciously and insidiously. Indeed, there is nothing that derails more spiritual seekers than the grasping at and attaching to personal relationships...

> Simply put, most people want to keep dreaming that they are special, unique, and separate, more than they want to wake up to the perfect unity of an Unknown which leaves no room for any separation from the whole. (Ref. 208)

Goals of Life

According to traditional Advaita, the "goals" of life can be categorized as follows:

> The scriptures declare four goals in human life and they are called the *puruShArtha*-s. The term *puruShArtha* not only denotes what the objectives of life should be but it also means what the objectives of life are as the result of the psychological tendencies of the individual. The *puruShArtha*-s consist of *dharma, Artha, kAma* and *mokSha* in that order.
>
> First, every human being needs to obey the law of nature by strictly following *dharma. dharma* is the stability of the society, the maintenance of social order, and the general welfare of mankind. And whatever conduces to the fulfilment of this purpose is called *dharma.*
>
> *Artha* is the acquisition of wealth; is regarded as the primary purpose of life as, without it, human existence is impossible. One has to live before one can live well. *Artha* is the foundation upon which the whole structure of life has been built and all the other *puruShArtha*-s can be achieved only by the fulfilment of this primary purpose in life. The acquisition of wealth is through dharmic actions and wealth needs to be used in the preservation of *dharma.*
>
> *kAma* means desires; desires of varying degrees. It is from *dharma* that *Artha* and *kAma* result. Man recognises here that *Artha* and *kAma* satisfy the psychological tendencies of man and they form essentially the two fundamental aspirations of every individual. It is implied what one desires needs to be within the threshold of one's wealth and within dharmic values!
>
> Now the word *mokSha* means the ultimate freedom from birth and

death or the deliverance of the soul from bondage. From the Advaitic point of view, *mokSha* results from the extinction of false knowledge (ignorance). Self-knowledge is the aim and end of man's misery and bondage. **Ram Chandran** (Ref. 161)

Ananda Wood sees these goals as a hierarchy of values, in a pyramid as it were, with the most limited, personal aims at the apex, widening out to the foundational "level" of unconditioned freedom at the base. *kAma* is the selfish, personal desire, transient and superficial. *Artha* is wealth or achievement in general, with ambition partially motivated by whatever cultural values obtain in the particular society:

> They are broader and more enduring than personal desires; because they are shared in common by different people, in a community that continues, while particular persons come and go. (Ref. 162)

The word *dharma* is a key one in Hinduism in general. Indeed, those adherents whom we might call "Hindus" often do not appreciate the appellation and prefer to call their religion *sanAtana dharma*. (The word "Hindu" was coined by Muslims to refer to the people in the Indus valley.) *dharma* means customary practice, conduct, duty, justice and morality. The favored meaning of most traditional teachers is, however, "nature, character, essential quality," which they often translate as "essence." *sanAtana* literally means "eternal" or "permanent." *sanAtana dharma* is thus used to refer to the traditional (also carrying the sense of "original" and "unadulterated") Hindu practices. **Ranjeet Sankar** gives a clear explanation:

> Loosely defined, *dharma* means "that which we have to wear/follow/practice." *dharma* is not something to be preached. It is something to be followed. It can be defined as the sum total of all the values which we should follow in our lives. The *RRiShi* in the *taittirIya upaniShad* (1.11.1) advises us - *satyaM vada, dharmaM chara*. (Speak

the truth, practice *dharma*)...

...But the definition which surpasses all of them in terms of lucidity, clarity and profoundness is given by the great *shaMkarAchArya* himself. He has given the definition of the word *dharma* in his introduction to his *gIta bhAShya*...

"*dharma* is that which is meant for the stability of the world and also as the direct means to both secular and spiritual welfare of living beings. That *dharma* which is so, is followed by *brAhmaNa*-s and others belonging to the other castes and stages of life, who aspire after the highest." (Ref. 163)

Ananda Wood goes on to show how this expands upon the sense of meaning for the individual but must ultimately fall short, since the "individual" is a mistaken concept, limiting our true nature:

[The Hindu sense of *dharma* is of] a universal harmony that is naturally expressed in the world outside and in our bodies and minds as well. The problem is that our bodies and minds are incomplete. As we see the world through them, they produce a superficial show that doesn't tell us everything. That leaves us uncertain and confused, in our physical and mental perceptions of the world. So we do not rightly see the harmony that is expressed. And we often get out of touch with it.

Through duty, ethics, virtue and religion, the aim of *dharma* is to get back in touch. This aim is inherently reflective, as can be seen from the English word "religion." It comes from the Latin "religare," which means to "bind back." It implies a reversal of direction: from the divided and passing aims of cultural value and personal desire, towards a secure grounding in the natural order of some more fundamental principle that different motivations share in common. (Ref. 162)

mokSha brings the final release from all limitations and is that ultimate freedom, which is the true aim of the deluded *jIva*, removing once and for all that veil of ignorance which apparently obscured his real nature. **Ananda**

Wood concludes:

> Thus *mokSha* (as pure freedom) is both goal and source. As the aim of
> *mokSha* is attained, all desires and values are returned to that originating
> ground from which they come. In that one origin, there are no divisions,
> no constraints. There are no partialities that cloud pure knowledge and
> obscure plain truth. There, knowledge is found free of ignorance, as
> unconditioned truth. And there is nothing further to desire or to value.
> That is the final aim: where unaffected freedom is realized, by returning
> back to source. (Ref. 162)

To most westerners, the ideas behind *dharma* and *mokSha* would mean
nothing. To the materialistic individual living in a democratic society,
kAma is the purpose of life and *Artha* the key to its attainment. "What I
want is personal happiness through the satisfaction of my desires and,
unfortunately, I need money in order to get it." (Of course, we also
frequently encounter the confusion of aims, in which happiness is believed
to be synonymous with wealth and is pursued as an end in its own right.)

We have to come to realize that the fulfilling of desires and
accumulation of wealth are going to bring only short-lived satisfaction.
The ultimate, though presently hidden, desire behind these aims is to
attain *eternal* happiness and the limited can never result in the limitless.
Only *mokSha* can bring us this. Once this truth is appreciated we have
become a seeker!

Pleasure and Happiness

Some further clarification of terms is necessary before talking too much
about happiness. Our true nature is *Ananda*. We gain glimpses of this from
time to time and give various names to it, of which happiness and bliss are
two. But even the most blissful experience is simply that – an event in time
with a beginning and an end. What we essentially are stands outside of time,
which is simply a concept used by the mind. To differentiate the words
"pleasure" and "happiness," I will use "pleasure" to mean the purely

mechanical element of the mind that gives rise to some degree of happiness:

> There is good evidence to suggest that pleasure is merely an evolutionary development – we feel it when we do something that is "good" for us, in the sense of liable to help us survive and thereby propagate the species. Hence eating and sex are good examples of pleasurable activities. Eating things that are bad for us is likely to be accompanied by opposite feelings such as nausea or disgust so as to discourage us. We will tend to choose those things that are likely to bring pleasure and avoid ones that are likely to bring pain.
>
> There appear to be areas in the brain which, when electrically stimulated, trigger feelings of pleasure. A recent theory suggests that pleasure is a function that enables us to choose between activities. Thus, an experiment with lizards shows that their favorite foods – i.e. the ones that give the most pleasure – can tempt them out of a warm environment into a cold one, whereas less enticing food will not.
>
> Essentially, however, pleasure seems to be a short-term emotion, working in an obviously mechanistic way similar to pain. In fact, there is good reason to suppose that pleasure and pain are effectively opposite ends of what is the same "thing" – an evolutionary brain mechanism for encouraging behavior optimal to survival. Happiness, on the other hand, appears not to function in this way. It does not seem to relate so clearly to "things" or "events." It seems much more related to me directly. I can say "I am happy," but not "I am pleasure." Drugs might bring about an extremely pleasurable state but they could never make me happy.
> (Ref. 165)

Happiness

To be happy is probably the fundamental purpose of all human endeavors, surpassing all other ambitions. Even those whom we perceive to be living in what we might think to be dire poverty, physically disabled or in a totalitarian regime can apparently still be happy so that those considerations must presumably be of a lower importance. **Dr. K. Sadananda** comments:

The fact of the matter is that I am propelled to interact with this universe, which sometimes is conducive to my likes and many times is not. I am forced to live out experiences from this world, day in day out, from birth to death. I find myself happy when my experiences and environments are favorable to my liking and unhappy when they are unfavorable or when I dislike them. The bottom line is, as long as I am here in this world, I want to be happy. This was true centuries ago; this is true now and will be true even in the next millennium. Hence I go on looking for environments or experiences that are conducive to my likes so that I can be happy. It is a continuous struggle since the environment keeps changing continuously and does not remain constant to my liking, and even if the environment remains the same, my likes and dislikes keep changing. (Ref. 172)

And there is nothing *wrong* with our wanting happiness, as Ramama Maharshi explained in the recollections of **A. Devaraja Mudaliar**:

Once I said to Bhagavan: "What do I know about liberation and all that? Really Bhagavan, I do not care for liberation or anything else. I only want to be always happy."

Frivolous as it might seem, this really was my attitude at heart. Bhagavan replied: "You are only asking for liberation or *mukti*, though you are not using that word. The uninterrupted and unmixed happiness which you want is possible only through salvation or *mukti*, that is through freedom from *aj~nAna* (ignorance)."

So again, Bhagavan taught me that there is nothing wrong in our desiring happiness. In fact, no one can help desiring happiness, since happiness is one's essential nature. What is wrong is only seeking for that happiness in the not-self instead of in the Self where alone it can be found.

...Sometimes however, Bhagavan said: "You want only good and happiness, but these terms can have no meaning at all without their opposites. Good and evil, happiness and misery, are very relative terms, and are inevitable on the relative plane, until you transcend the pairs of opposites and reach the Absolute. That is perfect happiness." (Ref. 179)

Happiness and the ego

How is it that, if our true nature is *Ananda*, we seem to experience relatively little in the way of happiness? The ultimate answer, as with all such questions, is that our true nature is covered over by ignorance. The problem is again one of identification or, to put it another way, the culprit is the ego.

The problem is, of course, that we are always looking to find happiness outside, in events, objects or people, when in reality it is our own nature.

The reason why we are frequently happy, albeit for a relatively short time, when we are pursuing what we might call "enjoyable" activities, is not because of any property intrinsic to the activity. It is because, as we sometimes put it, we "forget ourselves." What this actually means is that the sense of "I am doing this" or "I want that" or even "I am enjoying this" is momentarily forgotten. There is simply "doing" without any overlay of ego or mental commentary. In the absence of mind or ego, the natural happiness of the Self is able to shine through. Momentarily there is no duality - no enjoyer and enjoyed, subject and object - simply enjoyment of one's own Self.

The extent to which we fail to appreciate this is cause for the ultimate irony, however. The moment quickly passes. The ego returns and immediately claims "I am happy" and ascribes the happiness to a separate object or the result of an action. This is then stored in memory, reinforcing our false belief that happiness results from all of this "doing" etc. and then, inevitably, we feel that we have to seek to repeat the activity or search for something new in order to "bring back" the sense of joy. And we fear the loss of this happy state as it is now perceived. Such ideas immediately cover over the Self with ignorance and the happiness dissipates. And it is all quite untrue – at the moment of happiness the ego was not there at all. If it had been, there would not have been any happiness. Any thinking about happiness objectifies it as something other than ourselves and thus renders it unattainable.

So it is that we are forever searching in the wrong direction, for something "other" than ourselves in order to find that which can only be found within. (Ref. 165)

Swami Parthasarathy has a wonderful story that expresses this well:

Two men were traveling in a railway compartment. One was a wealthy merchant. The other was a thief... He wanted to steal the money.

...They were both in the same compartment with two sleeping berths. No one else was with them. The thief waited anxiously for the merchant to retire. To his surprise the merchant openly took out his wads of currency notes. He counted them in the presence of the thief and put them back. The thief's appetite was keen. He prepared his bed. The thief went first to the toilet to wash and change. He returned in a few minutes and pretended to sleep. The merchant next went out. He took his own time to wash and change. Meanwhile the thief got busy and searched the entire compartment for the money. He looked for it everywhere. He could not find it! He was wonderstruck - how could the money have disappeared? He knew for certain that the merchant did not carry it with him to the toilet. He could not sleep the whole night. The merchant slept peacefully.

The next morning they greeted each other. The thief could no longer contain himself. In desperation he confessed his malicious intentions to the merchant. He requested the merchant to satisfy his curiosity: "where did you hide the money?" The merchant smiled and reached for the packet under the thief's own pillow!

So it is with your life. You search and search for bliss everywhere in the world except your own self. (Ref. 123)

Even those directly seeking happiness, through religion or any other path are never going to find it "for themselves," the ego. The ego is the obstacle to finding it and any *experience* of bliss is only a passing phenomenon in time. **U. G Krishnamurti** says:

> Your natural state has no relationship whatsoever with the religious states of bliss, beatitude and ecstasy; they lie within the field of experience. Those who have led man on his search for religiousness throughout the centuries have perhaps experienced those religious states. So can you. They are thought-induced states of being, and as they come, so do they go. Krishna Consciousness, Buddha Consciousness, Christ Consciousness, or what have you, are all trips in the wrong direction: they are all within the field of time. The timeless can never be experienced, can never be grasped, contained, much less given expression to, by any man. That beaten track will lead you nowhere. There is no oasis situated yonder; you are stuck with the mirage.
> (Ref. 204)

The ego itself is never going to be happy because happiness is not part of its nature. I am sometimes this, sometimes that, wanting first one thing and then another. Like the mind that it effectively is, it is flitting constantly from one thing to another. And ultimately it is only effectively a process, a false identification of the real Self with something "other." As an entity in its own right, it does not exist.

…even if we conceded to the ego any kind of freedom, it would not be happy or fulfilled. Why? Because fulfillment is not in the *nature* of the ego, as this is only a false product or a false representation. What does not exist potentially cannot actuate or realize itself. Although the moon may wish to appropriate light from outside of itself, it will never become a sun. The human physical body, though it may live for any incredible length of time, will never become immortal because one cannot "become" but *is* immortal; and if one *is*, one does not seek immortality.

The empirical ego, because *it is not*, has to find its fulfillment, its *raison d'etre* and its realization *outside of itself*, and indeed it is obliged to, it needs to. This means that at best it may find some kind of gratification, but a gratification that comes from other than itself cannot be permanent bliss-fulfillment. If one is dependent and under the sway of the law of necessity one cannot be in harmony, pacified, blissful and fulfilled. If the empirical ego is searching, desiring and longing for, it means that it *is not* and every one of its realizations is a false realization, a false achievement. **Raphael** (Ref. 182)

Roy Whenary expresses the same truth as follows:

The ego, the "I," can never be happy. Emotional attachment, identification with objects of happiness, resistance and negativity, all deprive us of happiness. In the Hindu tradition there is a term, *nirvikalpa samAdhi*, which can be translated simply as "joy without object," which describes well what it feels like living from the silent emptiness of our true nature. It is a spontaneous happiness. It is our natural state of being, our birthright, which is not dependent on any object. Going into the feeling of every situation in life eventually brings about a transformation in our way of seeing and experiencing life. The mind cannot do this on its own. We have to go into the body, into the feeling, and then we may stumble upon this happiness which is our birthright. When we find the clarity of our true nature, all the obstacles to happiness fall away, revealing an inner joy which, like a flower, is always ready to respond to the light. (Ref. 207)

Another irony is that modern western society (and the rest of the world, too, to the extent that they seek democracy) is increasingly emphasizing the importance of egoism, colloquially known as "individualism" and encouraging us all to want more "things" which, it claims, will bring us happiness.

The root problem here, as far as modern western society is concerned, is the increased importance being placed upon the individual. We are all encouraged to pursue our own interests and endeavors in order to find fulfillment. All of the earlier values of family or workplace or community have been supplanted by values relating to self. We are now the selfish society and it is perfectly acceptable to much of the present generation that we can justify our behavior and aims in life simply on the grounds that it is something that *I* want to do. If I don't like my job, home or partner, I will go elsewhere. We are each unique, we are told and have a right to discover and express our individuality. Individualism is, of course, simply the modern euphemism for egoism. It is ironic that, on the basis of such beliefs, we are encouraged by pop-psychology to discover ourselves, realize our potential and so on when it is precisely these false conceptions that will prevent us from ever doing so. (Ref. 77)

Only when this erroneous view is recognized and the individualistic urge is dropped is there any chance of lasting happiness. Basically, the ego has to go! **Wolter Keers** († 1985) summarizes this:

We have to see very clearly that if we try to find Freedom while living in a cage we are crazy...

Love and happiness are centrifugal qualities, radiating qualities. Fear, egoism, greed, defensiveness, clinging are centripetal qualities. They are the source of the cramps in our bodies; of all fears and defensiveness. And no matter how we get there either philosophically or via the heart, when in one way or another we are ready to let go of our defences, only then can the cramp in the body also disappear. Then the centripetal, the cramping, the pulling in becomes centrifugal again. Then we feel that we are no longer lumbering and heavy, but that we are becoming light. "He danced with pleasure on the street," a sentence like that can be found in many books. He danced, he was light. But in order to get that happiness every day - and all our activities strive for that - we use all the means that make that happiness impossible, as sure as the night follows the day and the day again follows the night. Egoism is by definition a means, a course of action, a perspective that always misses its target. But in order to see that you have to learn to see well...

Only when I have given all, all that I have and I am, is the happiness complete. (Ref. 194)

Language

In the language of the neo-Advaita satsang teachers, the problems begin with the use of the word "I," which in a sense brings about the entire delusional edifice about which our hopes and fears are constructed. In reality, there is only ever *brahman*, whatever word may be used to refer to this in an age that is suspicious of traditional terms. Terms such as "being-ness," "aliveness," unconditional love etc. are all attempts to reference the non-dual reality in a non-confrontational way. Nathan Gill says that we could equally well call it "strawberry yoghurt" (Ref. 25). **Joan Tollifson**'s way of putting things is as follows:

Words weave stories. They create mental movies that seem entirely believable and real. In this movie-world of thoughts and stories, it appears that "I" am inside this skin, and everything else is "out there." It appears that "I" am incomplete, forever in need of improvement or modification. "I" seek happiness and enlightenment in the future, chase after bigger and better experiences, compare "myself" to "others," and idolize those imagined to possess something special that "I" lack...

The words are just words. The forms appear and disappear. It seems that "you" have a problem: the rent is due, your car needs a tune-up, you can't stop smoking, you want to get enlightened, you need to find a new guru, you need to be more awake, you need to relax, or pay attention, or let go, or get a grip. But see that these are all thoughts, and that the root-thought is the "you" who apparently "has" all of these problems. Yes, the rent may be due, and you'll either get the money and pay it, or you won't. You'll either stop smoking or you won't. And actually, "you" won't be doing any of this, or at least, not "you" as thought imagines you: the character in the story of your life, the separate person. You as the totality, the One Being, are doing (or appearing as) all of it. And actually, no-thing is happening. Where is last night? Or yesterday morning? Or a minute ago?

There is only one moment. Here. Now. This. This one eternal, timeless moment accepts everything, just as it is, even the resistance and the upset and the apparent non-acceptance. This one moment is all there is. This one moment is unconditional love. This one moment is inescapable, for there is no one to escape, and no-thing to escape from. (Ref. 195)

Instead of accepting whatever is happening now without question, we habitually filter it through our accumulated memory of desires and fears, turning away from the reality of the present into a "perpetually possible" future or a "might have been" past. As **T.S. Eliot** says: "Human kind cannot bear very much reality." (Ref. 196) **Isaac Shapiro** expresses it thus:

Not wanting the experience we are having feels uncomfortable in the body and this registers as a problem. Our thinking is the capacity to solve problems, so our thinking tries to help by projecting what the problem is and what the solution could be. When we don't want the experience we are having, I am going to call this resisting. All that happens is that our experience gets more intense or subjectively we call it worse. Now that it is worse we don't want it either, so we resist again, which makes it worse and now that it is worse we don't want it either, so we resist, ad infinitum. In a matter of moments we feel out of control, the experience we don't want is still there and we feel overwhelmed. Our experience feels bigger than us. Most people spend their entire lives feeling overwhelmed. There is a sense of too much to do and there is a constant underlying feeling of stress and the feeling that we have to run just to survive.

For most of us, the habit is to tighten up as soon as we wake, if we don't wake up already contracted, from what we have dreamt. We do this by thinking of what we have to do this day and unconsciously or consciously believing that this tightening up somehow helps us to survive.

Once we have tightened up, this registers as a problem and then our mind tries to help... Etc.

In western psychology, what we call the subconscious mind is everything we never want to experience again and everything we think we want to experience, in other words all our unfilled desires, that we think will make us happy. All of this is our resistance to our experience NOW. (Ref. 197)

Desire

I can't gain anything except burdens. A true gain is to lose something.
Robin Dale (Ref. 374)

Osho (Ref. 177) relates an old Sufi story about the insatiability of desire. It tells of a king who, encountering a beggar in the palace grounds, asks him what he wants. (Unbeknownst to the king, the beggar had been his teacher in a past life and had promised to return to enlighten him.) The beggar asks if the king really thinks he can fulfil the beggar's desire and the king, ruling a vast and rich empire claims that, of course, he can. So the beggar simply holds out his old wooden begging bowl and asks the king if he can fill it with something.

So the king tells his servants to top up the bowl with some coins, thinking that would be a simple matter. Needless to say, it wasn't. Coins were added, followed by gold and jewels but the bowl seemed to be bottomless. It swallowed everything that was added, leaving it still apparently empty. The king's honour being at stake, he did not stop until he had given away all of his treasure and possessions at which point he prostrated himself before the beggar, asking only that the latter explain how the bowl was able to do this. The beggar replied that the bowl was made out of human desire...

All desires are selfish, even the ones that might appear to be unselfish. As long as we persist in the mistaken belief that we are a separate individual, our search for happiness will be in vain. **Aja Thomas:**

You are the Bliss of Non-Being. However, you immerse yourself in your desires of selfishness. You identify with the river of thoughts and desires that arise in the ocean of consciousness. All desires are selfish. Your actions are based on desires that you think will make You happy. They are selfish. Even if you are trying to save the world, you do so out of selfishness. Even if you are feeding the hungry, clothing the poor, or worshipping God, you are doing it because you think that it is "right" to do so and it makes you happy to think that you are "right." Even those seeking enlightenment, freedom, salvation, liberation, are doing so because it is "right." They seek to end suffering, to attain eternal bliss, to be free from death and bondage. Surely these are noble causes, honorable beliefs, but they are still based on a person desiring something. They are the apparent effect of an apparent ego, struggling in an apparent world, attempting to gain apparent happiness, to counteract apparent suffering.

...You are the Bliss of Non-Being And when you are ready to give up your separateness, to abandon the vain and continuous searching for happiness, to free yourself from the limitation of personhood that appear to bind you, then you can again experience the bliss of non-being. (Ref. 93)

Even the desire for happiness or for self-realization is still a desire. It is *freedom* from desire that has been equated with self-realization, as in this extract from **Swami Nikhilananda**'s introduction to the Atmabodha:

The seeker after Truth must always remember the detached nature of the Self and give up all identification with the ego. It is the ego that brings the Self back again and again to the world of ignorance. It is the ego that aggravates desires. When desires increase activities also increase. And when there is an increase of activities there is an increase of desires. Thus desires and activities move in a vicious circle and man's imprisonment in the body is never at an end. The destruction of desires has been described as Liberation, and the man free from desires is called a *jīvanmukta*, one liberated in life. (Ref. 193)

Amber tells the story of an ostrich who wished to fly like a flamingo. Unable to dismiss this unattainable desire, which is disrupting his life, he seeks advice from a wise tiger. Having listened to the problem, the tiger suddenly turns on the ostrich with a terrible roar, as if about to eat him, subsequently saying: "Where are your questions now, foolish bird? That is my answer to you. Now go."

Many years later, now living a fruitful and rewarding life, the ostrich meets the flamingo and explains what happened:

"I knew that I could not fly, as I yearned to do, nor could I relinquish my responsibilities to the flock. But I was unhappy. So there was only one place left for me to turn, and that was within myself. The tiger showed me how to look. He showed me that whatever emotion or feeling was dominant in my mind temporarily suppressed all other needs or thoughts."

"So you knew that even the strongest yearning, your need to fly, was temporary?"

"Yes, and therefore it couldn't have been as vital as I had supposed. In my terror at the tiger's roar, all my deepest yearnings temporarily vanished... so I understood that they were passing things only. Instead I wanted something permanent and lasting."

"How did you come to realize that the only thing that lasts is the quiet of the mind?"

"I simply stopped chasing after that which was transitory. Then to my wonder and joy, I found that all that was left was my sense of being. My own consciousness."

"But not a consciousness of something...?"

"No, the simple fact of consciousness itself." (Ref. 167)

Desire for Objects

The accepted belief in the west is that people find happiness in things or states. We are all individuals and naturally want different things but, when we get what we want we are happy – for a while. The mechanism of desire is described in the *Atmabodha* v.23:

> *rAga* (interest in, affection for), *ichChA* (desire), *sukha* (pleasure) and *duHkha* (pain) come forth in the presence of the intellect (*buddhi*), not in its absence in deep sleep. Therefore, they must be related to the intellect and not to *Atman*. (My translation)

The idea is that we see something and develop an interest in it, an attachment or identification. This leads to a desire to possess it. If we succeed in getting it, there is pleasure. But this proves to be temporary only and leads on to misery or pain. If we fail to obtain the desired object, this too brings misery. As noted, it is the identification with *vij~nAnamayakosha* that leads us to think that we are the doer and also it is the intellect that claims to be the enjoyer when there is identification with *Anandamayakosha*. That this is so can be understood by appreciating that all of these emotions, from interest through to enjoyment or dejection, disappear in deep sleep, when the mind ceases to operate. If they had anything to do with our true nature, they would always be with us since that remains constant throughout.

The **Bhagavad Gita** is even more uncompromising about the consequences of this process:

> When a man thinks of objects, attachment for them arises. From attachment arises desire; from desire arises wrath. From wrath arises delusion, failure of memory, loss of conscience; from loss of conscience he is utterly ruined. **II 61-2**. (Ref. 28)

We have no control over the arising of thoughts but, in itself, this is not a problem. In theory we can simply observe them and let them go. When we perceive some object, it is quite natural that a thought such as "that is nice" may come; however, it is all too easy to follow this up with another thought such as "I would quite like it." This is the beginning of attachment and can so easily grow into a clear desire to obtain the object. This is usually not so easy to do and, when the desire is thwarted by obstacles, frustration and anger are the inevitable consequence and we are no longer able to reason logically – we are deluded. We forget that this sort of thing has happened before and led only to dissatisfaction or worse, and repeat the same debilitating patterns as before, paying no attention to the feelings of others. Clearly there is no meaning or happiness in any of this.

Here is an example in more detail:

Suppose, for the sake of an example, we say that X very much wants a surfboard. He lives close to the sea and spends hours watching others surfing, envying their control, poise and wishing he were feeling the excitement etc. Then, one day Y has a serious accident in a particularly large wave. Y decides he never wants to surf again (which he couldn't do anyway until all of his fractures have healed) and gives his board to X, who is now blissfully happy.

There are several points that may be made regarding this example. First, the happiness could not in any sense have been in the surfboard. Many people (e.g. me!) would never even want one and would feel no particular positive emotion to receive it. Even Y will now probably feel only negative emotions towards it. Happiness cannot be in any object. If it were, the manufacturer of such objects would rule the world. The increase in prosperity in the west over the past century has given us material possessions beyond the dreams of previous generations but it hasn't brought about any increase in happiness. People in the third world, without even electricity to fuel many of the things that we now consider essential, are frequently happier than we are. And money is nothing more than a means for obtaining objects.

Also, even though Y was presumably made happy by the surfboard when he originally obtained it, he is clearly no longer made happy by it. And if X were to be given another surfboard the next day by his favourite aunt, he would not be likely to be twice as happy. In fact, he might well feel a bit aggrieved.

And, if the surfboard were taken away, X could find something else the next minute, which could bring equivalent happiness.

Secondly, what we want is itself only an idea, a product of our own particular genetic make up and environmental upbringing. X may want a surfboard but Z, from a family that spent time listening to music rather than going out to play sports, may well want a violin. What I want, and what I think that I need, depends upon who I think I am.

Thirdly, the idea (of what I want or need) is only a thought and we cannot choose to have thoughts – they simply "arise." And we are not our thoughts or our emotions.

Fourthly, the happiness that results when the desire for the surfboard is satisfied does not last. As soon as we get used to having the desired object, we are back to our "baseline state" and ready for the next desire to kick in. (Ref. 168)

True happiness cannot be found in things that change and pass away. Pleasure and pain alternate inexorably. Happiness comes from the self and can be found in the self only. Find your real self (svarUpa) and all else will come with it. **Nisargadatta Maharaj** (Ref. 5)

Ananda Wood describes the teaching of Atmananda Krishna Menon with respect to desire and objects:

Why is the object desired? Evidently, the mind that desires feels a want or a lack. The object is desired to fulfill that want.

When a desired object is successfully attained, the mind feels fulfilled, in a state of happiness. But what exactly is that happiness? As it fulfils the wanting mind, from where does it come?

Habitually, as our minds desire objects, we think of happiness as something that is found in them. But of course this isn't true. An object may or may not bring happiness, depending on the time and the occasion...

But then, if not in objects, where in truth can happiness be found? Can it be in the mind? No, it cannot. For if it were, the mind would always be enjoying it. In that case, we'd never see our minds dissatisfied. We'd never see them wanting any object of desire. And we would never see a passing state of happiness, resulting from some object that has been achieved. We'd never see this state of happiness give way to a further state of wanting - as the mind turns restless again, with desire for some other object.

In a state of happiness, the mind is brought to rest. As a desired object is attained, the mind comes then to be at one with its desired object. Mind and object are no longer seen as two, but are resolved as only one. Each has subsided and dissolved into unmixed consciousness, where there is no duality. There, self is one with what it knows.

In a state of happiness, that oneness shines, showing the true nature of each person's self. From that self comes happiness. The very being of that self is its non-dual shining, which we call "happiness." (Ref. 170)

Happiness – the Absence of Desire

The key element in happiness is seen to be the absence of desire, as **David Jennings** points out:

Why are you not happy? The first answers that will suggest themselves will be along the lines of "I don't have enough money," "I don't have a nice husband or wife," or "I don't have a big house or a new car" or "an interesting job," and so on. Or, I have enough money to have anything I want, but I still feel a deep emptiness. Things of that sort. However, a careful investigation of these possibilities will reveal that happiness does not come from objects or experiences.

You can see this easily, as a matter of fact, in your ordinary experience. If your attention is completely focused on a loss, let us say the sudden loss of a sum of money or the loss of a friend, then the body-mind machinery will function in accord with what it is seeing and experiencing. That functioning is called suffering. If on the other hand your attention is fully taken by a sudden gain, such as the meeting of someone new whose company you enjoy, or a wished-for possession you have suddenly gained, then the body-mind machinery will function in quite a different way. In this case you will feel happy.

Now, without thinking, you may take it that it is the possession of a new friend, or new things that has led to happiness in the second case. That is not actually so. You cannot desire what you already have, so that having something is coincident with having no desire for it. To the extent that your attention is totally taken up with something that you already have, you are experiencing no desire for that thing at that time; and, if you look carefully you will see that this absence is what we ordinarily experience as happiness.

How can it be, you might ask, that the mere absence of some superimposed personal whim such as a wish for something could seem to be happiness? Happiness could only feel as if it were absent from you if some mechanism is seemingly superimposed upon it, so as to obscure it. It cannot actually be absent, because it is an aspect of what you fundamentally are. (Ref. 169)

Thus it is most people live out their lives, continually looking outside of themselves for something which, they imagine, will bring them happiness. Even after a lifetime of pursuing first this and then that, always discovering in the end that they bring at the best a temporary reward, still we continue with this fruitless search:

11. The pleasures and riches of worldly life are deceptive appearances. Understanding that they are all but a passing-show, be detached and dispassionate, cultivate renunciation and seek Brahman.

12. Day and night, dawn and dusk, winter and spring, all these are flitting across the stage of the world. While time thus is frolicking and befooling us, our life span is also running out; yet we do not, even a little, give up the clinging to our desires, nor do we let the desires loosen their grip on us.

13. Crazy man! Why do you worry so much about your wife and property? Why don't you seek out the Truth? Know that in these three worlds it is only the association with the good and holy that can help you in crossing safely the ocean of life.

14. The ascetic with matted locks, the man with the shaven head or one with hair pulled out, or the man parading in the ochre robes - they all have eyes but yet do not see. All these are but deceptions for cheating the world, for filling their bellies. (Renunciation does not lie in external appearance, but in inward thought, attitude and feeling).

15. The body has become decrepit, the hair on the head has turned completely gray; the mouth has become totally toothless; the back is bent down and the old man cannot take even a step without the aid of his stick; yet he does not loosen even a bit, his hold on the bundle of desires.

(**Bhaja Govindam**, attributed to **Shankara**) (Ref. 176)

Mechanism of Desire

To summarize then, from Ref. 168, our usual state is that we feel limited and insecure – i.e. we believe we are the ego. When we desire something, we have the feeling that we lack the desired object, that somehow we are incomplete without it. We want to feel 'full-filled' and complete. We identify with the desired object and mistakenly imagine that it will give us this completeness, however temporary. At the moment of obtaining it, that perceived emptiness is filled and we feel satisfied and completely ourselves. Momentarily there is nothing that we want. The phrase "satisfaction of the desire" is a key one – the obscuring influence of the desire is no longer there. Obtaining the object, we feel that we are temporarily made complete. The desire that obscured the knowledge that we are already complete is lost.

We are no longer looking outwards away from ourselves for some thing that we perceive as a lack. We are at peace and content in simple knowledge of our true nature – which is existence, consciousness and happiness. This is, and was, always our true nature. The imagined limitation and the lack, manifested as a desire, simply took us away from it. But objects can never "complete" us in this sense and we know it, even if only subconsciously. As soon as we look, we find that we still see the objects as separate and the spell is broken.

There is no end to desire whilst we consider ourselves to be limited. As one desire is satisfied another is born, continually adding fuel to the fire and taking us away from the happiness that we seek. As Swami Dayananda said, it is not *what* I want that is the problem, it is *that* I want. As long as we continue to perceive ourselves as limited, as lacking something that will make us complete, we will continue to search for this elusive (and, of course, non-existent) something outside of ourselves.

And we could never be content with "limited" happiness. We want the complete and everlasting variety. This is yet more proof, if more were needed, that we will never find it in anything in the outside world or in mind, thoughts or emotions. These are all finite and temporary. Happiness must transcend time, space and causation; must be beyond mind and intellect; cannot in fact be in anything outside of ourselves.

We must supplant all other desires with the single one of endeavouring to discover our true nature. This will also have the effect of turning our attention back towards ourselves instead of outwards to the illusory external "things." Of all desires, the desire for self-realisation is the highest. Along the way, there are two sources that can reliably remind us of our true nature – meditation and deep sleep. Meditation is a state of absence of thoughts, i.e. absence of mind or ego. And in deep sleep, there is Consciousness only – again no ego. It is those moments when we "forget ourselves" when we feel most alive and happy. Only forgetting ourselves permanently, i.e. eliminating the ego completely, can bring lasting happiness.

The true nature of the Self is without limit – effectively everlasting bliss. When the mind is absent, this state is temporarily experienced through the reflection in *Anandamayakosha*. Unfortunately its significance is not appreciated and, upon returning to our normal, mind-governed life, we again feel at the mercy of the supposed events going on around us. When the ego is dissolved and the unity of the Self is recognised, it will be known that this bliss is our true nature, our permanent condition.

Ananda

In fact, to be strictly accurate, we never experience true *Ananda*. *Ananda* is an aspect of *brahman* and, as such, is infinite and non-dual, not an object of experience and it doesn't come and go (as happiness does). **Swami Dayananda** explains this brilliantly, (if you concentrate for a moment in order to cope with all of the Sanskrit terms!):

> There are a lot of people who translate the word *Ananda* as bliss which is not correct. Bliss itself is a *vRRitti-visheSha* [particular mental disposition], whereas the *Ananda* is the nature of the *Atma* and not a *vRRitti*. In the sentence "*satyam j~nAnam anantam brahma*" [*taittirIya upaniShad* 2.2.1 – Brahman is truth, knowledge and infinite], the word *ananta* stands for *Ananda*. *ananta* means that which is free from any limitation. That is the nature of *Atma*. Therefore limitlessness, wholeness, fullness is the meaning of the word *Ananda*.

But if the meaning of the word *Ananda* is *ananta* which is clear, then why use the word *Ananda* at all and confuse the issue? The *shAstra* uses the word *Ananda* instead of *ananta* because it is the *lakShaNa* [indirect pointer] for *puruShArtha*. It indicates the *puruShArtha*, pursuit. What we are seeking by *dharma-artha-kAma* is *Ananda*. So by gaining *Ananda* there is *puruShArtha-lAbha*, fulfillment of the pursuit. The common experiential *Ananda* one gets is also a *mAtrA*, fraction of the *svarUpAnanda* [one's own *Ananda*] that is limitless. What is experienced as *Ananda* is a *vRRitti-visheSha*, a particular state of mind, and is limited in terms of time also. So it is time-bound. Again there are degrees in the experiential *Ananda*. Therefore we have different words like - pleasure, happiness, joy etc. All these are *vRRitti-visheSha*-s with different degrees of intensity. In the experience of any *Ananda*, the fullness of the *Atma* is manifest and that is what is sought after by all. Therefore *Ananda* becomes a *lakShaNa* for the nature of the *vastu* [the thing itself, i.e. *Atma*]. *Ananda* is also an experiential word to which you can relate immediately and it also indicates the *puruShArtha*, therefore the *shAstra* uses the word *Ananda*. (Ref. 58)

True *Ananda*, if it could be experienced, is of infinitely greater "magnitude of" happiness then the shadowy forms normally experienced through these body-minds, as is explained at tedious length in the *taittirIya upaniShad* (2.8). Here is a more palatable, modern interpretation by **Ananda Wood**:

Imagine someone who is young,
who's open, honest, full of fun,
well-educated, sensitive,
alert, adjusted, healthy, strong,
with all the comforts wealth can bring.
Take this as "normal" happiness.

Much more intense is happiness
of celebration, breaking free
from personal conditioning
that limits ordinary life.

And more than this, there's happiness
of settled, long experience:
which goes on bringing in rewards
for relatively many years.

But this depends on happiness
of cultivated faculties
inherited through family
and breeding in society.

And further, there is happiness
of capabilities achieved
by one's own work and discipline.

Supporting this is happiness
of mastering one's faculties:
co-ordinating and controlling
them, towards one's chosen goals.

All this is based on happiness
of aspiration to the truth,
beyond all mere appearances
of seeming objects in the world.

And greater still is happiness
of coming to creation's source
from which appearances arise.

But none of these compares at all
with unconditioned happiness:

where all desires are dissolved,
and simple truth is realized
that consciousness is all there is,
with self and object known as one. (Ref. 175)

The ultimate irony is that we all know this happiness for which we are looking. Why otherwise would we be continually searching? If we recognize it when we find it we must have had prior knowledge of it. That is the meaning of "recognize" – to "know again." The only way that this can be explained is that we once had it, believe that we have lost it and are seeking to find it again. Unfortunately, we insist in looking for it in the (apparent) outside world of objects and other people and situations.

It really is as simple as that, as **Brian Lake** and **Naama Livni** point out:

In our ignorance, instead of recognizing the immediate invisible pure-intelligence that enables us to register images, we focus on what the images (objects) mean to us and on the self-image (subject) of the one we believe sees them. When we identify with self-image we say, "It can't be that the truth of what I am is so simple and self-evident." Thinking that it is too simple, we look outward and reach for a high that seems to come with extra-ordinary phenomena. (Ref. 171)

Happiness is the Nature of the Self

Happiness is our natural state. That which comes and goes is the ego. We think we are miserable, because we forget our essential nature, which is Bliss. Even an emperor, in spite of his wealth and power, often suffers because of his disturbed mind. The sage, who does not know where his next meal will come from, is ever happy. See who enjoys Bliss. **Ramana Maharshi** (Ref. 181)

Thus it can be seen that happiness is not something to be found outside but is actually an aspect of our own nature that we mistakenly ignore. **Ramana Maharshi** explains:

Happiness is the very nature of the Self; happiness and the Self are not different. There is no happiness in any object of the world. We imagine through our ignorance that we derive happiness from objects. When the mind goes out, it experiences misery. In truth, when its desires are fulfilled, it returns to its own place and enjoys the happiness that is the Self. Similarly, in the states of sleep, *samAdhi* and fainting, and when the object desired is obtained or the object disliked is removed, the mind becomes inward-turned, and enjoys pure Self-Happiness. Thus the mind moves without rest alternately going out of the Self and returning to it. Under the tree the shade is pleasant; out in the open the heat is scorching. A person who has been going about in the sun feels cool when he reaches the shade. Someone who keeps on going from the shade into the sun and then back into the shade is a fool. A wise man stays permanently in the shade. Similarly, the mind of the one who knows the truth does not leave Brahman. The mind of the ignorant, on the contrary, revolves in the world, feeling miserable, and for a little time returns to Brahman to experience happiness. In fact, what is called the world is only thought. When the world disappears, i.e. when there is no thought, the mind experiences happiness; and when the world appears, it goes through misery. (Ref. 178)

After (or quite often during!) the experience of happiness, the ego makes an entrance and a claim (if the happiness is still there, it is quickly dispelled). We associate the happiness with whatever was happening at the time or with the object that had just been obtained. Thus it is that we seek to regain it by repeating the experience or obtaining some new, related object. In fact, at the moment of happiness, there is neither subject nor object, as **Atmananda Krishna Menon** explains:

At the point of enjoyment you were thrown into your real Nature. You went beyond even the ego. You were thrown into your real Nature and you were alone there, shining in your own Glory. And that was Happiness. Coming out of it, you immediately superimpose upon that real Nature of yours an ego on this side and the thing with which you came into contact on the other. And you bring in the mind also to say that you enjoyed. That is how it is. So, in every experience likewise you are thrown into your real Nature and you are alone there, without anything else. So, the object of your experience is always the 'I'-principle and the subject of the experience is also the 'I'-principle. Or, in other words, there is neither subject nor object in Experience. There is Experience alone. You stand as Experience, without the subject or the object. And that is what Happiness is. Yes. (Ref. 117)

There is no thinking when we are truly happy – the mind and ego are in abeyance and *Ananda* is reflected without obstruction in the *Anandamayakosha*:

What is more important here is that we have to confess that each time we were really happy, truly fulfilled, there was no thinking process going on. There is just "what is." The thinking mind only pops up *afterwards*. When there is no thinking process going on, there is no hope and no fear, no complaining, no desire and no guilt. Or in other words, there is no "me." Isn't that amazing, to see that each time there is real happiness, that there is in fact *nobody there*? No separation, no self-image, just pure joy. There is only pure "Is-ness" which is not disturbed by any concept or thought about our little me. **Jan Kersschot** (Ref. 180)

Purpose

The intuitive knowledge of the Ultimate Reality of brahman alone is the prime purpose of human life, its fulfillment. There is no human purpose whatsoever that is not gained from this knowledge (of the Self or Atman). **D. B. Gangolli** (Ref. 292)

"Meaning" could be thought of as filling the apparent holes in our lives, giving us something to occupy the mind from moment to moment – a tactical maneuver. "Purpose" is more of a strategic ploy, making our life seem "complete"; something for us to work towards, even if we never achieve it. (Indeed, it may be better if we do not succeed because there are many examples of people who became foremost in their own field of endeavor and then were forced to think: what now?) For most people the wish is that they may be able to look back at the end of their lives and feel that something worthwhile has been accomplished.

If related to one's job, it is likely that the target is continually being moved back. Goals that seemed unattainable early in one's career may be achieved so that their value is diminished and more challenging objectives must be set. If unrelated to work, aspirations are likely to be sidelined, considered as something to dream about or to tackle after retirement. They exist perhaps as an intermittent, background worry, like the household job that I must get around to doing some day.

It is natural that an ambition achieved should eventually be perceived as unfulfilling. As an event in time, it is limited. The moment of its achievement is similar to the moment that a desired object is gained. The feeling is much more intense since the effective desire may have lasted most of one's lifetime. But the moment inevitably passes. The ego reasserts itself and the natural happiness felt in its absence recedes. Though temporarily buoyed by the success, there is now also a void – what am "I" going to do now?

Ultimately, of course, all ego-related activities fail to deliver the goods. It is somewhat akin to playing a game. Whilst winning, it may seem fulfilling but after it is over, it is seen for what it always was – merely a game...

If "what I want" is just an idea then, if I get it, all that is going to be satisfied is this idea. And ideas are temporary things only, coming and going with terrifying rapidity. No idea is going to provide lasting satisfaction. What we truly are deserves much more than this. (Ref. 77)

It seems to be human nature to feel that there must be something more to life than the mundane day-to-day search for transient pleasures and avoidance of the inevitable pains. Even the most shallow, materially minded person must occasionally stop and wonder. **Swami Vivekananda** puts it thus:

Just as by the knowledge of one lump of clay we know all the clay that is in the universe, so what is that, knowing which we know everything else? This, expressed more or less clearly, is the theme of all human knowledge. It is the finding of a Unity towards which we are all going. Every action of our lives, the most material, the grossest as well as the finest, the highest, the most spiritual, is alike tending towards this one ideal, the finding of Unity.

...Irresistibly we are impelled towards that perfection which consists in finding the Unity, killing this little self and making ourselves broader and broader

...That is the foundation of all morality. It is the quintessence of all ethics, preached in any language, or in any religion, or by any prophet in the world. (Ref. 191)

The concept of "purpose" can only be relevant if there is some entity that can undergo change so that we can start from where we are and progress in some way to become something different later in life. Hopefully, it is now becoming clearer that we are not such an entity. The body, mind and intellect do change. The body inevitably grows older and dies. The mind and emotions change from moment to moment and hopefully the intellect grows wiser in being able to monitor and cope with these changes. But we are none of these, as will be addressed in detail in the chapter on "Who we really are." We are actually limitless and changeless so that any idea of purpose ceases to have meaning.

To the extent that there is any purpose to human existence, it must be for us to realize that the very concept of separate human beings is a mistake, to understand the nature of that mistake and thus to discover who we truly are. Hence the teaching of Advaita: that we should prepare the mind, look for a guru and seek self-realization. **Ramesh Balsekar** has said:

What is "Self-realization" or "enlightenment" supposed to do for the entity for the rest of his life? Being anchored in peace and harmony, while facing life from moment to moment. That is the "purpose" of seeking. (Ref. 198)

The **Kena Upanishad** II.5 has this to say:

If in this world (a person) knows the soul, then the true end (of all human aspiration) is (gained); if a person in this world does not know (the soul), there will be great calamity. The wise who discern in all beings (the one nature of Brahman) become immortal, after departing from this world. (Ref. 199)

The *shvetAshvataropaniShad* (VI.20) states that:

Only when men shall roll up the sky like a skin, will there be an end of misery for them without realizing God. (Ref. 351)

Of course, the idea of purpose itself assumes that there is a separate individual or a separate human race living in a world and that all of this has been created with a particular end in mind. None of this is the case, as will be seen in the chapter on the nature of reality:

The only sensible purpose for the presumed person must be to discover who they are, to realize the truth, to understand the nature of reality.

Practically all of the words in the above sentence should really be put into quotation marks, in recognition of the fact that they are concepts and, as such, do not correspond with the way things actually are. The fact of the matter is that we cannot *under*-stand reality, we can only stand *as* reality. It is only the mind or ego that seeks, that wants to reach somewhere and get something. And the mind and ego are nothing more than concepts themselves so the whole idea is a non-starter.

Yes, the fact of the matter is that all "things," including concepts, are nothing but Consciousness but until this is directly realized, we are in the position of the man seeing the rope but thinking it is a snake. (Ref. 201)

Therefore, the bottom line must be that life is purposeless, as is explained by **Swami Dayananda**:

Since the world is superimposed upon *Atman*, it does not require to be explained away in terms of purpose. So there is no real purpose or meaning for the world...

The *jIva* is asking the questions, "how come this world is created?"...

All these questions such as "who plants this *avidyA*?," "when did *avidyA* begin?" have no basis because the *vastu* [the thing that exists] is *brahman*, which is the *svarUpa* [own nature] of the *jIva*. That is the thing to be understood. (Ref. 58)

Review of the model of "layers" of reality

The model of the sheaths (the *pa~ncha-kosha-prakriyA*) and a similar model from the Chandogya Upanishad provide excellent metaphors for the search for meaning in our lives and for the notional steps in a "spiritual path" towards an understanding of our true nature.

The *taittirIya upaniShad* (in the third section, called the *bhRRiguvalII adhyAya* or "section in which Bhrigu is given a lesson") examines the successive layers of identification that could be imagined to take place in the model of the sheaths, from the grossest bodily level up to the subtlest level of *Anandamayakosha*. It explains how reflection and meditation upon the nature of who we are can reveal our mistaken identity.

The *annamayakosha* represents the grossest material level of our bodies, consisting as they do merely of the food that we eat. These lumps of matter, complex though they may be, are nothing more than this unless they are pervaded by the life-force that energizes them, the "vital air" or *prANamayakosha* that enables those bodies to breathe in and out. It effectively raises the inanimate body of matter to the level of vegetable. With it, we are at least "alive." This more subtle body permeates and "controls" the grosser and cannot be separately perceived in the combination. It leaves the body only at death. As **Swami Krishnananda** puts it:

> Just as in a live wire electric energy charges every particle or atom of the wire and you cannot know which is the wire and which is electricity (but if you touch the wire you will get a shock), likewise you cannot know which is the body and which is the *prANa*. They have become one, so that if you touch any part of the body it looks as if you are being touched. Your life has become one with the vehicle which is the body; the vehicle has become one with the driver. They are identical; you can-

not separate one from the other. (Ref. 214)

At a subtler level still, the mind permeates the living body, feeling and sensing the body itself but aware of much else besides through the medium of the other senses. The *prANa* may move the material body but it does so only under direction from the mind, operating through the "organs" of action and of perception. This happens at an instinctual level so that the *manomayakosha* effectively raises the plant-like body-and-*prANa* combination to the status of animal.

It is only when the intellect suffuses this at an even subtler level that it is able to impart intelligence to the actions and discrimination becomes possible. This is effected through the part of the mind known as *buddhi*, which determines what the mind should pay attention to. This presence of the *vij~nAnamayakosha* distinguishes man, who unlike the animal is now able to speculate upon the nature of the universe.

The most subtle sheath of all is the so-called "bliss" sheath, *Anandamayakosha*. It is the level associated with the deep-sleep state, wherein we are still aware but aware of nothing. Though effectively a state of ignorance, it is called bliss because, in deep sleep, we are completely at peace and forgetful of all of our waking worries and suffering. It represents the highest level of "control" in this model of man since happiness is what drives the intellect to differentiate between possible courses of action.

This method, whereby the teacher directs the student from his initial identification with something gross on to increasingly more subtle levels of understanding, is called *sthUla arundhatI nyAya*. It is the clearest example of the Advaitic method of teaching. *nyAya* means logical argument. *arundhatI* is the Indian name given to a star, Alcor, in the constellation of Ursa Major (Great Bear, Plough or Big Dipper). In marriage ceremonies in India, the star is pointed out to the bride as an example to be followed, since the star is "devoted" to its companion star, Mizar or *vAsiShTha* (*arundhatI* was the wife of *vAsiShTha*). Because the star is scarcely visible, it is necessary to lead the eye to it gradually. Thus one might first locate the constellation by reference to the moon. Then the attention can be directed to the bright star that is at the tail of the Great Bear. Finally, there is a companion star which is only 11 minutes distant and fourth magnitude that can only be seen by people with exceptional eyesight. This is *arundhatI*.

In the same way, the *taittirIya upaniShad* first points to the body as being the Atman but then indicates that the vital energy is more subtle and the body is, after all, only food. In this way, the disciple is guided through successive levels until he is able to recognize his previously mistaken identifications and understand his essential nature.

In the context of the *guNa*, the hierarchy of sheaths also represents a movement from the *tamas* of *annamaya* through the primarily *rAjasika prANamaya* up to the *sattva* of *Anandamaya*. In practical terms, it represents a rising in the level of consciousness; a progression as if from mineral to God. And it can be seen in everyday life how man is prepared to give up the lower in order to satisfy the higher. We sacrifice parts of the body in order that we may continue to live. We give up our lives in the cause of ideals. And, throughout all of our actions in this life, the search for eternal happiness is the constant background motivation.

It is because this drive for happiness is so pervasive that this final sheath can become a sticking point in the search for truth. There is a danger that the seeker may believe that happiness (or "bliss"), being his true nature, is the end-point of the search. This idea that eternal happiness is possible in the human form is the final level of identification. And it is a good reason why *brahman* should be thought of as *sat – chit* and *ananta* – limitlessness – rather than as the more usual *sachchidAnanda*, as is discussed below.

A similar but more comprehensive hierarchy is presented in the *chhAndogya upaniShad* (Chapter 7) in which the sage Narada (*nArada*) visits Sanatkumara (*sanatkumAra*), one of the sons of Brahma, the creator of the universe, to ask how to discover the truth of *brahman*. The purpose of the story is to spell out the apparent layers of reality, each successively more subtle, until *brahman* itself is uncovered as the only (true) reality. As the aspirant's understanding grows, the lower levels fall away as being of no further interest, signifying the progress of the seeker along the path to realization, and opening up the way for the consideration of more subtle levels.

Narada is already prepared to receive this knowledge, having studied the scriptures in depth but approaches Sanatkumara with humility knowing that all of this knowledge remains "only words" and that he is still miserable. This is also the paradigm of the guru-disciple relationship.

Sanatkumara begins by telling him that everything he has learned to date is only Name, the unspoken word. If that is the limit of what one values then the most one can hope for is to obtain anything capable of being named. Greater than that is Speech (*vAch*), which enables us actually to understand the scriptures and the meaning of good and bad, true and false etc. Mind is superior to this, capable of contemplating, desiring and initiating both action (name) and speech.

But mind itself is incapable of doing anything unless thoughts occur first, are weighed and considered, and then willed. This considered and purposeful desire or will is called *saMkalpa* and this is deemed to be a higher reality than mind. However, we do not will anything unless the pros and cons have been weighed by the intellect and a decision reached. This takes into account past experience as well as what is presented to the mind now, and exercises judgement irrespective of what might actually be desired. So intelligence is higher than *saMkalpa*.

Greater than mere logical discrimination, however, is meditation, where full attention is given with self-control and stillness of mind, bringing peace and clarity. Higher still is knowledge, wherein understanding of what began as mere "names" in the scriptures is now fully present. But, in order to gain this knowledge, strength of mind (*bala*) is needed – the capacity fully to comprehend all that is knowable.

It is known that man's ability to think straight deteriorates significantly after a few days without eating so that food is clearly necessary if we wish to have strength of mind. This means that Food must be higher in the hierarchy. Our need for water is greater still and food itself, in the form of grain, will not be available without adequate rainfall. Without the heat from the sun, there would be no rain and therefore no water to drink, so that fire is even higher. But greater even than fire is the space or ether that contains the sun and all of the stars and planets. Everything exists within space.

Greater than all of these is memory, without which all would be meaningless. Only with the aid of memory are we able to think, speak and learn. Without any aspirations or desires (*AshA* as opposed to *kAma*, which refers to "longing" or sexual desire), however, there would be no motivation for any action so that this must be greater.

But without the life force, *prANa*, none of the above would exist. *prANa* is the energy behind everything in the universe. At the level of the individual body, it is the force that breathes air in and out, animating the material body, which is otherwise nothing but food (*anna*). At the level of the universe, it binds everything together "just as the spokes of the wheel are fastened to the hub." Here we have finally reached the first level of differentiation in the sheath model, with the *prANamayakosha* suffusing and enlivening the *annamayakosha*.

After having been told all this, Narada does not ask any more questions but Sanatkumara does not want him to leave thinking that *prANa* is the final truth (*satyam*) and continues the teaching. Only one who knows the supreme reality, *bhUmA*, is able to speak the truth.

In order to understand *bhUmA*, you have to reflect upon it but, in order for reflection to take place, there must be faith (*shraddhA*), otherwise there will be no expectation of success. There is no faith without steadfastness and that is not gained except through activity, in the sense of sense-control and concentration.

Everything that we do is done, overtly or otherwise, because we imagine that the result will bring us happiness. In the absence of this expectation we would have no reason for doing anything. **Ananda Wood** explains:

How does the conditioned world relate to the unconditioned happiness of real self? In the following passage from the Taittiriya Upanishad, 3.6, happiness is described as the complete reality that underlies all experience of the entire world. For this "happiness" is the final principle of value which motivates all perceptions, thoughts and feelings; and it thus always underlies whatever is perceived or thought about or felt, through all experience of the apparent world.

Reality is nothing else
but unconditioned happiness:
where falsity has been removed
from consciousness, which is thus known
at one with all reality.
From unconditioned happiness,
rise all of our experiences.
On it, each one of them depends.
It's what they want. It's where they go.
It is the self that knows in us
and all we ever really know. (Ref. 216)

The same applies to our search for the highest truth. The large can never find satisfaction in the small. **Swami Swahananda** explains in his commentary on the above:

bhUmA is a profound term supplied by this Upanishad to Vedanta. Sri Shankaracharya renders the meaning of it by the words *mahat* (great, important, distinguished) and *niratishayam* (unsurpassed). *mahat* and *bRRihat* are synonymous. The word *brahman* is derived from the root *bRRi*, meaning to grow. Here, therefore, the terms *bhUman, mahat,* and *brahman* denote the same reality which includes all finite existences and outside which one cannot conceive anything greater in magnitude or value. Anything short of this infinite, all-inclusive reality is only limited, petty, and finite.

It is common experience that the human mind cannot choose anything small when something greater than that is within its knowledge. Man is not happy with the small, he wants something more than what he already possesses and until the very limit of expansion is reached he cannot find complete contentment. Limitedness and unlimitedness are relative. The former implies the latter. The latter is not obtained by the common man and hence we find that his restlessness and craving are expressed through his activities. The infinite alone transcends all relations and includes within its range all the desires, hopes, and inspirations of man. Hence this *bhUman* alone is declared to be unequalled, unlimited, and unsurpassed bliss. This is the summit of Vedanta and the goal of all religious and philosophical search. (Ref. 43)

Sanatkumara explains the nature of *bhUmA*:

> Do you want to know what Completeness is? And do you want to know what finitude is? Here is the definition," says Sanatkumara. "Where one sees nothing except one's own Self, where one hears nothing except one's own Self, where one understands nothing except one's own Self, that is *bhUmA*, the Absolute; and where one sees something outside oneself, where one hears something outside oneself, where one understands or thinks something outside oneself, that is the finite. (Ref. 23)

The absolute reality cannot be known in the objective sense of something known by the mind. It is that by which all else is known. When all of the lower "orders" of reality have been sublated the Atman, one's own true Self, is realized as identical with the non-dual reality, Brahman.

Summary

Motivation and Meaning

- The belief that we are an "enjoyer" (*bhoktRRi*) leads to striving to maximize pleasure and minimize pain.
- This is rationalized as the "desire to be happy" and may be seen as our purpose in life. The true aim of life is the end of all desire.
- This is already our natural state but, being covered over by ignorance, requires knowledge to "attain."
- All desires and actions are aimed at overcoming our sense of being

limited.

- The meaning of a map lies in its use of symbols; its purpose is to get you from A to B. Meaning in our lives is the day to day rationale; its purpose is our final aim.

- Death is a key motivator, causing us to fear those things that might hasten it and pursue those that might delay it.

- Since it is only the body that dies, death is ultimately no more significant than that of the character in a dream when we wake up.

- Good and evil are only relative terms in the phenomenal world; Brahman is beyond both. Evil arises as a result of ignorance.

- Following the "pleasant" leads only to fleeting satisfaction of material desires; the "good" refers to spiritual actions/beliefs that lead to happiness.

- Spiritual pursuits, though initially arduous, bring eventual consolation and ultimate realization of the eternal reality.

- Worldly pursuits cannot bring lasting happiness. They are limited while our true nature is unlimited.

- Beauty is seeing our Self in something (apparently) external.

- Love, in the lower sense of the word, is genetic and ego-related (Sanskrit *moha*). Unselfish and undirected love, e.g. of wisdom, is *prema*, ego-less and transcending the physical.

- Love of another is love of the Self in the "other" but this is distorted and misunderstood by the ego.

- The four traditional goals of life (*puruShArtha*-s) are *dharma* (following the natural laws of society), *artha* (acquisition of wealth), *kAma* (satisfying desires) and *mokSha* (liberation; realization of our true nature).

- Pleasure seems to be a mechanical and possibly evolutionary device to aid survival and propagation of the species.

Happiness
- Happiness is the perceived purpose of human endeavor.
- Happiness is not related to physical or environmental factors but we

think it is and pursue ever-changing ends with ever-changing
requirements.

- What we want, and think will make us happy, depends on our
upbringing.
- The idea of "what I want" is a thought and we have no control over
these.
- The ego will never be happy. Individualism and materialism take us
away from the happiness that is our true nature.
- Ideas, desires and fears take us away from the reality of the present
moment – which is all there is.
- Desires, pleasures and pain all disappear in sleep so cannot be an aspect
of our true nature. They relate to the intellect and the belief that we are
a doer.
- Language is a major cause of the apparent problem, generating the belief
in a separate entity seeking fulfillment in external things.
- In ignorance, we look to things for happiness to try to fill a perceived
lack in ourselves.
- Happiness does not reside in objects, or in the mind. Unlimited
happiness could never be found in transient things, only in our Self.
- Happiness results when the desired object is obtained, i.e. when desire
disappears. The key to happiness is renunciation of desire.
- In happiness, mind and object are dissolved and we rest in the unity of
the Self. Subject and object, mind and ego are all absent.
- *Ananda*, as an attribute of Brahman, should be translated as "limitless,"
not "bliss." The "intensity" of *Ananda* is infinitely greater than that of
happiness.

Purpose
- Knowledge of the Self must be the prime purpose in life.
- Meaning is tactical, a moment to moment satisfaction; purpose is
strategic, the long-term aim of our lives to confer a sense of
completeness.
- When a purpose is achieved, it is seen to have been limited and

therefore ultimately unfulfilling.
* Our essential nature is changeless so that "becoming" or "achieving" can only relate to the body-mind.
* Since there are no separate individuals or world in reality, the idea of purpose can have no meaning.

pa~ncha-kosha-prakriyA

* The model of the five sheaths represents an increasing level of sophistication from gross mineral matter (*annamaya*), through vegetable (*prANamaya*), animal (*manomaya*) to man (*vij~nAnamaya*).
* (The search for) happiness. (*Anandamaya*) drives the intellect to discriminate.
* The teaching leads the mind from identification with the gross body through successive levels until the essential nature is understood.
* The bliss of the *Anandamaya* is not the final aim, however. It is the last and most subtle sheath covering the *Atman*.

4. KNOWLEDGE AND IGNORANCE

This chapter is one of the more difficult but is central to an understanding of the philosophy. It will look first at how ignorance is at the root of all of our problems, causing us mistakenly to identify with our bodies and minds and to look for fulfillment in a supposed external and separate world. The mechanism of *adhyAsa* is analyzed to understand how we mix up real and unreal elements of our experience and thereby bring about our confusion. The crucial distinction between *satyam* and *mithyA* is examined, one which is apparently not understood by many modern teachers. Next, the status of opinions, belief and knowledge are considered, which leads onto a review of the various means (*pramANa*-s) by which we acquire knowledge. The process of *bAdha* or sublation is explained, whereby we advance our understanding in successive stages, with reality being that which cannot be sublated. Other methods, by which Advaita leads us to an understanding of the nature of reality, are also explained.

Chapters 1 to 3 have examined how it is that we identify with our bodies, minds or roles. Few would deny that they are definitely either a man or a woman, for example. In a work situation most people are clear that they are a "doctor" or a "teacher." And when we are ill, there is no question but that we are a body, frail and vulnerable, doomed one day to die. But in moments of quiet reflection, after reading material such as that in the previous chapters, we may confess that we are unsure of who we really are. And this is the root cause of all of our seeming problems. We do not know who we are – the truth, whatever it might be, eludes us. Or, as traditional Advaita would put it, the truth is apparently covered over by ignorance.

No god is a philosopher or seeker after wisdom because he is wise already. Neither do the ignorant seek after wisdom; for herein is the evil of ignorance, that he who is neither good nor wise is nevertheless satisfied with himself. **Socrates**

It is ignorance that is responsible for our delusion. It keeps us "in the dark" and without it we would be "enlightened." Yet it is part of the nature of ignorance that those who are ignorant are usually unaware of the fact and live out their lives searching for happiness and fulfillment amongst the worldly baubles that are part of the illusion. Thus it is that recognition of the *fact* of our ignorance is the first step in the apparent process of dispelling it. Our minds are full of opinions and beliefs that are almost certainly false, being merely a condensation of all of the stuff that happened to arrive there by way of parents, teachers and media. There is a **Zen story** that illustrates this very well:

A professor of philosophy is visiting a Zen monastery in Japan and goes to visit the Zen master to ask for explanations about the teaching. The master invites him to take tea. The professor holds out his cup and the master pours the tea... and carries on pouring, until the tea is overflowing onto the floor.

"The cup is full," complains the professor, "it will not hold any more."

"Just so!" replies the master. "You, too, are like the cup. How can I explain anything to you when your mind is already full of what you consider to be the truth?"

We have to empty our minds of all of our preconceptions and start again from the beginning. And no one is suggesting that you simply fill it up again with ideas such as the ones in this book. You must test each new idea in your experience. Reflect upon all new concepts in the light of silence, quietly exposing them to the discrimination of your true intellect, not to the tired old arguments that others have used, no matter in what regard you might hold them. (Ref. 77)

A metaphor that is often used in reference to ignorance is that of clouds covering the sun. The knowledge is there but hidden, just as the sun is there all of the time, even when the side of the earth on which our bodies happen to be located is facing away from it. **Robert Adams** explains this:

> You get caught in the world. It's like the sun in the clouds. The sun is always shining, it never goes away; but sometimes clouds block it. So the ignorant person says, *"There's no sun. What do I have to do to make the sun come out? I'll climb up on a ladder and push the cloud out of the way. I'll get a wind machine and blow the clouds away!"* The clouds are always there because of ignorance. When the clouds dissipate, the sun shines once again. It never stopped. The light within us is always bright and shining but we cover it up with ego and mind. When ego and mind are removed, we shine once again in all our splendor - like we're supposed to... The mind actually creates the ego. Those are just terms; but if you follow the I to its culmination, they both go. (Ref. 79)

The metaphor can be extended still further. We know that, on a cloudy day, the sun may be totally obscured, although the fact that we are able to see anything at all is only by virtue of the presence of the sun behind the clouds. In the presence of ignorance, we fail to see how things really are but the fact that we see anything at all is only due to the presence of Consciousness even if we are unable to appreciate this. The ignorance causes us to mistake who we really are. Furthermore, the clouds themselves only exist by virtue of the sun (i.e. causing the sea to evaporate). By analogy, the ego is effectively brought about by the Atman itself, through the process of identification with the limited body and mind.

The world of names and forms is the result of mental activity. Ignorance (avidyA) begins at the very moment when the ego takes names and forms to be separate realities. **Jean Klein** (Ref. 64)

Atman and jIva

The Sanskrit term that is used for our present condition is *jIva*, the "embodied Self." It literally just means "living" or "alive" but is often equated with the idea of an individual soul as encountered in Christianity. The word *jIvAtman*, the "personal or individual soul" is also sometimes used (as opposed to *paramAtman*, the supreme spirit). In the ***advaita bodha dIpaka*** (*dIpa* is a lamp, providing *bodha*, knowledge, through its illumination), this is explained as follows:

> In the body appears a phantom, the "false-I," to claim the body for itself and it is called *jIva*. This *jIva* always outward bent, taking the world to be real and himself to be the doer and experiencer of pleasures and pains, desirous of this and that, undiscriminating, not once remembering his true nature, nor inquiring "Who am I?, What is this world?," is but wandering in the *saMsAra* without knowing himself. Such forgetfulness of the Self is Ignorance. (Ref. 80)

Who we really are is the non-dual Self, the *Atman*, but because of this covering of ignorance, we believe ourselves to be limited to a separate soul, contained in a body and mind. The *jIva* could thus be thought of as the *Atman*, together with the *upAdhi* (limiting adjunct) of *avidyA* (ignorance). An *upAdhi* is something that appears to restrict or limit but does not really.

A metaphor that is used to explain this is that of a jar being an *upAdhi* for the space apparently contained within it. If we have a one-litre jar, then it can clearly only hold one litre of liquid and we might regard the space within it as being similarly limited. But space is really everywhere, totally unaffected by the presence of the jar. If we move the jar a foot to the right, the space that was previously occupied by the jar is now seemingly free but nothing has really changed from the point of view of the space. If you now place a plant pot where the jar has previously been, the space will now seem to be conditioned by the pot.

The **Atmabodha** explains this as follows:

> The All-pervading *AkAsha* appears to be diverse on account of its association with various conditionings (*upAdhi*-s) which are different from

each other. Space becomes one on the destruction of these limiting adjuncts: So also the Omnipresent Truth appears to be diverse on account of Its association with the various *upAdhi*-s and becomes one on the destruction of these *upAdhi*-s. † (Ref. 81)

The *jIva* is really the *Atman* but, because of the limiting form of body and mind, it appears to be a separate entity, just as the space appears to be limited by the jar. If the jar should break, the space that previously "occupied" it is found to be quite unaffected. Similarly, on the death of the body, the Atman remains untouched. This way of explaining the nature of the *jIva* is called *avachCheda vAda* (*vAda* is a thesis or doctrine; *avachCheda* literally means "cut off." It could be called the theory of limitation.) This is the theory held by one of the two traditional schools of Advaita, the *bhAmatI* school (*bhAmatI* means "lustrous" and is the word that was applied to the philosopher *vAchaspati mishra*'s brilliant exposition of Shankara's commentary on the *brahma sUtra*-s. The school is also called the *vAchaspati* school.

Another metaphor for explaining the *jIva* was also used by Shankara. This says that *avidyA* or ignorance acts like a mirror. Who we really are is the *Atman* but this is only normally seen in the mirror. The essence of the reflection is, of course, the *Atman*, our true Self. It is not the actual Self but effectively an illusion, just as the image of our body in the mirror is not the actual body. This theory is called *pratibimba vAda* and is associated with the *vivaraNa* school of Advaita. *pratibimba* means a "reflection." In logic, *bimba* is the object itself, with the *pratibimba* being the counterpart with which it is compared. *vivaraNa* means "explanation" or "commentary." This is from the *vivaraNa* on PadmapAda's *pa~nchapAdikA*, produced by *prakAshAtma yati* in the 13th century AD. PadmapAda was one of the four principal disciples of Shankara and his book, the *pa~nchapAdikA* was a commentary on Shankara's commentary on the first part of the *brahma*

---

† Atmabodha, Swami Chinmayananda, © Central Chinmaya Mission Trust, Mumbai.

sUtra. It can be understood how, with commentaries upon commentaries stretching through the ages, divergences of interpretation and understanding have developed.

Eliot Deutsch explains the consequence of this theory as follows:

AVIDYA = IGNORANCE

One attains the truth of non-difference, then, the moment one understands that one is a reflection of *Atman* that only *appears* to be different from it, but is identical with it in reality. And just as the reflection of a person in a body of water varies according to the state of the water, according as the water is calm or turbulent, clean or dirty, so the reflection of the Absolute varies according to the state of *avidyA* upon which it is reflected. The minds of men vary: some are more, some are less, under the influence of passion and desire; some are more, some are less, capable of intellectual discrimination and insight. The Absolute appears differently according to these differences among individuals.

(This) description of, or metaphor about, the appearance of the *jIva* has this advantage; it suggests that the clearer the mirror, the more perfect is the relation between the *jIva* and *Atman*. As the mirror loses its individual characteristics it reflects better what is presented to it. The *pratibimba vAda* suggests, then, that rather than being restless, anticipating, and desiring, our minds ought to be like a clear and calm mirror capable of reflecting truth. (Ref. 82)

The metaphor of dirty or colored water imperfectly reflecting the truth also occurs in many guises throughout the scriptures and commentaries of teachers. If you place the purest, clearest water in a colored glass vessel, it will appear to be the color of the glass when looked at from outside. The western world's metaphor of looking at the world through rose-colored spectacles has similar import. The colored glass in all cases is effectively obscuring the truth by forcing us to view the reality through a covering or reflection of ignorance. Beliefs and opinions act in just this way, distorting our vision of reality. Only when the mind is empty of all preconceptions, still and clear as in meditation, can we see things as they really are. (This is still only a partial picture of the situation, in that it is actually not possible for us – i.e. the perceptions or mind – to see or understand reality anyway, as will become clear later.)

Ignorance and identification

The ego is born out of ignorance and identification and gives rise to all of our subsequent problems. **Sri Ranjit Maharaj** said: *"Understand I am the root of happiness and the ego is the root of unhappiness."* His commentator, **Andrew Vernon** elaborates:

> It is the most extraordinary and inexplicable irony that you are happiness yourself and yet, because you do not realize it, you seek for it outside. The happiness (*Ananda*) that you naturally are, if you only knew it, is the ultimate happiness - a joy and fullness that never changes and is never diminished. What else could you possibly want? And yet even sincere seekers cannot accept that this happiness is already theirs. They continue to entertain doubts about that final understanding. Often, the ego takes the blame, as though the ego were some powerful demon that had its own strength and its own will. The ego is the source of unhappiness, yes, but you only give it greater strength by believing in its power. In fact, it has no power. It is a false God, the false "I" that is born out of ignorance of reality. Reality is the true "I," the existence that you already know as Being and as happiness itself. (Ref. 20)

As long as the ignorance remains, there will be identification of one form or another and we will believe ourselves to be other than our true nature. The ignorance is said to be *anAdi*, without any beginning, and it will continue until it is removed by knowledge and enlightenment dawns. As the **vivekachUDAmaNi** says:

> 149. One's true nature does not shine out when covered by the five sheaths, material and otherwise, although they are the product of its own power, like the water in a pool, covered with algae.

150. On removing the algae, the clean, thirst-quenching and joy-inducing water is revealed to a man.

151. When the five sheaths have been removed, the supreme light shines forth, pure, eternally blissful, single in essence, and within.

152. To be free from bondage the wise man must practise discrimination between self and non-self. By that alone he will become full of joy, recognising himself as Being, Consciousness and Bliss. (Ref. 340)

The question is: how can we break through or remove these coverings of the five sheaths so as to recognize or realize the Atman within? One of the lesser known Upanishads, the *sarvopaniShat* (verse 1), asks these questions (and many more!):   VIDYA – KNOWLEDGE

OM. What is *bandha* (bondage of the soul)? What is *mokSha* (liberation)? What is *avidyA* (nescience)? What is *vidyA* (knowledge)? What are the states of *jAgrat* (waking), *svapna* (dreaming), *suShupti* (dreamless sleep) and the fourth, *turIya* (Absolute)? What are the *annamaya*, *prANamaya*, *manomaya*, *vij~nAnamaya* and *Anandamayakosha*-s (vestures or sheaths of the soul)? What is the *kartRRi* (agent), what the *jIva* (individual self), the *kShetraj~na* (knower of the body), the *sAkShi* (witness), the *kUTastha* (the unchangeable), the *antaryAmin* (internal ruler)? What is the *pratyagAtman* (inner Self), what the *paramAtman* (supreme Self), the *Atman*, and also *mAyA*? – The master of Self looks upon the body and such like things other than the Self as Itself: this egoism is the bondage of the soul. The cessation of that egoism is *mokSha*, liberation. That which causes that egoism is *avidyA*, nescience. That by which this egoism is completely turned back is *vidyA*, knowledge. (Ref. 85)

Since it is obviously ignorance that is the cause of our confusion, it would seem logical that we need knowledge to remove that ignorance. The **Astavakra Gita** is very clear on the subject:

From ignorance of oneself, the world appears, and by knowledge of oneself it appears no longer. From ignorance of the rope it appears to be a snake, and by knowledge of it, it does so no longer. (Chapter 2 Verse 7) (Ref. 86)

And the **advaita bodha dIpaka** states that:

Though the Self is Brahman, there is not the knowledge of the Self (being Brahman). That which obstructs this knowledge of the Self is Ignorance. Just as ignorance of the substratum, namely the rope, projects the illusion of a snake, so Ignorance of Brahman projects this world. (Ref. 80)

Throughout the scriptures, ignorance is represented metaphorically in these two ways: as something which covers over or obscures the truth or as the projection of an unreal illusion. These are the so-called twin aspects of mAyA – the veiling power of *AvaraNa* and the projecting power of *vikShepa*. They are explained in the **vedAntasAra** (essence of Vedanta) of Sadananda:

51. This ignorance has two powers, viz., the power of concealment and the power of projection.

52. Just as a small patch of cloud, by obstructing the vision of the observer, conceals, as it were, the solar disc extending over many miles, similarly ignorance, though limited by nature, yet obstructing the intellect of the observer, conceals, as it were, the Self which is unlimited and not subject to transmigration. Such a power is this power of concealment. It is thus said: "As the sun appears covered by a cloud and bedimmed to a very ignorant person whose vision is obscured by the cloud, so also That which to the unenlightened appears to be in bondage is my real nature – the Self – Eternal Knowledge."

53. The Self covered by this (concealing power of ignorance) may become subject to *saMsAra* (relative existence) characterized by one's feeling as agent, the experiencing subject, happy, miserable, etc., just as

a rope may become a snake due to the concealing power of one's own ignorance.

54. Just as ignorance regarding a rope, by its inherent power, gives rise to the illusion of a snake etc., in the rope covered by it, so also ignorance, by its own power creates in the Self covered by it, such phenomena as *AkAsha* (space or ether) etc. Such a power is called the power of projection. It is thus said: "The power of projection creates all from the subtle bodies to the cosmos."

55. Consciousness associated with ignorance, possessed of these two powers, when considered from its own standpoint is the efficient cause, and when considered from the standpoint of its *upAdhi* or limitation is the material cause (of the universe). (Ref. 88)

The mechanism of superimposition – adhyAsa

So, not only do we fail to appreciate the true nature of ourselves but also we identify ourselves with the limited body, mind and intellect. Our bodies grow old and die so we think that *we* grow old and die. Our minds are confused and the intellect unable to discriminate so we say that *we* are dull and stupid. It is a combination of inapprehension – failure to see the Self – and misapprehension – seeing wrongly. We are the seer, not that which is seen but we confuse the two. We superimpose the changing body and mind upon the non-changing Self. This process is called *adhyAsa* or *adhyAropa* (wrong attribution or erroneous transferring of a statement from one thing to another). It is sufficiently important for Shankara to examine it in detail before he begins his commentary on the *brahmasUtra*-s (**brahmasUtra bhAShya**) as follows:

Preamble: It being an established fact that the object and the subject, that are fit to be the contents of the concepts "you" and "we" (respectively), and are by nature as contradictory as light and darkness, cannot logically have any identity, it follows that their attributes can have it still less. Accordingly, the superimposition of the object, referable through the concept "you," and its attributes on the subject that is conscious by nature and is referable through the concept "we" (should be impossible), and contrariwise the superimposition of the subject and its attributes on the object should be impossible. (Ref. 34)

And this extract illustrates, perhaps more than most, why many seekers today rebel against traditional teaching with its perceived excessive use of Sanskrit, emphasis on preparation and *sAdhana* and, as here, its over-intellectualizing. Very few are likely to have the slightest idea what is being said here and, unless some clear explanatory comment is provided elsewhere, they will simply give up. It has to be remembered, however, that Shankara was a philosopher trying rigorously to prove his points and overturn the views of his objectors. Anyone who has read (or tried to read) western philosophers such as F. H. Bradley will know that unreadability is an occupational hazard!

What Shankara begins by saying is that "I" am different from the perceived object. I make a fundamental mistake when either I see one thing and think it is something else (e.g. I see a rope and think it is a snake) or I think something has an attribute that it does not really have (e.g. I think that the mirage is actually a lake). There is always something real (the rope or the sand with shimmering air above it) and something illusory. The real part, is unaffected by our superimposition. What is effectively happening is that we partially see the real part, the substratum such as the rope and then overlay it with some recollected memory of something else, such as the snake.

Here, the rope-snake metaphor is examined in more detail (from material posted to the Advaitin E-group by **Dr. K. Sadananda** and edited by myself):

This example originates from the commentaries of *gauDapAda* on the *mANDUkya upaniShad*. Seeing a rope in the dark, it is mistaken for a snake - an error or *adhyAsa*. We mistakenly superimpose the image of an illusory snake onto the real rope. In just such a way we superimpose the illusion of objects etc. upon the one *Atman*.

If there is total dark, we would not see the rope so could not imagine it to be a snake. Hence "ignorance is bliss," as in deep sleep - there can be no error. Similarly, if there is total light we see the rope clearly - in complete knowledge, we know everything to be Brahman. Knowledge is also bliss! The error occurs only in partial light or when the eyes are defective. Then there is partial knowledge; we know that some "thing" exists. This part, that is not covered by darkness or hidden by ignorance is called the "general part" (*sAmAnya aMsha*) and is "uncovered" or "real." That the "thing" is actually a rope is hidden because of the inadequate light or knowledge. This specific feature of the thing, that it is a rope, is called the "particular part" (*visheSha aMsha*) and is covered. In place of the covered part, the mind substitutes or "projects" something of its own, namely the snake.

In the example then, when we say "there is a snake," there is a real part and an unreal part. The real part is "there is"; this is the "general part." The unreal part, the snake, only appears to be there because the "particular part" - the rope - is covered. If light (i.e. knowledge) is made available, the rope is now seen. The "general part" - "there is" - remains unchanged but the "particular part," which was previously projected by the mind, is now uncovered and revealed to be a rope. The snake has not "gone away" since it never existed, except in the mind of the observer, where it might have given rise to very real fears and physical effects (fast heartbeat, sweating etc.).

From the point of view of actual reality (*paramArtha*), only the rope is real, the snake does not exist. For a perceiver who sees a snake, that snake is "relatively" real (*vyavahAra*) and causes as much mental suffering as would a truly real snake. There only ever was a rope but the ignorance of this in the mind of the perceiver creates the illusion of a snake and the suffering follows. Once light (i.e. the light of knowledge) is introduced, the mistaken perception of the particular part is corrected; the unreal snake disappears and the real rope is revealed. The associated fear etc. also disappears.

What has happened is that a valid means of enquiry has been

undertaken into the nature of the particular part to reveal the truth of the matter. The valid means of enquiry in this example was the torchlight. It was appropriate because the mistake was brought about by the dim light. Prayer or meditation would not have been appropriate and would not have revealed the rope. The method has to be appropriate to the nature of the error. Since ignorance of our true nature is the reason for *saMsAra*, the appropriate means of enquiry for removing the error is self-knowledge.

Comparison with our own situation

The analogous statement that Shankara uses is "I am a *saMsArin*," i.e. one who is subject to the cycle of birth and death. He could just as well have said "I am a person" or individual. Here, "I am" is the general part and is true. It refers to a conscious and existent being. It is "uncovered." There is no doubt in our minds that it is true; we need no external means of knowledge to verify it. "A *saMsArin*" (or "a person" etc.) is the particular part and is unreal, like the snake. In this case, the truth of the situation is covered over, rather than projected, but is just as unreal. That we "are" (*sat*) and that we are "conscious" (*chit*) is known from the general part. What is hidden in the particular part is that we are bliss (*Ananda*) or unlimited, complete, infinite etc. (*ananta*). In its place, we perceive unreal aspects such as misery, limitedness, incompleteness etc. This error is the cause of all our suffering. In order to solve this problem, it is necessary to apply the torchlight of Vedantic knowledge to reveal the real particular part - not "I am a *saMsArin*" but "I am Brahman."

ADHYASA

Mixing of real and unreal

When a mistake of this type occurs, what is happening is that a real part and an unreal part are getting mixed up and this is effectively how Shankara defines *adhyAsa* - the mixing up of real and unreal. In the case of the rope and snake analogy, the error can be viewed as a "misperceiving of the rope" or as the "superimposition of a snake" or as "the mixing of part of a real rope and part of an unreal snake." When we say "there is a snake," "there is" is the general part, which could be viewed as belonging to the rope, which is real, while "a snake" is the unreal, mentally projected, particular part. The mixing up of real and unreal effectively creates a third entity that is partly real and partly unreal.

When someone refers to the "snake," he does not realize that there are two aspects, one real and one unreal. If he says, "there is a long snake," the adjective "long" in fact refers to the rope, which is real whilst, if he says "there is a poisonous snake," the adjective refers to the unreal part.

Similarly, when someone says: "I am a shopkeeper" (or whatever), he does not realize that the attribute "shopkeeper" refers to the unreal part. He does not know that there are two parts, only one of which (I am) is real. In the mind of the ordinary "person" these two things are mixed up and a single, false, *jIva* is created. It is this mixed-up *jIva* who is striving for liberation. The purpose of the *brahmasUtra* is to inquire into the nature of the *jIva*, by directing the knowledge of Vedanta so that we can discard the unreal part and become established in the knowledge of the real part. When this happens, realization takes place and *saMsAra* is dissolved as unreal. (Ref. 89)

The underlying truth of the unreal snake is the real rope and that of the unreal *jIva*, the real Self. It is not that a snake has to be removed in order for us to see the rope – the snake *is* the rope. Similarly, when the five sheaths are spoken of above, it is not that we have to remove each of these in order to find our way to the Self at the center – we are already the Self and the sheaths represent different levels of superimposition or identification. All that is required is a switch in the way that we look at ourselves and the world. Nothing will actually change yet everything will be seen differently. Currently we identify with body, mind, world etc., all of which are forever changing. Whilst I think I am these things, it seems that I am subject to change, too. In fact, I am the changeless in which all of these things simply arise as changing forms.

There are actually two "types" of *adhyAsa*. The above example of rope and snake is an example of *nirupAdhika adhyAsa*. The rope is mistaken for a snake and, once this has been realized, the snake is no longer seen. In the other type, *sopAdhika adhyAsa*, even after the mistake has been realized the "illusion" is still seen. An example of this would be the sunrise. Even when we have learned that the sun does not orbit the earth, it still appears to do so.

satyam and mithyA

The Sanskrit word for "truth" is *satyam* and this is also the word for reality. The only reality is *brahman*. Ignorance is ignoring (literally "turning away from") this truth through identifying ourselves with a body, mind, belief, cause or whatever. We mistakenly take these things to be real in their own right instead of simply a form of one essential reality.

Another frequently used metaphor in Advaita is that of clay and a pot made from the clay. The clay exists before the pot is made. Whilst the pot is in use to hold something, it is still clay. And after the pot has been broken, the clay is still there. Advaita defines "real" as being that which exists in or transcends all three periods of time (i.e. past, present and future) - *trikAlAtIta* – so that it is only actually the clay that is real by this definition. Yet whilst the clay is in the form of the pot, it would not be true to say that the pot does not exist. Clearly it has some reality but it cannot be described as real according to the definition. But neither is it false, since we can use it to carry water about, while the clay in the form of an amorphous lump is not much use for this purpose. The pot's reality is entirely dependent upon the clay and, moreover, it is always clay and nothing but clay whether it is in the form of the pot or not. Thus the pot has a "dependent reality." There is no English word to describe this – the Sanskrit word that is used is *mithyA*.

Similarly, the world did not exist a few billion years ago and will be swallowed up by the sun in few more. The reality upon which it depends is Brahman. Brahman exists before during and after the world. The world too, whilst it exists, is nothing but Brahman in essence. Brahman is the only reality; the world is neither completely real nor completely unreal – it is *mithyA*. And the same applies to every "thing" in the world, be it people, houses, minds, concepts, emotions etc.

With this explanation, then, another possible definition for ignorance is available: ignorance is pursuing *mithyA* instead of *satyam*. Having mixed up real and unreal, most people spend their lives trying to derive happiness from material objects or transient relationships instead of coming to the realization that our already existent essence is limitless consciousness. Because we already *are* That, there is not, strictly speaking, anything that we can do to *become* That. Once the ignorance of the fact is removed, the already existent truth is revealed. This means, somewhat surprisingly, that it is knowledge of *mithyA* that brings about enlightenment, not knowledge of *satyam*, because it is the *mithyA* that constitutes the apparent bondage.

The precise ontological status of the ignorance is impossible to pin down. **Swami Dayananda** puts it as follows:

> The confusion is due to ignorance, the aforementioned two-fold non-apprehension - misapprehension phenomenon. It is often asked, "When and why does this ignorance begin?" The answer has to be, "It doesn't begin; it has no beginning." If someone glances in the direction of a rope and imagines that he sees a snake, but we know exactly what has happened, can it be asked, "When did the rope ignorance begin and then the snake come?" You might be tempted to play with words here and say, "It came at the time when he glanced at the rope." But the ontological truth is it would have to mean that prior to that glance there was knowledge of the rope. The ignorance and the false appearance are due to a helpless, hapless state of being which is said to have no reason, it is inexplicable (*anirvachanIya*), incomprehensible and beginningless (*anAdi*). (Ref. 90)

[Note that a better translation of *anirvachanIya* is "not able to be categorized." These terms will be described in detail in the later chapter on the nature of reality but, essentially, we usually think that something is real, apparent, illusory or non-existent. Ignorance cannot easily be defined in this way. In fact most things are *mithyA* and therefore ultimately *anirvachanIya*.]

Opinions and Beliefs

Ignorance takes various forms and we usually fail to recognize its presence. In our more rational moments, we may acknowledge that our opinions are only provisional, based upon our experience to date and subject to revision if more persuasive ideas come along. Most of the time, however, we happily voice our opinions, feeling that they are associated with some form of truth. It is only when someone questions them or argues against them that the rise of discomfort in the form of indignation or resentment may make us realize that we are merely attached to certain ideas to the exclusion of other, equally plausible ones.

If we don't know something, and know that we do not know it, then although we are ignorant, we are open to enlightenment. When we have already existing opinions, however, we are often reluctant to alter them. If we believe something strongly we may be completely closed to alternative explanations or contradictory facts. In this way, opinions and beliefs can be much more dangerous than mere ignorance. This is one aspect of the meaning of verse 9 in the Isha Upanishad (quoted again shortly): "*Those who worship ignorance enter into the depths of darkness but those who are addicted to knowledge are as though in greater darkness.*" Admitting one's ignorance allows the journey towards true knowledge to begin.

Osho (Ref. 96) suggests that to recognize that we *are* ignorant is effectively to destroy that ignorance. He uses the metaphor of someone going into a dark room with a torch looking for darkness. Obviously shining the torch into the dark corners of the room itself removes the darkness so that we can never find it. Similarly, one who knows he is ignorant and is therefore constantly vigilant is already open to the dawning of knowledge.

Mark McCloskey puts it even more strongly. He claims that we have to consciously give up all of our opinions and beliefs if we are ever to experience reality as it is:

Faith or any belief system as a whole is the final hurdle to overcome in the human path towards freedom and joy. Let me say it on a very personal level. Until you, as a human being, are able to completely abandon what you believe, have been told or taught what to believe or believe in, you will never experience this moment of reality as it is. You will never be fully free. You will be conditioned to experience present reality through a veil of the past, because beliefs are traditions from the past. This is not a joke, not any agnostic or atheistic principle. I am trying to point you to your own total human freedom to be able to live in this world joyfully, in love and compassion until the day you die. (Ref. 251)

and **Aja Thomas** warns against confusing beliefs with truth:

I can tell you what I believe Truth is, what God is, what the world is. I can quote from great authorities and from scriptures around the world. I can present evidence with startling logic and reasoning, until you too are absolutely convinced and ready to give your life for my cause, but it will only be a belief, a concept, an objective perception or misperception of the Truth. I may or may not have experienced the Truth, but no matter how many people I convince through non direct means, they will be experiencing beliefs, not truths. (Ref. 93)

Jiddu Krishnamurti [†] asks:

Is it possible to live in this world without a belief - not change beliefs, not substitute one belief for another, but be entirely free from *all* beliefs, so that one meets life anew each minute? This, after all, is the truth: to have the capacity of meeting everything anew, from moment to moment, without the conditioning reaction of the past, so that there is not

---

[†]   Krishnamurti did not recognize any specific philosophy, though much of his teaching is common to Advaita. See website at www.jkrishnamurti.org.

the cumulative effect which acts as a barrier between oneself and that which *is*.

And continues:

> ...a cup is useful only when it is empty; and a mind that is filled with beliefs, with dogmas, with assertions, with quotations, is really an uncreative mind; it is merely a repetitive mind. To escape from that fear - that fear of emptiness, that fear of loneliness, that fear of stagnation, of not arriving, not succeeding, not achieving, not being something, not becoming something - is surely one of the reasons, is it not?, why we accept beliefs so eagerly and greedily. And through acceptance of belief, do we understand ourselves? On the contrary. A belief, religious or political, obviously hinders the understanding of ourselves. It acts as a screen through which we are looking at ourselves. And can we look at ourselves without beliefs? If we remove those beliefs, the many beliefs that one has, is there anything left to look at? If we have no beliefs with which the mind has identified itself, then the mind, without identification, is capable of looking at itself as it is - and then, surely, there is the beginning of the understanding of oneself. (Ref. 97)

For most, perhaps, living entirely without beliefs is an unattainable goal. The ordinary person living in a community of others, especially in the west, would be thought very strange indeed if she had no views whatsoever on any topic. Being realistic, perhaps constant vigilance is the optimum state, always aware that opinions and beliefs can only ever be partial or relative. **Charles Wikner**'s approach is much more pragmatic:

> An illustration may help: the sun rises in the East, travels across the sky, and sets in the West - this is valid knowledge at the level of the senses. Later one comes to know of the solar system and that the Earth in fact rotates - this is finer knowledge, but does not negate the validity of the sensory experience. If you now go about preaching that there is no such

thing as sunrise or sunset, well you deserve to be branded as a heretic and burned at the stake!

Given the geocentric and heliocentric views, you need to realize that both are correct - it just depends which you take as your reference point. To see them as mutually exclusive is limiting - it is far more useful to be able to change frames of reference according to circumstance. Then one may come to appreciate that the entire creation is relative to whatever is chosen as the reference point - usually the ego!

The search then continues until one realizes that absolute reference point that never moves: only from there can you know the true measure of anything with certainty. To stop short of that, simply means that any judgment will be made according to the limited measure of the ego.

To judge beliefs as right or wrong is ignorance: view them rather as useful or not, appropriate or not. (Ref. 98)

Knowledge

It is enough to know what you are not. You need not know what you are. For, as long as knowledge means description in terms of what is already known, perceptual, or conceptual, there can be no such thing as self-knowledge, for what you are cannot be described, except as total negation. All you can say is: "I am not this, I am not that." You cannot meaningfully say "this is what I am." It just makes no sense. **Nisargadatta Maharaj** (Ref. 5)

In order to overcome the darkness, light is needed. In order to dispel ignorance, knowledge is needed. **Swami Venkatesananda** explains in his commentary on the *yoga vAsiShTha*:

Even as the arising of the first thought disturbs sleep and ends it, the slightest awakening of inner intelligence destroys ignorance. When one approaches darkness with light in hand, wishing to behold it, the darkness vanishes; when the light of enquiry is turned on ignorance, ignorance disappears. When one begins to enquire: "What is 'I' in this body composed of blood, flesh, bone, etc.?" at once ignorance ceases to be. That which has a beginning has an end. When all things that have a beginning are ruled out, what remains is the truth which is the cessation of *avidyA* or ignorance. You may regard it as something or as no-thing: that is to be sought which IS when ignorance has been dispelled. The sweetness one tastes is not experienced by another: listening to someone's description of the cessation of *avidyA* does not give rise to your enlightenment. Each one has to realize it. In short, *avidyA* is the belief that "There exists a reality which is not Brahman or cosmic consciousness"; when there is the certain knowledge that "This is indeed Brahman," *avidyA* ceases. (Ref. 38)

And **Shankara**, in the *Atmabodha* (which means "knowledge of Self"):

2. Just as the fire is the direct cause for cooking, so without Knowledge no emancipation can be had. Compared with all other forms of discipline Knowledge of the Self is the one direct means for liberation.

3 Action cannot destroy ignorance, for it is not in conflict with or opposed to ignorance. Knowledge does verily destroy ignorance as light destroys deep darkness.

4. The Soul appears to be finite because of ignorance. When ignorance is destroyed the Self which does not admit of any multiplicity truly reveals itself by itself: like the Sun when the clouds pass away.

5. Constant practice of knowledge purifies the Self ('Jivatman'), stained by ignorance and then disappears itself – as the powder of the 'Kataka-nut' settles down after it has cleansed the muddy water. [†] (Ref. 81)

The metaphor of the *kataka* nut is a beautifully chosen one. It is also called the "clearing nut" and, as indicated, is used for purifying water. The ground seeds are sprinkled on top of the dirty water (or rubbed on the inside of the water jar). A film then forms on the surface and the particles of dirt are

---

[†] Atmabodha, Swami Chinmayananda, © Central Chinmaya Mission Trust, Mumbai.

attracted to the film, which slowly sinks taking the dirt and itself to the bottom of the jar and leaving the purified water above.

In the same way, the knowledge that is introduced by Advaita is not an end in itself. Its purpose is only to remove the ignorance. Once achieved, both are discarded. A more familiar metaphor is the use of a "thorn to remove a thorn" and an updated version of this is that of the pole vaulter. It is necessary to use a long pole in order to raise oneself to the high bar but, if one is to pass over the bar without knocking it down, one has to let go of the pole. Having achieved its purpose, it is no longer required.

You see the habit of mind? It wants always to know what's going on and then it's too late. It's lost instead of surrendering. Knowledge is really arrogance.
Ganga (Ref. 78)

This is a point that is often overlooked and the **Isha** (or *IshAvAsya*) **upaniShad** explains the danger of overlooking this (my translation):

9. Those who worship ignorance enter into the depths of darkness but those who are addicted to knowledge are as though in greater darkness.
10. It has been explained to us by the wise that knowledge and ignorance each produce their own different results.
11. He who knows both *vidyA* and *avidyA* overcomes death through ignorance and gains immortality through knowledge.

This is because knowledge is also *mithyA* and, as noted earlier, pursuing *mithyA* instead of *satyam* is ignorance. Thus it is possible for someone to have vast knowledge of the scriptures and the philosophy of Advaita but still to be attached to this in an egotistical way, therefore being no nearer realization of the truth of the Self than someone without this knowledge.

The greatest of all delusions is the conviction that knowledge is not a delusion. **Tripura Rahasya**, XVIII 156 9 (Ref. 95)

Different types of knowledge

Most knowledge is what might be called "worldly" knowledge – information or facts about a particular subject – and we accumulate this type of knowledge throughout our lives. It is highly regarded in western society and increasingly throughout the rest of the world. We go to university to soak up this knowledge and sit examinations or write papers at the end of several years to demonstrate our proficiency. And then, more often than not, we spend the rest of our lives forgetting it.

This type of knowledge in itself does not bring about any result. Having gained my Bachelor's degree in Chemistry, I would have actually had to get a job in that field in order to *apply* the knowledge and so gain some result, whether developing some new drug, teaching the knowledge to other students or simply earning money in Industry. The relationship (*sambandha*) between the subject matter (*viShaya*) and the motive or purpose (*prayojana*) is said to be a goal motivated one (*chodya*).

The knowledge that brings about Self-knowledge is quite different. The knowledge itself brings about the result without the need for any action. The relationship between the subject matter and the purpose is called *pratipAdya–pratipAdaka sambandha*. **Swami Sri Atmananda Saraswati** explains:

> The PPS is however completely different. Here no action whatsoever is required for attaining our cherished goal. The mere knowledge helps us attain the goal. Such a *sambandha* is only seen in cases where the thing to be attained is already with us, but just out of ignorance appears unattained. I have my specs on my forehead but just out of forgetfulness I search all over, then someone comes and tells me that the specs are right on my forehead. This statement brings a knowledge which helps me "attain" the specs, without any action on my part. In the case of knowledge of Self or truth, PPS alone can be applicable, for the simple reason that the "object" to be attained is already attained. *pratipAdya* means "that which is to be revealed," while *pratipAdaka* means "that which reveals." The moment we catch the real implication of the words

of *shastra*, that very moment the Truth is as though attained. (Ref. 92)

In this sense, the gaining of knowledge or the removal of ignorance is not something that is achieved through action. When it occurs, there is no choice involved. It is like perception in this respect. If someone asks us to close our eyes and holds an object in front of us, when we open our eyes again the object is seen, regardless of any desire on our part to see it or not. Knowledge is objective (*vastu-tantra*) as opposed to action, which is subjective, a matter of our will (*puruSha-tantra*). [*tantra*, here, just means the main or essential point; *vastu* is a thing or object; *puruSha* means person or spirit.]

The classic story of the tenth man is an example of this:

There is a party of ten men traveling together to a distant village in a remote and rugged area. They encounter a swollen river, which they are obliged to cross. They join hands and begin the perilous crossing but inevitably they lose their footing in the strong current and have to swim. Much later and wetter, they reassemble on the opposite bank. As each counts the number of men who have arrived, they can only find nine and conclude that one of their number has drowned.

As they are bemoaning their loss, a monk passes by and asks them what the matter is. They explain and, quickly assessing the situation, he recognizes their mistake. He asks them to line up and, taking a stick, he hits the first man once, the second twice and so on down the line, counting out the number aloud each time. Reaching the end, he hits the last man ten times and calls out 'ten'. What had happened, of course, is that each man had counted the others but forgotten to count himself, and so had only reached nine. (Ref. 84)

In the story, the acting out of this ritual is sufficient to bring about the understanding that no one has died. And the idea is that, in the one hearing the story, the hearing itself is sufficient to bring about the understanding that the listener has forgotten his true nature and that he is really the Self.

Shankara uses the story in the **upadesha sAhasrI** and explains that the knowledge transmitted by the *shruti* is direct when it relates to our own Self:

> 201. (Objection) The Bliss of liberation is not obtained by ascertaining the meaning of the sentence unlike the satisfaction which is felt by eating. Just as boiled milk-rice cannot be prepared with cow dung, so the direct knowledge of Brahman cannot be produced simply by ascertaining the meaning of the sentence.
>
> 202. (Reply) Indirect knowledge, it is true, is the result produced by the sentences regarding the non-Self, but it is not so in the case of those regarding the Innermost Self. It is, on the other hand, direct and certain knowledge like that in the case of the tenth boy. (Ref. 104)

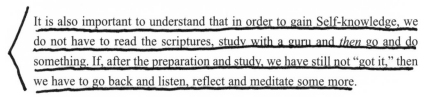

It is also important to understand that in order to gain Self-knowledge, we do not have to read the scriptures, study with a guru and *then* go and do something. If, after the preparation and study, we have still not "got it," then we have to go back and listen, reflect and meditate some more.

Stig Lundgren says:

> It is a common misconception that the *upaniShad*-s can give only intellectual conviction but no actual experience of the Self. Hence, people often believe that after studying the *upaniShad*-s, then we have to put its teachings into practice in order to gain enlightenment. But if your true Self is clouded by ignorance, then what really is the solution to our problem? The answer is: Knowledge. Ignorance can only be wiped away by knowledge. Knowledge - not mind-control, yogic *Asana*-s, detachment from possessions etc. etc. - is the antithesis and eradication of *avidyA*. And this knowledge is experienced at the very moment your *avidyA* is dispelled. And since the *avidyA* is yours, and the *upaniShad*-s are talking about your true Self, then what the

upaniShad-s say can actually make you experience your true Self. The *upaniShad-s* are dealing with what you actually are. Hence, *shruti* can give rise to direct knowledge of your Self. (Ref. 105)

There is no relevant, subsequent action apart from the reading, listening etc. (These aspects will be covered in detail in the next chapter.) The reason is that the knowledge is already there. The teaching is merely uncovering it. Self-knowledge is simply not about the accumulation of facts or the acquiring of more beliefs. **Aja Thomas** puts it more poetically and without the Sanskrit (though he is, himself a teacher of Sanskrit!):

> If you wish to fully appreciate the beauty of a rose, don't try to add to the rose. Remove that which obscures the pure vision of the rose and keeps you from experiencing it in its perfect roseness. Similarly, if you want to purely experience your own spiritual nature, you must subtract, not add. How can you add to what is already perfect? It is simply a matter of recognition, of stopping the search for something to add to make you more, better, greater...
>
> ...By adding more beliefs in the name of religiosity or spirituality, we are only furthering ourselves from the pure, simple, symmetry of our inherent Being. (Ref 93)

Some clarification is needed here before moving on. The key knowledge that we are talking about is that revealed by the scriptures, namely that "I am Brahman." This is something that I cannot automatically know and cannot easily discover. The basic fact that "I am," i.e. that I exist and am conscious, is on the other hand something that is self-evident. I do not need any external source of knowledge to reveal this. **Dr. K. Sadananda** explains:

> Suppose you are in a pitch dark room and cannot see anything. I call you: "Chandran, are you there?" What is your response? It cannot be: "I cannot see anything so I do not know if I am here or not"! You can only

say, "I do not see anything and I do not know if there is anybody else in the room or not."

Basically your existence is not proved or disproved by your perceptions. Perception is not the valid means of self knowledge. You also cannot use arguments such as "since I am able to hear you I must be here somewhere." That is, your existence is not proved by inference either. In fact one does not use any means of knowledge (*pramANa*) to prove ones' existence - all means of knowledge are valid only because you as a conscious entity are there to validate or invalidate them...

What everyone is looking for is neither self-knowledge nor Brahman. What everyone is looking for is only happiness... *shAstra* as *pramANa* tells me that I am that *Ananda*. (Ref. 94)

That I exist, then, is self-evident. That I am already perfect and complete, that there is *only* That (perfection, wholeness etc.) and that I *am* That – all of these are *not* self-evident. This "Self-knowledge" is what I seek and on the gaining of which I realize the truth and "become enlightened."

This is why experience alone is not enough to remove the ignorance, a fact that many modern teachers seem to ignore when they claim that we are already That, there is nothing to do and so on. If it were, we could presumably all simply take a dose of LSD and go and experience the truth directly, as used to be claimed could be done in the nineteen-sixties. But the point is that we are trapped in a mesh of misunderstanding and false belief and no amount of experience can change that.

One possibly misleading factor is in the translation of the Sanskrit word *anubhava*. The PPS knowledge described above was said to be immediate – we do not have to do anything. As soon as the information is transferred, the knowledge is there, as in the example of the spectacles on our forehead. Monier-Williams gives one of the meanings of the word *anubhava* as "experience" and it is often translated in this way, implying that something happens. Swami Dayananda points out in Ref. 112, that a much clearer definition is "immediate knowledge."

The example of the sun appearing to go round the earth was given earlier. This continues to be our experience but this does not affect our knowledge that the opposite is the case. **Swami Dayananda** has another example:

You think you are the physical body. Yet every night in a dream experience while that body is stretched out on a mattress with a pillow under its head, a "you" unconnected to the body works and eats and plays, is happy and sad. That dream experience does not shake your conclusion that you are the body. A teacher may use your dream experience as an aid to help you discover, through knowledge, that you are not the body, but the experience itself does not do the job of shaking off the wrong thinking. Wrong thinking can be shaken only by right thinking which comes from knowing, from seeing, not from experiencing...

The truth of oneself is not an intellectual conclusion, nor is it something to be "reached" by experiences. The student is not an elevator to go "up to Brahman" at the touch of a guru. Brahman is you — not a place to be reached. It is not through an experience that you become Truth. There is nothing to become. There is nothing to transform. You are the Truth that you are seeking. The teaching of Vedanta is simply a *pramANa*, a means of knowledge, an instrument that shows you what you are. (Ref. 112)

In our present state of identification, we are not in any position to appreciate the truth of our wholeness. We think we are a limited individual playing out insignificant roles in a vast universe. From a point of view such as this, how can we possibly appreciate our true stature? All of these mistaken opinions and beliefs have to be removed – the ignorant ideas shown to be false in the light of knowledge, before we can realize the truth.

That *Atman* = *brahman* is the purport of the entire scriptures and it is the purpose of the Advaita philosophy to explain this truth. There is only the non-dual reality (Brahman); the world has no separate existence and there are no 'others'; my own essence (Atman) is that Brahman. **Shankara** states in the *sarva-vedAnta-siddhAnta-sArasaMgrahaH*:

169. Liberation, consisting of the utter identity with Brahman, is unattainable except through the comprehension of the unity of the Atman and Brahman, through a process of rational enquiry into the two...

170. This is why the *shruti* says, "By knowledge alone doth one attain liberation." By proclaiming the unique nature of knowledge the *shruti* negates all other means. (Ref. 71)

The entire message of Advaita is said to have been summed up by Shankara in these words: *brahmasatyam jaganmithyA jIvo brahmaiva nA para -* Brahman is *satyam* (truth, reality); *jagat* (the world) is *mithyA;* the *jIva* is *nA* (not) *para* (different from) Brahman. In fact, it is not clear that Shankara did actually say this, although the first two parts of the statement appear in the *vivekachUDAmaNi:*

brahma satyam jaganmithyetyevaM rUpovinishchayaH
so.yaM nityAnityavastuvivekaH samudAhRRitaH (v.20)

"Brahman is the truth, the world is *mithyA*. It is the establishing of this nature that is declared to be discrimination between what is constant and unvarying (*nitya*) and what is only transient (*anitya*)." (My translation)

Means of acquiring knowledge (pramANa-s)

Having established that knowledge is needed in order to dispel the ignorance and having further established that only PPS knowledge is going to be of any use, the next question is "where do I find this knowledge?" Advaita recognizes six ways or *pramANa*-s in which we can gain knowledge. *pramA* means "true knowledge," as opposed to *bhrama*, which means "confusion, error or mistake." (NB. Do not confuse *bhrama* with *brahma*, the personal God or *brahman*, the non-dual reality!) Without a *pramANa*, nothing can be known. The mind is the instrument through which this takes place, in the same way as eyes are needed in order to see. And, just as we will not see very clearly if wearing spectacles with dirty lenses, so we are unlikely to understand using a mind cluttered with old, unexamined opinions. The mind needs to be still to operate effectively and it needs to understand the language and terminology. (Hence the need for preparation, as will be seen in chapter 5)

These six means of knowledge are as follows (the detail was culled from a combination of Refs. 27, 82, 89, 99, 100, 101 and 102):

1. Direct perception – *pratyakSha*. This includes the external senses – sight, hearing, touch, taste and smell - for perceiving so-called objects and the internal, mental perception of feelings or awareness of knowledge and so on. Everything that we are directly aware of is covered by *pratyakSha*.

According to traditional Advaita, in seeing something for example, awareness actually goes out through the eyes, makes contact with the object and assumes its form. This idea derives principally from the classical text *vedAntaparibhAShA* by DharmarAja AdhvarIndra and its literal interpretation has been disputed. Ref. 99 quotes a suggestion that it is only a figure of speech and should be compared to the English expression of our eyes "falling upon an object." But the idea fits in well with the basic philosophy since it means that we "directly know" the object by effectively becoming one with it.

It is spoken of as being immediate so that this process would occur just as quickly for a star, dozens of light years away as for the chair directly in front of us. Clearly this does not accord with modern scientific knowledge. This tells us that the mechanism of sight involves transmission of light from the star, at a strictly limited 186,000 miles per second and subsequent reception on the retina at the back of the eye, with onward nerve impulses to the brain. As will be seen later when we discuss the nature of reality, however, direct path Advaita describes the process rather differently.

Despite the power of this means of knowledge, as it is described by Advaita, it is actually quite limited since it can only act upon data that are within the scope of the sense organs or the mind. We cannot see the tiger around the corner and therefore have no knowledge of it. It is also not always reliable. When we do turn the corner and see the tiger, we probably will not immediately appreciate that it is only a very realistic projection on a screen...

2. Inference – *anumAna*. This is a very important tool in the philosophy of Advaita, precisely because of the limitations of *pratyakSha*. We are, after all, trying to learn about the nature of the Self and reality, neither of which are amenable to direct perception. Accordingly, it is worthwhile explaining the mechanism in more detail so that the arguments of the Sages can be more easily appreciated.

There cannot be any inference unless there is some prior knowledge gained from direct perception. We can suppose something to be the case, indulge in speculation or imagination, but none of these will give rise to knowledge. The classical example used by Shankara in the *brahmasUtra bhAShya* to describe the process is that of seeing smoke on a distant hill. We are used to seeing, in the kitchen for example, that when smoke arises it means that the pan has caught fire. We can therefore apply the analogy and infer that there must be a fire on the hill.

The formal logic used by Advaita here has a proposition, *pratij~nA*, (that there is a fire on the hill). It has a reason, *hetu*, for this (that one can see smoke on the hill). And it has an example, *udAharaNa* or *dRRiShTAnta*, (in the kitchen, where there is smoke there is also fire). The effective subject of the discussion (called the *pakSha*) is the hill. The thing that is to be inferred or concluded (called the *sAdhya*) is whether it is on fire or not. The *pakSha* has to be something that is already known about – i.e. from direct perception (*pratyakSha*) – otherwise we would not be able to talk meaningfully about it. Similarly, the fire in this example must *not* be perceptible - otherwise there would be nothing to infer. Finally, the *hetu* – the smoke on the hill - must also be perceptible (and must relate to the hill in question!) or we would not be able to make the inference. The object of the exercise is to prove the invisible part (the fire) by inference, based upon the similar example of the kitchen, where all of the elements kitchen, fire and smoke could be directly perceived, together with the visible smoke on the hill.

What effectively enables us to make the inference in this example is the knowledge we have from previous direct perception that smoke is invariable accompanied by fire. This is called *vyApti*, which means the "inseparable presence of one thing in another," "invariable concomitance" or effectively "a universal rule." The *vyApti* has to be proved through direct perception, ideally over many instances. Once this has been done it can be treated as a rule and thereafter we can use it to make inferences in similar situations.

The *brahmasUtra*-s make extensive use of inference but this differs from the strict interpretation above. As described, it is similar to what we would call scientific reasoning in the modern world. We make direct observations using our perceptions and then extrapolate or make inferences in a similar situation where we cannot use our perceptions directly. This is called *laukika anumAna*, where *laukika* means "worldly, everyday, common" (*loka* is the earth or world – there are other *loka*-s such as heaven and hell).

Unfortunately, when it comes to the nature of the Self, the *Atman*, worldly observations cannot be used to collect data. The only valid source for the data is the scriptures – *shAstra*-s. Therefore, what is found in the *brahma sUtra*-s are lots of references to quotations in the various *upaniShad*-s and inferences are then made from these. This is called *shAstrIya anumAna*.

Note that the *brahmasUtra*-s do also use *laukika anumAna* but for refuting the arguments of other schools of philosophy since that is the logic which the other schools use. Also, just as it is not possible to use scientific reasoning to discuss the *Atman*, it is also not possible to use it to refute the statements made in the scriptures themselves. It simply does not apply when talking about that which lies beyond the reach of science.

In the case of scientific inference, the observations upon which the conclusions are based are always taken as read – no one questions these; it is only the conclusions that may be wrong. This is obviously essential, otherwise the procedure would be pointless and new knowledge would never be gained. Similarly, in the case of the scriptures, it is necessary in order for the *pramANa* to be valid, that we must have accepted that the basic statements are true. I.e. we must have accepted the authority of the scriptures. More will be said about this in the discussion of the *shabda pramANa*, below.

[Vedanta Philosophy (see the breakdown in the Introduction) is one of the so-called *Astika* philosophies. This means that they acknowledge the authority of the Vedas. (*Astika* literally means "there is" or "there exists," referring to the existence of God.) Not recognizing this authority puts it into the category of *nAstika* philosophies, along with Buddhists and Jains (the word literally implies atheism).]

3. Comparison or analogy – *upamAna*. This effectively says the following: If A (which is directly perceived now) is similar to B (which is something perceived before and now remembered), then B is also similar to A. B's similarity to A is not actually seen *now* because B is absent so it is not a case of *pratyakSha*. Nor is it *anumAna*, since the form of the logic is different.

4. Non-apprehension – *anupalabdhi*. This states that not perceiving something is the same as perceiving that thing's non-existence. It is the only means of acquiring the knowledge of the non-existence or *abhAva* of a thing. We become aware of the absence of a chair in the room by going into the room and not seeing it there. I.e. we don't directly perceive the absence of the chair – we cannot see non-existence. Instead, we fail to see its presence. This might seem obvious but needs to be formally recognized in logic.

5. Postulation or supposition – *arthApatti*. This is the situation where we can directly observe something that is not explainable unless we assume something else to be the case. The classic example that is used is observing that someone whom we know does not eat during the day is nevertheless getting fat. We assume that he must be eating during the night when we are not watching.

6. Verbal authority or evidence – *shabda*. In the case of all of the other means of knowledge (except *shAstrIya pramANa*, which is dependent on *shabda*), our own direct perception is involved in one way or another. In the case of *shabda*, we rely on the testimony of others. *shabda* means "speech or language" as well and another term that is used is *Apta-vAkya*, which means a declaration from someone who is trusted.

Thus, in the example of the fire on the hill, we might see this with our own eyes – *pratyakSha* – or we might see the smoke and infer that there must be a fire – *anumAna*. Alternatively a friend, whose truthfulness we trust implicitly, may come and tell us that there is a fire. The fact that we have not seen it for ourselves does not make the report less reliable. After all, we sometimes see things ourselves that are not in fact true, such as a mirage. Verbal testimony can overrule what we see with our eyes, as in the example of the sun appearing to go around the earth.

In the west, accepting statements from scriptures is somewhat frowned upon and some modern teachers even seem to take the view that "in these enlightened times we should know better than to read this stuff." (See the Ref. 55 extract from Tony Parsons, for example, in the final chapter.) This is nonsense. The truth has always been the truth and this was undoubtedly better understood in the past than in this materialistic and egotistical age so that what is said there ought to be valued more, not less. Obviously scientific knowledge has progressed and such things as the descriptions of the world, with its five elements of space, air, fire, water and earth etc., are bound to seem strange But the worldly is not the matter about which we are seeking knowledge. If *shabda* leads to valid knowledge, then it is a valid *means* of knowledge. And if a degree of faith (*shraddhA*) is required to accept this, so be it. **Swami Satprakashananda** says:

According to Vedanta, implicit belief or faith (*shraddhA*) is the acceptance of, or the reliance on the words of the trustworthy, which need no verification. It is other than credulity or gullibility. It is conviction of truth and tantamount to valid knowledge. As such it is distinct from feeling, volition, imagination, or assumption. *shabda* as a source of valid knowledge means *Agama*, authentic word that is free from all defects. It is a canon of knowledge recognized by most Indian systems of thought that the words of such persons as are free from delusion, error, deceit, and defects of the senses and the mind are a source of valid cognition. Thus, reason is implicit in faith. It is not unreasonable to rely on the reliable. (Ref. 27)

Anantanand Rambachan explains the stance of Shankara in respect of *shruti* as the one valid means of knowledge regarding Brahman:

He (Shankara) is emphatic on the absolute inapplicability of all *pramANa*-s except *shruti* to the knowledge of *brahman*. Shankara is tireless in explaining the incompetence of sense perception in apprehending *brahman*. Each sense organ is naturally capable of grasping and revealing a quality which is appropriate to its own nature. Sound, sensation, form, taste, and scent are their respective spheres of functioning. *brahman*, however, remains unapproachable through any of them because of its uniqueness. *brahman* has neither sound, touch, form, taste, or smell. It is without qualities (*nirguNa*) and is therefore outside the domain of the sense organs. *brahman* is limitless, and to be an object of sense knowledge is to be finite and delimited, to be one object among many objects. A *brahman* that is sense-apprehended is therefore, in the view of Shankara, a contradiction.

And:

In addition to the inherent limitations of the sense organs and the absence in *brahman* of any quality that can be apprehended by any one of them, there is the impossibility of objectifying *brahman*. The process of empirical knowledge involves a distinction between subject and object, the knower and the known. We know things by making them the objects of our awareness, and in this way they are available for our scrutiny and analysis. Knowledge of an object presupposes the subject, the knower. *brahman*, however, is the eternal subject. As awareness, It illumines everything, and the entire universe, including mind, body, and sense organs, is Its object. It is impossible for the unchanging knower to be made an object of knowledge, like a pot or a thought. It is absurd to conceive of the subject as an object, for in its absence there is no subject to know the subject as an object. (Ref. 103)

Status of Knowledge and the process of sublation

Having looked at the various means that we have for acquiring knowledge, it is now necessary to look at the status of the knowledge that results. The attitude of Advaita is that the only reality is that of the non-dual Brahman. There is nothing apart from That. However, until the ignorance that prevents this realization is removed, there appears to be a world of separate objects and people and this is the realm in which the *pramANa*-s operate. Accordingly, Advaita accepts the validity of all knowledge gained through these mechanisms with a qualifying proviso. This is that it is quite prepared for some new knowledge to come along later that provides a new and more meaningful explanation. **Chittaranjan Naik** explains:

It is natural for us to ask questions about the world. A philosophy that seeks to answer these questions must explain the world and not negate the very thing that is to be explained. To negate the thing that is asked about is not answering the question. Experience is never negated. If I see a tree this morning, it is true for all time - for all of eternity - that I saw a tree this morning irrespective of the fact that any subsequent experience negates it or not. Sublation is the seeing of a different meaning in what was seen earlier and not the negation of the experience itself. (Ref. 106)

The process of *bAdha* is defined in **Monier-Williams** Sanskrit-English dictionary as "a contradiction, objection, absurdity, the being excluded by superior proof (in logic one of the 5 forms of fallacious middle term)" (Ref. 107). The word used in English is "sublation" (or occasionally "subration"), which the Oxford English Dictionary defines as "assimilate (a smaller entity) into a larger one." But these descriptions confuse and over-complicate what is actually a simple process. All that it means is that we held one explanation for a situation in our experience; then some new knowledge came along and we realized that an entirely different explanation made far more sense.

For example, it is supposed that people used to think that the earth was flat. If a ship sailed as far as the horizon, it would fall off the edge. Then some new knowledge came along – the earth is spherical. Now we can understand that the ship is moving further around the sphere and thus out of our sight. This new explanation has the added benefit of being able to explain how it is that a ship can return after having fallen off the edge! And it even explains why the horizon seems to be curved. So the old explanation – that the earth is flat – is said to have been "sublated" by the new one. It is said to be *bAdhita* – negated or shown to be contradictory, absurd or false.

The example most frequently used in Advaita is that of the rope and snake. We see the rope in poor light and erroneously conclude that it is a snake. Once a light (i.e. knowledge) has been shone onto the situation, we realize our mistake. If we encounter the situation again, we may still imagine we see a snake but the likelihood of being deceived is now much reduced because we no longer accord the same level of authenticity to our perception. It is this process of rejecting the appearance in the light of our experience or new knowledge that is called sublation or *bAdha*. This also provides a useful definition of "truth" in that the less able we are to sublate an experience, the truer it must be.

This stance, whereby, we accept as valid any satisfactory explanation we might have for the nature of our experience until something better comes along, is called *svataHprAmANyavAda* – the theory of the self-validity of knowledge. When a means of knowledge comes up with the goods, so to speak, it must necessarily be valid. If it subsequently turns out to be false, it is not because of any defect in the *pramANa*. Moreover, this validity is self-evident to the observer. When you see a chair, you don't usually have a philosophical debate with yourself about the nature of real and unreal before sitting down in it. If, when we do sit down, we fall on the floor, we might then infer that it was a holographic projection but, again, that is no fault of the *pramANa*. We would still see the chair on getting up but could now *infer* that it was a projection. **Eliot Deutsch** explains:

> An idea is held to be true or valid, then, the moment it is entertained (in the context of the theory no distinction is made between "truth" and "validity"), and it retains its validity until it is contradicted in experience or is shown to be based on defective apprehension. For example, according to the theory, if under the conditions of normal light and good eyesight I see an object and judge it to be a table, I immediately and rightfully trust my judgment that the object is a table and that I may safely place a book or a glass upon it. Whenever a cognition arises or a judgment takes place, it generates assurance about its truth. The judgment may be mistaken, but this is learned only later (e.g., the book falls through the "table"). *svataHprAmANyavAda* is thus a kind of perverse pragmatism. Instead of "truth" happening to an idea, it is "falsity" that happens. A cognition, in other words, is like the accused in court who is considered innocent until proven guilty; it is considered true until it is shown in experience to be false. (Ref. 82)

Ultimately, all knowledge proves to be sublatable, and therefore, untrue or invalid. The only knowledge that could not be sublated would be the knowledge of reality itself – and reality is not amenable to being "known" in any objective sense since that would make it dual.

The use of sublation as a technique is one of the most powerful aspects of the teaching. It is recognised from the outset that ignorance is our key problem. Simply telling us the answer as it were, would be of no use – our preconceptions and existing opinions and beliefs would simply force us to reject the truth. Accordingly, the method of traditional Advaita is to tell us something that we can accept and which allows us to revise our erroneous beliefs to some degree. Once that has been absorbed, the teacher tells us "well actually, that is not quite correct, it is actually more like this" and we can absorb a little more and destroy some more ignorance. Our original view is refined and supplanted by something that is still not the truth, since that cannot be spoken of, but is subtly "less false." It is complementary to the method of *adhyAropa-apavAda* described in the next section but, whereas that technique applies some attribute to the non-dual reality before taking it back, *bAdha* is the replacing of a whole paradigm or way of understanding the world.

Science

The scientific method is incommensurate with the means for obtaining higher knowledge. Science is in fact a hindrance on the path of self-knowledge. It is one of the pUrvapakSha-s [principal objection] that Vedanta must confront and demolish before the truth of Vedanta is seen.
Chittaranjan Naik (Ref. 314)

It is necessary briefly to mention the place of science in any investigation into non-duality. This can be very brief – it doesn't have one. Nevertheless, some modern writers have latched on to theoretical physics and its sometimes surprising postulates and discoveries as somehow validating the claims of Advaita. This is understandable in respect of such theories as Heisenberg's Uncertainty Principle, which shows that the observer is inextricably linked with the observed at the level of sub-atomic particles.

However, the point must always be borne in mind that science is a method of the phenomenal world of duality. There is invariably a subject studying an object, whether this is a supposed external, physical object or a subtle, internal concept. The non-dual truth is not available for objective research by definition. Thus it is that science can only ever find out more and more about *mithyA* and never anything about *satyam*, as was discussed above.

Knowledge of Reality

Knowledge, what is to be known, and the knower — these three do not exist in reality. I am the spotless reality in which they appear because of ignorance. **aShTAvakra gIta** 2.15 (Ref. 86)

Advaita states clearly that the non-dual reality cannot be spoken of. Any concept of it that could be formed would need a subject to understand that concept and this would necessarily be in the realm of duality, with the subject standing outside of it. Since there is *only* reality, every "thing" that could be perceived, thought or felt must be this same reality. Thus it is that some modern teachers – sometimes called "neo-Advaitins" – make statements such as "this is it," apparently believing that some useful and possibly enlightening information is being conveyed. Whilst undoubtedly true however, to anyone who understands the meaning of the term "Advaita," this can only ever be the truest truism of all time.

It can also be very misleading to someone who is unfamiliar with the teaching. If, for example, this "suffering" is "it," I might well be persuaded into complaining: "Well, then, I don't want it, thank you very much!" Ultimately, such a statement can only be accepted by someone who has already reached an intellectual appreciation of the tenets, in which case it will convey nothing that is not already understood.

Traditional Advaita employs more subtle techniques. One of the most fundamental of these is called *adhyAropa-apavAda*. You first "'impose" an attribute upon brahman in order to "describe" it in some way that is helpful to the seeker, i.e. that allows the intellect to gain some insight into its nature. Later, however, you have to take it back because, ultimately it is not actually true. Since you cannot say anything about the Absolute/ Consciousness/ Self whatever, you lead the listener towards understanding by saying something that is not actually true and then, once the import has been gathered, rescinding it.

Another technique uses what are called *lakShaNa*-s. **Swami Muni Narayana Prasad** explains the idea:

The goal of any search has to be clearly defined if it is to be successfully attained. In Sanskrit the definition of an object or objective is called *lakshaNam,* a word derived from the root *lakSh,* meaning to make something perceivable or to mark something out. The word *lakshaNam* therefore implies a precise description of something so as to make it perceivable, directly or indirectly, as distinct from other perceptions. The word is sometimes also used in the sense of science as, in the Indian view, science (*shastra*) should have a well-defined objective.

A proper definition will always clarify the object's essential content (*svarUpa lakshaNam*) and differentiating characteristics (*vyAvartaka lakshaNam*). As an object may have characteristics in common with others, a description of its general characteristics will not constitute a precise definition. The characteristics particular to that object alone have to be discerned and described without omitting any of them. This is how the definition (*lakshaNam*) of a thing is conceived in Indian thought. (Ref. 101)

Thus, another method of classical Advaita is called *taTastha lakShaNa.* (*taTastha* means "a property distinct from the nature of the body and yet that by which it is known.") This is the idea that since the truth cannot be spoken of; we can only point to it. This is why the statement "this is it" is unsatisfactory as an aid to appreciating the nature of reality. It is rather like looking at a forest of trees and saying something like "the treasure is buried under that tree there" and then simply pointing at the forest. There is no way that such a statement can really help the naïve listener. You have to give them some clearer indication so that they can understand what you are saying, such as: "see the oak tree over there which has its trunk split by lightning? There is a very old tree just to the right of it. The treasure is buried under that one."

Above all, the method of the Upanishads is one of negating what we are not so that we may come to a realization of what we are. I always think of this as the technique of Sherlock Holmes – when you have eliminated everything that you think possible, what remains, however improbable, must be the truth. It is epitomized in the words "*neti, neti*" in the *bRRihadAraNyaka upaniShad*, as already described in the first chapter. Here are some more words from **Swami Krishnananda** about our true nature, based upon II.iii.6 from this Upanishad:

What can we say about this glory? What can we speak of in respect of this great Reality which appears outwardly as that and inwardly this, which manifests itself as the five elements grossly as well as subtly, except that it is not anything that is conceivable to the mind or visible to the senses - *neti, neti*. It is not anything that is graspable either by the understanding or by the sense apparatus. Therefore, it is "not this," "not anything" that one can think of. It has no other definition except in this manner as has been put forth in this passage of the Upanishad. Its name is a secret. What is its name? It is the Truth of truth, Reality of reality, Being of being. It is the Soul of soul; it is the Self transcendent to the self. The individual self, of course, is real; anything connected with the individual self also is real. But, this is more real than the individual selves, more real than the mind and the understanding and the *prANa*-s and the senses. It is the ultimate Reality; it is the Supreme Being; it is absolutely Real, while others are only tentatively real, workably real and real only from a utilitarian point of view. So, this is a meditation, a means of spiritual at-one-ment. (Ref. 2)

And the *shvetAshvatara upaniShad* (Chapter 4) has this to say:

16. He who knows Brahman, who is all Bliss, extremely subtle, like the film that rises to the surface of clarified butter and is hidden in all beings; he who knows the radiant Deity, the sole Pervader of the universe, is released from all his fetters.

17. The Maker of all things, self-luminous and all-pervading, He dwells always in the hearts of men. He is revealed by the negative teachings of the Vedanta, discriminative wisdom and the Knowledge of Unity based

upon reflection. They who know Him become immortal.

18. When there is no darkness of ignorance, there is no day or night, neither being nor non-being; the pure Brahman alone exists. That immutable Reality is the meaning of "That." It is adored by the Sun. From It has proceeded the ancient wisdom.

19. No one can grasp Him above, across, or in the middle. There is no likeness of Him. His name is Great Glory.

20. His form is not an object of vision; no one beholds Him with the eyes. They who, through pure intellect and the Knowledge of Unity based upon reflection, realize Him as abiding in the heart become immortal. (Ref. 109)

The knowledge, once it has served its purpose of pointing towards the truth, is discarded too. Whichever technique was employed, once its significance has been appreciated, it has no further utility. Once the Self is truly known, knowledge and ignorance fall away, as **Ramana Maharshi** puts it in his **Ulladu Narpadu** (Reality in Forty Verses):

10. There is no knowledge without ignorance; and without knowledge ignorance cannot be. To ask, "Whose is this knowledge? Whose this ignorance?" and thus to know the primal Self, this alone is Knowledge.

11. Without knowing the Self that knows, to know all objects is not knowledge; it is only ignorance. Self, the ground of knowledge and the non-Self, being known, both knowledge and ignorance fall away.

12. True Knowledge is being devoid of knowledge as well as ignorance of objects. Knowledge of objects is not true knowledge. Since the Self shines self-luminous, with nothing else for It to know, with nothing else to know It, the Self is Knowledge. Nescience It is not. (Ref. 110)

The Self is the only "thing" that cannot be negated. When all that I think I am has been negated, that which cannot be negated (since it is itself "doing" the negating) remains. Even in deep sleep, I am the one that is aware of nothing. I am That. Ignorance apparently obscures this truth but when the light of knowledge is brought to bear, nothing is actually revealed that was not already there to begin with. Both the ignorance and the knowledge only affect the *jIva*; they do not touch the *Atman*. As **Ramesh Balsekar** puts it:

> *avidyA* (ignorance) arises on *vidyA* (knowledge) like ripples and waves arise on the surface of the ocean, and *avidyA* dissolves in *vidyA* just like the ripples and waves dissolve in the ocean. There is truly no difference between the waves and the water; similarly the distinction between ignorance and knowledge is notional and unreal. What exists, when ignorance and knowledge are no longer seen as two distinct entities, is Truth…

Ignorance vanishes as soon as it is examined critically. It is because of ignorance that one mistakes the silver in the mother-of-pearl. This ignorance can last only until the mother-of-pearl is seen for what it is. Ignorance vanishes as soon as it is apperceived that all that exists is the universal, infinite Consciousness. All phenomenal manifestations are merely appearances in Consciousness, like a mirror effect, and are therefore illusory. All that exists is Consciousness which can be represented by the personal subjective pronoun "I." (Ref. 111)

We are already 'That' – we just don't know it, i.e. the problem is one of ignorance. The only thing that can eliminate ignorance is knowledge. Accordingly, no practice or 'doing' of any kind is going to bring about enlightenment. Enlightenment is something that happens when the realisation is triggered in the mind that 'I am Brahman', I am not a separate, limited person but the undivided, changeless reality.

But, as will be discussed in the next chapter, this is not to say that things cannot happen to make this realisation more probable. If we continue resolutely along a path of selfish, desire-fulfilling, worldly pleasure, enlightenment is most unlikely. If, on the other, hand, practices such as Shankara's *chatuShTaya sampatti* are carried out, scriptures are read and reflected on, qualified teachers are consulted etc, then the state of the mind is likely to be more conducive to this mental modification occurring.

The precise realization 'event' is called *akhaNDAkAra vRRitti*. This is a *vRRitti* (thought) in the form of (*AkAra*) the formless or undivided (*akhaNDa*). It is a very special kind of knowledge, which is not knowledge as usually understood but that which removes ignorance of Self once and for all (see Chapter 8, topic 8). **V. Subrahmanian** explains the nature of this event:

> Knowledge has to come only in the locus of ignorance. Ignorance is present in the False Self, also called *jIva*. In Vedantic terminology this is called the *antaHkaraNa* where the reflection of the Real Self, Pure Consciousness, is available. It is this admixture of the *antaHkaraNa* (mind) and the Pure Consciousness that is called jIva. This is the false self. It is this *jIva* that experiences ignorance, *saMsAra*. It is this *jIva* that strives for knowledge. Ultimately it is this *jIva* that gets the Realization. It happens through a peculiar *vRRitti* (transformation of the mind) called *akhaNDAkAra vRRitti*. When due to prolonged practice, the mind takes on the form of Brahman, there occurs the destruction of the ignorance located in the *jIva* and thereby the *jIva* gets liberated. Once this happens that person is no longer *jIva*, but Brahman.
>
> If the above explanation is too complicated, just this much would suffice: It is the False Self that gets the realization. This marks the end of the 'false' and just the 'Self' remains. (Ref. 376)

VidyAraNya explains (in his Jivanmuktiviveka) how it is that the mind can take on the form of Brahman when Brahman has no form:

> A pot made of clay is full of the all-pervading space as soon as it is made. Filling it afterwards with water, rice or any other substance is due to human effort. Though the water, etc, in the pot can be removed, the space inside can never be removed. It continues to be there even if the mouth of the pot is hermetically sealed. In the same manner, the mind, in the act of being born, comes into existence full of the consciousness of the self. It takes on, after its birth, due to the influence of virtue and

vice, the form of pots, cloths, color, taste, pleasure, pain, and other transformations, just like melted copper, cast into moulds. Of these, the transformations such as color, taste and the like, which are not-self, can be removed from the mind, but the form of the self, which does not depend on any external cause, cannot be removed at all. Thus, when all other ideas are removed from the mind, the self is realized without any impediment. (Ref. 377)

Finally, an amusing and somewhat cynical description of the "path" of knowledge, otherwise known as *j~nAna yoga*, from **Wayne Liquorman**:

This path of *j~nAna,* this path of knowledge, requires a transcendence of the mind; and that can only happen when the mind is utterly, thoroughly, *completely* exhausted. After you have sought every *possible* avenue into which you might inquire and *know,* after you have thought again and again that you've GOT IT, only to find it slip through your fingers like jello; only then can there possibly be some kind of surrender, some kind of *acceptance* of the fact that the mind will not get you there. And it isn't enough to just pay lip service to the fact of, "The mind isn't gonna help; the mind isn't gonna know it"—That is something the mind KNOWS! (*Loud laughter*) That's the *new* truth that you're holding sacred!

It gets subtler and subtler. That which you think you *know,* gets subtler and subtler. It's really a process very much like a dog chasing its tail. Your mind is set in motion seeking itself, chasing itself, trying to catch itself. And if you have a mind that is strong, that has a lot of intellect behind it, you can get spinning VERY fast! And you can *catch up!* You can (*laughter*) *gain* on yourself! And the faster you get spinning, the closer that you gain on yourself and perhaps, if there is Grace, you will disappear up your own ass!

And this describes the path of *j~nAna.* I don't know what *veda* or *sUtra* it is in, but that is essentially what we've set out to do: to inquire deeply, to look at that which is asking the questions; to look at that which is seeking; and to find out: is there any substance there? And it's not something that I can do for you. I can sit up here all day and talk about it, and if you trust me... which is dicey to begin with... then you'll say, "He's telling the truth, what he's saying is valid, I believe him."

But I am NOT telling the truth. What I am saying here is NOT the truth. At the very best, these are pointers towards that truth, towards That which Is, That which is the Source and the Substance of everything; that Consciousness which is *all there is.* That which is our True Nature, That which we *Are.* (Ref. 113)

Conclusion

The topics in this chapter were brought together in an email from **Ananda Wood** recently, while commenting upon a later chapter. This sheds valuable light on the philosophy of Advaita as a whole and the method it uses in approaching the truth. The principal subject is the distinction between belief (*mata*) and faith (*shraddhA*).

Essentially, "belief" is a mental activity of supposing and imagining, oriented towards the dualistic realm of name and form. By contrast, "faith" is a deeper conviction - of inner trust and fidelity - to which a reflective enquiry returns, beneath the changing show of created names and forms.

Accordingly, the reasoning of Advaita refuses to take any beliefs for granted. It refuses to believe in anything. Its use of reason is essentially skeptical - as it examines all mind-created beliefs, in order to discern and thus to remove what's false from what is true in them.

This questioning examination cannot rightly aim at any preconceived objective, in the world of name and form. For any such preconception would inevitably prejudice the enquiry. The only proper aim must be a true knowing that is completely free from all preconceptions. The enquiry must aim reflectively, beneath all pre-conceptions of belief, towards a truth that's known beneath the mind's activities and all their physical or mental objects. Such an enquiry essentially implies a deep faith in the pure knowing of an objectless truth, beneath all mental and physical activity.

As implied by the word "philosophy," that faith is an uncompromising love of true knowing, quite distinct from the compromised desires which are formed from belief in partial objects of perception and conception through our bodies and our minds. In short, true faith is completely uncompromised, because it is purely subjective and spiritual (*AtmIya*), beneath all compromised belief in objective appearances that are made up by our partial and dubious faculties of mind and body.

So I would say that in all teaching methods of Advaita, it is our personal and cultural "beliefs" that are up for questioning, on the basis of an implied "faith" or "conviction" in the ultimate value of true knowing. (Ref. 347)

Summary

- The fundamental problem is that we do not know who we really are.
- Therefore, we are continually searching outside for meaning and happiness.

Ignorance and Identification

- We create the problem ourselves through identification.
- The *jIva* takes the world to be real and himself to be a doer-enjoyer.
- *jIva* = *Atman* + *upAdhi* of *avidyA*.
- The idea that the Self is limited in this way is called *avachCheda vAda*.
- The idea that ignorance reflects the Self like a mirror is *pratibimba vAda*.
- Clear untainted glass will reflect the Self and the world more clearly than colored or distorting glass. Similarly we should drop opinions and beliefs and look with an empty mind.
- Ignorance, and the ego that it engenders, will continue until it is removed by knowledge. Knowledge brings liberation.

- *mAyA* has two aspects – a veiling power *(AvaraNa)* that conceals the Truth and *vikShepa* that projects an illusion.

Mechanism of Superimposition

- *adhyAsa* or *adhyAropa* is the process of erroneous attribution, e.g. mistakenly seeing a snake instead of a rope.
- A part of the real is seen and known while part is hidden.
- We mix up the real with something unreal (from memory) and make the mistake of thinking that the combination is real.
- Once knowledge arises (or light in the metaphor), the hidden part is revealed and the mistaken perception vanishes.
- *jIva* is the mixing up of the real Self and a superimposed, unreal "person."

satyam and mithyA

- Advaita defines "real" as that which exists in all three periods of time (*trikAlAtIta*). This is the only "truth" *(satyam)*.
- That which is only a temporary form, but still has basis in reality, is called *mithyA*, a "dependent" reality, c.f. the pot which is really clay.
- Every "thing" in the world is *mithyA* (including us, the world, thoughts etc.)
- Ignorance is pursuing *mithyA* instead of *satyam*.
- It is not knowledge of reality (which is impossible anyway) that brings about enlightenment but knowledge of *mithyA*.

Opinions, beliefs and knowledge

- Opinions and beliefs may be more dangerous than ignorance since we are less open and view everything through their filters.
- An opinion is always one view out of many possible views. They are therefore dualistic and necessarily false.
- Ignorance is the belief in separate things and the finiteness of the Self.

- Knowledge is the realization that all is Brahman.
- When knowledge arises, ignorance disappears, just as darkness disappears when the light is switched on.
- Once ignorance has been dispelled, knowledge is discarded too. Knowledge is *mithyA*, not *satyam*.
- Worldly knowledge is for the purpose of gaining results through action. The knowledge that brings realization works directly without the need for action (*pratipAdya-pratipAdaka sambandha*). This is because we are already That.
- Advaita does not seek to add new beliefs but to remove old ignorance.
- That I exist (*sat*) and am conscious (*chit*) are self-evident. But *shruti* is needed to explain that I am also *Ananda*.
- Experience alone cannot remove ignorance, e.g. our dream experience does not persuade us that we are not the body.
- The scriptures are needed to reveal to us that *Atman* = *brahman*.

Means of knowledge (pramANa-s)

- Advaita recognizes six valid means of acquiring knowledge (*pramANa-s*):

  1 Direct perception (*pratyakSha*). This includes feelings and awareness of knowledge as well as sight, hearing etc.

  2 Inference (*anumAna*), e.g. fire on the hill.

  3 Comparison or analogy (*upamAna*).

  4 Non-apprehension (*anupalabdhi*).

  5 Postulation or supposition (*arthApatti*).

  6 Verbal authority (*shabda*). The testimony of others, especially scriptures, can be more reliable than *pratyakSha* or *anumAna*.
- Much of the reasoning in Advaita is inference from scriptural statements. These cannot be refuted by scientific reasoning.
- Faith (*shraddhA*) is accepting the words of the trustworthy, not credulity.

- Brahman is not accessible to the senses and cannot be objectified.
- The *pramANa*-s operate in the phenomenal realm; the reality of brahman transcends this.
- Accordingly, an apparently valid knowledge can be shown to be false and supplanted by another, higher knowledge. This is called sublation (*bAdha*).

Truth/Reality

- We assume our knowledge to be valid until a new experience shows it to be false. The ultimate reality is that which cannot be sublated.
- Traditional Advaita provides a series of "truths" supplanting ignorance a little at a time. The final truth could not be accepted straight away.
- Science is entirely objective, whereas we want to find out about the subject.
- Knower-knowledge-known do not exist in reality. Brahman cannot be "known" as such since this would then be duality.
- The technique of *adhyAropa-apavAda* gives attributes to reality but, once the point is understood, indicates that this is erroneous and takes it back.
- Although we cannot speak directly of Truth, we can point to it. This is the technique of *taTastha lakShaNa*.
- The method of "neti, neti" negates what we are not so that we may come to recognize what we are.
- Both the ignorance and the knowledge only affect the *jIva*; they do not touch the *Atman*.
- We are already the Self. The problem is that the mind is ignorant of this. The realization 'event' is called *akhaNDAkAra vRRitti*, when the mind 'takes on the form of the undivided' (i.e. Brahman).

5. SPIRITUAL PATHS AND PRACTICES

If you are looking for Liberation,
There is some bad news and some good news.
The bad news is that the person you think you are
will never find Liberation.
The good news is that what You really are
is already awakened. **Jan Kersschot** (Ref. 356)

This chapter will discuss the various spiritual practices advocated by traditional and modern Advaita in order to prepare the mind for realization of our (already existent) true nature. Effort is needed to remove the ignorance that prevents this understanding at the level of the intellect. Spiritual experiences have nothing to do with this process but "paths" are valid to the extent that they diminish the seeming dominion of the ego. Only when our mistaken view of the world has been corrected (something which practice can achieve), is there the opportunity to awaken from the delusion of *mAyA* (which no amount of effort can achieve).

The traditional *chatuShTaya sampatti* requirements are examined in detail, together with the various *yoga* techniques that have been advocated. Specific practices such as mind control, stillness, being in the present, meditation and attending satsang are looked at. The value of the scriptures and problems of language are examined and the traditional teaching of the origin of sound and words is described in passing. The nature of the guru-disciple relationship is analyzed and, finally, there is a brief look at the 'Self-enquiry' teaching of Ramana Maharshi.

Spiritual Practice
The easy way is hard. The hard way is easy. **Robin Dale** (Ref. 374)

If the preceding chapters have convinced you that there is logic and reason behind the assertions made by the Sages, the next question is likely to be "How do I realize this for myself?" You may have been persuaded by their reasoning into accepting intellectually that you are not the body, mind or intellect and that, rather than there being some meaning or purpose to be found in the outside world, your own essence is already eternal happiness but this is not your direct experience. Accordingly, the next step would seem to be to examine what has been said about what needs to be done. Alternatively, if we really are not able to "do" anything, what must happen to bring about the recognition of our true status?

There is a fundamental problem with the idea of spiritual practice being performed by someone who is seeking enlightenment. There are several aspects to this. Firstly, it is the ego that wants to be enlightened and, as was discussed in the first chapter, the ego does not actually exist – it is only a set of thoughts with which Consciousness identifies in this body-mind form. Secondly, our real and true nature necessarily is already present and "reality" is what it always was and will be. Thirdly, we have already discussed how we are not a "doer" and effectively have no free will. Consequently, on the face of it, no amount of effort or practice can change these facts.

Nothing whatsoever is required to be what you already are. **Nathan Gill** (Ref. 25)

If the divergence between traditional and so-called "neo-advaita" began with the considerations on action and free-will, it is on this subject that they part company irrevocably. The view of many of today's "satsang" teachers is that there is absolutely nothing that can be done and, moreover, nothing that *needs* to be done. We are already That and That is all there is. The modern mantra is, quite simply, "This is it."

The scriptures and traditional teachers for all time have also been perfectly aware of this. They have also acknowledged, however, that it does not *seem* to be like this for the confused seeker. And this is the crux of the matter. (The apparent contradictions in the teaching methods will be examined in detail in the final chapter.)

Ultimately, we cannot do anything to change who we are. Indeed, ignoring the fact that we are not actually "doers" anyway, there is a danger that all that we are likely to achieve is to change our self-image, substituting one set of ideas with another, probably stronger set. The reason that you are unable currently to accept this is that your misconceptions are superimposed upon the reality. **Andrew Vernon** explains:

> In the human being, the Self becomes identified with the false sense of "I" or ego. There is then the belief that "I" am seeking happiness for "my" benefit. When you become a spiritual seeker, that illusion remains so that you imagine "I am an aspirant" and "I am seeking liberation." When, through the grace of the Master, Self-realization actually occurs, it is understood that there never was any such seeker. It was the Self all along that was drawing Itself to Itself in a purely imaginary game of separation. When this happens, the game is over, and the Self rests contented in Itself, as far as that individual body-mind is concerned. However, the game goes on in all the other myriad forms. (4.25) (Ref. 20)

Sundance Burke explains clearly how it is our mind that is looking for an answer that can never be understood by the mind, as our infinite Being cannot be realized by means of the finite:

> Discovering your true nature is not like looking for your eye glasses when they are lost. Your eye glasses are an object and an object exists somewhere in time and space. Eye glasses can be found. Who you are can not be found objectively. (Ref. 211)

The mind, he says, is the wrong tool for the job. It is only good at finding *things*:

The snapshot of the investigator is not giving us what we seek. The snapshot is merely pointing to it. This is all that the investigator (mind) can do. The snapshot represents something but it can not be what it is representing. Certainly objects point to who we are. The body points to who we are. Our feelings and thoughts point to who we are. The world points to who we are. However, nothing we experience through the senses and intellect can equate to being who we are. (Ref. 211)

Who we are cannot be found in this way. Anything that could be found would necessarily be limited in some way:

You honestly cannot be located. You cannot know permanent fulfilment by being personally identified with a fleeting sense of this or that. Not one idea or feeling truly fits you as you are. Everything you try on is too small, too constricting and too fleeting. You can either keep shopping in the mall of the mind for the perfect and permanent fit or simply realize that you are naked in truth and simply free. (Ref. 211)

Again, if what has been said earlier has been accepted, this all makes perfect sense. But also it is effectively more of the same and the response is likely to be: "yes, I can follow that but how can I come to know it to be true instead of simply accepting the logic of it mentally?" Unfortunately, many modern teachers seem unable to provide a satisfactory response to this and are likely simply to repeat the same truth using slightly different words: "You are already what you are looking for. There is nowhere to go. This is it with knobs on." The point is that "I – the ego" can never "become realized" because "I – the ego" do not exist. A "category error" is being made, as will be explained in Chapter 7.

Part of the problem seems to be that neo-Advaita attempts to give you the final truth from the outset and this is in keeping with the modern western ethos of wanting everything now. We don't want partial truths or to be patronised with merely a glimpse of the whole picture. Unfortunately it is almost invariably the case that this "final truth" does not help. If an ego is still looking for meaning or happiness, it is not going to find it here. This is why another large group of modern teachers effectively aim their words at the psychological level, reducing fear and anxiety, bringing about acceptance and a more peaceful life – all very useful and valuable at the phenomenal level, but nothing to do with Advaita.

The Self is indeed always present, since there is only the Self. But the fact of the matter is that, from the vantage point of the *jīva*, there is ignorance and effort is needed to remove this. **Annamalai Swami**, a disciple of Ramana Maharshi, explains:

> A lamp that is lit may blow out if the wind is strong. If you want to see it again, you have to relight it. But Self is not like this. It is not a flame that can be blown out by the passing winds of thoughts and desires. It is always bright, always shining, always there. If you are not aware of it, it means that you have put a curtain or a veil in front of it that blocks your view. Self does not hide itself behind a curtain. You are the one who puts the curtain there by believing in ideas that are not true. If the curtain parts and then closes again, it means that you are still believing in wrong ideas. If you have eradicated them completely, they will not reappear. While these ideas are covering up the Self, you still need to do constant *sAdhana*. (Ref. 243)

Spiritual Experiences

> *The purpose of a spiritual experience is not to solve your problems or make "you" enlightened. Spiritual experiences come and go, and that is all you need to learn from them.* **Nirmala** (Ref. 254)

People following a spiritual path may sometimes have what is termed a spiritual experience. Indeed, having read or heard about the wonderful and possible life-changing experiences that others have had, there is a danger that these may explicitly be sought. The supposed epiphany of the "realization event" is the holy grail of the seeker, to mix a couple of metaphors. But the point that must always be borne in mind is that an event in time can have nothing to do with the reality of who we are. Experiences come and go while the Self is eternal, unchanging and must already be the case. This is the message that the neo-Advaitins constantly reiterate, usually to the exclusion of all others – and it is true. What we, as deluded *jIva*-s, are actually seeking is that the mental ignorance be dispelled so that there can be direct apperception of this already-existing fact.

Philip Mistlberger puts it as follows:

> Spiritual experiences - sometimes also called peak experiences - are not a problem in themselves, but they get used by the ego in order to maintain the appearance of time and the sense of separation. These peak experiences become memories, filed away, to be showcased, discussed, compared, or even bragged about. They happened in the *past,* and more of them are anticipated in the *future.*
>
> Our True Self exists in the timeless dimension of the present moment, and thus is not an experience. It is simply what is already the case. Spiritual experiences, when collected on the trophy case of memories, can actually serve to strengthen the ego's sense of separate identity. The ego identifies with these memories, and usually becomes proud of them, which is part and parcel of the spiritualized ego.
> (Ref. 134)

If spiritual experiences are pursued for their own sake, the whole point is missed. Neo-Advaitins claim that this is indeed what happens for many people, that the reality is already here now but, rather than acknowledge this, we prefer to go in search of some imagined goal and enjoy the path itself for whatever reason. **Leo Hartong** talks about this:

> That's absolutely fine. In itself it can be a beautiful game and there are plenty of people who would rather do that instead of seeing-what-is; to the mind this "seeing-what-is" may not seem very interesting. It is like space or silence and how would one describe that? The mind needs to be able to process words, sounds, pictures feelings or descriptions - and

how would you describe space? How to describe silence? The mind says "booooring, I would rather go and follow an interesting path, I will meditate and reach an exalted state and will have beautiful experiences."

Of course, wonderful experiences are available and possible, but that is not what this is about. Whatever experience arises, the stubbing of a toe or a wonderful meditation experience, there is something absolutely quiet that is aware of it. This silence is always one step before whatever it is that is perceived or experienced. To simply admit this and to say: "although it has been an interesting experience, all this seeking has been futile" - this is something not everybody is ready to admit. As long as you want to continue as an "I who has accomplished something" you're not ready to admit this. (Ref. 239)

The looking for and expectation of experiences associated with seeking means that the truth is effectively overlooked. We are always looking in the wrong place. The talks given by **Roger Linden** reflect this, being entitled "The Elusive Obvious" and he uses a metaphor to explain this:

An analogy would be that of looking at the drawing of a vase, where the outline of the vase can also be seen as two profiles. It is either two heads with the noses almost touching or it is a vase – do you know the picture I am talking about?

So you are trying to get the two heads but you only see the vase and you can spend a long time trying to do that but the reality is that what you are looking at is a bit of paper with a drawing on. There isn't a vase and there aren't two heads. It is just a piece of paper. Now, the fact that it was only a bit of paper was known the whole time wasn't it? But it was overlooked, taken for granted because there was an idea of there being something special to be got. What I am saying is that the assumption that there is something special makes it seem as if something is being obscured. What is being said is actually that there is nothing obscured. It was always a bit of paper. If you have spent years and years looking for the two heads then it is, "No, no, I know there are two heads. I have read about it, people have told me about it. I have seen people when they get it and it seems like a big deal. That is what I am after – I want the two heads not the bit of paper."

But the funny thing is that what's taken for granted turns out to be the diamond, turns out to be the jewel. What this is turns out to be absolutely what was being looked for but it is not what was assumed to be looked for. It is because there is the sense of lack that we assume that this couldn't be what is being described but I assure you it is. (Ref. 237)

Hans Laurentius describes how any seeking simply takes us away from who we are:

…what you are seeking is not an experience. The seeker is an experience, the meditator is an experience. And it is you who are the knower of these experiences. You, consciousness, cannot be experienced. Experiences belong to the mind, you are not the mind, but everything that the mind, and all its efforts and attempts witnesses. That is true knowledge. See through this and live by it, live in it and you are freed from every form of compulsion and discipline. What happens out of love never costs any effort, even though from the outside it might be seen as a great sacrifice.

Everything that costs effort takes you away from that, every effort adds another veil. Trying to understand this is also an effort and thus also leads you away from yourself. So don't try anything, see the trying. Make no effort. See the effort and the "effort maker." And realize at once, that you are the seeing and not what is seen. Because, every veil, every effort, every separation is known, and this knowing, that is you. (Ref. 244)

I think the problem here is one of language, as will be discussed later in this chapter. The idea of seeking certainly implies that some *thing* is being sought and this would certainly be a mistake. But this is not the actual purpose at all. The seeker is not looking for experience but endeavouring simply to eliminate wrong ideas about what is already the case. Whilst it is true to say that we are not the mind, it is nevertheless the case that these mistaken ideas *are* in the mind so that it is there that effort *does* have to be made. The body-mind mechanism will always act according to the conditioning of the mind. What needs to change is the idea that this has anything to do with who we are.

Spiritual Paths

Traditional Advaita states that the *jIva* can do something (at the phenomenal level) – whether this be to gain knowledge which will remove the ignorance or to aim to reduce the dominion of the ego. Neo-Advaita simply states that there is no one to do anything and, in any case, there is nowhere to go. Unsurprisingly, these contrasting views prevail on the topic of paths as well.

There is no path. Paths lead from here to there. How can a path lead from here to here? A path can only lead away from home. Home is awareness. Home is peace. Home is heaven. All paths to heaven lead to hell.
Wei Wu Wei and **Stephen Wingate** (Refs. 350 and 234)

There are two Sanskrit words that are used for "path": *mArga*, which also carries the sense of "way, method or means" and *upAya*, that by which one reaches ones aim. In reality, it must be the case that we are already who we really are. Who else could we be? It is the illusory ego that believes that we are in some way limited and that wants to become eternally happy. Whilst this state of affairs continues, the search is doomed to failure. Paths and practices are therefore needed not in order that we may find something new but in order that we may uncover what is already here now.

The reason why different paths are needed is that minds, bodies and egos function differently. All paths aim effectively to remove the obscuring effect of this ego. This can be done through the practices of devotion and surrender to a God, for example, in the case of *bhakti* yoga. It can also be achieved in simple day to day life of working, at whatever may be our particular job, by doing the work for its own sake and giving up any claim to the results, in the case of *karma* yoga. And it can be achieved by enquiry and reason, using the mind and intellect to appreciate the truth of the non-existence of the ego, in the case of *j~nAna* yoga.

There are two extremes of viewpoint on the need for or validity of a path. The orthodox view is represented by the following extract from **Vamadeva Shastri (David Frawley)**:

Recently I came across a statement to the effect that "anyone can realize the supreme truth." Perhaps, but the odds against it are astronomical if we are simply waiting for it to happen. As wonderful and inclusive as this statement sounds, it is a form of wishful thinking. All yogic traditions have clear guidelines about the preparatory disciplines and requirements for undertaking various levels of practice. There is a certain organic development to yoga that requires a step-by-step process, like learning to walk before attempting to run. In its fullest sense, yoga is an intense life discipline, and the further a student advances the more stringent these requirements become…

…people like to quote the example of Ramana Maharshi, who as a lad of sixteen, spontaneously and on his own asked himself the question, "Who am I?" and after a few moments of contemplation entered into a permanent state of self-realization. This could come about only because he was *able to die* on a psychological level, withdrawing all of his attention from the body and mind, and never looking back on them again. Only one in millions (if not billions) can do this. (Ref. 232)

And the neo-Advaitin view is presented here by **Nathan Gill**:

But this progression is not necessary for clarity to appear. Clarity could appear at any time in any character in the play. None of the apparent stages in the play of life has any ability to produce clarity. Advaitic knowledge has no more a special ability to create a condition for clarity to appear than does any other part of the play.

Spiritual life is based on the presumption of individuality, with reunion with the whole as the projected goal. And as a means to achieve this goal of reunion, an array of exotic techniques and methods are provided in the play, to "purify" the individual, to get rid of the "I"', to become enlightened, etc.

The fundamental point that is missed at every stage of the individual's quest is that the individual - being played by You, who are Consciousness - is already what he or she is seeking. Nothing can make the seeker any more what he or she already is.

The search and all the methods and techniques employed are there for no more reason than any other part of the play. They arise for their own sake, simply as part of the play. (Ref. 25)

The notion that there is no need for practice of any kind seems to be a relatively modern idea, in keeping with the western ideology of "wanting it now" and not being prepared to spend the whole of one's life, if necessary, working towards something that is known to be worth all of that effort. It seems likely that the principal source of this message is Sri Poonja, who is claimed as guru by a large percentage of the current teachers in the west. One of his disciples, **Pratima**, had this to say:

Papaji's message is simplicity itself. Nothing to attain anew, only a thin veil to be removed. He is totally revolutionary in this. The traditional paths of seeking the truth all seem so laborious and painstaking… maybe in 10 or 20 years or so or at the moment of death we will realize who we are all along! So why not wake up now! Why waste time?

We do not need to "seek" the truth anymore. We have matured beyond complicated rites and rituals, grown out of meditation, prayer and superstition. Mankind has done enough of this. It is clearly time for something totally simple, something that can be grasped equally by all people from all walks of life. Enough of wars over religion and particular belief systems. After all, we are all consciousness itself, inseparable, undivided. One throbbing beingness! It is time for us to wake up and roar this from the rooftops. (Ref. 78)

The justification for this message is not at all clear. Since it is the *jIva* doing the seeking, why should the general "progress" of mankind have anything to do with it? Indeed, on the face of it, spiritually speaking, it would seem that we are *more* ignorant now than in past ages.

There are two elements to the neo-Advaitin stance. Firstly there is no ego and secondly we must already be who we really are, i.e. there cannot be an enlightenment "event" in the future. **Jan Kersshot** explains this view:

> ...belief in a progressive path is very popular, but according to me it is completely contradictory to what liberation really is all about. The belief in a spiritual path that leads to the top of the mountain is based on two basic misconceptions:
>
> the importance you give to the personal part of the story (how can *I* reach "It"?);
>
> the belief that you still nurture in the phenomenon of time, your hope for a better future (*when* will I reach "It"?).
>
> As long as you have not understood that liberation is not personal and that it is timeless, you are like the donkey following a carrot. True liberation is impersonal, and therefore you can not claim "It" for yourself. I - as Jan - can never possess "It." Moreover, "It" is timeless (not "'here and now" but *beyond* time and space), and thus "That" can never be projected in the future. If you nevertheless do so, you are just fooling yourself - although in the end there is nothing wrong with fooling yourself either... (Ref. 236)

Wayne Liquorman, too, from the Navnath *sampradAya*, suggests that there is not actually any relationship between disciplines and "enlightenment":

> The point is, if you want to know what you can do, what I will say is that you can do a virtually endless number of things, none of which will necessarily provide that which you are seeking, but it may. If it happens, you causally link the two, you ignore the 10,000 other cases in which it

didn't. You say. "But I did that and then I got this — therefore I am living testimony! I did this and then got that, therefore there's a connection." The connection's notional of course. (Ref. 78)

The long-term seeker knows all this but does not see a way out. She acknowledges the identification with a mind that is pursuing this philosophy and the illusory ego that claims, paradoxically, to want enlightenment – but where to go from here? Such a person is very likely to become caught up in the seemingly irrefutable logic of the neo-Advaitins. **Shawn Nevins'** view is as follows:

Assuming you accept the notion that the ego is the great barrier to discovering our true nature and curing what ails us, you will eventually confront the ego of spiritual seeking. Egos are poses, beliefs about our self, which range from the ridiculous belief we are great lovers or unrecognized geniuses to the core belief that we exist. Many say that the ego of seeking is the greatest barrier to finding. There is a grain of truth in that, yet the untruth lies in trying to eliminate this ego. The ego of seeking will resolve itself at the proper time. As Ramana Maharshi says, the stick that stirs the funeral pyre is itself consumed by the fire…

Yet these mistaken seekers try to let go and stop seeking in hopes of finding. They attempt to do nothing, thinking that doing nothing eliminates the ego. Of course, they don't do nothing. They imagine doing nothing - they "do" doing nothing based on what they've read of letting go and acceptance. If they are really intelligent, they recognize they are "doing" doing nothing and really tie themselves into knots. All the while, other egos are growing to fill the vacuum. This is much ado about nothing. (Ref. 233)

There is also the fact that there are many who are actually more interested in the path itself than the goal. They enjoy the intellectual challenge of the philosophy, the feel-good sharing of satsang or simply the self-importance of the spiritual search rather than the materialistic values of the rest of society. **Aja Thomas** relates the following story:

> The situation is very much like an analogy that was recently shared with me. If you had two doorways, a doorway to heaven and a doorway to a lecture about heaven, you would find the vast majority of people lined up before the doorway to the lecture about heaven. Often we aren't as interested in experiencing the divine as we are in being able to "know" about it, talk about it, and impress people with our astounding depth of information about it. And what if you could actually open the doors and look in? In the doorway to the lecture about heaven, you would find a room full of beautiful people, drinking organic tea, talking about Gods & Goddesses, doing energy work, singing songs, meditating together, discussing the pros and cons of various paths and spiritual techniques - generally having a great time. On the other hand, when you opened the door to heaven, standing outside and peering in, you would see nothing. It would appear empty, dark, unattractive - because through that door there is nothing for the mind to know, nothing for the body to experience, no concepts or beliefs to grasp and certainly nothing that would "attract" our mind, unless annihilation was attractive. For to enter into the absolute is to be totally beyond the mind and ego. (Ref. 93)

Much of the confusion is brought about by language. It has led to the frequent practice of avoiding the use of the personal pronoun "I" in everyday usage so as to make it clear to the listener that the speaker is claiming that he has renounced the ego. Thus, **Wayne Liquorman** for example *does* acknowledge that there are paths, as long as the personal "doership" is excluded:

> Methods happen. People follow methods. Methods, we can say, are also the instruments of Consciousness so that things happen through people trying various methods. The point of the Teaching is that it is not the individual doing the method, it is Consciousness doing the method through that individual. And so these methods are different avenues

through which the doing happens. (Ref. 235)

In fact, since we "do" nothing, the fact that there is "seeking" is not a problem – the problem is the ignorance, in the form of ideas such as "I am a seeker" and that I, the ego, want to achieve some goal, as **Ramesh Balsekar** explains:

> It is the seeker who is the obstacle - not seeking; seeking happens by itself. Seeking happens because the body/mind organism is programmed to seek what it is seeking. So if the seeking for enlightenment is happening, then the body/mind organism has been programmed to seek. The obstacle is the seeker who says, "I want enlightenment." (Ref. 145)

Making Effort

You don't need to make a resolution to seek truth. Your perennial dissatisfaction is that resolution. **Robin Dale** (Ref. 374)

The need for effort at all seems to be paradoxical. We are already who we really are so obviously there is nothing we can do to become that. What is required is something to make us realize that this is the case, to remove the delusion that we are a body, mind, person etc. **Philip Mistlberger**:

> We need not worry about our true nature, actually. It's already there. We need only become aware of the ways in which the ego blocks our awareness of it, and the mind obscures it via deluded thinking. That is the sole value of all so-called methods. So we use these methods not with a view to attaining anything, rather only to see more clearly what is already the case—our natural state. (Ref. 134)

And...

> All efforts at work on oneself - spiritual growth - amount to wearing away layers of falseness to arrive at the truth of who we are. This truth

is situated outside of time. Once discovered, we understand that this truth can't be created, nor can it be destroyed - much as how modern science defines energy (energy can neither be created nor destroyed, it can only change form). And this is to be expected as the essence of the external universe, energy, is the outer expression of consciousness, which is our essential nature.

So while it is true that our essential nature, our natural state, cannot be created, it is also true that we must make efforts to realize our true nature anyway, as these efforts are crucial to the wearing away of illusions. Hence the paradox: spiritual growth itself is ultimately an illusion, and yet we must walk the spiritual path anyway in order to free ourselves from all illusions - including that of spiritual growth. Once free of illusions, what remains is our natural, awakened condition. (Ref. 134)

As long as we think of ourselves as limited, some investigation or enquiry is needed in order to remove this mistaken impression, as **John Wheeler** explains:

> Self-centered activity (like worrying, conflict, anxiety, fear and so on) is rooted in the belief in ourselves as isolated, limited personalities, localized and identified with the body. This stuff continues to plague you till you investigate the whole notion of being a person and a body. You need to put some solid inquiry into the question "Who am I?" You can't assume some statement as an ideal and expect your daily life to shift. You need to do the homework, cover the basics. (Ref. 70)

According to traditional scriptures, we have built up many *vAsanA*-s over countless lives. But whether we believe this literally or not, it is obvious that our minds have been conditioned to respond in particular ways in given circumstances; we have built up habits and we have rigid concepts on particular topics. If, as Advaita claims, we are completely mistaken in our view of the world and ourselves, we need to do something to break down these fixed patterns of behaviour. This is where the need for effort lies. The **Muktika Upanishad** says that:

> The destruction of impressions, cultivation of knowledge and destruction of the mind, when practised together for long will yield fruit. If not practised together, there will be no success even after hundreds of years, like mantras which are scattered. When these three are practised long, the knots of the heart surely are broken, like lotus fibre and the stalk. The false impression of worldly life is got in a hundred lives and cannot be destroyed without long practice. (II-ii-10-15, Ref. 240)

Arthur Osborne explains how the various practices act to eradicate the *vAsanA*-s:

> It is not actions that impede one's *sAdhana* nor spiritual strife, but the *vAsanA*, that is the deep-seated desires or tendencies giving rise to the actions. Indeed *sAdhana* is sometimes represented simply as the elimination of *vAsanA*-s, since it is these which turn the mind outwards, fling one into unnecessary activity, and drag the consciousness back to rebirth after this life has finished. Aloof or routine activity which does not nourish the *vAsanA*-s is harmless; only emotional activity is dangerous.
>
> Restricting activity is like trying to kill a tree by picking off the flowers and fruit; attacking the *vAsanA*-s is like breaking off the branches; Self enquiry is like uprooting the tree. The worst method is to try to destroy the *vAsanA*-s by gratifying them. That has the opposite effect, like trying to put a fire out by pouring oil on it. (Ref. 242)

One interesting viewpoint on this paradox is explained by **Wendy Doniger O'Flaherty**. She points out that we can prove that a dream is not real simply by waking up. But we cannot prove that the dream is real by never waking up. By analogy, we only realize the Self when we wake up from the waking dream that we are in – but there is nothing that we can *do* to achieve this. However, within the context of the dream, we make lots of mistakes – thinking that we are the body and mind, for example – and we *can* do something to realize these mistakes. She goes on:

> Is man helpless in the face of this dilemma? Is the process by which one is or is not drawn through the awareness of *bhrama* [confusion, perplexity, mistake] to the awareness of *mAyA* accidental or not? This argument was taken up in South India in the form of a debate about the nature of divine grace. The Cat School argued that one need not work at salvation, for God picks up the sinner as a mother cat picks up a kitten; all the kitten has to do is to go limp. (Indeed, according to certain extreme branches of this school, one *interferes* with the process of grace if one makes any effort at all to bring it about.) But the Monkey School argued that one did have to work at it, for God picks up the sinner as a mother monkey picks up a baby monkey: the baby monkey has to hang on for dear life. The problem of *bhrama* is a monkey problem: we can work hard, with good results, at ironing out our mistakes, at falsifying our theories, at testing our dreams. But the problem of *mAyA* is a cat problem; either we wake up from the dream - and there is no effort that we can make to do so - or we go on dreaming forever. (Ref. 241)

Spiritual Pre-requisites

Traditional Advaita recognizes that not everyone is willing to listen to the teaching and that certain qualities have to be engendered first. It was also pointed out earlier that, since it is ignorance that prevents us from appreciating the already-existing truth of our essential nature, knowledge is required to remove it. Before this knowledge can be assimilated, the mind must be prepared (otherwise we may "have the experience but miss the meaning" as T. S. Eliot put it in Ref. 196). The *brahmasUtra*, attributed to *vyAsa*, is the attempt to summarize the entire wisdom of the Upanishads and Shankara's commentary on this is authoritative for traditional Advaita. The first *sUtra* is *athAto brahmajij~nAsA* (now, therefore, the enquiry into Brahman), and from the first word *atha* -'now, then, moreover' - Shankara argues his list of pre-requisite characteristics for someone embarking on the search for their true nature.

atha i.e., after the attainment of certain preliminary qualifications such as the four means of salvation viz., (1) *nitya-anitya-vastu-viveka* (discrimination between the eternal and the non-eternal); (2) *IhAmutrartha-phala-bhoga-vairagya* (indifference to the enjoyment in this life or in heaven, and of the fruits of one's actions); (3) *ShaTsampat* (sixfold virtues viz., *shama* - control of mind, *dama* - control of the external senses, *uparati* - cessation from worldly enjoyments or not thinking of objects of senses or discontinuance of religious ceremonies, *titikShA* - endurance of pleasure and pain, heat and cold, *shraddhA* - faith in the words of the preceptor and of the Upanishads and *samAdhAna* - deep concentration); (4) *mumukShutva* (desire for liberation). (Ref. 40)

The mind has to be prepared before we begin the enquiry. Otherwise we will not understand the conclusions that are reached. Swami Dayananda compares it to the apocryphal story of Newton discovering the law of gravity. It was only because his mind was already oriented in the right direction that the supposed apple falling on his head triggered the realization. You have to be an *adhikArin*, one who is mentally prepared. These qualifying features that distinguish a seeker who is ready to receive the knowledge of the truth (*brahmavidyA*) are described in several of the works attributed to Shankara. In the *vAkya vRRitti* ("explanation of the aphorism" *tat tvam asi*), he merely says that:

Scorched by the blazing sun of the three miseries, a student – dejected with the world and restless for release, having cultivated all the means of liberation especially such virtues as self-control etc. – enquires of a noble teacher:

"Merely out of your grace and mercy, holy Teacher, please explain to me briefly the means by which I may easily get liberated from the sorrows of this bondage-to-change." [†] (Ref. 213)

These requirements have come to be called the *sAdhana chatuShTaya sampatti* – the fourfold (disciplines required) for success on a spiritual path. They are described in considerable detail in possibly the best known of the works attributed to Shankara – the *vivekachUDAmaNi*. He introduces it thus, in the translation by John Richards:

16. It is the wise and learned man, skilled in sorting out the pros and cons of an argument who is really endowed with the qualities necessary for self-realization.

17. Discriminating and dispassionate, endowed with peace and similar qualities, and longing for liberation - such is the man who is considered fit to practice seeking for God.

18. The wise talk here of four qualities, possessed of which one will succeed, but without which one will fail. (Ref. 4)

In detail, the four disciplines turn out to be nine, since one of them has six parts. They are described below.

I. Discrimination (*viveka*) (first of the *sAdhana chatuShTaya sampatti*)

The first of the four is viveka, discrimination. Traditional Advaita identifies a number of variants of this, such as: *nitya-anitya-vastu-viveka* – discrimination between the transient (*anitya*) and the eternal (*nitya*); *Atma-anAtma-viveka* – discrimination between the Self and non-Self; *dRRigdRRishya-viveka* – discrimination between the seer and the seen. But they are all essentially the same. The reality is the non-dual Atman, the eternal and unchanging. Everything "else" is an appearance only, name and form imposed upon that same non-dual reality. But, as a first "level" in

---

[†] Vakya Vritti, Swami Chinmayananda, © Central Chinmaya Mission Trust, Mumbai.

recognizing this, we must learn to differentiate between this seer-Self and the temporal, seen "not-Self" world of objects. We must reject all of this other as not-I – *neti, neti* as the scriptures tell us (not this, not this). Though this may initially be interpreted by the seeker as emphasizing a duality, it should be understood as a distancing of the mind from its tendency to identify with the various sheaths and to desire supposed external objects. It is ultimately seen to be the "naming" of "forms" of the non-dual Self as separate entities that is being rejected.

In the *prakaraNa grantha dRRigdRRishya-viveka*, attributed to Shankara, verse 20 states that every entity can be characterized by five aspects, viz. *asti* – existent, present; *bhAti* – light, splendor; *priya* – beloved, dear; *rUpa* – form; *nAma* – name. He says that, of these, the first three are *brahmarUpa* – features or characteristics of *brahman* – while the last two are *jagadrUpa* – characteristics of the world. The first three correspond to *sat, chit* and *Ananda* as has been discussed earlier - existence, consciousness and (unlimited) bliss. Thus, the differentiation that has to be made is to recognize that the name and form attributes are merely the transient appearance, in the same way that a lump of gold might currently be in the form of a necklace. This is *viveka*.

Swami Dayananda:

Knowledge does not come without viveka. It does not flash suddenly when you are sitting under a tree. The self is yourself, therefore it cannot flash any more than what it is doing now. Again as the self is all-pervasive, you do not have to "dive deep" to see it. Every perception is *Atman*; every thought is *Atman*. The object is *Atman*; the subject is *Atman*. The subject-object connection is also *Atman*. (Ref. 58)

II. Dispassion (vairAgya) (second of the *sAdhana chatuShTaya sampatti)* The word literally means to be "deprived of" (*vai*) "passion or desire" (*rAga*). It has also been defined as being *nirveda* - being indifferent towards or even having a loathing for worldly objects. It effectively means losing interest in anything other than Self-enquiry. Any other "thing" or knowledge, past or future, holds no appeal.

The *bRRihadAraNyaka upaniShad* (IV.4.6) says that those who remain attached to sense objects take nothing with them on death except for the *karma* that will force them to go through the same process again and again. The endless desires will thus never result in any satisfaction. Any fulfilled desire is only further fuel for the flames. On the other hand, if we become entirely desire-less, apart from the single desire to realize the Self, we then attain that desire. This is not some perverse law devised for the amusement of a malevolent God; it is simply the case that, since there is only the Self, the Self is all that *can* be attained – the rest is delusion. If we want what is not really there, we are doomed.

Ramana Maharshi has this to say:

Each one seeks happiness but is misled into thinking pain associated pleasures as happiness. Such happiness is transient. His mistaken activity gives him short-lived pleasure. Pain and pleasure alternate with one another in the world. To discriminate between the pain-producing and pleasure-producing matters and to confine oneself to the happiness-producing pursuit only is *vairAgya*. What is it that will not be followed by pain? He seeks it and engages in it. Otherwise, the man has one foot in the world and another foot in the spiritual pursuit (without progressing satisfactorily in either field). (Ref. 49)

Renunciation, *saMnyAsa*, is not explicitly mentioned in the context of the *chatuShTaya sampatti* but it is elsewhere and its purport is not really any different from *vairAgya*. In relation to Hinduism, it refers to "giving up the world" and becoming an ascetic, without belongings of any kind, dependent upon charity for food and shelter. What is significant about its intent, however, is the renunciation of all attachments – the giving up of desire for worldly things – i.e. *vairAgya*. **Ramana Maharshi** says about *saMnyAsa*:

> Renunciation does not imply apparent divesting of costumes, family ties, home etc., but renunciation of desires, affection and attachment, (Ref. 220)

As **Dr. K. Sadananda** points out, when a Hindu "takes *saMnyAsa Ashrama*," that action in itself cannot achieve realization. An action is an event in time and we are already the Self. Only knowledge can remove ignorance:

> Renunciation at the physical level - that is entering into a *saMnyAsa Ashrama* could be helpful in avoiding unnecessary entanglement with the world - but that is neither necessary nor sufficient for self realization. Self realization - realization of I am That and not this body, mind or intellect - has nothing to do with external renunciation. Taking up *saMnyAsa Ashrama* is an action. Action, no matter what it is, does not lead to knowledge. *karma* not being opposite to ignorance, it cannot eliminate it... But action purifies the mind. The mind became impure by indulging in action - willful egocentric actions - the *vAsanA*-s have been accumulated. It is natural that only by actions the mind can be purified - here action includes even thinking or *bhAvana* (reflection, contemplation). Hence path or action, including taking *saMnyAsa* or not taking *saMnyAsa*, may be a helpful means for purification of the mind, but not for realization. (Ref. 222)

III. *shamAdi ShaTka sampatti* (third of the *sAdhana chatuShTaya sampatti*)

The third of the spiritual preparations advocated by Shankara in fact consists of six qualities that should be cultivated (*ShaTka* means "consisting of six"). The word *sampatti* implies something of great value that has been attained or accomplished and *shamAdi* refers to the first of these – *shama*. They are summarized in Sadananda's **vedAntasAra** (meaning "essence" of the Vedanta, and not the same Sadananda quoted above!) as follows:

19. *shama* is the curbing of the mind from all objects except hearing etc.,
20. *dama* is the restraining of the external organs from all objects except That.
21. *uparati* is the cessation of these external organs so restrained, from the pursuit of objects other than That; or it may mean the abandonment of the prescribed works according to scriptural injunctions.
22. *titikShA* is the endurance of heat and cold and other pairs of opposites.
23. *samAdhAna* is the constant concentration of the mind, thus restrained, on hearing etc. of the scriptural passages and other objects that are conducive to these.
24. *shraddhA* is the faith in the truths of Vedanta as taught by the Guru. (Ref. 88)

It might be thought more logical to mention the need to control the senses (*dama*) before the need to control the mind itself (*shama*) but there is justification for this. The **Kanchi Maha-Swamigal** explains (translation by Professor V. Krishnamurthy):

The eyes and ears can close themselves and stop seeing or hearing. The hands and legs also can be tied so that they are incapable of any action. But even then the mind will be having its own goings-on without any discipline. Even though the senses are not experiencing anything, the mind can imagine them and go through all the rumblings and turbulences. When the senses act they act only by the promptings of the mind and for the satisfaction of the mind or fulfillment of the desires of the mind. So what is necessary is to immobilize the mind in order to stop all the multifarious activities of the senses.

It is because of this importance of mental control and discipline that *sAdhana* regimens talk first of *shama* and dwell on *dama* later. (Ref. 24)

Conversely, the mind may be still and apparently under control but the sight of something greatly desired can immediately destroy all of this and send it into a turmoil as **Shankara's** Sarva-Vedanta-Siddhanta-Sarasangraha points out:

127. When the senses pursue the objects of desire however unintentionally, that pursuit acts upon the mind like a wind that fans a flame.

128. But where the senses are held under restraint, the mind ceases to be agitated. The mind then regains its pure nature and attains tranquility. It is only when the mind is serene that liberation may be attained. It cannot be attained otherwise. (Ref. 71)

uparati means desisting from any sensual enjoyment, which only gives fleeting pleasure and aggravates desire. It also implies not thinking about things of the senses, dwelling upon memories of particular experiences or imagining possible future gratification. None of this is in the present moment so is all false and totally unhelpful to a spiritual aspirant.

titikShA means "endurance, forbearance and patience," which again relate to self-control and restraint. **Swami Vivekananda** says the following about this:

Then comes the next preparation (it is a hard task to be a philosopher!), *titikShA*, the most difficult of all. It is nothing less than the ideal forbearance – "Resist, not evil." This requires a little explanation. We may not resist an evil, but at the same time we may feel very miserable. A man may say very harsh things to me, and I may not outwardly hate him for it, may not answer him back, and may restrain myself from apparently getting angry, but anger and hatred may be in my mind, and I may feel very badly towards that man. This is not non-resistance; I should be without any feeling of hatred or anger, without any thought of resistance; my mind must then be as calm as if nothing had happened. And only when I have got to that state, have I attained to non-resistance, and not before. Forbearance of all misery, without even a thought of resisting or driving it out, without even any painful feeling in the mind or any remorse— that is *titikShA*. Suppose I do not resist, and some great evil comes thereby; if I have *titikShA*, I should not feel any remorse for not having resisted. When the mind has attained to that state, it has become established in *titikShA*. (Ref. 225)

samAdhAna means "contemplation, profound meditation" but is more usually translated as "concentration." According to the *vivekachUDAmaNi*, this means that the mind should always be inquiring into the nature of brahman; nothing else is worthy of its attention. "Single-minded" would be another way of putting it.

shraddhA is not so much another trait to cultivate as the constant background to all of the others. It is translated as "faith, trust or belief" (in the absence of direct personal experience); the student needs this initially in respect of what he is told by the guru or reads in the scriptures. If there is not implicit trust in the value of all of these disciplines, they are bound to come to naught. Initially, we cannot know the truth of what we are told – and what Advaita tells us is strongly counter-intuitive. A powerful faith is needed provisionally to accept all of this as true until we realize it for ourselves. As **Swami Dayananda** says: "*If shraddhA is there, everything else including mumukShutva can be accomplished.*" (Ref. 58)

IV. *mumukShutva* (fourth of the *sAdhana chatuShTaya sampatti*)

This is the desire to achieve enlightenment, to the exclusion of all other desires. This is what **Dr. Gregory Goode** is speaking of in the following extract:

This is the one that never lets go. This happens as soon as the motive shifts in a subtle way from wanting to *feel* a certain way, to wanting to *know the truth*. One wants to know the truth so badly that one is willing to die for it. It might seem an intellectual matter, but it is actually felt at every level of the inquirer's being. In the cells! No matter how the feeling state changes, one continues the inquiry because of the compelling desire to know... It's also very, very, very tenacious and gripping, and very sweet. And it remains in every waking moment when the mind/intellect is not involved in daily tasks. As soon as they are accomplished for the moment, the ultimately sweet inquiry is taken up once again. It continues until it reaches its natural conclusion. (Ref. 226)

In a sense, it is also key to the other disciplines in that it provides the basic driving force to submit to them rather than to the worldly desires that are forever enticing us away from the "path of the good." **Swami Budhananda** explains:

In seeking the control of our mind we must aspire to this absolute state of being. As long as we have more desires than one, or other desires than the desire for the realization of Atman, it will be difficult to control the mind, for it will then be in a scattered state. If we seek anything less than the highest, into which everything converges, as it were, the mind will be divided. It is hard to control a divided mind. In other words, those who seek anything less than perfect illumination, or realization of the Self, can never control their mind perfectly. They have some desire other than that for illumination and therefore they in effect vote for the perpetuation of *avidyA*. Thus they render themselves incapable of doing things needed for controlling the mind. (Ref. 227)

Ultimately, of course, even this desire is a mistake as **Nirmala** points out:

Longing for the truth can be a profound fire that burns away all the other desires, but fundamentally it is the same lie dressed up in spiritual clothing. Longing for Oneness is based on the lie of separation, that you are not already Oneness itself. (Ref. 254)

In fact, there is a useful point to be made here in that it is not actually a *lie*. A lie is something that we tell, to ourselves or others, knowing what is in fact the truth. Here, we have not yet realized the truth. Instead, we are making an *error*, in good faith as it were.

Yoga-s

The literal meaning of the word *yoga* is "the act of yoking or joining." It refers to the "union" of *jIvAtman* and *paramAtman* (and is nothing to do with body and mind). It is also used to refer to any path or system that aims to achieve such union. On its own, it is generally used for the system outlined by Patanjali in the "Yoga Sutras," called either *aShTA~Nga yoga* or *rAja yoga*, but more generally it refers also to the other three main "paths" of *j~nAna, karma* and *bhakti yoga*. The aim is forever to reconcile the level of appearance with that of reality, bringing to an end any sense of ego or separateness so that there is always full knowledge of the non-dual truth of *sachchidAnanda*.

The **Kanchi Maha-Swamigal** says the following about the three main yoga-s:

> The advaita *sAdhana* that the *AchArya* has taught us is the path of *j~nAna*. But the person who wants to go in this path must have purified his mind to such an extent that he should have the capability of one-pointedness (*ekAgratA*); only then he can traverse the path of *j~nAna*. If the mind is full of dirt it cannot go the path of *j~nAna-sAdhana*. For *j~nAna-yoga* the mind has to become one-pointed; a vacillating and vibrating mind cannot hold on to anything. It is for these twin tasks of purification of mind and of making it one-pointed that the *AchArya* has prescribed *karma* and *bhakti* as preliminary to *j~nAna yoga*. The prerequisite to starting *j~nAna yoga* are *karma yoga* and *bhakti yoga*.
>
> The barren land of the mind has to be tilled through *karma yoga* and then watered through *bhakti yoga*. Without this tilling and watering, nothing can be made to grow in that barren land of the mind. When one keeps on doing his *svadharma*, meticulously and according to the

shAstra-s, the impurities of the mind slowly disappear. When our mind becomes one-pointed in its devotion to the Lord, this training in one-pointedness towards one form leads it to do the one-pointed enquiry into the formless *Atman*. Thus when the mind is purified by *karma yoga* and gets the habit of one-pointedness by *bhakti yoga*, it can easily ascend the steps of *j~nAna yoga*. (Ref. 224)

Karma Yoga

It is not really a yoga of action, it is a yoga of attitude with reference to the action and the result. **Swami Dayananda** (Ref. 112)

This is the "yoga of action" but it has nothing to do with action per se or with the proficiency with which we act or with the amount that we do. *karma yoga* is concerned with the *attitude* we have towards those actions that we are obliged to perform. The attitude that we must have if we are to make progress spiritually is to acknowledge that "we" effectively do nothing, that we have no control over the outcome and we must happily accept whatever results from the action, irrespective of whether this was the "desired" result.

When we act in this way, no *saMskAra* is accumulated. This can easily be understood in that such an attitude means that there will be no mental reaction to the result of the action whether elation, in response to a desired result, or dismay and disappointment if the outcome was contrary to what we wanted. The mind remains still and open to whatever happens, thus also able to learn from the experience. It is often said that we "surrender the fruits of the action to the Lord" and this is where *karma yoga* meets *bhakti yoga*. In this, it also relates to *saMnyAsa* mentioned above in that it means renouncing the fruits of action, accepting that "I do nothing."

It is also about responding to whatever is in front of us – performing a task because it is there now and needs doing rather than because it is something that we *want* to do. Ego and personal desires have to be removed from all actions. We should aim to serve others. These types of action are called *niShkAma karma*, neither selfish nor unselfish, simply responding to the need of the moment [*niShkAma* means without desire]. This also relates to *dharma*, the first of the *puruShArtha*-s that was discussed in the chapter on Meaning and Purpose.

It is not what you do that counts but your real motive behind it. Your motive must be pure. **Swami Sivananda** says: *"Man generally plans to get the fruits of his works before he starts any kind of work. The mind is so framed that it cannot think of any kind of work without remuneration or reward. A selfish man cannot do any service. He will weigh the work and the money in a balance. Selfless Service is unknown to him."* (Ref. 228)

karma yoga is often regarded as a practice suitable for those who are not yet ready to embark upon a serious, i.e. contemplative, spiritual pursuit, and for whom the attitude of surrender and devotion appropriate for the *bhakta* is contrary to their nature. Over time, assiduous practice will develop a steadier, more introspective mind and lead naturally to *j~nAna yoga*.

Bhakti Yoga

According to Swami Chinmayananda (Ref. 230), the word *bhakti* does not occur anywhere in the Vedas. (In fact it occurs in the *muktikopaniShad* from the *shukla yajur veda*, but this may not be considered altogether valid since it is the last of the main 108 Upanishads and self-importantly references itself as the 108th. The word does occur twice in the Bhagavad Gita, which is *smRRiti*.) Instead, the word that is used for devotion is *upAsana*, meaning homage, adoration, worship or literally "sitting or being near or at hand." **Ramana Maharshi** says of it: *"upAsana is the uninterrupted meditation upon a deity or a form or a word like OM until one becomes that deity or form or word. It is a technique which is not generally followed nowadays. Its modern equivalent is bhakti (devotion)."* (Ref. 231)

Strictly speaking, in the Upanishads only two paths are specified as such. The idea of *bhakti* as a separate path came much later, possibly not until the sixteenth century, with the Hindu ascetic, Caitanya. **James Swartz** explains:

> Actually, there are only two paths prescribed in the Vedas: *karma yoga* for householders and *j~nAna yoga* or *sAMkhya yoga* for *saMnyAsin*-s. The idea of *bhakti* as a special path came later. The reason for this is that *bhakti* is native to any and every path, even worldly endeavors, *bhakti* being a positive, some say loving, motivation toward a particular object. *bhakti*, therefore falls under the category of *karma* in so far as "*bhakti yoga*" is a group of practices, rituals. In the Vedas ritual is considered *karma*. The *karma kANDa* of the Vedas deals with rituals which are for doers who want to achieve certain results. (Ref. 354)

The following verses (of words of **Ramana Maharshi**) and commentaries from Guru Vachaka Kovai - The Garland of the Guru's Sayings - by Muruganar clearly set forth the essence of bhakti yoga:

> Those who have one-pointed devotion towards God, like the magnetic needle [of a ship's compass] which always stands facing towards the north, will never be perplexed and go astray in the ocean of attachment of this world.
>
> Those who live in the world, clinging whole-heartedly to God, are like children who whirl round and round a pillar holding it firmly. Since they have a strong and unshakeable hold on God, they are devoid of ego and therefore will never fall a prey to the delusion of the world.
>
> If one fixes one's mind firmly on that pure Supreme Reality which pervades all activities, one will not be affected by any number of activities that are done.
>
> **Sadhu Om:** Just as the cinema screen, which is the base pervading all the pictures, is not burnt by a picture of fire or drenched by a picture of a flood, so Self, the Supreme Reality which is the base pervading all activities, is not affected by any number of activities. Therefore, since the one who attends to Self remains as Self itself, he is not affected by any number of activities he may appear to be doing.

Sri Muruganar: (i) The words "all activities" include both worldly activities and religious activities. (ii) Since he who abides in the reality [Self] loses his doership, it is said "he will not be affected." Therefore, though [it may appear as if] he does everything, in fact he does nothing.

Among all the rice grains, only those which move here and there will be crushed by the hand-mill, while those which do not move away from the foot of the axle will not be crushed.

Michael James: Likewise, among all the people in the world, only those who stray into worldly desires, leaving the thought of the Feet of God, will be ruined by *mAyA*, while those who do not leave His Feet will not be so ruined. (Ref. 229)

In *karma yoga*, one attempts to dissolve the ego by relinquishing all claims to actions and their results, accepting everything as effectively the will of God. In bhakti yoga, the idea of God comes very much to the fore, with an active love directed towards the chosen deity and any idea of ego surrendered in that love. **Swami Dayananda:**

Absolute love resolves duality. Even in the love between two persons, separation ends; the two are fused in emotional identity. If love for the Lord is total, it liquidates the individual. In perfect love or surrender, the individual is dissolved in the Lord not like a salt crystal in water, but like water in water. There is only one Lord who expresses the inside and outside of you. The individual is a notion; all is the Lord. You dissolve as the wave dissolves into the ocean; what goes is only your notion – that you are different. It is dissolved in the ocean of knowledge. (Ref. 31)

This highlights a fundamental point with all *sAdhana* and all "paths," namely that they begin in duality and end in non-duality. It is clearest of all in the case of the *bhakta*, who begins with an "I" worshiping a "God" and ends with the total surrender of that "I" to the point of an actual merging or realization of identity – the dissolution of the ego in love, as it is put. The ultimate surrender or renunciation is of our self, not of belongings, feelings or concepts.

Ramana Maharshi explains the real nature of self-surrender:

> All that one needs to do is to surrender oneself to the Source of oneself. There is no need to get confused by calling that Source God and assuming that it is somewhere outside. One's Source is *within* oneself. To that Source the surrender should be made; that is, *one should seek that Source and by the very force of that search merge into It*. The question "Where is the Source?" can arise only if it be thought that the Self is different from the Source. If the ego becomes merged into its Source, then there is no ego, no individual soul; that is, the seeker becomes one with the Source. That being the case, where is surrendering? Who is to surrender and to whom? And what is there to be surrendered? This loss of individuality - which even now does not really exist - is devotion, wisdom and the Quest. (Ref. 39)

Care must be taken that the act of surrender does not lead to hubris. There is a danger of feeling oneself to be in some way important if following spiritual pursuits rather than material ones and this will obviously have a counter-productive effect. In this connection, it is useful to consider this memorable quotation from **Sri Poonja**: "*You are ripe for enlightenment when you want nothing else. In order to be born as a baby you have to spend 9 months getting bigger and bigger. For enlightenment you have to get smaller and smaller until you disappear completely*" (Ref. 255)

And this brings us to the meeting point with *j~nAna* yoga, as **Nirmala** points out that both paths involve the dissolution of the illusion of the ego:

> The devotional path unravels the ego by continually surrendering to love and by loving more than the ego can withstand, while the path of inquiry accomplishes this by questioning so deeply that our illusions, especially the illusion "me," don't hold up. (Ref. 254)

j~nAna yoga

j~nAna yoga, too, involves devotion but, as **Sri Atmananda Krishna Menon** explains, this is devotion to the truth, which is higher than that to any notional God:

> The j~nAna path looks from a broader perspective and comprehends within its scope both *yoga* and devotion. It takes into consideration the whole of life's experiences - comprised in the three states - viewed impartially. It demands a high degree of real devotion, in the sense that the aspirant has to have a high degree of earnestness and sincerity to get to the Truth. This is *real devotion, to Truth*; and it is infinitely superior to devotion to anything else, which can only be less than the Truth. (Note 63, Ref. 13)

This essential relationship with the Truth also makes it different from the other paths, as he further explains:

> The j~nAna path does not claim to take you to the Truth or to illumine the Truth. You are always the Truth, and the Truth is self-luminous. So the j~nAna path claims only to remove the obstacles in the way – viz. the sense of separateness and its objects – by applying the correct tests of Reality, such as changelessness and self-luminosity. When all obstacles are thus removed, the self-luminous "I" remains ever shining in all its glory. This is called visualization or realization. j~nAna alone is *vastu-tantra* [governed by Truth]. But devotion, yoga, karma and all other paths are *kartRRi-tantra* [governed by doership]. (Note 1275 Ref. 13)

This book is effectively a manual of j~nAna yoga, aiming as it does to "explain" intellectually what Advaita is about, discussing the various models and levels and the process of sublating these to move towards an ultimate realization of the nature of reality. Through an understanding of the errors that we make in our outlook on life and the world, we endeavor to dissolve the ignorance and reveal the *j~nAna* - knowledge.

Ultimately, all paths lead to the same end and each embodies elements of the others. As **Ramana Maharshi** puts it:

Whatever path one may choose, the "I" is inescapable, the "I" that does the *niShkAma karma*, the "I" that pines for joining the Lord from whom it feels it has been separated, the "I" that feels it has slipped from its real nature, and so on. The source of this "I" must be found out. Then all questions will be solved. (Ref. 174)

Raja Yoga

This specifically delineated path, devised by Patanjali and expounded in his "Yoga Sutras," comprises eight steps or members. Hence, it is also called *aShTA~Nga yoga*, where *aShTan* means "eight" and *a~Nga* is a limb of the body. It could strictly be thought of as an extension of *karma yoga* (as noted above, the scriptures effectively only identified two paths) but, by the time of Vivekananda, the four paths of *karma*, *j~nAna*, *bhakti* and *rAja* were recognized as constituting modern or "Neo" Vedanta.

Swami Sivananda summarizes the method as follows:

According to Raja Yoga, there are three types of aspirants - *uttama*, *madhyama* and *adhama AdhikArI*. To three classes of aspirants Raja Yoga prescribes three kinds of *sAdhana*. To the *uttama adhikArin* (first-class aspirant) Raja Yoga prescribes *abhyAsa* ["the effort of the mind to remain in its unmodified condition of purity (*sattva*)"] and *vairAgya*. He practices meditation on the Self; he practices *chitta-vRRitti-nirodha* (restraining the modification of the mind-stuff) and soon enters into *samAdhi*. This is practice (*abhyAsa*) sustained by *vairAgya*. To the *madhyama adhikArin* (middling aspirant) Raja Yoga prescribes the *kriyA* Yoga - *tapas*, *svAdhyAya* and *Ishvara praNidhAna*. *tapas* is austerity. Egolessness and selfless service are the greatest forms of *tapas*. Humility and desirelessness are the greatest forms of austerity. Practice these through ceaseless, untiring, selfless service. Practice the three kinds of *tapas* mentioned in the Gita. Disciplinary practices like fasting, etc., also come under *tapas*. *svAdhyAya* is study of spiritual literature and also *japa* of your *iShTa mantra* [repeating your favorite mantra in meditation]. *Ishvara praNidhAna* is self-surrender to the Lord and doing all actions as *Ishvararpana*, as offering unto the Lord. These three form the *sAdhana*-s of the *madhyama adhikArin* who enters into deep meditation very soon and attains *kaivalya mokSha*. To the *adhama adhikArI*, lowest kind of aspirant, Raja Yoga prescribes *aShTA~Nga* Yoga or the eightfold *sAdhana* - *yama, niyama, asana, prANayAma, pratyAhAra, dhAraNA, dhyAna* and *samAdhi*. (Ref. 245)

The "steps" are as follows (Refs. 11, 107, 218, 219):

1. The *yama*-s. *yama* literally means a rein or bridle so that these constitute "self-restraints" or moral injunctions, also interpreted as how we should behave with respect to others. There are five of them: *ahiMsA* – not injuring anything; *satyam* – truthfulness, sincerity; *brahmacharya* – moderation, chastity; *asteya* – not stealing; *aparigraha* – renouncing of all possessions.

2. The *niyama*-s. *niyama* refers to an obligation or standard of behavior to which one should adhere, also interpreted as conduct to oneself. Again, there are five of these: *shaucha* – purity of mind, integrity; *saMtoSha* – satisfaction, contentment with one's life; *tapas* – austerity, living a simple life without comforts; *svAdhyAya* – self-study or more specifically studying the scriptures, literally reciting the Vedas in a low voice to oneself; *Ishvara praNidhAna* – meditation on/contemplation of/devotion to Ishvara, surrender to God.

3. *Asana* – adopting a comfortable posture, especially for meditation.

4. *prANayAma* - usually understood to mean control of breathing in advanced yoga techniques or as a prelude to meditation. But strictly

speaking, *prANa* refers to the life-force or life-principle in general rather than simply breath so that *prANayAma* really means all of those activities concerned with regulating life at its basic level. They are referenced in many of the Upanishads. Thus *prANa* involves perception as well as taking in air. *apAna* refers to rejection of irrelevant material gained from perception etc. and to the formation of limited views as well as to simply excretion. *vyAna* alludes to the discriminatory faculties, evaluating and judging etc. rather than merely the circulatory system. *samAna* relates to assimilation and integration of perceptions with existing knowledge rather than just the digestive system. *udAna*, in addition to that vital air associated with the throat, relates to the understanding that has been gained from past experience. *Asana*-s and *prANayAma* together constitute what is usually referred to as *haTha yoga*, the physical aspects of the practice of yoga, which has unfortunately become an end in itself in the west.

5. *pratyAhAra* - withdrawal of the senses from external objects.

6. *dhAraNA* – concentration of the mind.

7. *dhyAna* - meditation, usually in the sense of the mechanical act using a mantra as opposed to *nididhyAsana*.

8. *samAdhi* – the experience of non-duality when body and mind have been transcended.

tapas, mentioned above as being appropriate for the intermediate student in *kriyA* yoga, means "religious austerity, special observance." It is usually thought of as referring to physical asceticism, such as that of fakirs but it also relates to mental self-discipline and to speaking the truth and avoiding speaking about anything unpleasant. It is really about purification of the mind again, as with all of these practices. The literal meaning of the word is warmth or heat. This traditionally refers to the ascetic deliberately exposing his body to a fire when the climate is already hot so as to discipline himself into accepting pain rather than pursuing pleasure. But metaphorically, it points to the purification through fire in the sense that metals are extracted and purified from their ores.

Swami Satchidananda refers to the classical metaphor of the charioteer:

> *tapas* also refers to self-discipline. Normally the mind is like a wild horse tied to a chariot. Imagine the body is the chariot; the intelligence is the charioteer; the mind is the reins; and the horses are the senses. The Self, or true you, is the passenger. If the horses are allowed to gallop without reins and charioteer, the journey will not be safe for the passenger. Although control of the senses and organs often seems to bring pain in the beginning, it eventually ends in happiness. If *tapas* is understood in this light, we will look forward to pain; we will even thank people who cause it, since they are giving us the opportunity to steady our minds and burn out impurities. (Ref. 11)

bhaja govindam

Another variant of the practices that should be followed as preparation for following a spiritual path is presented in the *bhaja govindam*, also attributed to Shankara. Govinda is the disciple to whom the teaching is addressed and each verse concludes with the instruction: "Practice, Govinda; practice, Govinda." (The verb *bhaj* means to pursue, practice or cultivate, also translated as to seek.)

The disciplines to be followed are divided into two aspects, those relating to the external world, *bahira~Nga sAdhana* and those that are internal, *antara~Nga sAdhana*. The former constitute the early stages of embarking upon a spiritual path, when the seeker is developing distaste for the mundane elements of worldly life, while the latter form the more advanced disciplines. There is a general progression and a parallel with Patanjali's *aShTA~Nga yoga*, with the first four or five steps of this being equated with *bahira~Nga* and the remainder with *antara~Nga*.

In Ref. 6, **Swami Chinmayananda** [†] summarises the Outer Disciplines as "study of the Gita, worship of the Lord, satsang and charity, along with the elimination of all the wealth-hunting distractions by a process of correct thinking." The Inner Disciplines are said to be *prANayAma*, *pratyAhAra*, *nitya-anitya-viveka*, *japa* and *samAdhi*. These are the "active departments of manifested life in a living intelligent man."

prANayAma, *pratyAhAra* and *samAdhi* are as mentioned above with respect to *rAja yoga*. *viveka* has been discussed under Discrimination. *japa* refers to the repetition of a *mantra* in meditation and will be dealt with later in this chapter. **Swami Chinmayananda** says of *samAdhi*:

> The state of Final Beatitude is never as such expressed in any *shAstra* – only the last stage of human effort, called the practice of *samAdhi*, is indicated. The final experience is not gained by anyone; it is already with all of us. Practice of *samAdhi* only lifts the veil and reveals what was, is and shall ever be: the Eternal Nature of the Infinite: "That Thou Art," roars the teacher in Chandogya Upanishad. (Ref. 6)

Kundalini yoga

Kundalini is mentioned in the Sandilya and the Yoga Kundali Upanishad but is not normally considered to be an aspect of Advaita and is rarely mentioned by any text or teacher. **David Godman** says of Ramana Maharshi: *"Sri Ramana never advised his devotees to practice kundalini yoga since he regarded it as being both potentially dangerous and unnecessary."* (Ref. 17)

Specific Practices

Apart from the traditional disciplines discussed above, there are a number

---

[†] Bhaja Govindam, Swami Chinmayananda, © Central Chinmaya Mission Trust, Mumbai.

of useful practices and almost certainly more than I am covering below. Some practices, such as meditation, form part of several overall approaches – meditation is said to be suitable for the *madhyama adhikArin*, the intermediate student. Others, such as *shravaNa*, *manana* and *nididhyAsana* are specific to one path only, *j~nAna* yoga in this case, being difficult and only for the advanced student – *uttama adhikArin*.

Controlling or Stilling the Mind

It is the mind that frees us or enslaves.
Driven by the senses we become bound;
Master of the senses we become free.
Those who seek freedom must master their senses.

When the mind is detached from the senses
One reaches the summit of consciousness.
Mastery of the mind leads to wisdom.

Amritabindu Upanishad (Ref. 295).

Mind control is something of a contradiction in terms, implying as it does that there is an entity separate from the mind that will do the controlling. The witness-self plays no part in any of this. The Self does not act; all activity, thinking and feeling is simply the movement of the *guNa*, all taking place according to the natural law of cause and effect at the level of the phenomenal world.

Ramana Maharshi used the metaphor of a policeman, himself guilty of a theft, being charged with the task of catching the thief. Alternatively, it is like the eye trying to see itself without the benefit of a mirror. There are no levels of self within the individual, whatever Freud may have claimed. All of this is simply ideas in mind, including the ego-notion itself.

Whether you want to concentrate your attention, suppress a desire or rid the mind of thoughts so that you can meditate, a direct "command" to the mind to obey "your" wishes will be fruitless. Such wishes and demands themselves originate in the mind. Who you really are does not have any requirements and is equally at home with a restless mind as with a quiet mind. If we attempt to use the ego-mind to come to a realization of this, it is bound to fail. **Robert Powell** puts it as follows:

> If you use your mind, your thought process, to try to grasp it, it will ever elude you for the simple reason that the mind that is always active, is itself the hindrance, the stumbling block, the barrier to knowing, to finding oneself with what is. And it is the *only* barrier. Now the mind can trick itself and say: I am not really there, I am in a state of abeyance, I am quiet, I am silent. But it is still the mind that says it. If there is a real subsidence of that mind activity, there is nothing being said because there is no one to say it. (Ref. 116)

Thus, the idea of mind control should not be understood in the literal sense. As will be seen in the discussion of meditation below it is not possible to stop thoughts. It is, after all, the nature of the mind to think. **Swami Dayananda** says that:

> Dealing with the mind is like how the modern management deals with employees. The modern management does not go into the private affairs of the employee. It does not try to control their life. What it wants is that during the working hours the person should work. One should handle the mind similarly. As long as it is available to you when you want it, it is a good deal. (Ref. 58)

It is more a matter of gently redirecting the attention away from unhelpful thoughts or of giving attention to the silence between them. Whenever we are aware of a thought, this means that the thought is illuminated by Consciousness and this is the key. With practice, instead of allowing the natural tendency of the mind to turn outwards to the thought or external object of perception, we can turn inwards to the source of the thought. **A. R. Natarajan** explains how Ramana Maharshi tackled the problem:

So, the first step without which one cannot proceed at all is to arm one-self with a technique which sterilizes the past and renders it impotent. For achieving this, Ramana suggests an approach which leaves all desires, all thoughts severely alone. He would say, "Do not run with the running mind." For, any effort in which the attention is paid on the thoughts themselves, good, bad or indifferent, is no better than shadow chasing. It is said that when a child tries to catch a shadow by running after it and is distressed at not being able to do so, the mother prevents it from running. Similarly, one should closely look into the essence in any thought formation and not deal with the shadow, the rest of the thoughts. In this light, it is only the thinker, it is only the individual, who matters. Shifting the mind's attention to its core, to the first person, is what is to be attempted. The second and the third person thoughts would no longer have the power to damage, since the attention of the "I" is not cast on them. An analogy would serve to highlight this point. To say "do not have desires is like asking one to take medicine without thinking of the monkey." Sure enough the dominant thought would then be the monkey. Instead Ramana's method gives a positive turn by saying, "drink the medicine thinking of the elephant." In other words it is like advising one who has to "abandon the east" to "go west"…

An early seeker said in dejection, "What can I do? If I reject one thought, another thought takes its place." Ramana promptly advised, "cling to the I-thought. When your interest keeps you to that single idea, the other thoughts automatically vanish." The past in the form of the thought power flowing from *vAsanA-s*, the inherent tendencies, is pulverized by attention. Those thoughts just wither and fade away. "Thought grows with thought as fire with fuel. When attention is withdrawn thoughts die like flame without fuel." True, to begin with they distract and one has to repeatedly bring the attention back to the thinker. Soon one is off the outward mental movement. The shifting of attention to the subject does the trick. (Ref. 246)

There are many forms of exercise for stilling the mind but all are very similar, relying upon consciously giving attention to particular sensations or perceptions to the exclusion of all others so that the usual chaotic activity becomes increasingly restful and eventually still. This first is a good example of this, source unknown:

Right now in this moment:
close your eyes.
Be still.
Be silent.
Rest in this stillness.
Rest in this silence.
This is all that there is
to find freedom.

All of your
trying to figure it out,
adopting teachings
and philosophies,
seeking ways
to make this moment better
are just ways
you struggle in distraction.

You are perfect as you are.
Your life is perfect as it is.
This moment is divine.

So be still.
Be silent.
Rest in this stillness.
Rest in this silence.

Consciousness is always here,

always aware.

Consciousness is what you are. (Ref. 247)

An interesting variant, that aims to trick the mind into being silent, is presented below from **Dr. Hubert Benois**:

Alone, in a quiet place, muscularly relaxed (lying down or comfortably seated), I watch the emergence within myself of mental images, permitting my imagination to produce *whatever it likes*. It is as though I were saying to my image-making mind, "Do what you please; but I am going to watch you doing it."

As long as one maintains this attitude - or, more exactly, this relaxation of any kind of attitude - the imagination produces nothing and its screen remains blank, free of all images. I am then in a state of pure voluntary attention, without any image to capture it. I am not paying attention to anything in particular; I am paying attention to anything which might turn up, but which in fact does not turn up. As soon as there is a weakening of my voluntary effort of pure attention, thoughts (images) make their appearance. I do not notice the fact immediately, for my attention is momentarily asleep; but after a certain time I perceive what has happened. I discover that I have started to think of this and that. The moment I make this discovery, I say to my imagination, "So you want to talk to me about that. Go ahead; I'm listening."

Immediately everything stops again, and I become conscious of the stoppage. At first the moments of pure attention are short. (Little by little, however, they tend to become longer.) But, though brief, they are not mere infinitesimal instants; they possess a certain duration and continuity.

Persevering practice of the exercise gradually builds up a mental automatism which acts as a curb on the natural automatisms of the imagination. This curb is created consciously and voluntarily; but to the extent that the habit has been built up, it acts automatically. (Ref. 248)

Once the principle has been understood – namely that the mind has to be naturally still, unruffled by all of the thoughts, worries and desires that habitually trouble the unprepared mind – then the benefit of other attributes can also be appreciated and those can be cultivated too. Thus, the **Astavakra Gita** (I.2) mentions other aspects:

> If you aspire for liberation, my child, reject the objects of senses as poison, and seek forgiveness, straight-forwardness, kindness, cheerfulness and truth as nectar. (Ref. 12)

"Rejecting the objects of senses" is *dama*, as discussed above, but other forms of behaviour can also affect the tranquillity of the mind. Thus, harbouring resentment against another for prolonged periods disturbs our own mind (and probably affects the other not at all), whereas forgiving them brings instant peace. Behaving deviously towards others with the intention of benefiting ourselves at their expense involves us in lies and self-justification and other mental turmoil, whereas acting honestly and openly leaves us with no subsequent concerns. Similarly with acting generously and considerately, maintaining a happy and optimistic demeanour. All of these positive traits help establish and sustain a peaceful mind whereas their opposites will certainly not.

Since an undisturbed mind is essential for listening, reflecting and meditating, it is obvious that all such virtues need to be cultivated if we are to progress on our notional path towards realization.

It is worth mentioning, in passing, the idea of teaching through silence. It is said that Ramana Maharshi often practised this. In the mythology of Hinduism and Shaivism, Dakshinamurthy (*dakShiNAmUrti*), who is the iconic guru and represents the god Shiva, is supposed to have taught in silence. There is a certain logic in this, given that it can be argued that language is the source of all of our problems (see Chapter 7). Clearly silence avoids all of the paradoxes that arise once we begin to use words.

Swami Dayananda, however, says that this is a misunderstanding (Ref. 112). When it is said that *dakShiNAmUrti* taught by silence, the word actually used is *mudrA*, meaning a sign made by the position of the fingers and should be interpreted as "language." He says that if He was silent, all our Upanishads would be in the form of blank pages! Silence is the appropriate response only when an answer might be misleading.

Being in the Present

Since the source of everything doesn't come and go, it must be here right now, in this very moment. **Nirmala** (Ref. 254)

As T. S. Eliot has pointed out in The Four Quartets, the future is futureless and the past is all deception. There is only the here and now – the rest is delusion or imagination. *This* is it, as the Neo-Advaitins say. Thought and action can only take place in the present so that for any change to be made to the ignorance that makes us misperceive the world and the nature of ourselves, we must be in the present. The more frequently this happens and the longer the duration, the greater the opportunity for realizing how things really are; the better the chance of seeing the rope instead of the snake.

Most of the time, we are only partly paying attention to what is in front of us. Another part of the mind is somewhere else entirely, worrying about whether we switched off the cooker or wondering what to wear for the party next week. Being in the present means *simply* being. The mind is still, without thoughts or expectations. Thinking about what is there only comes afterwards, when the "being in the moment" has past. Although thinking itself obviously occurs in the present, the content of those thoughts is always necessarily about what is now in the past or anticipation about what might be in the future. By the time that a thought about the present can arise, it has already gone. **Philip Mistlberger** points out what a difference being fully in the present can make:

> To witness a wild flower on a hillside - simply to witness it without any mental interpretation at all - is to begin to realize and see its natural form, and, at the same time, to begin to realize our own natural state.

That is because if I'm only twenty-five percent present when looking at the flower, then the flower is only going to be twenty-five percent present as well - dull, with hardly any fragrance. However, if I manage to be one hundred percent present when witnessing this flower, then so too is the flower one hundred percent real - vivid, brilliant, with wonderful fragrance.

Such direct experience imposes no mental forms or concepts on the flower, and makes no attempt to interpret the bare experience of witnessing it. Only then is the true magnificence of the flower revealed - its natural form. And, it is a magnificence that in no way depends on the belief of the observer. Any thoughts about whether the rose is the true flower, or the marigold is the only way to God, are rendered meaningless in the tremendous light of simply witnessing the truth of the flower in the moment, free of mental filters. (Ref. 134)

Thoughts dilute the attention and reduce the feeling of aliveness. We are all familiar with the sudden jolt back to awareness when we have been "miles away" in a daydream. Less frequently we may experience the intensity of being fully in the moment without any distraction, perhaps when caught by the sudden beauty of a sunset or when faced by a life-threatening situation. We are temporarily free of the habitual clutter of mental trivia. It is as though the brightness and contrast controls have been adjusted and we can see the world clearly for once. **Katie Davis:**

In the Now, nothing is broken and nothing needs to be fixed. You are whole and pure. The Now is forever new, innocent and enhanced with a fresh sense of adventure. You are free from the robotic cycle. On the other hand, while you are reliving the past and practicing for the future, you are missing the aliveness of Now and the Joy of Being. As Eckhart Tolle points out, it is the quality of your consciousness here and now that determines future moments. This quality is your ability to remain still and keenly present, free of past and future, while all else comes and goes. Free of resistance, the Current of Life runs through you.

(Ref. 249)

Alan Watts is more usually associated with Zen than with Advaita, though he was at home with all non-dual approaches. He points out that all knowledge, as well as the tools of thought and language

> ...are of real use to men only if they are awake - not lost in the dreamland of past and future, but in the closest touch with that point of experience where reality can alone be discovered: this moment. ...But to see and understand it at all, the mind must not be divided into "I" and "this experience." The moment must be what it always is - all that you are and all that you know. (Ref. 250)

To be fully in the present means that there must be no desire for what *is* to be any different. There is total acceptance, total surrender, and effectively no ego. Simple though this might sound, few achieve it and, if it should happen, it is known to be special, as **Mark McCloskey** explains:

> Allowing the pure silence, the emptiness, the openness within you to be experienced, relaxing into the space of no thought, need, want, desire or belief you will soon realize that you are what you have believed in for so long and perhaps tears will come, or emotional jolts at the magnificence of this. That is wonderful. That is the moment you have waited for your entire life. You will have come home to here, now and this. And that is love itself. In the words of Krishnamurti, the great spiritual teacher "Stop believing in anything and you find that which is love and truth itself." This is so. (Ref. 251)

Desire/fear means to want things to be different from how they are, to escape from the present. Although not usually thought of in this way, it also means to want to escape from the reality of now into an imaginary future (or often the past – equally imaginary if we would only admit it). Accordingly, if we could eliminate desires we would be a long way towards the goal of being in the present.

Nirmala points out that no desire can ever satisfy, since the attention is always on something that is not present. If it *were* present, we wouldn't be desiring it. He says that our awareness is narrowed onto the object that we desire so that we are not actually aware at that time of the experience of desiring itself. If we just direct our attention to the desire itself, we will see the lie and the fact that this experience is not itself desirable at all.

It becomes obvious that desiring is the cause of suffering, not the absence of the desired object... The suffering is equal to the distance between here-and-now and what you have given your heart to... And if you look deeper, wanting comes from believing you are separate from the whole... The only thing that really satisfies is uncovering the truth of this moment. (Ref. 254)

In the present, there is no ego and consequently no problems. This is why people pursue dangerous sports, such as car racing and mountain climbing. When a wrong move can literally make the difference between life and death, there is no room for ego and we live from moment to moment *in the moment.* **Eckhart Tolle**:

If you walk the tightrope of now, you have to be totally present, every step. There's no little me. You can't remember your problems on a tightrope, or you would fall off immediately. Even fear. You can't fear the next step or you would fall off immediately. There's only this step. And there's a total presence with every step. This is the state that is arising, and it's only in that utter and complete presence that the little me dissolves and all the problems that cling to it - in fact, which make up its very existence - fall away. They cannot survive in intense presence. (Ref. 252)

Meditation

Meditation is the epitome of being in the present, without distractions of any kind, yet with nothing to do. In the danger-triggered present there is no ego but this is because the body and mind are on full alert, responding automatically to the needs of self-preservation, according to genetically programmed imperatives. In meditation, there is total stillness and silence, irrespective of would-be, outside distractions. External sounds and internal thoughts may arise but are effortlessly ignored. We become still, at the center of the turning world.

The usual western view of meditation is that it is a technique for relieving mental stress, with possible benefits for physical health, too. Most people probably accept that it is generally beneficial but think that it is not for them. They do not need it and, anyway, they do not have the time. Another view is that it is a mental exercise for reflecting on problems and perhaps coming up with creative and novel solutions. The view that was probably prevalent in the nineteen sixties and seventies – that it was something only for dropouts and hippies as a cheap substitute for drugs – is now generally more enlightened.

But none of these have anything to do with the true purpose and benefit. Meditation, in the sense that it is used here, is not for "me" in any way, neither the physical body nor the mental faculties nor imagined personality. It is not even a means for speculating on the purpose of "life, the universe and everything." All of those things relate to the level of appearance only and have nothing to do with our true nature, the nature of reality. Meditation aims to transcend all of these and bring about this recognition.

The best known method of meditation in the west is TM, Transcendental Meditation, propagated by Maharishi Mahesh Yogi. In fact, meditation achieved by any method is transcendental, in that past and future are transcended and we remain as pure awareness in the present. Time, space and causation are only mental concepts for use in the phenomenal world. The various techniques are akin to the mental preparation discussed earlier – they do not actually bring about meditation but make the mind more conducive. We eventually find ourselves in meditation in much the same way as we fall deeply asleep, except that awareness is now totally clear instead of totally opaque.

This clarity is effectively a merging with our true Self (*yoga*), though of course we were never actually separate, the fact only being obscured by the egotistic thoughts. Transcendental Meditation and others use the repetition of a *mantra* as the method. [A *mantra* is a sacred formula or incantation.] This is called *japa* and the technique in general is called *japa yoga*. Other techniques involve looking at an object, such as the idol of a favorite deity, a candle flame etc. or simply watching the breathing.

The purpose of them all is to concentrate the mind to a single point so that all extraneous details are eliminated. Once this has happened, the practice continues until the single object too becomes superfluous and bare awareness remains. During the early stages, thoughts arise and we become aware of external or internal distractions but these are simply ignored and attention is brought back to the chosen object.

Swami Dayananda (Ref. 256) has a beautiful metaphor to explain the different functioning of the mind during meditation. He says that it usually operates in an analogous manner to eating spaghetti – we lift the fork with one mouthful and another comes with it. It is a continuous process with one thought triggering the next in an uncontrolled way. Meditation is more like eating peanuts – we put one in our mouth, we eat it, we pick up another one and so on. *japa* meditation is a discrete process like this – we mentally sound the *mantra*, there is a period of silence, we mentally sound the *mantra*. Key to the whole exercise is the period of silence between the sounding. These periods increase as meditation progresses and the pace slows until ultimately there is only silence and the mind is still. This is then "pure" meditation (*yoga*), the *japa* having fallen away.

We are in control of the mind with *japa* meditation, whereas the mind is usually controlling us. When a thought arises, no one can guess what thought will occur next; it depends upon each person's history, conditioning, present emotional state etc. When practicing *japa*, we always know what is coming – another repetition of the *mantra*.

In theory, any word, phrase or even something much longer will work as a *mantra*. However, words carry meaning and are always likely to trigger associative thoughts in the mind. Traditionally, meditation is *dhyAna*, which also means "mental representation of the personal attributes of a deity" and *mantra*-s are often associated with Gods or with phrases from the scriptures. Indeed, meditation on the form of a God can be done without *japa* at all. If the name of a God is used as a *mantra*, then it should be understood that name and form are considered to be inseparable in this respect. This is why the *mantra* is held in reverence and reserved for use in meditation, not being spoken of to others.

The TM organization and others surround the "initiation" into mantra meditation with much ritual and charge considerable sums of money in the west. Practically speaking, this does have benefits for the individual, however. It is likely that the typical westerner would not have the *bhakta* sentiments for the *mantra* and would therefore not naturally have the appropriate reverential attitude. If he has paid a significant portion of his salary, however, he will normally have made a definite commitment and this will ensure that initial practice at least will be undertaken with due consideration.

In Hinduism, *mantra*-s often take the form of invocations and the vibrations are believed literally to manifest the power and form of the related God. *japa* may take the form of repeating the *mantra* aloud, silently in the mind or even written repeatedly in silence. All help cultivate *dhAraNA* (concentration) and *tapas* (self-discipline) quite apart from the mental stillness and any incidental physical benefits. A particularly well known one is the *aShTAkShara* (eight syllables) *mantra* of Vishnu – *OM namo narAyANAya*. This is a short, direct invocation (*nArAyaNa* is Vishnu, son of the original man). Another, even better known one is the much longer **gAyatrI mantra** (*gAyatri* refers to the meter of 24 syllables, arranged in a triplet of 8; it originated in the *RRig veda but is found in all four*). It is a prayer to the sun God, *sAvitrI*, to lend His powers to our meditation. It is said to develop a brilliant intellect (illuminated by the sun):

AUM bhUrbhuvaH svaH (separate prefix from Yajur Veda)
tat saviturvareNyaM

bhargo devasya dhImahi

dhiyo yo naH prachodayAt (three lines of 8 syllables – these are from the *bRRihadAraNyaka upaniShad* V.I.3.6 and also the *chhAndogya upaniShad* 3.12.)

A literal translation of the mantra is as follows:

Oh matter-energy-mind (triple universe); Upon this worthy source of divine spiritual light, meditate: thus enlighten our intellect. (Ref. 257)

The simplest, shortest yet most powerful mantra of all is "OM." It is usually written as: ॐ when it is called the *praNava shabda* (either word separately or both together mean "mystical or sacred symbol").

You will probably recognize it (certainly Indians will since it is prominently displayed on all of the buses amongst other things!) This symbol is generated in ITRANS by the characters *OM*.

praNu means "to make a humming or droning sound." If you have heard monks repeating it, you will understand why – the "m" sound at the end is continued with a resonating humming sound. *OM is the symbol for God and its purpose is to convey the sense of God's universality*. Names are used to represent those objects, concepts etc. about which we wish to speak. All words are necessarily limited – after all, they invariably contain only a few letters of the alphabet. The name we give to God would ideally contain all letters and all ways of sounding them. OM achieves this by utilizing the scientific way in which the Sanskrit language is constructed. All of the sounds originate with the basic sound of *a*, sounded by simply moving the vocal chords with the mouth wide open. All of the remaining letters use this with the mouth, tongue and lips being progressively modified. In fact, only the vowels actually sound; the purpose of the consonants is to curtail the sounding of the vowels in different ways.

Now, if the sound *a* is made and continues to sound while the mouth is slowly closed, the sound made at the "mid-point" as it were, is "u." If these two sounds are made together or, more practically speaking, if the sound corresponding to the mid-point between these two is made, the sound that emerges is *o* (as in "boat"). If the mouth continues to close while still making the basic sound, the ultimate sound when the lips come together is "m." Thus, bringing all of these aspects together, the sound that encompasses the entire range of possible sounds is "*a – u – m*." When sounded in practice, this is *OM*.

It is not just a word, devised by someone in antiquity to represent a concept so that he could speak about it to another. It is THE word, as in "In the beginning was the Word, and the Word was with God, and the Word was God." One of the major Upanishads - the *mANDUkya* – has the whole of its few twelve verses about this word. It says that the syllable *OM* **is** Brahman, reality itself. Each part of the word is identified with a different aspect of consciousness. *a* is the waking state, *u* the dreaming state and *m* the deep sleep state. Together, *OM* represents that consciousness that forms the substratum of all three, effectively a fourth "level" of consciousness called *turIya*. The word also represents the union of the three gods, *vishNu* (a), *shiva* (u) and *brahmA* (m) in the Hindu religion.

Because the sound includes all possible sounds, it is effectively present in or behind all other words – it can be regarded as the source of all other words; the seed from which they arise. This single word has the capacity to create all other words and thus represents the capacity of God to create all things in the world. It is a universal sound, not restricted to any religion. It is the "AMEN" in Christianity. If you listen to the word being correctly sounded, the vibration continues after the sound of the word itself ends. This "unspoken" sound is always there in the absence of other sounds (and of mental activity of any kind!) – *prANa*, the basic vitality of life itself. It is the sound at the end of meditation when the mind is perfectly still; the sound to which **T. S. Eliot** refers in his magnificent work "The Four Quartets" (Ref. 196): -

But heard, half-heard, in the stillness

Between two waves of the sea.
(Ref. 114)

Thoughts arising during meditation are not a problem. This is natural and there is nothing "I" can do about it, especially since "I" am just a group of those thoughts anyway. The technique of coping with them is simply to watch them without attaching to any and chasing after them. **Osho** (Ref. 48) compares it to a muddy stream, stirred up by someone walking through it. We cannot jump in and try to clear the leaves and debris that have been stirred up – this will only make it worse. All that we can do is to sit silently, without concern, and wait for it to clear naturally. Here is what **Leo Hartong** says about meditation:

> Formal meditation may spin a mantra around the brain to silence the continuous stream of thoughts. In true meditation, thoughts are seen to occur freely and are not viewed as problematic interruptions that need to be controlled by an imaginary ego, which claims to be bothered by them. The key here is to see that this ego is itself part of the stream of thought it wants to control and that it has no reality independent of thought. Clearly, there is no need for this ghostly helmsman of an ego to steer the mind to a single point of concentration. All is freely arising and welcomed, including mantras, the ego illusion, thoughts and emotions. None of this activity is able to affect the silent space of Pure Awareness in which it has its moment and - without leaving a trace - dissolves.
(Ref. 22)

Attending Satsang

satsa~Nga means "association with" (*sa~Nga*) the "wise" as well as "the real" (*sat*). It is the effort made with the support of other like-minded individuals to discover the truth, by turning away from the false. It is especially beneficial when such a group is guided by a Sage (another meaning of *sat*). The Self is, of course, already *sat* but in our ignorance we fail to realize that. So, pedantically, we are always in *satsa~Nga.*

Verse 9 of the **Bhaja Govindam**:

> Company of the good develops detachment, detachment leads to removal of delusion, and when the delusion is removed the mind becomes calm and serene, and the serene mind leads to liberation, while living. (Ref. 30)

Today it is also possible to associate with other seekers via the Internet and there are many so-called Egroups on which people discuss Advaitic topics via email (some of these are referenced in Appendix F on Internet Resources and a number of the extracts in this book are taken from them). These cannot really be called satsang, however. There may be considerable information provided and often learned argumentation. Much of this is provided in an earnest and self-effacing manner with all due respect and devotion, though some contributions are bound to be invested with a little ego, too. But such discussions are lacking the direction of an acknowledged teacher, able to resolve contentions and provide authoritative statements when needed.

Accordingly, overall clarity is usually not present and beginners especially may be confused. The following extract from **Sri Ramakrishna** is relevant:

> To drink pure water from a shallow pond one should gently take the water from the surface without disturbing the pond in the least. If it is disturbed, the sediments rise up and make the whole water muddy. If you desire to be pure, have firm faith, and slowly go on with your devotional practices, without wasting your energy in useless scriptural discussions and arguments. Your little brain will otherwise be muddled. (Ref. 50)

One aspect of the value of satsang and listening to a guru is that our habitual identification with elements of the world and involvement in the various activities may be temporarily broken. **Nathan Gill** uses the metaphor of going to the cinema. We are very likely to become totally involved in the film. If, however, someone nearby is continually unwrapping sweets with the associated crackling of the wrappers, this is likely to distract us and bring us back into the present. He says that what is happening in satsang is that "someone is constantly crackling sweet wrappers." (Ref. 25)

shravaNa, manana and nididhyAsana

Key to practice in *j~nAna* yoga is what is called *shravaNa, manana* and *nididhyAsana*. These three alone may provide a complete, though steep path to realization. This practice is for the *adhama AdhikArI*, the best qualified students only. *shravaNa* is the hearing of scriptures, primarily *shruti* and ideally read and then explained by an enlightened guru, who is also a *shrotriya* – well versed in the scriptures.

The *bRRihadAraNyaka upaniShad* states that:

> The Self, my dear Maitreyi, should be realized – should be heard of, reflected on and meditated upon. By the realization of the Self, my dear, through hearing, reflection and meditation, all this is known. (II.4.5 Ref. 1)

Even a single *mahAvAkya* such as *tat tvam asi* – thou art That – theoretically has the power to awaken a *jIva* but it usually takes much more than that. Having heard the truth spoken and explained, the next step is *manana* – thinking about what has been heard and subjecting it to reason based upon one's own experience. This will usually involve asking questions of the guru to obtain further clarification. The final stage is *nididhyAsana*, where that which has been understood intellectually is meditated upon until it is directly realized for oneself. *nididhyAsana* should be differentiated from *upAsana* or *dhyAna* as described earlier, which are rather meditation upon a *mantra*.

In fact, in the extract just quoted, the Upanishad uses the word *vij~nAna* for meditation in the second sentence, meaning "discerning, understanding, right apprehension." Rather than directly meditating upon the truth, it is more a case of rejecting all untruths and therefore coming to a realization of what, therefore, must be true.

(The primacy of *shravaNa* is emphasized by the *vivaraNa* school of Advaita. The *bhAmatI* school believes that it is only a stepping stone to the later practice of *nididhyAsana*, in which the indirect knowledge gained from *shravaNa* is intuitively realized.)

Cee presents a modern interpretation of this practice, though the last step has now been revised to Ramana Maharshi's Self-Enquiry method described later:

Listen: You may have noticed that all great spiritual traditions are talking about the same truth. All rivers lead to the ocean, but if you keep changing rivers it may take you a very long time to get there! After you have checked out the spiritual supermarket, pick one teaching and stick with it. Then read sacred texts and associate with wise sages. Use all of your time wisely toward your own liberation.

Ponder: Contemplate and fully consider the teachings. Don't just believe them. See if they hold true for you. Use your mind like a sword to cut through illusion. Keep the teaching always in mind. Try to get to the deepest meaning of the words.

How can this be so? How does it apply to me? Eventually you will cut through ALL limiting ideas and concepts. The true meaning of the words will be understood directly without the limiting adjunct of the mind. The teaching will be your own.

Meditate: Set time aside every day just to sit and be with yourself. Sit comfortably in a position such that you will not fall asleep in. Bring your attention inward, away from all worldly distractions. In our way, being with yourself involves finding out who that self is! We ask ourselves the question "Who Am I?" It is called self inquiry. It is not watching thoughts. It is diving directly into who has the thoughts. It is a systematic looking at who you believe yourself to be. Are you really a body? Are you always a body? Are you any of your thoughts, or all of your thoughts put together? If something arises in meditation, to whom is it arising? Who you are has to be true ALL the time. If something comes and goes (like a body) it can't be you. If you hold onto your sense of "I" and keep eliminating the "I" that is seen as an object—you will always come to a vaster, more formless "I." (Ref. 258)

Reading Scriptures – svAdhyAya

Anyone who has read, or attempted to read, the Upanishads, the Bhagavad Gita or any of the later *prakaraNa*-s in direct translation will know that this is not always an easy task. We know that reading Shakespeare or Chaucer is difficult and those writers lived only hundreds of years ago and spoke English. It is hardly surprising then that translations from Sanskrit written in an alien culture thousands of years ago should often be confusing and occasionally impenetrable. But then if we only read commentaries or poetic translations by westerners, it is inevitable that any misunderstandings on their part will only compound the problem further.

The problem with merely reading the scriptures is that there is the opportunity, with every word, for the mind to go off at a tangent, thinking related thoughts triggered by the word. Very quickly, the intended sense of a passage may be lost completely as we impose upon it other ideas already in the memory. **Atmananda Krishna Menon** explains how this problem necessitates the presence of a *guru*:

When you listen to the spoken word of the Guru, even on the first occasion your ego takes leave of you and you visualize the Truth at once, being left alone in your real nature. But when you read the same words by yourself, your ego lingers on in the form of the word, its meaning etc., and you fail to transcend them. To visualize the Truth, the only condition needed is the elimination of the ego. This is never possible by mere reading, before meeting the Guru. Therefore listen, listen, listen and never be satisfied with anything else. After listening to the Truth from the Guru direct and after visualizing the Truth in his presence, you may well take to thinking deeply over what the Guru has told you. This is also another form of listening and takes you, without fail, to the same experience you have already had in his presence. (From Note 1015, Ref. 13)

Reading is therefore fraught with danger and far superior is to hear the scriptures expounded by one who does know and understand them and who has direct experience of the subject matter (such a one is called a *shrotriya*). There is another word of warning here, however. This is that the *guru* speaks to the disciple (*shiShya*) at the latter's level of understanding. Thus he, the *guru*, may say one thing to one disciple and something apparently contrary to another. This is in keeping with the fundamental teaching method of Advaita whereby one level of understanding is successively sublated by higher ones as the student progresses.

Because of this, if a question of authority has to be resolved, one should always go back to the scriptures and not to the *guru*. *shruti* is always the ultimate authority. This is also a key reason why one should find a suitable *guru* and then stay with them. The *guru* then takes full responsibility for leading the student to the truth via the appropriate levels of half-truths. Only further confusion can come from consulting many teachers on a casual basis. **Chittaranjan Naik** explains this below:

The instructions given by a Master are prescriptive and not necessarily descriptive whereas in *vAda* [discussion, explanation] what we are more often than not debating is the descriptive aspect of a *darshana* [viewpoint, philosophy]. The descriptive aspect of a *darshana* for any *darshana* of Vedanta is obtained from the *prasthAna traya bhAShya*-s of the *bhASyakAra* [various commentators] of the *darshana* which over-rides the sayings of a Master if there is a conflict seen between them.

There is never any conflict really between the *darshana* and a Master in the tradition of the *darshana*, but the Master's words are sometimes directed to the individual depending on the time, cultural setting and the specific pre-conditioning of the individual concerned and it is not meant to be used as the correct standpoint of the *darshana* even though it is not incorrect in the context of the utterance. It is because of this reason that the aspirant in the path is advised to give precedence to the *shruti* over what any Master or any other scripture says, but when an aspirant becomes a disciple of a Guru through initiation, then the Guru's sayings are supreme for the aspirant because they are the specific cure for the illness of the disciple and because the disciple is now in the hands of the Guru.

Since we are here debating the standpoint of Advaita Vedanta, the *bhAShya*-s of Sri Shankaracharya on the Vedas, the Bhagavad Gita and the Brahma Sutras (*prasthAna traya*) are the supreme authority for resolving any issue that may come up. (Ref. 259)

It has already been pointed out, and will be discussed at much greater length in the next chapter, that we are already That – the truth, reality or whatever other word is preferred. We do not need to (nor can) do anything to bring about this already existing fact. One aspect of the value of the scriptures, therefore, is in their ability to bring about the realization of this already existing fact.

As things stand at present, I know that I am "I" and that Brahman is "That" – it is unthinkable that I can be Brahman. I think I am an insignificant, limited, body-mind which is a created thing whereas Brahman is the unlimited, all-powerful, ubiquitous creator. How can we be the same? But the mahAvAkya *tat tvam asi* cancels out all of these contradictory elements and tells me that "I" am "That," i.e. Brahman. This canceling out of contradictory elements, leaving an equality of the non-contradictory parts is called *bhAga tyAga lakShaNa*. The oneness that is pointed to (*lakShaNa*) is understood by "giving up" (*tyAga*) the contradictory parts (*bhAga*).

There is an excellent metaphor that explains how this works. Suppose that you and a friend, A, both went to school with a third person, X. Although you were not particularly friendly with X, you knew him quite well but, since leaving school you lost touch and have forgotten all about him. Today, you happen to be walking along with A and see Y, who is a famous film star, walking by on the others side of the street. You have seen films starring Y and admire him very much. A now makes some comment such as "Y has come a long way in the world since we knew him, hasn't he?" You are mystified since you have never even spoken to Y as far as you know and you ask A to explain himself. A then makes the revelatory statement: "Y is that X whom we knew at school."

All of the contradictory aspects, that X is an insignificant, scruffy, spotty oik that you once knew at school, while Y is a rich, famous and talented actor, are all cancelled out, leaving the bare equation that X and Y are the same person. Furthermore, the knowledge is *apArokSha* – immediate. We do not have to study the reasoning or meditate upon it for a long time.

In the example of *tat tvam asi*, the canceling out of body, mind etc. is possible because of what has gone before. We have investigated these beliefs and exercised our reason, negating the false impressions (*neti, neti*), as we did in Chapter 1. Without this preparation, there could not have been the sudden understanding that *tat* and *tvam* are indeed the same. On the face of it, the Neo-Advaitin teaching of "This is It" is also an example of *bhAga tyAga lakShaNa*. Here, however, the vital difference is that the mental preparation and reasoning to undermine our initial belief (that this is certainly *not* it) has not taken place. Although the true situation is already the case, the layers of ignorance have to be uncovered before this can be clearly seen. This is why there remains a need to follow the traditional "path," even in today's climate of supposedly superior understanding and fast-track capability.

(See also Verbal Authority or Evidence (*shabda*) in the section on *pramANa*-s in Chapter 4 for justification for accepting what the scriptures tell us.)

Sound, Words and Language

Having discussed the power of the *mantra* in meditation and the value of hearing about the scriptures in *shravaNa*, it is necessary to take a brief diversion to look at sound and language in more detail.

The speaking of a word is the result of a four-stage process according to Advaita. (Actually, this classification began with just three steps - *parA* was added later. It was devised by the poet and grammarian *bhartRRihari* in the 7th century AD and explained in his book *vAkyapadIya*.) **Swami Muni Narayana Prasad** explains:

> The *RRiShi*-s of India, who were also psychologists, saw the process of expressing an idea as having four stages. They are called *parA* (the transcendent), *pashyantI* (visualization), *madhyamA* (medium), and *vaikharI* (the uttered word). The causal Truth which is of the essence of Consciousness is *parA* or the transcendent. Without it nothing happens. In that Consciousness happens the formulation of an idea or experience which has a specific form. The visualization of that form is called *pashyantI*. This vision has to be brought into the mould of a medium in order to express it. This medium could be a language, mere sound (music), color, or even concrete forms as in sculptures. This is the third stage called *madhyamA* or medium. The last stage is the expressed form of it, either as words or music, or any other form of expression. This stage is called *vaikharI* which means the uttered word. The word stands here for all the forms of expression as it is the commonest way of communicating ideas.
>
> What a word can do is to express an idea or an experience, which belongs to the second stage of *pashyantI*. Word cannot contain the transcendent as its meaning. It is that transcendent that made the specific vision find expression through words. (Ref. 260)

It is suggested that the mechanism of language formation in the mind and its subsequent expression actually brings about the apparent transformation of the non-dual Consciousness into the seeming differentiation of name and form. The creation is said to be the manifestation of OM (c.f. the statement in the Gospel according to St. John that "In the beginning was the Word").

The effective intent of spiritual practice is to reverse this process and take us "back" to the state of unmanifest, pure Consciousness. **HH Sri Shantanand Saraswati** says that:

> Most of the worldly communication is materialized in the *vaikharI* state and some in *madhyamA*. The spiritual activities of meditation, reflection etc., comprehend and make use of *madhyamA* and *pashyantI*. When the union is made and the being is himself then he is in *parA*. (Ref. 261)

(See Refs. 262 and 263 for a detailed exposition on this topic.)

We make use of words, then, via the scriptures, to point us back to the truth. Words cannot themselves describe Brahman or tell us directly about the nature of reality. The words that we have acquired during in our life have been acquired in order to help identify things, talk about feelings etc, i.e. they refer to objects, external or internal, real or abstract. **Swami Dayananda**:

> Known words cannot reveal Brahman because all known words are words that we have gathered to describe things that we already know, which are all limited in nature, like a pot, for example. All these known words are words which deal with genus or species (*jAti*), attributes (*guNa*), actions (*kriyA*), and relationships (*sambandha*). (Ref. 264)

Over the thousands of years in which language has been developing, it has shaped more and more the way in which we look at the world and think about reality. Distortions in the meaning and use of words has led to similar confusion and mistaken thinking in the mind and some of these have been crucial in leading us away from the truth. The way in which a word such as "person" has come to mean the exact opposite of its original intention is but one example. **Steven Harrison** describes how this happens:

> Understanding language is integral to understanding thought and reality.

As we observe the nature of what we are, we also describe the obser-vation. This naming process is necessary for us to function in the world. It is what a child learns as it grows with the primary learning being the difference between "me" and "not me." The use of language or naming is the very thing that differentiates objects, actions, and qualities in the world. This distinction or separation is the basis of intellect and consequently the basis for the apparent manipulation of the world around us. It is not however, the basis for true intelligence.

What is lost in the learning of differentiation is the underlying unity from which this world of names and of separate objects grew. As the "me" center is established and the world that appears to be outside of "me" is learned and described through language, the actuality of the undifferentiated pre-linguistic nature of life is forgotten...

Implicit in the development of language is the "me" and the "me-object" relationship. There is no named without a namer, and no namer without a named. As language develops, we are swallowed by the reality that language creates. (Ref. 265)

Even something as basic as the distinction between adjectives and nouns leads to confusion. The nature of the world as *mithyA* was discussed in chapter 4. The example of a "ring" being only the name for a particular, temporary form of "gold" was used to highlight the distinction – gold being the "reality" and "ring" being *mithyA*, always having gold as its essential nature. **Swami Dayananda** (Ref. 112) similarly takes the example of a table. He says that, when we use a name such as this, it should refer to an actual object. If I am not using the alleged table for that purpose, however, the name is no longer appropriate.

Strictly speaking, the name should always refer to the actual substantive object which, in the case of the alleged table, is actually "wood." "Table" just happens to be the form in which the wood is currently held. Perhaps the joints are not actually fixed and I can dismantle it in an instant and re-assemble it into a shelf. Form is the "attribute" of the object and should be expressed as an adjective and not a noun. Thus, rather than talking about a "wooden table," we should really say "tably wood." Similarly, we would say "ringy gold" instead of "golden ring," "potty clay" and so on.

He goes on to say:

> Wood becomes substantive for the time being. But wood itself is an attribute because we can call it earth. It is endless. It will end up only in *nirguNa*, the attributeless. Whenever you describe something, the description requires a substantive. All definitions are descriptions. All descriptions are attributes. All attributes require a substantive. If the substantive is discovered to be an attribute, definitely it requires another substantive. Therefore final substantive should be *nirguNa*, it should be free from attributes. (Ref. 112)

In other words, everything is Brahman – *sarvam khalvidam brahma*. By following back all of the relative appearances in the world, we eventually return to that from which it is all manifest. **Hans Heimer**:

> The *bRRihadAraNyaka* [verse I.4.7] states that in the beginning and now, what is called "the world" consists only of relative (i.e. not ultimately real) distinctions, distinctions of name and appearance (or form). In reality it is all the *Atman*, the real Self. The name is that distinction which arises from language, and the appearance is that distinction which arises from our sensory perceptions. By "the world" is meant all percepts and concepts, as is made clear when reference is made to body, breath, speech, activities, etc. Now the term "beginning" is also a word, a concept, so that too is relative and a manifestation of the *Atman*. The beginning is always now, in the ever-present.
>
> The last part of [the verse] gives us a wonderful metaphor, of cattle who have disappeared from view, but who left a trail on the ground which enables the farmer-owner to find them. This metaphor shows that to find the Self, by the trail of all aspects of the entire world, we have to follow to the source of the trail made by that which we value, represented by the cattle. All manifestation is the clue to the source, and

it needs reflection and searching before the source can be found. The source is ever present, but it is hidden by name and appearance. (Ref. 266)

Swami Krishnananda's commentary on this verse is:

> The world that we see is nothing but the form of God, and it is He that is fully present in every form. Whenever we touch any object, we are coming into contact with that Being only. If this awareness could be awakened in a person, at that very moment there could be liberation – here and now. (Ref. 2)

But, from early childhood, we learn to name each object, thereby irrevocably separating it out from its surroundings and making it exceedingly difficult to return to a virgin perception without the mind leaping in and claiming it, thus preventing the recognition of this truth.

Becoming the disciple of a guru

Strictly speaking, the *guru* is not directly responsible for bringing about the realization of truth in a disciple. The knowledge arises from within. This is often referred to as *sadguru* (literally "a good teacher"). The real Self is prior to the idea "I am" which is the beginning of all of the apparent manifestation. As the levels of mistaken understanding are whittled away, this truth is able to reach out, as it were, and clear away the final barrier of the ego itself. The **Yoga Vasishtha** says:

> Self-knowledge or knowledge of truth is not had by resorting to a *guru* (preceptor) nor by the study of scripture, nor by good works: it is attained only by means of enquiry inspired by the company of wise and holy men. One's inner light alone is the means, naught else. When this inner light is kept alive, it is not affected by the darkness of inertia. (Ref. 38)

John Wheeler makes this point even more strongly:

There is no teacher outside and independent of us who "has the understanding," has awakened, is enlightened or what have you. This kind of assumption leads to mistaken beliefs that just cloud the simplicity of what is being pointed to. There are a couple of problems with this way of thinking. First, the idea that teacher "so-and-so" is realized has the implicit assumption for most of us that "therefore, I am not." Thus the belief in the sense of separation from our own presence is subtly strengthened. Second, talking about teachers who have it (or not) reinforces a belief that what is being pointed to is outside of ourselves - again emphasizing a sense of separation. Third, the teachers being discussed are usually not in our immediate environment and we are simply spinning in conceptual thought about people that are figments in imagination in that moment. Even if there were such a being as an enlightened teacher, if you approached them, the most you would find is a physical form composed of matter, chemicals and cells - which are just transient appearances in awareness. So the whole notion of beings who are awake or have the understanding is a complete fiction when looked at head on...

At best, a teacher is simply a sign post that can point back to what is real and present within you. There is no enlightened sign post. There is only the fact of being-awareness itself. As soon as we begin to talk about others who have it or not, we overlook the fact that it is fully present and shining as our own real nature here and now. (Ref. 270)

There is a story in the Yoga Vasishtha that explains how it can be that a *guru* is needed yet is not actually the cause of the enlightenment (if it should arise) in the end. It concerns a miser who loses a small coin whilst he is walking in the forest. Worried that the loss of this will incur further losses through inability to invest it, he spends three days searching for it. He fails to find it but, instead, finds a jewel. Clearly it was the miserliness of the man and his determination to recover this small coin that led to his finding something truly valuable. In the same way, it is said that the disciple, having been instructed by the guru, spends all his time searching for something. He thinks that the search is for something for himself – peace of mind, meaning in his life or whatever. But he fails to find this. Instead, if he perseveres, he finds something of much greater value – his true Self. This cannot be found directly as the result of anyone's teaching. Nevertheless, had it not been for the guidance of the guru, he would not have continued looking.

Alexander Smit († 2000) warns about the dangers of pursuing a path such as Advaita without the guidance of a guru, by simply reading:

> The objection to books about Advaita, including the translations of Nisargadatta's words is that too much knowledge is given in them. That is an objection. People can use this knowledge, and especially the knowledge at the highest level to defend and maintain their self-consciousness. That makes my work more difficult. Knowledge, spiritual knowledge, can when there is no living master, be used again to maintain the "I," the self-consciousness. The mind is tricky, cunning. And I speak out of my own experience! Because Advaita Vedanta, without a good *living* spiritual master, I repeat, a *good one*, can become a perfect self contained defence mechanism. It can be a plastic sack that leaks on all sides, but you can't find the leak. You know that it doesn't tally, but it looks as if it does tally. That is the danger in Vedanta. Provided there is a good *living* master available, it can do no harm. But stay away from it if there is no master available! Provided it is well guided Advaita can be brilliant. (Ref. 267)

There are many teachers of Advaita in the west today – over 200 are listed in Appendix D, with links to their websites – and many more in India. But there are few well-known ones of the stature of Ramana Maharshi, Nisargadatta Maharaj or Atmananda Krishna Menon. And it is certainly the case that many seekers are not actually interested in Self-realization as it is understood by Advaita. Rather, they are concerned with finding peace in their lives, minimizing psychological stress and so on. **Vamadeva Shastri (David Frawley)** points out that:

> Only great disciples can have great gurus. Ordinary disciples, such as most of us are, require ordinary gurus. Today, good disciples are harder to find than those who claim to be great gurus. We want instant enlightenment, preferably without having to do any practices or give anything up. We want both God and the world, enlightenment and all the good things of life. This causes us to select teachers who tell us what we want to hear. (Ref. 268)

The traditional guru-disciple relationship involves total surrender on the part of the latter and this is not something that can be accepted by most westerners. The casual basis of satsang attendance means that there is not usually any commitment on the part of either so that the fundamental basis of the association is lacking. Even the idea of "guru" has negative connotations, being linked with cults and malpractice.

Alan Jacobs, former chairman of the Ramana Maharshi Foundation in London, who has vast experience of many teachers through hosting their visits, has this to say:

> The Contemporary Teachers often adapt their teaching to psychotherapy to meet their audiences' demands, as they earn their livelihoods by itinerant teaching wherever an audience may be found. They marginalize Self Enquiry, as being too difficult, or ignore it. At the best it is given in an attenuated form. They do however, succeed in undermining the sense of personal doership and teach "surrender" by sleight of hand through terms such as welcoming, embracing, being ok, accepting "what is" etc. These terms strip the teaching of its necessary Devotional implications such as are felt as "God" or the "Real Self". Devotion is essential to open the Heart. Intellectual understanding alone is arid and leads nowhere except as a precursor to necessary sAdhana. To imply "all is only consciousness so do whatever you like," is a truncation of the

Maharshi's great Teachings. The injunction to give up spiritual practice is dangerous, as it allows the *vAsanA*-s full permission to indulge, and leads to a dead-end of Hedonism, or at best a parking space until the next "satsang fix." There is no Grace without effort. One either wants an illusory but comfortable self-calming quietness, or one wants Enlightenment. (Ref. 269)

The psychological bias is understandable. I already know that I exist (sat) and I know that I am conscious (chit) so that what is lacking is the realization that I am happy. We are searching for happiness outside of ourselves in the belief that we are lacking this. We look to the guru for help. Anything that he or she can do to assist will be seen as successful. In fact, the true function of the guru is to bring us to the realization that our own nature *is* happiness. We are already perfect and complete.

Choosing a teacher can be seen as a significant problem, especially when the material in a satsang may not even be immediately identifiable as Advaita. A 'threefold-verification' is sometime spoken of to assist in this: Does the teaching match that given in the scriptures? Does it match the teaching of a known Sage? Is what is spoken of verifiable in one's own experience?

There is more on this subject in the last chapter, comparing Teaching Methods.

Self-enquiry (Atma vichAra)

Self Enquiry is the term usually given to the technique advocated by Ramana Maharshi in which the question "Who am I?" is repeatedly asked. We are not looking for an answer. Any answers that may arise will be from the mind and necessarily untrue. It might seem to be a variant on the "*neti, neti*" practice in the *bRRihadAraNyaka upaniShad* but Ramana denied this, claiming that "*neti, neti*" was an intellectual exercise and effectively saying that the ego could never eliminate the ego.

Nisargadatta Maharaj says:

The mind must learn that beyond the moving mind there is the background of awareness, which does not change. The mind must come to know the true Self and respect it and cease covering it up, like the moon which obscures the sun during solar eclipse, first realize that nothing observable or experienceable is you or binds you. Take no notice of what is not yourself. (Ref. 5)

Self-enquiry begins with the realization that "I am not the body" and progresses along the lines explained in the early chapters of the book. Recognizing what I am not is part of the process of discovering who I am. It is all about bringing the light of Consciousness to bear upon the subject to dispel the darkness of ignorance. Self effort channeled into self-enquiry ultimately brings self-knowledge.

The theory is that, as has been explained earlier, the Self does not "do" anything. All thinking and apparent action is through the medium of the mind. The very notion of "I" is itself only such a modification. Ramana Maharshi calls it *aham vRRitti*, mental disposition or modification of "I" – usually translated as the "I"-thought.

The technique itself involves putting the question "Who am I?" (*koham*) to oneself mentally. Note that the "I," here, is not the real Self. The mind cannot know the true Self. The purpose of the exercise is to try to discover the ego. The question is not used as a *mantra* but as a simple enquiry. Having asked it, we wait for the mind to throw up an answer. This is examined and ultimately rejected and the question posed again. Any concerns, doubts, fears etc. that may arise are not followed up. We simply ask to whom these worries are occurring, as **Ramana Maharshi** explains:

Ask yourself, "To whom do these doubts, fears and worries occur?" - and they will vanish. Cease to pay attention to them. Pay attention to the Self within. Fears etc. can only arise when there are two, or when anybody else exists apart from, or separate from, or outside of you. If you turn the mind inward towards the Self, fears etc. will disappear.

If you try to remove a doubt or fear, another doubt or fear will arise.

There will be no end to it. The best method of annihilating them is to ask, "To whom do they occur?" and they will disappear. Destroying a tree by plucking its leaves one by one is impossible - other leaves will grow by the time you pluck a few. Remove the root of the tree - the ego - and the whole tree with its leaves and branches will be destroyed. Prevention is better than cure...

Look at your Self or *Atma*, rather than anywhere else. The eyes may be kept open or closed - it is immaterial. There is only one I, whether you spell it "I" or "EYE." There is no point in opening or closing the eyes. Attention must be focused on the inner "I." You are not "I" that can be opened or closed. You may close or open the eyes according to your liking for you will cease to think of the world when you think of the Self. If you are in a room and do not look out, it is immaterial whether you close the windows or keep them open. (Ref. 271)

Whenever an apparent answer is thrown up by the mind, it is turned around into another question. By separating the idea of "I" from the objects with which identification is occurring, the intention is to undermine the seeming reality of the ego. When the questioning and answering finally ceases, what remains must be the Self, from which all this arises:

Wherefrom is the "I" thought? Probe into it. The "I"-thought will vanish. The supreme Self will shine forth of itself. No further effort is needed. (Ref. 49)

When the *aham vRRitti* disappears, there is no longer any identification of any sort – no feeling that "I am a doer, thinker etc." or a person. All is seen as Self. This is Self-realization.

It has been suggested that the technique of Self-enquiry has the advantage over meditation in that it helps dissolve the process of identification, which is maintaining the illusion of separate existence. Meditation, since it depends upon the deliberate, initial concentration on a separate object, might be thought subtly to be maintaining it. In reality, I do not think that this is a reasonable criticism since true meditation only begins once *japa* has ceased and the object is essentially of no further interest.

In fact, it seems that the end result of both practices is the same, namely that a state is reached in which the sense of an individual self has disappeared. It is only a state – *samAdhi* – until such time as there is no return of the ego following practice. Self-enquiry differs from meditation in that it is intended that it should be practiced all of the time. It is not necessary to adopt a special position in silence for a prolonged period.

Finally, a comment on the practice from a modern teacher, **Satyananda**:

"Who am I?" is the question that the mind cannot answer. In that impossibility it stops. You know, it's like computers - when you put something in that they cannot handle, they just crash. It's the same with the mind. If the mind asks itself "Who am I?," it cannot solve it. It cannot solve it because all that it knows is name and form. That which is the source of the mind is completely beyond name and form, so it cannot put it into a box. In that impossibility, the mind just stops. That which remains as consciousness is the real you. That is the way home, cutting through everything that is there - passion, fear, pain, whatever. The real you is all that remains. (Ref. 78)

Conclusion

Neo-Advaitin teachers claim that no reading or practicing of any kind can be helpful; there is no path and no one to tread it. It will be found, however, that most spent years reading and following gurus before they realized this. It is certainly the case that, for most "apparent" seekers, preparation *is* necessary; that this knowledge needs to be acquired in one way or another before we can let it go as being ultimately mistaken. It is the signpost that points the way. Once we have passed it and moved in the right direction it makes no difference if the signpost crumbles into dust – it has served its purpose.

The real clarity comes from seeing the absence of the person. It is the person that gums up the works and creates all the problems and supposed solutions. Just keep coming back to the fundamentals. Your nature is luminous, ever-present, radiant, perfect, being-awareness. This is fully realized and complete right now. There is literally nothing you need to do or practice...

All problems are for the "I." See that there is no "I" and all problems must resolve. There is a logic to it that you can confirm by direct experience. **John Wheeler** (Ref. 70)

Summary

Spiritual Practice

- It is the ego that wants to become enlightened... and there is no ego.
- We are already the non-dual Self.
- If there is no doer and we have no free will, clearly we can't do anything.
- But it does not seem like this to the apparent person.
- We can investigate the apparent self and world to see through the illusion.
- But we can only investigate the objective, not the investigating subject.
- The mind is usually ill-prepared and misses the simple truth.
- Some teachers only provide the psychological benefit that the seeker wants.
- Whilst ignorance remains, effort is need to remove it.

Spiritual Experience

- Spiritual experiences have nothing to do with Self-realization.
- Who we are is prior to any experience. The Self cannot be experienced.

Spiritual Paths

- Effort is needed to eliminate the mistaken ideas that obscure the Truth.

- Neo-Advaita claims that nothing can help bring about enlightenment. We must already be who we are so there can be no future realization event.
- Doing nothing does not bring about enlightenment either.
- There are dangers of the "seeker ego" and following a path for its own sake.
- As long as we think we are limited, effort is needed to break down habit.
- Within the phenomenal realm, we can eliminate ignorance (bhrama) by knowledge but not voluntarily awaken from the dream (mAyA).
- Neo-Advaita confuses bhrama and mAyA.
- Traditional Advaita says the mind must be prepared before it is able to accept the wisdom that will eradicate ignorance.

Prerequisites

- The preliminary requisites are:
  - discrimination (*viveka*)
  - indifference (*vairAgya*)
  - the six-fold virtues: mind control (*shama*), sense control (*dama*), shunning sense-objects (*uparati*), equanimity towards opposites such as pleasure and pain (*titikShA*), faith in the scriptures (*shraddhA*) and concentration (*samAdhAna*)
  - desire for liberation (*mumukShutva*).
- If we are not mentally prepared (an *adhikArin*), we will not recognize the truth (when it falls on our head like Newton's apple).
- Discrimination is needed between transient-eternal, Self and not-Self, seer-seen, equivalent to seeing the ring and knowing it to be really gold.
- The only acceptable desire is to realize the Self. This provides the energy to submit to the above disciplines. All else leads to *saMsAra*.
- Renunciation (*saMnyAsa*) is an action and cannot itself bring realization.

- *vAsanA*-s were created by action so action is needed to remove them.

Yoga-s

- karma yoga is action without attachment to the result in response to the need.
- bhakti yoga is meditation on a deity or mantra. It involves one-pointed devotion to a god, surrendering the ego and attachment to the world.
- The purpose of *j~nAna* yoga is to remove the obstacles to Truth.
- *rAja* yoga is the method of Patanjali, which recognized three levels of aspirant. *aShTA~Nga* yoga, the eightfold path, was for the lowest level.
- *aShTA~Nga* yoga comprises the five *yama*-s or restraints, five *niyama*-s or standards of behavior, posture control (*Asana*), breath control (*prANayAma*), withdrawal of the senses (*pratyAhAra*), concentration (*dhAraNA*), meditation (*dhyAna*) and ultimately *samAdhi*.
- *tapas* is self-discipline of the mind, not allowing it to be distracted.

Mind control

- It is not really possible to "control" the mind since it is only thoughts and feelings proceeding automatically at the phenomenal level.
- It is the nature of the mind to think. The key is in directing attention. Thoughts die without attention.
- Positive traits such as honesty and forgiveness help still the mind whereas negative ones prolong its turmoil.
- The idea of teaching "through silence" is a misunderstanding.

Being in the Present

- There is only ever the present moment.
- "Being in the present" means just being, i.e. not thinking about it. The object of a thought cannot be in the present.

- The clarity and intensity of the experience is proportional to the level of attention and to the absence of thoughts, desire and ego.
- No desire can ever satisfy since the attention is on something that is not present.

Meditation

- Meditation needs a still mind in the present moment without distraction.
- Its traditional purpose is not for "me," nor to relieve stress or improve health.
- The technique of mantra repetition is called japa but contemplation on an object or watching the breathing has the same effect.
- It is effectively mind control, since we know what is coming next – another repetition of the mantra.
- The objective is "bare awareness."
- *OM* is Brahman, representing the Consciousness (*turIya*) that underlies all three states – waking, dreaming and deep sleep.

Satsang

- Satsang (*satsa~Nga*) is association with the wise, seeking truth in the company of like-minded people, ideally guided by a Sage.

shravaNa, manana and nididhyAsana

- The key practices in *j~nAna* yoga are *shravaNa, manana* and *nididhyAsana.*
- *shravaNa* is listening to the scriptures, ideally unfolded by a Sage who fully understands them (*shrotriya*).
- *manana* is reflecting upon what has been heard and *nididhyAsana* is meditating deeply on its meaning, rejecting all untruth.

Scriptures

- Reading scriptures is difficult and prone to error from translation and commentators. It also involves the ego. Hence the need for a *shrotriya.*

- A good teacher speaks at the level of the student's understanding. Listening to a guru allows Truth to arise directly, dissolving the ego.
- *shruti* is the ultimate authority.
- The method of *bhAga tyAga lakShaNa* cancels out the apparent contradictions between "I" and "Brahman" and demonstrates that I must be that – *tat tvam asi.*

Sound and Language

- Words manifest at *vaikharI* (spoken or written level), express the visualized ideas of *pashyantI* in the medium (*madhyamA*) of sound or vision. The transcendent, causal truth (*parA*) behind the idea cannot be expressed.
- Language differentiates the underlying unity by applying names to forms. Naming also implies a "namer."
- Our use of nouns and adjectives is frequently confused.
- Adjectives describe attributes of an underlying substantive. "Wooden table" should really be "tably wood." A true substantive cannot be an attribute.
- Ultimately, everything is Brahman. The source is always present, simply hidden by name and appearance.

Guru-Disciple Relationship

- There is no independent, enlightened teacher separate from ourselves. The guru merely guides us to the truth that is already present.
- There is a danger of the disciple using the knowledge to bolster the ego in the absence of a guru.
- Most seekers don't want "enlightenment" but (psychological) improvement to their lives.
- The traditional relationship involves surrender of the disciple to the guru. Most western relationships are casual and lacking commitment.

- The purpose of the teacher is not to make us happy but to bring about the realization that we are happiness.

Self-Enquiry

- Self-enquiry is asking the question "Who am I?" but not in expectation of an answer at the level of the mind.
- The notion of "I" is only a mental disposition; the mind cannot know the true Self.
- The purpose of self-enquiry is to uncover the ego and thereby eliminate it.
- When the "I thought" disappears, that is *samAdhi*. When it disappears forever, that is Self-realization.

6. WHO I REALLY AM

This chapter briefly reviews who we are not before discussing what is meant by enlightenment. It is recognized that we must already be who we are, so that the idea of doing something to realize this at some future date must be in error. We need not and cannot do anything. Enlightenment seems to happen as a result of "grace" and subsequently everything is known to be the Self. The notion of "levels" of enlightenment is examined and the three states of consciousness are analyzed to see what light they shed on our true nature. It is shown how the states arise within the Self but do not affect it. Our true nature is the background to these states - *turīya*. The behavior of a "realized man" is considered. Ultimately, the Self cannot be described, being prior to mind. The reality is unmanifest.

The insight, the final, supreme insight that you are not just a little fragment is called "Self realization" in the Advaita tradition. **Jan Koehoorn** (Ref. 151)

If you have ever been asked whether or not you believe in God, you may well have realized that it is impossible to answer this question without first establishing what the questioner means by the word "God." The same applies when you consider the question "Who am I really?" This is a question that almost requires an understanding of the answer before it can be asked. If what is meant is "Who am I, the ego, that which I have always thought myself to be?" the answer has to be: "You do not exist, and never have." This is why many seekers encounter difficulties when they visit a teacher. What they actually want is to feel good about themselves or to discover how to ensure that they will survive the death of their bodies.

Traditional Advaita understands these problems and the teaching aims to disenchant such seekers of their mistaken beliefs in a gradual manner so as not to cause unnecessary suffering. There is another danger here, however, in that the modern ego does not like to be told that it is in some way "not ready" for the final teaching and must approach it gradually. "What is the bottom line?" is a popular cliché; "Give it to me straight" is another. And neo-Advaitin teachers do just this: "This is it; you do not exist; there is nowhere to go; there is nothing to be taught." All this is true from the standpoint of the absolute truth but of no help whatsoever to the majority of *jIva*-s, identified with their idea of being individual persons, seeking some truth about the world and their life and death.

Hence the practical value of models such as that of the *kosha*-s or sheaths discussed in the early chapters. As part of the process of finding out who I really am, it is natural to progress through these levels of understanding. Initially, I genuinely believe that I am the body and that I will cease to exist when the body of food becomes food for something else. Ultimately it is revealed that there is no *thing* that is essentially me; that the ego is no more than an idea, a set of thoughts/emotions/desires etc. that is constantly changing and which is given significance only as a result of ignorance.

To the extent that the question has any meaning, then, the answer is not at all palatable to the ego and has to be approached circumspectly. We will begin with a brief review.

Review of Who We Are Not

The one which is listening, which you do not know, is you, and the one which you know as you, you are not. **Nisargadatta Maharaj** (Ref. 129)

In chapter 1, we looked at the various identifications that we have mistakenly formed with body, mind and intellect and established that we are not the body, feeler or thinker. Then we examined the ideas of karma and free will and concluded that we are not a doer, either. Finally, in the chapter on meaning and happiness, we were hopefully convinced that we are not an enjoyer. Behind all of these identities, there is an ever-present, unchanging witness, and (at least for the moment), it is that which most nearly approaches who we truly are. We see the body getting older and less healthy but that which sees this happening is the same as it always was. The memory becomes less reliable; the processing of data becomes more laborious, reactions slower and the intellect less incisive. Yet throughout all of this, the essential "I" remains as young-old as it ever was, unaffected by the coarse body or subtler senses and brain mechanisms. As **Atmananda Krishna Menon** explains, we are fundamentally not a "human being":

Are you a human being? Define a human being. A human being is an incongruous mixture of body, senses and mind with the "I"-principle. All except the "I"-principle are changing every moment. But you will admit that you are that "I"-principle. You, as that "I"-principle, stand as the permanent background connecting all these changes that come and go. That "I"- principle is distinct and separate from the changing body, senses and mind. Where is the human being in your deep sleep, when you have no body, senses or mind? Certainly nowhere. Still "you" are there, as that "I"-principle. Therefore you are not a human being but a changeless, permanent principle. As such, you can very well understand that Truth, beyond. (Ref. Note 1085)

The problem of language was introduced in the last chapter where it was pointed out that we use adjectives and nouns in a misleading way, thereby imputing substance to what are really only attributes (as in the example of "gold ring" instead of "ringy gold"). We do the same when we name these bodies. This accords a spurious individuality to what is nothing more than a form of earth. **Monica Alderton**:

Having created this fictitious person/ego/psychological sense of self, the Source/God then proceeds to further muddy the waters and expand the silliness by allowing us each to have a name. As Michael suggests, I am hot, I am not, I am cold, I am depressed, but Michael is always Michael?? The name seems to cement the character; give it a continuity it does not deserve. The "I"-s and the "Me"-s are legion. If we dispensed with the name of the character the game would be more transparent. (Ref. 272)

According to traditional Advaita, as expounded by **Swami Chinmayananda**, the mistakes that lead us into the assumption of duality take place at three levels. The body takes on the role of a "perceiver" through the sense organs and this leads to the belief that there are separate "objects" in the "outside world." The mind acts as a "feeler" sensing internal "emotions" and the intellect believes itself to be a "thinker" of "thoughts." Both feelings and thoughts are, of course, identified as being "mine" and they are different from "yours."

Thus, traditional teachings actually differentiate the "gross," "subtle" and "causal" bodies. Since "everything is Brahman," this must apply to bodies too, dead or alive, but the gross body, *sthUla sharIra*, referring to the physical body made of food, is not in itself sentient. That aspect which is responsible for sensing, doing, feeling and thinking is called the subtle body, *sUkShma sharIra*. This is also called the *li~Nga sharIra*, where *li~Nga* means "mark, sign, badge etc." because its presence is a sign that the *jIva* is present in the body. All activities take place through the medium of the subtle body, although this is only possible because of the *Atman*. A metaphor for this is that of the light bulb and electricity - on its own, the light bulb can do nothing. It is the electricity together with the bulb that enables the light. (The causal body, *kAraNa sharIra*, is *mAyA* but this is one of the subjects of the next chapter.)

The cause of all of this is the accumulation of *vAsanA*-s from our past *karma* and this mistaken outlook on life will continue until these *vAsanA*-s are exhausted.

Thoughts of bondage and of freedom last only as long as one feels, "I am bound." When one inquires of oneself, "Who am I, the bound one?" the Self, Eternal, ever free, remains. The thought of bondage goes; and with it goes the thought of freedom too. **Ramana Maharshi** (Ref. 110, verse 39).

The bottom line is that we are not any of these "things" that we may think ourselves to be. We are the subject, mistakenly taking ourselves to be an object. The attitude has to be that, if we can perceive or conceive it, then we cannot be it. As we progress through the successive levels of the sheath model, the sensed object becomes increasingly subtle and more intimate so that the identification is more ingrained and difficult to overcome. But all of this must be seen through if the intuition into our true nature is to grow. **Aja Thomas** explains:

> Guess What? It's all an illusion - the ego, the world, the suffering, the happiness. It is all a dream state, being dreamed in a cosmic dream. When you abandon the body/mind, what is left? When you give up all identification, what remains? It is only I Am, without any identification. It is the I Am that becomes identified. So first revert to the I Am without identification. Dwell in that and see where it comes from. From what does I Am arise? Even the I Am has no location. It is not located within space and time. You cannot find its beginning or end. It is only consciousness without objects. It is the infinite subjective state without a sense of other. Remove all else and dwell in that. Do not think about it, but simply reside in that absolute consciousness. As one sinks deeper (surrenders) into that pure awareness, even the sense of I Am begins to dissolve, for even it is a part of the dream. There is only empty awareness of non-being. It is pure existence, awareness and, yes, bliss. This is the state which you actually are, always have been and always will be. (Ref. 93)

Becoming Enlightened

Enlightenment is the sudden recognition that non-duality is, has always been, and will always be the reality of our experience. **Francis Lucille** (Ref. 274)

To the extent that "becoming enlightened" has any meaning, it refers to the transition from the position of believing oneself to be a person – body, mind etc. as already described earlier – to the position of knowing that there is only the non-dual Self; that there are no persons, objects, world, thoughts etc. that are ever separate from That. This is a very crude picture that necessarily falls short of the truth. There will be many more quotations from more worthy sources in this chapter so that perhaps the many inadequate attempts will add up to something slightly less inadequate.

The Self is already "enlightened." There is nothing that can or need be done to alter this fact. The problem is simply the mind and, in its ignorance, the identification with something limited, be it mind, body, role or whatever. Accordingly, to remove that ignorance, knowledge is needed and this process is all at the level of mind in the phenomenal world. When sufficient knowledge has been acquired, the ignorance is dissolved and the mind realizes that already existent truth. But nothing has actually changed.

Possibly a metaphor from the Zen tradition is as good as any, describing enlightenment as "the gateless gate." From the viewpoint of the seeker, there appears to be a gate through which one must pass in order to "become enlightened" but, from the viewpoint of the "realized man" looking back, there never was a gate. Enlightenment is gaining the knowledge that we are already free.

Advaita is not about attaining any state. Its path leaves no trace because it is going from Here to Here. **Chittaranjan Naik** (Ref. 276)

Believing that we are not enlightened, we are necessarily imagining enlightenment to be a "state," something that will be achieved or gained at some future time (if we are good, practice meditation regularly etc. or if we meet the right guru who will somehow transmit the knowledge to us). But we have already seen that Advaita defines reality as that which is not bound by time. It must already be the case and therefore cannot be a state. If, during the process of seeking, we encounter novel states of heightened awareness, mental clarity and so on, these can have nothing to do with enlightenment. **Hans Laurentius** explains:

…the realization-experience is often accompanied by one or more sensational "states" that are naturally temporary, as is every state. An experience of realization is after all an experience, and what it is really about is to realize that which is not a temporary, experiential state. Often, the experience that can be seen as a guiding phenomenon is mistaken for the realization. Periods of great clarity or being soaked through by intense joy or love are of course very impressive, but too soon we have the idea that having similar experiences is the permanent state of the "'realized," which is naturally not correct. (Ref. 275)

As the neo-Advaitins continually remind us, we already are. That, as is everything else. Becoming "enlightened" does not change this already-existing fact. All that changes is the way that "we," i.e. the mind that we currently think we are, looks at things. **Ranjit Maharaj** explains:

You have become the gross body because only one body is the object of your concept. The servants and the attendants should be considered as God. There is no other Brahman with or without quality. All is Govinda (God). Because we categorize all objects, there is the ego (*jIva*). You perceive the wife as wife, the daughter as daughter, the horse as horse or the dog as dog. They are all Brahman only. There is no need to change the form of the objects. Only the attitude of the seer must change. Brahman is the same even when it is in a state with attributes. You should see Brahman in whatever state He exists. Even the atoms and molecules of a chair are all Lord Krishna (Brahman). Once this attitude is taken, then he himself is Brahman. Even though one sleeps, awakens, or goes about, one has not slept, awakened, gone about or taken a meal. When all is Brahman who is eating and sleeping? The one who is without quality and the one who is speaking (i.e. with quality) are both God. Whether a king is sitting on the throne or hunting, he is always a king. (Ref. 277)

In a very real sense, there is nothing to be done. Advaita means "not two" – the non-dual reality must be now; it cannot be any "state" to be attained through practice at some time in the future. This fact is reiterated by all sources. Here is **Ramana Maharshi** on the subject:

Realization is nothing to be gained afresh; it is already there. All that is necessary is to get rid of the thought "I have not realized." Stillness or peace is realization. There is no moment when the Self is not. So long as there is doubt or the feeling of non-realization, the attempt should be made to rid oneself of these thoughts. They are due to the identification of the Self with the not-Self. When the not-Self disappears, the Self alone remains. To make room, it is enough that objects be removed. Room is not brought in from elsewhere. (Ref. 278)

The metaphor of space is a useful one and many other teachers have referred to it. Here is another example from **Justus Kramer Schippers**:

The problem lies in the fact that enlightenment is not something that is added, but is the state that remains when non-enlightenment falls off or is dropped. What remains after you move all the furniture out of your room? Right! Space, emptiness, which is needed in order to place furniture. Where was this space? The space was always already present in the room: with or without furniture, the space and emptiness are always there. But, we only notice the space when the furniture is removed.

Something like that happens with enlightenment. Enlightenment is always there, it is the background, the space, the emptiness, that we are and from which we witness the non-empty. Nothing can be said about emptiness: it has no dimensions, you can't take hold of it, you can't understand it, or contain it, it has no properties, doesn't weigh anything, there is absolutely no way to perceive it. But nevertheless, it is a necessary condition for creating objects in the emptiness, if we want to perceive anything at all. (Ref. 279)

There is not therefore anything that we can actually do to bring about this already existing fact. **Anthony De Mello** amusingly relates this paradoxical situation:

"What can I do to attain Enlightenment?" asked the eager disciple.

"See Reality as it is," said the Master.

"Well, what can I do to see Reality as it is?"

The Master smiled and said, "I have good news and bad news for you, my friend."

"What's the bad news?"

"There's nothing you can do to see - it's a gift."

"And what's the good news?"

"There's nothing you can to do see - it's a gift." (Ref. 280)

Anything that is perceived or conceived is objective; a transient event in time and/or space. Who we actually are is the subject. We are already That. There is nowhere to go. In order to know something, we have to stand apart from that which is known. If we claim to have some "knowledge" of the truth (of self-realization) therefore, this must be false since the claim is still at the level of duality. Here is **Karl Renz**:

People come to find a way out and I show them that there is no way out. They may come to see that the idea of a way out occurs because of the belief that there is one "who needs a way out." If I show them that what they are has no need of anything, and that there is no necessity to leave what they already are, they may directly see that whatever they cognize is not what they are. Without the absolute perceiver nothing would be present. Even the relative perceiver, the person, is part of the act of perception. The ideas of a perceiver, the act of perceiving, and the object perceived is only just a part of this realization. Although the unfolding is a functioning of the Self, the Self is always absolute stillness and is untouched by any unfolding. Ultimately, there is no unfolding of anything, even this is a concept. Ramana Maharshi said that you use one concept to remove another concept, and then both are discarded. All of this is just to see that what you are is not a concept. And this absolute experience is seen when you are in total emptiness; then there is no second. When there is nothing to perceive, what remains is still what you are. In this total emptiness, it is not possible to say if you are or you are not. So you exist even without an idea or perception of anything. You remain what you are even when the sensation of being "you" no longer exists. (Ref. 284)

Ultimately, there can be no totally satisfactory answer to explain why it is that we do not realize this truth that must necessarily already be the case now. Any answer would be at the level of mind and it is mind that is the problem. It is only when this mistaken view of the world is sublated, and the delusion of *mAyA* is seen through that there is seen never to have been a problem. Here is **Ramana Maharshi** again:

Our real nature is *mukti* (liberation). But we are imagining that we are bound and are making various strenuous attempts to become free, while we are all the time free. This will be understood only when we reach that stage. We will be surprised that we frantically were trying to attain something which we have always been and are.

An illustration will make this clear. A man goes to sleep in this hall. He dreams he has gone on a world tour, is roaming over hill and dale, forest and country, desert and sea, across various continents and, after many years of weary and strenuous travel returns to this country and walks into this hall.

Just at that moment he wakes up and finds he has not moved an inch, but was sleeping where he lay down. He has not returned after great effort to the hall but is and always has been in the hall. It is exactly like that. If it be asked why being free we imagine we are bound, I answer "Why being in this hall did you imagine you were on a world adventure, crossing hill, dale, desert and sea?" It is all mind or *mAyA* (the world illusion). (Ref. 302)

Is simply hearing the truth sufficient?

Only when we realize that we are free can we appreciate that we were never bound. The immediate experience of the seeker is that he *is* limited, trapped in a body and mind with desires and suffering, and no amount of simple repetition of the truth is going to make any difference. Telling me that I am enlightened does not make me enlightened. There is a fundamental and seemingly impenetrable layer of ignorance obscuring the truth and the only sure way of removing it is to chip away at it from as many angles as possible. This is why the slow but sure approach of the traditional methods may succeed when the blunderbuss attack of modern teaching does not.

Furthermore, what a traditional teacher says is invariably reinforced by relevant quotations from the scriptures, whereas modern teachers often openly despise scriptures and stand on their own authority alone for what they say. When what they say is so contrary to everyday experience – my own experience – why should I believe what they say? The real purpose of a teacher, according to traditional Advaita is to enable me to bridge the gap between who I currently think I am and what the scriptures say I truly am. Simply being told that I am already the non-dual reality does not achieve this.

All of this points back to the need for the spiritual practices that were outlined in the previous chapter. We need to prepare the mind, find a teacher, listen to the truth of the scriptures with a quiet, attentive mind, reflect on these at length, discuss further with an enlightened teacher and meditate on the ideas that have been revealed. Slowly, through such a process, the false ideas are overturned and eventually the truth stands revealed.

Reality is (by definition) that which does not change in any of the three periods of time. (Time is, in any case, an invention of the mind, which is also non-real.) Enlightenment is always and irrevocably knowing that there is only the non-dual reality and that the world is simply an appearance - the bracelet that is always only gold. There can be no slipping in and out. And of course, since reality does not change, it is already the case. We are already realized (we just don't realize it). "Becoming" enlightened is simply gaining this knowledge or, to be pedantic, uncovering the ignorance that obscured it.

Realization is not *of* the mind but *from* the mind. Otherwise realization would cease in dream and deep sleep and would therefore come and go and therefore, by definition, would not be real.

Grace

Another way in which traditional teachings differ from those of neo-Advaita is in the belief that divine intervention or dispensation is required in order to promote enlightenment.

From the standpoint of reality, there can be no meaning to any such concept (but then there are no meanings and no concepts there either). In the relative or phenomenal realm, where there still appears to be a separate person, there is also the delusion that there is duality. Within that seeming state of ignorance, there may also be occasional glimpses of how things must really be. These can be interpreted as momentary falling away of the ignorance or as momentary illumination by Consciousness, in much the same way as temporary sunny spells in an otherwise cloudy day may be seen as clouds breaking up or sun breaking through.

"Grace" is a word frequently used for such an occurrence, whether the illumination is temporary or permanent. Even in the case of those for whom religious connotations are repugnant it is not altogether unhelpful because it does carry the sense of something that is outside of our control. The Christian sense is of "the free and unmerited favour of God," according to the Oxford English Dictionary. It is understandable that the strength of feeling that may accompany such revelations can easily conjure up the sense of a divine intervention. Descriptions of these experiences are frequently given in religious terms throughout traditional teachings. The point is that the sense of ego has to be surrendered before the true nature of Self can be realized and surrender to a provisionally assumed God admirably serves this purpose. **Sri Ramakrishna** explains:

> However much you may try, without God's grace nothing can be attained; He cannot be realized without Divine grace. But Divine grace descends not so easily. You shall have to banish your ego completely from the heart. If you have the egoistic feeling, "I am the doer," you can never see God. If there is somebody in the store-room, and if the owner of the house is asked to fetch a certain thing from the store, he at once says, "Well, there is someone already in the store; please ask him to get

it. There is no need of my going there." God never appears in the heart
of him who thinks himself to be the doer. (Ref. 50)

In reality, enlightenment amounts to the Self "revealing himself to himself,"
since there is only That, temporarily manifesting as ignorance to obscure the
truth. This is expressed in the **Katha Upanishad** (I.ii.23):

> This *Atman* cannot be attained by study of the scriptures, nor by sharp
> intellect, nor by much hearing; by him is It attained whom It chooses –
> to him this *Atman* reveals its own (true) form. (Ref. 285)

Commenting on this verse, **Swami Ranganathananda** provides another
explanation as to why it is not possible to gain enlightenment as the direct
result of spiritual practices alone. He points out that the Atman would have
to be considered an "effect" if it could be brought about as a result of
meditation or other practice. If this were so, then it could not be eternal,
since effects do not exist prior to their causes. Furthermore, to use the
metaphor of light, a torch could never illuminate the sun. Similarly, a no
matter how powerful the mind or profound the meditation, these could never
reveal the Atman.

The implication is that, effectively, the Atman "reveals itself" when the
moment is right or, as **Ram K. Piparaiya** puts it (commenting on the
Mundaka Upanishad III.ii.3) (Ref. 286): "the Self naturally chooses one
whose heart is wholly purified and ready to receive the revelation."

S. Radhakrishnan, commenting on the verse from the Katha
Upanishad, says that, although spiritual practice is of value in the early
stages, the "experience" of the Self only comes about as a result of Grace:

> If man becomes aware of God's presence in the soul, it is due to God's
> own working in the soul. It is beyond the power of unassisted nature...
> If a man is to escape from himself as he actually is and reach the
> perfection for which he is made, he needs a transforming force within.
> The seeker feels that this force issues not out of his own natural self but

enters into him from beyond. (Ref. 287)

As with much of the teaching of Advaita, there is a paradox and, despite observations to the contrary, the clear advice of traditional teachers to seekers whose understanding is, after all, still very much at the phenomenal level, is that self-effort *is* necessary. **Swami Venkatesananda** comments as follows:

> When engaged in an enquiry into the nature of the truth concerning the world, oneself, relationship and why the relationship exists, where does the answer come from? In olden days especially, it was usual to insist upon revelation. The truth was always revealed through a divine mystery, a divine dispensation, divine grace. Vasishtha has one of the most brilliant responses to this. He says: "What do you know about grace? Nothing. Do you believe in the existence of God who whispers into your ears? Nonsense! Drop it. Did some God serve you dinner, or did your wife or somebody else prepare it and give it you? Self-effort - that is what counts, nothing else counts. Dismiss all these speculations and enquire into it afresh." (Ref. 288)

The "Experience" of Enlightenment

> *(Enlightenment) is not a personal event because it is the disappearance of the person, like awakening after a dream. Sages say this is a non-event because it does not happen in time and space since they both disappear upon awakening. The sage knows that space-time is nothing but a concept that is part of the dream.* **Stanley Sobottka** (Ref. 304)

When the realization "event" (or as neo-Advaitins often refer to it – "non-event") occurs, it has to be said that, really, "nothing ever happened," a phrase often associated with Sri Poonja. **Wayne Liquorman** says:

> Yes, that point, that moment when the ME completely dissolved is a historical moment in the history of the organism. What happened in that

moment we can point to and allegorically say, "There was then the realization; there was then seen that there is no separation." But that is not really accurate! In that moment the whole paradigm, the whole question, is dissolved! A false idea disappears, and nothing literally changes. And so the most precise thing you can say is that nothing happened! (Ref. 235)

But what can be said is that the various levels of identification that might have been present before this (non-)event are no longer present afterwards. Every "thing" is then seen as merely another form of the Self, arising in the Self. This is experienced as a loss of all previously perceived limitations. **Adyashanti** says that:

As long as you identify yourself with the projection of separateness, you will continue to deny that you are the Source of all projections. When you truly and absolutely awaken to this fact, and comprehend the overwhelming implications inherent within this awakening, you will continually experience that all apparently personal relationships are in truth nothing other than the play of your Self. To realize that the personal me is an illusion born of false identification with the body, thoughts, and emotions, brings a profound sense of freedom. This is fundamentally the realization of emptiness, of what you are not. But contained within the realization of emptiness (formlessness) is also the realization of what you ARE. In the most absolute sense you ARE this conscious emptiness which is the source of all appearances (existence). But you are the appearance as well. Not just one part of the appearance called "me," but all of it, the entire whole. This is the challenge, to let your view get this vast. To let your view get so vast that your identity disappears. Then you realize that there is no other, and there is nothing personal going on. (Ref. 208)

Some of the clearest descriptions of what it means to be "enlightened" are to be found in the last chapter of Ref. 311, by **Ken Wilber**:

You might be looking at a mountain, and you have relaxed into the effortlessness of your own present awareness, and then suddenly the mountain is all, you are nothing. Your separate-self sense is suddenly and totally gone, and there is simply everything that is arising moment to moment. You are perfectly aware, perfectly conscious, everything seems completely normal, except you are nowhere to be found. You are not on this side of your face looking at the mountain out there; you simply are the mountain, you are the sky, you are the clouds, you are everything that is arising moment to moment, very simply, very clearly, just so...

In other words, the ultimate reality is not something seen, but rather the ever-present Seer. Things that are seen come and go, are happy or sad, pleasant or painful - but the Seer is none of those things, and it does not come and go. The Witness does not waver, does not wobble, does not enter that stream of time. The Witness is not an object, not a thing seen, but the ever-present Seer of all things, the simple Witness that is the I of Spirit, the center of the cyclone, the opening that is God, the clearing that is pure Emptiness.

There is never a time that you do not have access to this Witnessing awareness. At every single moment, there is a spontaneous awareness of whatever happens to be present - and that simple, spontaneous, effortless awareness is ever-present Spirit itself. Even if you think you don't see it, that very awareness is it. And thus, the ultimate state of consciousness - intrinsic Spirit itself - *is not hard to reach but impossible to avoid.* †
(Ref. 311)

Leo Hartong uses the metaphor of two puppets having an argument about whether or not they exist. Of course they do not exist at all as separate entities. The words that they seem to speak to each other are those of the puppeteer. He goes on to explain that:

---

† From The Eye of Spirit, by Ken Wilber, ©1997. Reprinted by arrangement with Shambhala Publications, Inc., Boston, www.shambhala.com

The above is not meant to say that we are mere puppets. It says that we are *that* which appears *as* the puppets. To use another metaphor, you are the actor and not the role. Someone who sees his limited role or ego as reality is like a hypnotized actor playing a villain and becoming so absorbed in his play that he has forgotten who he really is. When he is released from the hypnotic illusion, he sees that the villain never existed. It would be incorrect to say that the villain has realized that he is, in fact, the actor. It is the actor who sees that he is not, nor ever was, the villain. Nothing will prevent him from continuing in his role, but he will no longer think of himself as the villain. (Ref. 22)

The mistaken ideas that we are bodies or minds are lost and replaced by the clear knowledge that we are That in which all of the perceptions and conceptions arise. This is not to say that the mind disappears – the so-called realized man could hardly continue to function in life if this were the case. It is simply that the ignorant ideas that previously held sway have now been dissolved. The knowledge is now there, in the mind, that we are not those ideas. There remains a functional instinct that will act to preserve the body if threatened. Preferences will continue to arise as before but there is now no attachment to any of these thoughts nor any vested interest in particular outcomes. The ego has disappeared. Instead, there is the clear understanding that I am That which pervades everything – body, mind, intellect and universe.

There can be no real "levels" of enlightenment - this would be a contradiction of the teaching – but there may appear to be so from the standpoint of the mind. Reality is not a "state," which by definition has a beginning (and an end) in time. Therefore something that could happen in the future, but is not already the case, could not be enlightenment. Similarly, so-called levels of *samAdhi*, the experiences reached in deep meditation, are not enlightenment. There may be a temporary awareness of the non-dual reality but, on return to normal waking consciousness, the ignorance that obscures self-knowledge is still present. Technically, Ramana Maharshi referred to the natural condition of full self-awareness without effort as *sahaja nirvikalpa samAdhi* but *sahaja sthiti* is a less confusing term, omitting the word *samAdhi* altogether since this carries the sense of deep meditation (i.e. a state).

Similarly, many teachers talk about the "witness" or "witnessing Consciousness" as enlightenment. This, too, cannot be correct since a witness implies something that is witnessed and this is still in the realm of duality. **Dr. Gregory Goode** had the following to say about it:

The witness is a very intuitive and flexible teaching. It is intuitive because it takes advantage of the existing structure of our beliefs, according to which we are limited and separate. It is flexible because it works at every level to dismantle this structure.

The witness teaching can be used to experience that the body does not sense anything, but is instead a collection of witnessed sensations. At that point you can no longer take yourself as limited to a body.

The witness teaching can also be used to experience that the mind does not actually think or believe anything. Rather, thinking and believing are themselves witnessed objects, as is the mind. When you see that the mind is *witnessed* instead of being the witness, you can no longer take yourself as limited to a mind. Your being no longer feels physically or psychologically limited.

In a more subtle way, the teaching can be used to experience that you are never separate or localized. In this sense the word "witness" can never be plural! And as inseparable from everything, you lack nothing.

The different kinds of witness teachings can be distinguished as levels of what I'd call a "thin witness" and a "thick witness." A thin witness is the kind spoken of above. It is effortless, it has no psychological characteristics, it can never be lost, and it never needs to be maintained or practiced. For many people, this teaching sounds very impressive, but too subtle to get hold of.

A less subtle version is the "thick witness." This is a witness with psychological characteristics. This is the kind of witness spoken about by many neo-advaita teachers. The thick witness sees what arises. But it has other properties as well. It takes effort to maintain, like a state of mind. It feels like you're in the flow, as long as things are going well. It feels like you lost something, when things are not going well. To hear some teachers speaking, it sounds like each person has his own separate witness. This is easier to understand than the thin witness teaching, but also leaves more of a residue that needs to be investigated later.

Of course the witness teaching is a dualistic model. But the brilliance of the model is its own self-destruction. As soon as it is understood deeply and intuitively, then the model collapses under its own weight. With total clarity that there can be no objects outside of awareness, then it truly makes no sense to speak of "witnessed" objects in the first place. The subtle dualistic structure of witness/witnessed dissolves into awareness – which is your nature itself, shining with no subjects or objects. (Ref. 355)

The appearance of "levels" of enlightenment in the mind is spoken of by **Nisargadatta Maharaj**, referring to the story of King Janaka and his dream. On awakening, Janaka wondered whether he was a king who had dreamt that he was a beggar or a beggar who was now dreaming that he was a king. After talking to his guru, he realized that he was neither, being instead the unchanging witness of these transient states. But Nisargadatta goes on to point out:

This is your last illusion that you are a *j~nAnI*, that you are different from, and superior to, the common man. Again you identify yourself with your mind, in this case a well-behaved and in every way an exemplary mind. As long as you see the least difference, you are a stranger to reality. You are on the level of the mind. When the "I am myself" goes, the "I am all" comes. When the "I am all" goes, "I am" comes. When even "I am" goes, reality alone *is* and in it every "I am" is preserved and glorified. Diversity without separateness is the Ultimate that the mind can touch. Beyond that all activity ceases, because in it all goals are reached and all purposes fulfilled. (Ref. 5)

The first "level" is that with which everyone is familiar – believing that we are the ego or mind with a separate outside world. Once this teaching is encountered, the mind may come to understand that "everything is brahman" and "I am That" – but this is initially only at the level of the mind. **Möller de la Rouvière** points out that:

> Mind then projects a vision of what it believes wholeness is and comes to the conclusion that "I am all." Here the delusion of separation is not so apparent because while we are absorbed in the mind, any projection of mind as wholeness appears to us as wholeness itself. (Ref. 303)

This is a subtler stage of mental delusion, which may be erroneously perceived as enlightenment. But thoughts are forms of Consciousness and not reality itself. **De la Rouvière** asks: "Does your enlightenment exist as a living truth when thought is not around to confirm its own projection about 'your' (note the dualism) non-dual state?'"

The third "level" is when we cease to identify with this thought of being everything and rest simply in the thought "I am." This is the subtlest thought of all – but still only a thought. As has been mentioned above, being a "witness" is still in the realm of duality. The mind is still in control and further resolution is required. **De la Rouvière** concludes:

> They begin to observe the workings of thought, attention, awareness, identification and so on. And with correct guidance and a dedicated heart, it may gradually dawn on such a person that mind is the slayer of truth; that no aspect of mind could be trusted to allow for the revelation of the natural non-dual condition of the living moment. This has to be re-cognized, understood and gradually transcended. At this point the whole thing begins to relax and when the entire process of seeking and projection begins to fragment and starts to fall away by non-use, and the instruments of delusion no longer function in unawareness, "reality alone" begins to shine through the fog of confusion and self-delusion. Here no sense of "I" exists. "There is only This." (Ref. 303)

States of Consciousness

This is a topic that has not yet been discussed and which may at first sight appear out of place in this chapter. However, an analysis of this does in fact throw much light on the subject of who we really are. It is called *avasthA-traya prakriyA* – "the method of the three states of consciousness."

Waking and Dreaming

The key fact to appreciate is that, whenever we think or talk about this subject we inevitably do so from the vantage point of the waking state, so that what we say about dreaming and deep sleep is biased to say the least. We all naturally believe that we exist in a real world and, indeed, this is how it appears in our waking state. But, in dreaming, the external world is replaced entirely by one that clearly originates in our mind, whilst in deep sleep there is no world at all.

A more logical stance is that taken by the western philosopher, Bishop George Berkeley, who argued that there is no world independent of ideas. The very concept of a physical substance that can be "known" by the mind makes no sense so is not worthy of consideration. (Note that this not the position of Advaita.) After all, our sensory experiences all take place within the brain after conversion of supposed external data by the sense organs. We do not see an apple. Instead, light (which is assumed to have been reflected from the putative apple) is translated into nerve impulses and these are then deciphered by various functions in the brain. It is not at all unreasonable to claim that the world is in the mind rather than the other way round. (This is the western theory of Idealism, recognized in Hindu philosophies hundreds of years earlier as *vij~nAna vAda*.)

When we begin to look at things in ways such as this, it no longer seems entirely absurd to suppose that the world ceases to exist when we sleep or dream. We do not, after all, claim that the worlds of our dreams continue to exist when we wake up. Waking and world go together – it is not meaningful to speak of one without the other. When we go to sleep, the world invariably disappears and only appears on waking (we cannot say "re-appears," since we only have the waking state to argue that it is the same one that was there before). And why should we rely upon the reports of others, since they too only exist in the waking state? We could equally well say, from the standpoint of the deep sleep state, that no world ever appears there so that therefore no world appears in the waking state either.

If we look at it objectively, the characteristics of waking and dreaming are similar. In both, there are apparent objects and apparent individuals performing actions according to laws of cause and effect and benefiting (or not) thereby. It may well be that, from the standpoint of the waking state, we deem the actions and outcomes in the dream to be illogical but they were perfectly acceptable and "normal" at the time of the dream. In fact, we would never accept (in the dreaming state) any claim that we were "only dreaming" and that there was some higher state of reality that was the "real" waking state.

"Sailor" Bob Adamson was asked if the apparent reality is no more substantial than a dream. His response was:

> No! It is not. It is no more substantial. You carry on in the dream, doing all sorts of activities, but where is the dream figure when you wake up? If you went to sleep every night and then dreamed, and the dream carried on from where it left off the previous night, would you be able to tell the difference between this and the waking state? (Ref. 9)

Any object or benefit gained in the dream world is certainly not carried over to the waking world but then this applies in the other direction, too. **Radhakrishnan** comments on the Chandogya Upanishad VIII sections 2 - 5:

> All these fulfilled desires are real at their own level. They are not to be dismissed as false or unreal. Even dreams are unreal only in relation to what we see when we are awake. (Ref. 287)

The notion of the world being a "projection" of the mind is often represented by the metaphor of a cinema screen, as **Ramana Maharshi** explains:

Just as the pictures appear on the screen as long as the film throws the shadows through the lens, so the phenomenal world will continue to appear to the individual in the waking and dream states as long as there are latent mental impressions. Just as the lens magnifies the tiny specks on the film to a huge size and as a number of pictures are shown in a second, so the mind enlarges the sprout-like tendencies into tree-like thoughts and shows in a second innumerable worlds. Again, just as there is only the light of the lamp visible when there is no film, so the Self alone shines without the triple factors when the mental concepts in the form of tendencies are absent in the states of deep sleep, swoon and *samAdhi*. Just as the lamp illumines the lens, etc., while remaining unaffected, the Self illumines the ego (*chidAbhAsa*), etc., while remaining unaffected. (Ref. 290)

The three states are unarguably separate states from the standpoint of the phenomenal world, with each having its own characteristics and apparent "ego." The waking state is called *jAgrat*, with its waking ego of *vishva* (literally meaning "whole, entire," because the individual person seems to be "complete"), also referred to as *vaishvAnara* (literally "relating to or belonging to all men"). The dreaming state is *svapna*, with the dreaming-ego *taijasa*, literally "consisting of light." *svapna* also means sleeping but it is only the body that sleeps in this state – the mind is very active, constructing its own world out of itself, complete with its own space, time and causality. The true sleeping state – deep sleep - is called *suShupti* and the sleeper is *prAj~na*. In this state, both body and mind are inactive and time apparently stands still. It is the mind that, upon waking, claims that the deep-sleep experience was a blank since it was not present at the time. But clearly the Self must have been there – indeed it is never absent.

These three states, then, are a well know fact of life and, if we are to know who we truly are, they must all be taken into consideration. It would not do to consider the waking state alone – this would merely be *vishva* doing the considering. We say that "I" continue to exist in all three states but what we usually mean is that I, the waking ego, seem to re-appear on awakening and to be the same "me" as the one who went to sleep. But this belief stems from memory and in any case relates to the ego that is only a construction of the mind. What of the *taijasa* – the ego that dreams its seemingly self-consistent worlds that differ radically from this waking appearance? And can we say anything at all (from the vantage point of the waking ego) about *prAj~na*?

This viewpoint explains many seeming paradoxes in Advaita. One of these is the problem of the seeker looking for the truth. Both seeker and his supposed truth are within the waking world – a subject and objects in a necessary and perennial duality. "Who we are" is not this waking ego, nor a sleeping ego, nor the *prAj~na*. We are that which witnesses all of the states or rather, to avoid yet another paradox of duality, that in which all states arise.

Deep Sleep State

The states can be regarded as levels of increasing subtlety. The waking state represents the grossest, physical level with the body looking outwards towards the world of objects in physical space. In dreaming, this physical body is absent and the much more subtle mind creates its own world which occupies no space but changes only according to its own time frame. The imputation of subtlety may be understood in the sense that such activities of the mind as reflection and imagination enable insight into what cannot be directly perceived at the gross level of perception. Deep sleep is yet more subtle without manifestation of any kind and with neither outward nor inward perception. **Ananda Wood** describes this, commenting on the *mANDUkya upaniShad*:

> In the experience of deep sleep, no desires are felt, no objects are conceived, no mental or physical appearances are seen. Viewed through our minds and bodies, the depth of sleep seems blank and dark and empty.

But the Mandukya Upanishad doesn't see it like that. Instead (in stanza 5), it describes the deep sleep state as having come to unity (*ekIbhUta*), as filled with consciousness (*praj~nAna-ghana*), as made of happiness (*Anandamaya*), and as knowing in itself (*prAj~na*). Here, deep sleep is seen from its own point of view, as a positive experience in its own right.

In the waking and dream states, body and mind see differing and changing things. But in deep sleep, body and mind have disappeared. There are no different objects, no conflicting activities. In order to experience anything, body and mind need difference and action. So, from a physical or mental point of view, there is nothing in deep sleep. It seems to be a blank, without experience.

And yet, in actual fact, we do experience deep sleep. It is just that state where our experience is neither physical nor mental. We experience it where all differences and conflicts are dissolved in peace. In its own experience, it is just peace: with no difference or conflict to disturb its unity.

In the peace of sleep, there are no appearances that partly cover knowledge, leaving gaps of ignorance. There is just pure experience: in which no cover up, nor any gaps are known. In that pure consciousness, no desires are frustrated, no dissatisfactions are found. Its essence is unclouded happiness: which all beings seek, through their actions in the world.

For that happiness, all acts are done. (Ref. 291)

We do not lose our consciousness or knowledge, nor do we cease to exist. If we really thought that, is it likely that we would willingly seek sleep? In fact, deep sleep is something to which everyone looks forward. **D. B. Gangolli**:

No one believes too that in deep sleep we become devoid of knowledge or consciousness just like a dry or withered block of wood. Even now the block of wood is not sentient, in the future too, despite whatever attempts, it will not get either its own knowledge or the knowledge of the external objects. But as soon as we wake up from deep sleep we get the knowledge or consciousness of the divisions or distinctions of the type - "I" and "another." Therefore, it cannot be accepted that in deep sleep we existed in an insentient nature or state. To say also that – "There in deep sleep we ourselves became non-existent" - is a ridiculous statement. If anyone had such feeling about deep sleep, why were people showing or entertaining so much eagerness or fervor for such a thing like deep sleep? No one, whosoever he may be, keeps thinking in the manner - "Oh God; If by chance deep sleep accrues to us and if we ourselves become non-existent, then what will be our plight or predicament?" (Ref. 292)

The "experience" of deep sleep is therefore one of non-duality and this is so regardless of whether the person is enlightened. Duality is associated with the mind, with its seeming subject and objects and this is absent in deep sleep. On re-awakening, the seeming duality reasserts itself in the mind of the ignorant because they identify with this mind. It requires an intuitive leap beyond the limited waking ego to see beyond this.

The fact that we still exist in deep sleep (and no one doubts this to be the case) tells us that we cannot be the thoughts or emotions, which are no longer present. This also includes the "I" who seems to have those experiences. That is not present in deep sleep either so that we cannot be that – it, too, must be another thought, belonging to the mind. **Ramana Maharshi** answered an enquiry on the topic as follows:

The man awake says that he did not know anything in the state of sleep. Now he sees the objects and knows that he is there; whereas in deep sleep there were no objects, no spectator, etc. The same one who is now speaking existed in deep sleep also. What is the difference between these two states? There are objects and the play of senses now which were not there in sleep. A new entity, the ego, has risen up in the meantime; it plays through the senses, sees the objects, confounds itself with the body, and says that the Self is the ego. In reality, what was in deep sleep continues to exist even now. The Self is changeless; it is the ego that has intervened. That which rises and sets is the ego; that which remains changeless is the Self. (Ref. 49)

This argument also applies to the world. The classical metaphor, already mentioned, is that of clay and pots. When the pot exists, so too does the clay. But when the pot is broken, the clay still exists. Therefore, we conclude that the clay is real while the pot is only *mithyA*. Similarly, when the world and thoughts are present, we exist and when these are absent, as in deep sleep, we still exist. Consequently, we must conclude that who we really are – the Atman - is real, while the world, including body and mind etc. is *mithyA*. This logical process is called *anvaya vyatireka* (*anvaya* means "connection, association"; *vyatireka* means "distinction, separateness, exclusion").

Pedantically, deep sleep should not really be considered a state since that implies position in space or beginning and end in time. The beginning and end in time relate only to the waking and dreaming states. Though we may later say, in the waking state, that we were in deep sleep between such and such a time, during the deep sleep itself there was no experience of time at all. It is the waking ego who calls it a state. During deep sleep itself, there is no experience at all. Nor does that mean that we experience "nothing." In reality, there is no subject present in deep sleep either. We exist as pure Consciousness.

The *kauShItaka upaniShad* explains how we become one with *brahman* (referred to here as *prANa*, the vital breath) when we sleep and the world etc. springs forth on awakening:

When a person is so asleep that he sees no dream whatever, then he becomes one with that vital breath. Then speech together with all names goes to it; the eye together with all forms goes to it; the ear together with all sounds goes to it; the mind together with all thoughts goes to it. When he awakes, as from a blazing fire sparks would fly in all directions, even so from this self the vital breaths proceed to their respective stations;

from the vital breaths, the gods (the senses); from the gods, the worlds. This same vital breath, the self of intelligence, seizes hold of the body and raises it up. This therefore one should worship as the *uktha* [*verses recited in praise*]. This is the all-obtaining in the vital breath. (Ref. 300)

The fact that we become one with *brahman* in deep sleep is, of course, unknown to most. This has been compared with someone who, having no knowledge of geology etc., walks over a field containing buried gold every day without realizing it. Because, in the waking state, we are bound by *avidyA*, we go into sleep like someone being taken into a beautiful palace wearing a blindfold, says **Gangolli**.

And yet we invariably go willingly into sleep, doing our best to ensure we will be comfortable and undisturbed. Someone who sleeps "well" appears refreshed and at peace, whereas one who slept "badly" or not at all is ill at ease, fractious and impatient for the opportunity to sleep. Though there is no subject or object in deep sleep and therefore no enjoyer and enjoyed in the waking sense, nevertheless we all speak of enjoying sleep and it does seem as though happiness is something that somehow occurs during it. Since this happiness does not come from anything external, it must be an intrinsic aspect of our own nature – *Ananda*.

States, Self and Ego

D. B. Gangolli (Ref. 292) points out that the word "state" is commonly used in two particular ways. It is used to refer, for example, to the degree of ripeness of a fruit. We recognize the fruit when it has just begun to form from the flower and progressively as it grows to full size and then begins to change color and become soft as it ripens. It may then fall from the tree, become over-ripe and finally rot. There is a continual process here but with conventionally identifiable stages. The other way in which we use the term is to denote the position of an object when it moves from A to B, whether this is a bird leaving a tree and flying to another one or the theoretical energy level of an electron. Neither of these seems applicable to the change between waking, dream and deep sleep.

Instead, he says that it is like having a certain sum of money. This might be in the form of a single, high-denomination note, several notes of smaller denomination or in lots of small coins but it is still the same sum of money. Similarly, Brahman appears as waking, dream and deep sleep. Each is nothing but Consciousness alone but appears as a different condition.

There is neither a spatial nor a temporal relationship between the states. It might appear that they take place sequentially in time but, again, this is from the vantage point of waking. The time frame in a dream is totally different from that in waking, with possibly days or years of experience passing in a single dream and there is no sense of time at all during deep sleep. This being the case, it is not reasonable to even speak of a "number" of states – the concept of number only applies in the context of a spatial or temporal frame of reference.

In reality, the apparent states are nothing but the non-dual Self, misperceived in ignorance by the waking mind. *gauDapAda* refers to the metaphor of the rope and the snake in his *kArikA* on the *mANDUkya upaniShad*. The rope might be wrongly seen, not just as a snake, but also as a stream of water or as a crack in the ground. When it is seen as one of these, it is not simultaneously seen as either of the others, just as, when we seem to be awake, we do not at the same time believe ourselves to be dreaming or asleep. But, once it is realized to be a rope, immediately the misperceptions of snake, stream or crack disappear. Similarly, upon Self-realization, the states are no longer witnessed as separate. The waking, dreaming and deep-sleep egos are known to be just appearances.

The *vivekachUDAmaNi* (verse 55) says that, just as the process of identification takes place at the level of the intellectual sheath, *vij~nAnamayakosha*, and it is effectively this that is the thinker, doer, enjoyer, etc., so it is for this alone that the three states exist. Although the Atman enables all of this to take place, it is not affected by any of them. In deep sleep, body mind and the entire universe cease to exist but the Atman remains to witness their absence. Using the definition of "reality" as that which exists in all three periods of time, only the Atman can be real.

There is an excellent metaphor, which I have only encountered in the book by **Arvind Sharma** (Ref. 293), which helps to understand all of this. He supposes that a girl, very much in love, buys a dress to please her boyfriend. While the dress remains lying untouched on a table, she imagines wearing it to go out for a meal with this man, possibly spilling her drink down it, and how he will propose to her. She further imagines keeping it and showing it to her daughter many years later. Throughout all of these daydreams, he says, the experiences relate not to the dress itself, which is still on the table, but to a dress-thought. Similarly, he says, in our experiences of life, those experiences relate to an "I-thought" and not to the real Self. This "I-thought" derives from the real "I" and is powered by it. But it rules our lives, not just for the few minutes of a daydream but often for the entire duration. This "I-thought" is what we usually refer to as the ego.

The metaphor can be extended to shed light on the three states. The girl can have different thoughts about the dress. There is the thought about spilling wine down it and the thought about showing it to her daughter. These thoughts are quite unrelated and, significantly, do not affect the actual dress lying on the table. Similarly, we have the waking ego, the dream ego and the deep-sleep ego. These are similarly independent and do not affect the real Atman that exists throughout. The "ego thoughts" derive from the Atman in the same way that the dress thoughts derive from the dress. Just as the thought about spilling wine does not spoil the actual dress, so the trials and tribulations of the waking ego do not affect the real Self.

turīya

That which is the unchanging basis for the appearance of the states of consciousness is called *turīya*. The word itself means "consisting of four parts" and is usually interpreted as "fourth" but this is not another state. It is the only reality, to which we "awaken" when the truth is realized.

It is described in the **Mandukya Upanishad** (verse 7) as follows:

That is known as the fourth quarter: neither inward-turned nor outward-turned consciousness, nor the two together; not an undifferentiated mass of consciousness; neither knowing, nor unknowing; invisible, ineffable, intangible, devoid of characteristics, inconceivable, indefinable, its sole essence being the consciousness of its own Self; the coming to rest of all relative existence; utterly quiet; peaceful; blissful; without a second; this is Atman, the Self; this is to be realized. (Ref. 373)

Swami Sharvananda (Ref. 296) clarifies that, in this verse, "cognizing the internal subject" refers to the dream state – *taijasa* – and "external objects" refers to the waking state – *vaishvAnara*. *turIya* is not an intermediate state between waking and dream; it is not an indefinite mass of cognition, as deep sleep might be described. Finally, it "should not be identified with God or *Ishvara* who experiences the whole of phenomenal existence in one act of cognition."

turIya is also referred to as the "egoless state" or the "transcendental state." Unlike the deep sleep state, in which our true nature is covered over by ignorance, in *turIya* this is not the case. The *sat-chit-Ananda* is present as before but now it is *known* to be present. There is no longer any ego-process and the three states are seen to be mere appearances upon the one reality of the Self. This is what is referred to by the superficially cryptic verse in the **Bhagavad Gita** (II.69) which states that what is night for all beings is day for the sage and while the rest of the word is awake, it is night for the sage. To the ordinary man, deluded by ignorance, reality is comparable to the darkness of night though the Sage can comprehend it clearly. What the ordinary man perceives as being awake, i.e. seeing the duality and separation of the world is perceived by the Sage as the night of ignorance.

One of the clearest descriptions of *turIya* is given in the anonymous text, highly recommended by Ramana Maharshi, **Ellam Ondre** (originally written in Tamil, this means "All is One"):

6. If you ask what that is, it is called *turIya*, which means the fourth state. Why is this name used? This name is proper because it seems to say the three states of your experience - waking, dream and deep sleep - are foreign to you and your true state is the fourth, which is different

from these three. Should the three states, waking, dream and deep sleep, be taken to form one long dream, the fourth state represents the waking from this dream. Thus it is more withdrawn than deep sleep, also more wakeful than the waking state.

7. Therefore your true state is that fourth one which is distinguished from the waking, dream and deep sleep states. You are that only. What is this fourth state? It is knowledge which does not particularize anything. It is not unaware of itself. That is to say, the fourth state is Pure Knowledge which is not conscious of any object, but not unconscious itself. Only he who has realized it even for a trice, has realized the Truth. You are that only.

8. What is there more for him who has gained the fourth state? Practically, it is not possible for anyone to remain forever in that state, that is, the state of no particular knowledge. He who has realized the fourth state later wakes up in this world, but for him this world is not as before. He sees that what he realized as the fourth state, shines forth as all this. He will not imagine this world as distinct from that Pure Knowledge. Thus what he saw within, he now sees without in a different form. In the place of the differentiation of old, he is now established in the state of non-differentiation everywhere. Now, he is all. There is nothing distinct from himself. His eyes closed or open, howsoever the things may change, his state remains unchanged. This is the state of Brahman. This is the natural eternal state. You are that ever-true state. (Ref. 297)

The Enlightened Man

Liberation does not concern the person, for liberation is freedom from the person. **Jean Klein** (Ref. 19)

It should, by now, be appreciated that the idea of an "enlightened man" is a contradiction in terms. A person cannot become enlightened. For many, this is seen as the ultimate paradox. "I" am studying Advaita in order to gain true knowledge of the Self. The scriptures and sages provide this knowledge. After it has been conveyed and assimilated, there will be a sudden flash of understanding, changing my entire outlook on life and I will be said to be "enlightened." So it seems.

But it cannot be like this. If there is only the Self and no duality, there cannot be an "I" and a "knowledge to be gained." Self must be knower, knowledge and the process of knowing, just as it must be the apparent ignorance that currently exists. Language creates this paradox by misleading us into believing in the duality that is necessarily created by the use of separate words. Fortunately, the judicious use of language may also help us to appreciate how this can be. Here, **David Godman** addresses the question of a realized man or *j~nAnI*:

> The hidden premise behind all such questions is the belief that there is a person (the *j~nAnI*) who experiences a state he calls the Self. This assumption is not true. It is merely a mental construct devised by those who have not realized the Self (*aj~nAnI*-s) to make sense of the *j~nAnI*'s experience. Even the use of the word *j~nAnI* is indicative of this erroneous belief since it literally means a knower of *j~nAna*, the reality. The *aj~nAnI* uses this term because he imagines that the world is made up of seekers of reality and knowers of reality; the truth of the Self is that there are neither *j~nAnI*-s nor *aj~nAnI*-s, there is only *j~nAna*. (Ref. 17)

It is often said that the ego must die before realization can occur. This idea treats the ego as an existing thing, which it is not. As was explained in the first chapter, *ahaMkAra* is rather a process of identification, whereby the Self is mistaken for a body-mind. This "mistaking" is of course being done by the Self, functioning through the body-mind. It is only through the mind that perceiving, imagining and conceiving takes place. The saying (*kAra*) of the word "I" (*aham*) by the body-mind causes the mind to jump to the conclusion that I **am** the body-mind. The realized man (assume the presence of quotation marks henceforth) does not cease to function in the world; it is simply that this process of identification no longer occurs. **Atagrasin** explains:

> For the Sage, the ego is seen through. The assumed ego is known for what really is an expression of totality *as* a particular body/mind mechanism, not *through* a particular body/mind mechanism. The ego story is part of, let's say, the life landscape rather than a filter as it appears to be when there is identification as the exclusive "me." The point is that the ego is only a function and not a separate entity. The identification with the body aspect of this function doesn't die in the Sage. For example, if you call a Sage by his name he responds. That sense of separation is functional. It is functional within the play as part of the play. Without seeming distance and separation the play wouldn't work. For the Sage Oneness is the whole thing, including the seeming separation. (Ref. 307)

Similarly, it is often said that the realized man will behave in certain ways, showing tremendous compassion for example. **Adyashanti** says that:

> Enlightenment can be measured by how compassionately and wisely you interact with others; with all others, not just those who support you in the way that you want. How you interact with those who do not support you shows how enlightened you really are. (Ref. 309)

This may well be the case, for it is now known that there are no others – that the apparent person in front of him is his own Self. But there is also the matter of *prArabdha karma*, mentioned in the chapter on Action, karma and Free Will. Whether or not this principle is accepted, there will still be the tendency for the body-mind to behave in the ways to which it had become accustomed to behave. Desires will still arise, though there will now be no attachment to them and whether or not they are fulfilled will not impact on an ego. **Jan Koehoorn**, for example, speaks about the emotion of anger:

Now if anger arises, every inclination to "do" something about it is gone, it does not have to be repressed and neither does it have to be expressed. The label "rage" might appear, but pales totally in comparison to what is actually being experienced at that moment. It is bubbling, sparkling, living and wants to be seen. It is not as if the anger itself wants anything, but the liveliness and the actuality of it is a kind of a "celebration" of myself in action. And I see that all happening, not as-a-person, but I as-what-I-am. What a difference from the past. (Ref. 308)

This topic will be revisited in the final chapter since both traditional and direct path Advaita believe that the behavior of a realized man is relevant whereas neo-Advaitins deny this.

Describing the Self

The entire play of solving the "hard problem" of consciousness takes place in Consciousness Itself. There is no problem except the problem posed by the illusion that Consciousness exists within bodies. Rather it is bodies that exist in Consciousness. Change pertains to bodies and not to Consciousness that is akShara, immutable. **Chittaranjan Naik** (Ref. 305)

To be "enlightened," then, is to have gained sufficient knowledge to dispel the ignorance that we are *not* enlightened. What we are then left with is what was there at the beginning – what we really are. This sounds deceptively simple and, of course, essentially nothing could be simpler. The problem lies in the genuine dispelling of ignorance. Simply reading books or listening to a teacher may indeed provide knowledge and we may think that we believe it. Deep down, however, there usually remains a subtle identification, which is incredibly tenacious – the ego's existence as an apparently separate entity depends upon it. The mind's various successive visions of reality have to be sublated before we can reach what Zen has referred to as the "state" of "No Mind." "Thinking" that we are enlightened is, by definition, not being enlightened. The Self simply IS, prior to mind.

If you understand Advaita truly, there are no riddles and no questions arise at all. The essence of Advaita is to Know Thyself. This knowing is not the knowing of answers to questions but the Self-Knowing that swallows the mind which raises questions. **Dr. Harsh K. Luthar (Harsha)** (Ref. 310)

The Mandukya Upanishad (verse 2) states that everything is Brahman and that (one of the four *mahAvAkya*-s) "This Self (Atman) is Brahman" (*ayam AtmA brahma*). One of the key "descriptions" or "definitions" of Brahman is *satyam j~nAnamanantaM brahma* (Taittiriya Upanishad II.2.i), meaning limitless existence and knowledge. As **Swami Dayananda** points out (Ref. 58), although Brahman is knowable, it is not describable, in just the same way as sweetness is something that we can experience but not describe to another. Neither can Brahman be experienced since all experiences are limited in time. This is the purpose of the teaching of Advaita – to point to that which cannot be explained.

The essence of enlightenment extinguishes subjectivity. When the subject disappears, the separation from the object is impossible. **Katie Davis** (Ref. 249)

Adjectives are inappropriate

The usual purpose of adjectives in qualifying a noun is to differentiate between members of the same group. Thus there are roses, for example, and a "red" rose differentiates amongst all roses of differing color and a "fragrant, red rose" contrasts this from another red rose which doesn't have any smell. This relationship of adjective to noun is called *visheShaNa-visheShya-sambandha*, where *visheShaNa* is the differentiating aspect (i.e. adjective) and *visheShya* is that which is to be distinguished from something else (i.e. the noun).

In the case of Brahman, the function of the words *satyam*, *j~nAnam* and *anantam* cannot be like this, since there are no other Brahmans to differentiate between. Instead, the relationship of adjectives to noun is one of pointers to that which is to be characterized or defined – *lakShya-lakShaNa-sambandha*. If what is being described is unknown to us then the description gives us indirect knowledge, so that if we do come across it, we are then likely to recognize it. In the case of Brahman, however, although we may not realize it, we are directly aware of it already, since it is our own nature. Accordingly, this definition may give us direct knowledge of ourselves.

I exist and this existence is without limit i.e. in all periods of time, all space and all objects. Similarly, the knowledge is unlimited – I am the knower, the knowledge and the known, i.e. the Consciousness that is present in all. **Swami Dayananda** points out:

It is true that everything is *Atman*, but *Atman* is free from everything. That is how it has to be recognized. Only then can *Atman* be everything. If *Atman* has its own characteristics then it becomes another object like a pot. Even *satyam j~nAnam anantam* are not the characteristics of the *Atman*, they are words revealing the nature of *Atman* by implication…

Atman and *anAtman* are not two parallel realities. *anAtman* is *mithyA* depending entirely upon *Atman*. The "I" sense in *anAtman*, the gross subtle and causal bodies, is the mistake which is the cause of all the problems. The *anAtman* is time-bound, finite and subject to a variety of afflictions. All these problems are superimposed upon *Atman*. Then you the infinite as though become finite. (Ref. 58)

Consciousness

"Consciousness" is possibly the most frequently used western word for Atman, Brahman or the Self. Nisargadatta Maharaj made the pithy quotation; "Consciousness is all there is" in Ref. 129 and since then variations are very frequently stated by modern satsang teachers. As noted at the beginning of this section, consciousness is seen as possibly the final and most difficult scientific problem by many western scientists, with many still believing that it is an epiphenomenon arising once brains reach a certain level of complexity. Hopefully, it is now appreciated that science will never succeed in pinning it down because there is no "thing" to be analyzed in this way. The reason that scientists find it so hard to explain is that they insist on assuming that consciousness is something that arises in us rather than the other way round.

(Consciousness) is the common principle of illumination in all experience. In our personalities, it is seen mixed with our limited faculties of mind and body, where it is found expressed. In the world outside, it is seen mixed with the limited objects and happenings that our faculties perceive. But in itself, it's quite unmixed, beyond all limitations.

Found thus unmixed, beneath its mixed appearances, it is the same everywhere: the one complete reality that all experience shows. It is one single consciousness, expressed in everything, throughout the universe.

This conclusion presents us with an immediate difficulty. If the whole universe expresses consciousness, then it is all alive. How can we make sense of that? We recognize that consciousness can be expressed in the feelings, thoughts and actions of living creatures. But how can we find any such expression in objects that are inanimate, like a rock or a mountain?

...In the personalities of living creatures, nature's expression is personal, through personal faculties of body and mind. In objects like a rock, where no such faculties are found, nature's expression is impersonal. There nature speaks impersonally, but it speaks all the same. All order, meaning and value are natural expressions of consciousness, whether in personality or outside world. All nature is alive, as it expresses consciousness throughout the world.

...Since consciousness is pure light, it doesn't wish nature to do anything; it doesn't tell nature what to do; it doesn't interfere at all in what takes place. As consciousness shines unaffected through experience, it is the knowing ground beneath all acts and happenings. Unmoved itself by any act, it is the final ground of our experience. From it, all actions rise. On it, all actions take place. Back into it, all actions must return and be absorbed. **Ananda Wood** (Ref. 306)

I am

"I am" is our self-evident, direct experience, requiring no justification or explanation, known to us immediately through the *pramANa* of *pratyakSha*. **Ramana Maharshi** speaks of it here:

> **Bhagavan:** "I exist" is the only permanent, self-evident experience of everyone. Nothing else is so self-evident (*pratyakSha*) as "I am." What people call "self-evident" viz., the experience they get through the senses, is far from self-evident. The Self alone is that. *pratyakSha* is another name for the Self. So, to do Self-analysis and be "I am" is the only thing to do. "I am" is reality. "I am *this* or *that*" is unreal. "I am" is truth, another name for Self. "I am God" is not true.
>
> The Swami thereupon said, "The Upanishads themselves have said 'I am Brahman'."
>
> **Bhagavan:** That is not how the text is to be understood. It simply means, "Brahman exists as 'I'" and not "I am Brahman." It is not to be supposed that a man is advised to contemplate "I am Brahman," "I am Brahman." Does a man keep on thinking "I am a man," "I am a man"? He is that, and except when a doubt arises as to whether he is an animal or a tree, there is no need for him to assert, "I am a man." Similarly the Self is Self, Brahman exists as "I am," in every thing and every being. (Ref. 174)

The *mahAvAkya* "*tat tvam asi*" tells us who we are – "Thou art That." *tat*, in the scriptures, refers to *brahman*, while *tvam* refers to the limited *jIva*. It is certainly not immediately apparent how these two can be identical. *tvam* refers to something about which I am directly aware (*pratyakSha*) while *tat* refers to something remote (*pArokSha*). Clearly, the meanings of the words cannot be immediate but must be implied. *vivekachUDAmaNi* (verse 244) uses the simile of a glow-worm and the sun. Both emit light but there is a vast difference in degree. Thus *Ishvara* can be all-powerful and omniscient whilst the *jIva* is weak and relatively ignorant.

vivekachUDAmaNi goes on to explain that the apparent dissimilarity results from their respective *upAdhi*-s. *Ishvara*'s *upAdhi* is *mAyA*, whilst the *jIva* is limited by the five sheaths. But these are only like the different costumes worn by an actor, with *Ishvara* being the role of the king and the *jIva* being that of the beggar. The actor is the same – *brahman*. Advaita, then, pursues the path of negating each of the five sheaths which we mistake ourselves to be, as was discussed in the first part of the book. This process leads us to the understanding that "I" am that Consciousness that is present in everything. Similarly, the finite, time-bound objects of the world are negated so that *Ishvara* is realized to be that same Consciousness. Then it is seen that I am That.

When everything has been negated, what remains is that which is doing the negating. That which witnesses all does not itself change. **Swami Dayananda** explains how this works:

> The physical body is an object. The subject is I. The "I" cannot be negated. Everything else can be negated. Your body can be negated, your thought can be negated, but you cannot negate yourself. Time can be negated, space can be negated, *Atman* cannot be negated. All that is negated is in time and space.
>
> What is negated? A thing that is right now is negated now - now it is, now it is not. It is purely time bound. Every negation is time bound. If I can negate the time itself and still be, where is the question of negation for me? Time swallows everything, but you swallow time itself. In sleep there is no time. In a moment of joy there is no time. Between two thoughts there is no time really speaking and still you are. Then where is the problem? That is *mokSha*, to know that I am immortal. I should know that very clearly, without doubt. That is called *mokSha*. *mokSha* is not a thing; it is yourself. You are liberated by yourself. You are ever free.

For him who knows he is immortal, there is no birth or death. What more? (Ref. 112)

Even Consciousness is not the Final Reality

Ultimately, though, Consciousness too has to be seen as not the final reality and this subject is addressed particularly in the later books of Nisargadatta Maharaj and will be covered in the next chapter. **Robert Powell** uses the analogy of an object and its shadow. Consciousness points to the reality in the way that the shadow accompanies the object but is not the object:

> Similarly, the consciousness foreshadows the Self, but the Self is not the consciousness. The manifest only points to the Unmanifest. (Ref. 116)

In the end, any descriptions have to be negative ones, as was stated at the outset. Here is **Shankara**:

> I am without any change, without any form, free from all blemish and decay. I am not subjected to any disease, I am beyond all comprehension, free from all alternatives and all-pervading. I am without any attribute or activity, I am eternal, ever free, and imperishable. I am free from all impurity, I am immovable, unlimited, holy, undecaying, and immortal (*apArokShAnubhUti* Verses 25 – 8) (Ref. 212)

The Self is everything and this is neatly summarized by the word for "I," *aham* in the Sanskrit language - *a* is the first letter and *ha* the last – as is noted in the *Yoga Vasishtha*:

> We contemplate the self which is the very basis of all language and expression, being the alpha and the omega, which covers the entire field from *a* to *ha* and which is indicated by the word *aham*. (Ref. 38)

Summary

- We are not the body or mind; not a doer etc; we are not a human being.
- We are not the gross, subtle or causal bodies.
- Enlightenment is realizing this and understanding that we are already That.
- Enlightenment is not a state and, in reality, not something to be attained.
- The Self is already "enlightened."
- Consequently, in reality, there is nothing that we need to do or can do.
- At the phenomenal level, ignorance prevents the mind from realizing this. Enlightenment is the removal of this ignorance at the level of mind.
- Enlightenment seems to happen when the seeker is "ready" – this is "grace."
- Subsequently, there is no identification and everything is seen to be the Self.
- "Levels" of enlightenment are in the mind, including the idea of a "witness."
- Idealism and the dream state suggest the waking world may be an illusion.
- All three states need to be considered in a treatment of the nature of reality.
- In deep sleep, body and mind disappear and we exist as pure Consciousness.
- The states of consciousness arise within the Self but do not affect it, in the same way that thoughts about a dress do not affect the dress itself.
- *turIya* is the ever-present background reality and our true nature – *Atman*.
- At the phenomenal level, there is no *ahaMkAra* in the "enlightened man." He still plays his role in the play, experiences desire etc. but

there is no attachment.
- The Self is not describable. It is prior to mind and language can only point to it. It is what remains when all else has been negated.
- Even Consciousness is its manifestation. The reality is unmanifest.

7. THE NATURE
OF REALITY

*When we insist that the unreal is **really** unreal, we ground ourselves further into duality **thinking** that we have got to Advaita. When we see that there really is no unreal, then All is Real. That is Advaita that is pUrNa [full, perfect, complete].* **Chittaranjan Naik** (Ref. 316)

A ll that we can know and experience is necessarily limited and temporary. Reality must somehow "contain" all knowledge and experiences; is beyond the intellect, inconceivable and unapproachable. It can only be spoken of tangentially or by use of pointers (*lakShaNa*-s), which suggest without being explicit. Here is an attempt by **Alexander Smit** († 2000) to address the ineffable:

All ups and downs are temporary experiences. Any experience whatsoever is subject to change, marvelous experiences as well as terrible experiences. But, there is something that actually includes everything, that stands completely apart from whatever experience. That means that the peak experiences, that the ego or the person are so eager to have, and the valley experiences all last for very short times and are finally not important enough to try to build your life on. That, within which the peak and valley experiences become manifest, stands apart from my attention, and simultaneously my attention can not take hold of it, because attention takes place in That. Therefore it is seen and at the same time not seen - the paradox.

Everything that I can see and that disappears again must be temporary in nature. And I am neither in nor out of that unchanging being in which things happen. Finally I only know that there is Knowingness, Awareness, Consciousness. And that knowing gives immediate joy and immediate rest, immediate fulfillment that needs nothing more. The temporary, no matter how beautiful or how terrible can never be the truth. Because the experience needs something else. The experience is carried by something else, and that can not be experienced. Because if it could be experienced it would not be That. Therefore the truth is without experience. It is thus the experienceless that makes experience possible. Every feeling dissolves itself in something that knows no feeling, but which makes every experience possible. Everything will disappear in something that does not disappear, that cannot disappear. Everything dies in something immortal. (Ref. 315)

It has been mentioned earlier that the definition of "real" according to Advaita is that which exists in all three periods of time – past, present and future. If this is the starting point, then it follows that there cannot be much around us that is real. Even mountains rise up from the sea bed under volcanic action or collision of tectonic plates and are gradually eroded by wind and rain. Even the earth will eventually be swallowed up as the sun becomes a supernova.

Shankara says:

...a thing is said to be *satya*, true, when it does not change the nature that is ascertained to be its own; and a thing is said to be unreal when it changes the nature that is ascertained to be its own. (*bhAShya* on *taittirIya upaniShad* II.i.1 Ref. 336)

This was put into a more memorable form by **Sri Poonja**, when he said: "What changes is not real and what is Real cannot change." (Ref. 15)

Essentially, everything which is manifest must be unreal if the adjective is applicable, since to be manifest implies that it was at some time in the past unmanifest. If the universe was brought into being through a "big bang," it clearly did not exist prior to this (ignoring the fact that this concept has no meaning if time itself also originated with the Big Bang).

It follows that, according to this definition of the word, the only "thing" that can be real is that which is unmanifest, which takes us clearly into the realm of metaphysics (looking for a black cat in a cellar without a torch... when it is not there, as someone once said).

Advaita Vedanta, then, must labour under this fact, which it explicitly acknowledges, that whatever is expressed is ultimately non-Brahman, is ultimately untrue. **Eliot Deutsch** (Ref. 82)

The Taittiriya Upanishad states later (II.9) that *brahman* is beyond words or concepts. Even the attributes of existence (*sat*), consciousness (*chit*) and bliss (*Ananda*) have limited use. (After all, they are meaningful only to the waking mind, which is relevant only to the waking state.) **D. B. Gangolli** summarises what *brahman* is **not**:

> It is not a substance (*dravya*), not a quality (*guNa*), not any relationship (*sambandha*), neither the category of genus (*sAmAnya*) nor the particular (*visheSha*), not non-existence (abhAva); it is not a knower (*j~nAtRRi*), not a known object (*j~neya*); not a doer (*kartRRi*), not an action (*kriyA*), not a means of action (*kAraka*), not a result or fruit of action (*phala*). It being so, how can it at all be proper to call it by any name? All words are the names of objects or phenomena that exist in the waking. But the ultimate reality does not exist in the waking; the waking itself is a certain appearance that is "illumined" or that "shines" in the ultimate reality. The objects that appear in the waking and their names are nothing but the false appearances only that are manifested in it, i.e. the ultimate reality. Therefore, that entity which is apart from these two phenomena of the name and the object having the name and which is their essence alone – that alone is the Ultimate Reality. (Ref. 292)

Since the real is beyond description, it is referred to in various ways by Advaita, reflecting what could be called "attributes" (if reality were something which could have attributes). Most widely, it is *brahman*, in its universal aspect and *Atman* as it applies to the essence of the apparent individual. *Ishvara* does not, strictly speaking, refer to *brahman* but to its seeming function as controller of the universe. It is also called *akShara*, the imperishable and unchangeable; *avyakta*, the unmanifest; *prANa*, in the sense of pure energy; *AkAsha* (again slightly misleading, since ether is the first of the traditional elements, but in the sense that it pervades the entire universe). In more modern texts and satsangs, words such as "Absolute" "Self" and "Consciousness" are often used but other less obvious terms like "Source," "Presence," "Oneness," "Pure Awareness" and "Truth" also occur. (If a word has a capital letter, you can begin to get suspicious – for example "Knowingness" or "Beingness"!)

Brahman may also be referred to as God, in the west, but this is certainly misleading as Hinduism has many gods, which are really only aspects of *Ishvara*. There are gods to control the elements, e.g. *prANa* becomes *vAyu*, the God of the wind; there is a goddess of learning (*sarasvatI*) and a god of death (*yama*), to mention just a few. Accordingly, concepts of God really relate to attempts to rationalise the creation, maintenance and dissolution of the universe and have nothing to do with reality.

It is said that the use of names such as these act as reminders. The knowledge of our true nature is always there, temporarily covered over by ignorance. Just as, when asleep, we awaken if someone calls our name, so these words help us to remember the truth of our real Self. It is also interesting to note that a name does not necessarily represent a specific, individual god. In his commentary on the Brahma Sutras (I.iii.28), Shankara suggests that Indra, for example, might refer to a rank, like commander so that it relates to the position of a god in the hierarchy. Similarly, the positions of god of wind, fire etc. would be held by different individual gods at different times, since gods are not immortal and, indeed, must traditionally be reborn in human form before they can achieve enlightenment and escape *saMsAra*.

We will continue to experience a separate world as long as there is ignorance but, irrespective of this, the truth is always that of the non-dual *brahman.* Accordingly, we have to differentiate between apparent "levels" of reality. There is the (true) reality of brahman and there is the apparently true (whilst in a state of ignorance) reality of the world. This is the distinction between *paramArtha* and *vyavahAra* discussed below.

As always, Advaita approaches the topic of reality using successive levels of understanding, with one theory replacing another when it has served its purpose. Thus, for example, there are theories of cause and effect to satisfy the seeker in the early stages of their search because this is our everyday experience. Similarly in respect of the phenomenal world itself and the notion of a creator-God. Initially put forward as facts, these are later retracted once the aspirant is ready to appreciate the more subtle teaching.

Because the various concepts – of creation, *Ishvara*, *mAyA* and the theories that attempt to provide explanations – all go together, it is inevitable that there will be some overlap and a little duplication in the discussions below, where an attempt has been made to discuss them under separate headings. Perhaps any repetition may help to clarify what is actually quite a complex subject!

The World

O Rama, the unreal jIva perceives the unreal world on account of the unreal influence of the unreality. In all this what can be considered as real and what as unreal? **Yoga Vasishtha** (Ref. 38)

When asked whether the world was a reality or an illusion, **Ramana Maharshi** replied as follows:

Both statements are true. They refer to different stages of development and are spoken from different points of view. The aspirant [*abhyAsI*] starts with the definition: that which is real exists always. Then he eliminates the world as unreal because it is changing. The seeker ultimately reaches the Self and there finds unity as the prevailing note. Then, that which was originally rejected as being unreal is found to be a part of the unity. Being absorbed in the reality, the world also is real.

There is only being in Self-realization and nothing but being. (Ref. 49)

When we begin our spiritual search in ignorance, we have to differentiate between a "real" and an "unreal," practising *neti, neti* to persuade the mind that we are not the body, not the mind and so on. It is only as our understanding grows that the earlier statements can be taken back and we can truly understand the statements of Shankara (see Chapter 4) to the effect that "*brahman* is the (non-dual) reality; the world is *mithyA*; the world is brahman." Having forgotten our true nature, we remind ourselves of it by first discovering what we are not. While we genuinely believe that the world is real, with ourselves as separate individuals in it, it is necessary to teach that the world is an illusion. Only much later can we accept that, not only are we the *Atman* but that this *Atman* is also *brahman* and, moreover, every "thing else" is also *brahman*. The *neti, neti* method is itself negated in the final sublation of all levels.

Brahman in itself is unmanifest (*avyakta*) and we cannot perceive or conceive it in any way. The world is obviously manifest (*vyakta*) and accessible to the senses. Thus, the metaphors that have been used, such as gold being the essential reality of the *mithyA* ring, cannot be taken all the way - gold is just as visible as the ring that is formed out of it.

It is the names and forms that we see around us and mistakenly think to be reality. We are the unchanging witness of the constantly changing manifestation, as **Jean Klein** points out:

The world you perceive is none other than a figment of the imagination founded on memory, fear, anxiety and desire. You have locked yourself away within this world. See this without jumping to conclusions and you will be free. There is no need whatsoever for you to free yourself from a world which exists only in your imagination.

What you take to be reality is only a concept arising from memory. Memory arises from the mind, the mind from the witness, the witness from the Self. You are the witness, the onlooker standing on the bank watching the river flow on. You do not move, you are changeless, beyond the limits of space and time. You cannot perceive what is permanent, because you are it. (Ref. 19)

Atmananda Krishna Menon has a useful story to indicate how we fail to appreciate the non-dual, essential nature of the world and instead concentrate only on the form:

> There was a palace cook who usually diluted the milk for the king, keeping a portion of the milk for himself. The king got accustomed to it and believed it was pure milk. Subsequently, a new cook came and gave the king pure milk instead. This upset the king's stomach. At first, the king thought that the new cook was in the wrong and scolded him for negligence. But eventually the king understood that the old cook had regularly cheated him. This is exactly the nature of our view of the Reality. We are so accustomed to its perverted form that we take the form alone as real and take no note of the substance. At last, when the Truth is revealed to us by the Guru, we look back and recognize our long-standing mistake. (Note 276 Ref. 13)

paramArtha and vyavahAra

The world and the rest of "creation," including all of these apparently separate people, belong to what Advaita calls *vyavahAra*, the phenomenal realm. It all seems very real but is also continually changing so that, according to the definition above, cannot be real. There is a seeming paradox, here, since Advaita means "not two" and this is resolved later in the teaching, when it is made clear that the unreality of the world lies in its *apparent* separateness. It *seems* as though there are many things but this is mere appearance, just as the snake is mistakenly seen in the rope. In fact, what is happening is that there is only ever *brahman* and we impose the apparent separateness through the naming of the continually changing forms. The unchanging essence is *brahman*, out of which these forms arise, stay a while and then return. This is the only reality – *paramArtha*.

Everything that we do is at the vyAvahArika level only and even the description and explanation of pAramArthika are also at the vyAvahArika level... TRUTH (Self-Realization) can never be described in words. Everything that is written, spoken or remembered will fall into the vyAvahArika level. **Ram Chandran** (Ref. 331)

The non-dual reality in Advaita is usually termed *brahman*, deriving from the Sanskrit root *bRRih*, meaning to grow great or strong. It carries the sense of that which is greater than anything and encompasses all. As with all language, however, this is misleading in that the concepts of time and space themselves apply only in the realm of *vyavahAra*. Attributes such as size simply have no applicability at the level of *paramArtha*.

The unmanifest is non-dual, without form so that we cannot directly perceive it but it is the essence of all the appearances, the manifest forms of the world of apparent duality. The metaphor that has now been used several times is that of gold and ornaments. When we look at bracelets and necklaces, we perceive the forms without usually appreciating that the reality is always only gold. The form cannot exist without the essence but the unmanifest essence can only be seen through its form. All forms in the world, including all of the apparent people point to the non-dual reality that is *brahman*. The forms in themselves are neither real nor unreal – they are *mithyA*, dependent reality.

It is worth briefly revisiting this topic since it is so important. **Swami Dayananda** uses the example of a shirt. We might (since we are wearing it and it is keeping us warm and dry) claim that it is a real shirt. But if we are pedantic about it, the reality is the cotton out of which it is made – the shirt is *mithyA*, "dependent reality." But clearly the shirt is not illusory. Further analysis would then force us to concede that the cotton is only *mithyA*, too – the reality is the unwoven fiber that was taken from the plant. And so on, back via chromosomes and molecules to sub-atomic particles and energy. Ultimately, only *brahman* is *satya*, the rest is *mithyA* – name and form only.

This is where the Sanskrit word *anirvachanIya* is appropriate. It is usually translated as "indescribable" but a better way of understanding it is as "that which cannot be categorically stated as either real or unreal." (Ref. 186)

It is the failure to understand *mithyA* that causes most of the problems in respect of creation. If the universe is taken for *satyam*, then we conclude that we live in a world of duality. If it has been created by a God, then He too is a separate entity we suppose, just as the artist who makes the necklace is separate from his creation. It is the taking of the *jIva* and the world as real that necessitates the existence of a real God, *Ishvara*, to create them. All of this constitutes the phenomenal realm of *vyavahAra* – the level at which we appear to exist until knowledge arises to eliminate the ignorance that obscures the reality. In fact, none of these are real as separate entities; there is only the non-dual reality of *paramArtha* in which each of these apparent names and forms rise and fall, manifest and transcend.

The world, therefore is not unreal but neither, as will be seen, has there been any creation. It is real in that it is *brahman*. Similarly, God exists so long as we take the world as real in its own right just as we are real as separately existing *jIva*-s. But, once this mis-taking of separate existence has been resolved, the reality is known to be unchanged and unchanging. There is no creation and therefore no need to posit a God who created it; there is no *jIva* and no birth or death.

It is often said by some that, once self-realization occurs, the world will somehow cease to exist. This is a serious mistake. (And in any case, as Shankara points out, since it never came into existence in the first place, it cannot cease to exist either.)

No, there never has been anything new created. There is just the continual, ever-changing, ever-new, yet always the same - simply different names and forms of the non-dual reality. Bangles changing into bracelets but always still gold. To this extent, the neo-Advaitins have always been right – This is it! Already.

What is there "after realization" cannot be anything new – it is That already; always has been and always will. Upon realization, outwardly everything remains the same – still the same house and garden, still the same getting up to go to work, still the same poverty-stricken starvation in Africa. The point is that it is now known, irrevocably, that this is all simply an outward form of the Self, whose essence has always been perfect and complete. It is *avidyA*, ignorance, that veils the truth and projects the illusion of suffering. Subtract the *avidyA* from the *jIva*, the apparent individual, and what you are left with is *Atman*. (Ref. 342)

The world is an illusion in the sense of the illusions performed by magicians. We might see a woman being sawn in half, for example. As a child we might believe this to be literally happening and be frightened – this is analogous to the person's belief in a separate world. As a mature adult, we still see the lady apparently being sawn in half but we know that it is only a trick, even though we may not know how the illusion is brought about. This is the situation in respect of the enlightened response to the world. People and objects are still seen but it is known that they are only names and forms of the non-dual reality. **Dr. K. Sadananda** explains:

There are two terms: one is illusion and the next is delusion. Seeing the plurality is the illusion. There is no ignorance in that. There can be knower-known, the movement, the change etc. – all are illusion.
The delusion is taking the illusion as real - that is the ignorance part. Hence, realization is not the absence of knower-known distinctions but taking the distinctions as real. Bhagavan Ramana was transacting like every body - eating, sleeping, helping in the kitchen etc. yet he had no misunderstanding that the plurality was real. By knowledge, the illusion does not disappear, only the delusion, since the delusion is in the individual mind while the illusion is due to the projection of collective mind (objective illusions). These distinctions have to be clear. Other wise we tend to jump from one reference to the other. (Ref. 30)

Another useful metaphor is the sunrise. Because the sun apparently rises every morning in the east, traverses the sky and sets in the west, people naturally used to believe that the sun went around the earth. This was shown by scientists to be wrong and today, no educated person would make this mistake. Nevertheless, the sun still appears to everyone to rise in the east...

Until the distinction between *paramArtha* and *vyavahAra* is fully understood, and continually borne in mind when discussing Advaita, confusion will easily arise. This is especially the case in respect of some neo-Advaita discussions, where a seeker will almost always be asking questions from a *vyAvahArika* standpoint. If the teacher always responds from the *pAramArthika* standpoint, the seeker is very likely to fail to understand and become frustrated. What he or she fundamentally wants to know is "what should I do in order to realize the truth." A response of "there is no seeker and nothing to be sought; there is no 'you' who can do anything" is certainly true from a *pAramArthika* standpoint – but it is not very helpful!

Professor V. Krishnamurthy uses the metaphor of television soap operas. He supposes that there are two independent programs, X and Y. Actor A plays the *brother* of actress B in X and, quite coincidentally, happens to be playing the *husband* of B in Y. Now he supposes that some unsuspecting viewer, who has not been watching either program, happens to see X followed by Y on the same day, without realizing that they are two   different programs. He gathers that A is the brother of B but then sees them in bed together and immediately writes a letter of complaint to the television station. (Clearly this scenario happened some years ago!).

The mistake is obvious when explained – the viewer has simply mixed up the roles in the two series. **Professor Krishnamurthy** goes on to explain:

> This is exactly the case with our initiate in Advaita, who asks: "If there is only one non-dual reality, then what is the need to pray or worship or do *bhakti*?" The existence of the one non-dual reality is in the absolute level, whereas the praying or worshipping or doing *bhakti* is in the *vyAvahArika* level...
>
> In the absolute plane there is only one non-dual reality. There is no

mAyA there. But in the *vyAvahArika* plane, everything is *mAyA*. The *vyAvahArika* plane itself is *mAyA*; but mark it, not to somebody in the *vyAvahArika* plane, but to some one who is outside of it! To be outside of it, you have to surrender to Him when you are inside of it. Those who surrender to Me when they are in the *vyAvahArika* plane, I will take them out of the *vyAvahArika* plane to My Absolute Plane - says the Lord, very explicitly in Bhagavad Gita 7-14 and 18-66. (Ref. 332)

David Carse (Ref. 375) thinks of this problem as a "category error". Our experience is entirely at the level of duality, in the apparent world as an apparently separate individual. Then, along come Advaita and starts talking about the non-dual reality (whilst at the same time acknowledging that this is not possible, since language is dualistic). It is hardly surprising that confusion arises. He gives the following as an example of the conflict in concepts:

Our Experience	**Teaching of Advaita**
sense of being an individual	no individuals anywhere
source works through me	all is perfect presence; no source; no me
sense of doership	nothing is done; everything happens
control, responsibility	everything happens spontaneously
time, cause/effect	appearances in the unfolding
purpose, meaning	⟨ Emptiness; "entertainment" ⟩
evolution, progress, change	Absolute; all is as it is
movement, restlessness, motivation	Perfect; brilliant; stillness

At any intermediate stage between the non-seeker, who has never encountered these ideas, and the "realized" one, for whom they are the ever-present truth, there is likely to be confusion. Our experience will be as it always was but is now likely to be overlaid with partly digested understanding of the philosophy. As an example:

> ...to say that "all there is, is consciousness" (an Advaita concept); and then to turn around and say that "I am not the doer; it is source working through the individual instruments" (a concept from the Experience column, which comes from still taking the separate individual self seriously.) (Ref. 375)

As he says, "this is why a conversation with a teacher who does not compromise can be quite short." The questions that we ask are from the standpoint of a presumed person so that it is understandably difficult for the teacher to respond with answers that are from the standpoint of reality. A frequently asked question, for example, is "why is there so much suffering in the world?" which can probably be translated, for most people, into "why do I have to suffer?" This is a category error in that the suffering is related to body-mind in *vyavahAra*, whilst who I really am is in the non-dual *paramArtha*.

This is why the teaching of neo-Advaita is really only suitable for relatively mature seekers who are less likely to make this mistake. It will never make any sense to someone still enmeshed in egoism to be told (in whatever modern terminology) *tat tvam asi*. All that will result is a category error.

Heaven and Hell

The scriptures (*shruti* as well as those of other religions) mention heaven (*svarga*) and hell (*pAtAla*) as actual places of happiness and suffering to which souls may go after death of the body according to whether they have accumulated *puNya* or *papa* (good or bad karma as fruit of actions performed). These are concepts indicative of value judgments made by man, as are the ideas of the gods (*deva*) and demons (*asura*-s) which supposedly inhabit these worlds (*loka*-s). These concepts are clearly of value to the ignorant man who is striving for happiness and wishes to avoid suffering. From the standpoint of reality, no separate thing has any meaning since all is *brahman*. Accordingly, it is not useful to talks of whether gods or heaven "really" exist – clearly they do not. At the level of *vyavahAra* they are at best, like everything else, *mithyA*. The most that we can say is that they do not exist as separate from the non-dual reality.

For those natures that are suited to *bhakti yoga* as a path, the notion of a personal God to whom the ego can be surrendered is a useful one. It is similarly useful to accept that their path may take many lifetimes and that a moral life will take them in the right direction (via interludes in a heaven) whilst a dissolute one will lead to interim stays in hell. None of this can ever be amenable to proof one way or the other for obvious reasons.

Cause and Effect

How, then, does the phenomenal realm arise? In the case of a gold bracelet, we know that it is only ever gold but, nevertheless, a goldsmith has, at some time, to forge and mould the gold to make it into the form that is now visible. If the smith is the creator of the bracelet, who is the creator of the universe?

Before looking into this topic in more depth, it is necessary first to consider how Advaita addresses the subject of cause and effect.

The western philosophical treatment of the subject stems from Aristotle, who differentiated four elements relating an "effect" to its presumed "cause." It will be helpful to consider the making of a pot from clay, since this example is often used in the Scriptures from which Advaita derives.

Aristotle called the first of these four causes the *material cause* – in the example, this is the clay from which the pot has been made. Supposing that the pot is a mug for drinking out of, someone at some time would have thought of the basic design for this – a cylindrical container with a handle by which the mug can be comfortably held by a human hand and so on. This basic design constitutes the definition of the "form" of the pot and Aristotle called this the *formal cause*. Someone, namely the potter, has to collect together the materials and be in possession of the design knowledge and physically construct the pot - he is called the *efficient cause*. Finally (in Aristotle's analysis), there is the actual purpose for which the pot is made, typically in order that someone may use it to drink his coffee – this is the *final cause*. There are also further refinements possible to this model, such as for example, the identification of *instrumental cause*, as the potter's wheel on which the mug is thrown. And this might be powered by electricity and so on.

Later western philosophers have questioned this model, even suggesting that the whole idea of cause and effect is illusory. David Hume thought that it was simply the case that, on repeated observation, an event always appears to succeed another event but that it might not do so the next time we observe it, e.g. applying heat to a kettle of water might cause it to freeze instead of boil. Immanuel Kant believed that our ideas of cause and effect, as well as of time and space, are simply concepts that we have devised in order to make sense of the phenomenal world, which is in reality beyond the ability of the mind to understand.

Advaita agrees with such a view to the extent that causality is a concept, depending on time, which is also a concept – one thought arises and then another; the concept of time then arises as the interval between those thoughts. That which is aware of the thoughts, that which stands outside of both cause and effect is the *Atman*, unaffected by either.

The Sanskrit terminology can be confusing and it is made worse if you attempt to clarify the definitions by using the dictionary, since there seems to be considerable overlap. The word *kAraNa* is defined in Monier-Williams (Ref. 107) as "a cause (in philosophy i.e. that which is invariably antecedent to some product)" but can also mean "instrument, means" and "agency, instrumentality." Note also that the word *karaNa*, with a short "a" as the second letter, has as one of its definitions "the means or instrument by which an action is effected, i.e. the instrumental cause, but it is frequently and potentially misleadingly used interchangeably with *kAraNa*.

The Sanskrit word for "effect or result" is *kArya*.

Lest I introduce unnecessary confusion by describing the various misuses, here are the terms that *should* be used:

Material cause - *upAdAna kAraNa*

Efficient cause – *nimitta kAraNa*

Instrumental cause - *karaNa kAraNa*

The material cause is further subdivided in Hindu philosophies. *Arambha* refers to the situation where the effect is clearly distinguishable from its material cause, as a garment is different from the fibres from which it has been woven. *pariNAma* is used when there has been a change or transformation of the material cause into the effect. The example usually given is that of milk being transformed into butter – the change is irreversible. *vivarta* refers to the situation where there is only an appearance of the effect with the cause remaining unchanged. (Refs. 138, 139)

Dr. K. Sadananda says the following about *vivarta*:

vivarta is an apparent transformation only, as in the gold becoming ring or bangle. Ontologically the realities are slightly different from the cause to the effect. The ring is a dependent and the gold an independent entity. The effects are apparent while the cause is more real. It is actually a transformation-less transformation or a creation-less creation. The cause is of higher reality compared to the effects. The cause permeates the effects. One can remove the effects but the cause still remains. That is the secret of *neti, neti*. On the other hand, if we remove the cause, there will not be any effects either. Thus, the effect has a dependent reality and the cause an independent reality. (Ref. 371)

Causation-related Theories of Creation

The following definitions are actually of more relevance to the subject of creation, which will be discussed later, but will be covered briefly now so as to keep the material on causality together in one section.

There are three theories about creation (as it relates to the discussion here – in fact the ultimate truth according to Advaita is that there has never been any creation – *ajAti vAda*).

1. **Arambha vAda** (*Arambha* literally means "beginning, commence-ment" and *vAda* means "thesis, proposition, argument, doctrine" etc.) is the

theory that the world (i.e. universe) is the result of the coming together of atoms. This is not much different from modern science and the theory was held by the *naiyAyika*-s, the followers of the *nyAya* philosophy, and by the *dvaitin*-s, the followers of *dvaita*. It can be considered to be "real causality," with something different – an effect – resulting from the process.

This theory is also called ***asatkArya vAda***, i.e. the doctrine (*vAda*) that the effect (*kArya*) is not real (*asat*), i.e. is not pre-existent in the cause. The following two theories, which effectively *do* claim this are therefore special cases of the more general doctrine of ***satkArya vAda***.

2. ***pariNAma vAda*** (*pariNAma* literally means "change, transformation into") states that the world is the result of the evolution of *prakRRiti*, i.e. a transformation of one thing into another. This is the belief of the two *sAMkhya*-related schools as well as *vishiShTAdvaita*.

3. ***vivarta vAda*** states that the world is only an apparent projection of *Ishvara*, brought about by the power of *mAyA*. This turns out on closer examination to be a denial of causality. It is the belief of Advaita (and, incidentally, of *mAdhyamika* Buddhism).

The teaching of Advaita begins with the general theory of *satkArya vAda* and, in the *brahma sUtra bhAShya*, Shankara argues the common sense of this through such examples as our expecting to get butter from milk and not from clay (BSB II.i.18). "If everything be equally non-existent everywhere before creation, why should curds be produced from milk alone and not from clay?" he asks. (Ref. 34) Clearly milk has some special property not possessed by clay that enables it to be used for producing curd. Therefore, he argues, the effect pre-exists in the cause.

The theory is only relevant, however, in the phenomenal realm – the practical world – and the theory has to be sublated to make way for the more subtle theory of *vivarta vAda*. As discussed below, this involves the postulation of the forces of *mAyA*, wielded by *Ishvara*, leading us into a consideration of the fine distinction between appearance and reality. Ultimately, that theory too must be sublated to be replaced by *ajAti vAda*, which claims that there has never been any creation at all.

The rationale behind this process is explained by **Swami**

Satchidanandendra:

...a doctrine of cause and effect is accepted as a preliminary device to help induce the mind to understand the unity and sole reality of the Self. The Veda does not teach that the effect is real... It is therefore laid down clearly and with utmost emphasis that the doctrine that there exists a universe of effects is only admitted at all in order to teach the existence of a cause as its ultimate ground. (Ref. 24)

The idea that there is no such thing as causality is difficult to accept for a western mind. *gauDapAda* in his *kArikA* to the *mANDUkya upaniShad* devotes quite a number of verses to enumerating the various possibilities and destroying them one by one. Some of these arguments had been used by the early *mAdhyamika* Buddhist philosopher, *nAgArjuna*. **Douglas A. Fox** discusses this in Ref. 141. Nagarjuna said that if the effect was the *same* as the cause, then it was meaningless to call it by a different name, their being no change. If, on the other hand, it was completely *different, with no connection* to the cause at all, then any "effect" might occur from any "cause" in a random fashion and the concept of cause would be meaningless. The idea that cause and effect are both the same *and* different is not meaningful. The only other possibility is that they are *neither* the same nor different. This presumably implies that there is no relation between them so that an "effect" is self-generated. This also does not make any sense.

For those who want to work through the detailed arguments, the relevant verses are 11 – 23 in the fourth *prakaraNa* (subject or topic) of the *kArikA* (a concise philosophical statement in verse) on the *mANDUkyopaniShad*, entitled *alAtashAnti* ("On the quenching of the firebrand"). For Shankara's comments on these as well, see Ref. 35. For a more readable and understandable presentation, see Ref. 33. But, in the interest of not sending you to sleep, I will move on!

One final aspect of causality worth mentioning at this point is that of the "chicken and egg" situation, which becomes relevant in respect of the *jIva*. How does the *Atman* become apparently limited by *avidyA*? **Dr. K.**

Sadananda addresses the question:

> In Advaita Vedanta, the *jIva* is the product of *avidyA* and yet at the same time the *jIva* is the locus of *avidyA*. I.e. it appears that the *jIva* has the *avidyA*. He cannot be the locus of *avidyA* if he is the effect, since *avidyA* must be there before the *jIva* is born. However, when the *jIva* is not there, there is only Brahman and He cannot have *avidyA*, since if he has it, he cannot be Brahman. Bhagavan *rAmAnuja* uses these arguments to dismiss the Advaitic thesis. Shankara rightly says just as in the chicken-egg situation *avidyA* is *anAdi* (beginningless), and the relationship between the *jIva* and *avidyA* is unexplainable, *anirvachanIya*. (Ref. 30)

This situation is called *anyonya Ashraya* – mutual dependence. Because of the interdependence, it is not possible to determine any cause-effect relationship. Another way of looking at this is that each individual chicken and individual egg has a beginning, no matter how far back one goes. What is actually "beginningless" is the mathematical series but then this does not have a physical existence.

The bottom line is that causality is a necessary concept at the level of the world-appearance in order to function in the world. It is part of the foundation of science and a constant assumption in everyday life. From the standpoint of *paramArtha*, however, it has no meaning. As the **Maitri Upanishad** (VI 7) states: "*Where knowledge has attained non-duality, devoid of effect, cause and action; inexplicable, incomparable, indescribable; what is it? It is ineffable.*" (Ref. 101)

The notion of *satkArya vAda* - that the effect pre-exists in the (material) cause – explains how an apparent universe of multiplicity can arise out of the non-dual reality. The traditional elements of the Vedas have a clear hierarchy with space or *AkAsha* being the first to be created. It is associated with sound and this relates to the idea that the universe was "spoken" into existence. Each successive element then arises out of the former by a process of differentiation with air or *prANa* first, then fire, water and earth. Each successive level represents a greater degree of "grossness."

Thus it is that each subsequent element is not created out of nothing but is an "effect" that is already contained in its preceding "cause." Furthermore, every seemingly separate thing is only ever the non-dual reality, only differentiated by name into form as a result of our ignorance. A word in the mind, representing an object, is projected as an image and vice versa. In a sense, an object *is* its name, and all names ultimately reduce to OM, the "original" sound, which in turn is nothing but the Absolute.

As regards creation, Shankara treats the apparent objects rather as a "manifestation," by which he means that something not previously perceived is now perceived. As such, the so-called effect is clearly pre-existent. An example he uses is of an object that becomes visible when the sun rises. Just because it was not seen earlier does not mean that it did not exist. If it did not exist, it would not be seen in light either.

We will continue to see the world with its separate, apparently real objects as long as our ignorance persists. Once that is removed by knowledge, it will be realized that there was only ever *brahman*. This is explained here by **Swami Tapasyananda** translating and commenting on the **Srimad Bhagavata** - The Holy Book of God:

58. The reflection of an object is actually observed as existing, though in the eye of logic it is not there where it is seen. In the same way, the objects experienced are not existences independent in themselves, as it is contrary to fact. (They are the expression of the will of the Supreme Being appearing to be independent existences so long as the *jIva* does not realise his oneness with the Supreme.)

61. Even though there is no difference in the *Atman*, the sense of recognition based on difference would persist so long as there is *aj~nAna*. Then the question will arise whether the scriptural prohibitions and injunctions based on the sense of difference will not be unreal and not binding. The answer is that they are binding only so long as there is the spell of ignorance. It is just like sleeping and waking experienced in

the course of a dream. After the basic dream breaks, they have no relevance. Such is the case with the Vedic injunctions and prohibitions. (Ref. 298)

Creation

As with most scriptures, the Upanishads provide creation myths. These can satisfy the naïve mind, which needs a rational context in which to make sense of itself and the world until such time as knowledge can be acquired to erode the ignorance. But they may also serve as metaphors to the more mature mind to reveal subtle truths not amenable to direct communication. These stories of a "gradual creation" are called *krama sRRiShTi*, where *krama* means "progressing step by step." The converse theory, *yugapatsRRiShTi*, says that creation is simultaneous with the perception of it and that there is no related process involved (*yugapad* means "together, at the same time"). This is really another name for the more commonly encountered *dRRiShTi sRRiShTi vAda*, below. It only becomes plausible when we can begin to see through the illusion of cause and effect.

The *aitareya upaniShad* has one of the most detailed descriptions of creation. It describes how the Atman decided to create the worlds. He created the worlds of "celestial waters," the sky, earth and waters below the earth. Then he created a "cosmic person" as a lump from the waters. As a result of meditating upon this, a hole opened up in the lump in the form of a mouth... And so on. And there are other, contradictory descriptions in other sources.

Bhaskar explains how it is that we have such accounts, which clearly do not accord with the essential philosophy of Advaita:

It is clear that *shruti* is not so particular about giving the correct account of creation. If the creation is real, *Ishvara* is really its creator; how can *shruti mata* [doctrine] give incorrect information about it?

The *prashna upaniShad* says that the *puruSha* created *prANa* etc. but it is not clear out of which substance he created them. The *Aitareya* says differently: that all this universe was *Atman* before creation. The *muNDaka* says Atman himself became all this in the process of creation... and it seems all the created things appeared at a stretch like hair out of a person! And the *chhAndogya* says *Atman* itself modified and transformed into the universe, though we know that this sort of self transformation is repugnant to the *shruti* and its *siddhAnta* of *nirvikAra Atman* [its conclusion that Atman is uniform and unchangeable]. It is also to be noted that, with regard to the *jIva*, *shruti* gives different description at different places.

So, if *shruti* is not giving us the "correct" order and process of this creation in order to attribute the same to *Ishvara*, what is the intention in advocating creation, *jIva* etc?

Since both *jIva* and *jagat* are easily accessible to us, *shruti* is adopting this method in order to teach us the "reality" which is beyond this *nAma rUpAtmaka* [composed of name and form] *jIva-jagat*. It is all a device for the purpose of teaching the absolute non dual reality, using the traditional method of superimposition (*adhyAropa*) and rescission (*apavAda*).

It would not be out of context if I repeat here the *paramArtha* in Advaita as stated by Sri *gaudapAdAchArya* in his *kArikA* on the *mANDUkyopaniShad*:

"There is neither creation nor dissolution; no one bound nor one who undergoes spiritual discipline; no one who intensely desires to be released nor one who is released - this is the **absolute truth**."

If we understand the above declaration properly, it is not difficult for us to discern that the method of creation is presented in all the *shruti* texts as a variety of the *adhyAropa* and *apavAda* method. All apparent differences in *sRRiShTi*, *jIva svarUpa* and *brahma svarUpa* can easily be reconciled once we know how this method works throughout the *prasthAna traya*.

The *kArikA* also states (3-15):

"The creation which is taught in various ways by means of illustrations like that of clay, metal and sparks is only a **device** (*upAya*) for the purpose of leading the mind to the truth. There is no diversity on any account." (Ref. 325)

Shankara explains (Brahma Sutra *bhAShya* II.i.32-33) that:
...the texts teaching that there was a creation are not concerned with proclaiming the ultimate truth. For their subject-matter falls within the realm of practical experience consisting of name and form imagined through nescience, and their ultimate purpose is only to indicate how one's true Self is the Absolute. (Ref. 335)

And (Bhagavad Gita *bhAShya* XVIII.67):

They [i.e. the scriptures] say what is good for the student and will help him to understand the unity at the back of all variety even when what they say is not literally true, just as we say "This will make your hair grow" to recalcitrant children when we want to induce them to drink milk. (Ref. 335)

Ramakrishnan Balasubramanian explains why it is that the theories are often conflicting:

It is actually quite natural that we have differing theories of creation. The world is *anirvachanIya* and descriptions of it are based on the assumption of its reality and also causality. Since these fundamental assumptions are flawed, conflicting theories abound. Thus, as *shrI gauDapAda* shows in a different context, *ajAti vAda* only is *avivAda* and *aviruddha* [free from dispute and non-contradictory].

The main points of *advaita vedAnta* are *jIva-brahma aikya* [identity], the world is *mithyA* and that *j~nAna* alone gives *mokSha*. Whatever theory... is found the most satisfying to help understand these main points of advaita, can be adopted by the *sAdhaka*. (Ref. 323)

Perception-related Theories of Creation

The view of the majority of people, at least in the western world, is that the universe exists as an objective reality independent of ourselves as observers. (More will be said about this later when we consider whether "objects" exist at all.) This is the case whether we think that it was created by a God of whatever variety or whether we believe that it was brought into existence by a "big bang." This "common-sense" theory is called *sRRiShTi dRRiShTi vAda*. *sRRiShTi* means "creation" and *dRRiShTi* means "seeing" so that this is the theory that creation occurs first and then we see it.

Advaita, of course, means that there is only the non-dual reality. Brahman could not create a universe without introducing duality. Therefore, if Advaita is true, the world cannot be real and Brahman cannot be a god in the usual sense of the word (all-powerful, all-knowing etc.) because there is nothing to control or know. Nevertheless, it is accepted that there appears to be a world and this world appears to consist of complex things that could not have originated by accident. In our initial state of ignorance, we are unable to appreciate the highest reality. Accordingly, the Upanishads teach (what is effectively) an 'argument from design' (teleological) for the existence of a creator-god, in a similar way to the currently popular resurgence of this concept in the United States.

But this is only a temporary sop to the naïve mind. The argument is effectively an analogy, as the western philosopher David Hume pointed out. We know that complicated things like watches were designed by an intelligent being so we assume that the much more complex world must have had an even more intelligent designer. Hume suggested that, in order to highlight the deficiencies of the argument, the world resembles a vegetable more than it does a watch. He proposed that it results from a process of generation rather than one of design. After all, we have lots of experience of reasoning-things resulting from generation but none of generating-things resulting from reason.

Nevertheless, to the western mind, it seems that *sRRiShTi dRRiShTi* is the *only* option but of course this is not the case. Advaita begins with that theory for the seeker who believes he or she is a separate body in an alien world. To such a mind, it is necessary to provide a "cause" for the apparent "effect." But, once teachings such as *neti, neti* have begun, and the seeker begins to realize that the Self is only identifying with body and mind as a result of ignorance, it is possible to begin to see beyond the apparent. We know, for example, that the dream world is a complete creation of the mind, regardless of the amount of detail. All of its peoples and places, space and time, color and sound exist only in our dream and vanish on awakening. We ought therefore to be equally skeptical about the apparent waking world.

As was noted when we discussed the states of consciousness in the last chapter, Advaita does not differentiate waking and dream to quite the same degree as common sense would dictate. Accordingly, it should come as little surprise that there is a theory which sublates the one above and which suggests that the world is effectively a product of the perceiving mind. This is called *dRRiShTi sRRiShTi vAda*. Note that this was not a theory prevalent in Shankara's time. It does not really fit in with the ideas of Advaita but it is one which is mentioned in later writings, such as those of Ramana Maharshi. According to **David Godman**, Ramana justified this by saying that: "if one can consistently regard the world as an unreal creation of the mind then it loses its attraction and it becomes easier to maintain an undistracted awareness of the 'I'-thought." (Ref. 17)

Sri R. Visvanatha Sastri explains how the process of postulating a creation takes place in the mind:

9. The concepts of "I" and "Thou" as well as of "(this) universe" are a fancy of our ignorance. What is seen as the pot, etc. is not there (from the Absolute sense); it is only a play of words.

10. Was the pot there before it was seen? What was it then and how was it there? From where did it come into our perception? How is it that it is a pot and not a non-pot?

11. When the mind cognizes the pot, or for that matter any entity, a process of cognition goes on in the mind to recognize the pot.

12. That awareness of the pot pervades the intellect and terminates in the declaration: This is a pot. It is only a re-cognition of the "appearance" of

what was occupying only the intellect.

17. When a pot has not yet been fully made, when does the "clay"-stage end and when does it get the name of a "pot"? Nobody can precisely answer this.

18. Even the one who knows by previous association what a pot is, cannot specify at what stage the so-called "pot" leaves its previous state and becomes a "pot." (Ref. 341)

As noted earlier, the theory used by Shankara to supersede the naïve theory of a "designed" actual creation, that was nevertheless already present in its cause, was *vivarta vAda*. This is the theory that the world is only an apparent projection – *vivarta* means an "error or illusion," brought about by ignorance. It would obviously contradict the notion of *brahman* as the non-dual reality if creation were accepted as real. Transformation means change which, in turn, means limitation and this would therefore imply that *brahman* is not infinite. This train of thoughts leads on to the notion of *mAyA*. Although the "act" of creation is described in the Upanishads, Shankara claims that this is not an actual transformation but only an appearance – the *adhyAsa* as a result of *avidyA* as described in the chapter on Knowledge and Ignorance. Gaudapada's *kArikA* on the *mANDUkya upaniShad* (III.21) says that what is immortal cannot become mortal nor vice versa because it would be a contradiction for something to change and yet remain the same. Only those statements of the *shruti* which are corroborated by reason should be accepted, says Gaudapada (III. 23).

Anand Hudli explains how the concept of *mAyA* relates to the theory of *vivarta vAda*:

The whole universe is explained by Advaita along the lines of a classic case of illusion, such as the illusion of the snake in the rope. What is seen under the influence of illusion is the snake which has been superimposed on the rope. The whole illusion is the result of two powers of *avidyA (aj~nAna)* called the *AvaraNa-shakti* and the *vikShepa-shakti.*

Two phenomena happen in this illusion. First, the reality, the rope, is obscured or concealed. This is done by the *AvaraNa-shakti*. Second, the illusory object, the snake, is projected by the *vikShepa-shakti*. The *AvaraNa shakti* is called the power of concealment and the *vikShepa-shakti* the power of projection.

Nevertheless, the rope is the substratum of the illusion. In the illusion process, the rope gets *apparently* transformed into the snake. Similar is the case of the brahman-universe illusion. It is only admitted by Advaita that the universe (world) is an *apparent* transformation of the substratum Brahman, not a *real* transformation... Such an apparent transformation is called *vivarta*. So you may say that advaita upholds *vivarta vAda*. (Ref. 322)

ajAti vAda – the 'No-creation' Theory

The final sublating theory in this scheme of development is the same as that which succeeded *vivarta vAda* in the cause and effect discussion above, namely *ajAti vAda*. It is the only truth at the level of *paramArtha*, all other theories being used as teaching aids in *vyavahAra* according to the level of understanding of the aspirant.

Vidyasankar Sundaresan describes it as follows:

As the question of creation does not even arise when the identity of *Atman* with *brahman* is known, it follows that nothing either comes into being nor goes out of being - it is always self-existent. This is *ajAti vAda*. The *Atman* is eternal, unborn and undying, admitting of no divisions. (Ref. 337)

It must be emphasized that this theory does not mean that the world is unreal or merely an illusion as some would maintain. It simply means that there has been no creation – the apparent world of name and form is nothing other than *brahman*. And it is not the "effect" of any "cause." But it must nevertheless be "real" – because it is none other than the Self, which is all that there is.

Ramana Maharshi explains why it is that we are told at an intermediate level of the teaching that the world is an illusion:

> At the level of the spiritual seeker you have got to say that the world is an illusion. There is no other way. When a man forgets that he is Brahman, who is real, permanent and omnipresent, and deludes himself into thinking that he is a body in the universe which is filled with bodies that are transitory, and labors under that delusion, you have got to remind him that the world is unreal and a delusion. Why? Because his vision which has forgotten its own Self is dwelling in the external, material universe. It will not turn inwards into introspection unless you impress on him that all this external material universe is unreal. When once he realizes his own Self he will know that there is nothing other than his own Self and he will come to look upon the whole universe as Brahman. (Ref. 173)

Having previously discussed the topic of *mithyA*, the claim that there has never been any creation ought not to come as any surprise. The necklace does not exist as a separate entity but is only a transient form of the gold that is its essential nature. It is temporarily "necklacey gold" as opposed to "ringy gold." You may "separate" the gold from the necklace by application of heat but to separate the necklace from the gold is impossible. Similarly, everything in this supposed creation is only a temporary form with a particular name. Brahman will be "separated" from you on death of the body but "you the person" can never be separated from Brahman. In essence, there is always and only the non-dual *brahman*.

The Bhagavad Gita (IX.4) states that "*All this world is pervaded by Me in my unmanifest form (aspect); all beings exist in Me, but I do not dwell in them.*" [†] (Ref. 122) This parallels the metaphor, whereby all necklaces and

---

[†] The Holy Geeta, Swami Chinmayananda, © Central Chinmaya Mission Trust, Mumbai.

rings are pervaded by the gold. All necklaces are gold but gold does not have to be in the form of a necklace. Gold is *satya*, the necklace is merely *mithyA*.

In the following verse (IX.5), Krishna says: "*Nor do beings exist (in reality) in me...*" Although the above analysis is valid at the level of *vyavahAra*, in reality nothing is ever created, nothing changes. It is only ever an appearance as a result of ignorance.

Creation has also been compared to a dream. When we enter our dream, the dream world is created and we exist for a time in what may appear to be the most detailed and comprehensive environment no less complex than the waking world. It has its own apparently self-consistent laws of time, space and causation and our life there seems full and natural. And yet the entirety exists in our own mind while the physical, waking body lies inert in bed. To the dreamer, the dream world is perfectly real and is rarely questioned. It is only realized to have been a fabrication upon awakening. In just the same way, this waking world appears and disappears but is never separate from or other than *brahman* – it is as though the day-dream of *brahman*. Nothing is ever created.

From the standpoint of the dream, I am the creator. The dream world manifests within me, is sustained by me and dissolves back into me. I am both the efficient and the material cause. Though the dream world is nothing but me, the dreamer-ego believes it to be real. Similarly, the waking world manifests within *Ishvara* and the waking ego, the *jIva*, believes it to be real. In reality, nothing ever happened.

Creation is real only to the extent that it is a manifestation of *brahman*. The Yoga Vasishtha uses the metaphor of the wind. It appears to be real when in motion and to cease to exist when the movement stops. Similarly, the world-appearance can be regarded as neither real nor unreal – *mithyA*. It is only ignorance – *avidyA* – that causes us to see it as separate from *brahman*.

The **Yoga Vasishtha** states that:

Nothing has ever been created anywhere at any time; and nothing comes to an end either. The absolute *brahman* is all, the supreme peace, unborn, pure consciousness and permanent. (Ref. 38)

Here is a modern take on *ajAti vAda* from **Cee**:

> There are many modern spiritual teachings that say "now is the reality," but it (now - as it appears to human senses) is a far, far cry from the truth of your own Existence. Go deeper than what you see. Go deeper than what you hear. Don't take even "now" as the Reality. The now comes and goes. The final perfect enlightenment in the Advaita is called "no creation." There is no birth or death. There is no bondage and no liberation, nothing has been created. No human forms and no world. That doesn't leave a void. That leaves perfect consciousness. It's silent. It's vast. And it is perfect, unutterable bliss. And you will see that past is just mind, the future is just mind, the now is just mind, and mind as such does not exist. But the perfection of your self, THE Self, IS. (Ref. 258)

And she (**Cee**) explains the basic concepts of there being no creation and no cause and effect in everyday terms as though it were the most obvious thing in the (non-existent) world:

> Then the obvious question to "No Creation" is, "Well, then why is there all this stuff?" However, there really is not any "stuff" when you actually inquire in this way and rest as pure Being because all this "stuff" is actually made up of pure Being, your own Being. It is all the same. It is all your Self. One explanation for that question would be to say, "Everything is gold and all these things are ornaments. All these objects are ornaments. It is all the same pure Consciousness. It is all the same gold. It all melts down to the same thing. It is all made out of the same thing." Nothing is created. How could something be created when it is all the same stuff? Nothing could be created within something that is just what it is. There is no second thing that ever occurs. You can see how cause and effect cannot even happen. How could there be a something that causes a something else when there are no two things to

begin with? Even just looking at nature, obviously everything changes and dissolves and reoccurs out of the same stuff. How can there really be cause and effect when everything is that same pure Consciousness? It is actually very logical and very literal, this Existence. How could there be any other teaching? It is Existence Itself that we are talking about, our own Existence. There is no other Truth to find. There are no words good enough for it because it is just this Being, just this pure Existence. (Ref. 258)

Such an explanation holds true only from the vantage point of reality, of course. From the point of view of the *jIva*, there is plainly a world out there and he or she believes it to be true, just as the dreamer believes in the reality of the dream world. And, just as the dream objects are real to the dreaming mind, so are the worldly objects real to the *jIva* (being in the mind of *Ishvara*). Even the *j~nAnI* still sees the manifestation, though it is no longer taken as real. Nevertheless, the creation eventually proves to be largely irrelevant to the seeker of Truth because such a one is ultimately only interested in *paramArtha* and not *vyavahAra* as **Shankara** explains (Commentary on *gauDapAda*'s *kArikA* to the *mANDUkya upaniShad* I.7):

> The noble ones, the seekers of liberation, are preoccupied only with the ultimate reality, not with useless speculations about creation. Hence the various alternative theories about creation come only from believers in the doctrine that creation is real. (Ref. 335)

Metaphors for Creation

There are a number of metaphors relating to the apparent creation.

Creation and the supposed separate objects are said to be like waves in the ocean. Though each wave might appear to have its own unique characteristics of height, temperature, amount of spray and foam and so on, they are all nevertheless simply water, as is the ocean itself. As the Yoga Vasishtha says, when the whirlpool in the ocean "dies," nothing is really dead.

Taking *brahman* (or more accurately *Ishvara*) as both the effective (*nimitta kAraNa*) and material cause (*upAdAna kAraNa*) of the universe, another very appropriate metaphor is that of the spider spinning a web. The web is spun at the instigation of the spider and the material originates from the spider's own body, being reabsorbed into it when the web is later eaten. The implications of this metaphor should be clearly seen – the web effectively *is* the spider in the same way that the pot *is* clay and the ring *is* gold. Likewise, the whole of this universe, including you and me, *is brahman*.

The metaphor can be taken even further in the case of a silk moth spinning a cocoon, in that the cocoon effectively binds and imprisons the caterpillar until such time as it is ready to emerge as a moth. In the same way, although we are ourselves *brahman*, we believe ourselves to be separate individuals trapped in the world.

The apparent diversity of the world is also like the multicolored rainbow produced when sunlight is diffracted by drops of rain. (This is not such a good metaphor in the light of modern scientific knowledge, given that the pure white light of the sun's rays does actually consist of many colors of different wavelength electromagnetic radiation. If this modern "truth" is taken for the actuality, then it might seem as though the apparent non-duality is being shown in the world in its true multiplicity.)

Space is that which pervades everything but which is unaffected by anything. Electricity empowers all varieties of electrical equipment but is unaffected by any of them. Light illuminates all activities, good, bad or indifferent without being influenced. Similarly, *brahman* is the sine qua non of everything, yet it does not interfere in any way and remains unchanged. It has been described as the unmoved mover.

Perhaps the clearest metaphor of all, however (which is why I keep using it!), is that of gold and the ornament – ring or bracelet – made from it. I remember the first time I was presented with this metaphor and the difficulty that I had in understanding how it was that the "ring" that was held up was not in fact a ring but was only gold. And I remember thinking that this would mean that one would have to point to a Rembrandt and say that it was "only paint." But this is undeniable, also. It merely emphasizes how completely the ideas of society have been inculcated into our minds.

We are so mesmerized by the world and our supposed separateness from other persons and objects that it is habitual to see the form and believe it to be the thing itself; to refer to the attribute and think we are talking about the noun. We see the appearance and take it to be the reality.

But the form changes while the gold remains unchanged. From the standpoint of the gold, there is only ever gold. Once this has been realized, it can then be seen that *even the appearance is only ever Gold.* It was only the use of the word "ring" that deluded us into thinking that there was ever anything else present.

In the case of the Rembrandt, the same applies in essence. What is different is that the form of the painting embodies the skill and insight of the artist and so enables the resultant beauty to point us more clearly towards the truth than would the random daubs of a novice. But this has now moved beyond the bounds of the original metaphor. In fact, both are equally *brahman* and moreover both are pointers to *brahman.* It is only the ignorant mind that requires the prompting of beauty to help overcome that ignorance.

Similarly, once we have negated the five sheaths and acknowledged that we are the *Atman*, we can look back at the world and see that there is only the Self everywhere. It is merely the convention of names applied to the various forms that delude us into thinking that there is multiplicity.

Swami Satprakashananda uses the metaphor of a stained-glass window (Ref. 27). If we look at such a window in a cathedral when the sunlight is shining through it, each of the elements in the scene is brightly lit and stands out in brilliant color. As the sun dims, however, the picture becomes dull and lifeless, disappearing completely when the light fades entirely. In fact, the image consists only of the sunlight itself, temporarily modified by the variously colored glass. Similarly, all subjects and objects are manifest purely by the light of Consciousness, temporarily modified by the various *upAdhi*-s (limitations).

The most frequently encountered metaphor in the whole of Advaita is that of the rope and the snake. When used in connection with the notion of creation, it does help to illustrate how the world might be unreal and only appear because of our failure to "see" the non-dual reality. It can also bring out another valuable point, however, namely how this reality is not the "cause" of the universe but the "ground," as **Arvind Sharma** explains:

> One may therefore now ask: in what sense, if any, can the relationship between the rope and the snake be regarded as one of causation, if the effect is only *apparent*? We may say that the appearance of the serpent was the *cause* and the fear in the person generated by it an *effect* thereof, but in what sense was the rope the cause of the snake? If anything the defective vision or poor lighting was the cause, not the rope. The rope was the *ground* of the appearance of the snake rather than the cause. Similarly, the Reality is properly spoken of as the ground of the universe rather than its cause. (Ref. 326)

One last example, particularly popular amongst modern teachers, is that of the movie screen, where the "reality" is the screen itself with all else mere appearances in the movie. Whether "The Towering Inferno" or "Waterworld" is the movie being shown, the screen is totally unaffected. Here is **Chuck Hillig**:

> No matter *what* activities are, seemingly, "happening" in the movie, the fundamental reality beneath It all is still *only* the unbroken and seamless Screen that's supporting all of the dramas being played out.
>
> Although the world *appears* to exist, the only thing that's really *real* is Consciousness, Itself. So, as the historical ego-self, you're *always* looking directly into the cosmic mirror of Life and beholding the wondrous and multifaceted face of God. And here's the great miracle: It's always been *your* face! (Ref. 320)

Ishvara

God has not created the universe like a poet creates a poem, the relationship is just like a dancer and the dance; they remain one. **Osho** (Ref. 166)

The concept of *Ishvara* often poses a problem for the western mind. Having rejected the idea of a Christian God in heaven (and a separate, created world with the descendents of Adam living in inherited sin) and embraced the non-dual concept of Advaita, it somehow seems to be a retrogressive step to start talking about *Ishvara*.

It seems that the only intellectually acceptable idea is that there has been no creation. If the world exists as separate from the Absolute, then that would mean duality, irrespective of whether or not He created it. Alternatively, if the Absolute has transformed Himself into the world, then He is subject to change and no longer Absolute. Creating something implies a desire to create, in turn implying that He lacks something, which is a limitation, again meaning that the Absolute is not "infinite."

Instead of a creation, the rational explanation if one is needed is that the apparent world is a superimposition – the snake on the rope mistakenly perceived as a result of ignorance. But it is only meaningful to talk about creation in the phenomenal realm, where causality appears to exist. Once this has been transcended, the question no longer arises, just as it is no longer meaningful to ask whether the snake is poisonous, once we have realized it to be a rope.

The appearance is the world; the reality is *brahman*. But it does not make sense to say that *brahman* is the cause of the world, just as one cannot say that the rope causes the snake. Causality and change have no meaning at the level of *paramArtha* – there is no relationship between *Ishvara* and the world because "both" are *brahman*. There is a "creator" only as long as the world is believed to be real. Or, to put it another way, if you believe in the reality of the world, you are obliged to invent God.

At the level of the individual, the ignorance that prevents the *jIva* from seeing the truth is called *avidyA*. At the level of the world, the "force" which obscures the reality and projects the apparent world is called *mAyA*. Since it would not make sense to talk of such a force without also talking about an "entity" which wields the force, it is necessary to postulate one. This entity, which as it were, carries out the creation on behalf of *brahman* is *Ishvara*. *Ishvara* and *mAyA* have the same ontological status. Unlike the *jIva*, however, who is at the mercy of *mAyA*, *Ishvara* is its controller.

> *God is only a concept, though the highest the human mind can make. But you are not a concept.* **Atmananda Krishna Menon** (Note 1310 Ref. 13)

Thus, the following equations can be formed to help understand the various relationships:

jIva = *Atman* + *avidyA*

Ishvara = *brahman* + *mAyA*

This is expounded in the *pa~nchadashI* (III.37):

> Brahman who is existence, consciousness and infinity is the reality. Its being *Ishvara* (the omniscient Lord of the world) and *jIva* (the individual soul) are (mere) superimpositions by the two illusory adjuncts (*mAyA* and *avidyA*, respectively). (Ref. 52)

Atman in the form of an individual body-mind is the *jIva*; *brahman* in the form of the totality (including all individual body-minds) is *Ishvara*. Thus it is that the individual can be a part of the totality, in the same way that a wave is a part of the ocean, and yet *Atman* can be *brahman*, in the same way that both wave and ocean are water. The reality, *satyam*, is always only *Atman-brahman*; the person and the world are *mithyA*, though their essence, too, is *brahman*. **Swami Dayananda** explains further:

> Between the wave and the ocean, the difference is obvious. If the wave is enlightened, it gives up the *mithyA* difference, having recognized its

oneness with the ocean. The ocean – *satyam* (what is real) – transcends *mithyA*. But this transcendence does not imply any physical separation. That is why we use the word "transcend." It is both immanent and transcendent. It remains in and through, and it is more than; it goes beyond. It is exactly like when you say "touch wood." Whatever wooden object happens to be in front of you, you touch… transcending the door, table, chair or desk, I recognize wood.

…As *satyam*, there is only one limitless *brahman*, and that I am. The little enlightened wave can as well say, "There is only one limitless ocean, and that I am. I am the cause of all these waves and breakers; they are all from me." But the other waves must be enlightened to understand that. (Ref. 186)

Once we have removed the ignorance that causes us to identify our true self with a body and mind (*ahaMkAra*), we are left with the realization that we *are* the *Atman*. It is not that we have acquired something new (knowledge) that has changed us into the *Atman* – we always were That. Our experience has changed but the reality has not – who we are transcends the experience. It is only the body, mind, thoughts etc. that change but as long as I think I am those, it seems as if I am subject to change, too. It is this *avidyA upAdhi* – concealment of ignorance – that effectively makes me, the *Atman*, into a limited person. Who I really am is free from all limitations.

Another way of looking at it is through a consideration of *vAsanA*-s, the impressions that we accumulate as a result of action, according to the theory of *karma*. Each of us has his or her own *vAsanA*-s that we bring into this life and these form our individual (*vyaShTi*) *upAdhi* of ignorance, which in turn dictates how we react to situations in life. Effectively, they might be considered to bring about the sort of life we lead or the world in which we live – they are held in our *kAraNa sharIra* or "causal body." The world is the total of all of these "individual worlds," the sum (*samaShTi*) of all of the individual *vAsanA*-s. Thus it is that *Ishvara* can be considered to create the world according to these *samaShTi vAsanA*-s in order that all of the individuals have the optimum opportunity to "work out" their *prArabdha saMskAra* and thereby realize their true nature.

This is somewhat different from the "argument from design" considered under the topic of creation. It is assumed that action gives rise to "fruit of action," as was discussed in Chapter 2. Often the fruit is immediate or occurs in the near future. If we eat, we feel immediately satisfied. If we plant a seed, it eventually sprouts and grows. Sometimes, the fruit depends upon others, as for example when we work for an employer and they are then responsible for paying us. The argument is that there are no examples where the fruit is not dependent either on our own actions or on the actions of another. Therefore, there must be a God who keeps record of all of the fruits due to us that need to be carried over to a future life if not given later in this one. This is also the argument for performing religious rituals, the idea being that these generate *saMskAra* in *Ishvara* in the same way that the work of a servant causes *saMskAra* in the mind of his master. (These arguments stem from Shankara's *vAkya bhAShya* on the *kenopaniShad*, as related in Ref. 335.)

Remember God is not the future, not heaven, God is "I am," present tense, this moment. **Mark McCloskey** (Ref. 251)

But it must never be forgotten that *Ishvara* IS *brahman, simply being looked at from the point of view of the world*. It is all a question of trying to make words perform tasks for which they are inadequate. Brahman cannot create as discussed above. Since, in our ignorance, there appears to be a creation, we postulate a creator, *Ishvara*, and a power derived from *brahman*, *mAyA*, to account for it provisionally until the truth is realized. Similarly, subsidiary explanations are offered to account for more detailed aspects such as that the *mAyA* of *Ishvara* is predominantly one of projecting the illusion (*vikShepa*) while the *avidyA* of the *jIva* is predominantly one of covering over (*AvaraNa*) the truth. (*mAyA* is said to consist of pure *sattva*, whilst *avidyA* is impure *sattva*, contaminated by *rajas* and *tamas*.)

All the words such as omnipotent, all-seeing, omniscient etc. apply to *Ishvara* but not to *brahman* – *brahman* is beyond description

Similarly, *mAyA* and reality are the same. As **Ramana Maharshi** said (Ref. 49), it is simply that "the universe is real if perceived as the Self, and unreal if perceived apart from the Self."

saguNa and nirguNa

There are further ways in which traditional Advaita speaks of reality. The *bRRihadAraNyaka upaniShad* (II.3) addresses the "two forms of reality" – the finite and the infinite, the immanent and the transcendent, the formed and the formless, the mortal and the immortal, the moving and the unmoving. The infinite, true, noumenal, formless, immortal, unmoving and changeless is perhaps best referred to as the "unmanifest" – *amUrta* or *avyakta*. The finite, empirical, phenomenal, perceptible and ever-changing is then the "manifest" – *mUrta* or *vyakta*.

The active principal in manifestation, which we might call "God" is *Ishvara*, also called *shabda-brahman*, differentiated from the unmanifest, non-acting principal, called *para-brahman* or *paramAtman*, which we might call the "Absolute."

The unmanifest, non-dual reality of brahman is said to be without qualities or attributes of any kind – *nirguNa* (*guNa* – the three qualities of *sattva*, *rajas* and *tamas*). The apparently manifest, controller/creator of the universe, *Ishvara*, is said to be with qualities – *saguNa*. **Paul Tillich** spoke of this as follows:

> When Brahman is said to be the efficient and material cause of the world's existence, it is *saguNa brahman*, not *nirguNa brahman*, that is so described. To speak of Brahman as the cause of the world presupposes a duality of Brahman and world, and such dualistic thinking is grounded on ignorance of the true nature of Brahman and Atman. Although Brahman is characterized in various Vedic texts as the efficient and material cause of the universe, Shankara holds that these texts refer to *saguNa brahman* and that thinking of Brahman as *saguNa* ("with attributes") constitutes only a preliminary view of Brahman, a view based on the human need to explain the apparent existence of the

universe. However, in order to understand the true nature of Brahman, we must go beyond this preliminary view and understand Brahman as it is in itself, not in relation to the universe, i.e., in non-dualistic terms. At that level of comprehension, it is seen that the entire universe is nothing but a superimposition upon and mere appearance of Brahman, the underlying reality of all that is. (Ref. 333; extract included as an introduction to Ref. 324)

nirguNa is thus the *paramArtha* view, the unspeakable, unthinkable Truth of *ajAti vAda*. *saguNa* is the interim assumption of *vyavahAra*, made by the *jIva* in his ignorance, prior to enlightenment. The topic of language, and in particular the conflict between adjectives and nouns, was discussed in Chapter 5. Thus, for example, the wooden table was seen to be really "tabley wood," with the wood simply having been formed into a shape that we name "table." This applies to all "objects" – they all turn out to be forms of something more subtle. The ultimate "object" (which is no object at all) is that which is itself formless – this is *nirguNa brahman*.

Microcosm and Macrocosm

I do not intend to discuss this here. The key source for anyone interested is the *mANDUkyopaniShad* (not the *kArikA*) - see Refs. 35, 230, 286, 287, 296 for example. The diagram in Appendix E summarizes the essential details, relating this with states of consciousness, sheaths, gross-subtle-causal bodies and the symbolic letter OM.

mAyA

mAyA is beginningless (anAdi), for time arises only with it; it is unthinkable (achintya), for all thought is subject to it; it is indescribable (anirvachanIya) for all language results from it. **Eliot Deutsch** (Ref. 82)

Advaita is all about coming to an intellectual understanding and then an intuitive realization about the nature of the non-dual reality. But this cannot be achieved without accounting for the apparent duality of the world. If the truth is *Advaita* (not two), then there can be no duality, in which case the world, as currently perceived, cannot exist. Whatever the world is, *brahman* must be its cause and yet that implies change and *brahman* cannot change if non-dual. Thus, the artificial mechanism that is introduced in order to "explain" creation is a creator god (*Ishvara*), that is nevertheless not other than *brahman*, and a power (*mAyA*), that is also not independent of *brahman*. As before, *mAyA* is *mithyA*, neither real nor non-existent – it is *anirvachanIya*, not able to be categorized.

The word "illusion" is often used in relation to *mAyA* but this is not really correct, as **Professor Gummuluru Murthy** relates:

Quite often, the word illusion, or unreal is used as an equivalent of *mAyA*; but illusion is not the right equivalent. As far as I understand, there is no equivalent word for *mAyA* in the English language. I would like to expand on this by using the following *upaniShad*-ic statements.

[*muNDaka* U. II.2.12] All this (manifested) universe is verily the supreme Brahman.

[*bRRihad*. U. II.4.6] All this (manifested) universe is this *Atman*. (Because everything springs from this *Atman*, is dissolved in It and remains imbued with It during continuance, for it cannot be perceived apart from the *Atman*. Therefore everything is the *Atman*). [Yajnavalkya's teachings to Maitreyi]

[*bRRihad*. U. II.5.19]

This Brahman is without a prior or a posterior (cause or effect), without interior or exterior (no other species within It or without It), this *Atman* is Brahman, the perceiver of everything.

All the above statements say unequivocally that everything is *Atman* (Brahman) i.e. the universe (*jagat*) that we see cannot be an illusion.

But the *jagat* is a product of *mAyA* i.e. *mAyA* is not illusion. *mAyA* is a statement of fact of what we are and what we see around us. It (*mAyA*) refers to the inner contradictions (pairs of opposites) we see all around us. All our experiences in the realm of *mAyA* are experiences coming through the sense organs. They are not illusory, but true. Knowledge of the not-Self (the *jagat*) is still truth. But the Self or *Atman* or *brahman* is the "Truth of the truth." *bRRihadAraNyaka* (II.1.20) says

Its (Atman's) intimate name is the Truth of the truth. The cosmic energy (*prANa*) is verily truth, and This (the *Atman*) is the truth of that.

The best understanding of *mAyA*, apart from *upaniShad*-s, (it is debatable whether the word *mAyA* appeared in the *upaniShad*-s or not) is Shri VidyAraNyaswamI's *pa~nchadashI* verse:

If one correctly understands the *veda*-s (*shruti*), it (*mAyA*) does not exist (*asat*); by reasoning (*yukti*) using intellect, we conclude that it is indeterminate (*anirvachanIya*); but for the worldly-minded (*laukika*), it is real (*vAstava*) indeed. (Ref. 329)

The description "Truth of the truth" comes from the *bRRihadAraNyaka upaniShad* (II.1.20), which gives the analogy of the creation being brought about by Brahman in the same way that a web emerges from a spider. The world is relatively true, to be sure but it is Brahman that is the essence of everything that we see - the Truth of that relative truth. Brahman is the actual reality of the apparent reality that we take for granted. It is the absolute reality because it is changeless, unaffected by time or space, whilst the universe "bangs," evolves and ultimately decays and dies.

As usual, the concept of *mAyA* creates some apparent paradoxes. These are explored here by **Professor V. Krishnamurthy**:

Unless *mAyA* is already present, neither concealment nor projection can take place. Is *mAyA* then coeval with *brahman*? Do they exist side by side? Does this not contradict the non-dual status of *brahman*? Where does *mAyA* operate? What is its base of operation? These questions raise very profound issues.

The base of activity of *mAyA* cannot be *brahman* because the latter is Absolute luminosity and there is no place in it for ignorance or darkness. Nor can the *jIva* be the base of operations of *mAyA*. For *jIva* itself cannot come into existence until *mAyA* has operated. There seems to be an irresolvable logical difficulty here.

But the difficulty will vanish once we realize that we are here making an implicit assumption that is not valid. We are actually assuming the prior reality of time and space before the appearance of *mAyA*. Otherwise we could not have asked the questions: Where does *mAyA* operate? When does it come into existence? These questions are valid only if you have a frame of reference in time and space independent of *mAyA*. But time and space, says Shankara, are themselves creations of *mAyA*.

"I am ignorant" is a common expression, within anybody's experience. Hence *mAyA* is not completely unreal. But it disappears with the onset of knowledge. So it is not real either. Thus it is different from both the real and the unreal. In Sanskrit it is therefore called *sad-asad-vilakShaNa*, meaning that it is different from both the real and the unreal. And for the same reason it is said to be *anirvachanIya*, meaning "that which is undecidable or that which cannot be defined one way or the other." It is in this sense we say that the world of perception, the common world of experience, cannot be rejected out of hand as totally false, like the hare's horn or the lotus in the sky; nor can it be taken to be totally real because it suffers contradiction at a higher level of experience.

It is real in the empirical sense and unreal in the absolute sense. (Ref. 327)

Once a full understanding of all of the above has been gained and served its purpose of dispelling the mistaken belief of a separate self in an alien world, the interim assumptions of *Ishvara*, *mAyA* and the like can all be dropped. **Swami Krishnananda** explains, in his commentary on the *pa~nchadashI*:

...on a careful investigation, we understand that Brahman, in its pristine purity, is utterly unattached, and *Ishvara*, endowed with the power of *mAyA* is the direct cause of creation. There is, in fact, no necessity to engage oneself in any argumentation in regard to the relation subsisting between

Ishvara and *Brahman*, since from the standpoint of *Brahman*, there is neither creation nor the world, and the explanation of the process of creation is afforded only to the *jIva*-s who consider the world as real and creation as a fact. The creation-theory is a help to the *jIva* in understanding the all-pervading nature of Reality, and the necessity to realise its identity with it. *Brahman* and *Ishvara* are one, as the pure canvas is one with that stiffened with starch. (Ref. 138)

pralaya

The opposite face of creation is dissolution – *pralaya* – when the universe is destroyed at the end of a *kalpa*. All *jIva*-s and *Ishvara* cease to (apparently) exist. As usual, attempts to "explain" this logically are difficult. This is discussed in the **Advaita Bodha Deepika**:

> In dissolution there remains only the non-dual Brahman and no *Ishvara*. Clearly there cannot be His will. When it is said that in dissolution all are withdrawn from manifestation and remain unmanifest, it means that the *jIva-s*, all the universe, and *Ishvara* have all become unmanifest. The unmanifest *Ishvara* cannot exercise His will. What happens is this: just as the dormant power of sleep displays itself as dream, so also the dormant power of *mAyA* displays itself as this plurality, consisting of *Ishvara*, His will, the universe and the *jIva-s*. *Ishvara* is thus the product of *mAyA* and He cannot be the origin of His origin. *mAyA* therefore has no antecedent cause. In dissolution there remains only Pure Being devoid of will, and admitting of no change. In creation *mAyA* hitherto remaining unmanifest in this Pure Being, shines forth as the mind. By the play of mind, plurality appears as *Ishvara*, the worlds and the *jIva-s*, like magic. *mAyA* manifest is creation, and *mAyA* unmanifest is dissolution. Thus of its own accord, *mAyA* appears or withdraws itself and has thus no beginning. Therefore we say there was no antecedent cause for it. (Ref. 80)

Just as the *jIva* continues to exist in "latent form", as it were in sleep (and this can be shown since calling someone's name whilst they are deeply asleep will still awaken them), so *Ishvara* exists in latent form in *pralaya*. The macrocosm mirrors the microcosm.

[According to the creation mythology, *laya* is the sleep of the *jIva*; *pralaya* the sleep of *brahma*, the creator. A *kalpa* is the complete cycle of creation and dissolution and lasts one day in the timescale of *brahma*. He then rests for the night and starts again the following day. This goes on for about a hundred years (*brahma* time), after which *brahma* dies and another takes over the role, beginning the entire process again. Supposedly, this will continue until all *jIva*-s realize their identity with *brahman*.]

lIlA

lIlA is the concept that God created the universe in order to "enjoy" Himself (since it is only through the medium of body-minds that He is able to "know" Himself at all). Since we have already seen that there has never been any "creation" and both *Ishvara* and *mAyA* are *mithyA*, it will hopefully be realized that this is yet another idea aimed at providing an "explanation" for seekers at an interim level of understanding. The notion becomes redundant once a more subtle appreciation of the subject has been gained.

Ramesh Balsekar says the following:

The *lIlA* is the only answer to the question, "Why has God created this universe?" You can either say "Why not?" or you say "It was just a game God is playing." Just a game of hide-and-go-seek. Just a game of the observer and the observed, each considering itself the subject, and therefore there are human relations and the problems of human relations. Basically, it simply means it's a game that is going on. And we ask, "Why?" There is really no answer.

You can see this if you watch a couple of children on the seashore with a spade and a bucket. They create a castle or whatever and they spend a lot of time over it, a lot of trouble over it and at the end of the day, when the parents say that it's time to go home, they just kick it and go! You ask the child, "Why did you build the castle and then demolish it?" The child wouldn't understand your question! If you persist, he would say, "Because I like to create. I created a castle because I like to create the castle. I demolished it because I like to demolish it." (Ref. 334)

Existence of Objects

As was pointed out by Berkeley and discussed briefly earlier, so-called objects are not known as such, i.e. as gross matter. Perception only occurs at the level of mind, where the subtle transactions of nerve impulses are interpreted. If there is such a thing as gross matter, we can never know it directly. All reference is indirect, via the realm of thought and language. Effectively, there is no such thing as matter; all so-called objects exist as thoughts, feelings or concepts.

If this sounds too abstruse, just consider a simple object such as a flower. What is a flower? Suppose we take a fragrant red rose. We hold it in our hand and feel the stem and the petals, smell the heady perfume and see the intense crimson color. Surely, we know what we mean by a rose and cognize it as a separate and distinct object?

But suppose we dip the rose in some chemical solution, which leaches out the color and destroys the smell. Is it still a rose? And what if we start removing the petals one by one? At what stage does it cease to be a flower? We call an apparently separate thing by a distinctive name in recognition of a particular form and specific properties. The color of the rose in this example is only apparent to the eyes and its perfume to the nose. We say that it is the rose that has these properties. Which sense is able to detect the rose itself, as opposed to one or two of its properties? We are only ever aware of attributes – the "thing itself" always eludes us. Does the "flower" or the "rose" exist at all? If there is something that is the substrate, as it were, for all of these qualities of color, fragrance, texture and so on, but which does not itself have any such qualities, how could we ever know of its existence? What would it even mean to suppose such a thing?

The classical Advaitin view of the mechanism of perception it that the mind effectively "goes out" via the senses and "separates out" a part of the essentially formless reality. It is claimed even by modern science that an infant does not recognize himself as separate from others or from things. All is a formless, nameless whole. It is through the learnt process of language that the world comes to be seen as a multiplicity of separate entities. Thus, regardless of any literal interpretation of the traditional description, it is effectively the case that duality arises through the action of the mind in separating out forms and naming them. The duality collapses, along with the other mental concepts of time, space and causality, when we fall into deep sleep and the mind ceases to operate.

As was seen in the first chapter, who I really am is not the mind, body or intellect. Just as perception occurs at the level of mind and not in the gross world, so "I" exist above the realm of thoughts and, by analogy, cannot know thoughts etc. at the level of mind. As Krishna Menon puts it (Note 1429 Ref. 13), thoughts have to be transformed into pure Consciousness in order to be witnessed by the I-principle. Effectively, therefore, the subtle level of mind does not exist either. Only Consciousness exists.

Another way of looking at it is to recognize that what actually happens when "I" see an "object" is that there is only "seeing." The ideas of subject and object are both subsequently occurring concepts in the mind. **"Sailor" Bob Adamson** explains:

> For example, take seeing. You're seeing right now. Then the thought comes up, "I see." But the actual seeing was happening before the thought. With the thought you have created a pseudo-seer. When you say "I see the tree," you've created a pseudo-object – a subject and object in form. (Ref. 346)

The analogy of dreams is also useful, as it is in so many aspects of the philosophy. In our dreams, we "see" external objects and we "think" and "feel" what are evidently internal thoughts and feelings. From the waking standpoint, it is evident that both the supposed external objects and internal states were equally illusory and only imagined. Consequently, it is no longer a convincing argument to suppose that external objects in the waking state are more real than mental imaginings.

Sufficient has been said earlier for it to be appreciated that objects do not exist as separate entities but only as name and form superimposed in our ignorance upon the non-dual brahman. Again, the idea of "tabley wood" instead of "wooden table" helps to see this clearly. When we say that this computer on the table in front of me "exists," I need to see that it is really a form of its composite parts – monitor, CPU, hard drive and so on. Each component is itself a complex form of other parts. The electric wires, for example, consist of strands of metal covered by fibers and plastic. They are not "plastic covered wire" but "wiry plastic and metal." Plastic is a polymerized form of a fractional distillate from oil. Oil results from vegetation, compressed over millennia. Vegetation is a complex form of proteins, sugars, RNA etc. Proteins are complex organic molecules. Molecules are combinations of atoms, which are made up of protons, neutrons and electrons. These are wave-particle forms of energy, which itself is the manifest expression of *brahman*. Only *brahman* "exists" in the final analysis.

Dr. A. J. Alston, commenting on Shankara's view of objects, says that:

Objects are illusions, entirely dependent on their names. They are the mere illusory appearance of a plurality of isolated units in the Absolute that result from the arbitrary activity of naming. In this sense, the object is entirely dependent for its existence on, and therefore identical with, its name. (Ref. 335)

The **Srimad Bhagavata** says that:

The reflection of an object is actually observed as existing, though in the eye of logic it is not there where it is seen. In the same way, the objects experienced are not existences independent in themselves, as it is contrary to fact. (They are the expression of the will of the Supreme

Being appearing to be independent existences so long as the *jIva* does not realise his oneness with the Supreme.) (Ref. 298)

Having determined that there are no separate objects, that everything we see is mistakenly "named" as a thing, rather than as an attribute of some more universal "thing," there is a danger in being reduced to an attitude of solipsism, concluding that "I" am the only reality. This is another level of mistake and the solution is that the "I" has to be treated in exactly the same way. This is not to conclude that nothing exists but that I am another attribute of that same non-dual reality. **Michael Reidy** explains:

It is occasionally mentioned without further analysis that "nature is *jaDa*" [inert]. Yes that is apparently the case but if we take it to be the ultimate truth then we may be backed into a position of solipsistic idealism. Before going into that, it is important to state the Vedantic position on the perceptuality of objects or clarify how it is that the apparently inert object comes to be an item of awareness of that object as it really is, "out there"...

What is happening is that the same Consciousness is inflected in 3 ways as knowing, the knower and the known. What brings them all together is what has been called connaturality i.e. they share the same nature. If that connaturality is neglected then the only consciousness in the picture will be that of the perceiver and the shining in the consciousness of the perceiver of the object will be due to the perceiver's consciousness alone. Thus the object will remain trapped in the magic circle of the subject alone, *solus ipse* (sole itself). You cannot from there go, as some do, to claim that all is consciousness because by virtue of your base position there is no exterior reality.

"I could be bounded in a nutshell and count myself the king of infinite space" (Hamlet, Prince of Denmark and Patron of Solipsism) (Ref. 330)

As in so many other aspects of Advaita, there is a progression of understanding in respect of objects; successive layers, which must be sublated. We begin with the everyday understanding that objects exist separately from each other and from us, the subject who sees them in an alien and indiscriminate world. This is objectivity. Under the *AvaraNa*, concealing force of *mAyA*, the truth has become obscured. The initial teaching of Advaita is that the world has been created by Ishvara out of His own substance – that we are watched over and justly rewarded for our actions. The world exists within Brahman. The ultimate realization is the identity of the world as Brahman, where nothing is separate but only a form of the same non-dual reality, arbitrarily partitioned off by naming. As **Govindagopal Mukhopadhyaya** puts it:

> The Upanishads thus solve the problem of the subject and the object not by a denial of the one and an affirmation of the other, neither by a denial of both, but simply through a transcendence of both the terms. (Ref. 344)

Conclusion

We have to accept that language can never describe reality. It can only be used in two main ways, namely to clarify mistaken concepts so as to remove ignorance and to point towards the truth, much as a signpost points the direction towards a destination. **Justus Kramer Schippers** says the following:

> Language can create many misunderstandings because words always refer to an experience or an object that can be experienced. A word is therefore a label with which an object or phenomenon is indicated, never the phenomenon itself. The menu (word) is never the dish (the object that can be experienced). How can you explain in words how rosemary tastes? That can not be explained with words. Taste a bit and we (think) we know what rosemary is. Naturally we know absolutely nothing; we have only had an experience that we call tasting...
>
> Language is certainly useful for practical existence, where we want to, or have to, give each other concrete messages such as "can you hand

me that book," or "watch out there's a car coming." But to let each other know with the use of language what Unity or Truth is, or the Source of all Being out of which all phenomena arise is impossible. But we have no other tool, we have to make do with it. (Ref. 319)

Coming full circle

I do not expect to prove that London exists with words, but with words I can chart a course that will bring all to London. **Richard Rose** (Ref. 209)

As regards the nature of reality and the seeming world, the teaching of Advaita effectively returns us to where we started from, but with a radically different vantage point. We begin by thinking that there is a real world "out there." In particular, we believe that there is a body and a mind that are somehow uniquely mine. We have to be disillusioned of these mistaken views and Traditional Advaita begins by telling us that we are *not* these things – *neti, neti*. We are told that the world is an appearance only, imagined like the snake on the rope in ignorance. Once the lesson has been learned, as it were, such not-strictly-accurate teachings can be taken back, to be replaced with more accurate metaphors. Truth is beyond words and concepts but is non-dual. All is *brahman* – including, necessarily, the world and our body-minds. Here is **Chittaranjan Naik**, a freely admitted "realist" amongst Advaitins:

An important distinction needs to be made here. This is the distinction between the *upAya*, the means to the end, and the assertion of truth. The one is the method prescribed for the *sAdhaka*, the other is the statement of the Advaitic Ontological Truth. And then everything seems to fall into place almost magically. Truth is not a matter of a step-by-step process. The Truth is eternal. It is always the same, both when we are blinded to it, and when our eyes are open to see it. This truth is the *pAramArthika satya* that All is *brahman*; the world is *brahman*; *brahman* is the Real; the world is therefore real.

The prescription of "*neti, neti*" is the *upAya*, a provisional means for the *sAdhaka* to free himself from the bondage of the limited to awaken to the light of the Unlimited. Again, it may be noticed that *"neti, neti"* is used with a greater emphasis on the denial of the seen as constituting the Self than on the denial of the world itself. The mind is naturally directed outward towards objects and does not "see" the Self, and it must return from being outward bound to its source by a denial of the objects that attract its attention. The entire process is one of dispelling the false notion of the objects it clings to as being the Self. (Ref. 321)

Brahman is spoken of throughout the scriptures in various ways, to try to get around the fact that it cannot be spoken of at all. Here is one of the better attempts from the *muNDakopaniShad* 2.2.11, followed by the commentary by **Swami Parthasarathy**:

11. Verily, this is the immortal *brahman* Reality. *brahman* is in front and behind. *brahman* is on the right and on the left, above and below, all-pervading. This world is indeed the supreme *brahman*.

brahman, the supreme Reality is said to be immortal. Immortal means deathless. Deathless means birth-less. Birth-less and deathless together mean changeless. *brahman* is therefore changeless. The changeless substratum upon which the manifold changes take place in the world. The world is ever in a flux of change. For changes to take place there needs to be a changeless background. Trains move on fixed rails. Motion pictures are projected on a static screen. Likewise, the changing world appears upon the changeless *brahman* .

brahman alone exists. Nothing else. A Self-realized Soul recognizes this truth. Having identified with the changeless Reality he remains unaffected by the fluctuations of the external world. Others are caught up, enmeshed in the changing phenomena. Suffer the sorrows thereof.

People are lost in the affairs of the world. Have hypnotized themselves to project the world on the immaculate *brahman*. And need to be retrieved from self-hypnosis. The *guru* tries to dehypnotize them through powerful suggestions that *brahman* is everywhere. *brahman* is in front of you. *brahman* is behind you. *brahman* is on your right. *brahman* is on your left. *brahman* is above you. *brahman* is below you. *brahman* is all-pervading. This world is indeed *brahman* and *brahman* alone. (Ref. 282)

Another famous verse from the *taittirIya upaniShad* (III.1.1) has an effective "definition" of brahman in the words (quoted because it is one of the more famous Sanskrit passages):

yato vA imAni bhUtAni jAyante
yena jAtAni jIvanti
yatprayantyabhisaMvishanti
tadvijij~nAsasva
tad brahmeti

This is loosely translated as: "Crave to know that from which all things are born, by means of which they live, towards which they move and into which they return upon death. That is *brahman*." Rather than being a clear and distinct definition, which is impossible, this is meant to be a series of pointers on which we may meditate and thereby come to a realization of the truth. And if you are unable to remember the whole of the quotation, you can always make do with just the last part – *tad brahmeti*, "That is brahman" or, as will be reiterated in the next and final chapter on Teaching Methods, from the neo-Advaita viewpoint, "This is it."

We cannot know or experience Truth or reality. That which knows and experiences – the mind – is itself only a manifestation within Consciousness. Awareness of knowledge or existence is duality. Only awareness of awareness is beyond mind and could be said to be an aspect of *brahman* rather than of the *jIva*. As **Nisargadatta Maharaj** says:

[Reality is] whatever is permanently there, immortal, unchanging. The eternal ever is, a non-experiential state. Subsequent to that is the consciousness, "I Amness," the body experience and life. Your experiences are in the realm of consciousness. In the realm of consciousness you cannot have the experience of truth. As a matter of fact, there can be no experience of the truth because you are That in the ultimate analysis. How can there be the experience of the truth? It is prior to the beingness. (Ref. 345)

Summary

- What we can know is necessarily limited. Since reality is unlimited, it cannot be known or experienced.
- Reality is that which does not change, which exists in all three periods of time.
- Brahman is beyond name or attribute. Gods relate to attempts to rationalize creation and have nothing to do with reality.

The World

- The world is initially treated as illusory, later as *mithyA* and finally acknowledged to be *brahman*.
- Creation belongs to *vyavahAra*, the phenomenal realm of apparent separation. Its unchanging essence is *brahman*, the realm of *paramArtha*.
- All forms point to the unmanifest, formless reality that is their essence.
- Taking the world as real and separate necessitates the existence of a God who created it.
- The illusion of the world continues after enlightenment; the delusion that it is separate disappears.
- Heaven and hell are also *mithyA*, useful concepts for those with a *bhakta* nature.

Cause and Effect

- Advaita differentiates between material cause (*upAdAna kAraNa*), efficient cause (*nimitta kAraNa*) and instrumental cause (*karaNa kAraNa*) but only at the level of *vyavahAra*. In *paramArtha*, there is no causality.
- An effect may be distinguishable from its material cause, e.g. a woven garment (*Arambha*); it may be an actual transformation, e.g. milk to butter (*pariNAma*) or it may simply be an appearance, e.g. snake on rope (*vivarta*).

Creation Theories

- *satkArya vAda* is the preliminary teaching of Advaita, that the effect (creation) is pre-existent in the cause (*brahman*), i.e. effectively denying causality. Elements come into existence by successive differentiation (naming) of the preceding cause.
- This is sublated by *vivarta vAda*, which states that creation is an apparent projection of *Ishvara* through the power of *mAyA*.
- This, in turn, is sublated by *ajAti vAda* – nothing has ever been created.
- Causality is necessary within *vyavahAra* but meaningless in *paramArtha*.
- Creation myths satisfy the naïve and provide metaphors for the more advanced. They are a device (*upAya*) for leading the mind to Truth.
- *sRRiShTi dRRiShTi vAda* says that there is an actual creation, which we then experience.
- This is sublated by *dRRiShTi sRRiShTi vAda*, a post-Shankara theory that the world is effectively a product of the mind.
- *ajAti vAda* is the truth from the standpoint of *paramArtha*.
- The world is *mithyA*; its essence is *brahman*, the only *satya*.
- Theories of causation are irrelevant when concerned with ultimate reality.
- The world is name and form of the non-dual reality as a ring is only gold.

- Reality is the ground of the universe as rope is ground for the snake.

Ishvara and mAyA

- While the world is believed to be separate, *Ishvara* is needed to create it.
- He creates it using the force of *mAyA*.
- *jIva = Atman + avidyA; Ishvara = brahman + mAyA.*
- Ignorance obscures the fact that *jIva* and *Ishvara* are brahman, just as the wave and ocean are already water.
- The world is "created" according to the sum of individual's *vAsanA*-s. *Ishvara* keeps a record of all the "fruit" that is due.
- The finite, manifest, immanent form of reality is termed *saguNa brahman* (with qualities); the unmanifest, infinite, transcendent and formless is termed *nirguNa*.
- Since everything is *brahman*, the world must be *brahman*. Our experiences of the world must be truth. *brahman* is said to be the Truth of the truth.
- Since time and space are creations of *mAyA*, it does not make sense to ask when or where it originated. *mAyA* is *anirvachanIya* – we cannot categorize it.
- Consideration of *pralaya*, cosmic dissolution, shows that *mAyA* can not have any antecedent cause so that *Ishvara* is effectively a product of *mAyA*.
- *lIlA* is the idea that God created the universe for enjoyment. It is only of value at an intermediate level of understanding.

Objects

- What is a "rose" apart from a collection of attributes detected by several senses? It is the process of "naming" through language that tricks the mind into presuming a dualistic world.
- There is only "seeing," not a "seer" or a "seen." These ideas only occur subsequently, when the thought "I see X" arises in the mind.

- Any supposed "object" is seen to be only a form of something more basic. Ultimately, everything reduces to a form of *brahman*. Objects are an illusion resulting from "naming."
- "I" am also another named attribute of *brahman* and not a solipsistic entity. Both subject and object are transcended in the non-dual reality.
- Language is the cause of most of our problems but is a valuable tool to help remove ignorance.
- In the end, it is realized that the world and ourselves are also real, since there is only the non-dual Truth.
- *tad brahmeti* – "This is it."

8. THE TEACHING METHOD

I have delayed explicit discussion of this topic until the end since it is necessary to understand the subject thoroughly before the subtleties of the distinctions between the various approaches can be appreciated. Hopefully, most of these differences could be deduced by careful reading of what has gone before but, by highlighting them, this chapter may serve as a good summary of the whole book.

The truth of Advaita can only ever be one. The very meaning of the word Advaita tells us that the purport of any teaching must be the same. Any difference lies solely in the way that this message is transmitted. And any method is valid if it leads to the truth, as pointed out in the **Siddhantabindu of Madhusudan Saraswati**: *"Whatever are the means by which the inner-self is realized by men, those should be regarded as flawless, and they are endless."* (Ref. 281)

I would like to differentiate five "methods" of teaching Advaita, for the sake of clarity: Traditional Advaita Vedanta, Neo-Vedanta, Direct Path Advaita, Neo-Advaita and Pseudo-Advaita. There is a distinct danger of confusion between the terms 'Neo-Vedanta' and 'Neo-Advaita' since these are often used interchangeably in India. Throughout this book I have used neo-Advaita to refer to the modern western style of teaching epitomized by Tony Parsons and Nathan Gill. I have not used the term neo-Vedanta and I have not explicitly attempted to differentiate between it and traditional Advaita.

There is also a danger that these teachings will be seen as some sort of progression, with neo-Advaita as the latest, streamlined version of an outmoded, archaic traditional system. If they are seen as equivalent, then neo-Advaita is certain to seem more attractive to many Westerners, claiming as it does that no effort is needed and that "you (can) have it now." Finally, as **Greg Goode** says, "it often seems that neo-Advaita presents its own hard line stance as the type of Advaita for those tough and clear enough to take their whiskey straight, no chasers."

None of these views is correct, as the reader will hopefully now appreciate. Greg goes on to say:

> Every path has its way of presenting itself as an alternative. A traditional way to look at the differences among paths might be in terms of the energy or *guNa* balances, none more correct or privileged than the others.
>
> Traditional: more inclusive and active, for those who resonate with *karma* and *j~nAna yoga*, or who have a balance of *rajas* and *sattva*, with less *tamas*.
>
> Direct: more intellectual and less active, for those who resonate with *j~nAna yoga*, or who have lots of *sattva*, some *tamas* and less *rajas*.
>
> Neo: more emotional and less active, for those who resonate with *bhakti yoga*, or those who have lots of *sattva* and *tamas*, and less *rajas*. (Ref. 370)

Traditional Advaita

This is regarded as that defined by Shankara in his *bhAShya*-s (interpretation and commentaries) on the Upanishads, the Bhagavad Gita and the Brahma Sutras (together called the *prasthAna traya*). Shankara formalized the traditional method around the 8th century AD, according to most modern authorities. Swami Satchidanandendra, in his very scholarly book "The Method of the Vedanta: A Critical Account of the Advaita Tradition" (Ref. 24), believes that Shankara's essential method depends upon the technique called *adhyAropa – apavAda* or "false attribution followed by subsequent denial." Thus for example, it provisionally teaches such things as the five sheaths of being or the three states of consciousness. Later, however, once the implications have been taken on board, it acknowledges that all such ideas are only part of the superimposition that we make upon the non-dual reality in our ignorance. It describes the two aspects of *vyavahAra* and *paramArtha* that were discussed in the chapter on Reality and recognizes the interim validity, indeed necessity, of talking about people and objects, concepts and practices even though none of these *really* exist.

The Traditional approach is defined by the scriptures, which are claimed to be the ultimate source of the truth. All traditional teachers refer, and invariably defer to them. Traditional Advaita recognizes various "paths" that "seekers" may follow to help them on their way to enlightenment. Amongst these are the way of action (*karma yoga*), the way of devotion (*bhakti yoga*) and the way of knowledge (*j~nAna yoga*) as discussed earlier.

Neo-Vedanta

This is not a term that I have used in this book. It refers particularly to Advaita as taught by Swami Vivekananda and his followers. It is argued that Traditional Advaita was, in a sense, "watered down" and adapted so as to be more palatable to the western temperament, when Vivekananda brought the message (of Ramakrishna) to the west in 1893. It aimed to be a philosophy in the sense that this was understood in the west, perhaps equated with a sort of Absolute Idealism, rather than *shruti* – the "unauthored" message contained in the scriptures.

The stance of traditional Vedanta is that the teacher "unfolds" the scriptures so that the student (eventually) gains immediate apprehension of the Truth (see Chapter 4 on *pratipAdya-pratipAdaka sambandha*). In this sense the *shruti* are the direct *pramANa*. There is the sense that Neo-Vedanta, instead, treats the subject as a philosophy that is studied and then the student goes out into the world, applies the knowledge gained and (eventually) realizes the Truth. The scriptures are then only indirect or even incidental.

Some traditionalists argue that key elements of Advaita have been lost in this process, which now concentrates almost exclusively on *j~nAna yoga* rather than *bhakti* or *karma*. For example **Bithika Mukerji**, in her book "Neo-Vedanta and Modernity" (Ref. 348), says that in particular the principle of renunciation and the concept of bliss (*Ananda*) have been ignored at the expense of more intellectual aspects which themselves belong in the realm of *mAyA*. This might have resulted, she suggests, because traditional adherents were anxious to refute possible accusations that Advaita was in some way "mystical" and also lacked an ethical foundation. All this is understandable but has not been taken as a specific issue in this book. Certainly the emphasis has been on the intellectual aspects of Advaita – the knowledge that is required to remove the ignorance that obscures Truth. The "attributes" of the non-dual reality have also been considered rather as *satyam-j~nAnam-anantam* (unlimited existence-knowledge) than as *sat-chit-Ananda* (existence-consciousness-bliss).

Since the principal audience of the book will be western, a fine distinction is not really required. There is, however, a potential danger that is raised in the extract below by **James Swartz**. He suggests that another consequence of Vivekananda's teaching was that westerners began to look, through the teachings of Advaita, for an enlightenment "experience," a concept that does not occur in the pure Traditional Advaita but rather from the various *yoga*-s that derived from Patanjali's method. Whereas *yoga* used to be treated as a spiritual practice and preparation, it now became in danger of being pursued as an end in itself:

Before Yoga sullied the pure teachings of Vedanta, enlightenment was considered to be the removal of ignorance about the nature of the Self. But with the ascendancy of the Yoga teachings enlightenment came to be considered a "permanent experience of the Self" in contrast to the mundane experiences of everyday life, which it obviously can't be if this is a non-dual reality as the Upanishads claim. It can't be a permanent experience, first because there is no such thing as a permanent experience and second, it can't be an experience in a non-dual reality because the subject object distinction necessary for experience is missing in a non-dual reality. If this is true then the quest for a permanent enlightenment experience is pointless and what is needed, as traditional Vedanta says, is the knowledge of reality since the craving for experience, including the experience of the Self, is *mAyA*, the consequence of seeing oneself a doer who is separate from reality.

(Ref. 349)

He further says this about the different styles of teaching:

> The reason why Vivekananda is considered a Neo-Vedantin by the traditionalists is because of the way he taught Vedanta. He taught it as a philosophy, as an intellectual discipline. His lectures were lectures. Lecture is not the method of teaching in traditional Vedanta although many who call themselves traditionalists lecture because they are not enlightened or did not learn how to wield the means of knowledge. Vedanta is a *pramANa*, a means of knowledge. It directly reveals the Self according to an ancient method of teaching. It does not talk "about" the Self. When you talk about the Self you inspire *bhakti* and a desire to know or experience it (*yoga*). When you teach It directly you reveal it. It is an art. (Ref. 354)

These topics of the Self "knowing" or "being known" are considered below. If it is considered that Neo-Vedanta believes that the Self can *become* enlightened or *experience* enlightenment, then the views expressed by this book are Traditional and not neo-Vedanta.

All of this notwithstanding, in the discussion below, when I use the term "Traditional Advaita," this should be understood to mean Traditional and/or Neo-Vedanta, although pedantically and academically these approaches may differ slightly. It should be noted also that others deny that Vivekananda is in any way not "traditional." Certainly many of his lectures are clearly Advaita in the traditional sense. It is possible that some later disciples have emphasized the yoga element of his teaching to the detriment of the Advaita.

Direct Path

This approach effectively asks: "Why bother with all of these interim ideas, when they have eventually to be rejected anyway? Why not get straight to the meat of the subject?" Nevertheless, it provisionally acknowledges the seeker and the *guru* even though proclaiming unambiguously that, ultimately, there is only the Self. The need for transmission of knowledge is still accepted together with the need for a teacher to provide this. **Atmananda Krishna Menon** defines the term as follows: "*vichAra-mArga* (the direct path) is removal of untruth by arguments, leaving over the Truth absolute as the real Self." (Note 1281 Ref. 13)

Francis Lucille (influenced by both Atmananda Krishna Menon and Jean Klein) has possibly used this term more than most, actually publishing a journal called "The Direct Path" in 1995. In an email discussion with him at the time, I made the comment: "The idea of just carrying on with one's everyday life (or not) and awaiting 'Grace' does not seem very encouraging! And what exactly is the Direct Path if not this?" His response was:

> We don't have to carry on with anything. Life carries on with itself, by itself, without our intervention. Everything that comes to us unexpected is grace. Why wait? Why postpone it? Why fail to welcome it? Simply be open to the possibility that whatever the present moment is bringing to you is a gift from grace. That is the direct path. (Ref. 72)

This more direct method of teaching became prevalent through teachers such as Ramana Maharshi, Nisargadatta Maharaj and Atmananda Krishna Menon, though it is not strictly speaking a new approach - the uncompromising stance of Gaudapada in his *kArikA* on the *mANDUkya upaniShad* could be said to be Direct Path. Ramana Maharshi, though still referring frequently to what might be called a *bhakti* approach, established the method of *AtmavichAra* or Self-enquiry as the principal means of realizing the Self. In the case of Nisargadatta, and increasingly with his disciples Ramesh Balsekar and Wayne Liquorman, there is the emphasis on there not being any doer and on predestination. Krishna Menon demonstrates through rigorous logic that there are no objects, thoughts etc. separate from awareness. (As Greg Goode points out, it therefore follows that it is not really meaningful to talk about beliefs in respect of the direct approach, since beliefs themselves are also deconstructed.) None of these latter approaches advocates any practice as such, though all emphasize the need for a *guru*.

John Wheeler (a disciple of Bob Adamson, who was taught by Nisargadatta Maharaj) effectively provides a good description of Direct Path teaching when he says:

> ...this is not about practices, techniques, etc. It is about seeing directly what is true within you now. This removes the cause of ignorance and annihilates self-centered thought patterns (like doubt, suffering and confusion).
>
> ...This approach is just looking deeply into what is here and now and realizing that what you are is, in fact, already free.
>
> ...A little bit of investigation and clear seeing clears up the mistaken ideas, and the feeling of limitation is replaced by the natural freedom of your true nature.
>
> (Ref. 70)

Possibly the most authoritative living expert on the Direct Approach is **Dr. Gregory Goode**. Academically trained in western philosophy, he has studied all the branches of eastern non-dual philosophies, regards Atmananda Krishna Menon as his *sadguru* and is an enlightened teacher of Advaita. His description of Direct Path Advaita is as follows:

> As described by Sri Atmananda, the direct path consists of taking one's stand as the awareness that you already are, and seeing how all experience confirms this stand. The direct path is not goal-oriented or prescriptive. Instead of prescribing practices, it attempts to point to how things are. Using present experience as its data, the direct path deconstructs the existing body of presumptions, beliefs and psychological structures – all of which make one feel separate, vulnerable, and cut off from the world. How does it do this? Not by trying to disbelieve these structures, but by testing their claims against

one's present awareness. When held up to the light of awareness, these structures peacefully dissolve. This awakening is experienced as a sweetness, an immediacy, a gapless clarity, which is awareness itself. And quite often, there's laughter! (Ref. 53)

The Direct approach does not prescribe paths, instead attempting to deconstruct our everyday view of the world and ourselves to demonstrate that "all there is" is Consciousness.

Neo-Advaita

The teachers of neo-Advaita officially do not acknowledge any need to practice, investigate, or inquire in any way whatsoever. Outwardly, they acknowledge *only* the reality. They make no concessions at all to the ignorant seeker. There is no seeker and nothing to be sought. There is no teacher and nothing to be taught. There is only This. Of course, since they necessarily use language in their teaching, they cannot avoid talking about ideas of Self, misconceptions, recognizing and so on – and all of these imply the existence of a person. This may lead to statements such as "It was seen by no one," which in turn may give rise to confusion in the (non-existent) listener! Furthermore, any implication that the seeker "just needs to understand this" and can do so by attending satsang and listening to such statements immediately contradicts their position.

Neo-Advaita denies that any path can be of any help or that any knowledge can dispel ignorance because everything that appears, including ourselves, is nothing more than a story or a program on the television screen.

Neo-Advaita is a relatively new term. It is not known who coined it and some (at least) of those teachers to whom the term is applied do not recognize it. Nevertheless, amongst the seekers on the Internet, it is a commonly used designation and key teachers who are so classified are Tony Parsons, Nathan Gill and Roger Linden. There are also a number of Dutch teachers such as Leo Hartong and Jan Kersschot and others are springing up around the world. Whilst Direct Path teachings still draw much of their wisdom from the scriptures, Neo-Advaita does not perceive any value in them. Below is an essay by **Tony Parsons** in which he discusses his perception of the differences:

It has recently been argued that Traditional Oneness is somehow better than 'Neo-Oneness', or even 'Pseudo-Oneness'. The strangeness of this idea exposes the foolishness of trying to give title to that which is limitless.

The cunning and manipulative guru mind inevitably objectifies verbal expression, and out of that objectifying arises a plethora of dogmatic movements all claiming supreme understanding of that which cannot be understood.

As a consequence, so-called Traditional Advaita, for instance, is just another established religion with a proliferation of teachings and literature, all of which very successfully and consistently miss the mark. It stands alongside Christianity and Buddhism as one of the many systems of personal indoctrination promising the eventual spiritual fulfilment.

The teaching of "Traditional Advaita" has no relevance to liberation because it is born out of a fundamental misconception. Its logical and sensibly progressive recommendations include meditation, self-enquiry, self-restraint, and to quote "the renunciation of the ego and all desire." Of course there is nothing right or wrong with the idea of desiring to renounce desire. However, these idealistic recommendations and teachings are based on the fundamental misconception that there is such a thing as a separate individual with free will and the choice to become.

The belief that there is a separate seeker (subject) who can choose to attain or become worthy of something called enlightenment (object) is a direct denial of abiding oneness (Advaita).

Within the hypnotic dream of separation, the prevailing perception is that of the seeker and the sought. The ignorance of this perception continues in the search for enlightenment, and inevitably the dream-seeker is attracted to a dream-teaching which upholds and encourages the same premise of personal discipline and sacrifice (seeking) leading to the eventual goal of enlightenment (the sought).

The recommendation to cultivate understanding and refine something called "the mind" (?) is hugely attractive to the dream-seeker because it prolongs the very worthy search and thrives on logic, detachment, complication, endeavour, hierarchy and exclusivity.

This confusion is of course as much an expression of oneness as the clarity which exposes it.

When it is suddenly and directly rediscovered by no one that liberation brings with it the realisation that there is nothing to seek and no one to become liberated, then there is much laughter. (Ref. 55)

This view is not confined just to those teachers, however. Even **Gangaji**, the principal of Sri Poonja's disciples, has this to say:

The Advaita theory in general? Well, forget it! Advaita fundamentalists everywhere! They're caught in a box and it's the fundamentalism in every religion that causes the most problems because it demands conceptually a freedom and a perfection. But freedom and perfection are not conceptual. Anything that is conceptual is bound by mind...

And I don't speak in Advaitic terms because I find them very stilted, like if I were speaking in biblical terms or some other religious terms. (Ref. 78)

Following an email discussion with **Tony Parsons** about the content of this chapter, he offered the following as an explanation of the position of so-called neo-Advaitins:

The term Neo-Advaita is a misnomer conjured up by those wishing to pigeon-hole this particular communication as nothing more than a modern, westernized message offering fast-track enlightenment.

Strangely, the uncompromising and paradoxical expression of this particular message is generated directly out of a clear and uncompromising perception of the meaning of the word Advaita. The essence of its singular message is interwoven into and throughout the scriptures, and can be discovered within the core of most religious a spiration. Its expression in words can only point to the mystery that is beyond all words. However, there is also an energetic element which is not mentioned in this chapter.

The simple nature of this message confounds the mind, which will inevitably retreat into dogma. To quote [from a meeting given in London in 2005]:

"All there is is not two . . . there is no other. There is no separate entity with free will, choice or the ability to follow a path, scripture or belief. Being (Brahman) appears as confusion (ignorance) together with the clarity (knowledge) that can expose it. But clarity (knowledge) does not bring liberation. Knowing that there is only being (Brahman) is not being."

To quote the scriptures:

In the Brahma Sutra Bhasya of Shankara 1.1.4 [from Ref. 34] Shankara argues that Mukti (liberation) is not a thing to be acquired, for it is ever-present. ". . . and no dependence on work can be proved by assuming liberation to be a thing to be acquired; for it being essentially one with one's very Self, there can be no acquisition. Even if Brahman be different from oneself, there can be no acquisition, for Brahman being all pervasive like space, it remains ever attained by everyone . . ." (Ref. 368)

I pointed out that it did not seem reasonable to use the scriptures to support the Neo-Advaitin position, when these are usually denigrated. Also, the reference quoted is part of an answer by Shankara arguing the validity of the scriptures. His response to this was as follows:

Referring to the Shankara quote there is clearly a misunderstanding between us. We consider that those parts of the scriptures that presume the reality of a separate entity that can, through personal choice and endeavor, attain something called enlightenment, are based on a misconception about the very meaning and nature of Advaita. However, we also accept that, interwoven into these and other scriptures, is a deeper, more hidden message that points to another possibility that is beyond dogma and a path of becoming. I therefore feel that it is very important to include the Shankara quote which supports this uncompromising expression of Advaita because it adds another side to the balance of comparisons. (Ref. 369)

Pseudo-Advaita

This is included only for completeness and it is a term that would not be recognized by its adherents (for obvious reasons). It refers to those teachers who exploit the philosophy for their own financial gain and who cynically misuse the teaching. It can be summed up in the attitude "I am enlightened and I can enlighten you too (if you give me lots of money)." I will not speak any more about pseudo-Advaita. This clearly has nothing at all to do with the philosophy proper.

Comparison of Beliefs

In the table below, I make a number of statements regarding aspects of Advaita and indicate whether Traditional (T), Direct Path (D) and Neo-Advaita (N) approaches agree with them. There is some overlap in these – belief in an individual person obviously implies belief in a separate world, for example. It can be seen that Neo-Advaita differs from the other approaches on virtually every count. In the end, most of these come down to the distinction between *paramArtha* and *vyavahAra* and the bottom line is that Neo-Advaita differs from other approaches in denying that there is such a distinction.

Note that the ticks against the various beliefs and paths are based on my understanding, which in turn is based upon the past 20 years of reading and discussion. **Tony Parson**'s initial suggestion was that the two ticks against

8 and 9 for Neo-Advaita be removed and a tick placed against 3 (Ref. 368).

My response to this was to observe that "If you tick 3, accepting ignorance and the validity of its removal by knowledge, surely this entails accepting the possibility of a 'path' (to eliminate ignorance), which also implies a seeker and a teacher who can help to provide the knowledge. I understood that all of these things were denied."

Tony replied that "*Again this is a question of interpretation, but for us it seems that clarity (knowledge) can expose confusion (ignorance) but this all arises in the appearance (story) and can only lead, or be an apparent path, to something called absolute knowledge without ignorance. But, and this is a big but, and probably where we do not agree, absolute knowledge or clarity is not enlightenment.*" (Ref. 369)

Lest there should be any doubt, this is the view of Traditional Advaita: Who we really are is the non-dual *brahman* – already. It is in the mind that the idea-belief occurs that "we" are unenlightened so, yes, enlightenment can be nothing other than the removal of this ignorance in the mind. And this can only be achieved via knowledge. The **Brihadaranyaka Upanishad** (IV.4.19) states that "*It is only through the mind that the truth can be realized.*" And when so-called realization occurs, it is seen that nothing has actually changed. It is simply that the mistaken view of a "world" and "separation" has now disappeared. And **Raphael** comments on the Atmabodha:

2. As fire [is necessary] for cooking so, among the different types of discipline (*vinA*), only Knowledge (*bodho*) is the direct means for liberation (*sAdhana mokSha*): without Knowledge there can be no Liberation.

Why is it that only Knowledge can set us free? Because, according to Advaita *vedAnta*, *avidyA*, metaphysical ignorance, is what keeps us captive. Therefore only *vidyA*, metaphysical Knowledge, can defeat the ignorance as to the nature of Being. Darkness can be dispelled only by the splendor of light, and error can be resolved only by truth. (Ref. 372)

Accordingly (Ref. 369), Tony suggested that all of the ticks/crosses be removed "in order not to confuse the reader." Instead, he wishes to make the following statement:

From the so-called Neo-Advaita perception all of the items listed from 1-12 below simply refer to transient, personal beliefs or attained states that apparently arise and fall away in the story or dream of seeking.

The very idea of there being something called Advaita that could be rightly or wrongly approached is as dual as the idea that there are right or wrong scriptures. Our message exposes the futility of looking for an approach of any kind to that which is already nothing and everything. (Ref. 369)

	Comparison of beliefs	T	D	N
1.	Provisional acceptance of world-appearance as real (i.e. distinction between *paramArtha* and *vyavahAra*)	✓	✓	×
2.	Provisional acceptance of *jIva* as real	✓	✓	×
3.	Provisional acceptance of existence of ignorance, capable of being removed by knowledge	✓	✓	×
4.	Acceptance that it is man's purpose to achieve realization	✓	✓	×
5.	Acceptance of value of *guru*	✓	✓	×
6.	Acceptance of the value of effort in a path to enlightenment	✓	✓	×
7.	Behavior of a realized one relevant	✓	✓	×
8.	The Self identified as that which is a known object of any action	×	×	✓
9.	The Self identified as that which knows or experiences	×	×	✓
10.	Acceptance that the scriptures are of value	✓	✓	×
11.	Use of the concept of Brahman	✓	✓	×
12.	Other Differences in Beliefs	-	-	-

1. Provisional acceptance of world-appearance as real

The entire world of Form exists nowhere but in your own present formless awareness. **Ken Wilber** (Ref. 339)

> According to traditional teachings, we see the world-appearance as a result of ignorance. When this veil is removed, it is seen to have been only name and form falsely superimposed upon the non-dual Brahman. This does not mean that the world disappears but that the false knowledge is dissolved so that it is seen for what it always was, in the same way that the rope is seen when the delusion that it was a snake is dropped. Until this realization takes place, there is no denying our perception and experience of the world in its usually understood sense and it seems that attempts to perceive it as unreal are of little value.

Traditional Advaita only makes provisional statements about the nature of reality, and then later retracts them. Perhaps one of the clearest and most recognizable to today's satsang attendees is from the **Chandogya Upanishad** (III.14.i): *sarvaM khalvidaM brahmA* – all this (universe) is verily Brahman. (This is not one of the four *mahAvAkya*-s but is a close runner!) It bears a striking resemblance to "This is it," which might be claimed to be one of the mantras of neo-Advaita. **Swami Krishnananda** says of the traditional version: "It requires a tremendous psychological preparation and an extraordinary type of purity of mind to appreciate what this instruction is." (Ref. 23) And this, I think, applies equally to the modern version.

And there are numerous other instances for example:

> All this that is in front is but Brahman, the immortal. Brahman is at the back, as also on the right and the left. It is extended above and below, too. This world is nothing but Brahman, the highest. *muNDaka upaniShad* II.ii.11 (Ref. 26).

> This *brahman* [Brahmin, member of the Brahminical caste], this *kShatra* [warrior, member of the military caste], these worlds, these gods, these beings - everything is this Self. *bRRihadAraNyaka upaniShad* II.iv.6

That Being which is this subtle essence (cause), even That all this world has for itself. That is the true. That is the *Atman*. That thou art. *chhAndogya upaniShad* VI.xiii.7 (Ref. 43)

But, prior to realization, the world seems to be real; it seems that we are separate individuals trapped in a body-mind and our experiences of pleasure and pain seem to be perfectly valid. **Shankara** says:

So long as the oneness of the true Self is not realized, nobody entertains the idea of unreality when dealing with the means of knowledge, objects of knowledge, and the results; rather, as a matter of fact, all creatures discard their natural oneness with Brahman to accept through ignorance the modifications themselves as "I and mine" - that is to say, as one's Self or as belonging to oneself. Hence all common human dealings or Vedic observances are logical (and valid) prior to the realization of the identity of the Self and Brahman, just as much as knowledge with the stamp of conviction, supposed to be attained through direct perception, does occur, before waking up, to an ordinary man when he is asleep and dreams of things high and low. The idea that these are semblances of perceived things does not occur to him during that dream. *brahmasUtra bhAShya* II.i.14 (Ref. 34)

Until knowledge comes along to dispel the ignorance, our experience of a real, separate world cannot be argued against since all our senses, society and science tell us it is so. Shankara says that "unless there be an exception, the general rule prevails" BSB II.ii.31.
Swami Nityaswarupananda says that:

The admission of grades in reality, lower and higher, is a methodological device and is a concession to lower intellects. It is always recognized that the apparent (*prAtibhAsika*) and the conventional (*vyAvahArika*) orders of reality are rather phases of unreality, as absolute reality is denied to them. All things other than the Self are only an appearance, no matter how persistent and consistent some of them may appear to be. The admission of provisional reality is not in conflict with the central doctrine of Vedanta that only one Self exists, as the reality accorded to the phenomenal world is only vicarious, it being recognized that it shines in borrowed light and, apart from the substratum of the Self over which it appears, it has no existence whatsoever. (Ref.12)

Ramana Maharshi said, in response to a question about the supposed unreality of the world:

> The Vedantins do not say the world is unreal. That is a misunder-standing. If they did, what would be the meaning of the Vedantic text: "All this is Brahman"? They only mean that the world is unreal as world, but it is real as Self. If you regard the world as not-Self, it is not real. Everything, whether you call it world or *mAyA* or *lIlA* or *shakti*, must be within the Self and not apart from it. (Ref 174)

Having said that the world is not unreal, however, this is not the same as saying that Brahman *is* the world. The statement "This is it" of the Neo-Advaitins implies that Brahman *is* the totality of this world-appearance but this is *not* what the scriptures say (in fact this is the stance of the western philosopher, F. H. Bradley). Brahman is the unmanifested, non-dual reality. The world of appearances is simply a manifestation of name and form, appearing to Consciousness through the medium of a body-mind. A metaphor that is used by Shankara to explain this is that of multiple reflections of the sun in different vessels of water. The sun is effectively present in the reflections but is not actually the reflections. Although the quality of the reflection may change by disturbing the container to make ripples on the surface, the sun itself remains unaffected.

The concept of *lIlA* is that the Absolute created the world in order to "enjoy Himself" and that it is only through the mind-body of the *jIva* that the Absolute, in a sense, knows Himself. Thus, **Eckhart Tolle** says:

Hence, the ultimate purpose of the world lies not within the world but in transcendence of the world. Just as you would not be conscious of space if there were no objects in space, the world is needed for the Unmanifested to be realized. You may have heard the Buddhist saying: "If there were no illusion, there would be no enlightenment." It is through the world and ultimately through you that the Unmanifested knows itself. You are here to enable the divine purpose of the universe to unfold. That is how important you are! (Ref. 45)

Neo-Advaita denies the existence of levels of reality. There is only this and "it knows itself" as all there is. Teachers of the approach are becoming increasingly direct and uncompromising regarding this position. Here is a quotation from one of the newest, **Unmani Liza Hyde**:

This is not going anywhere. This is the beginning and the end. This is it. There is nothing more or less. This is the whole of Life and Death. There is no journey. This is it. There is nowhere else. This has always been it. There never has been a past and will never be a future. This is all that has ever been longed for. This is it. (Ref. 301)

In discussions in the traditional teaching, it is often said that confusion arises because the discussants begin to talk at one level and then unconsciously switch to the other, i.e. they mix up *vyavahAra* and *paramArtha*. One very articulate neo-Advaitin, **Tanya Davis**, on an Internet discussion list responded to this as follows:

It is not that there is confusion because I am "mixing levels." It is that confusion arises when there is the idea of levels, or the idea that there is something to "get" or the idea that it has to be a particular way in order for that to be "it" - basically, the idea of separation and duality. (Ref 56)

2. Provisional acceptance of jIva as real

Traditional and Direct Path Advaita both acknowledge the apparent existence of separate entities, called *jIva*-s, as described in earlier chapters.

In the *brahma sUtra bhAShya*, **Shankara** states that, although in reality there is only the *Atman*, whilst there is ignorance there seems to be a separate, embodied *jIva*. In reality, our true nature is brahman irrespective of our beliefs or delusions. But, for that to be realized, the identification with body and mind needs to be dropped:

As long as the individual soul does not free itself from *avidyA* (ignorance) in the form of duality and does not rise to the knowledge of the Self or Brahman, whose nature is unchangeable and Satchidananda which expresses itself in the form "I am Brahman," so long it remains as an individual soul. The ignorance of the *jIva* may be compared to the mistake of a man who in the twilight mistakes a post for a man, a rope for a serpent.

When it gives up the identification with the body, sense organs and mind, when it realizes its identity with the Supreme Brahman it becomes Brahman itself whose nature is unchangeable and Satchidananda, as is declared in Mun. Up. III-2-9. "He who knows the highest Brahman becomes even Brahman." This is the real nature of the individual soul by means of which it arises from the body and appears in its own real form. I.iii.19 (Ref. 36)

This view is re-iterated by later interpretations of the scriptures, such as the *pa~nchadashI*, written by *vidyAraNya* in the 14th Century. Here he makes clear that there are not really *jIva*-s but that these appear to exist as a result of *adhyAsa* – the confusion of real and unreal. They can be considered as reflections of the real substratum of Brahman:

The substratum of illusion is Brahman, the immutable, association-less, pure consciousness, the Self of all beings. When, through mutual superimposition, Brahman becomes associated with the intellect, an association which is phenomenal and not real, He is known as *jIva* or *puruSha*. *pa~nchadashI* VII.5 (Ref. 52)

Ramana Maharshi uses an excellent metaphor to explain how it is that there are apparent *jIva*-s and they do *separately* become enlightened. (This is one of the aspects most emphasized by neo-Advaitins: that there are no individuals to become enlightened.)

> Again, there is the moon. Let any one look at her from any place at any time; she is the same moon. Everyone knows it. Now suppose that there are several receptacles of water reflecting the moon. The images are all different from one another and from the moon herself. If one of the receptacles falls to pieces, that reflection disappears. Its disappearance does not affect the real moon or the other reflections. It is similar with an individual attaining Liberation. He alone is liberated.
>
> The sectarian of multiplicity makes this his argument against non-duality. "If the Self is single, if one man is liberated, that means that all souls are liberated. In practice it is not so. Therefore Advaita is not correct."
>
> The weakness in the argument is that the reflected light of the Self is mistaken for the original Light of the Self. The ego, the world and the individuals are all due to the person's *vAsanA*-s. When they perish, that person's hallucinations disappear, that is to say one pitcher is broken and the relative reflection is at an end.
>
> The fact is that the Self is never bound. There can therefore be no Release for It. All the troubles are for the ego only. (Ref. 49)

Whilst we are still deluded and see the *vyAvahArika* state as a reality, we are bound by the seeming rules of that delusion, just as the dreamer has to operate within the confines of his dream world. Thus, for example, **Swami Agamananda**, in his introduction to Shankara's *sarva vedAnta siddhAnta sara saMgraha*, says that:

> We may logically say that we are one with the eternal Substance and that we are of the same substance of which the sun and the moon are made. But such a conception does not satisfy our present needs. To take a

concrete example ice, water, and vapor are in reality the products of one element. But if we should be put into a room that is full of vapor without any apparatus to quench our thirst, we will find ourselves in a difficult position. It is true that everything is Brahman. God, man, dog, cat and tree are in reality one. But for all pragmatic purposes, we accept that God is God and man is man. This distinction lasts so long as we feel our identity with our body. (Ref. 71)

Neo-Advaita claims that there is only ever the non-dual Awareness, which "knows itself" as this present appearance. This present appearance is simply whatever is now appearing – objects, thoughts, feelings. The idea that there is a separate seeker, ignorant and searching for the truth about reality is just part of this - a story. Whether or not the story develops into the "enlightenment" of this apparent seeker makes not the slightest difference to anything. And, of course, the characters in the story cannot influence the outcome in any way.

The belief that there is an individual (who needs to find out who he really is) is part of the problem, as is explained by this excellent metaphor from **Leo Hartong**:

As long as we believe that there is an ego to either improve or remove, and as long as we work toward the betterment or elimination of that ego, the more the illusion is perpetuated. It's like looking in the mirror and seeing your face. Trying to remove your face by cleaning the mirror is useless. If you simply walk away, it's not there anymore; but you don't see that. All you know is that every time you look it's still there, and you may decide that more cleaning is needed. During the course of the day we often "forget" to look and, in such moments, we are totally without a sense of ego. We don't realize this since, during these moments, there is no "I" to notice its absence. (Ref. 22)

As soon as language is used, we are in the realm of duality. Words themselves are intrinsically dual – "naming" the "forms" of supposed objects and concepts – and communication takes place between an assumed speaker and an assumed listener. The refusal of Neo-Advaita to recognize the seeker as valid during the seeming process of overcoming his mistaken view of the world and himself invalidates it as a coherent teaching method. If the neo-Advaita teacher truly believes everything that he says, he gives lie to it as soon as he speaks, for this assumes another to whom the words are addressed.

Of course, this does not mean that it cannot "work." Since reality can never be described as such, all teaching methods are ultimately artificial devices to bring about the death of the misconceptions. Thus it can certainly be the case that the uncompromising statements of some modern teachers can act as the final trigger for those who have already been steeped in these ideas for many years.

Neo-Advaita, then, apparently recognizes neither the existence of a *jīva* nor of an event called "enlightenment." It is nevertheless usually implied that the seeing-through of the story brings with it a sense of freedom, light, love, etc. The inference is that there is a "condition of mind" in both cases "prior" to this, when there is the condition of being an individual and a state "after" it, when there is no longer any sense of separation. It does seem that this event in time could usefully be called "enlightenment," for want of a better word, and the connotations of the word "*jīva*" do seem to apply to the state prior to this event. So perhaps the "X" should be removed from the table for this topic.

3. *Provisional acceptance of existence of ignorance, capable of being removed by knowledge*

avidyA is the disease and the rise of the ego is the symptom of the disease. Tackling the ego is simply treating the symptoms only while the disease remains untreated. The disease can be eradicated by Knowledge alone and not by action. **Professor Gummuluru Murthy** (Ref. 68)

Both knowledge and ignorance belong to the phenomenal realm and, as such, ultimately have no separate existence. For there to be a knower, there must be something that is known. Ignorance could be defined as the state of not knowing (something) so that knowledge must arise, or be conveyed from elsewhere, in order to dispel that ignorance. All of this is necessarily dualistic.

Neo-Advaita cannot accept that the non-dual reality could have anything to do with ignorance and the traditional view agrees that it doesn't – *in reality*! Paradoxical though it may seem however, from the standpoint of the *jIva* in *vyavahAra*, it is all too real. **Shankara** confirms this as follows (*bRRihadAraNyaka upaniShad bhAShya* I.iv.10):

> We agree that the Absolute is not the author of Ignorance and that it is not deluded by it either. Even so, there is nothing other than the Absolute which is the author of Ignorance, and no other conscious being apart from the Absolute that is deluded by it. (Ref. 24)

As long as the knowledge that we are That has not yet arisen to dispel the ignorant belief that we are bodies or minds, the apparent world with its passing pleasures and constant threat of suffering carries on as usual. The analogy with dreaming is often used: the fact that the entire dream world is a product of our own mind simply does not occur to us while we are dreaming, unless the "realization" of lucidity occurs (and even this is a delusion, as was explained in the chapter on the Nature of Reality).

Traditional Advaita defines *adhyAsa* as the root of all our problems – the mixing up of real and unreal, Self and not-Self, the classical metaphor being the superimposing of the imaginary snake on the rope. Its stance is that, once knowledge has been conveyed by scriptures and *guru*, light is effectively shed on the rope of reality, making the falsely superimposed snakes of ego and world vanish into the air. The snake never really existed, as neither did the ego or world. The knowledge and ignorance are effectively part of this snake illusion, too. On realization ego, mind and ignorance all disappear. In reality, there was and is only Brahman. But this explanation provides a sop to the pre-enlightened mind and a potential aid to its destruction. Neo-Advaita accepts only the final truth and attempts to use a dualistic statement of this to "enlighten" "seekers" (although it also denies the existence of enlightenment and seekers).

Even as a shadow vanishes when it turns to see the light, this ignorance perishes when it turns towards Self-knowledge. **Yoga vAsiShTha** (Ref. 38)

It has to be appreciated that it is not knowledge that is being acquired in the traditional teaching process but ignorance that is being removed. In the metaphor of the scum being removed from the surface of a pond, or dust from a mirror, nothing is being added. Initially the water or reflection cannot be seen at all. As more of the contaminant is removed, that which was obscured becomes clearer until, finally, the water or mirror which was always there sparkles once more. Knowledge is the nature of the Self and is always present beneath the layer of ignorance.

Ramana Maharshi explains that it is ignorance that hides the truth of the Self from the *jIva* - this is the *AvaraNa*, or "veiling" power of *mAyA*. But again, at the end, there is the reminder that these "explanations" are not how things *really* are but are merely presented to satisfy the mind of the seeker:

AvaraNa (veiling) does not hide the *jIva* in entirety; he knows *that* he is; only he does not know *who* he is. He sees the world but not that it is only Brahman. It is light in darkness (or knowledge in ignorance).

In a cinema show the room is first darkened, artificial light is introduced; only in this light are the pictures projected. For differentiation a reflected light is thus necessary. A sleeper dreams, he is not out of sleep: only in the darkness or ignorance of sleep can he see the unreal dream objects.

Similarly the darkness of ignorance gives rise to the knowledge of the perceptions of the world.

This veiling is a characteristic of ignorance; it is not of the Self; it cannot affect the Self in any manner; it can veil only the *jIva*. The ego is insentient. United with the light from the Self, it is called *jIva*. But the ego and the light cannot be seen distinct from each other; they are always united together. The mixed product is the *jIva*, the root of all differentiation. All these are spoken of to satisfy the questioners. (Ref. 49)

He says that:

What is called Self-Knowledge is that State in which there can be neither knowledge nor ignorance; for what is commonly regarded as knowledge is not true knowledge; the Self is Itself true Knowledge, because It shines alone — without any other that could become an object of Its knowledge or a knower of It. *Ulladu Narpadu* v.12 (Ref. 110)

Neo-Advaita denies the existence of ignorance as an "obstacle" to enlightenment and hence the need for any knowledge to remove it. **Nathan Gill** explains this (note that, when he uses the word "You," with a capital letter, this refers to the real you (i.e. *Atman*) as opposed to "you" with a small letter, the illusory ego):

As Consciousness You are already awake and aware. In the play of life when there is exclusive focus as the individual, Your true nature is forgotten and there is complete involvement in searching for enlightenment or awakening. But You already *are* aware, already completely awake; it's simply that this is veiled by appearances, the story of 'me' as an individual.

Whenever Your true nature is remembered the spell is broken. The pursuit of enlightenment is clearly seen as nothing more than the cosmic *lIlA*. Awakeness is already the case under all circumstances, regardless of contrary appearances in the play. (Ref. 338)

At the level of the creation, the obscuring power of *mAyA* (*AvaraNa*) appears to limit *brahman* – and there is nothing that we can do about that. The *jIva*, however, appears to be limited by *avidyA* (ignorance) (or *bhrama*, confusion) – and that is something that we *can* do something about. In the above extract, it would appear that the latter is being spoken of, since "me as an individual" is specified. One is then bound to ask how "veiled by appearances" differs from "ignorance." Once the existence of ignorance is admitted, then it seems to follow necessarily that knowledge is required to remove it. In turn this implies the need for a teacher or material to impart that knowledge and consequently, effectively a path and a seeker etc.

Certainly this is all within the context of the play and who we are talking about is the role of a seeker in the play. But, from the point of view of You playing that role, this is not appreciated. The actor believes he is the role.

4. Acceptance that it is man's purpose to achieve realization

The scriptures tell us that a man may have been through many rebirths as lower life forms before he becomes sufficiently mature to be born in human form. Human form is unique in that it is only from this state that enlightenment, and consequent freedom from *saMsAra*, may be gained. Good actions may gain sufficient merit (*puNya*) that a man may be born as a god and spend a long period in heaven but eventually, he must return to human form on earth in order to proceed on his journey back to the Self. [Higher (gods) and lower forms are said not to have free-will so that they are only enjoyers and not doers.]

This view is expressed by **Shankara** at the beginning of his *vivekachUDAmaNi* (NB not all academics are agreed as to whether Shankara was actually the author of this book):

19. These three things are hard to achieve, and are attained only by the grace of God - human nature, the desire for liberation, and finding refuge with a great sage.

20. He is a suicide who has somehow achieved human birth and even manhood and full knowledge of the scriptures but does not strive for self-liberation, for he destroys himself by clinging to the unreal.

21. Who could be more foolish than the man who has achieved the difficult attainment of a human body and even manhood but still neglects his true good? (Ref. 340)

The human birth is rare to obtain. After having obtained it, if man does not aspire for the realization of Ishvara, he is born in vain. **Sri Ramakrishna**

Thus it is that traditional Advaita argues that it is our purpose and destiny to escape from this cycle of birth and death and that we should take every advantage of this golden opportunity of human form to make the necessary effort.

Swami Viditatmananda Saraswati, a disciple of Swami Dayananda says:

Life is not meant for acquiring things; it is meant for getting rid of the ignorance, getting rid of *rAga*-s and *dveSha*-s, passions and aversions, likes and dislikes which actually deny me what I am. Getting rid of them is called *tyAga*, renunciation; *tyAga* means renouncing that which is false, which is useless. (Ref. 32)

Dr. Gregory Goode's comment on this, in respect of the Direct Path approach, is that: "If a student has to have an overall purpose, this is one of the least occluding and most inspiring. Of course it serves only until the felt need for purpose spontaneously melts away." (Ref. 57)

Not recognizing the *jIva* or the notion of enlightenment, neo-Advaita also does not agree with this concept of a purpose to move beyond life, as it were. Life is its own purpose as **Tony Parsons** puts it:

It seems that our attachment to purpose is born from our need to prove something to ourselves. But life is simply life and is not trying to prove anything at all. This springtime will not try to be better than last springtime, and neither will an ash tree try to become an oak.

By letting go our fascination with the extraordinary and spectacular we can allow ourselves to recognize the simple wonder that lies within the ordinary.

For life is its own purpose and doesn't need a reason to be. That is its beauty. (Ref. 47)

5. Acceptance of value of guru

The *muNDaka upaniShad* says:

Let a *brAhmaNa* (an aspirant), after he has examined the worlds gained by *karma*, acquire freedom from all desires, reflecting that nothing that is eternal can be gained by *karma*. Let him, in order to obtain the knowledge of the eternal, take sacrificial fuel and approach that preceptor alone who is versed in the Vedas and is established in Brahman. I.2.12 [†] (Ref. 33)

Swami Chinmayananda clarifies:

In order to know That, in order to realize the Self, the scripture advises that a Brahmin must approach a *guru*. In this mantra, we get the clearest definition of a perfect *guru*. It is noteworthy that nowhere else in the bulk of our scriptures have we such a complete and exhaustive definition of a *guru*.

A *guru* should have two great qualifications: (a) a mastery over the entire scriptural literature and (b) a complete personal experience of the Absolute Reality. (Ref. 33)

(Incidentally, the word "Brahmin" here does not to refer to cultural status but to mental and spiritual maturity, sincerity, desire to realize the truth etc.)

Further than this, there is also a third requirement, namely the teaching method – the ability to convey the knowledge to another. Simply reading the scriptures, even with knowledge of Sanskrit, is not enough. What is really

---

[†] Mundakopanishad, Swami Chinmayananda, © Central Chinmaya Mission Trust, Mumbai.

needed is someone who already understands the truth to explain this in terms that we will be able to appreciate. This is where the idea of *sampradAya* or teacher-pupil lineage comes in, the particular style of teaching, fund of stories, metaphors etc. found to be effective by one teacher and passed on directly and indirectly to the disciple who subsequently becomes a teacher himself or herself.

Ramana Maharshi says that a *guru* is a "very powerful aid" and that "so long as you consider yourself a separate ego, a *guru* is necessary" but he reminds us that "the *guru* does not bring about Self-Realization. He simply removes the obstacles to it. The Self is always realized." (Ref. 49)

Nisargadatta Maharaj says that: "In the initial stages you must have an external *guru*. That *guru* initiates you with the inner *guru*." But that:

Your own Self is your ultimate teacher (*sadguru*). The outer teacher (*guru*) is merely a milestone. Only your inner teacher will walk with you to the goal, for he is the goal. Look within and you will find him. The greatest *guru* is your inner self. Truly, he is the supreme teacher. He alone can take you to your goal, and he alone meets you at the end of the road. Confide in him and you need no outer *guru*. (Ref. 5)

Ananda Wood, a disciple of Atmananda Krishna Menon, explains his teacher's viewpoint as follows:

A teacher is needed to deepen the enquiry, and thus to broaden it from narrow technicalities of reason and prescription by the head. The teacher is a living expression of truth, spontaneously expressing feelings from a depth of heart that is quite missing in mere books or words or arguments or discussions with other egos. The teacher seems to be another person and hence another ego, but that seeming is somehow proved untrue, through the relationship of teacher and disciple.

Sri Atmananda did insist that a living teacher was essential. When asked why, he would explain that by reading, by discussions with fellow seekers and by thinking on one's own, one can see what one is not - that one is not body, nor senses, nor mind. Such means are suitable for "clearing away the rubbish." But only the truth itself can show exactly what one is. And it does so by expressing itself in the form of a living teacher.

If pressed further, Sri Atmananda would say that this is not a subject to which the mind should be applied, through explanations and reasoning. A seeker need not worry about it, for it would take care of itself. If necessary, a teacher would spring up from the ground when the seeker was ready. (Ref. 54)

Amongst teachers that can be classified as belonging to Direct Path lineages, those in the Navnath lineage from Nisargadatta Maharaj onwards seem to have been taking an increasingly neo-Advaitin stance. **John Wheeler** has this to say on the subject of teachers, practices and levels of understanding:

> If there is any such thing as a teacher, I would say that it is someone who has realized their true nature as presence-awareness and does not support any of the concepts and ideas that are based on the idea of the existence of separate person. The best teachers point out that this understanding is immediate and available, here and now. They do not encourage the seeker to engage in protracted processes that subtly support the idea that understanding is in the future or the result of a practice.
>
> ...The direct understanding of who we are requires no time, no effort, no practice and no maintenance.
>
> ...There are no levels of understanding; there is nothing to maintain or cultivate; there are no levels of awakening; there is nothing to bring into daily life; there is nothing which needs to deepen. All of these things imply time, which is simply a mental concept. They also imply a separate individual to traverse through the various stages and experiences. None of these things exist in the presence-awareness.

Existence can never become more existent. Awareness can never become more aware. The absence of a separate "I" can never become more absent. It is all about seeing clearly what is present. (Ref. 70)

And yet, at the same time, he disparages the "nothing to do" approach of Neo-Advaita:

...this approach differs in style and emphasis from other approaches. I am particularly referring to those teachings that maintain that there is nothing to do, that everything, including suffering, doubt, confusion, and even the dreaded ego, are simply an expression of what is, that is, the perfection itself. (Ref. 70)

Thus, whilst still acknowledging that a teacher can be invaluable, the utility of practice or effort of any kind is downgraded and the notion of the *jIva* is deprecated. (It should be noted that he does say elsewhere in the same book that: "You need to put some solid inquiry into the question 'Who am I?' You can't assume some statement as an ideal and expect your daily life to shift. You need to do the homework, cover the basics." So, clearly *some* practice is still believed to be valuable.)

Nathan Gill denies that a teacher can transmit enlightenment or that it could happen by "grace" in the presence of a *guru*:

The guru and the disciple appear as images in the cosmic *lllA* - the play of life. Maybe the storyline in the play is that through grace the disciple receives the blessing of the guru, and for as long as there is entrancement with the story of 'me' this can be an enthralling drama. In actuality though there is no transmission of anything from one to another because there simply *isn't* anyone. (Ref. 338)

It is true that the guru knows that the seeker does not really have any problem but he has to recognize that the seeker thinks he has a problem and show compassion in helping him to see through the ignorance. Of course, this compassion may sometimes take the form of the Zen master's timely wielding of a large stick...

6. Acceptance of the value of effort in a path to enlightenment
The supreme truth is this: there is neither birth nor dissolution, nor aspirant to liberation nor liberated nor anyone in bondage. **Gaudapada** (Ref. 69)

Firstly, it must be noted again that all true teachers always acknowledge that in reality there is only the Self, so that the ideas of seeker, sought and path must ultimately be meaningless. The *mahAvAkya "tat tvam asi"* – That thou art – tells us that we are *already* the non-dual Self. There is nothing to do to get there. Anything we can do would be a finite event in time – it could never bring about something that is timeless and infinite. Thus it is that Shankara, for example, states unambiguously that: "The Self is not a thing unknown to anybody at any time, is not a thing to be reached or got rid of or acquired." *bhagavadgItA bhAShya* XVIII.50 (Ref. 28). And **Swami Dayananda** says:

> Knowledge of yourself as the limitless being is not an action to be accomplished by you; there is no effort, no motion required... You can reach ends by paths, but you cannot cut a path to reach yourself. (Ref. 31)

But he goes on to clarify:

> There are various techniques to make your mind purer, more abiding, subtler: but the real goal is not merely to improve the mind – it is to recognize yourself. For that there is no path.
>   Darkness cannot meet light; as light comes, darkness goes. Similarly ignorance and knowledge are opposed to each other. The Lord says, "I am the easiest to reach as I am the most difficult. If you search for Me, you cannot find Me. But for one whose mind is ready, who has the

blessing of the teaching, I am easy to know." (Ref. 31)

The problem is not that we are not directly acquainted with the reality of who we are but that our reason is distracted by the phenomenal world of name and form that has effectively been "created" through ignorance. It is because it so difficult for the mind to accept that "there is only Brahman" and "I am That" that Shankara advocated his *chatuShTaya sampatti* – fourfold requisites – for a spiritual seeker, as was discussed in the chapter on practices. The mind has to be prepared and purified before the final message of the teaching can be appreciated. Traditional teachings allow you to appear to be a body-mind, with *karma* and *saMskAra*-s to be worked out before you can attain self-realization. They advocate practices that can be followed to aid in this and initially emphasize the need for following *svadharma* (i.e. fulfilling your own particular destiny) and behaving in the appropriate manner. Only later, once those levels of understanding have been sublated, do they explain that our real nature is beyond all of this.

Dr. K. Sadananda, a disciple of the traditional Swami Chinmayananda says:

> If you ask me whether everybody needs to do *sAdhana*... the answer is yes or no and it depends on the type of the student. It is just like teaching quantum mechanics. If he has already taken the preparatory courses including math, then he can take the course right away. But for those who are only familiar with simple physics, they have to do many preparatory courses before they enter the quantum mechanics class. If this is true for objective studies, the subjective course is even more difficult, since the object of inquiry is the very subject itself. One cannot objectify the very subject of inquiry. Hence it is extremely subtle....
>
> Conditioning of the mind is done by deliberate actions, and to decondition the mind one has to have the appropriate detergent depending on the nature of the dirt. We do not want the detergent on the plate either - it is needed only as a tool and should leave the plate clean

and free from both dirt and detergent. The kind of detergent one needs depends upon the dirt one has. Hence, there is no one path, one yoga or one way. The teacher, after studying the student's tendencies and inclinations, generally recommends the path for that particular student. Hence a proper teacher is required. That is what we call a *sampradAya* teacher, who not only knows the truth but knows how to teach that to the student who has deeply rooted notions of his own. Also, a proper teacher is one who directs his disciples to the scriptures as the authority and not to himself since this is a subjective science. (Ref. 30)

Ramana Maharshi says that:

Divine Grace is essential for realization. It leads one to God realization. But such grace is vouchsafed only to him who is a true devotee or a yogi. It is given only to those who have striven hard and ceaselessly on the path towards freedom. There is a state beyond effort and effortlessness. However, until it is realized, effort is necessary. (Ref. 61)

Nisargadatta Maharaj is as unequivocal as the Neo-Advaitins in his condemnation of paths:

All paths lead to unreality. Paths are creations within the scope of knowledge. Therefore, paths and movements cannot transport you into Reality, because their function is to enmesh you within the dimension of knowledge, while the Reality prevails prior to it. To apprehend this, you must stay put at the source of your creation, at the beginning of the knowledge "I am." So long as you do not achieve this, you will be entangled in the chains forged by your mind and get enmeshed in those of others. (Ref. 62)

In neo-Advaita, of course, the mind is just the term applied to the thought that there is somewhere in which thoughts arise and are processed. There is neither mind nor ignorance to be dispelled; it is all just a story on the screen of awareness. The very concept of enlightenment is just that – a thought arising in awareness, which is itself unchanging and unaffected by any ideas, be they of joy or suffering, ignorance or Self-realization. Basically, once the "appearance" (of world and individuals) has been denied, any further discussion about ignorance and paths etc. is pointless. Anything that only has meaning in the phenomenal realm is treated as irrelevant; simply part of the story that is known by awareness. The status of the person is reduced to that of the actor in a play or, even worse the character-in-a-novel, who does not even have the scope to act well or badly. It is simply meaningless to talk of someone doing something to become enlightened – if that is what the story says, it will happen; if not, it won't – but either way this makes no difference to Consciousness.

No one becomes enlightened because in actuality there isn't anyone. Only within the story in the play of life does striving to transcend individuality appear to have validity. **Nathan Gill** *(Ref. 338)*

No practice could ever achieve anything. **Nathan Gill** says:

> There is no individual that could become enlightened; no one that needs to attain or realize anything. The drama of striving to achieve enlightenment through various practices is limited to the play of appearances. What practice is needed to simply *be*? (Ref. 338)

And **Tony Parsons** effectively puts the opening quotation of this section (from Gaudapada) into a modern context:

> For I am already that which I seek. Whatever I seek or think I want, however long the shopping list may be, all of my desires are only a reflection of my longing to come home. And home is oneness, home is my original nature. It is right here, simply in what is. There is nowhere else I have to go, and nothing else I have to become. (Ref. 47)

7. Behavior of a realized one relevant

Behavior, here, refers to the standards of morality imposed by society – and everyone knows that these vary according to era and country, in what to an alien might seem to be a totally arbitrary manner. As an extreme, slavery used to be thought normal and morally defensible in a number of cultures whereas few would now consider it ever to be acceptable.

The traditional view is that, in the case of a realized man or woman, the *saMchita saMskAra* (that accumulated from past action), apart from the *prArabdha* element (that which has reached fruition in this life) has been burnt up. (Strictly speaking, some argue that the *ichChA* part of this, personal desire is the one that no longer exists – see Chapter 2.) The Bhagavad Gita says that: "Even the man of knowledge acts in conformity with his own nature." (BG III 33, Ref. 28) Naturally, the realized man will not incur any (*AgAmin*) *saMskAra* in future actions so all that is left is the *prArabdha*. This is said to continue *from the point of view of other jIva-s* until it has run down, like a spinning wheel from which the motive force has been withdrawn. From the *j~nAnI*'s point of view, as **Ramana Maharshi** puts it, "There is no body or *karma* apart from the Self, so that the actions do not affect him." (Ref. 49)

Swami Krishnananda's comment is that:

> The *prArabdha* in the *jIvanmukta* is not experienced by his conscious-ness; it is not a content of the Absolute-Consciousness; it is existent only to the other ignorant *jIva*-s who perceive the existence or the movements of his body. (Ref. 67)

Ramakrishna suggests that the nature of the realized man returns effectively to the innocent status of that of a child, i.e. prior to the ignorant overlay of attachments that results in desire for objects and frustration and anger when they are not obtained:

> When a leaf of the coconut tree drops off, it leaves a mark on the trunk. This helps us to understand that there was once a leaf there. In the same

way he who has attained God keeps only the marks, the withered scars, of anger and passion. His nature is just like that of a child. (Ref. 50) and he adds that:

He who has acquired spiritual Knowledge can be never poisoned by the venom of lust and greed... Good and evil cannot bind him who has realized the oneness of Nature and his own self with Brahman. (Ref. 50)

The Direct Path view, as one might expect, makes fewer concessions to any cultural concepts on the relative plane. *"In conventional, interpersonal terms, the principle is that enlightenment consists of a deep, established, nonintellectual understanding of one's true nature as awareness, as permanent peace."* (**Dr. Gregory Goode** – Ref. 370) So anything that fosters this understanding is of value. Any moral law that is imposed by society acts as a restriction upon what I (the ego) might ideally desire to do. It is only in this sense that behavior is relevant. Nevertheless, **Krishna Menon** is unambiguous about the need for a realized man to adhere to social conventions for the sake of others:

From the spiritual standpoint, it might be immaterial to you whether you observe them or not. But then you have an obligation to the less fortunate members of society, who are really in need of every one of those customs and conventions to help them through the moral and righteous way of life. If a man respected in society – for whatsoever reason – were to break such laws of society, many others would follow him regardless of consequences; and society would disintegrate. An enlightened man will not violate any of the healthy conventions and customs insisted upon by *shAstra*-s and the great men of old. (Note 821 Ref. 13)

Robert Adams says that:

If we have a clear understanding of ourselves, we become the happiest people on earth. We become compassionate, kind, peaceful, we no longer have anything to fight. We no longer wish to change anybody or anything. We leave everything alone just the way it is, including ourselves especially. (Ref. 42)

Ramesh Balsekar claims that the body-mind mechanism is effectively programmed and that, following enlightenment, it will continue to act as before, the key difference being that there will now be no sense of ownership or "doership." The person obviously doesn't dissolve – it continues as before, but is now known simply to be an actor in the play - it is known that that "I am not the person." Consequently, if the nature of the person was to express things in a particular way, that is likely to continue. He says that:

Self-realization, to me, is merely the acceptance of whatever happens as the will of God according to Cosmic Law; and that no one is responsible for any actions. (Ref. 60)

Robert Adams disagrees with this. He says that there is a "transmutation" upon realization. He says that the "brain chemical changes" and the brain cells become servants of the mind. *"They no longer have their programming. All the programming disappears."* (Ref. 66)

Wayne Liquorman may perhaps be regarded as intermediate between Direct Path and Neo-Advaita. Here is what he has to say on the expected versus actual behavior of the realized man:

The tendency among most spiritual aspirants is to idolize and idealize the *guru*. He is dehumanized, placed in a distant and exalted position and then expectations are heaped upon him. He is held to a variety of standards of Enlightened Behavior that are quite impossible to fulfill if for no other reason than the fact the standards vary depending on the values of the evaluator. The irony is that enlightenment and behavior are not linked. All of the great sages have pointed to the fact that

Enlightenment is transcendent. It is not personal. Still, the emphasis of most seekers is on the personal. The perpetual satsang question revolves around, "What will I be like when I (the seeker) gain enlightenment?" The perpetual hope of this "personal enlightenment" vision is that the seeker turned enlightened being will now live a perfect life. "I will never again hurt anyone or be hurt by anyone. I will always act in accordance with my values" (whatever they might be) which is simply another way of saying I will become what I am not now... a Perfect being.

This teaching suggests we are ALL already perfect beings. Even what we call our flaws are perfect in that they are the product of Universal forces. We did not create these aspects of ourselves we don't like and most importantly others did not create those aspects of themselves we don't like. As this understanding deepens there is less and less room for guilt and blame, hatred and self-loathing... this is Peace. (Ref. 29)

One final word on this topic that is, perhaps, telling is that the Sanskrit word often used for a Sage is *sAdhu*. This means a holy man, saint, sage or seer but its literal meaning is straight or right and it is variously translated as kind, peaceful, good, virtuous and honorable. This is surely no accident.

8. The Self identified as that which is a known object of any action

Only two kinds of people can attain to Self-knowledge: those whose minds are not encumbered at all with learning, that is to say, not overcrowded with thoughts borrowed from others; and those who, after studying all the scriptures and sciences, have come to realize that they know nothing.
Ramakrishna

That the Self is not knowable in the usually understood sense of this word is made clear throughout the scriptures. Neither can it be experienced since all experiences are limited in time. This is the purpose of the teaching of Advaita – to point to that which cannot be explained. The reason this is not appreciated is because of ignorance in the mind and the only way to dispel this is by knowledge. This is the path of *j~nAna* and, yes, it is intellectual/analytical. And of course it is discarded along with everything else once the penny drops. **Swami Sivananda** explains in his commentary on the Brahma Sutra *bhAShya*:

> Brahman is not an object of the action of knowing. "It is different from the Known and again it is beyond the Unknown." (*kena upaniShad* I-3) "How should he know him by whom He knows all this?" (*bRRihadAraNyaka upaniShad* II-4-14) Brahman is expressly declared not to be the object of an act of devout worship (*upAsana*). "Know that alone to be Brahman, not that which people adore here. (*kena upaniShad* I-5). I.i.4 (Ref. 36)

Shankara tells us that the world of name and form is revealed to us through the "self-effulgent" light of Brahman, in the same way that visible things are revealed to sight through the light of the sun. But, whilst Brahman reveals all other objects, no object reveals Brahman. (BSB I.iii.22).

The statements in the scriptures have to be understood in the context in which they occur. In the *bRRihadAraNyaka upaniShad*, the seeker, Usasta, asks his teacher, Yajnavalkya, to explain further the nature of Brahman, having just effectively been told "This is it." He asks for clarification. As **Swami Krishnananda** loosely translates:

> You have only told me, this is your inner Self in the same way as people would say, "this is a cow, this is a horse," etc. That is not a real definition. Merely saying, "this is that" is not a definition. I want an actual description of what this internal Self is. Please give that description and do not simply say, "this is that." *bRRihadAraNyaka upaniShad* III.iv.2 (Ref. 2).

Swami Krishnananda goes on to explain Yajnavalkya's response:

Nobody can know the *Atman* inasmuch as the *Atman* is the Knower of all things. So, no question regarding the *Atman* can be put, such as "What is the *Atman*? Show it to me" etc. You cannot show the *Atman* because the Shower is the *Atman*; the Experiencer is the *Atman*; the Seer is the *Atman*; the functioner in every respect through the senses or the mind or the intellect is the *Atman*. As the basic residue of reality in every individual is the *Atman*, how can we go behind It and say, "this is the *Atman*?" Therefore, the question is impertinent and inadmissible. The reason is clear. It is the Self. It is not an object. (Ref. 2)

Swami Satprakashananda states that:

The Knower is contrary to all that is known including the body and the mind. While the known are many, limited, changeful, and non-conscious, the knower is one, unlimited, changeless, and self-aware. (Ref. 27)

And he quotes from Sureshvara (one of the four principal disciples of Shankara):

The inmost Self, which is perpetual awareness, which is not dependent on any other proof [being self-evident], which is without attributes, such as sound, form, etc., as to whose existence there is no room for doubt, which is supreme blessedness, which is immeasurable, which is the innermost being, cannot be determined by such means of knowledge as perception and the rest engendered by despicable desire. (Ref. 27)

In reality, the Self is "self-luminous" or self-evident and does not require to be "known" in the usual sense of the word. What the scriptures seek to teach us is not the self-evident nature of the *Atman* but the fact that this Atman is *brahman*.

Atmananda Krishna Menon agrees that we cannot "know" That, in any normal sense of the word. It is more a case of "identity":

"I know I am" is a single experience, recognized by all persons. It consists of two parts: "I know" and "I am." The "I am" can never be an object of "I know." Therefore both mean the same thing, and together are an experience in identity. When knowledge is objectless, it is not the subject either. These are the only two statements that require no proof. (Note 654 Ref. 13).

And later: "Knowledge of Self is knowledge as Self." (Note 1320).

Francis Lucille asks:

How can we know this presence? We can only be it. We cannot touch, feel, comprehend, or see it. That is why we can never say that it is finite, or in time. What can the mind say about something that escapes it? We are knowingly this presence, the moment we know nothing about it, or about what we are; and thus, the moment we "know nothing" about anything. To meditate knowingly, means to take our stand in unknowing, to make "unknowing" our home...

Do not try to know what you are. You would catch only a shadow. Simply understand that you are this mirror, the abode of all things, and also peace and happiness. (Ref. 59)

The mental 'thought' that occurs at the moment of realization, when Brahman is *effectively* 'known' is called *akhaNDAkAra vRRitti* but, as was explained in Chapter 4, this is not a knowing as such but the mind 'taking on the form of the undivided.'

9. The Self identified as that which knows or experiences

Be still, and you will know. You will know there is no one to know; that there is nothing to know. **Robert Adams** (Ref. 42)

This is effectively the same as the previous belief, but viewed from the other side, so to speak. Since there is *only* the Self, knower and known must be identical. But it is worth considering so as to throw yet more light on the differences in the teaching methods.

The traditional view is that the Self only knows anything by virtue of the body, mind and senses of the individual. These do not really exist of course, but from the phenomenal point of view they are what are called "limiting or conditioning adjuncts" (*upAdhi*-s) apparently existing as a result of ignorance. Thus, **Shankara** says, in his commentary on the *kaThopaniShad* (I.iii.4):

> Rightly do the wise, the discriminating ones, speak of the Self associated with body, senses and mind as the experiencer, the one undergoing transmigration. For the Self alone is not an experiencer. It only appears to become an experiencer through association with such apparent conditioning adjuncts (*upAdhi*) as the intellect (*buddhi*), etc. (Ref. 24)

The Self neither knows nor is known in any literal sense. In his *bhAShya* on the *bhagavadgItA*, **Shankara** says: "Because the Imperishable is unmanifest, He is not accessible to words and cannot therefore be defined. He is unmanifest, not manifest to any of the organs of knowledge." (BG XII 3 Ref. 28)

In the *vivekachUDAmaNi*, the Self is described as *agochara*, meaning "not perceptible" or "not objectifiable" (Ref. 58). It cannot be experienced as an object – that 'I am' is our direct experience; perhaps 'recognition' is a better word. It is self-illuminating like the sun. The Direct Path view given by **Greg Goode** is similar:

> Seeing the Self as a knower of something is a teaching metaphor. It still leaves the subtle residue of the subject/object paradigm, which eventually gives way. "Knowing your True Nature" sounds beautiful and inspirational, but it is not meant to be taken literally. This Self-knowledge is not cast towards an object, as is perception. It's not like mirrors, images, or reflections. It's more like the shining of the sun. (Ref. 57)

Nisargadatta Maharaj points out that the Absolute only becomes conscious and thus aware "of" anything at all in the context of a phenomenal world, with time, space and mind:

> As Absolute, I am timeless, infinite, and I am awareness, without being aware of awareness... Unless there is space and duration I cannot be conscious of myself. (Ref. 129)

This is the thinking which justifies the idea of *lIlA*, the manifestation of a creation in order that the Absolute can experience Himself.

10. Acceptance that the scriptures are of value

Tradition would have it that the Scriptures are not merely of value but virtually essential. In fact, a teacher is not considered truly authentic unless he refers everything he says back to the scriptures for authority. A true teacher is expected to be a *shrotriya* – well versed in the scriptures. Similarly, the disciple has to have faith in both scriptures and in the guru's ability to explain them. Otherwise the teaching will remain at the level of theory only.

The Brahma Sutra states right at the beginning: "But that (Brahman is to be known only from the Scriptures and not independently by any other means is established), because it is the main purpose (of all Vedantic texts)." I.i.4 (Ref. 37)

Shankara's view is as follows:

> True, it (i.e. Self-knowledge) is unattainable to those who have not been properly initiated into the traditional knowledge by the *guru*-s (the Great Ones), who have not learned and studied the (teachings of the) Vedanta, whose intellect is quite engrossed in the external objects of senses, and who have not been trained in the right sources of knowledge. *bhagavadgItA bhAShya* XVIII.50 (Ref. 28)

But it is not intended to imply that reading the *shruti* can bring about

Self-realization. Suggesting that this might be so is another example of the *adhyAropa* – *apavAda* method and it does not really contradict the statements made earlier that Brahman cannot be an object of perception or knowledge. Once the scriptures have served their purpose, they are discarded as unreal, along with every "thing" else. They only have validity in the apparently dualistic world of ignorance and knowledge, *guru* and seeker. **Shankara** makes it clear that:

> These ideas, namely, the ideas of teacher, taught, and scripture are for the purpose of teaching which are (therefore appear) true till one realizes the Highest Truth. But duality does not exist when one, as a result of the teaching, attains knowledge, i.e., realizes the Highest Reality. (Commentary on Gaudapada *kArikA* on the *mANDUkya upaniShad* I.7 (18). Ref. 35)

Nor is it any contradiction to suggest that the Scriptures can help, having just argued above that the Self can never be known. **Shankara** explains this in the *brahma sUtra bhAShya* (I.i.4):

> If you object that, if the Absolute is not an object of knowledge, it cannot be known through the Veda, we reply that this is not so. For the aim of the Veda here is to put an end to distinctions imagined through Ignorance. The Veda does not aim to expound the Absolute as if it were an object characterizable as this or that. What, then, does it do? What it does is to eliminate distinctions such as those of knower, knowledge and known, which are imagined through Ignorance. And it does so by teaching that the Absolute, because it is the inmost Self, is *not* an object of knowledge. (Ref. 24)

The way in which the scriptures work is explained by **Swami Satchidanandendra**:

> Thus the means of knowledge called the Veda is (ultimately seen to be)

an illusion. And its power to effect release through destroying Ignorance is also an illusion. And on this basis one might wonder whether direct knowledge of the supreme Self was itself also an illusion, or whether it was real. If it were an illusion, then the liberation it effected would also be illusory, and in that case what would be the point in the Upanishadic discipline? If, on the other hand, we say that direct knowledge of the Self is real, then how could real direct knowledge arise from illusory Upanishadic texts?

If this objection is raised, we must draw attention to two different ways in which it can be answered. If we take the phrase "direct knowledge arises through the holy texts" to mean that such direct knowledge consists in the mere mental idea to which the texts give rise, then such knowledge would be illusory. It would be as illusory as a dream-sword used to slay a dream-tiger. Still, it will be enough to destroy illusory Ignorance. And being itself inseparable from Ignorance, it will be destroyed with the latter. Liberation, which will mean becoming established in one's own nature, will be attributed figuratively to one who was never involved in erroneous knowledge and its destruction, just as waking up is attributed to a dreamer who was never really involved with sword or tiger.

But is it not the case that, on this view, bondage will be an illusion and liberation, therefore, also an illusion? Let it be even so. No harm will result to the supreme reality. (Ref. 24)

Any teaching that advises you that you need to be serious or honest or purified or changed through some process is simply not relevant. **Tony Parsons** (Ref. 63)

Neither Direct Path nor Neo-Advaita accepts the authority of the scriptures. This actually means that they cannot call themselves Vedanta in the true sense, since they are not *Astika* (deferring to the authority of the Vedas).

Greg Goode's short comment on the subject is that: "*If anything can have value, such as a poem, a walk in the woods, or the smile of a loved one,* *then why not scripture?"* (Ref. 57)

11. Use of the concept of Brahman

It might have been thought that the acknowledgement that "who I really am" is That (Brahman, Absolute, etc.) is fundamental to Advaita. The belief is clearly stated by the four great statements (*mahAvAkya*-s), one in each of the four Vedas. In the *aitareya upaniShad* in the *RRig veda*: *praj~nAnaM brahma* (Consciousness is Brahman). In the *ChAndogya upaniShad* from the *sama veda*: the most famous – *tattvamasi* 'You are That'. In the *mANDUkya upaniShad* from the *atharva veda*: *ayamAtmA brahma* (This Self is Brahman). In the *bRRihadAraNyaka upaniShad* from the *yajur veda*: *aham brahmAsmi* (I am Brahman).

To Shankara, it is a self-evident fact that "I" exist - something that direct experience can never deny. Since the purport of the traditional teachings is that there is only Brahman, what is needed is to remove the false superimpositions that have been made upon this. I erroneously think that there are objects, other people etc. and that I am separate. The *guru* imparts knowledge through the scriptures so that discrimination can remove this ignorance and reveal the truth that was there from the beginning – I am Brahman.

The denial of the existence of the *jIva* by neo-Advaitins means that these statements do not really make any sense to them. Of course, they argue, since there is only Consciousness it must be the case that this non-existent appearance of "me" (the "story") is also Consciousness but that is really not saying very much.

Direct Path teachers, as noted, largely bypass the preparation and set about explaining the nature of reality straight away but the bottom line is still "You are That." "Who we essentially are" is not a body or mind. Objects and concepts are an aspect of the illusory phenomenal realm only. When I refer to "I," all ideas of the personal have to be discarded. Nevertheless, that ultimate "feeling of unchanging existence" remains. That is what I am. That is the non-dual reality. As **Greg Goode** puts it: *"Awareness, a non-traditional synonym for Brahman, is the being of everything. All notional "I"s are nothing but it. It is I-ness itself."* (Ref. 57)

Neo-Advaita teachers have no time for the personal – the person does not exist; it is only a story appearing in awareness (to no one). "Who I essentially am" is also relegated to a concept or apparent actor in the story. Thus, all that there really is, in the end, is this impersonal "awareness of itself" with the phenomenal reduced to a lifeless projection on a cinema screen in an empty theatre.

As was discussed in the first chapter, most normal (!) people think of themselves as bodies. Thus we might say, for example, "I am walking." It is only when this is investigated closely that it comes to be understood that it is actually the body that is walking and not "I." If the legs were amputated and the body had to move about in a wheelchair, "who I actually am" would remain unaffected. A more accurate way of describing the situation is "there is walking."

As the next step, we might say "I see the body walking," in recognition of this. But, again, closer examination reveals that what is happening here is that the eyes are registering the movement and the mind is interpreting this. I am still not actually doing anything. Instead, "there is seeing."

But this analysis can continue as far back as you may try to take it. Some teachers use the concept of witnessing to get across the idea of a totally detached observer of all that seemingly takes place to this person that we once thought ourselves to be. Thus there can be witnessing of thinking and feeling etc. and I might initially say "I am the witness of these." But, again, this is another limited view, and we cannot be that. Again, it has rather to be phrased as "there is witnessing." It is not possible to pin down "who we are" using words or concepts.

This situation is recognized by all approaches. With traditional teachers and students, it is not usually a problem, however. In the beginning, when a student uses the word "I," she genuinely believes that she is referring to her body or mind. Once it has all been understood and assimilated, the word is used simply as a linguistic convenience. It is understood that the person talking is not really who I am but speaking itself is meaningless unless the provisional existence of the person is accepted. In neo-Advaita, however, students attending satsangs for a month or two cannot be expected fully to appreciate the teaching.

As an example of misunderstanding of the teaching, some years ago, in some satsang circles, it was not uncommon to encounter people habitually referring to their bodies and minds as totally "other" than themselves. "The body is experiencing aches" may not seem too strange but "the desire to visit the bathroom was observed" is positively arcane. This mode of expression became known as the "Lucknow Syndrome," in honor of the location in India where Sri Poonja used to hold his meetings.

Nevertheless, if there are to be teachers attempting to pass on the message to apparent seekers of truth, words and concepts *do* have to be used and it seems that they should be used sensibly. In traditional teachings, the nature of Brahman is communicated largely by a process of negation – *neti*, *neti*. And although recognizing that it is beyond words, the disciple can be given some appreciation of the reality - That. Once this has been gained, the final message is "you are That, too."

12. Other Differences in Beliefs

There are a number of other differences of opinion regarding some fundamental beliefs in Advaita but these have been dealt with earlier in the book in the appropriate chapters. For example, traditional Advaita allows that *jIva*-s have a limited degree of free-will, whereas this is denied by Neo-Advaitins (and most modern Direct Path teachers). Traditional teachings talk of reincarnation, heaven, gods and demons and some will insist that the subtle body does continue across lives. Everyone else acknowledges that there is no entity that is born in the first place so it cannot die to be reborn either.

Accordingly, I will not pursue this examination of the differences any further. It can be seen that Direct Path teachings represent a move away from the Traditional and away from allowances of meaningful interactions at the level of *vyavahAra*. Neo-Advaita makes no concessions at all and attempts to make all of its statements at the level of *paramArtha*, a stance that is somewhat illogical, since all language is necessarily dualistic to begin with. The essential difference seems to me to be that Neo-Advaitins do not recognize the validity of the supposed statement of Shankara (mentioned in Chapter 4) summing up the essence of Advaita to Gaudapada, the teacher of his own guru:

brahma satyam jaganmithyA
jIvo brahmaiva nAparaH

(Brahman alone is real. The world is *mithyA*. The *jIva* is identical with Brahman.)

In making the claim that "This is it," Neo-Advaitins are effectively stating that "this" (i.e. the world) is *satya*, truth, whereas in fact it is *mithyA*, neither real nor unreal. It is the **essence** of the world-appearance that is *brahman* or *satya*. The world appears as the world, along with all of its apparent duality to the realized man just as to the seeker. Just as the sun still appears to circle the earth, though we know that this is not in fact so. (The ignorance of this fact is the *sopAdhika adhyAsa* referred to in the chapter on Knowledge, as opposed to the rope-snake type, *nirupAdhika adhyAsa*.)

Since the table shows that the views of Neo-Advaita differ on all counts from those of Traditional Advaita and since it is a *nAstika* system, it might be concluded that it has been wrongly named. Whatever system it might be "new" of, it doesn't seem to be Advaita. However, it must be acknowledged that the "bottom line" understanding is the same – there is only the non-dual reality. In fact, the Neo-Advaitin claims quite simply that there is only the non-dual reality and that this is it. There is nothing else, no seeker, no ignorance, no path etc. But **Govindagopal Mukhopadhyaya** comments as follows:

To state in the terms of the classical example of *vedAnta*, it will not do merely to know that the snake is nothing but the rope, but one must fully know how, through what process of misapprehension, the rope had appeared as the snake. Till then the illusion will not be dispelled, the fear will not be removed, the truth will not be revealed. True transcendence thus implies a knowledge in detail of the entire process of manifestation.

(Ref. 344)

Summary

- Any method is valid if it leads to the truth (though neo-Advaitins would presumably not accept this).
- Traditional is gradual; practice and interim beliefs are later rescinded.
- In theory, Neo only recognizes the non-dual reality. In practice, once they acknowledge that this truth can be "discovered", they are committed to much more.
- Traditional and Direct recognize the seeming reality of the world as *vyavahAra*; neo-Advaita claims recognizes only *paramArtha*.
- Traditional and Direct provisionally acknowledge the jIva; neo does not.
- Mistaking the Self for a person as a result of ignorance and needing knowledge to remove this is a teaching device for Traditional/Direct. Neo does not recognize the existence of ignorance.
- Traditional argues that it is man's purpose to seek enlightenment and renounce the world. Neo believes that life is its own purpose.
- Traditional/Direct claim the need for a guru. Neo denies the existence of either seeker or guru.
- Traditional/Direct believe that the mind must be prepared and effort made before "Grace" may enter. Since Neo does not accept mind or enlightenment, the idea of effort is meaningless.
- Traditional/Direct believe that the realized man naturally behaves morally within societies' conventions. Again, these concepts are not relevant to Neo.
- Traditional/Direct do not believe that the Self can be "known," as they regard "knowledge" as pertaining to the mind. And the true Self is unmanifest. Neo makes such claims as that we are "knowingness" and that we know and are known "as This."

- Traditional believes that Scriptures are essential, along with a guru to unfold them. They act like a dream tiger to awaken us. Neither Direct nor neo accept their ultimate authority, though Direct frequently makes use of them.
- Traditional/Direct use the teaching that "I am Brahman." Since Neo denies the *jIva*, this statement has no meaning for them.
- The fundamental difference of Neo seems to be its failure to recognize the world as *mithyA*. (It also confuses *bhrama* or *avidyA* and *mAyA* – see chapter 4.)

Conclusion

It is certainly the case that traditional Advaita does not "sit comfortably" with the western mind. Those brought up in a western society and culture are bound to feel more at home with the impromptu liveliness and lack of ritual associated with modern Direct Path and Neo-Advaitin teachers. But it is the enquiring mind that is both the problem and the solution to seeing how things really are in respect of us and the world. I began my own seeking on a traditional path and then moved into Direct Path, also dabbling in a neo-direction. Ultimately, however, I found it necessary to go back to the roots in order really to understand what is being said (not always clearly) by *all* teachers. "In reality" there is no ignorance, but then there is no knowledge either. From the viewpoint of the seeker, however, both are very relevant and knowledge is the only way to remove the ignorance that is ultimately found never to have existed. The entire subject is riddled with paradox as far as the mind is concerned.

Much of the problem has to do with language, as was pointed out in the chapter on Spiritual Paths. It therefore seems to me that there is a danger of compounding confusion by introducing new words or using them in unfamiliar ways. This seems fine in creative writing but not in a book that is attempting to convey understanding. Also, I am never sure that I know what people mean when they use words in a novel context. It seems that writers can use this technique when they don't really know themselves what they are trying to say. If the language is imprecise, the reader may think she has understood but perhaps it was actually the case that the writer wasn't making a clear statement in the first place.

Language is necessarily dualistic and this is bound to lead to paradox. But these are paradoxes only to the mind. As long as we remain trapped in endless mental deliberations, the seeming paradoxes will continue. In reality there are none – there cannot be because there are not two things.

Accordingly, I do not hesitate to recommend that the serious "seeker" should follow a traditional path, even to the extent of learning some Sanskrit! What is always happening in the apparent world is that we are continually looking outwards, trying to discover new things, ideas and pleasures; aiming "to boldly go where no one has gone before." This is moving in the direction of increasing differentiation of name and form, further into the realms of ignorance, away from the essence that is forever unchanging.

Instead, we need to work backwards to discover that out of which all of this manifest creation arises, that which is the absolute essence of all. Yes, the creation is wonderful and a never-ending source of amazement, diversion and entertainment. But that is the point – that it is always changing and therefore, according to the definition, unreal. If we want to discover that which is the only unchanging reality, the apparent cause of all this diversity, we need to undertake the voyage – back to the truth.

CODA

There seems no better way to end this book than to comment briefly on the famous prayer - *shAnti-pATha* (peace study or reading) - appearing at the beginning of the *IshA upaniShad*. (It also occurs in the *bRRihadAraNyaka upaniShad*.):

OM. That is Fullness. This is Fullness. This Fullness comes forth from that Fullness. When this Fullness is taken away from that Fullness, Fullness alone remains.

"That" (*adah*) is the unmanifest, formless absolute (*nirguNa brahman*) – *adah* means "that," as opposed to "this" and is used to refer to something remote, not available for direct knowledge. "This" (*idam*) is the manifest universe (*saguNa brahman*) - *idam* means "known, present" and refers to everything that is here, now, in front of me, having form and available to my perception. The manifest apparently proceeds from the unmanifest but the Absolute is totally unaffected.

adah represents the subject, the eternal witness of everything else, the *idam* objects. This experience of difference is resolved in this verse, as explained by **Swami Dayananda**:

> When I turn to the Upanishads for an answer to my problem of limitation, *shruti* tells me that I am the limitless being who I long to be. But, at the same time, *shruti* recognizes my experience of difference. In this *shAnti-pATha*, the two separate pronouns *adah* and *idam* (together comprising everything in creation) are used to indicate *pUrNam*, not for the sake of a riddle, but to recognize the experience of duality. *adah* recognizes I, the subject - I who seems to be a being separate and distinct from all else; *idam* recognizes all known and knowable objects which appear to differ from me and from one another. Thus, *shruti* says there is nothing but fullness, though fullness appears to be *adah*, that (I), and *idam*, this (objects). In this way, *shruti* acknowledges duality - experiences of difference - and then, accounts for it by properly relating experience to reality. *shruti* accounts for duality by negating experience as non-real,

not as nonexistent.

...Therefore, when it is said that aham, I, am *pUrNam* and *idam*, this, is *pUrNam*, what is really being said is that there is only *pUrNam*. *Aham*, I, and idam, this, traditionally represent the two basic categories into one or the other of which everything fits. There is no third category. So if *aham* and *idam* represent everything and each is *pUrNam*, then everything is *pUrNam*. *Aham*, I is *pUrNam* which includes the world. *Idam* this, is *pUrNam* which include me. The seeming differences of *aham* and *idam* are swallowed by *pUrNam* - that limitless fullness which *shruti* (scripture) calls *Brahman*. (Ref. 352)

The world that is initially claimed to be separate is eventually seen to be the same non-dual reality. We deny the world only in order to realize our own Self. The seeming separation is only a mistaken view of the mind yet causes untold suffering. It is therefore necessary, provisionally to distance ourselves from it until more knowledge has been gained. Finally, it is seen that the world is not "other." The Self is complete - unlimited existence-knowledge - and the world is but a manifestation of that same reality, also necessarily perfect and complete. Since nothing has been created, there is no diminution of the whole despite the seemingly endless variety of form in the universe. Similarly, *brahman* remains unaffected by bliss and suffering, births and extinctions, just as the sun is unaffected by the multifarious events on the earth that it illuminates.

Sri Ranjit Maharaj says that "The illusion cannot give something more to reality, because reality is at the base of everything that is," and **Andrew Vernon** comments:

All the fascinating places and magnificent scenery in the world, all the beautiful plants and flowers, the enormous variety of species of animals and the multitudes of human beings - none of them have any effect on the Self. They do not add anything to reality when they appear and they do not take anything away from reality when they go away. Reality, the Self, is the base of all that appears, the source. It remains full and complete in Itself if there are a billion worlds, and it remains full and complete if there is no manifestation at all. The Sanskrit prayer at the beginning of the Isha Upanishad expresses this great truth. (Ref. 20)

Govindagopal Mukhopadhyaya is commenting on this verse when he says:

> Thus "ne 'ti ne 'ti" does not deny the reality of existence, it "denies all the empirical characterization of reality." It just signifies that Reality is something unique and distinct from the empirical. If we keep this sense of denial in mind, then it will be clear that "the denial of attributes and qualifications to Brahman does not reduce it to a void" but on the contrary, points to its inexhaustible fullness, which remains absolutely undiminished even after the whole of creation streams out of it, because it is not touched by this process of continuous ebb and flow at all, being absolutely distinct from all this. Here, by a strange mathematics, even after the subtraction of the full from the full, the remainder still remains the full! (Ref. 344)

As **Madathil Nair** points out, this single verse effectively sums up the whole of Advaita Vedanta:

> Let the mountains, rivers, stars, and all the beings therefore remain as they are. What does it matter? If I am fullness, for which *shruti* is my guarantee, the mountain cannot be outside me or other than me. Therefore, the mountain is me. Thus, the river is me, the star is me, everything is me. I am the fullness that pervades all of them. They are not parts of me or in me (*bhagavad gIta* – IX.5), because as fullness I can't have parts or contents. They are all verily me! When I am 'looking' at them, I am 'face to face' with infinity – the reality that I am!
>
> Thus the *pUrNamadah* verse has all *vedAnta* encapsulated in it!
>
> The deluded and limited me is just an appearance like all the rest of the things in this perceived universe. They are just non-real (*mithyA*)

superimpositions on the reality that I am. Take them away or bring them back – the fullness that I am remains unaltered and undiminished, whether the seeming me is awake, asleep or dead! (Ref. 318)

OM pUrNamadaH pUrNamidaM
pUrNAt pUrNamudachyate
pUrNasya pUrNamAdAya
pUrNamevAvashiShyate
OM shAntiH, shAntiH, shAntiH

OM. That is Fullness. This is Fullness. This Fullness comes forth from that Fullness. When this Fullness is taken away from that Fullness, Fullness alone remains. OM. Let there be peace.

[*shAntiH* is repeated three times to symbolize freedom from *adhidaivika* problems – from supernatural sources; from *adhibhautika* problems – from elemental or material sources, wars, disagreements etc; from *adhyAtmika* problems – relating to ourselves, physical and mental health etc.]

Finally, if it is thought that all that has gone before has been understood, it is perhaps best to finish with the following observation from **Nisargadatta Maharaj**:

The ultimate point of view is that there is nothing to understand, so when we try to understand, we are only indulging in acrobatics of the mind... Whatever you have understood, you are not. Why are you getting lost in concepts? You are not what you know, you are the knower. (Ref. 129)

APPENDIX A - ITRANS TRANSLITERATION OF SANSKRIT

In the West, Sanskrit is rarely represented in its correct Devanagari form since few people would be able to make any sense of it. Instead, it is usually written in what is called a transliterated form, which means that the actual characters of a given word are converted into an Anglicised form using the Roman alphabet. There are several methods for doing this but the one most frequently used on the Internet is called ITRANS and was devised by Avinash Chopde. His software, and details about the system, may be downloaded from his website at *http://www.aczoom.com/itrans/*. The problem was that the previously most widely used scheme used symbols called macrons (lines above letters) and dots above and below letters, so that it was quite unsuitable for computer keyboards with basic letters and the normal fonts provided with word processors. Accordingly, ITRANS was devised to use only the usual letters of our alphabet, together with the occasional special character such as the tilde ~.

The five basic vowels

The first letter of the alphabet forms the fundamental sound from which all others are derived simply by moving the tongue and lips. It is made by opening the mouth wide and letting the vocal chords operate. The sound which emerges sounds like a cross between the short "a" in cat and "u" in but. It is written as *a* in ITRANS but the correct letter in the proper script, called *devanAgarI* (meaning city of the gods), is: -

अ *a*

This is the first letter of the alphabet and the first vowel or, to use its correct term, *svara*, meaning sound.

If the back of the tongue is now raised slightly towards the back of the roof of the mouth, keeping the front of the tongue down against the back of the lower teeth, and the same short movement of the vocal chord is made, a slightly different sound emerges. This sounds a bit like the short "i" in bit. It is written as *i* in ITRANS.

इ *i*

The next two vowels seem strange to Westerners but follow the logic of the development. The underlying sound for both of these is the *i* sound just covered but the tip of the tongue is first moved further forward in the mouth. If you raise the tip of the tongue until it is almost touching the roof of the mouth and then, make the *i* sound as before, the next vowel sound emerges. Modern students often actually flick the tongue downwards as the sound is made so that the result sounds something like "ri" in the word rip, though the rolling "r" beginning is not clearly enunciated because the tongue never actually touched the roof of the mouth. However, strictly speaking this is not correct. It is written *RRi* in ITRANS (or, in old releases, *R^i*).

ऋ *RRi*

This procedure is repeated but now the tip of the tongue moves further forward still, to just behind the front teeth, before the "i" is sounded. Again, modern speakers often flick the tongue up towards the roof and down so that the sound that actually comes out is "lri." Again, not strictly correct but it hardly matters since there is only one word in the language that uses this letter! It is written *LLi* in ITRANS (or, in old releases, *L^i*).

ऌ *LLi*

Continuing the development, the emphasis finally shifts to the lips (labial position), having begun in the throat (guttural position), moved to at the back of the mouth (palatal), then to the roof of the mouth (cerebral) and then the teeth (dental). If a circle is formed of the lips but without any tension and the basic sound is made, a short "oo" sound comes out as in soot or cut. This is the last of the simple vowels, written *u*.

उ *u*

These five vowels with their characteristic mouth positions effectively head up the five main groups of consonants. Consonants all still sound the basic "a" but "stop" it from coming out in that simple way by varying the position of the tongue and lips in the way dictated by the vowel at the head of the group.

The long vowels

The basic five vowels above are all short vowels - *hrasva*. This means that, when pronounced, the sound is made as short as possible whilst still being distinguishable - really quite short! Each of these vowels can be sounded long. The length is actually very precise. If the short form is treated as one measure, then the long form should be two measures. The long form is called *dIrgha*. In ITRANS, the vowel is shown as long either by putting two of them, as with the ii in diirgha or by capitalising it thus: - dIrgha. The latter form has been used as standard in this book.

When the vowels become long, the pronunciation naturally changes slightly, too. Thus, the short *a* becomes *aa* or *A* and sounds like the "a" in calm. The short *i* becomes *ii* or *I* and sounds like the double "ee" sound in words like sleep. The short *RRi* becomes *RRI* (or *R^I* in old releases of ITRANS). Here there is no option of having two small I's. The *dIrgha* vowel is sounded as for the *hrasva* form but with the ending "ee" instead of "i." Similarly, the short *LLi* becomes *LLI* (or *L^I* in the old releases of ITRANS) but, since there are no words at all known to contain it, this hardly seems to matter! Finally, short *u* becomes long *uu* or *U* and sounds like the double "oo" in root.

The vowels can be sounded for longer than two measures, in which case they are called *pluta* - prolonged. In this case they are written with a number "3" below and just to the right of the letter, both in *devanAgarI* and in the Romanised version. This form cannot be represented in ITRANS.

A	*I*	*RRI*	*LLI*	*U*
आ	ई	ऋ	ॡ	ऊ

The compound vowels

Now, if the sound *a* is made and continues to sound while the mouth is slowly closed, the sound made before the lips come together is *u*. If these two sounds are made together or, more practically speaking, if the sound corresponding to the mid-point between these two is made, the sound that emerges is *o* (as in "boat"). This new letter is called a compound vowel. Similarly, when a combines with *i*, it forms the compound vowel *e*.

If you sound a prolonged a_3, and then raise the back of the tongue towards the *i* position, but stop before you get there, you should hear the *e* sound. It's a bit like the "a" in "hate" but not as open as we would pronounce this.

If, after making the above sound for *e*, you relax the tongue back towards the *a* position but again stop before you get there, there is another sound formed as a compound between *a* and *e* which sounds like the "ie" in "die." It is written *ai*.

In a similar way to that described above, if the mouth moves from the *a* (open-mouthed) position to the *o* (partially closed) position but stops half-way, there is a sound similar to "ow" in "brown." This is written *au* in ITRANS.

These, then are the fourteen vowels but there are two final letters to be added to complete the group of sixteen, so-called *mAtRRikA*. They are not really part of the alphabet but act as modifications to a preceding vowel. (Note that, because of this, if they are sounded as letters in their own right, they assume an "a" before rather than after.)

The first of these is called an *anusvAra*. It is written as *M* and causes the preceding vowel to be sounded through the nose. In the Devanagari, a single dot is added over the preceding letter. The precise nasal sound is determined by the consonant that follows it, in that it uses the mouth position corresponding to that for the consonant so that the effect is something like the nasal consonant (*anunAsika*) described below.

The other special letter, not really part of the alphabet, also modifies the sound of the preceding vowel, is written *H* and it has the effect of adding a brief, breathing out, "unvoiced" sound after the vowel. It is as though there were a word beginning with "h" immediately following and you start to sound it as soon as you finish the preceding letter (i.e. without changing the mouth position) but then realise your mistake and stop before the word itself starts to sound. It is called a *visarga*. In the Devanagari, two dots are added to the right of the preceding letter.

e	ai	o	au	aM	aH
ए	ऐ	ओ	औ	अं	अः

Table of Vowels

So, to recap, the 16 vowels, or *mAtRRikA*, are as follows: -

a	A	i	I	u	U	RRi	RRI
अ	आ	इ	ई	उ	ऊ	ऋ	ॠ

LLi	LLI	e	o	ai	au	aM	aH
ऌ	ॡ	ए	ओ	ऐ	औ	अं	अः

The first group of consonants (guttural)

The Sanskrit term for consonants is *vya~njana*, meaning a "decoration" (of the basic vowel sound). Twenty-five of these are grouped in five sets of five "underneath" the five basic vowels described above. They are formed by positioning the mouth (tongue or lips) in such a way as to "stop" the sound of the vowel in some way. The first group uses the mouth position of the *a* sound for decorating. This all takes place at the back of the mouth where it becomes the throat - the "guttural" position.

Strictly speaking it is not possible to pronounce a consonant on its own. It is in itself only a positioning of the mouth to "stop" the sound made by a vowel. Accordingly, when speaking the alphabet, the sound of *a* is used by default after each letter. The first consonant of this group is written *k*, sounded (with a) "ka" as in cat.

When talking about the letter on its own, the sound "a" is automatically assumed. Clearly it could occur at the end of the word (as "k" in "rack" for example). In this case it would have an additional mark under the letter, called a "halant," which means "don't make any vowel sound after this." (The Sanskrit word is *halanta*, meaning ending in a consonant.) This used to be written *k.h* where *.h* after any consonant in ITRANS means that it is followed by a halant and therefore "a" is not sounded after it. In fact, it is no longer necessary in ITRANS to do this - if the letter is written on its own, a halant is inserted automatically.

The second consonant in the guttural group is written *kh*. Its pronunciation is much like the preceding one but with the addition of a slight breathy sound caused by actually letting out some air immediately following the "k" sound. It is often sounded as though it were "k-h" in an imaginary word "k-hat" but there is much too much emphasis in this - it is really more subtle. Consonants such as *k* are said to be "with little breath" (*alpaprANa*) while ones like *kh* are "with much breath" (*mahAprANa*).

The third in this group is written *g*, sounded "g" as in gap (*alpaprANa*). The fourth is written *gh* and, like "kh" is *mahAprANa* and sounds like "gh" in doghouse.

The final consonant in this group is the first of the type mentioned briefly above - *anunAsika*, meaning that the sound is made through the nose. It is written *~N*. There are four n-related sounds; hence the need for the tilde and capitalisation. It has the sound of "ng" made at the back of the throat and sounding through the nose, like "sing" but with the ending further back in the throat like someone being strangled rather than singing!

k	kh	g	gh	~N
क	ख	ग	घ	ङ

The second group of consonants (palatal)

This second group forms the sounds in the back part of the mouth but not the throat. Based on the *i* vowel, these use the back of the tongue and the rear of the mouth; they are called "palatal." They follow the same pattern as the previous group (as do all five of these groups of consonants, you will be pleased to know!) in that the first and third members are *alpaprANa*, the second and fourth are *mahAprANa*, and the fifth is *anunAsika*. The first, then is written *ch* and is sounded like the "cha" in chap but, whereas English pronounces this by using the front of the tongue near the front of the roof of the mouth, Sanskrit uses the rear parts.

The second character is written *Ch* (or *chh* in older versions). Since I have already said that the pattern of the first group is repeated in the others, you might guess that this is sounded pretty much like *ch* but with some added breath - and you would be right! Just remember not to make it too pronounced so that it comes out like "ch-ha" and it should be fine.

The third is written *j* and pronounced more or less as would expect, like the "ja" in "jam" spoken as far back in the mouth as you can without injuring yourself. It uses minimum breath again as for all in this third "row" of the main consonants. The fourth is written *jh* and you can work out now how it should sound - like "j-ha" but not too much so.

The final letter in this group the second of the anunAsika characters (the "n" type sounds made through the nose). It is written *~n* and has a sort of "ny" sound, as in canyon. However, whereas the latter is made by the front of the tongue at the front of the mouth, you have to try to make this sound with the back of the tongue at the rear of the mouth.

ch	*Ch*	*j*	*jh*	*~n*
च	छ	ज	झ	ञ

The third group of consonants (cerebral)

This third group has now moved the mouth position another step forward so that the tip of the tongue is used, pointing up to the roof of the mouth. To construct the main consonants, the tongue actually touches the roof. It is called the cerebral position. The first is written *T*. All of this third, (middle) group are written as capital letters to differentiate them from the fourth group. (In the Romanised transliteration, the letters have a dot beneath them.). *T* is pronounced as the "t" in tub but instead of having the tongue forward of the roof of the mouth, put it right up to the roof as you say it. That should have been spoken "with only a small breath" as usual (*alpaprANa*). The second letter is the same but with more breath as you make the sound (*mahAprANa*), a bit like "po-th-ole" (pothole). It is written *Th*.

The next is written *D* and pronounced like "d" in dot but, as before, with the tip of the tongue right up in the roof of the mouth. The fourth letter sounds the same as the third but with more breath (e.g. go-dh-ead) and is written *Dh*. The last in the group is another "na" sound but with the tongue in the roof of the mouth. Written, as you already know, *N*.

T	*Th*	*D*	*Dh*	*N*
ट	ठ	ड	ढ	ण

The fourth group of consonants (dental)

This group of consonants are sounded just behind the teeth and called, unsurprisingly, dental. The first is *t*. It is sounded just like our t, as in "tip." Then comes the equivalent letter, but with more breath (*mahAprANa*), *th*, as in "butthead." Next is *d* as in "dog" and the breathy equivalent *dh*, as in "redhead." Finally, in this group, is the one sounded through the nose (*anunAsika*) *n*, as in er... "nose."

t	*th*	*d*	*dh*	*n*
त	थ	द	ध	न

The fifth group of consonants (labial)

And so, at last, the final group of the main consonants sounded at the lips and called labial. The first is *p* just like our p, as in "put." Then comes the corresponding breathy *ph*, as in uphill. Next is *b*, as in "bad" and the *mahAprANa bh*, as in "clubhouse." And finally the *anunAsika* in this group is *m*, as in "man."

p	ph	b	bh	m
प	फ	ब	भ	म

Table of basic consonants

The table of the five groups of consonants, with the corresponding vowel shown in Column 1 for reference, is as shown below: -

Guttural	*a*	k	kh	g	gh	~N
Palatal	*i*	ch	Ch	j	jh	~n
Cerebral	*RRi*	T	Th	D	Dh	N
Dental	*LLi*	t	th	d	dh	n
Labial	*u*	p	ph	b	bh	m

The semi-vowels

There are two small groups of letters left. The first of these is the group of four so-called "semi-vowels." They are formed by combining the four main vowels other than *a* with *a*. Thus, if you sound *i* and then immediately move to the *a* sound, what emerges sounds like "ya" and this is the first semi-vowel or *antaHsthA*: - *y* as in "yap." If you sound *RRi* and move to *a*, you get *r* as in "rap." If you sound *LLi* and move to *a*, you get *l* as in "lap." Finally, if you sound *u* and move to *a*, you get *v* as in "wag." Note that Americans seem to prefer to ignore this logical derivation and pronounce it as "va" in "van." Since it is somewhat illogical to write it as beginning with a "v" while sounding it as a "w," I suppose both sides of the Atlantic have a case.

y	*r*	*l*	*v*
य	र	ल	व

The sibilants

Almost last of all, there are three sibilants or sss-sounds. (A sibilant is called *UShman* in Sanskrit.) These are in the palatal, cerebral and dental positions. (In theory there are also ones in the other two positions but these are so rare that they are usually ignored). In the palatal position, there is *sh* sounded by making a shh sound in that mouth position; it comes out like the ending of a soft German "ich" with the default *a* ending of course. The second, in the cerebral position, is *Sh* (or *shh* in older releases) made by sounding "sha" with the tongue up to the roof of the mouth. Finally is the dental *s*, sounding like the normal "s" in "sand."

sh	*Sh*	*s*
श	ष	स

h

This leaves the last letter in the alphabet, *h*, sounding, as you would expect, as "h" in "hat." It is sometimes considered to be another sibilant and is also called *UShman*, which literally means "heated."

h ह

The complete alphabet

The order of the alphabet, if you want to look up a word in the dictionary, is pretty much the order used here in introducing the letters. The 16 *mAtRRikA* are at the beginning, followed by the basic consonants - guttural, palatal, cerebral, dental and labial. Then come the 4 semi-vowels (*antaHsthA*) and the three sibilants and finally *h*.

Further study

As you will certainly have realised by now, in order to learn how to sound these correctly, you really need to listen to someone who knows. Since it is unlikely that you will be sufficiently interested to go into it this deeply, however, just follow the instructions and don't worry about how it feels. We are unused to making full use of our mouth and tongue in speaking and, since Sanskrit makes almost scientific use, we will find much of it peculiar and initially uncomfortable.

If you want a more thorough introduction, with little in the way of expense or commitment, there is a truly excellent one available off the Internet. You can download this free of charge and the only cost is the subsequent printing. It is called "A Practical Sanskrit Introductory" and was produced by Charles Wikner. You can access it from one of the sites devoted to Sanskrit – see my website at http://www.advaita.org.uk/sanskrit/sanskrit_resources.htm. As well as describing the alphabet in much more detail and teaching the Devanagari script, this introduces the grammar and some vocabulary.

Alternatively, you can buy my book, on which this appendix is based - details at Ref. 114 or http://www.advaita.org.uk/sanskrit/sanskrit.htm. This aims to teach you just enough Sanskrit to be able to read and pronounce the script and then break it down into words so that you can look them up in a dictionary. There is no grammar to learn and no declensions or conjugations. Note that it will still take you several months of dedicated effort and practice to learn the essentials.

Finally, if you are really serious, an excellent book - "*devavANIpraveshikA* - An Introduction to the Sanskrit Language" by Robert P. Goldman and Sally J. Sutherland can be purchased from the Center for South and Southeast Asia Studies, University of California, Berkeley.

Conclusion

If you read through this a few times and refer to it when in doubt, you should be able to make a creditable attempt to pronounce most words. Of course, such a brief introduction cannot give you any real idea of the language, which is extremely beautiful in more ways than one. Here is what a well-known Vedic prayer looks like in the original Sanskrit: -

असतोमा सद्गमय ।   *asato mA sadgamaya |*
तमसोमा ज्योतिर्गमय ।   *tamaso mA jyotirgamaya |*
मृत्योर्मा अमृतंगमय ॥ः   *mRRityormA amRRitaM gamaya ||*

Lead me from the unreal to the real,
Lead me from darkness into light,
Lead me from death to immortality.

APPENDIX B – ADVAITA TIMELINE

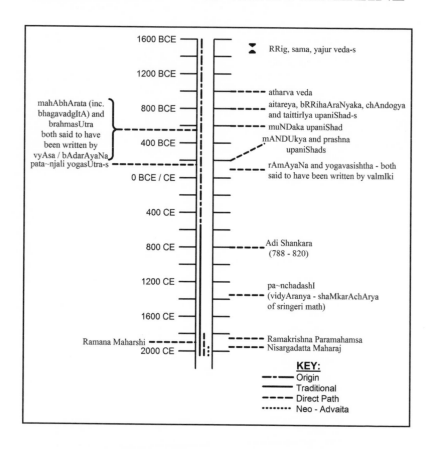

APPENDIX C – TEACHER LINEAGES

Note that, as regards western teachers, these charts represent principal influences and it should not be understood that the teachers necessarily teach according to the traditional *sampradAya* in which they are listed. This applies especially to the Navnath *sampradAya*, which is (strictly speaking) 'grossly inaccurate'.

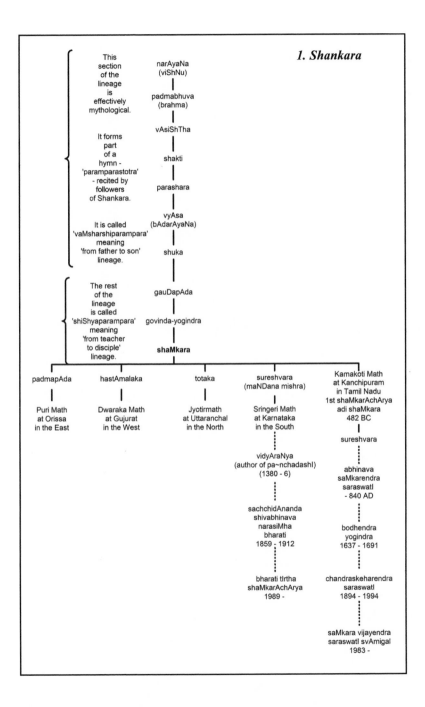

1. Shankara

This section of the lineage is effectively mythological.

It forms part of a hymn - 'paramparastotra' - recited by followers of Shankara.

It is called 'vaMsharshiparampara' meaning 'from father to son' lineage.

narAyaNa (viShNu)

padmabhuva (brahma)

vAsiShTha

shakti

parashara

vyAsa (bAdarAyaNa)

shuka

The rest of the lineage is called 'shiShyaparampara' meaning 'from teacher to disciple' lineage.

gauDapAda

govinda-yogindra

shaMkara

padmapAda
Puri Math at Orissa in the East

hastAmalaka
Dwaraka Math at Gujurat in the West

totaka
Jyotirmath at Uttaranchal in the North

sureshvara (maNDana mishra)
Sringeri Math at Karnataka in the South

vidyAraNya (author of pa~nchadashI) (1380 - 6)

sachchidAnanda shivabhinava narasiMha bharati 1859 - 1912

bharati tIrtha shaMkarAchArya 1989 -

Kamakoti Math at Kanchipuram in Tamil Nadu 1st shaMkarAchArya adi shaMkara 482 BC

sureshvara

abhinava saMkarendra saraswatI - 840 AD

bodhendra yogindra 1637 - 1691

chandraskeharendra saraswatI 1894 - 1994

saMkara vijayendra saraswatI svAmigal 1983 -

2. Swami Sivananda

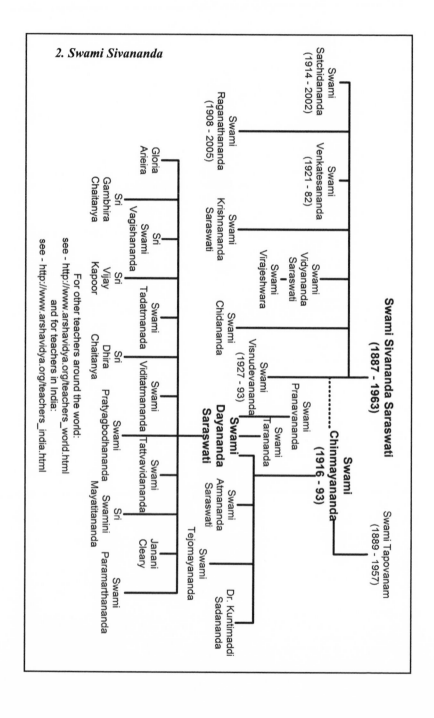

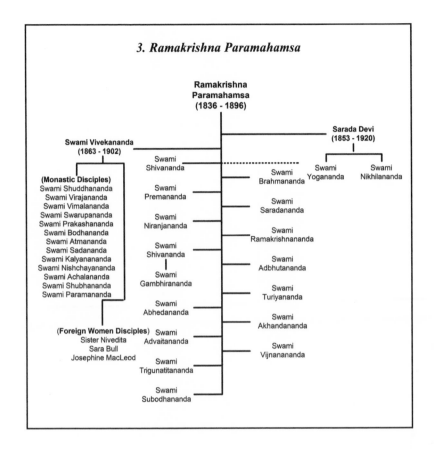

3. *Ramakrishna Paramahamsa*

Ramakrishna Paramahamsa (1836 - 1896)

Sarada Devi (1853 - 1920)

Swami Vivekananda (1863 - 1902)

(Monastic Disciples)
Swami Shuddhananda
Swami Virajananda
Swami Vimalananda
Swami Swarupananda
Swami Prakashananda
Swami Bodhananda
Swami Atmananda
Swami Sadananda
Swami Kalyanananda
Swami Nishchayananda
Swami Achalananda
Swami Shubhananda
Swami Paramananda

(Foreign Women Disciples)
Sister Nivedita
Sara Bull
Josephine MacLeod

Swami Shivananda
Swami Premananda
Swami Niranjanananda
Swami Shivananda
Swami Gambhirananda
Swami Abhedananda
Swami Advaitananda
Swami Trigunatitananda
Swami Subodhananda

Swami Brahmananda
Swami Yogananda
Swami Nikhilananda
Swami Saradananda
Swami Ramakrishnananda
Swami Adbhutananda
Swami Turiyananda
Swami Akhandananda
Swami Vijnanananda

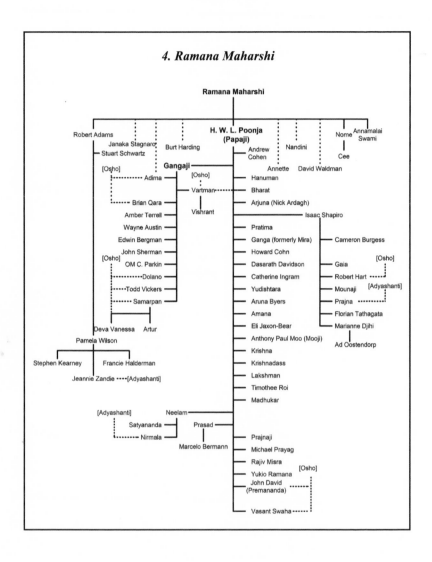

4. Ramana Maharshi

Ramana Maharshi

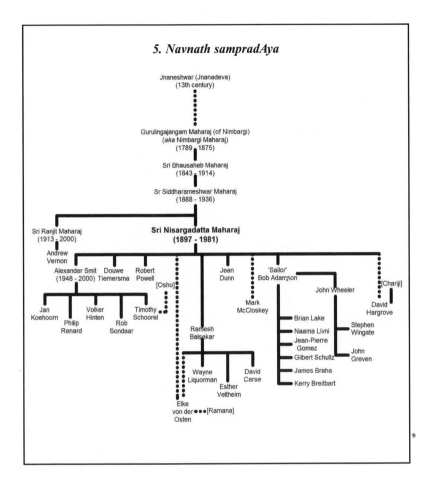

5. *Navnath sampradAya*

Jnaneshwar (Jnanadeva)
(13th century)

Gurulingajangam Maharaj (of Nimbargi)
(*aka* Nimbargi Maharaj)
(1789 - 1875)

Sri Bhausaheb Maharaj
(1843 - 1914)

Sr Siddharameshwar Maharaj
(1888 - 1936)

Sri Ranjit Maharaj
(1913 - 2000)

**Sri Nisargadatta Maharaj
(1897 - 1981)**

Andrew
Vernon

Alexander Smit
(1948 - 2000)

Douwe
Tiemersma

Robert
Powell

[Osho]

Jean
Dunn

'Sailor'
Bob Adamson

John Wheeler

[Chariji]

David
Hargrove

Jan
Koehoorn

Volker
Hinten

Timothy
Schoorel

Philip
Renard

Rob
Sondaar

Ramesh
Balsekar

Mark
McCloskey

Brian Lake

Naama Livni

Jean-Pierre
Gomez

Gilbert Schultz

James Braha

Kerry Breitbart

Stephen
Wingate

John
Greven

Wayne
Liquorman

Esther
Veltheim

David
Carse

Elke
von der ●●●[Ramana]
Osten

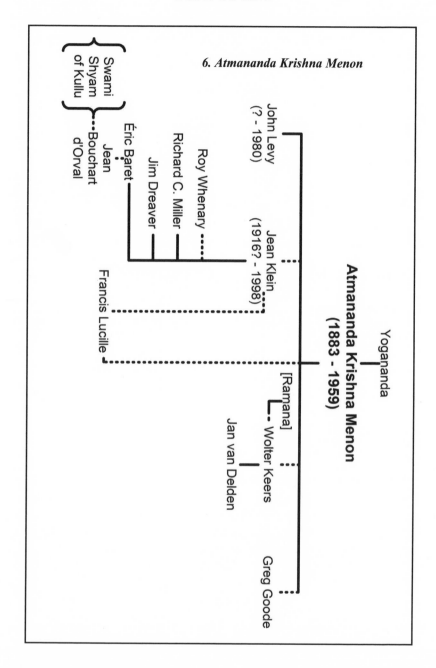

6. Atmananda Krishna Menon

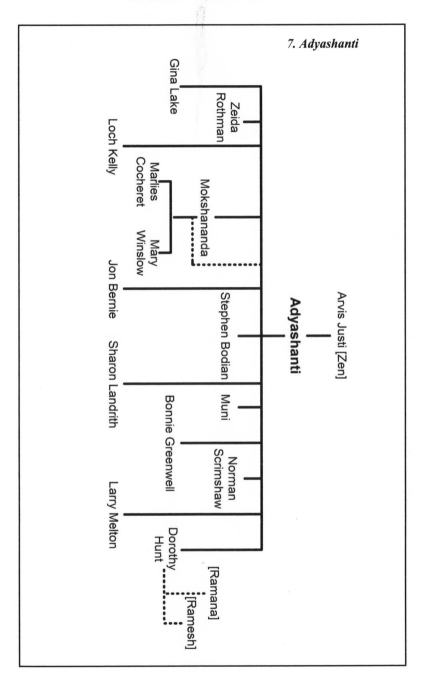

7. *Adyashanti*

8. Narayana Gurukula Line

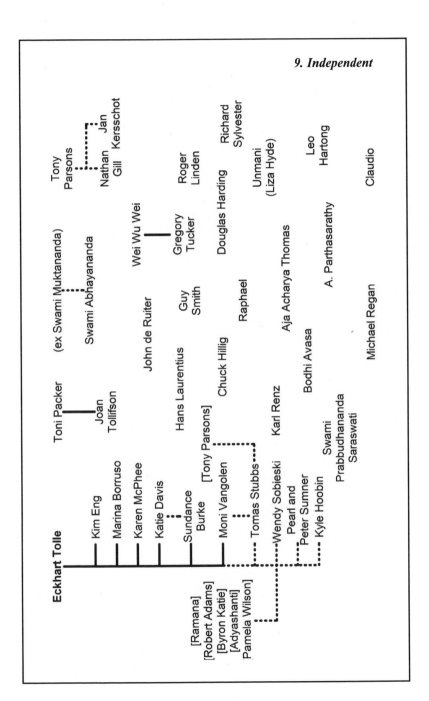

9. Independent

APPENDIX D – MODERN TEACHER LIST

I have endeavored to list all current teachers of Advaita. My sincere apologies if anyone who ought to have been listed has been excluded. Please let me know and I will update for any future reprint.

Each entry is in the following format:

Name of teacher; date of birth - date of death (if known); principal guru or influence; related lineage chart (Appendix C); URL of (main) website.

Abhayananda, Swami (Stan Trout); 1938 - ; ex Swami Muktananda; Independent; http://www.swami-abhayananda.com/

Abhedananda, Swami; 1866 - 1939; Ramakrishna; Ramakrishna; http://www.geocities.com/Athens/Acropolis/1863/abed.html

Adbhutananda, Swami; d. 1920; Ramakrishna; Ramakrishna; http://www.geocities.com/Athens/Acropolis/1863/adbhut.html

Adams, Robert; 1928 - 1997; Ramana Maharshi; Ramana Maharshi; http://www.robertadamsinfinityinstitute.org/

Adamson, 'Sailor' Bob; ; Nisargadatta Maharaj; Navnath; http://members.iinet.net.au/~adamson7

Adima (Brigitte Brüning); 1959 -; Osho, Papaji, Gangaji; Ramana Maharshi; http://www.adima.net/english/start_e.html

Advaitananda, Swami; 1828 - 1909; Ramakrishna; Ramakrishna; http://www.geocities.com/Athens/Acropolis/1863/advait.html

Adyashanti; ; Justi, Arvis (Zen); Adyashanti; http://www.zen-satsang.org/

Aja Acharya (Thomas); 1954 -; ; Independent; http://www.atmainstitute.org/index.htm

Akhandananda, Swami; 1864 - 1937; Ramakrishna; Ramakrishna; http://www.geocities.com/Athens/Acropolis/1863/akhand.html

Amana (Aile Shebar); ; Poonja, H.W.L. (Papaji); Ramana Maharshi;

http://home.earthlink.net/~aileamana/aileamanahome.htm

Annamalai Swami; 1906 - 1995; Ramana Maharshi; Ramana Maharshi;
http://www.angelfire.com/realm/bodhisattva/annamalai.html

Annette; ; Ramana, Bon Lineage; Ramana Maharshi;
http://www.thefreeheart.com/

Arieira, Gloria; ; Swami Dayananda; Sivananda;
http://www.arshavidya.org/teachers_world.html

Arjuna (Nick Ardagh); ; Poonja, H.W.L. (Papaji); Ramana Maharshi;
http://www.livingessence.com/

Artur; ; Samarpan; Ramana Maharshi; http://www.artur-sein.de/

Austin, Wayne; ; Gangaji; Ramana Maharshi; http://endofthesearch.com/

Balsekar, Ramesh S.; 1917 -; Nisargadatta Maharaj; Navnath;
http://www.advaita.org/

Baret, Éric; ; Jean Klein; Atmananda Krishna Menon;
http://www.bhairava.ws/english/eric-eng.html

Bergman, Edwin; ; Gangaji; Ramana Maharshi;-

Bermann, Marcelo; 1952 -; Prasad; Ramana Maharshi;
http://awakenedself.org/

Bernard, Wolfgang; 1951 -; Osho; Osho; http://www.finaldialogue.com/

Bernie, Jon; ; Adyashanti; Adyashanti; http://www.sf-satsang.org/

Bharat (Melvin Rochlin); 1948 -; Poonja, H.W.L. (Papaji); Ramana
Maharshi; http://www.poonja.com/Satsang.htm

Bodhi Avasa (Adrian Meyers); ; -; Independent;
http://www.avasa.net/whoisavasa.html

Bodian, Stephan; ; Adyashanti; Adyashanti;
http://www.stephanbodian.org/

Borruso, Marina; ; Eckhart Tolle; Independent;
http://www.marinaborruso.net/

Bouchart d'Orval, Jean; 1948 -; Éric Baret; Atmananda Krishna Menon;
http://www.omalpha.com/english.html

Braha, James; ; Bob Adamson; Navnath;
http://www.jamesbraha.com/home.html

Brahmananda, Swami; 1863 - 1922; Ramakrishna; Ramakrishna; http://www.geocities.com/Athens/Acropolis/1863/brahm.html

Breitbart, Kerry; ; Bob Adamson; Navnath; -

Burgess, Cameron; ; Shapiro, Isaac; Ramana Maharshi; http://www.cameronburgess.org

Burke, Sundance; ; Tolle, Eckhart; Gangaji: Katie Davis; Independent; http://www.sundanceburke.org/

Byers, Aruna (Rea); ; Poonja, H.W.L. (Papaji); Ramana Maharshi; http://www.arunabyers.com/eng/index.htm

Carse, David; ; Ramesh Balsekar; Navnath, -

Cee; ; Nome; Ramana Maharshi; http://www.presentnonexistence.com/

Chaitanya, Sr Dhira; ; Swami Dayananda; Sivananda; http://www.arshavidya.org/teachers_uscan.html

Chaitanya, Sri Gambhira; ; Swami Dayananda; Sivananda; http://www.arshavidya.org/teachers_world.html

Chidananda, Swami; ; Sivananda; Sivananda; http://www.sivanandadlshq.org/home.html

Chinmayananda, Swami; 1916 - 1993; Tapovan Maharaj; Sivananda; http://www.chinmayamission.org/

Claudio; ; ?; Independent; http://www.effortlessbeing.org/

Cleary, Janani; ; Swami Dayananda; Sivananda; http://www.arshavidya.org/teachers_uscan.html

Cocheret de la Moriniere, Marlies; 1959 -; Osho, Adyashanti; Adyashanti; http://www.freewatersangha.org/

Cohen, Andrew; 1955 -; Poonja, H.W.L. (Papaji); Ramana Maharshi; http://www.wie.org/

Cohn, Howard; ; Poonja, H.W.L. (Papaji); Ramana Maharshi; http://www.poonja.com/Satsang.htm

Dasarath (Let Davidson); ; Poonja, H.W.L. (Papaji); Ramana Maharshi; http://www.letwisdomwork.com/8bio.htm

Davis, Katie; ; (Eckhart Tolle); Independent; http://www.katiedavis.org

Dayananda Saraswati, Swami; ; Chinmayananda; Sivananda;
http://www.arshavidya.org

Devamarg; ; Osho, Vartman; Osho; http://www.devamarg.com/

Djihi, Marianne; ; Isaac Shapiro; Ramana Maharshi; www.djihi.nl/

Dolano; 1952 -; Gangaji, Osho; Osho/Ramana; http://www.dolano.com/

Dreaver, Jim; ; Jean Klein; Atmananda Krishna Menon;
http://www.jimdreaver.com/

Dunn, Jean; ; Nisargadatta Maharaj; Navnath, -

Eng, Kim; ; Eckhart Tolle; Independent; http://www.eckharttolle.com/

Gaia; ; Isaac Shapiro; Ramana Maharshi;
http://www.gaia-satsang.com/home.htm

Gambhirananda, Swami; 1899 - 1988; Swami Shivananda;
Ramakrishna; http://www.geocities.com/bibhasde/swami.html

Ganga (Mira Decoux/Pagal); 1947 -; Poonja, H.W.L. (Papaji); Ramana
Maharshi; (http://www.gangasatsang.com/) - now closed

Gangaji (Antoinette Roberson Varner); 1942 -; Poonja, H.W.L. (Papaji);
Ramana Maharshi; http://www.gangaji.org/

Gill, Nathan; 1960 -; Tony Parsons; Independent;
http://www.nathangill.com

Gilman, Jim; ; Chinmayananda; Sivananda, -

Gomez, Jean-Pierre; ; Bob Adamson; Navnath;
http://www.you-are-that.com/

Goode, Greg; ; Atmananda Krishna Menon; Atmananda Krishna Menon;
http://www.heartofnow.com

Greenwell, Bonnie; ; Adyashanti; Adyashanti;
http://www.kundaliniguide.com/

Greven, John; ; John Wheeler, Bob Adamson; Navnath;
http://www.onenessjustthat.com/

Halderman, Francie; ; Pamela Wilson; Ramana Maharshi;
http://www.franciesatsang.com/

Hanuman; ; Poonja, H.W.L. (Papaji); Ramana Maharshi;
http://www.poonja.com/hanuman.htm
Harding, Burt; ; Ramana Maharshi; Ramana Maharshi;
http://members.shaw.ca/burtharding/
Harding, Douglas; 1909 -, -; Independent; http://www.headless.org/
Hargrove, David; ; Parthasarathi Rajagopalachari (Chariji); Navnath;
http://hometown.aol.com/zmann07/
Hart, Robert; ; Osho, Barry Long, Isaac Shapiro; Ramana Maharshi;
http://www.antiguru.org/
Hartong, Leo; , -; Independent; http://www.awakeningtothedream.com/
Hillig, Chuck; , -; Independent; http://www.chuckhillig.com
Hinten, Volker; ; Alexander Smit; Navnath; http://www.advaitaweb.nl/
Hoobin, Kyle; ; Eckhart Tolle, Don Miguel Ruiz; Independent;
http://www.kylehoobin.com/
Hunt, Dorothy S.; ; Ramana, Ramesh, Adyashanti; Adyashanti;
http://www.dorothyhunt.com/

Ingram, Catherine; 1952 -; Poonja, H.W.L. (Papaji); Ramana Maharshi;
http://www.catherineingram.com

Jaxon-Bear, Eli; 1947 - ; Poonja, H.W.L. (Papaji); Ramana Maharshi;
http://www.leela.org/
Jivanjili; ; Osho, Shantimayi; Osho; http://www.jivanjili.org/

Kapoor, Sri Vijay; ; Swami Dayananda; Sivananda;
http://www.arshavidya.org/teachers_uscan.html
Kearney, Stephen; ; Pamela Wilson; Ramana Maharshi; http://www.true-
bozo.com/
Keers, Wolter; -1985; Ramana, Krishnamenon; Atmananda Krishna
Menon; http://www.ods.nl/la-rousselie/bron.htm
Kelly, Loch; ; Adyashanti, Buddhism, Dzochen etc.; Adyashanti;
http://www.lochkelly.org/
Kersschot, Jan; ; Tony Parsons; Independent; http://www.kersschot.com/

Klein, Jean; 1916? - 1998, -; Atmananda Krishna Menon;
http://www.jeanklein.org/index.html
Koehoorn, Jan; ; Alexander Smit; Navnath;
Krishna; ; Poonja, H.W.L. (Papaji); Ramana Maharshi;
http://www.satsangteachers.com/krishna.htm
Krishnadass; ; Poonja, H.W.L. (Papaji); Ramana Maharshi;
http://www.krishnadass.com/sub21/index.htm
Krishna Menon, Atmananda; 1883 - 1959; Yogananada; Atmananda
Krishna Menon; http://www.geocities.com/skknair_tvm/philo.htm
Krishnananda Saraswati; 1922 - 2001; Sivananda; Sivananda;
http://www.swami-krishnananda.org/

Lake, Brian; ; Bob Adamson; Navnath;
http://www.awarenessthatsimple.com/
Lake, Gina; ; Adyashanti (and wife of Nirmala); Adyashanti;
www.RadicalHappiness.com
Lakshman; ; Poonja, H.W.L. (Papaji); Ramana Maharshi;
http://www.beingthat.com/
Landrith, Sharon; ; Adyashanti; Adyashanti, -
Laurentius, Hans; ; various; Independent;
http://home-1.worldonline.nl/%7Efengcons/engels.htm
Levy, John; ; Atmananda Krishna Menon; Atmananda Krishna Menon;
http://www.ods.nl/am1gos/am1gos5/index.html?jl_vriend_us.html%7EmainFr
Linden, Roger; ; Tony Parsons; Independent; http://www.rogerlinden.com
Liquorman, Wayne; 1951 -; Ramesh Balsekar; Navnath;
http://www.advaita.org/
Livni, Naami; ; Bob Adamson; Navnath;
http://www.awarenessthatsimple.com/NaamaLivni.html
Lucille, Francis; ; Jean Klein; Atmananda Krishna Menon;
http://francislucille.com/

Madhukar; ; Poonja, H.W.L. (Papaji); Ramana Maharshi;
http://www.madhukar.org/

Mayatitananda, Sri Swamini; ; Swami Dayananda; Sivananda;
http://www.wisearth.org/bri_maya/index.html

McCloskey, Mark; ; Krishnamurti, Nisargadatta; Navnath;
http://www.puresilence.org/

McPhee, Karen; ; Eckhart Tolle; Independent; http://www.livingnow.ca/

Melton, Larry; ; Adyashanti; Adyashanti, -

Miller, Richard C.; ; Jean Klein; Atmananda Krishna Menon;
http://www.nondual.com/rcm.html

Misra, Rajiv; ; Poonja, H.W.L. (Papaji); Ramana Maharshi;
http://www.satsang.nl/rajiv/

Mistlberger, Philip (Teertha); ; Osho, Gangaji, Hanuman; Osho;
www.geocities.com/annubis33/

Mokshananda (Joe Sussa); 1958 -; Gurumayi, Adyashanti; Adyashanti;
http://www.freewatersangha.org/

Mooji (Anthony Paul Moo-Young); 1954 -; Poonja, H.W.L. (Papaji);
Ramana Maharshi; http://www.mooji.org/

Mounaji; ; Isaac Shapiro; Ramana Maharshi;

Muni; ; Adyashanti; Adyashanti; http://www.meetingwithmuni.com/

Nadeen, Satyam (Michael Clegg); ; Osho; Osho;
http://www.satyamnadeen.com/

Nandini (Dalia Bishop); 1947 -; Ramana; Ramana Maharshi;
http://www.advaitaspirit.org/

Narayana Guru; 1854 - 1928, -; Independent;
http://www.narayanagurukula.org/

Neelam; 1963 -; Poonja, H.W.L. (Papaji); Ramana Maharshi;
http://www.neelam.org/

Nikhilananda, Swami; 1895 - 1973; Sri Sarada Devi; Ramakrishna;
http://www.ramakrishna.org/SN.htm

Niranjananda, Swami; d. 1904; Ramakrishna; Ramakrishna;
http://www.geocities.com/Athens/Acropolis/1863/niranj.html

Nirmala (Daniel Erway); ; Neelam; Ramana Maharshi;
http://www.Endless-Satsang.com

Nisargadatta Maharaj; 1897 - 1981; Siddharameshwar Maharaj; Navnath; http://www.advaita.org/

Nome (Jeffrey Smith); ; Ramana Maharshi; Ramana Maharshi; http://www.satramana.org/

OM C. Parkin (Cedric Parkin); ; Gangaji; Ramana Maharshi; http://www.om-c-parkin.de/

Oostendorp, Ad; ; Marianne Djihi, Isaac Shapiro; Ramana Maharshi; http://www.geocities.com/mahamounam/Satsang.html

Osho; 1931 - 1990, -; Osho; http://www.osho.com

Packer, Toni; 1927 -, -; Independent; http://www.springwatercenter.org/

Parsons, Tony; 1933 -, -; Independent; http://www.theopensecret.com/

Parthasarathy, A.; , -; Independent; http://www.vedanta-edu.org

Poonja, H.W.L. (Papaji); 1910 - 97; Ramana Maharshi; Ramana Maharshi; http://www.poonja.com/

Powell, Robert; 1918 - ; Nisargadatta Maharaj; Navnath, -

Prabbudhananda Saraswati, Swami; , -; Independent; http://www.vedanta-philosophy.com/

Prajna; 1961 -; Isaac Shapiro, Adyashanti; Ramana Maharshi; http://www.prajna-satsang.org/prajna.htm

Prajnaji (Zaida Gates); 1946 -; Poonja, H.W.L. (Papaji); Ramana Maharshi; http://www.prajnaji.de/

Pranavananda, Swami; , -; Sivananda, -

Prasad; ; Poonja, H.W.L. (Papaji); Ramana Maharshi; -

Pratima (Michèle Mumford); 1952 -; Poonja, H.W.L. (Papaji); Ramana Maharshi; http://www.poonja.com/Satsang.htm

Pratyagbodhananda, Swami; ; Swami Dayananda; Sivananda; http://www.arshavidya.org/teachers_swamiprat.html

Prayag, Michael; ; Poonja, H.W.L. (Papaji); Ramana Maharshi; http://www.neti.ws/index.html

Premananda (John David); ; Poonja, H.W.L. (Papaji), Osho; Ramana Maharshi; http://www.premananda.de

Premananda, Swami; 1861 - 1918; Ramakrishna; Ramakrishna; http://www.geocities.com/Athens/Acropolis/1863/prem.html

Qara, Brian; ; Gangaji, Osho; Ramana Maharshi; http://theopenflame.org/

Raganathananda, Swami; 1908 - 2005; Sivananda; Sivananda, - **Ramakrishna Paramahamsa**; 1836 - 1886, -, -; http://www.sriramakrishnamath.org/

Ramakrishnananda, Swami; 1863 - 1911; Ramakrishna; Ramakrishna; http://www.geocities.com/Athens/Acropolis/1863/ramak.html

Ramana, Yukio; ; Poonja, H.W.L. (Papaji); Ramana Maharshi; http://radicalawakening.org/

Ramana Maharshi; 1880 - 1950, -; Ramana Maharshi; http://www.ramana-maharshi.org/

Rani; ; Osho; Osho; no longer giving satsang

Ranjit Maharaj; 1913 - 2000; Siddharameshwar Maharaj; Navnath; http://www.sadguru.com/index.html

Raphael; ; -; Independent; http://www.vidya-ashramvidyaorder.org/

Regan, Michael; ; Pamela Wilson?; Independent; http://www.michaelregan.us/

Renard, Philip; ; Alexander Smit; Navnath; http://www.advaya.nl

Renz, Karl; ; -; Independent; http://www.karlrenz.com/

Roi, Timothee; ; Poonja, H.W.L. (Papaji); Ramana Maharshi, -

Rothman, Zeida; ; Adyashanti; Adyashanti, -

Ruiter, John de; 1961 -, -; Independent; http://www.johnderuiter.com/

Sadananda, Kuntimaddi; ; Swami Chinmayananda; Sivananda, - **Samarpan (Sam Golden)**; 1941 -; Osho, Gangaji; Osho/Ramana; http://www.samarpan.de/indexeng.html

Sarada Devi; 1853 - 1920; Wife of Ramakrishna; Ramakrishna; http://www.srv.org/sarada.html

Saradananda, Swami; 1865 - 1927; Ramakrishna; Ramakrishna; http://www.geocities.com/Athens/Acropolis/1863/sarad.html

Saraswati, Swami Atmananda; ; Swami Chinmayananda; Sivananda; http://www.vmission.org/

Satchidananda, Swami; 1914 - 2002; Swami Shivananda; Sivananda; http://www.swamisatchidananda.org

Satyananda (Bernardo Lischinsky Arenas); 1964 -; Neelam; Ramana Maharshi, -

Satyaprem; ; Osho, Dolano ; Osho; http://www.satyaprem.com/lifeing.html

Scrimshaw, Norman; ; Adyashanti; Adyashanti; http://whitemountainsangha.org/

Schoorel, Timothy; ; Osho, Alexander Smit; Navnath; http://www.7freedom.com/index.htm

Schultz, Gilbert; ; Bob Adamson; Navnath; http://www.shiningthroughthemind.net/pages/home.aspx

Schwartz, Stuart; ; Robert Adams; Ramana Maharshi; http://www.satsangwithstuart.com/

Shapiro, Isaac; 1950 -; Poonja, H.W.L. (Papaji); Ramana Maharshi; http://www.isaacshapiro.de/

Sherman, John; 1942 -; Gangaji; Ramana Maharshi; http://www.riverganga.org/john.shtml

Shivananda, Swami; 1854 - 1934; Ramakrishna; Ramakrishna; http://www.geocities.com/Athens/Acropolis/1863/shiv.html

Siddharameshwar Maharaj; 1888 - 1936; Bhausaheb Maharaj; Navnath; http://www.angelfire.com/realm/bodhisattva/sadguru.html

Sivananda; 1887 - 1963, -; Sivananda; http://www.sivanandadlshq.org

Smit, Alexander; 1948 - 2000; Nisargadatta Maharaj; Navnath, -

Smith, Guy; ; -; Independent; http://http://www.guisemyth.com/

Sobieski, Wendy; ; Tolle, Katie, Ramana, Adams, Adyashanti, Wilson; Independent; http://www.beinggrace.com/index.htm

Sondaar, Rob; 1951 -; Alexander Smit; Navnath; http://home.hccnet.nl/r.sondaar

Stagnaro, Janaka; 1960 -; ; Ramana Maharshi; http://www.janakastagnaro.com/

Stubbs, Tomas; ; (Eckhart Tolle); Independent;
http://www.livingpresence.ca/tomas

Subodhananda, Swami; 1867 - 1932; Ramakrishna; Ramakrishna;
http://www.geocities.com/Athens/Acropolis/1863/subod.html

Sumner, Pearl & Peter; ; Eckhart Tolle; Independent;
http://peterspearls.com.au/

Susan (Deva Sarovara); ; Osho; Osho; http://www.isness.de/

Swaha, Vasant; ; Osho, Papaji, Ramesh; Osho/Ramana;
http://www.vasantswaha.net/

Swarup; 1964 -; Osho, Ramesh Balsekar, Dolano; Osho;
http://www.swarup.net/

Sylvester, Richard; ; (Tony Parsons); Independent;
http://www.richardsylvester.com

Tapovanam, Swami; 1889 - 1957, -; Sivananda, -

Taro (Gerritson); 1949 -; Osho, Dolano, Prem Rani; Osho;
http://www.tarossatsang.com/home.htm

Tadatmananda, Swami; ; Swami Dayananda; Sivananda;
http://www.arshabodha.org/

Tathagata, Florian; ; Isaac Shapiro; Ramana Maharshi;
http://www.tathagata.de/start_noflash_en.html

Tattvavidananda, Swami; ; Swami Dayananda; Sivananda;
http://www.arshavidya.org/teachers_swamitat.html

Tejomayananda; ; Chinmayananda; Sivananda;
http://www.chinmayamission.org/

Terrell, Amber; ; Gangaji; Ramana Maharshi;
http://www.truelightpub.com/

Thompson, Madhukar; ; Osho, Papaji, Ramana, Ramesh, D. B. Gangolli;
; http://www.madhukarthompson.com/

Tiemersma, Douwe; ; Nisargadatta Maharaj; Navnath;
http://www.advaitacentrum.nl/

Tolle, Eckhart; ; - ; Independent; http://www.eckharttolle.com/

Tollifson, Joan; ; Toni Packer, Zen influence; Independent;

http://home.earthlink.net/~wakeupjt/

Trigunatitananda, Swami; 1865 - 1914; Ramakrishna; Ramakrishna;
http://www.geocities.com/Athens/Acropolis/1863/trig.html

Trolle; Pyar; 1960 -; Osho, Samarpan; Osho; http://www.pyar.de/

Tucker, Gregory; ; Wei Wu Wei; Independent;
http://www.thespiritworks.com/

Turiyananda, Swami; 1863 - 1922; Ramakrishna; Ramakrishna;
http://www.geocities.com/Athens/Acropolis/1863/turi.html

Unmani (Liza Hyde); ; -; Independent;
http://www.not-knowing.com/index.html

Vagishananda, Sri Swami; ; Swami Dayananda; Sivananda;
http://www.arshavidya.org/teachers_world.html

van Delden, Jan; 1951 -; Wolter Keers; Atmananda Krishna Menon;
http://www.ods.nl/la-rousselie/

Vanessa, Deva; 1941 -; Samarpan, Osho; Osho/Ramana, -

Vangolen, Moni; ; Eckhart Tolle; Independent;
http://www.livingpresence.ca

Vartman, Chetan; 1967 -; Gangaji; Osho/Ramana;
http://www.vartman.com/

Veltheim, Esther; ; Ramesh Balsekar; Navnath;
http://www.parama.com/index.html

Venkatesananda, Swami; 1921 - 1982; Sivananda; Sivananda;
http://www.sivanandadlshq.org/saints/venkates.htm

Vernon, Andrew; ; Ranjit Maharaj; Navnath;
http://www.wayofthebird.com/

Vickers, Todd; 1968 -; Osho, Papaji, Gangaji; Osho/Ramana;
http://www.spiritparadox.com/

Viditatmananda, Swami; ; Swami Dayananda; Sivananda;
http://www.arshavidya.org/teachers_swamivid.html

Vidyananda Saraswati, Swami; ; Sivananda; Sivananda, -

Vijnanananda, Swami; 1868 - 1938; Ramakrishna; Ramakrishna;

http://www.geocities.com/Athens/Acropolis/1863/vijna.html

Vimalananda, Swami; ; Vivekananda; Ramakrishna, -

Virajeshwara, Swami; ; Swami Vidyananda Saraswati; Sivananda;
http://www.swami-virajeshwara.com/

Visnudevananda; 1927 - 1993; Sivananda; Sivananda;
http://www.sivananda.org

Vivekananda, Swami; 1863 - 1902; Ramakrishna Paramahamsa, -;
http://www.vivekananda.org

Vishrant (Vincent Cooper); 1954 -; Osho, Ramana, Vartman; Ramana
Maharshi; http://members.iinet.net.au/~vishrant/

von der Osten, Elke; 1944 - ; Ramana, Nisargadatta, Ramesh Balsekar ;
Navnath; http://www.ost-seminar.de/

Waldman, David; ; Ramana Maharshi; Ramana Maharshi;
http://www.davidwaldman.org/

Wei Wu Wei (Terence Gray); 1895 - 1986; Buddhism, Taoism;
Independent; http://www.weiwuwei.8k.com/

Wheeler, John; ; Bob Adamson; Navnath;
http://www.employees.org/~johnwhee/

Whenary, Roy; ; Jean Klein; Atmananda Krishna Menon;
http://www.lotusharmony.com/index.htm

Wilson, Pamela; 1954 -; Robert Adams; Ramana Maharshi;
http://www.pamelasatsang.com/

Wingate, Stephen; ; John Wheeler, Bob Adamson; Navnath;
http://www.livinginpeace-thenaturalstate.com

Winslow, Mary; ; Adyashanti, Mokshananda; Adyashanti;
http://www.marywinslow.org/

Yogananda, Swami; 1861 - 1899; Sri Sarada Devi; Ramakrishna;
http://www.geocities.com/Athens/Acropolis/1863/yog.html

Yudishtara; ; Poonja, H.W.L. (Papaji); Ramana Maharshi;
http://www.poonja.com/yudishtara.htm

Zandie, Jeannie; ; Pamela Wilson, Adyashanti; Ramana Maharshi; http://www.jeanniezandi.com/

Special Thanks to:
Sarlo's Guru Rating Service -
http://www.globalserve.net/%7Esarlo/Ratings.htm
and Nonduality Salon: Gurus, Teachers, Realizers -
http://nonduality.com/morea.htm

APPENDIX E – MICROCOSM – MACROCOSM

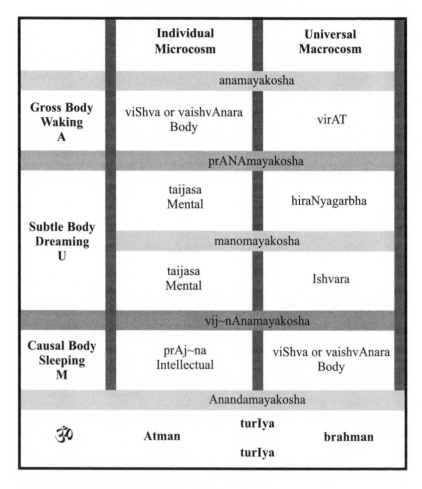

	Individual Microcosm	Universal Macrocosm
	anamayakosha	
Gross Body Waking A	viShva or vaishvAnara Body	virAT
	prANAmayakosha	
Subtle Body Dreaming U	taijasa Mental	hiraNyagarbha
	manomayakosha	
	taijasa Mental	Ishvara
	vij~nAnamayakosha	
Causal Body Sleeping M	prAj~na Intellectual	viShva or vaishvAnara Body
	Anandamayakosha	
🕉	**Atman** turIya turIya	**brahman**

Acknowledgements to Refs. 286 296 and 343

APPENDIX F - INTERNET RESOURCES

I n the past ten years, the information relating to Advaita that is available on the Internet has multiplied dramatically. In 1995, a few discussion groups enabled interested seekers to share their understanding and discuss their experiences but there were few actual web sites. Web search technology was also in its infancy, so that it was not easy to discover the little information that might be found. Today, 23rd August 2006, typing the keyword "advaita" into the most popular search engine (Google) returns 936,000 results and this is three times more than last year. More careful selection of search criteria can recover information about virtually any aspect of the subject. Even entire classical works can be downloaded for study off-line, such as the unparalleled 'Talks with Sri Ramana Maharshi', recently made available at Sri Ramanasramam.

This appendix aims to provide a very brief introduction to the sort of material that may be found. The source is my own web site – www.advaita.org.uk – part of whose purpose is to link to those sites that I have found to be particularly good in their related classification. As editor of the Advaita category for the Open Directory Project - http://dmoz.org/Society/Religion_and_Spirituality/Advaita_Vedanta/ - the aim is that I should be aware of *all* sites dedicated to Advaita, whether about specific teachers, organizations, publications, philosophy or history. [Note that, because site owners may change their web hosts, or even cease to maintain a site altogether, the addresses given below may change and it is always best to check with site directories such as the one above to ensure that the most up-to-date address is used.]

A. Organizations

These are locations which provide specific teaching on Advaita, usually in the form of regular talks or discussion groups. They may also publish their own books or at least provide a bookstore from which books on Advaita may be purchased. Some of the larger ones may operate from many locations, possibly throughout the world. Whilst their principal aim is to advertise their facilities and encourage new members, many also provide information on-line for the casual "browser." This may be anything from biographical information of founders to complete downloadable books (usually in PDF format for ease of reading on-line).

1. UK-Based
Shanti Sadan was founded by Hari Prasad Shastri in London in 1929. Free talks are organized on most Wed and Fri Evenings at W11 as well as One-Day Courses at other venues in Central London. They publish a wide range of books, both translations of Advaita classics and original works by Hari Prasad Shastri. These include the six-volume Shankara Source Book, and a quarterly journal, Self-Knowledge. http://www.shanti-sadan.org/

School of Economic Science
Also known as the School of Practical Philosophy in the US, this is one of the most widespread organizations, with centers in a number of countries around the world, and especially in the UK. There are branches in Belgium, Canada, Cyprus, Greece, Malta, the Netherlands, Ireland, Australia, New Zealand, Spain, Trinidad, Venezuela and South Africa. The principal emphasis is on karma yoga.

Most of the ideas are presented in the first term of 12 lectures but students are encouraged to continue attendance indefinitely. Eventually, stable groups may form to practice and discuss the philosophy, attending regular 'residential' courses of 2 - 10 days at a time, in addition to their 36 weekly meetings per year, to enable more concentrated practice. Transcendental Meditation is introduced after two years. It is also a world-class center for the study of Sanskrit.

The school provides a valuable introduction to Advaita and can be highly recommended. There are several shortcomings but these only become apparent after some time, namely the absence of a 'residential sage', an obsession with conquering the ego and the confusing of

Shankara-based Advaita with teachings from other traditions.

The school is now affiliated with Shri Vasudevananda of Allahabad. http://www.schooleconomicscience.org/

The Saraswati Society has held satsang in Sutton, Surrey for the past 15 years. They combine Sufi teaching with Advaita and practice Mevlevi whirling (Sema) to traditional music along with meditation and teaching from the Bhagavad Gita. http://www.saraswati.soc.btinternet.co.uk/

School of Meditation
Another organization based in London, this also has branches in several parts of the UK as well as in Greece and Holland. Its origins are in the same tradition from which the Maharishi Mahesh Yogi's Transcendental Meditation school derives. It adheres to the tradition however, whereas the TM organization has adapted the original techniques. It is the School of Meditation that "initiates" members of SES into meditation. The principle of this School used to be a senior member of SES and visited the same Shankaracharya for guidance. Contact is still maintained between these schools along with the Study Society. They hold weekly meetings, primarily to discuss the practice of meditation and its background. Guidance is available for life for all who have learnt meditation with the school. There is also the opportunity to attend two residential weekends each year.

Vedanta Institute UK is effectively the UK branch of the Vedanta Cultural Foundation established in 1976 in India by Swami Parthasarathy. Annual lectures, management seminars, study groups, talks, workshops and retreats are organized. Activities take place in various parts of London, Manchester, Nottingham and Birmingham. http://www.vedanta.org.uk/

2. US-Based
Arsha Vidya Gurukulam is an institute for the traditional study of Vedanta and Sanskrit, located in the Pocono Mountains, at Saylorsburg,

Pennsylvania. It offers studies in the Upanishads, Bhagavad Gita, Brahma-sutras, and other classical Vedic texts. It was established in 1986 by Swami Dayananda Saraswati. There is also a home study course for Bhagavad Gita ($210 in US) and for Sanskrit ($55 in US) and an excellent bookstore. http://www.arshavidya.org/

Arsha Bodha Center is a similar organization in central New Jersey founded by Swami Tadatmananda, a disciple of Swami Dayananda. There are regular classes in Vedanta and Sanskrit and numerous other events. Payment is by donation. http://www.arshabodha.org/index.htm

Transcendental Meditation

This main site provides details of what TM is, scientific research carried out to validate its benefits and where you can be initiated (you submit an online form and someone from your nearest branch then contacts you). There is information about Maharishi Mahesh Yogi, the TM program and frequently asked questions and answers. It is very much advertised as a means for achieving relaxation and as a benefit to bodily and mental health, with no obvious references to Advaita or any other philosophy. i.e. it appears to be for 'me', not for realizing the Self. You may also enroll in the Maharishi Open University, which offers Internet Video Broadcasts and courses in "Yogic Flying" amongst other things. http://www.tm.org

Meditation Station

The Meditation Society of America has produced these pages, which look likely to contain everything you ever wanted to know about meditation, including descriptions of 108 different techniques, concepts, words of wis-dom and a message board. There are also newsletters, CDs... and a tee-shirt! http://www.meditationsociety.com/

The **Advaita Yoga Ashrama** was set up to spread the teachings of yoga and Advaita according to the lineage of Sri Swami Sivananda. The site introduces many aspects of Advaita and gives details of activities and

retreats at affiliated centers throughout the world.
http://www.yogaadvaita.org/

The School of Practical Philosophy is affiliated to the UK SES organization above. There are classes and weekend retreats. Students are eventually
initiated into mantra meditation. There are branches in NYC, Boston and
San Francisco. www.practicalphilosophy.org

The Philosophy Foundation is a School of Advaita in Waltham,
Massachusetts, offering classes, seminars and retreats in Advaita philosophy, meditation and related subjects. The faculty includes senior students
who have been studying and practicing together for over 30 years, and
welcomes anyone who is interested in Advaita, whether beginner or experienced. The School is affiliated with the *Sringeri Sharada Peetham* in
Sringeri, India, the Southern Seat established in 820 CE by Shankara, and
is guided by His Holiness Shri Bharati Tirtha Swamigal.
http://www.PhilosophyFoundation.org

The **Narayana Gurukula** was established in Kerala State, SW India by
the successor of Narayana Guru but there are now branches in the US,
Australia, Fiji, France, Singapore and England. It is devoted to studies of
Advaita and other teachings of wisdom, reflected by its use of the term
East-West University. There are details of its publications here and brief
biographies of the gurus in the lineage. The website is maintained by the
US branch. http://www.narayanagurukula.org/

Swami Satchidananda was the founder of "Integral Yoga," which now
has institutes throughout the world. This is a huge site which contains
details of his life, work and publications with photos, audio and written
extracts of his teaching. Sri Gurudev, as he was known, was the author of
the excellent commentary on the Yoga Sutras of Patanjali - see
Recommended Books. http://www.swamisatchidananda.org
Satchidananda Ashram Yogaville is the international headquarters for

Integral Yoga and there are details about the ashram, courses and retreats. Publications may also be purchased here. (Note that the emphasis throughout is on practical yoga techniques and not primarily Advaita theory, though j~nAna yoga is also addressed.) http://www.yogaville.org/. Integral Yoga publications may be ordered from http://www.shakticom.org.

3. India-Based

The **Official Website of the Divine Life Society** at Uttaranchal, India. This is a huge website containing well organised articles from Swami Sivananda on many aspects of spiritual practice and yogas, pdf books to download by Swamis Sivananda, Chidananda, Krishnananda, Venkatesananda and others, information about the DLS and the Sivananda Ashram, a multimedia centre, bookstore, e-magazine and much more. http://sivanandaonline.org/html/

The **Divine Life Society**, Sivananda Ashram, Rishikesh, Himalayas, India. This organization, led by Swami Krishnananda until his death in 2001, has books by Swami Krishnananda on yoga, meditation, spiritual practice, Gita, Upanishads, mysticism and philosophy. Many books and discourses may be downloaded free of charge.
http://www.swami-krishnananda.org/

Another Divine Life Society site -
http://www.sivanandadlshq.org/home.html - dedicated to Swamis Sivananda, Chidananda and Krishnananda has much information available for free download: teachings, "inspiring messages," saints and mystics, Gods and scriptures together with many discourses. A large number of the full-length books have already been made available in html or pdf format for free download. (The former are readable by any web browser, the latter by Adobe's free Acrobat Reader.)

A related organization is the **Yoga Vedanta Center**, established by Swami Vishnudevananda, a disciple of Swami Sivananda.
http://www.sivananda.org/

Swami Omkarananda Ashram, Rishikesh

There are lots of articles and information to download, including a comprehensive summary of Western Philosophical thinking on the nature of reality, with definitions of all of the "isms" etc. This is the organization that produces the excellent, free PC utility for generating Sanskrit script from ITRANS text for copying into any word processor.
http://sanskrit.bhaarat.com/Omkarananda

Vedanta Mission

This huge, professionally produced website has a wealth of information on the Vedantic scriptures and Advaita philosophy. The mission itself was established in 1992 by Poojya Guruji Sri Swami Atmananda Saraswati. There is an ashram at Indore where a free three-year course in Advaita may be taken, with donations at the conclusion. There are centers at other locations in India offering week-long courses. There is a free monthly "ezine" (i.e. electronic magazine), containing various articles and details of talks, camps etc. All back issues may be downloaded. A glossary of common Sanskrit words and an FAQ (Frequently Asked Questions) are under construction. There are also two on-line courses based upon Shankara's Tattva Bodha and on the Bhagavad Gita. There is a further channel containing information relating to Hinduism.
http://www.vmission.org/

Yoga Malika

This is an institution in Chennai, India, guided by Swami Dayananda Saraswati and Swami Paramarthananda Saraswati. It provides classes in Vedanta, trains teachers, maintains a library of books and cassettes etc. Some talks by Swami Dayananda and Paramarthananda may be downloaded , including an excellent one on japa. A few are also available in Real Audio format. There is a year-long "self-help" program that can be studied at the site for ten-minutes per day with a different practice each month. http://www.yogamalika.org/

Vedanta Life Institute

Founded by Sri Parthasarathy, who has been touring the world for the past 20+ years giving the most wonderful lectures on the Bhagavad Gita, full of profundity and humor and illustrated by many excellent metaphors and stories. The 'Vedanta Academy', near Mumbai in India, offers a three year residential course on Vedanta, based on study, contemplation and practice. It is open to those aged 16 - 30. Short-term, practical residential courses are also available for business men and professionals on topics such as stress and time management. Books may also be purchased (though not by credit card) and there are Vedantic Centers at various locations around the world. http://www.vedanta-edu.org/

Mathas

Shankara, the Sage who formalized classical Advaita, established four "seats" in India in the N, E, S and W of the country, their purpose being to provide living Sages throughout history to pass on the teaching and answer questions from any seeker of the truth. These four mathas or monasteries still exist today at Puri in the East, Sringeri in the South, Dvaraka in the West and Jyotir Math at Badari in the North, and a fifth math, Kanchi Kamakoti Peetham, at Kanchipuram.

The **Sringeri matha** is currently headed by His Holiness Shri Bharati Tirtha Swamigal. The site contains lots of information about the area, temples, branches, functions and its history and *guru paramparA*. The site appears to be still under development with an area set aside for downloads of photos and audio/video. http://www.sringerisharadapeetham.org/

Also see http://www.srisharada.com/welcomefinal.htm where there is an on-line book by M.K.Venkatarama Iyer (1976), entitled "Contribution of Bharati Tirtha and Vidyaranya to Development of Advaitic Thought" with chapters on metaphysics, *jIva*, *mAyA*, knowledge, truth and error, ethics and religion, and *moksha*. A commentary on the *vivekachUDAmaNi*, by Sri Sri Chandrasekhara Bharati Mahaswamigal, is also under construction.

The **Self Realization Fellowship** - http://www.yogananda-srf.org/ - established by Swami Paramahamsa Yogananda, maintains traditional links with the **Puri matha**.

Shri Kanchi Kamakoti Peetham - http://www.kamakoti.org/index2.html - has more than 1000 pages of information on Hinduism and Advaita. See their site map for links to everything about Hindu dharma, together with many articles and tributes to Shankara and his lineage.

The Jagannath Puri Site - http://www.jagannathpuri.com/index.html - is essentially a tourism site and contains details about such things as the architecture and the worship that takes place at the temple.

The **Jyotir matha** - http://www.templenet.com/Tamilnadu/df067.html is briefly described here, one of the pages of "TempleNet" - http://www.templenet.com/, that has information on Indian Temples in general.

The **Adi Sankara Advaita Research Center** - http://advaitacentre.org/index.htm - is related to the Kanchi Kamakoti Peetham. It is concerned, as the name suggests, with carrying out studies relating to Advaita as taught by Shankara. It publishes a newsletter and journal and organizes talks and seminars. There are several articles on-line and a number of publications may be purchased.

4. Related to Swami Chinmayananda

The **Chinmaya Mission®** is an International Non profit Organization that "helps people bring the essence of Vedanta and Upanishads into their daily lives." It was established by Swami Chinmayananda, a disciple of Swami Sivananda and Tapovan Maharaj. Its mission statement is "To provide to individuals, from any background, the wisdom of Vedanta and practical means for spiritual growth and happiness, enabling them to become positive contributors to the society." Chinmaya Mission® has centers in

Africa, Australia, France, Canada, Hong Kong, India, Singapore UK, USA, and many more. The site at http://www.chinmayamission.org/ contains links or email addresses to some of the major centers and retreats. Books and tapes, magazines etc. may also be purchased from within the organization.

One of the local centers, for example, is the **Chinmaya Mission Washington Regional Centre** at http://www.chinmayadc.org/. They organize talks, study groups, lectures on Sanskrit, dance, etc. in various locations in Maryland and Virginia. The UK branch of the organization at http://www.chinmayauk.org/ has study groups on the Bhagavad Gita, Atmabodha and on Swami Chinmayananda's own book on Self-Unfoldment at various locations in London. There is also an excellent html-based package for studying the Bhagavad Gita, containing the complete commentaries of Swamiji. Many other local branches are listed at http://dmoz.org/Society/Religion_and_Spirituality/Hinduism/Gurus_and_S aints/Swami_Chinmayananda/

5. Related to Sri Ramakrishna and Swami Vivekananda
There are even more organizations throughout the world established in the names of **Sri Ramakrishna and Swami Vivekananda**. Sri Ramakrishna Math at Chennai is perhaps the root site for all of the others. It has biographies, books, news, events, audio and video and articles from the English version of the magazine "The Vedanta Kesari."
http://www.sriramakrishnamath.org/

The **Vedanta Society of Southern California** - http://www.vedanta.org/ - has information about Vedanta in general and the Ramakrishna order in particular. There are links to other centers around the world, a calendar of events, recommended reading and pointers to bookstores, and photographs for purchase.

The **Vedanta Centre UK** at Bourne End in Buckinghamshire - http://web.onetel.net.uk/~suman11/index.htm - began its life in London in

1948 but moved to its present location in 1977. Discourses are held on Sunday by its head, Swami Dayatmananda. Lectures are also held at Bharatiya Vidya Bhavan in London. A wide selection of books may be purchased from this site and, being mostly published in India, these are very reasonably priced.

Addresses and telephone/ fax/ email addresses for all of the centers throughout the world are obtainable from http://www.sriramakrishna.org/foreign_c.htm.

The Ramakrishna and Vivekananda site at http://www.geocities.com/neovedanta/ contains more general information on Advaita, as well as specific material on these two sages. There are lots of articles to read on such subjects as the upanishads and gita, maya, states of consciousness etc. and there is also a poetry section.

See http://www.ramakrishna.org/ and http://www.vivekananda.org/ for information specifically on Sri Ramakrishna Paramahamsa and on Swami Vivekananda, respectively.

Disciples of Sri Ramakrishna - http://www.geocities.com/Athens/Acropolis/1863/disciples.html - provides biographies of all the direct disciples and brief extracts from their teaching.

The Complete Works of Swami Vivekananda are available at http://www.ramakrishnavivekananda.info.

For many more sites, see the Open Directory listings at http://dmoz.org/Society/Religion_and_Spirituality/Hinduism/Gurus_and_S aints/Sri_Ramakrishna,_Sri_Sharada_Devi,_and_Swami_Vivekananda/ .

6. Related to Bhagavan Ramana Maharshi

The main organization related to **Ramana Maharshi** is **Sri Ramanasramam**, the ashram at the foot of Mount Arunachala at Tiruvannamalai in India, where he lived for practically the whole of his life. The mountain is believed by his followers to be the oldest and holiest place on earth, itself capable of bringing about self-realization to one who stays there. http://www.ramana-maharshi.org/

There are links to books, videos, photographs etc., relating to Ramana Maharshi and most of his works may be downloaded for study offline. There is information for those wishing to visit Sri Ramanasramam and about the ashrams in New York, US and Bridgetown, Nova Scotia, Canada.

The **Society of Abidance in Truth** (SAT) is in Santa Cruz, California under the supervision of Master Nome. There are events, lectures, retreats etc. based on the teaching of Ramana Maharshi. http://www.satramana.org/

Vidya Bharata - http://www.vidya.org/ - founded by Raphael, Ashram Vidya Order, Italy, is another organization based upon the teachings of Ramana Maharshi. Note that this site is principally in Italian - see the New York based **Aurea Vidya Foundation** - http://www.vidya-ashramvidyaorder.org/ - for an English site about Raphael.

The **Ramana Maharshi Foundation UK** was affiliated to Sri Ramanasramam but is now independent. There are members throughout the world but meetings are principally held at Hampstead in London on the afternoon of the second Saturday of each month. There are short readings on a particular theme, interspersed with periods of silence and followed, in the second half, by an open, moderated discussion. Topics alternate between bhakti and jnana emphasis. http://www.ramana-maharshi.org.uk/

The organization publishes an informal A4 newsletter two or three times per year containing general information about the group and lists of forthcoming talks and residential retreats with Sages.

The **Ramana Maharshi Center for Learning** at Bangalore publishes a monthly magazine, "The Ramana Way," as well as a number of other books and pamphlets on the teachings of Ramana, principally by A. R. Natarajan. http://members.tripod.com/~rmclb/index.htm

David Godman is the author of possibly the best book relating to Ramana Maharshi – "Be As You Are." This site contains interviews, a biography of Ramana and details of David's books amongst other things.

http://www.davidgodman.org/

There are a number of pages covering Ramana's biography and extracts from his teaching at the **Gnostic and Mystical Philosophy** site. http://www.hermetic-philosophy.com/ramana_maharshi1.htm

Books may be borrowed from the **Ramana Maharshi Online-Lending-Library** for Europe. Biographies and Teachings etc. may be borrowed for 4 weeks. Cost is the forwarding postage to the next borrower. Books are available in English, German and French. http://www.geocities.com/ramana_library

Ramana Maharshi and Us has articles about Ramana, personal stories and a free lending library. http://www.ramanamaharshi.info/

Finally, there is a very useful page of links to Ramana related sites and Egroups, etc. at http://www.geocities.com/bhagavanramana .

For even more sites, see the Open Directory listings at http://dmoz.org/Society/Religion_and_Spirituality/Hinduism/Gurus_and_S aints/Ramana_Maharshi/.

B. Internet-specific resources
1. General information on Advaita
http://www.advaita.org.uk/ is the website of the author of this book. It contains all of the (up to date) information contained in Appendices A, B, C, F and G. In addition, there are well over 100 essays by teachers and writers and a section devoted to informative links to current satsang teachers and past sages.

http://www.advaita-vedanta.org/avhp/ is the **Advaita Vedanta** site maintained by S. Vidyasankar. Based around Shankara, it is a very authoritative site, winner of several awards and cited by the Encyclopedia Britannica (though it does use a non-standard transliteration scheme for the Sanskrit). There are general descriptions of Advaita with detailed information on many aspects accessible through comprehensive hyperlinked references. There is a biography of Shankara and details of his lineage with scholarly discussion of many related aspects, such as dating his birth and death. The teachings of pre- and post-Shankara philosophers are also discussed in the same rigorous, academic manner. The many schools of philosophy that cite the Upanishads as their source are discussed and their relationships explained. Overall, the site is excellent as a source of reference material and very professionally produced. It is clearly aimed primarily at the serious student.

http://www.advaitin.net/ is the home page for the email discussion group called the **Advaitin** List. There is information about Shankara and extracts from his works, general information about Advaita and Hinduism, details of history, terminology and Vedantic scriptures. The site also contains a number of related links and the opportunity to join the Advaitin E-Group (see below).

There is an excellent set of bookmarked links, available only to members of the Advaitin E-Group. http://groups.yahoo.com/group/advaitin/links is maintained by Sunder Hattangadi, who seems able to provide references to any Advaita related topic imaginable.

Non-Duality Salon is maintained by Jerry M. Katz. Amongst other things it has some extremely useful pages listing living teachers, alphabetically or by location. Each entry contains a few quotations, together with a pointer to the teacher's own website, if applicable. There are also many personal accounts of satsangs with various teachers. The links can keep you surfing for some considerable time! http://nonduality.com/

Realization.org is a very professionally produced site with a wealth of information and articles on many topics with regular updates. There are biographies of sages and excerpts from books, articles on Advaita, bhakti and j~nAna yoga, meditation, Sanskrit and much more. Each page has links to associated material. The editor of the site is a Ramana Maharshi devotee. http://www.realization.org/

Sentient.org is based around Ramana Maharshi, his teaching and teachers who have been influenced by him. There are also essays on awakening and on teachers in general. http://www.sentient.org/index.html

Wikiverse - http://advaita-vedanta.wikiverse.org/ - has a number of pages of general description on aspects relating to Advaita in an encyclopaedic style.

Pathways to Metaphysics - http://geocities.com/egodust/ - is the site of Frank Maiello (egodust), who has been principally influenced by Ramana Maharshi. It presents the teaching of Vedanta for "novices" to "sadhus" and is a large site containing lots of information and valuable insights.

3rd Millennium Gateway is a large site with only some of the content directly relating to Advaita. There are links to current and past teachers, resources, articles and books. In addition, there are pages on spirituality, cosmology, religion in general, new age, frontiers of science, scriptures, social issues and environment. There are articles, interviews and reviews. Everything is supported by lots of annotated links.
http://www.thirdmg.com/

Amigo - http://www.ods.nl/am1gos - is a free Web magazine about Non Duality. There are articles by the editor Wolter Keers, a disciple of Ramana Maharshi and others such as Douglas Harding, Krishna Menon and Tony Parsons. Dutch teachers such as Jan van Delden and Hans Laurentius also have essays and satsang extracts translated into English. New issues come available several times per year. They are professionally produced and some of the articles are excellent. See Issue 2, for example, for lucid discussions on the topic of free will (or not!).

Another web magazine is published less frequently by **Harsha Satsangh**, another of the Advaita E-Groups hosted by Yahoo.
http://www.nonduality-advaita.com/

Dancing with the Divine is an on-line magazine containing articles and poems of non-dual wisdom. http://www.dancingwiththedivine.com/

Pure Silence is the website of Mark McCloskey, who is selflessly (!) spreading the message of non-duality without thought of personal gain. There are a large number of short articles on various aspects of life, emphasising the need to live in the present from the silence that is our true nature. There are also several audio extracts from his acclaimed "Pure Silence" CD. http://www.puresilence.org/

When I awoke - http://www.wheniawoke.com/ - contains tales of awakening in various non-dual traditions (though principally Advaita). Essays from a number of teachers describe their enlightenment experience and there is a practical exercise from Ken Wilber.

Wide Awake Living is about enlightenment and waking up to what is already here, now. There are essays, poetry, links and an offer to participate in the creation of personalised journals with questions and answers to act as a practical tool. http://www.wideawakeliving.com/index.html

Benjamin, who is interested in Buddhism and Western Idealist philosophies as well as Advaita, maintains a website - **SunyaPrajna: Nondual Spirituality** - containing a collection of readable and literate articles on consciousness and other topics. http://www.sunyaprajna.com/

There are some interesting musings on aspects of Advaita as well as some autobiographical stories from **Michael Reidy** and a number of quotations. Not a high-tech website (!) but well worth a visit. http://homepage.eircom.net/~ombhurbhuva/

If pictures help you to understand new concepts and you have the Shockwave plugin Flash 5.0 installed, you may be interested in **Who Are You?** This poses a set of visually stimulating questions on the nature of ourselves and the world of appearances. http://www.ods.nl/ikben/gb/

There is an e-book **Introduction to Advaita** by D. Krishna Ayyar that can be read in full on-line. Despite claiming to be "a presentation for beginners" this is very comprehensive covering practically any topic that you might think of. This is a classical treatment that uses all of the correct Sanskrit terminology.
http://www.katha.org/Academics/Advaita-FrontPg.html

Another e-book is partially presented at "**Garland of Advaitic Wisdom**." This advertises the complete book by Ajati, a devotee of Ramana Maharshi. With an emphasis on ajati-vada, the theory that nothing has ever been created, a number of pages are available on line. There are quotations from a number of classic Advaita scriptures as well as from Ramana Maharshi, Zen and Tao. http://www.ajati.com/

An excellent, step by step, **Introduction to Advaita**, presented in the form of a dialogue (of 1008 single lines) has been written by Professor V.

Krishnamurthy (see below).

http://www.geocities.com/profvk/advaitadialoguepage1.html presents the pages for viewing on-line. Alternatively, the complete dialogue may be downloaded as a PDF file from the Advaitin site at http://www.advaitin.net

Ananta Yoga Learning Center presents essays, poetry and links which are a mixture of Kashmir Shaivism, Patanjali's Yoga and Advaita. A number of classics from the scriptures may also be viewed on-line or downloaded. http://www.upnaway.com/~bindu/anantayogaweb/

Ahwan - The Spiritual Approach to Life has a large number of articles based on the lectures of Sri Bimal Mohanty expounding the traditional teaching of Vedanta. Subscription requested for access to further articles. http://www.ahwan.com/

Philip Teertha Mistlberger - Teachings and Writings on the Spiritual Path. A wide selection of writings from various traditions, including Zen, Tibetan Buddhism and Tantra. A book is advertised, entitled "A Natural Awakening: Realizing the Self in Everyday Life" with the first two chapters on-line and the first of these provides a crystal clear description of the seeker's situation and the nature of enlightenment as described by Advaita. (Several extracts that I have chosen from the book may also be read at my own website.) Another short article lists the "Nine Essential Points of Spiritual Enlightenment." http://www.geocities.com/annubis33/

Being - the home you never left - Correspondence, Audios, Essays, Books and Links from Charlie Hayes, a former professional racing driver, who is influenced by the Navnath sampradAya. Charlie offers frequent meetings and personal consultations at his home in Santa Ana, California. http://www.awake-now.org/.

Arsha Vidya Satsangs has details of satsangs held by Arsha Vidya Gurukulam at various locations in the US as well as Australia and Canada. Also, there are many pdf file and mp3 audio files of satsang excerpts from Swamis Dayananda, Viditatmananda, Tattvavidananda and Pratyagbodhananda. These can all be downloaded and contain a wealth of material on assorted topics. http://www.avgsatsang.org/

The **shAstraprakAshikA Trust** in Chennai, India sells audio cassettes of recordings of lecture and discourses by Swami Dayananada, Swami Paramarthananda, Swami Omkarananda and Swami Guruparananda. You may also pay on line and download mp3 files. http://www.sastraprakasika.org/

Self Knowledge is a journal (of Adhyatma Yoga and Advaita Vedanta) produced by Shanti Sadan. There are articles on key yoga teachings and a selection from the archives. http://www.self-knowledge.org/index.htm

Jean-Pierre Gomez, a student of 'Sailor' Bob Adamson, answers a number of questions that frequently arise for the 'seeker of enlightenment' at http://www.heartsongflutes.com/HERE-&-NOW-YOU-ARE.html .

Advaita Vedanta - An extensive site containing quotations from Sivananda and others, explanations of key aspects of Advaita, articles by a number of authors, excerpts from scriptures, glossary of Sanskrit terms, a bulletin board and links. It also provides a tourist based introduction to Rishikesh. http://www.geocities.com/radhakutir/ .

It Is Not Real is the website of Edward Muzika. Principally a homage to his teacher, Robert Adams, it contains a biography of and satsang extracts from Robert Adams along with details of their relationship. There are also sections on spiritual practices, Nisargadatta Maharaj, Zen Buddhism, psychoanalysis, book recommendations and a philosophical essay on Self and Consciousness. http://www.itisnotreal.com/

Living in Peace: The Natural State - Stephen Wingate, a disciple of Bob Adamson and John Wheeler provides essays, poems, dialogues and links. Correspondence is invited. http://www.livinginpeace-thenaturalstate.com/

Non-Identity - A record of essays, dialogues and quotations from Nishkama Naishkarmya Asamvedi, a *j~nAnI* who lived in Madras from 1930s to 1990s. The author was associated with Asamvedi from 1981-1987. http://www.mounam.org

Vedantaquest is the website of Dr. Narendra Tulli, who is seeking to unite science with the teaching of Advaita according to Shankara. There are details of his books on the Srimad Bhagavad Gita and Brahmasutra (with extracts) and of prospective projects. He also gives courses on

Introductory and Advanced Vedanta covering the *prasthAna traya* with the commentaries by Shankara (in English at the Delhi branch of Kailas Ashram). http://www.vedantaquest.ind.in/

This is Presence - writings and selected quotations from Jeff Foster, who offers non-dual counselling and therapy, email discussions etc. http://www.geocities.com/thisispresence/

Reflections is the website of Dr. Haramohan Mishra and contains a number of articles on aspects of Advaita as well as details of his books, including Advaita Epistemology, Sadananda's Vedantasara and commentaries on the Isa and Katha Upanishads. http://www.reflectionsindia.org/

shiningworld.com is the website of James Swartz. There is much to read here - and it looks very good! Many perennial questions on Advaita are addressed in 12 different categories and opinions are expressed on a number of issues. Books and essays may be read on-line or downloaded as PDF files. Some may be purchased as hard copy and the entire site is available on CD. There is also a large section on dream analysis. A tour of temples in India is organised annually. There are galleries of artwork, some of which may be purchased as cards and hi-res images. http://www.shiningworld.com

2. Hinduism

One of the best general sites on **Hinduism** and related topics has pages on many topics with an easily accessible index to all of the pages. Both philosophical and practical aspects are covered. http://www.hinduism.co.za/

Many of the classics of Hinduism and Advaita are available as public domain downloads at the **Internet Sacred Text Archive**, including the Vedas, Upanishads, Mahabharata and Ramayana. http://www.sacred-texts.com/hin/

India Divine - has general information on Hinduism and scriptures with articles, downloads, screen-savers etc. Audio lectures on Vedanta may be heard on-line or downloaded. There are bi-monthly newsletters published by Bhaktivedanta Ashram in India and much more. http://www.indiadivine.com/

Hinduism Online is another large site specialising in all topics relating to Hinduism. http://www.himalayanacademy.com/

Science and Spirituality - http://www.geocities.com/profvk/

Prof. V. Krishnamurthy has made extracts from his books available here. There are a wide range of topics relating to Hinduism in general and Vedanta in particular - and new topics are being added all the time!

Shri Kanchi Kamakoti Peetham (also listed under Indian Organisations) - contains lots of general information on Hinduism. In particular, there is an English translation of two volumes of "Hindu Dharma" from the Tamil, containing talks on many subjects by Sri Sri Sri Chandesekharendra Saraswati Mahaswamiji. There are also a number of articles by various people on, for example, the life and teaching of Shankara. Five hours of audio and video are also offered. http://www.kamakoti.org/

An excellent hierarchical index of a great many sites may be found at the **Khoj India Directory**. http://www.khoj.com/Society_and_Culture/Religion_and_Spirituality/Hinduism/

Advaya is the website of Philip Renard, who has been influenced by a number of teachers but principally by Nisargadatta Maharaj and Alexander Smit. He teaches in the Netherlands (Bilthoven) but his site has a parallel stream in English, where there are a number of articles, including a series on Ramana, Nisargadatta and Atmananda. - http://www.advaya.nl/

3. Indian Philosophies

Indian Philosophy and Religion provides links to sites of general interest on Indian religions; publishers of related books and relevant E-Groups. There is a list of pointers to sites containing texts of many of the Upanishads, the Gita and the Brahmasutras and other texts such as the Astavakra Gita and Patanjali Yoga sutras. There are links to traditional schools and temples etc. as well as modern schools. http://www.geocities.com/gokulmuthu/

4. E-Groups

These are discussion groups in which the participants communicate via email. Someone will write on a specific topic or question in which they are interested and this message will be sent to all members. Anyone may then respond and these responses are similarly copied to everyone. E-Groups (E for "Electronic" presumably) have evolved from the original "Listservs," "Newsgroups" and "Bulletin Boards" that provided a similar function in the early days of the Internet (and which still exist in some case).

A group may be organised by an individual through his or her own website but, more usually, a central facility makes many different groups available. The biggest of these is Yahoo at http://groups.yahoo.com/. There are thousands of such groups, including 73 related to Advaita (as at 24th Aug 2005). Usually anyone may join but the owner of a group is always able to exclude or ban members. Sometimes the posted messages are "moderated," which means that the owner of the group will read messages before allowing them to be posted to everyone else. This enables the filtering out of abusive or off-topic messages. Many groups, however, are un-moderated and this can often result in a majority of messages consisting of irrelevant chat or so-called "flame" mail, in which two or more members are simply very rude to each other! Unfortunately, this has happened on otherwise very good, supposedly non-dual discussion groups.

Because there are so many, I have personally only sampled a few and currently belong to only four. Accordingly, my recommendations here are not based upon extensive familiarity at all.

Advaita-L is probably the most authoritative group available for Advaita philosophy in the tradition of Shankara. Much of the material posted can be very academically biased however and is often related to Hindu ritualistic aspects. Naïve posts or observations not strictly within the guidelines for the list are not well tolerated.
http://lists.advaita-vedanta.org/cgi-bin/listinfo/advaita-l

Advaitin is the group that I would most recommend. It exists to discuss any Advaita-related topic, on any level. Though it takes the teachings of Shankara as its baseline, followers of Direct Path methods are not at all frowned upon! There are 1250 members as of August 2005. Many of its senior members are very knowledgeable and able to comment learnedly on all topics. There are also numbers of relative newcomers, both from traditional Indian backgrounds and from other Western traditions. Questions from newcomers to the philosophy are always treated with respect and never answered patronizingly. There are clear guidelines for behavior in the group and intervention by the moderators is very rare. Disrespect or posts that are outside of the subject matter are not tolerated, however. In the 7 years of my membership there have been many excellent discussions. There are also ongoing expositions, with discussion from time to time, on topics such as the Bhagavad Gita and on Shankara's *bhAShya* on the *brahmasUtra*. http://groups.yahoo.com/group/advaitin

NonDualitySalon is a long-established group (the first of its kind) which, after a period of rest has now re-opened and has 859 members at Aug. 2005. It is run by Jerry Katz, who also has one of the largest web sites on Non-duality, listed above under "General Information on Advaita." http://groups.yahoo.com/group/NondualitySalon/

NonDualPhil - I left this group in October 2004 after a prolonged period of heated exchanges between several members. Accordingly I do not know how it is going at present. With 142 members in August 2005, this could certainly be worth trying again.
http://groups.yahoo.com/group/nondualphil

SatsangDiary was set up in April 2004 primarily for those who attend satsangs of Advaita teachers living in or visiting the UK. There have been good discussions on aspects relating to the nature of enlightenment and, in particular, the different approaches of traditional and neo-advaita. As at August 2005, there has been very little activity for the past few months, though there are still around 100 members.
http://groups.yahoo.com/group/satsangdiary

Million Paths - There is intentionally not a lot of discussion on this list, which exists primarily for members to post extracts and quotations from the Sages. Principal amongst the sources are Ramana Maharshi and

Nisargadatta Maharaj, though any Advaita material (actual or effective) is acceptable. This list provides an excellent opportunity to discover ideas, and ways of expression, that strike a chord. 348 members at August 2005. http://groups.yahoo.com/group/millionpaths

Harsha Satsangh discusses the teachings of Ramana Maharshi and others. It is a busy group with about 925 members as at August 2005. http://groups.yahoo.com/group/HarshaSatsangh

NDhighlights provides daily posts from 1 or 2 of the 4-5 members who run this group; there are no discussions on the material. The extracts that are posted draw on other sources on the Internet, including many non-dual E-Groups and websites. News articles, discourses, poetry and random information that has caught the interest of the poster - anything may appear. If you do not know where to look for inspiration, something here is likely to appeal eventually. 802 members at August 2005. http://groups.yahoo.com/group/NDhighlights

There are several E-groups specifically devoted to Ramana Maharshi. The two largest are **Ramana Maharshi** (788 members Aug. 2005 - http://groups.yahoo.com/group/RamanaMaharshi) and **Ramana_Maharshi** (196 members - http://groups.yahoo.com/group/Ramana_Maharshi/). And there is a "silent group" (107 members - http://groups.yahoo.com/group/SriRamana), which simply emails members with a short quotation from Ramana each day.

Others - Note that there are many other E-Groups that I have not investigated, including ones that are concerned with only a single teacher, e.g. Nisargadatta, Vivekananda. Many now operate through yahoo and the complete list of those may be searched at http://groups.yahoo.com/. Many of them are also described at http://www.nonduality.com/list.htm

5. Web Logs

Web logs, now better known as "Blog Spots" or simply "Blogs," began as transient web sites on which the owner was able to change information very quickly, often on a daily basis. Typically, these allowed people with lots of opinions on current affairs and the ability to express these in amusing ways to run what amounted to their own electronic newspaper or diary. There are now sites that provide the software to allow anyone to set up such a facility very easily. Of course, only those sites belonging to people who genuinely have something interesting to say survive, since the others never accumulate frequent visitors.

There are now a number of such Blogs devoted to Advaita-related topics and several of these may have "staying power." The ones that have come to my attention are as follows:

http://advaitavedantameditations.blogspot.com/ from Floyd Henderson.

http://www.atmainstitute.org/ajablog.htm from Aja Thomas.

http://nondualitynotes.blogspot.com/ from Gilbert Schultz.

http://acalayoga.blogspot.com/ - Acalayoga and http://talksandconver sations.blogspot.com/ - Talks and Conversations. These last two are devoted to Bhagavan Ramana Maharshi with links to downloads and extracts, up-to-date information on events and other relevant thoughts.

KrishnaViswaroopam is apparently a more traditionally based blog, drawing on the teachings of the Upanishads and Swami Vivekananda. http://krishnaviswaroopam.blogspot.com/

Non-duality Cartoons has a number of... well, cartoons depicting various aspects of non-duality from illustrator Bob Seal. http://advaitatoons.blogspot.com/

12 Step Liberation is the blog of E J Shearn. The title refers to his suggested program of Self-Enquiry using the model of Alcoholics Anonymous' Twelve Step Program. http://12stepliberation.blogspot.com/

6. Upanishads

There are many sites specifically relating to the scriptures – *shruti*, *smRRiti*, *brahmasUtra*-s and *prakaraNa grantha*. Some of these concentrate on just one element, especially those on the Bhagavad Gita in the next section but others are more eclectic. The following are particularly useful for upanishads.

Celextel's Online Spiritual Library has translations of more Upanishads than I have have found elsewhere (108 of them!), including many that I have not even heard of before. There are also translations of the *gIta*, *brahmasUtra*, *pa~nchadashI* and a number of works by Shankara. http://www.celextel.org/

The **Sanderson Beck Foundation** has lots of background information to the Upanishads and translations of a number of them. http://www.san.beck.org/EC7-Vedas.html

You can download a PDF format file of 11 of the major Upanishads, translated by **Swami Nikhilananda** at http://sanatan.intnet.mu/upanishads/upanishads.htm. Recommended (but there is no Sanskrit text).

sankaracharya.org also has Swami Nikhilananda's translations as well as translations of the Vedas and Shankara's works and bhASya-s on the gIta and brhama sutra-s. http://www.sankaracharya.org/

Max Muller translations may be downloaded at http://www.sacred-texts.com/hin/upan/

Vidya Vrikshah has word-by-word translations, together with the original Sanskrit for a number of the main Upanishads and other scriptures, as well as presentations on the main concepts of Vedanta and discussions of music and poetry. (Note that these will be found in the "Presentations" section and you may need to download and install the fonts from the "Software" section before you can see the script correctly.) http://www.vidyavrikshah.org/

The **Advaita Vedanta Library** has English translations of the principal and many of the minor Upanishads, together with other major texts such as Bhagavad Gita, aShTAvakra gIta, pa~nchadashI, brahmasUtra and the writings of Shankara. An excellent collection of valuable resources! http://www.geocities.com/advaitavedant

You can **search** eleven of the major Upanishads for key words (in English) at http://atomicshakespeare.com/word/

7. Bhagavad Gita

The **Gita Supersite** has various translations and commentaries available, including the English version of Shankara's commentary.

http://www.gitasupersite.iitk.ac.in/

Swami Krishnananda's translation, with summaries of each chapter and extensive commentary may be downloaded at http://www.swami-krishnananda.org/gita_00.html

A modern translation by **Ramanand Prasad** may be downloaded at http://eawc.evansville.edu/anthology/gita.htm

The dvaita commentaries of **Swami Prabhupada** can be read at http://www.bhagavad-gita.us/ and chanting of the complete Gita may be purchased on CDs.

The **International Gita Society** has a comprehensive site with study lessons, stories and other scriptures. http://www.gita-society.com/

http://in.geocities.com/gitabykrishna/ contains much valuable information relating to the Gita, including a translation for every word of Sanskrit, complete text and meaning and a number of separate commentaries.

A suite of hyperlinked study notes may be downloaded from the UK Branch of the Chinmayananda Foundation. These contain the complete text of **Swami Chinmayananda's commentary** and also show the Devanagari script for each verse. The package downloads as a zip file whose contents include an executable that sets up the files and installs the font. Excellent! http://www.chinmayauk.org/Resources/Downloads.htm

There is a general commentary on the Gita by **Nataraja Guru** at the German Advaita Vedanta site. http://www.advaitavedanta.de/contents_gitaintro.htm

Acharya has an on-line Gita and a Sanskrit word list containing all words in the Gita with a reference to the verse(s) in which they occur. http://acharya.iitm.ac.in/online/gita.html

8. Sanskrit Resources

Anyone who studies traditional Advaita is certain to encounter Sanskrit terms from time to time. Whether such a student wishes merely to look up the word in a dictionary or is more ambitious and would actually like to learn a little of the language, there are many suitable resources on the

Internet.

The basics of the language and an introduction to ITRANS – the transliteration scheme that is most frequently used on the Internet and for communication via email – are described at my own site: http://www.advaita.org.uk/sanskrit/sanskrit.htm. There is also a glossary of the most frequently encountered spiritual terms in Advaita and an extract from my book "An Essential Guide to Sanskrit for Spiritual Seekers."

http://sanskrit.gde.to/ is one of the best sites for all Sanskrit-related information. Many documents may be downloaded in a variety of formats: PDF, PS, ITX, GIF, TXT, Sanskrit98, Sanskrit99, XDVNG. There are links to dictionaries and grammar-related tools and many exercises relating to conversational Sanskrit. Fonts etc. are available for download and links are provided to ITRANS and postscript tools. Finally, there are links to many other academic and personal Sanskrit-related projects around the world. There are even news broadcasts in Sanskrit, in Real Audio format.

A regularly updated page of useful information and links is also maintained as **Sanskrit Studies Links and Information**. http://sanskritlinks.blogspot.com/

There is a similar site at **http://sanskrit.bhaarat.com/**. Unfortunately, this is not always accessible. Again there is a wide selection of tools, documents etc. and the site itself is professionally presented. (The "Documents" section is a mirror of the previous site.) There is also a "Forum" section.

Another huge list of links to sites in many languages may be found at http://www.languages-on-the-web.com/links/link-sanscrit.htm.

Samskrita Bharati offers numerous publications to help in the learning of Sanskrit as well as some on-line audio. It has news about related events and details of how to help. http://www.samskrita-bharati.org/

If you want to learn Sanskrit, the Argentinean site Sanskrit & Sánscrito produced by Gabriel Pradiipaka & Andrés Muni at http://www.sanskrit-sanscrito.com.ar is simply excellent. It takes you from the basics of learning to write and pronounce the letters up to a very comprehensive set of instructions and examples for combining letters (vowel, *visarga* and consonant *saMdhi*). Scriptures are translated and there are audio files of Patanjali's Yoga Sutras that may be listened to alongside the other material. A tremendous amount of effort has clearly gone into this project and it shows. It is well presented and easy to read.

Sudhir Kaicker has provided a freely downloadable tutor (nearly 38MB when I downloaded it) at **Sanskrita Pradipika**. This is aimed at providing adults learning on their own with a 'leisurely introduction'. It runs under Java run-time environment (so should be computer independent) in a small window that displays a small page of information at a time. It seems to do exactly what it claims. It is interactive to the extent that words may be constructed by typing at the keyboard. It can also sound out the letters but this facility is not included in the downloaded software to keep the size to a minimum. A CD can be mailed at the cost of the recipient. Later chapters explain *saMdhi*, declension and conjugation and sentence construction but not all of these are available yet. http://www.sanskrit-lamp.org/

There is also a very comprehensive set of on-line lessons produced by the **Systems Development Laboratory** at Chennai, India. Some of them may be downloaded for study off-line. There is also a free multilingual editor, for use in generating web pages containing Devanagari (and other) scripts. This is needed in order to be able to make full use of the lessons. http://acharya.iitm.ac.in/sanskrit/lessons/lessons.html

Another good site is maintained by **Gerard Huet** at http://sanskrit.inria.fr/. Though the dictionary tools are aimed primarily at French speakers, most of the information is also in English. There is also an on-line tool whereby you can specify the stem of a noun (*prAtipadika* form), together with its gender and it will provide you with a tabular listing of all of the cases. There is also a "sandhi analysis" utility that will attempt to break a sentence into words. There is an extensive page of categorized links at http://sanskrit.inria.fr/portal.html.

Chitrapur Math is in the process of providing graded lessons in Sanskrit. At the time of writing, this is up to month 12 with (at least) 2 more months to go. Having had a quick look, they appear comprehensive

and approachable. The later lessons have the student translating quite complex English sentences!
http://www.chitrapurmath.net/sanskrit/step-by-step.htm

Wikipedia, a well-known Internet encyclopaedia, now has a good page of history, general information and links at http://en.wikipedia.org/wiki/Sanskrit.

ITRANS is the transliteration scheme, developed by Avinash Chopde for communicating Sanskrit on the Internet. Full details of the scheme are given on his site at http://www.aczoom.com/itrans/. ITRANS itself is used with another tool called LaTeX. Since this is not at all straightforward, beginners or casual users are advised to use the **web-interface** at http://www.aczoom.com/itrans/online/ (since its .ps and .pdf files are transportable for all platforms) or the special tool below.

For easy ITRANS representation of Sanskrit, I recommend the use of the excellent software package **Itranslator 99**, developed by the *saMnyAsa*-s of Omkarananda Ashram Himalayas, Rishikesh, India. This program, compatible with the latest versions of Windows, is downloadable free of charge. Words can be typed in ITRANS and converted into Devanagari and Roman diacritical forms. These can then be copied and pasted into any Windows package. There is also a Unicode version called "Itranslator 2003," which will only run on systems supporting this (e.g. Windows XP). http://www.omkarananda-ashram.org/Sanskrit/Itranslt.html

The ITRANS transliteration and Devanagari script for the alphabet may be viewed, and the correct pronunciation of each letter heard at the **Sarasvati** site http://members.tripod.com/sarasvati/devanagari/alphabet.html.

Charles Wikner's excellent **Sanskrit tutorial** may be downloaded in its entirety or viewed chapter by chapter at http://www.danam.co.uk/Sanskrit/Sanskrit%20Introductory/Sanskrit%20Introductory.html

A downloadable pdf docment and an mp3 file teach you basic pronunciation at the **Devasthanam** site.
http://www.sanskrit.org/Sanskrit/sanskrit.htm

If you would like to hear some Sanskrit being chanted, there are a number of sites, which offer such facilities, e.g. http://bhaarat.com/SANSKRIT/dale/Audio.html provides the complete Isopanishad and a chapter from the Bhagavad Gita amongst other things and has links to other sites.

umd_samskritam is a group established in 2005 in the US to promote the speaking of Sanskrit. The site aims to provide resources, act as a link for Sanskrit-related activities around the world and promote Sanskrit forums and blogs. Free weekend workshops are organized in the Washington-Maryland area. http://speaksanskrit.freepgs.com/

A list of recommended books, divided up into Introductory Grammar and Readers, Reference Grammars, Dictionaries Sanskrit-English and Dictionaries English-Sanskrit, is provided by the Columbia University **Inventory of Language Materials**.
http://www.realization.org/page/doc0/doc0078.htm

The dictionary that is essential if you are seriously interested in pursuing the language is that by **Monier-Williams**. It can be purchased from Amazon.com (for a mere $155) but if you are prepared to wait for it you could obtain it much more cheaply from India. The University of Cologne has done an incredible job of digitising much of the Monier-Williams Sanskrit to English dictionary. This may be used on-line and you can also enter a search word in English to find all of the Sanskrit words that may translate to this. http://webapps.uni-koeln.de/tamil/.

The dictionary may also be downloaded in its entirety (19Mb compressed to 7Mb) together with a superb utility for accessing the content. This facility has been provided by **Louis Bontes** at http://members.rott.chello.nl/l.bontes/. A CD version of the dictionary can be purchased for $1 from http://www.thekrishnastore.com/Detail.bok?no=2295&bar= (the dictionary itself is freeware and occupies 421MB). It consists of TIF images of all of the pages together with a simple search tool to locate the relevant page.

C. Buying Books

The Internet is an excellent resource for buying books on Advaita simply because bookstores that stock these books are so difficult to find unless you live in India. You will be fortunate indeed if you happen to have such a store within easy access of your home. Buying off the Internet using a credit card is very easy and, providing that the web site has a secure facility, also very safe.

Large organisations such as Amazon are excellent in that they have huge stocks and a very efficient service. Prices are also often lower than you will find elsewhere. Because Advaita is such a specialist subject however, and many books are printed without ISBN by small Ashrams, you will not always find the books listed. In this case it is often necessary to buy direct from the publisher.

Buying books from India is also very easy. The quality of the printing and binding is not always as good as you would expect from western publishers and books usually have a unique smell (which you will grow to love!). Delivery often takes a long time too (over a month is not unusual). The very big point in favour of this route, however, assuming there is any choice, is that books are usually extremely cheap compared to buying in the west. As an example, the Bhagavad Gita with Shankara's commentary translated by Swami Gambhirananda was $20 from Amazon.com in Aug. 2005 and Rs110 = $2.51 from Motilal Banarsidass.

1. In the UK

Watkins Books is the bookshop that I visit whenever I travel to London in the UK. It has a large section downstairs devoted to Advaita, both traditional and modern. It is in the process of building an on-line purchase facility and this may well be available by the time that you read this. http://www.watkinsbooks.com/

Non-Duality Books is a mail-order outlet now specialising in books on neo-Advaita. http://www.non-dualitybooks.com/

Teeran's Booksellers at the Bhavan is also based in London (West Kensington). They also sell CDs, videos, musical instruments, statues and art but specifically stock books from India. It is associated with the teachings of the Sri Lanka sage Yoga Swami 1872-1964.

http://mysite.wanadoo-members.co.uk/teerans

Motilal Books (UK) is the UK branch of the Indian Publisher and Booksellers Motilal Banarsidass below. The site supports on-line ordering, prices are quoted in £ sterling and books presumably shipped from the UK. http://www.mlbduk.com/index.asp

2. In the US

The **Awake Bookstore** in Washington has a wide range of books on Advaita and other non-dual teachings that may be ordered securely worldwide. http://www.awakebookstore.com/

Blue Dove is a non-profit making bookstore based in San Diego, California. Containing a number of good books on Advaita and related topics, it also provides an excellent world-wide delivery service. It is also able to supply copies of Atmananda Krishna Menon books "Atma Darshan" and "Atma Nirvritti," both difficult to obtain. http://www.bluedove.org/

Note that this may have ceased trading as of Oct 2006.

Chimaya Publications are able to supply all the books by Swami Chinamyananda that are currently in print. http://www.chinmayapublications.org/

Arsha Vidya Gurukulam has already been mentioned in the Organizations section but must have another mention here since it is the principal (sometimes only) source for the excellent books by Swami Dayananda. http://www.arshavidya.org/

Inner Directions publish numerous books, videos and audiotapes on non-duality. http://www.innerdirections.org/

Nataraj Books at Springfield, Virginia have an extensive collection of books from India (over 5,000 titles) on various subjects, including some that are difficult to obtain elsewhere. There is a facility to order online. https://www.natarajbooks.com/main.aspx

The **Vedanta Press** of Southern California has a huge selection and on-line ordering providing that you live in the US. http://www.vedanta.com/

Sentient Publications publishes all of the works of Wei Wu Wei and Steven Harrison amongst others. http://www.sentientpublications.com/

3. In India

Vedams Books are good for buying books on Vedanta (or anything else to do with India). There is a detailed description of nearly every book so you can check whether it sounds like what you are looking for before you order. http://www.vedamsbooks.com/

Zen Publications of Pune and Mumbai, India publish the works of Ramesh Balsekar and stock most of his works together with a number of others. There is no on-line ordering facility, however. http://www.zenpublications.com/

Motilal Banarsidass publishes many books on Advaita, both traditional and modern and it is surprisingly cheap to buy these for export to the UK or US, much cheaper than buying the equivalent books from your local bookstore. They have a detailed on-line catalogue and you can purchase books using credit cards. Instead of doing this on-line, you print out a form, fill in the details and fax this. Alternatively the form is emailed after completion. http://www.mlbd.com/

Sundeep Books also publishes a wide range of material relating to India, including a good selection of books on Advaita. Books may be purchased on line via credit cards and prices are quoted in US $. http://www.sundeepbooks.com/

Samata Books publish the complete works of Shankara as well as his commentary on the Bhagavad Gita. http://www.samatabooks.com/

Indian Books Centre are publishers of Indological Books. Books may be ordered on-line but there are, as yet, no credit card facilities. http://indianbookscentre.com

Saujanya Books have a large number of relevant books with prices, including airmail, in US $ and payment by Visa or Mastercard. http://www.saujanyabooks.com/index.htm

Some books published by Ashrams can only be purchased from them directly and, in the case of some books, this is very worthwhile. The

Advaita Ashrama at http://www.advaitaashrama.org/ is one such example, publishing such books as Swami Nikhilananda's translation of the Mandukya Upanishad. **Sri Ramakrishna Math** at http://www.sriramakrishnamath.org/ is another specialist publisher, of the recommended Upadesha Sahasri by Shankara, for example.

APPENDIX G –
RECOMMENDED
READING

Before letting you peruse the list below, I cannot resist recounting a story I read recently (from the Ramana Maharshi organization) indicating what he said about reading lots of books. He asked whether, on looking in the shaving mirror in the morning and seeing that we needed a shave, we would then go to look in lots of other mirrors for confirmation. Similarly, if we read a book explaining that we are not who we thought ourselves to be and that we should endeavor to find the real "I," why then read lots of other books telling us the same thing? We should simply start to do something about it now! Just as the mirror cannot shave us, the book cannot enlighten us.

Note that some of the books recommended below may be difficult to find. Many are published by Ashrams in India and some of the ones I have purchased in the past were in very limited editions (one as low as only 200 copies). One compensating factor is that the vast majority of these books are published in India and consequently they tend to be relatively cheap.

Buying these books: There are direct links from my website (www.advaita.org.uk) to purchase these books from Amazon in both the US and the UK. Often, the books are only available from other sources such as direct from publishers in India, in which case links to these are provided.

I. Traditional

There are traditionally three "types" of scriptures referenced by this philosophy. They are called the *prasthAna-traya* (*prasthAna* means "system" or "course" in the sense of a journey; *traya* just means "threefold"). The first of these is *shruti*, which refers to the Vedas, incorporating the Upanishads. *shruti* literally means "hearing" and refers to the belief that the books contain orally transmitted, sacred wisdom from the dawn of time. The second is *smRRiti* and refers to material "remembered" and subsequently written down. In practice, it refers to books of law, in the sense of guidance for living, which were written and based upon the knowledge in the Vedas. Most often it is used to refer to just one of these books - the Bhagavad Gita. Finally, there is *nyAya prasthAna*, which refers to logical and inferential material based upon the Vedas, of which the best known is the Brahmasutra of Vyasa. This work was extensively commented on by Shankara in the *brahmasUtra bhAShya*, which analyses the theory and arguments behind Advaita and counters all of the objections that might be posed to that mode of interpretation.

1. Upanishads

There are very many translations and commentaries on these, either singly or in groups. There are not very many versions of the "Complete" Upanishads, if it could be agreed what this means exactly, since there are certainly more than 100 separate ones. Upanishads such as the *bRRihadAraNyaka* or *ChAndogya* can run to as many as 1000 pages, including commentary, while some like the *tejabindu* are only a few pages. Because there are so many, it is difficult to recommend specific ones. The best thing to do is to visit a specialized bookshop and browse. See Section C on "Buying Books" in Appendix F.

There are a number of collected works of the major Upanishads:

i. A version, with no Sanskrit, no literal translation and no commentary is **The Ten Principal Upanishads** put into English by Shree Purohit Swami and W. B. Yeats. (Ref. 74) This can definitely be recommended but should be read as poetry rather than as an aid to finding out about Advaita.

ii. The best value for money I have discovered is a little book **Four Upanishads** by Swami Paramananda. (Ref. 14) It covers four of the principal Upanishads - Isha, Katha, Kena and Mundaka. There is no Sanskrit and not all verses are commented but the commentary that is provided goes straight to the heart of the matter.

iii. The definitive version of eight of the major Upanishads is probably that translated by Swami Gambhirananda and with the commentary by Shankara, entitled unsurprisingly **Eight Upanishads** (Ref. 336). It comes in two volumes.

iv. **The Message of the Upanishads** (Ref. 285) contains a series of lectures given by Swami Ranganathananda, of the Ramakrishna Order in the 1960's. They are based upon the Isha, Kena and Katha Upanishads but contain quotations from many other sources, east and west, philosophic, scientific, mystical and poetic. A very substantial read!

v. If you enjoy a rigorous, philosophical presentation, which is nevertheless still approachable by the non-academic, **Studies in the Upanishads** by Govindagopal Mukhopadhyaya (Ref. 344) is excellent. If you enjoyed Eliot Deutsch's western treatment of Advaita (as I did), then this might be considered to be the eastern version (though western philosophers are also quoted). It is divided into three sections: the goal, the way and the attainment and is packed with erudite references. The chapter on "The problem of reality" is excellent.

vi. **The Principal Upanishads** by Alan Jacobs (Ref. 121) is what he calls a "poetic transcreation." It covers twelve of the most well known, with abridged versions of the Brihadaranyaka and Chandogya Upanishads. It is not a literal translation but a modern, free verse interpretation, interspersed with informative comments and quotations from other sources. For those who find the traditional versions difficult, this is much more approachable.

If you want to look at individual Upanishads, the major ones are the Kena, Katha, Isa or Isavasya, Mundaka, Mandukya, Prasna, Taitiriya, Aitareya, Chandogya and Brihadaranyaka. Of these, I would recommend the first three to begin with. The last two are very long. The Mandukya is possibly the most important, with its commentary (*kArikA*) by Gaudapada, but it is quite difficult so should not be attempted straight away.

vii. For the **Kenopanishad** (Kena), I would recommend the one with commentary by Swami Muni Narayana Prasad (Ref. 260). It is not examined verse by verse as most treatments are. Instead there are many topics, such as "What is Mind?," "The Unknowability of Truth," and the meaning of the text is unfolded in a wider context. Although the correct Sanskrit terminology is used, it is a more modern interpretation.

viii. Swami Chinmayananda has commentaries on most of the Upanishads, and all can be recommended as reliable, traditionally presented resources. Quoted in this book are extracts from the **Katha** (Ref. 156), **Mundaka** (Ref. 33), **Kena** (Ref. 75), **Isha** (Ref. 343) and **Mandukya** (Ref 230). The books are usually transcriptions of his discourses but are authoritative and fairly readable, with Devanagari and word by word translations followed by extensive interpretation.

ix. The **Mandukya** and its *kArikA* by Gaudapada are essential if you want to learn about OM, states of consciousness or the *ajAti* theory of creation. Ref. 35 has Shankara's commentary and is translated and commented by Swami Nikhilananda. It is very good but really only for the serious student. If you wanted to read only one book to discover the "bottom line" on Advaita philosophy, this would probably be it. A much more approachable version is the one commented by Swami Chinmayananda (Ref. 230). The book **Dispelling Illusion** by Douglas Fox (Ref. 141) is a more general (Westerner's) look at Gaudapada and his ideas as presented in the *kArikA*.

2. Bhagavad Gita

There are many different translations and commentaries on this classic work, where "'many" = tens if not hundreds. Some merely translate the

Sanskrit, with varying degrees of accuracy and artistic license. Others provide several pages of commentary on each verse. I have only 9 different versions so it is perfectly possible that many of those I have not seen are excellent.

i.   The most authoritative version is probably the one that includes all of Shankara's commentaries - translated by Alladi Mahadeva Sastry (Ref. 28). Unfortunately, though undoubtedly authoritative, it is not the most readable. Although I would unhesitatingly recommend it to serious students, beginners would almost certainly prefer one of the others below.

ii.   Swami Dayananda has written **The teaching of the Bhagavad Gita** (Ref. 31). This is really using the Gita to present an overview of Advaita and it gives verses as illustrations rather than covering the entire book, verse by verse. It is, nevertheless, a very good book and I can thoroughly recommend it. (Indeed, anything by Swami Dayananda can be recommended.) He also provides a study course on the Gita, using extensive notes, which are excellent (available from http://www.arshavidya.org/).

iii. The version by Winthrop Sargeant must be mentioned since this is the only one of which I am aware that has both original and Romanized Sanskrit, together with the *meaning and grammar for each word*. There is no commentary however. Nevertheless, if you want to study the Gita in depth, this is probably an essential buy.

iv. Swami Chinmayananda has a voluminous edition published by Chinmaya Publications (Ref. 122). Unfortunately, I have not yet read this but it is likely to be very good, albeit possibly a little verbose. It does suffer from a slight drawback in not having the original Sanskrit presentation of each verse. See also III.1.iii below for an even better free version.

v.   A supremely readable commentary for the modern reader is **The**

Living Gita by Sri Swami Satchidananda (Ref. 357). Strictly speaking, this is Yoga rather than Advaita but that really does not matter - it is full of clearly expressed wisdom. I have only recently acquired this and it is a book that I will enjoy reading rather than treating it as work.

vi. For a modern treatment, I can recommend this version from Alan Jacobs. It is not a straight translation - the title is **The Bhagavad Gita: A Poetic Transcreation** (Ref. 358) - and the verses themselves are updated into a modern, yet evocative free-verse form. Much more than this, however, Alan has biased the wording towards a clearer Advaitic expression. And he has provided a commentary which draws upon his extensive experience of Advaita and incorporates valuable quotations and observations from others, such as Ramana Maharshi and Ramesh Balsekar. Extremely readable, too!

vii. If I had to choose just one version, I would probably pick the version with commentary by Swami Chidbhavananda (Ref. 118). Each verse is given in Devanagari, followed by Romanized Sanskrit and then a word for word translation. A full commentary is then given, often using excellent metaphors. Frequently, relevant quotations from Sri Ramakrishna are then presented.

3. Brahma Sutra bhAShya

This is the third branch of the *prasthAna-traya* - you will need a specialist bookstore to locate it. Note that, since you will presumably only be interested in the Advaitic interpretation, you will want the one with the *bhAShya* by Shankara.

i. The most popular version is probably the one with commentary by Swami Gambhirananda (Ref. 34). It is an exceedingly difficult book to read and, though it contains some of the most profound philosophical analysis, it is certainly not for the beginner.

ii. Rather than a direct translation, this version is paraphrased by the

Advaita scholar V. H. Date (Ref. 40) and is much more readable. Unless you really want the most accurate rendition, this is probably the best choice, though you may have difficulty finding a copy.

4. Other Classics of Advaita

i. **Astavakra Gita** (*aShTAvakra gIta* or *aShTAvakra saMhitA*) Not *shruti* and not really *smRRiti* either but a classic nonetheless. It is not known when, or by whom, the original work was written. It is named after the mythical Sage who appears in the Mahabharata and the Vishnu Purana, both very old scriptures. It is thought, however, that it was probably written more recently, either around the 8th Century or even as late as the 14th, by a follower of Shankara.

I would recommend the version translated and commented by Swami Nityaswarupananda (Ref. 12). A relatively small, thin and cheap version, easily fitting into the pocket, this can be carried around and is a source of the most wonderful uncompromising statements on pure Advaita. Complete with Devanagari Sanskrit and word for word translations.

Again, Swami Chinmayananda has a commentary (Ref. 18). A much weightier tome, this version may be easier to find.

There is a modern translation by Dr. Thomas Byrom (Ref. 87) with simple yet luminous prose.

ii. The **Atmabodha** (Knowledge of Self) is one of the classic works on Advaita attributed to Shankara. Shankara is the nominal author of a number of books that are considered classics, almost of value comparable to those in the *prasthAna traya*.

Highly recommended, though only available from the Author's organization "Vedanta Life Institute," Sri Parthasarathy provides original Sanskrit with word for word translation (Ref. 16). The book is also liberally sprinkled with excellent metaphors and stories. The nature of the Real Self is dealt with at length.

The version by Raphael (Ref. 372) is short, with a good, clear, modern translation and commentary. It lacks Devanagari but has Romanized

Sanskrit and uses Sanskrit terms throughout. There is an extensive glossary.

iii. The *vivekachUDAmaNi* (Crest-jewel of discrimination). This is probably the most famous of the books attributed to Shankara.

A simple but useful book that is not exactly a commentary, since no actual verses are presented, is that by Swami Prabhavananda and Christopher Isherwood (Ref. 65). It is eminently readable and presents the material with great clarity. Suitable for those new to Advaita.

Swami Dayananda Saraswati - **Vivekacudamani: Talks on 108 Selected Verses** (Ref. 58). This is the book that I would recommend to all those who think that they already understand Advaita. I have learned more from this book than any other that I have read. The explanations are crystal clear, often entertaining and presented with the deep wisdom of probably the greatest living sage. There is only one possible problem in that there is a lot of Sanskrit and no glossary, so you have to note carefully as each new word is introduced. (Most of the terms used are in the Glossary.)

iv. **Upadesha Sahasri** (*upadeshasAhasrI*) (A thousand teachings): This is one of the few books that all scholars seem to agree was definitely written by Shankara. It requires some effort on the part of the reader but covers the subject of knowledge of the Self with thoroughness and obvious authority.

The version from Sri Ramakrishna Math, translated by Swami Jagadananda (Ref. 104), presents the Devanagari and English translation. One very useful extra is that footnotes are provided listing the Upanishads from which each of the very many references in the text derives.

v. A somewhat more obscure book, also attributed to Shankara, is worth looking out for. It is very small, easily carried around in one's pocket, yet merits re-reading and study. Its title cannot even be written satisfactorily in the Roman alphabet, so here it is in ITRANS: **dRRigdRRishyaviveka**, translated as "an inquiry into the nature of the 'seer' and the 'seen'." It addresses the topics of the illusory self, the universe, *mAyA* and *samAdhi*.

The version translated and annotated by Swami Nikhilananda (Ref. 73) is the version with which I am familiar and can highly recommend. It is available from the Vedanta Society of Northern California for a mere $1.75.

vi. The **Yoga Sutras of Patanjali** recommended in the translation by Swami Satchidananda (Ref. 11). The "yoga" here refers to Raja Yoga (*rAja* = royal), is also called *aShTA~Nga* (eightfold) Yoga, defined as "the system of concentration and meditation based on ethical discipline." Though not strictly Advaita teaching, there is much overlap and the readable style of Swami Satchidananda, with many stories and metaphors, is able to communicate the ideas very clearly. Each sutra is given in Sanskrit, with word by word translation, followed by extensive commentary where necessary to bring out the meaning. There is much of practical value in this book as well as clarity of theory.

vii. **The Yoga Vasishtha** is another classic. It is available in a number of editions, most of them transcribed by Swami Venkatesananda, and of varying sizes. I have recently completed one of the more abridged versions, called "The Supreme Yoga" (Ref. 38), formatted into 365 pages, the idea being that you read one page per day. However, I (and others) would recommend the complete version.

It addresses principally the more metaphysical questions of Advaita, i.e. the nature of reality and the world-appearance and the need to overcome the desires of the mind. It does so through a large number of dream metaphors, some of which are incredibly convoluted. Some take the form of large-scale creation myths and may become a little tedious but many are short, sharp and very effective. Highly recommended!

The book **Dreams, Illusions and Other Realities** by Wendy Doniger

O'Flaherty (Ref. 241) is an analysis of many of the dream stories from the Yoga Vasishtha. I found myself skimming some of the more detailed parts relating to dreams within dreams within dreams... but if you are interested in the mythology and its psychological and philosophical intricacies, this is definitely the book.

5. Philosophical Treatments

There are many books which address specific philosophical aspects of Advaita in an academic manner. Most of these are probably only attractive to those actually studying the subject at university but some are so well written and approachable and contain so much useful background material that they are worth attempting by anyone wanting to understand Advaita.

i. **Methods of Knowledge According to Advaita Vedanta** by Swami Satprakashananda (Ref. 27). The cover description states: "The book deals with an exposition of the six means of valid knowledge leading to Self-realization."

This is excellent - very readable, yet comprehensive and authoritative. I have not come across such lucid explanations of the most abstruse aspects of Advaita before. It also explains the differences between Advaita and other branches of Indian Philosophy. Everything is set out in point by point explanation. And it has probably the most comprehensive index of any book I have seen!

ii. **The Method of the Vedanta**: A Critical Account of the Advaita Tradition by Swami Satchidanandendra, translated by A. J. Alston (Ref. 24).

This is a huge book, requiring considerable commitment but, if you want to understand clearly what Shankara believed and how his message has been modified or even distorted by subsequent interpreters, then it is indispensable reading. Shankara's essential method is presented as that of *adhyAropa - apavAda*, attribution and subsequent denial. His commentaries on the *prasthAna traya* are examined in detail. Then, following a brief look at pre-Shankara Advaita, there are chapters on each of the major teachers and schools that followed him, in which the same topics are re-examined and the differences outlined.

Fortunately, the translation is by A. J. Alston - see below - so is always understandable. This book will be republished by Shanti Sadan when existing supplies run out so that they are the point of contact if you are unable to obtain it.

iii. Most of Shankara's writing is scattered through his various commentaries on the *prasthAna traya*, the only major authenticated work being the Upadesha Sahasri (see above). These writings are available in a number of translations with commentaries by others but the translations are often difficult to follow and rarely what might be called "readable." A. J. Alston (died 2004) was the brilliant translator of "The Method of the Vedanta" (see above). His ability to render the often abstruse philosophical arguments of Shankara into comprehensible and readable English is without parallel in my experience. Accordingly, this set of books – **"A Shankara Source Book Vols. 1 – 6"** - is invaluable to serious students of Advaita. I have only read one of these - Vol. 2 Shankara on the Creation (Ref. 335) - but am prepared unreservedly to recommend them all on the basis of this.

Each book is divided into clear sections and sub-sections. Each topic is introduced and explained by the author, who then selects relevant passages from Shankara's text which address the topics. It took Alston 37 years to complete this task and Advaitins everywhere can now reap the rewards.

iv. **Advaita Vedanta: A Philosophical Reconstruction** by Eliot Deutsch (Ref. 82).

This reads like an academic Western Philosophical text and presents Advaita from an objective analytical viewpoint. This might tend to put off many potential readers but should not necessarily do so. Whilst it may seem dry at times and does require some effort to read, it presents some difficult concepts in a very clear manner and is an essential addition if you are building a library of key texts on the philosophy.

II. Modern and Neo-Advaita

These cover the now classic dialogues of sages such as Nisargadatta Maharaj and Ramana Maharshi and selections from the growing numbers of books written by present day satsang teachers, including the more radical, absolutist neo-Advaitins. Ideally, there would be (at least) two sections here, since some teachers would not wish to be associated with the other "camp," so to speak. But the dividing lines seem to be becoming increasingly hazy these days with some teachers, who might have been considered generally traditional, making statements more usually attributed to neo-Advaitins. Accordingly, I have grouped them all together and hope that I don't upset anyone!

1. Books by recent Sages

i.   The main works of the Sage **Atmananda Krishnamenon**, who influenced both Jean Klein and Francis Lucille, are **Atma Darshan** (Ref. 360) and **Atma Nirvritti** (Ref. 361). Both are very short, originally in verse form in the Malayalam language, and translated by the author. So simple, straightforward and logically presented, yet presenting all of the key issues of Direct Path Advaita. Excellent!

ii.   **I Am** by Jean Klein (Ref. 19). There are a number of books available by Jean Klein, all in the form of short questions followed by longer answers on topics typically raised by those seeking answers to spiritual questions. Most are available in at least English, French and Spanish. His teaching is very much Direct Path but attempts to provide answers that can give some satisfaction to the intellect. He often brings a refreshing lightness to the mind with its tendency to become mired in irresolvable logical analysis. This book in particular is full of insightful observations. All his books may be purchased at the Jean Klein Foundation. N.B. the Website has been down for some time (early 2006) and I have been unable to obtain any response by mail either. N.B. Non-Duality Press have now taken over reponsibility for publishing Jean's books from Element and two have been published July 2006 - 'Who Am I?' and 'Be Who You Are'.'

iii. **I am That – Discourses by Nisargadatta Maharaj** (Ref. 5). This is probably the best known book by any modern day Sage and justly so. It consists of short dialogues that he had with visitors, who traveled from around the world to listen to his blunt and forceful answers to questions on a variety of topics of concern to those still trapped in the illusory world. There are many wonderful, direct and unambiguous statements from this illiterate seller of cigars in the back streets of Bombay. It is an essential buy.

iv. **Pointers From Nisargadatta Maharaj** - Ramesh S. Balsekar (Ref. 7). Though based upon actual discourses, these have been supplemented by other material so as to present each topic in more depth. Presentation is mostly in the third person rather than the question and answer format of most of the books of Nisargadatta's teaching. Ramesh also ensures in his translation that the intended meaning comes across much more clearly than a simple literal rendition would achieve. Accordingly, this is a very worthwhile addition to anyone's library.

v. Some will take exception to including **Osho** in a list of "recent sages" but there is no denying that some of his recorded material is extraordinarily perceptive. He is also capable of transmitting it in a very clear manner, interlaced with many (often rude) jokes to keep one awake. There are so many books by him that it is very difficult to recommend just one or two (even assuming that one has read them all). They are principally transcriptions of the talks he gave over many years or of the question and answer sessions that he held with his disciples or "sanyasins," as he called them. Many are based around a particular classical work such as an Upanishad. Whilst the philosophy that he propounded was usually commensurate with that of Advaita, he drew his inspiration from many other sources, including Buddhism, Sufism, Hassidism.

The Mustard Seed (Ref. 166) is based upon the Gospel according to St. Thomas, the Christian work discovered amongst the Dead Sea Scrolls. Although this document may not be universally accepted amongst Christians, he uses it to bring out very clearly the non-dual teachings of Christ. It is quite a long book - nearly 500 pages - but it is nevertheless amazing how many topics are covered. Always readable and provocative, it is often very funny too. Extremely good.

Also highly recommended are **Heartbeat of the Absolute**, Ref. 96 and **I Am That**, Ref. 83. Both are discourses on the Isha or Ishavasya Upanishad. The former is based on talks given in April 1971. The latter is published under Osho's previous pseudonym, Bhagwan Shree Rajneesh and is based upon talks in October 1980. If asked to choose between them, I would probably prefer "Heartbeat" (although "I am That" contains more jokes!).

Finally, **What is Meditation?** (Ref. 202) unlike most of his books, is very short. It consists of brief extracts from his other work, which are relevant to the subject of meditation, telling us what it is and what it isn't, how to deal with thoughts, the nature of silence and much more. He is a master of metaphor and example and, if you are learning to practice meditation, this is an ideal prompt for relevant issues.

vi. **Talks with Sri Ramana Maharshi** (Ref. 49). This is the classic book of conversations recorded by Sri Munagala S. Venkataramiah over the period 1935 - 9. Previously published in three volumes, they are now available in a single book of over 600 pages, published by Sri Ramanasramam. Very readable, yet full of wisdom. It has a comprehensive index and glossary. Another essential buy! Also available for free download – see section III.

vii. **Be As You Are**: The Teachings of Sri Ramana Maharshi, edited by

David Godman (Ref. 17). Short, but full of the wonderfully clear teachings of probably the most important teacher of the past millennium. This can be recommended whole heartedly as one of the very best books on Advaita. David Godman researched many sources and combined the material so as to provide fuller answers to the various questions, which are sorted into topics.

viii. The **Gospel of Sri Ramakrishna** by M (Ref. 120), translated and with an introduction by Swami Nikhilananda documents the teaching of this 19th Century Self-realized saint through his dialogues recorded during the last four years of his life. There is an extensive introduction providing biographical details. I have only read this abridged version (the full version is over 1000 pages) but can highly recommend it. His words are full of compassion and wisdom and many of his stories are used in modern Advaita teachings.

2. General Books on Advaita

i. **Vedanta Treatise: The Eternities** by A. Parthasarathy (Ref. 123). Swami Parthasarathy has written several books, including one on the Gita, one on Shankara's Atmabodha and a commentary on several of the Upanishads. The Vedanta Treatise was his attempt to summarize Vedanta from his readings of the classical texts and from his studies with his own guru, Swami Chinmayananda. A new edition was produced in 2004. He still travels the world giving lectures on the Gita and also runs a school in Bombay, which provides a three-year residential course on Vedanta. An excellent introductory book, it tends to be more practical than theoretical, emphasizing *bhakti* and *karma yoga* aspects more than those of *j~nAna*. This is in line with the quotation on all of his cassettes that "The Bhagavad Gita is a technique, a skill for dynamic living, not a retirement plan."

ii. **The Science of Enlightenment** by Nitin Trasi (Ref. 149). This provides a comprehensive coverage of the subject in an informed manner. It reads like a school textbook on the subject (though this is in no way intended to be a criticism) and has, indeed, been selected by the Department of Education in India for university libraries. It quotes very extensively from the works of Ken Wilber. It is thus particularly useful if you wish to acquaint yourself with the latter's work but, like me, find him not particularly readable.

iii. **Introduction to Vedanta** (Understanding the Fundamental Problem) by Swami Dayananda (Ref. 363). Exactly what it says - an introduction to some of the key concepts, explained in simple terms for the beginner. "The fundamental problem," "The Informed Seeker" and "Ignorance and Knowledge" form the core of this very clear exposition. It also uses all of the correct Sanskrit terms so that these will be understood when moving on to more general reading.

iv. Two more general books on Advaita by Swami Dayananda, both highly recommended, are **Self-Knowledge**, Ref. 186, and **Dialogues with Swami Dayananda**, Ref. 112. The former is based on nine talks on *Atma vidyA* given in May 2003 while the latter is collected from various sources and was originally published in 1988. Both are very readable and suitable for any level of student. They are both short but contain key topics presented with original lucidity. Swami Dayananda is, in my view, the best living teacher of traditional Advaita and one of the few to teach in the west. He is able to explain the most difficult aspects clearly, using modern language and often amusing metaphors.

v. **Vedanta Sutras of Narayana Guru** by Swami Muni Narayana Prasad (Ref. 101). Based upon twenty-four short sutras from Narayana Guru, Swami Muni has provided a commentary that is both lucid and informative. It is authoritative, yet eminently readable, covering many of the topics of this book. Despite its unpromising title, this is certainly one of the better books on Advaita, traditional or modern. Full references are provided and there is a comprehensive glossary of Sanskrit words.

vi. **Raphael** is an Italian writer, also very popular in Germany, who inaugurated the Aurea Vidya Foundation in New York, which is now publishing his books. He writes of non-duality in the Orphic tradition (a secret religious movement in Greece, which began in the 6th century BC), Plato and the neo-Platonists as well as Advaita. **Tat Tvam Asi**, That Thou Art by Raphael (Ref. 365) is an unusual book, which contains some excellent material on the nature of reality. The style of presentation, as a fictionalized dialogue between a reformed drug addict, now spiritual seeker, and his guru makes Raphael's teaching much more accessible, with only occasional lapses into mystical confusion.

vii. **The Rope and the Snake** by Arvind Sharma (Ref. 326). All students of Advaita will be aware of the famous metaphor of the rope and the snake, used amongst other things to explain the theory of *adhyAsa*. However, this book presents many other uses from pre-Shankara Buddhist times through to modern interpretations of Advaita. The purpose of metaphor is of course to make difficult concepts easier to understand and makes this particular one the metaphor par excellence. Highly recommended (but only for the relatively advanced)!

viii. **The Magic Jewel of Intuition** by D. B. Gangolli (Ref. 292). This is one of the few books that specifically attempts to investigate the nature of reality from the standpoint of all three states of consciousness, on the grounds that to do so from only the waking state is necessarily partial and incomplete. Accordingly, this is an important book. It is written by a disciple of Swami Satchidanandendra, the author of "The Method of the Vedanta" (I.5.2 above) and the investigation is therefore conducted rigorously using the methods of Shankara. Unfortunately, in addition to being a difficult topic, the book is unedited and suffers from stilted use of English. Consequently, it is often difficult to read and even more difficult to understand. Also, it was published in 1986 with a print run of only 1000, so it is very difficult to obtain.

ix. **Vedanta or The Science of Reality** by Krishnaswamy Iyer (Ref. 378). This is the only other book I am aware of that specifically discusses the *avasthA traya prakriyA*. It is written by the guru of Swami Satchidanandendra and is much more readable than the above book, though not so detailed. It also addresses many Western philosophies looking for correspondences with and differences from Advaita. I am still reading this at the time of writing so that there are no extracts from it. But it is definitely an important book and recommended.

x. **The Book of One** by Dennis Waite (Ref. 84). Someone pointed out that I was not recommending my own book in this section and that I really ought to be. Modesty aside, I obviously think that what is said here is worth reading or I wouldn't have written it. I will not try to write a subjective-objective review of it however and refer anyone interested to the section of my website devoted to extracts, endorsements etc. Suffice to say that it is a general introduction to Advaita as opposed to this book's more detailed examination. http://www.advaita.org.uk/discourses/the-book/thebook.htm.

xi. **How to Meet Yourself (and find true happiness)** by Dennis Waite (Ref. 77). This is effectively my introductory book on Advaita. Disguised as a 'self-help' book, it provides a very gradual introduction to Advaita without any overt philosophy and without any Sanskrit. It uses the findings of sociological surveys, evolutionary psychology and western philosophy to point towards the truth. Again, for details and extracts from the book, see the website.
http://www.advaita.org.uk/discourses/meet_yourself/meet_yourself.htm

3. Books by Modern (satsang) Teachers and writers
There are quite a number of western teachers holding satsangs regularly

around the world and many of these are selling the recorded material subsequently on CD or even DVD as well as transcribed into book form. Dialogues in books may or may not be edited and, consequently, the quality of questions and answers is variable.

Given that a good teacher will be addressing responses directly to a specific seeker at his or her level of understanding, it necessarily follows that these may not be suitable for any particular reader and the context may also be lacking. Accordingly, "satsang dialogue" books are intrinsically not a good medium for teaching Advaita.

The redeeming facts are that there are many basic questions that repeatedly arise in satsang and such answers are generally understood by all. Also, some teachers are very good at explaining even difficult topics so that their material is usually worthwhile regardless. The books recommended in this section are not all of this type but, where they are, they do not suffer too much from these drawbacks.

i. **Living Reality**: My Extraordinary Summer with **"Sailor" Bob Adamson** by James Braha (Ref. 346). This book does contain dialogue but is superior to most of them on at least four counts. Firstly, the teacher is "Sailor" Bob Adamson, possibly the clearest and most authentic living western teacher. Secondly, instead of questions from many different seekers, those here are mainly from a single person, the author, and hence are much more coherent and focused. Thirdly, James Braha has provided valuable commentaries between sections, in which he is able to summarize and express his own extensive understanding of the topics under discussion. Finally – and this is the factor that especially recommends it – the whole book is presented as a real-life adventure, in which we share the excitement of a prolonged visit by an enlightened teacher. Sailor Bob spent a full five weeks in the author's home giving private and public talks, and we get an intimate and fascinating account of the entire experience.

ii. **Eternity Now - Dialogues on Awareness** by Francis Lucille (Ref.

8). This is not a published work, but is available from specialist bookshops or from his own website. It contains transcriptions from some of his audiocassette discussions with David Jennings (who utilizes the teachings of Advaita in his psychotherapy practice) together with additional material, such as answers to my email questions. As noted earlier, his approach is direct path and, as such, there is nothing of the traditional *bhakti* or *karma* methods here. The questions are answered in an incisive and unarguable manner that will appeal to those who feel that they have to use their minds and intellects to analyze everything.

iii. **Acceptance of What Is - A Book About Nothing** by Wayne Liquorman (Ref. 113). This book presents much of the material that you will hear if you attend one of his talks and in the same style - humorous yet uncompromising. It is possibly the best book to read for an entertaining introduction to the key principles of Advaita as taught by Ramesh Balsekar, with its emphasis on "non-doership."

iv. **Awakening to the Dream** by Leo Hartong (Ref. 22). Leo's teaching is usually regarded as neo-Advaita, influenced as he has been by both Tony Parsons and Nathan Gill (below). Nevertheless, it retains some of the best traditional metaphors and styles. It is a marvelous exposition of non-dual teachings, straight from the heart. Though drawing on quotations from a wide variety of sources (not just Advaita), it is principally a crystal clear presentation from the author's own experience. Highly recommended!

v. **Tony Parsons** is possibly the most widely recognized of the modern neo-Advaita teachers (though this term is not one which they themselves use). His first book was **The Open Secret** (Ref. 47), a short book relating the experiences of the author in a candid and unpretentious manner. It is a refreshing antidote to the tendency of many books to over-intellectualize the topic. It is repeatedly made clear that there is "no separate identity."

vi. **The Texture of Being** by Roy Whenary (Ref. 207). A practical guide to living the spirit of non-duality amidst the vicissitudes of the apparent world. Roy appeals from the heart directly to the heart for us to recognize our true nature and abandon once and for all the traditional pursuits of pleasure, prestige and prosperity, which can never lead to happiness. Instead we should open ourselves up to the silence and clarity, there to discover the beauty and fulfillment of the reality that is already here and now.

vii. **The Teachers of One Living Advaita**: Conversations on the Nature of Non-Duality by Paula Marvelly (Ref. 78). All seekers will empathize with this sincere and beautifully written, personal search for the truth of the Self, as the author traverses the world to interview a number of modern teachers of Advaita. There is much to learn about their personal backgrounds, teaching styles and content and gems of wisdom are elicited by the penetrating questions. But for me it was the interludes between these, where the author writes about her own feelings and reactions that make this book special. The reader shares her moments of confusion, loneliness and yearning as well as those of peace, understanding and acceptance, culminating in a samAdhi experience in Ramana's Virupaksha cave at Arunachala. Wonderful!

viii. **The Wisdom of Balsekar** (Ref. 366) is a compilation of extracts from Ramesh's other books, themed by topic (e.g. action, bondage, death, desire, effort, ego etc.). A wonderful selection presenting an overview of his clear and logical approach to the teaching. Edited by Alan Jacobs, president of the Ramana Maharshi Foundation UK and approved by Ramesh.

ix. **Silence of the Heart: Dialogues with Robert Adams** (Ref. 155). Robert Adams did not write books or give lectures. Towards the end of his life he attracted a small group of students who would come to him for satsang. After Robert's death in 1997, some of these students transcribed some tapes of Robert's talks, and this book consists of these transcriptions. The style is simple and direct. Robert, like Ramana, advocated self-inquiry:

x. **A Natural Awakening** by Philip Mistlberger (Ref. 134). Many students of Advaita think that to become enlightened is to attain a permanent state of peace and happiness in which they no longer have any worries or fears.

It seems that many teachers attempt to subvert the traditional teachings by diluting them with ideas from western psychology in order that they may satisfy this need. If they can make the person feel good (instead of undermining their idea that there actually is a person), they claim to have succeeded. This completely misses the point and invariably the student ends up confused and dissatisfied. The reason that this can happen is that the teacher is usually poorly trained in psychology and has not correctly understood the philosophy himself (irrespective of whether or not he is himself 'enlightened').

In order to address the perceived needs of these western students, what seems to be needed is a teacher who fully understands both. He will then be able to address the psychological issues authoritatively in their own context whilst at the same time expanding the students' awareness into being able to see the truth behind their seeming problems.

In my own studies and research, I have read many books on Advaita from all traditions and I have never encountered anyone with the ability to teach in this way - until now. I invariably pencil in notes in the margins of books whenever I encounter particularly useful explanations or helpful metaphors so that a very good indicator of the value of a book can be gained by the number of such annotations. Based upon this, I can state categorically that this is a very good book indeed!

xi. **Already Awake**: dialogues with Nathan Gill (Ref. 25). Nathan is another teacher of Neo-Advaita and this book is an excellent example of the style. For the most part, what he says is clear and (that adjective applicable to many modern teachers) "uncompromising." One can certainly imagine that a mature seeker might have some remaining vestiges of confusion removed by these words. Unfortunately, it does occasionally fall foul of that bane of neo-Advaita – gobbledygook – when there is an attempt to pass off the duality of *vyavahAra* as the non-duality of *paramArtha*. (e.g. "The seeing through is not dependent on any happening in the play, although it may appear that understanding arises in the story of the character prior to *knowing* being revealed.") As long as this problem is recognized, I can definitely recommend this book.

xii. **Simply This** by Liz Jones (Ref. 367). I don't read very much poetry at all. Apart from T. S. Eliot, I have never really appreciated any, probably because anything worthwhile needs to be read many times before you start to appreciate it. Having been sent this, however, I did make the effort and found it not very much effort at all. These were easy to read, yet clever, perspicacious and enjoyable. Sharp, clear, neo-Advaitin observations on life – its delusions and its resolution in non-duality. Simply This!

xiii. **Awakening to the Natural State** by John Wheeler (Ref. 70). This is not drawn from satsang material but from emails and from personal discussion of the author with "Sailor" Bob Adams. Additional comments and clarification have been added and the quality is generally high so that this book can definitely be recommended.

xiv. **Presence-Awareness**: Just This and Nothing Else, Talks with "Sailor" Bob Adamson, edited by John Wheeler (Ref. 9). Another book of dialogues with "Sailor" Bob, this benefits greatly from being divided up into clear chapters of just two or three pages each on specific topics.

xv. **Perfect Brilliant Stillness** by David Carse (Ref. 313). The Self cannot be described but David Carse makes a very good effort. Quoting from Sufi and Taoist sages as well as Advaitin ones, he helps uncover the non-dual truth that is the essence of the phenomenal appearance. The language he uses is direct and carries the conviction of experience. In many books on Advaita there is the distinct feeling that what is said is in the realm of theory or based upon what has been read elsewhere; one is left in no doubt that this is not the case here. Although nothing new is being said, the material comes across so clearly, simply and self-evidently. And I think this is the key to why the book succeeds. The words carry the understanding to those seeking the explanations but they cannot prevent the heart-felt, mind-less, direct 'knowing' from shining through and piercing the merely intellectual.

Although much is said about the inadequacy and ultimate failure of language to speak of reality, David's writing is very good. I have said in my own books that it is not possible to talk clearly about this subject without using the correct Sanskrit terminology but this book seems to give the lie to that statement. There are some very original metaphors and many brilliant, quotable observations. Sometimes, every other paragraph seems to contain a new profundity.

David is not a teacher of Advaita and specifically states that he does not teach. Beginners will probably not benefit and should perhaps look elsewhere to begin with. But, if you think you know it all already yet feel that 'it' has still not clicked, this is definitely for you. It is the book for those who want to differentiate between intellectual understanding and realization. I have also noted that it seems to receive praise from both traditional and neo-Advaitins – and that is praise indeed!

I have mentioned elsewhere that I always pencil in the margins of any Advaita books that I read these days. Positive comments are marked: 'good', '!' and Q (for 'quote'); things that I don't understand are marked '?' or, if I disagree, 'x'. There are very few '?', only a couple of x's and many Q's and good's. What more can I say? The only adverse comment that I would make – and it is a warning for potential readers as much as anything else – is that the early chapters do go on a bit! So, if you find that, don't be put off and give up; keep reading – it just gets better… and better!

4. Books which are not strictly Advaita

i. **The Book** (on the taboo against knowing who you are) by Alan Watts - (Ref. 359). This is a very readable book, written by the man who started out as a Christian in England and became a popular speaker and writer on most Eastern philosophies, especially Zen, during the 1960's. The teaching espoused by this particular book is predominantly Advaita and it is advertised as the book that you give to your children when they set out to make their own way in life, answering all of the questions that they will ask about meaning and purpose. A large number of his talks are available on CDs, videos and audiocassette, mostly from his son's web-site at http://www.alanwatts.com. There are also a number of Internet "radio stations" that broadcast these talks on a regular basis.

ii. Another highly recommended book by Alan Watts is **The Wisdom of Insecurity** (Ref. 250), subtitled "a message for an age of anxiety." Not just about the impossibility of finding certainty or security in our lives but about the meaninglessness of past and future, memory and desire.

iii. With respect to meditation, the most widely known and practiced method in the west is that brought over by Maharishi Mahesh Yogi in the 1960's. The movement still flourishes though we may hear less about it these days and the method remains a simple and readily accessible one. It can be used simply to reduce stress or as part of a more structured spiritual "path" (if you believe in such things). **The TM Technique**: An Introduction to Transcendental Meditation and the Teaching Method of Maharishi Mahesh Yogi by Peter Russell (Ref. 364) is an excellent presentation of the topic, its history, practice and benefits.

iv. **Ken Wilber** has written many books and, though I have periodically looked at some of them in bookshops, I have always been put off by what appeared to be an overly intellectual treatment of the subjects.

However, the last chapter of The **Eye of Spirit** : An Integral Vision for a World Gone Slightly Mad (Ref. 311) was recommended to me by Greg Goode so I bought it. And I can confirm that this last chapter is amazing. It is the clearest exposition I have ever read of how we are already "it" and how nothing we can do can ever change this. So clear is it that it is totally unarguable. (N.B. I haven't read the rest of the book, which looks overly intellectual...)

v. **Radical Happiness: A Guide to Awakening** by Gina Lake (Ref. 203). Although not following Advaita philosophy in respect of theory, this book should nevertheless prove valuable to all serious seekers of truth, no matter what their background. It is a very practical guide to coming to terms with such topics as ego, desire and suffering and it is filled with the wisdom of someone obviously skilled and knowledgeable in the field of psychology. There are many astute observations about the human condition and the mistaken views of ourselves that bring about all of our problems. These points are driven home effectively and in a very readable manner. Highly recommended.

vi. **Women of Wisdom: The Journey of the Sacred Feminine through the Ages** by Paula Marvelly (Ref. 353) presents a vast panorama of spirituality, seen through the writings of key women in religion and mysticism. Meticulously researched and eruditely presented, this covers the relevant history and mythology of over twenty major figures from a diversity of backgrounds, providing insight into the origins of religions and showing how women have triumphed over persecution and repression to realize the non-dual nature of reality. If you like poetry as well, you will treasure this book.

vii. **Noticing What you Already Know (And That You Already Know It)**, Robin Dale. (Ref. 374). I initially viewed this book with some suspicion, seeing that it consisted mainly of pages with very little writing. It soon became apparent however that these few sentences were usually thought provoking and often profound. There is little in the way of explanation here; rather the material prompts reflection and simply points towards the truth. It is really a book for the mature seeker who already has the theory but lacks the final insight. The more I read, the more I was reminded of Wittgenstein - if you like your philosophy straight and presented with an apt and clever turn of phrase, this is definitely for you. If you simply like aphorisms, these are much less obscure than Zen koans and may just shake the dust from your mind. By the end, I realized that you don't need lots of words to say things worth hearing.

III. Free Books

There are an increasing number of books being made available for free download on the Internet and some of these are excellent. Most are in Adobe's PDF format, which is clear and readable on a good computer monitor and, of course, printable if you prefer to read in bed or whilst eating your lunch. An outstanding example is the "Notes" of Atmananda Krishna Menon (Ref. 13), long unavailable but currently being prepared for a second edition and available for download at my website. Books by Swamis Sivananda and Krishnananda have long been available but Sri Ramanasramam have recently made books on the conversations of Ramana Maharshi available. Also, some modern western teachers make edited satsang material available in this way – Nirmala is a notable example. Below are listed some of the best that I am aware of, together with link information. (Again, it should be noted that there is a section at my website containing details of all these together with links.)

1. Traditional

i. **From The Upanishads** by Ananda Wood (Ref. 175) – This is a free translation of selected passages from a number of the Upanishads into blank verse, along with some occasional prose. Divided up according to clear topic headings. An original adaptation to make them more accessible to the modern reader.

www.advaita. org.uk/discourses/ananda_wood/ananda_wood.htm

ii. **Interpreting The Upanishads** by Ananda Wood (Ref. 216) - This focuses on particular ideas from the Upanishads, and explains how these ideas can be interpreted. For each idea, selected passages are translated and placed for comparison beside much freer retellings that have been taken from the first book. The Sanskrit is often referenced with explanation of alternative translations.

www.advaita.org.uk/discourses/ananda_wood/ananda_wood.htm

iii. A number of other essays by **Ananda Wood**, covering language, states of consciousness, OM, science, mind and knowledge are available for download at

www.advaita. org.uk/ discourses/ ananda_wood /ananda_wood.htm.

iv. **Swami Chinmayananda**'s commentary on the **Bhagavad Gita** is available as an excellent html-based package, containing the complete text. It is available for download from http://www. chinmayauk. org/Geeta_download.shtml. This does contain the Sanskrit (unlike the book version) as well as additional study notes.

v. At the time of writing (March 2006), **Dr. K. Sadananda** has just begun posting his notes on the **Mandukya Upanishad** and Gaudapada's *kArikA*. By the time you read this, archives of the material should be available to members of the Advaitin E-group. As noted above, this is not the easiest of the Upanishads and this opportunity should not be missed.

vi. See Appendix F B.6 for links to Internet resources for downloading Upanishads and B.7 for the Bhagavad Gita.

vii. At http://www.swami-krishnananda.org, you can download complete books by **Swami Krishnananda** on the Upanishads (including the Chandogya and Brihadaranyaka) and the Panchadasi. Swami Sivananda's book on the Brahma Sutras may also be downloaded in its entirety. The hardcopy versions may also be ordered from the same website.

viii. A translation of the *aShTAvakra gita* by John Richards is available at http://www.realization.org/page/doc0/doc0004.htm.

ix. The commentary on the *aShTAvakra saMhitA* (a different name for the same work) by V. Subrahmanya Iyer may be downloaded from http://www.wisdomsgoldenrod.org/publications/.

x. "**Self Realization** (*brahmAnubhava*): The Advaitic Perspective of Shankara: Indian Philosophical Studies IV" by Vensus A. George covers the work of Shankara in considerable depth. It is written in a scholarly manner with detailed references but is nevertheless very readable. It is. It may be purchased but is also available for free download for personal study from http://www.crvp.org/pubs.htm.

xi. Most of the Upanishads, works by Shankara and a large number of other classics are available electronically at http://www.celextel.org/. Only the English translation (i.e. no Sanskrit), without commentary, is provided but this is a tremendous resource.

xii. Shankara's commentary on the Brahma Sutras, in the translation by George Thibaut, can be read on-line at http://www.sankaracharya.org/

2. Books by Recent Sages

i. **Notes on Spiritual Discourses of Shri Atmananda**, taken by Nitya Tripta (Ref. 13). This is Krishna Menon's magnum opus. Long unavailable, because a weighty tome originally published only in small numbers, the copyright has now been transferred and the new holder wishes to make this wonderful document available to all seekers, as easily as possible. It consists of 1,450 notes of varying length, covering a wide range of subjects in his unique pithy and logical style. There is also a detailed biography. A version of the second edition may now be downloaded from www.advaita.org.uk/discourses/downloads/notes_pdf.zip. Most of the proofing and scholarly checking has been done in the latest version. The file has been zipped for minimum size (1.7Mb), 500+ pages including a comprehensive index with hyperlinked page numbers.

ii. **Maha Yoga** by "Who" (Ref. 39). This is essentially a book about Advaita as taught by Ramana Maharshi who, to my mind, bridges the gap between traditional and direct path methods. The author, only identified as "Who" on the title page, was Sri K. Laksmana Sarma, who studied for over twenty years with Ramana. He defines Maha Yoga as "the Direct Method of finding the Truth of Ourselves." The key topics addressed are happiness, ignorance, world, soul, god, the nature of the Self and the means for realizing this, and the role of the Sage and devotion. Some difficult concepts are explained with transparent clarity and the entire book is readable and authoritative yet written with obvious humility. Highly recommended. It may be downloaded from http://www.ramana-maharshi.org/downloads/maha_yoga.pdf.

iii. **Talks with Sri Ramana Maharshi** (Ref. 49). This is the classic book of conversations recorded by Sri Munagala S. Venkataramiah over the period 1935 - 9. Very readable, yet full of wisdom. It has a comprehensive index and glossary. It is downloadable as three separate zipped files, the first at
http://www.ramana-maharshi.org/downloads/talks_part_one.zip.

iv. Other classic collections of material by or about Ramana Maharshi are available from the same site - http://www.ramana-maharshi.org/ - including **The Collected Works,** edited by Arthur Osborne (Ref. 362) and **Day by Day with Bhagavan.** (Ref. 174).

v. All (?) books by **Osho** are available at http://oshoworld.com/. They are displayed about 250 – 300 words at a time and could theoretically be copied and printed. But this would take a very long time – they are clearly intended to be read on-line. The website also appears to have a distinct preference for Internet Explorer over other browsers at the time of writing.

3. Books by Modern (satsang) Teachers and Writers

i. **Nothing Personal**: seeing beyond the illusion of a separate self by **Nirmala** (Ref. 254). As with most modern books on Advaita, this is a psychological rather than a metaphysical presentation but it is full of sincere love, wisdom and humor. It is highly practical and readable with many original ways of looking at the situation in which the seeker finds him/herself. I highly recommend this book and there is no excuse for anyone not to read it when it may be freely downloaded as a PDF file. A wonderful gift to the Advaita community. Alternatively, if you want to be able to read it anywhere, it may be purchased in the usual format. Nirmala is a disciple of Neelam, in the lineage of Ramana Maharshi and Sri Poonja.

ii. **Who You Are**: Contemporary Dialogues on Non-Duality by Jean-Pierre Gomez. I have yet to read all of this but there is an extract at my website. The complete book by this disciple of "Sailor" Bob Adamson is available from http://www.theeternalstate.org/.

iii. **The Way of the Bird**: Commentaries on the Teachings of **Sri Ranjit Maharaj** by **Andrew Vernon** (Ref. 20). This should perhaps be in the previous section. Ranjit Maharaj was the less well-known disciple of Siddharameshwar Maharaj, along with the famous Nisargadatta Maharaj. This book consists of his terse words on a wide range of topics but, fortunately, these are elaborated and explained by Andrew

Vernon in an exceptionally lucid manner making the whole book a mine of valuable knowledge. Available from http://www.wayofthebird.com/.

4. Others

A retired philosophy lecturer and author, Jonathon Bennett, is in the process of performing the most tremendous service to lovers of philosophy everywhere - that of rendering a number of classics of western philosophy into comprehensible, modern language (without changing the essence). He has already "translated" works by Berkeley, Descartes, Hobbes, Hume, Kant, Leibnitz, Locke and Spinoza. These may be downloaded from http://www.earlymoderntexts.com/ as PDF files for private use or for teaching purposes.

REFERENCES / BIBLIOGRAPHY

1. Brihadaranyaka Upanishad, Translated by Swami Madhavananda, Advaita Ashram, Kolkatta. Electronically available from http://www.celextel.org/ebooks/upanishads/brihadaranyaka_upan ishad.htm.

2. The Brihadaranyaka Upanishad, Swami Krishnananda, The Divine Life Society, 1984. No ISBN. Also Electronically available from http://www.swami-krishnananda.org/.

3. Narada-Parivrajaka Upanishad, Translated by Prof. A. A. Ramanathan, The Theosophical Publishing House, Chennai. Electronically available from http://www.celextel.org/ebooks/upanishads/narada_parivraja ka_upanishad.htm .

4. Vivekachudamani, attributed to Adi Sankara, translated by John Richards. Electronically available from http://www.celextel.org/ebooks/adi_sankara/vivekachudamani.htm .

5. I am That. Sri Nisargadatta Maharaj. Chetana (P) Ltd., Bombay, 1981. ISBN 085655-406-5.

6. Sri Sankaracharya's Bhaja Govindam, Swami Chinmayananda, Central Chinmaya Mission Trust, 1991. No ISBN.

7. Pointers from Nisargadatta Maharaj, Ramesh S. Balsekar, Chetana (P) Ltd., 1983. ISBN 81-85300-19-4.

8. Eternity Now: Dialogues on Awareness, Francis Lucille, Truespeech Productions, 1996. No ISBN.

9. Presence-Awareness: Just This and Nothing Else, Talks with 'Sailor' Bob Adamson, edited by John Wheeler, Non-Duality Press, 2004. ISBN 0-9547792-4-X.

10. The Book of Secrets, Osho, St. Martin's Griffin, 1998, ISBN 0312180586

11. The Yoga Sutras of Patanjali, Translation and Commentary by Sri Swami Satchidananda, Integral Yoga Publications, 1990,

ISBN 0-932040-38-1.

12. Astavakra Samhita, Swami Nityaswarupananda, Advaita Ashrama, 1990. No ISBN.

13. Notes on Spiritual Discourses of Shri Atmananda taken by Nitya Tripta, 2nd Issue not yet published. Electronically available from http://www.advaita.org.uk/.

14. Four Upanishads, Swami Paramananda, Sri Ramakrishna Math, 1974. ISBN 81-7120-233-0.

15. The Truth Is, Sri H. W. L. Poonja, Yudhishtara, 1995. No ISBN.

16. Atmabodha (Knowledge of Self) by Sri Adi Sankarachaya, A. Parthasarathy, Vedanta Life Institute, 1980. No ISBN.

17. Be As You Are. The Teachings of Sri Ramana Maharshi, edited by David Godman, Arkana 1985. ISBN 0-14-019062-7.

18. Astavakra Gita, Commentary by Swami Chinmayananda, Central Chinmaya Mission Trust, 1997. No ISBN.

19. I am, Jean Klein, compiled and edited by Emma Edwards, Third Millennium Publications, 1989. ISBN 1-877769-19-3.

20. The Way of the Bird - Commentaries on the Teaching of Sri Ranjit Maharaj, Andrew Vernon, 2003. Electronically available from http://www.wayofthebird.com/.

21. The Upanishads, translated by Juan Mascaro, Penguin Books, 1965. ISBN 14 044163 8.

22. Awakening to the Dream: The gift of lucid living, Leo Hartong, Trafford, 2001. ISBN 1-4120-0425-X.

23. ChhAndogya Upanishad, Swami Krishnananda, The Divine Life Society, 1984. No ISBN. Electronically available from http://www.swami-krishnananda.org/.

24. The Method of the Vedanta: A Critical Account of the Advaita Tradition, Swami Satchidanandendra Saraswati (Holenarasipur, Karnataka, India), Translated by A. J. Alston, originally published by Kegan Paul International, 1989. ISBN 0-7103-0277-0, edition now listed and distributed by Shanti Sadan, www.shantisadan.org.

25. Already Awake, Nathan Gill, Non-Duality Press, 2004.

ISBN 0-9547792-2-3.

26. Mundaka Upanishad, Translated by Swami Gambhirananda, Published by Advaita Ashram, Kolkatta. Electronically available from http://www.celextel.org/ebooks/upanishads/mundaka_upanishad.htm.

27. Methods of Knowledge according to Advaita Vedanta, Swami Satprakashananda, Advaita Ashrama, 1965. ISBN 81-7505-065-9.

28. The Bhagavad Gita with the Commentary of Sri Sankaracharya, translated by Alladi Mahadeva Sastry, Samata Books, 1977. No ISBN.

29. Advaita Fellowship News - February 2005, sent out by subscription from fellowship@advaita.org.

30. Discussions on Advaita Vedanta, Dr. K. Sadananda, Unpublished Manuscript, 2005.

31. The Teaching of the Bhagavad Gita, Swami Dayananda, Vision Books Pvt., 1989. ISBN 81-7094-032-X.

32. Jiva - a Seeker, Swami ViditAtmananda Saraswati, extract from satsang, Electronically available from www.AVGsatsang.org.

33. Mundakopanishad, Swami Chinmayananda, Central Chinmaya Mission Trust, 1988. No ISBN.

34. Brahma Sutra Bhasya of Shankaracharya, Translated by Swami Gambhirananda, Advaita Ashrama, 1996. ISBN 81-7505-105-1.

35. The Mandukya Upanishad, with Gaudapada's Karika and Shankara's Commentary, Translated by Swami Nikhilananda, Advaita Ashrama, 1987. No ISBN.

36. Brahma Sutras, Swami Sivananda, The Divine Life Society. Electronically available from http://www.swami-krishnananda.org/bs_00.html.

37. Brahma Sutras, Unknown Translation. Electronically available from the Advaita Vedanta Library: http://www.geocities.com/absolut_ism/brahmasutra.htm.

38. The Supreme Yoga: Yoga VasiShTha, Swami Venkatesananda, Chiltern Yoga Trust, 1976. ISBN 81-208-1964-0.

39. Maha Yoga or The Upanishadic Lore in the Light of the Teachings of Bhagavan Sri Ramana, "Who", Sri Ramanashramam, 1937. No ISBN.

Electronically available from http://www.ramana-maharshi.org/.

40. Vedanta Explained: Shankara's Commentary on the Brahma-sutras, V. H. Date, Munshiram Manoharlal Publishers Pvt. Ltd., 1973. No ISBN.

41. Self Enquiry, Autumn 1997, Vol. 5 No. 3. (Quarterly Review of the Ramana Maharshi Foundation UK.) ISSN 1357 0935.

42. Self Enquiry, December 1999, Vol. 7 No. 3. (Quarterly Review of the Ramana Maharshi Foundation UK.) ISSN 1357 0935.

43. Chandogya Upanishad, Swami Swahananda, Sri Ramakrishna Math, 1980. No ISBN.

44. Shankara and Bradley: a Comparative and Critical Study, S. N. L. Shrivastava, Motilal Banarsidass, 1968. No ISBN.

45. The Power of Now: A Guide to Spiritual Enlightenment, Eckhart Tolle, Hodder and Stoughton, 2001. ISBN 0 340 733500.

46. Self Enquiry, September 2002, Vol. 10 No. 2. (Quarterly Review of the Ramana Maharshi Foundation UK.) ISSN 1357 0935.

47. The Open Secret, Tony Parsons, The Connections, 1995. ISBN 0 9533932 0 9.

48. The Ancient Music in the Pines, Osho, The Rebel Publishing House, 1998. ISBN 8172610793.

49. Talks with Sri Ramana Maharshi, Sri Ramanashramam, 1955. No ISBN.

50. Sayings of Sri Ramakrishna, Sri Ramakrishna Math, 1987. No ISBN.

51. Nathan Gill, Self Enquiry, August 2001, Vol. 9 No. 2. (Quarterly Review of the Ramana Maharshi Foundation UK.) ISSN 1357 0935.

52. pa~nchadashI of Sri VidyAraNya SwAmi, SwAmi SwAhAnanda, Sri Ramakrishna Math, 1980. No ISBN.

53. Overview for Vedanta Class, Dr. Gregory Goode, Private communication.

54. Post to the 'Direct Approach' Egroup, Ananda Wood, Jul. 2003.

55. The Divine Misconception: Traditional Advaita (Oneness) versus Neo-Advaita, Tony Parsons, April 2005. Complete essay may be viewed at www.advaita.org.uk/discourses/trad_neo/neo_parsons.htm.

56. Post to the 'SatsangDiaryGroup' Egroup, Tanya Davis, April 2005.

57. Private email, Gregory Goode, Apr. 2005.

58. vivekachUDAmaNi - Talks on 108 Selected Verses, Swami Dayananda Saraswati, Sri Gangadharesvar Trust, 1997. No ISBN.

59. Francis Lucille, Self Enquiry, April 2000, Vol. 8 No. 1. (Quarterly Review of the Ramana Maharshi Foundation UK.) ISSN 1357 0935. From a retreat in Dorset, May 1999.

60. No Escape, Ramesh Balsekar, Self Enquiry, December 2000, Vol. 8 No. 3. (Quarterly Review of the Ramana Maharshi Foundation UK.) ISSN 1357 0935. Reprinted from London & South East Connection, Issue 27 (Aug/Nov 2000). ISSN 1357 0935.

61. Sayings of Sri Ramana Maharshi, compiled and edited by A. R. Natarajan, Ramana Maharshi Centre for Learning, March 1994. ISBN 81-85378-14-2.

62. The Nectar of Immortality: Sri Nisargadatta Maharaj Discourses on the Eternal, Robert Powell, North Atlantic Books, 2001. ISBN 1884997139.

63. Self Enquiry, August 2000, Vol. 8 No. 2. (Quarterly Review of the Ramana Maharshi Foundation UK.). ISSN 1357 0935.

64. Be Who You Are, Jean Klein, Element, 1989. ISBN 1-85230-103-1.

65. Shankara's Crest-Jewel of Discrimination, translated by Swami Prabhavananda and Christopher Isherwood, Vedanta Press, 1947. ISBN 0-87481-038-8.

66. Self Enquiry, Winter 1997, Vol. 5 No. 4. (Quarterly Review of the Ramana Maharshi Foundation UK.). ISSN 1357 0935.

67. The Realisation of the Absolute, Swami Krishnananda, The Divine Life Society, 1947. Electronically available from http://www.swami-krishnananda.org/realis_0.html.

68. Post to the 'Advaitin' Egroup, Professor Gummuluru Murthy, November 2001.

69. gauDapAda mANDUkyakArikA: The Metaphysical Path of Vedanta, Raphael, aurea vidyA Foundation, 2002. ISBN 1-931406-04-9.

70. Awakening to The Natural State, John Wheeler, Non-Duality Press, 2004. ISBN 0-9547792-3-1.

71. The Quintessence of Vedanta of Sri Sankaracharya: A Translation of Sankara's Sarva-Vedanta-Siddhanta-Sarasangraha, Swami Tattwananda, Sri Ramakrishna Advaita Ashrama, Kalady, 1960. No ISBN.

72. Personal email communication from Francis Lucille, 12th April 1995.

73. dRRig-dRRishya-viveka - An Inquiry into the Nature of the 'Seer' and the 'Seen', with English translation and notes by Swami Nikhilananda, Sri Ramakrishna Ashrama, 1976. ISBN 090247927X.

74. The Ten Principal Upanishads, Put into English by Shree Purohit Swami and W. B. Yeats, Faber and Faber, 1937. ISBN 0 571 09363 9. Extract reprinted with permission of A P Watt Ltd on behalf of Michael B Yeats and Benares Hindu University.

75. Discourse on Kenopanishad, Swami Chinmayananda, Central Chinmaya Mission Trust, 1952. No ISBN.

76. Already Awake, Nathan Gill, Self Enquiry, Decemner 1999, Vol. 7 No. 3. (Quarterly Review of the Ramana Maharshi Foundation UK.). ISSN 1357 0935.

77. How to Meet Yourself (and find true happiness), Dennis Waite, O Books, 2007. ISBN 1-84694-041-9.

78. The Teachers of One. Living Advaita. Conversations on the Nature of Non-duality, Paula Marvelly, Watkins Publishing, 2002. ISBN 1 84293 028 1.

79. My Confession, Robert Adams, Self Enquiry, July 2003, Vol. 11 No. 1. (Quarterly Review of the Ramana Maharshi Foundation UK.). ISSN 1357 0935.

80. Advaita Bodha Deepika [Lamp of Non-dual Knowledge], Sri Karapatra Swami translated into English by Sri Ramanananda Saraswathi, Sri Ramanasramam, 2002. Electronically available from http://www.ramana-maharshi.org/.

81. Atmabodha, Shankara, translated by Swami Chinmayananda, Central Chinmaya Mission Trust. Electronically available from http://www.geocities.com/absolut_ism/.

82. Advaita Vedanta - A Philosophical Reconstruction, Eliot Deutsch,

East-West Center Press, 1969. ISBN 0-8248-0271-3.

83. I Am That: Discourses on the Isa Upanishad, Bhagwan Shree Rajneesh, Rajneesh Foundation International (Now Osho International Foundation), 1984. ISBN 0-88050-580X.

84. The Book of One: The Spiritual Path of Advaita, Dennis Waite, O Books, 2003. ISBN 1 903816 41 6.

85. Minor Upanishads, Swami Madhavananda, Advaita Ashrama, 1980. No ISBN.

86. Astavakra Gita, Translation by John Richards, Electronically available from http://www.realization.org/home.htm.

87. The Heart of Awareness : A Translation of the Ashtavakra Gita, Thomas Byrom, Shambhala, 2001. ISBN 1570628971.

88. Vedantasara of Sadananda (The Essence of Vedanta), Sadananda Yogindra, translated by Swami Nikhilananda, Advaita Ashram, 1941. No ISBN. Electronically available from http://www.celextel.org/index.htm.

89. AdhyAsa: Notes on Shankara's exmination of the nature of Error in the introduction to the brahmasUtra, K. Sadananda from lectures by H. H. Swami Paramarthananda, edited Dennis Waite. Electronically available from http://www.advaita.org.uk/discourses/real/adhyasa.htm.

90. Commentary on Pa~nchadashI Ch. 7 v. 5, Swami Dayananda Saraswati, Arsha Vidya Gurukulam. Electronically available from http://www.AVGsatsang.org.

91. Spirituality Without God, Möller de la Rouvière, Llumina Press (March, 2005) ISBN: 1-59526-141-9. Extracts electronically available from http://www.spiritualhumanism.co.za/.

92. Lessons on Tattva Bodha-1, Poojya Swami Sri Atmananda Saraswati, Vedanta Mission. Electronically available from http://www.vmission.org/.

93. In This Moment! Teachings on the Nature of Consciousness, Aja Thomas, Extracts electronically available from http://www.atmainstitute.org/index.htm.

94. Post to Advaita List (Internet Email Group), Dr. K. Sadananda, 22 Apr

1998, modified by email discussion Jan 2006.

95. Tripura Rahasya or The Mystery Beyond The Trinity, translated by Swami Sri Ramanananda Saraswathi (Sri Munagala S. Venkataramaiah), Sri Ramanasramam, Fifth Edition, 1989. Reprinted 1994. Electronically available from http://www.ramana-maharshi.org/.

96. Heartbeat of the Absolute: Commentaries on the Ishavasya Upanishad, Osho, Element Books, 1994. ISBN 1-85230-490-1.

97. The Penguin Krisnamurti Reader, edited by Mary Lutyens, Penguin Books, 1954. ISBN 14 003071 9. © 1954,1963,1964 Krishnamurti Foundation of America, PO Box 1560, Ojai, California, 93024, email: kfa@kfa.org, url: www.kfa.org.

98. Post to the 'Advaita' Egroup, Charles Wikner, 23rd March 1998.

99. Perceiving in Advaita Vedanta: Epistemological Analysis and Interpretation, Bina Gupta, Associated Universtiy Presses, Inc., 1991. ISBN 81-208-1296-9.

100. Notes On brahmasUtra - II, post to the 'Advaitin' Egroup, Dr. K. Sadananda, Aug. 2000.

101. Vedanta Sutras of Narayana Guru, Swami Muni Narayana Prasad, D. K. Printworld (P) Ltd., 1997. ISBN 81-246-0085-6.

102. Six Pramanas, Poojya Swami Sri Atmananda Saraswati. Electronically available from http://www.vmission.org/.

103. Shankara's Rationale for shruti as a Definitive Source of Knowledge of brahmaj~nAna: A Refutation of Some Contemporary Views, Anantanand Rambachan. Electronically available at http://www.pramana.org/.

104. upadesha sAhasrI of shrI shaMkarachArya, translated into English with expanatory notes by Swami Jagadananda, Sri Ramakrishna Math, 1989. ISBN 81-7120-059-1.

105. The role of scriptures in enlightenment, Stig Lundgren, Based upon a discussion on the Advaitin Egroup April - May 2004. Electronically available from www.advaita.org.uk.

106. A Realist view of Advaita, Chittaranjan Naik (extracted from a discussion on "The Real and the Unreal" on the Advaitin Egroup July

- August 2004). Electronically available from www.advaita.org.uk.

107. A Sanskrit English Dictionary, M. Monier-Williams, Motilal Banarsidass, 1899. ISBN 81-208-0065-6. See Appendix F, B.8 for Internet resources.

108. Consciousness in Advaita Vedanta, William M. Indich, Motilal Banarsidass, 1980. ISBN 81-208-1251-9.

109. The Upanishads - A New Translation, Swami Nikhilananda in four volumes, Ramakrishna-Vivekananda Center of New York Publications, 1987. ISBN 0911206140. Electronically available from http://sanatan.intnet.mu/upanishads/upanishads.htm.

110. Ulladu Narpadu (Reality in Forty Verses), Ramana Maharshi, From "The Collected Works of Sri Ramana Maharshi", Sri Ramanasramam. Electronically available from http://www.ramana-maharshi.org/.

111. Final Truth: A Guide to Ultimate Understanding, Ramesh S. Balsekar, Advaita Press, 1989. ISBN 092944809X.

112. Dialogues with Swami Dayananda, Sri Gangadhareswar Trust, 1988. No ISBN.

113. Acceptance of What IS - A Book About Nothing, Wayne Liquorman, Advaita Press, 2000. ISBN 0-929448-19-7.

114. An Essential Guide to Sanskrit for Spiritual Seekers, Dennis Waite, Black and White, 2005. ISBN 81-89320-00-9.

115. Why Me and not that Chair?, Dr. J.R. Millenson, Self Enquiry, Dec 02/January 2003, Vol. 10 No. 3. (Quarterly Review of the Ramana Maharshi Foundation UK.). ISSN 1357 0935.

116. Dialogues on Reality: An Exploration into the Nature of Our Ultimate Identity, Robert Powell, Blue Dove Press, 1996. ISBN 1-884997-16-3.

117. Atmananda Tattwa Samhita: The direct approach to Truth as expounded by Sri Atmananda, compiled and edited by K. Padmanabha Menon, Advaita Publishers, 1973. No ISBN.

118. The Bhagavad Gita, Commentary by Swami Chidbhavananda, Sri Ramakrishna Tapovanam, 1986. No ISBN.

119. The Geeta: The Gospel of the Lord Shri Krishna, put into English by Shri Purohit Swami, Faber and Faber, 1935. ISBN 0 571 06157 5.

120. The Gospel of Sri Ramakrishna (Abridged Edition), Translated into English with an Introduction by Swami Nikhilananda, Ramakrishna-Vivekananda Center of New York Publications, 1980. ISBN 0-911206-02-7.

121. The Principal Upanishads: A Poetic Transcreation, Alan Jacobs, O Books, 2003. ISBN 1 903816 50 5.

122. The Holy Geeta, Commentary by Swami Chinmayananda, Central Chinmaya Mission Trust, 1992. No ISBN. An Electronic Study Guide 'Geeta Vaatika', which includes the complete text, may be downloaded from http://www.geocities.com/Athens/Troy/7641/.

123. Vedanta Treatise: The Eternities, A. Parthasarathy, 2004. ISBN 8187111577.

124. Jnana Yoga: The Yoga of Knowledge, Swami Vivekananda, Advaita Ashrama, 1992. No ISBN.

125. The Problem of Evil, Chandi, forwarded to the Advaitin Email list by Naren, Sept. 2001.

126. Your Questions Answered, Swami Krishnananda, The Divine Life Society. Electronically Available from http://www.swami-krishnananda.org/ans_00.html.

127. Ramana Smriti, from "The Maharshi", March/April 2002, Vol. 12 - No. 2. Electronically available from http://www.ramana-maharshi.org/.

128. De Vreungde van Verlichting, Hans Laurentius, Ankh-Hermes, 2000. Extract (translated from Dutch) published in Amigo Mar. 2002. Electronically Available from http://www.ods.nl/am1gos.

129. Prior to Consciousness: Talks with Sri Nisargadatta Maharaj, Edited by Jean Dunn, The Acorn Press, 1985. ISBN 0-89386-024-7.

130. Karma and Reincarnation, Swami Muni Narayana Prasad, D. K. Printworld (P) Ltd., 1994. ISBN 81-246-0022-8.

131. You Are That! Satsang with Gangaji, Gangaji, Gangaji Foundation, 1995. ISBN 096321943X.

132. The Ease of Being, Jean Klein, Acorn Press, 1986. ISBN 0893860158.

133. Interview of Wayne Liquorman by Blayne Bardo, May 1998.

Electronically available at http://advaita.org/blayneinterview.htm.

134. A Natural Awakening: Realizing the True Self in Everyday Life, P. T. Mistlberger, TigerFyre Publishing, 2005. ISBN 0-9733419-0-4.

135. Post to the Advaitin Email group, Professor V. Krishnamurthy, May 2005.

136. The Soul: Further explanations by Swami Nikhilananda, Ramakrishna-Vivekananda Center of New York Publications. Electronically available from http://www.hinduism.co.za.

137. Myth and Ritual in Christianity, Alan W. Watts, Beacon Press, 1971. ISBN 0807013757.

138. The Philosophy of the Panchadasi, Swami Krishnananda, The Divine Life Society. Electronically Available from http://www.swami-krishnananda.org/panch_00.html.

139. Monograph on "Age of Vidyaranya - Contribution to Vedanta Philosophy", M.K.Venkatarama Iyer (1976). Electronically Available from http://www.srisharada.com/Vedanta1.html .

140. The Essential Teachings of Hinduism, Edited by Kerry Brown, Rider 1988. ISBN 0 09 978530 7.

141. Dispelling Illusion: gauDapADA's alAtashAnti, Translation and Introduction by Douglas A. Fox, State University of New York Press, 1993. ISBN 0-7914-1502-3.

142. Prize Essay on the Freedom of the Will (Cambridge Texts in the History of Philosophy), Arthur Schopenhauer, Cambridge University Press, 1999. ISBN 0521577667.

143. The Riddle of Fate and Free-Will Solved (A dialogue between His Holiness Shri Chandrashekhara Bharati Mahaswami and a Disciple): [His Holiness was the Sringeri Mathadhipati 1912-1954.] Electronically Available from http://www.advaita-vedanta.org/ articles/The_Riddle_of_Fate_and_Free.htm.

144. The Key to Discovery, Swami Venkatesananda, The Divine Life Society. Electronically Available from http://www.dlshq.org.

145. Close Encounters of the Advaita Kind, Chris Parish. Reprinted with permission from What Is Enlightenment? magazine; Fall/Winter 1998.

© 1998 EnlightenNext, Inc. All rights reserved. http://www.wie.org.

146. Ramesh Balsekar, Transcript of Satsang held at Bombay, India, January 12, 2001, posted to ANetofJewels Egroup, http://groups.yahoo.com/group/ANetofJewels/.

147. The Play of Consciousness, Burt Harding. Electronically Available from http://members.shaw.ca/burtharding/.

148. Jan Kersschot, Amigo Mar. 2002. Electronically Available from http://www.ods.nl/am1gos.

149. The Science of Enlightenment, Nitin Trasi, D. K. Printworld (P) Ltd., 1999. ISBN 81-246-0130-5.

150. Essay from the Karmayogin (1909-1910), Sri Aurobindo, Electronically Available from http://www.sriaurobindoashram.org/.

151. Jan Koehoorn, Amigo Mar. 2002. Electronically Available from http://www.ods.nl/am1gos.

152. Post to the Advaita-L Email group, Swami Vishvarupananda, Mar 1998.

153. Post to the Advaitin Email group, Dr. K. Sadananda, Jul 2005.

154. Post to the Advaitin Email group, Dr. K. Sadananda, Apr 2001.

155. Silence of the Heart, Robert Adams, Acropolis Books, 1999. ISBN 1-889051-53-5.

156. Kathopanishad, Swami Chinmayananda, Central Chinmaya Mission Trust, 1994. No ISBN.

157. The Merry-go-round, From The Myth of Enlightenment, by Karl Renz. Copyright 2005 by Karl Renz. All rights reserved. Reprinted by arrangement with Inner Directions, Carlsbad, California. www.InnerDirections.org. Electronically available from http://www.advaita.org.uk/discourses/teachers/merry_renz.htm.

158. The Bhagavad Gita: A Scripture for the Future, Translation and Commentary by Sachindra K. Majumdar, Asian Humanities Press, 1991. ISBN 0-89581-896-5.

159. Tony Parsons, As It Is (US Edition), quoted in Amigo Mar. 2002. Electronically Available from http://www.ods.nl/am1gos.

160. Meaning and Purpose, Dennis Waite, Feb. 2004. Electronically

available from www.advaita.org.uk .

161. Objectives of Life - puruShArtha and karma, Ram Chandran, posted to the Advaitin Email group Dec 2003. Electronically available from www.advaita.org.uk .

162. The purusharthas: Four aims of human motivation, Ananda Wood. Electronically available from www.advaita.org.uk.

163. dharma and guNa, Ranjeet Sankar. Electronically available from www.advaita.org.uk.

164. Peace and Harmony in Daily Living, Ramesh Balsekar, Yogi Impressions, 2002. ISBN 81-901059-8-1.

165. Pleasure and Happiness, Dennis Waite, Feb. 2004. Electronically available from www.advaita.org.uk.

166. The Mustard Seed, Osho, Element Books, 1994. ISBN 1-85230-498-7. Reprinted with permission of Osho International Foundation, Switzerland. www.osho.com. All rights reserved.

167. The Purple Flamingo and the Ostrich, Amber, © 1992. Posted to Advaita-L Egroup, July 1996.

168. Desire for Objects, Dennis Waite, Feb. 2004. Electronically available from www.advaita.org.uk.

169. Meetings without persons: psychotherapy and non-duality, David Jennings, Direct Path (Electronic publication of Truespeech Productions), April 1995.

170. The Teaching of Sri Atmananda Krishna Menon - Prakriya 6 - Happiness, Ananda Wood. Electronically available from www.advaita.org.uk .

171. Actual Seeing, Brian Lake & Naama Livni. Electronically available from http://www.awarenessthatsimple.com/.

172. Fundamental Human Problem, Dr. K Sadananda, Electronically available at www.advaita.org.uk.

173. Letters from Sri Ramanasramam, Suri Nagamma, Sri Ramanasramam, 1995. ISBN 8188018104.

174. Day by Day With Bhagavan, A. Devararaja Mudaliar, Sri Ramanasramam, 2002. ISBN 8188018821. Electronically available

from http://www.ramana-maharshi.org/.

175. From the Upanishads, Ananda Wood, Full Circle Publishing Ltd, 2003. ISBN 8176210005. Electronically available from www.advaita.org.uk.

176. Bhaja Govindam, attributed to Shankara, translated by Balakrishna Kumthekar. Electronically available from http://home.nctv.com/omganesh/sankara.html.

177. Zen: The Path of Paradox, Osho, St. Martin"s Griffin, 2003. ISBN 0312320493.

178. Who Am I? (Nan Yar?): The Teachings of Bhagavan Sri Ramana Maharshi, Translation by Dr. T. M. P. Mahadevan, Sri Ramanashramam, 1982. No ISBN.

179. My Recollections of Bhagavan Sri Ramana, A. Devaraja Mudaliar, Sri Ramanasramam, 1960. No ISBN.

180. Beyond the Mind, Jan Kersschot, published in Amigo Edition 4, Oct. 2002. Electronically Available from http://www.ods.nl/am1gos.

181. Ramana Smrti Souvenir, T. N. Venkataraman, Sri Ramanasramam, 1980.

182. The Pathway of Non-Duality, Raphael, Translated from the Italian by Kay McCarthy, Ashram Vidya, Rome, 1988. ISBN 81-208-0929-7.

183. The Questions of Life, Fernando Savater, translated by Carolina Ospina Arrowsmith, Polity Press, 2002. ISBN 0-7456-2629-7.

184. The Indestructibility of our True Being by Death, Arthur Schopenhauer, Self Enquiry, Dec 2000, Vol. 8 No. 3. (Quarterly Review of the Ramana Maharshi Foundation UK.). ISSN 1357 0935.

185. Enlightenment May Or May Not Happen: Talks on Enlightenment with Ramesh S. Balsekar, Edited by Madhukar Thompson, Neti Neti Press, 1999. ISBN 0-9665245-1-9.

186. Self-Knowledge, Swami Dayananda Saraswati, Arsha Vidya Gurukulam, 2003. ISBN 0-9748000-0-7.

187. Conscious immortality: Conversations with Ramana Maharshi, Ramana, Sri Ramanasramam, 1984. No ISBN.

188. Post to the Advaitin Email group, Chittaranjan Naik, Nov. 2004. Electronically available from http://

www.advaita.org.uk/discourses/chittaranjan/evil_chittaranjan.htm.

189. A Concordance to the Principal Upanishads and Bhagavad-Gita, Colonel G. A. Jacob, Motilal Banarsidass, 1999. ISBN 81-208-1281-6.

190. Sreyas and Preyas, Pujya Swami Atmanandaji, Electronically available from http://www.vmission.org/vedanta/articles/index.htm.

191. Complete Works of Swami Vivekananda, Swami Vivekananda, Advaita Ashrama, 1999 (8th Ed.). ISBN 8185301468.

192. Bhagavad Gita, Dr. Ramanand Prasad, American Gita Society, 1988. Electronically available from http://eawc.evansville.edu/anthology/gita.htm.

193. Self Knowledge: Shankara's Atmabodha with Notes, Comments, and Introduction, Swami Nikhilananda, Sri Ramakrishna Math, 1947. ISBN 0911206116. (Introduction electronically available from http://www.anandamayi.org/om/ab2.htm).

194. Wolter Keers, Conversation with Wolter Keers in Gent, April 25, 1973 Amigo Mar 2002. Electronically Available from http://www.ods.nl/am1gos.

195. The Simplicity of What Is, Joan Tollifson. Electronically available from www.advaita.org.uk.

196. Four Quartets, T. S. Eliot, Faber and Faber Limited, 1979. ISBN 0-571-04994-X.

197. Awareness and Experience, Isaac Shapiro. Electronically available from www.advaita.org.uk.

198. Ramesh Balsekar, A letter to Self-Enquiry journal Vol. 10 No. 3 Dec 02/Jan 03, (Quarterly Review of the Ramana Maharshi Foundation UK.) ISSN 1357 0935.

199. The Twelve Principal Upanishads Vol. 1, Dr. E. Röer, D. K. Printworld (P) Ltd., 1906. ISBN 81-246-0167-4.

200. Upanishads Retold, V. H. Date, Munshiram Manoharlal Publishers Pvt. Ltd., 1999. ISBN 81-215-0894-0.

201. Purpose, Dennis Waite, Email response, June 2005. Electronically available from http://advaitavedantameditations.blogspot.com/.

202. Zen: Zest, Zip, Zap, Zing! Chapter 11, quoted in What Is Meditation?,

Osho, Element Books, 1995. ISBN 1-85230-726-9.

203. Radical Happiness: A Guide to Awakening, Gina Lake, iUniverse, 2005, ISBN 0-595-348336-5.

204. The mystique of enlightenment: The unrational ideas of a man called U.G, U. G Krishnamurti, Dynamic Living Press, 1984. No ISBN. Electronically available from http://www.well.com/user/jct/.

205. A Course in Consciousness, Stanley Sobottka, 2000 - 5. Electronically available from http://faculty.virginia.edu/consciousness/.

206. What is it that you really want? A dialogue with Om C. Parkin. Electronically available from www.om-c-parkin.de.

207. The Texture of Being, Roy Whenary, Lotus Harmony Publishing, 2002. ISBN 0-9543100-0-4.

208. The Heart of Relationship, copyright ©1999 by Adyashanti. Electronically available from http://www.adyashanti.org/.

209. Deposition of Conclusions of Life's Philosophy, Richard Rose, 1955. Reproduced in TAT Forum Oct. 2005. Electronically available from www.tatfoundation.org/forum.htm.

210. The Question to Life's Answers: Spirituality Beyond Belief, Steven Harrison, Sentient Publications, 2002. ISBN 0-9710786-0-2. Extract published in Amigo Jul 2003. Electronically Available from http://www.ods.nl/am1gos.

211. Simply Being Free: The Radiant Wisdom of the Heart, Sundance Burke, not yet published (2005). Extract electronically available from www.advaita.org.uk.

212. Aparokshanubhuti: Or Self-Realization of Sri Sankaracharya, translated by Swami Vimuktananda, Vedanta Press, 1997. ISBN: 8175051078. Electronically available from http://www.geocities.com/absolut_ism/index.htm.

213. Vakya Vritti, translated by Swami Chinmayananda, Central Chinmaya Mission Trust. Electronically available from http://www.geocities.com/advaitavedant/index.htm.

214. The Essence of the Aitareya and Taittiriya Upanishads, Swami Krishnananda, The Divine Life Society, 1982. Electronically available

from http://www.swami-krishnananda.org/.

215. Hinduism & Gandhi, Jagmohan, from the Statesman, Calcutta, 2nd Oct. 2005. Posted to the Advaitin Egroup.

216. Interpreting the Upanishads, Ananda Wood, Full Circle Publishing Ltd., 2003. ISBN 8176210013. Electronically available from www.advaita.org.uk.

217. Unpublished material presented by the School of Meditation, Sri Shantanand Saraswati, personal email from M. Alderton, September 2005.

218. The Eight Limbs of Raja Yoga. Electronically Available from http://www.sivananda.org/teachings/philosophy/eightlimbs.html.

219. An Inspiration, Danielle Arin. Electronically Available from http://indigo.ie/~cmouze/yoga_online/inspiration.htm .

220. Crumbs from his table, Ramananda Swarnagiri, Sri Ramanasramam, 1969. No ISBN. (Quoted in Ref. 17)

221. Kaivalya Upanishad, Translated by Swami Madhavananda, Advaita Ashram. Electronically Available from http://www.celextel.org/index.htm.

222. Post to the Advaita-L Email group, Dr. K. Sadananda, November 1996.

223. This is Unimaginable and Unavoidable, Guy Smith, Non-Duality Press. ISBN 0-9547792-5-8 .

224. Discourses on Advaita sAdhana, Kanchi Maha-Swamigal translated by Professor V. Krishnamurthy, posted to the Advaitin Email group, October 1996.

225. Sadhanas or Preparation for Higher Life, Swami Vivekananda, Advaita Ashrama, 1982. No ISBN.

226. Post to the Advaitin Email group, Dr. Gregory Goode, May 2001.

227. The Mind and its Control, Swami Budhananda, Advaita Ashrama, 1971. No ISBN.

228. Principles of karma yoga, Swami Sivananda, Electronically available from http://www.sivananda.org/teachings/karma/karmayoga.html.

229. Guru Vachaka Kovai (The Garland of the Guru's Sayings), Muruganar.

Electronically available from
http://davidgodman.org/rteach/gvk_intro.shtml.

230. Mandukya Upanishad, Swami Chinmayananda, Central Chinmaya
Mission Trust. No ISBN.

231. Vichara Mani Mala (Jewel Garland of Enquiry), Ramana Maharshi.
From "The Collected Works of Sri Ramana Maharshi", Sri
Ramanasramam. Electronically available from
http://www.ramana-maharshi.org/.

232. The Adhikara: To Form a Vessel, Vamadeva Shastri (David Frawley),
Self Enquiry, Volume 8 No. 2, August 2000. (Quarterly Review of the
Ramana Maharshi Foundation UK.) ISSN 1357 0935.

233. Shawn Nevins, The TAT Forum (Monthly Journal founded on the
writings of Richard Rose), July 2005. Electronically available from
http://www.tatfoundation.org/.

234. Reflections, Stephen Wingate. Electronically available from
http://www.livinginpeace-thenaturalstate.com/Reflections.htm.

235. Wayne Liquorman, Interview by Belle Bruins & Kees Schreuders
(June 2002) in Amigo Edition 5, Feb 2003. Electronically Available
from http://www.ods.nl/am1gos.

236. An e-mail conversation with Jan Kersschot, Amigo Edition 5 Feb
2003. Electronically Available from http://www.ods.nl/am1gos.

237. Unpublished Extract, Roger Linden, posted to the SatsangDiary Email
Group by Tanya Davis, March 2005.

238. No one Becomes Enlightened, Tony Parsons, Self Enquiry, December
2000, Vol. 8 No. 3. (Quarterly Review of the Ramana Maharshi
Foundation UK.) ISSN 1357 0935. Reprinted from London & South
East Connection, Issue 27 (Aug/Nov 2000). ISSN 1357 0935.

239. Discussion with Leo Hartong, Amigo 6, July 2003. Electronically
Available from http://www.ods.nl/am1gos.

240. Muktika Upanishad, Translated by Dr. A. G. Krishna Warrier, The
Theosophical Publishing House, Chennai. Electronically available
from http://www.celextel.org/index.htm.

241. Dreams, Illusions and Other Realities, Wendy Doniger O'Flaherty, The

University of Chicago Press, © 1984 by The University of Chicago.
ISBN 0-226-61854-4.

242. My Life and Quest, Arthur Osborne, Sri Ramanasramam, 2001. ISBN
8188225207.

243. Annamalai Swami - Final Talks, Edited by David Godman, Annamalai
Swami Ashram. Extract posted to MillionPaths Email Group, Jan.
2005.

244. De Vreungde van verlichting, Hans Laurentius, Ankh-Hermes, 2000.
Translated and published in Amigo Mar. 2002. Electronically
Available from http://www.ods.nl/am1gos.

245. Raja yoga, Swami Sivananda, Electronically available from
http://www.sivanandadlshq.org/teachings/rajayoga.htm.

246. The Silent Mind - The Ramana Way, A. R. Natarajan, Ramana
Maharshi Centre for Learning, 2004.

247. Post to the MillionPaths Email Group, Anon.

248. Notes in Regard to a Technique of Timeless Realization, Dr. Hubert
Benoit, Translated by Aldous Huxley, From "Vedanta and the West"
(March-April 1950). Electronically available from
http://www.selfdiscoveryportal.com/bztech.htm.

249. Awake Living Now, Katie Davis, Unpublished Manuscript, 2005.

250. The Wisdom of Insecurity: A Message for an Age of Anxiety, Alan
Watts, Rider, 1992. ISBN 0 7126 9588 5.

251. Mark McCloskey, Essays electronically available from
http://www.puresilence.org/.

252. The Great Work of Fiction Created by the Little Me, Eckhart Tolle,
Extracts from a talk at the Inner Directions Gathering 2000 in
California, Self Enquiry, Vol. 8 No. 3, December 2000. (Quarterly
Review of the Ramana Maharshi Foundation UK.) ISSN 1357 0935.

253. Japa yoga, Swami Sivananda, Electronically available from
http://www.sivanandadlshq.org/teachings/japayoga.htm.

254. Nothing Personal: Seeing Beyond the Illusion of a Separate Self,
Nirmala, Endless Satsang Press, 2001. No ISBN. Electronically
Available from http://www.enlightenedbeings.com/nirmala.html.

255. An Interview with Sri Poonjaji, Shraddha, Lucknow, India 26th August 1994. Electronically Available from http://www.firehorse.com.au/philos/papaji/.

256. Japa, a talk by Swami Dayananda. Electronically Available from http://www.yogamalika.org/yogahome.html.

257. Gayatri, Wikpedia, the free encyclopedia. http://en.wikipedia.org/wiki/Gayatri_Mantra.

258. Transcripts of Some Talks - Extract from website, Cee. Electronically Available from http://www.presentnonexistence.com/teaching.htm.

259. Authority of Scriptures, Chittaranjan Naik, posted to the Advaitin Email group, November 2005.

260. Kena Upanishad, Swami Muni Narayana Prasad, D. K. Printworld (P) Ltd. 1994. ISBN 81-246-0034-1.

261. Conversations, H H Sri Shantanand saraswati1973, unpublished material from the School of Economic Science.

262. Old Ideas of Language, Ananda Wood. Electronically available from www.advaita.org.uk.

263. Levels of Language: from an old philosophy, Ananda Wood. Electronically available from www.advaita.org.uk.

264. Words and What They Reveal (extract from satsang). Swami Dayananda Saraswati, Arsha Vidya Gurukulam. Electronically available from http://www.AVGsatsang.org.

265. Doing Nothing, Steven Harrison, Jeremy P. Tarcher/Putnam, 1997. ISBN 1-58542-172-3.

266. Returning to the Source, Hans Heimer, Self Enquiry, Winter 1998, Volume 6 Number 3. (Quarterly Review of the Ramana Maharshi Foundation UK.) ISSN 1357 0935.

267. Experiences with Nisargadatta Maharaj, Alexander Smit, Amigo Mar. 2002. Electronically Available from http://www.ods.nl/am1gos.

268. All Gurus (& Disciples) Great and Small, Vamadeva Shastri (David Frawley), Self Enquiry, Summer 1998. (Quarterly Review of the Ramana Maharshi Foundation UK.) ISSN 1357 0935.

269. Western Advaita Teachers - An Overview, Alan Jacobs, Self Enquiry,

Feb 2004. (Quarterly Review of the Ramana Maharshi Foundation UK.) ISSN 1357 0935.

270. Shining in Plain View, John Wheeler, Non-Duality Press, 2005. ISBN 0-9547792-6-6.

271. A Practical Guide to Know Yourself: Conversations with Sri Ramana Maharshi, A. R. Natarajan, Ramana Maharshi Centre for Learning, 1995. ISBN 81-85378-09-6.

272. Post to the OpenAwareness Email Group, Monica Alderton, October 2005.

273. Bhagavad-Gita: The Song of God, translated by Swami Prabhavananda and Christopher Isherwood, with an introduction by Aldous Huxely, Signet Classics, 2002. ISBN 0451528441. Introduction electronically available from http://members.tripod.com/~parvati/perennial.html.

274. A Primer on Advaita, Francis Lucille. Electronically Available from http://www.francislucille.com/.

275. Hans Laurentius, Amigo Nov 2001. Electronically Available from http://www.ods.nl/am1gos.

276. Post to the Advaitin Email Group, Chittaranjan Naik, October 2005.

277. From a talk at Amrutlaya, Ranjit Maharaj. Electronically available from http://www.sadguru.com/index.html.

278. Maharshi's Gospel: The Teachings of Sri Ramana Maharshi, T. N. Venkataraman, Sri Ramanasramam, 1979. Extract recorded in Ref. 17.

279. Justus Kramer Schipper, Costa Rica, May 2002, Amigo 4, Oct 2002. Electronically available from http://www.ods.nl/am1gos.

280. Anthony De Mello, quotation posted to NDHighlights Email Group, July 2005.

281. The Siddhantabindu of Madhusudan Saraswati, translated by K.N. Subramanian, Rishi Publications, Varanasi.

282. Choice Upanishads, A. Parthasarathy, A. Parthasarathy, 2001. No ISBN.

283. Dissolving versus Seeker, Kyle Hoobin. Downloaded from http://www.kylehoobin.com/ (but no longer available at time of

writing).

284. Interview, Reprinted from The Inner Directions Journal, (Spring / Summer 2004), Copyright 200? by Karl Renz. All rights reserved. Reprinted by arrangement with Inner Directions, Carlsbad, California. www.InnerDirections.org. Electronically available from http://www.karlrenz.com/english/index.html.

285. The Message of the Upanishads, Swami Ranganathananda, Bharatiya Vidya Bhavan, 1968. No ISBN.

286. Ten Upanishads of Four Vedas, Researched and Edited by Ram K. Piparaiya, Bharatiya Vidya Bhavan, 2003. ISBN 81-7276-298-4.

287. The Principal Upanishads, S. Radhakrishnan, HarperCollins Publishers India, 1994. ISBN 81-7223-124-5.

288. Discourse, Swami Venkatesananda, The Divine Life Society. Downloaded from http://www.sivanandadlshq.org/discourse/dec98.htm.

289. Post to Direct Approach EGroup, Dr. Gregory Goode, Sept 2002.

290. Spiritual Instruction of Bhagavan Sri Ramana Maharshi, Sri Ramanasramamam, 1974. Electronically available from http://www.prahlad.org/gallery/spiritual_instruction_of_ramana.htm.

291. Dreaming, sleep and awakening, (Mandukya Upanishad - stanzas 3-7), Ananda Wood. Electronically Available from www.advaita.org.uk.

292. The Magic Jewel of Intuition (The Tri-Basic Method of Cognizing the Self), D. B. Gangolli, Adhyatma Prakasha Karyalaya, 1986. No ISBN.

293. The Experiential Dimension of Advaita Vedanta, Arvind Sharma, Motilal Banarsidass, 1993. ISBN 81-208-1058-9.

294. Erase the Ego, Swami Rajeswarananda (compiler), Bharatiya Vidya Bhavan, 1974.

295. The Upanishads, Eknath Easwaran, Penguin Books, 1965. ISBN 0-14-019180-1.

296. mANDUkyopaniShad, swami sharvAnanada, Sri Ramakrishna Math, 1982. No ISBN.

297. Ellam Ondre (All is One), Anon. Electronically available at several sites, including http://www.cosmicharmony.com/EllamOndre/EllamOndre.htm.

298. Srimad Bhagavata: The Holy Book of God, Swami Tapasyananda (Translator), Sri Ramakrishna Math.

299. Contribution of Bharati Tirtha and Vidyaranya to Development of Advaitic Thought, M.K. Venkatarama Iyer, 1976. Electronically available from http://www.srisharada.com/Vedanta1.html.

300. Kaushitaki-Brhamana Upanishad, Dr. A. G. Krishna Warrier, The Theosophical Publishing House. Electronically available from http://www.celextel.org/index.htm.

301. I Am Life Itself: the absolute paradox of nothing as everything, Unmani Liza Hyde, Non-Duality Press, 2005. ISBN 0-9547792-9-0. Extract available from http://www.not-knowing.com/book.html.

302. The Three States: Waking, Dream & Sleep, Ramana Maharshi. Extract available from http://www.truthisone.org/docs/insights/three-states.htm.

303. Levels of Mind, Möller de la Rouvière. Posted to NDHighlights Email Group, Aug 2005.

304. Stanley Sobottka interview with Ivan Frimmel. Electronically available from http://harshasatsangh.com/Frimmel.htm.

305. Post to Advaitin EGroup, Chittaranjan Naik, Oct 2005.

306. God in the Upanishads, Ananda Wood. Electronically available from www.advaita.org.uk.

307. Ego death and the sage, Atagrasin. Posted to Advaitin EGroup, Sept 2005.

308. Realization; a surprise!!! Jan Koehoorn, Amigo 1, Sept 2001. Electronically Available from http://www.ods.nl/am1gos.

309. How You Treat Others, copyright ©1998 by Adyashanti. Electronically available from http://www.adyashanti.org/.

310. Why Advaitins say Jagat/World is mithyA, Dr. Harsh K. Luthar (Harsha). Posted to Advaitin EGroup, Dec 2004.

311. The Eye of Spirit: An Integral Vision for a World Gone Slightly Mad, Ken Wilber, Shambhala Publications, Inc., Boston, 1997, www.shambhala.com. ISBN 1-57062-871-8.

312. Passionate Presence: Experiencing the Seven Qualities of Awakened

Awareness, Catherine Ingram, Gotham Books, 2004.
ISBN 1592400493.

313. Perfect Brilliant Stillness, David Carse, Non-Duality Press, 2005.
ISBN 0954779282.

314. Post to Advaitin EGroup, Chittaranjan Naik, Nov 2005.

315. The Middleman, Amigo, Nov 2001 (with permission of the Advaita
Foundation). Electronically Available from http://www.ods.nl/am1gos.

316. ajAtivAda and vivartavAda, Post to Advaitin EGroup, Chittaranjan
Naik, Dec 2004.

317. Knowing the Self, To Being the Self, Ram in dialogue with
Premananda (John David). Downloaded from
http://www.johndavid.org/index.htm.

318. Purnamadah Purnamidam Revisited, Madathil Nair, basis of a
discussion topic on the Advaitin Egroup, April 2004. Electronically
available at www.advaita.org.uk.

319. Responsibility, Justus Kramer Schippers (February 2003, Costa Rica),
Amigo 6, July 2003. Electronically available from
http://www.ods.nl/am1gos.

320. Twenty Questions About "It", From The Way "It" Is, Chuck Hillig,
Black Dot Publications, 2001. ISBN 0964974010.

321. The Real and the Unreal, Chittaranjan Naik, derived from posts to the
Advaitin Egroup 19th Jan. 2004. Electronically available at
www.advaita.org.uk.

322. The Powers of mAyA, Anand Hudli, Edited from a discussion on the
Advaita-L list April 1998. Electronically available from
www.advaita.org.uk.

323. Theories of creation - their place in advaita, Ramakrishnan
Balasubramanian, Post to Advaita-L EGroup, Jun 1998.

324. Commentary On The Vedanta Sutras (Brahmasutra-Bhashya),
Rendition and editing by George Cronk, © 1998. Electronically
available from http://www.bergen.edu/phr/121/ShankaraGC.pdf.

325. Creation - an adhyArOpa on brahman, Bhaskar, Post to Advaitin
EGroup, Nov 2005.

326. The Rope and the Snake: A Metaphorical Exploration of Advaita Vedanta, Arvind Sharma, Manohar, 1997. ISBN 81-7304-179-2.

327. What is the nature of maya?, Professor V. Krishnamurthy, from a discussion on the Advaitin Egroup Dec. 2003. Electronically available from www.advaita.org.uk.

328. From Self to Self: Notes and Quotes in Response to Awakening to the Dream, Non-Duality Press, 2005. ISBN 0954779274.

329. mAyA - illusion - unreal, Professor Gummaluru Murthy, Post to Advaita-L List Nov 1998.

330. Solipsism, Michael Reidy, Post to Advaitin EGroup, Nov 2005.

331. Truth, Appearance and Reality, Ram Chandran, posted to the Advaitin Egroup in Dec 2003. Electronically available at www.advaita.org.uk.

332. Vyavaharika and Paramarthika, Professor V. Krishnamurthy, Post to Advaitin EGroup, August 2005.

333. Paul Tillich, "Theology and Symbolism", in Religious Symbolism, ed. F. Ernest Johnson, Harper and Row, 1955.

334. Consciousness Speaks: Conversations with Ramesh S. Balsekar, Edited by Wayne Liquorman, Advaita Press, 1992. ISBN 0-929448-14-6.

335. Shankara on the Creation (A Shankara Source Book Vol. 2), Compiled and Translated by A. J. Alston, Shanti Sadan, 2004. ISBN 0-85424-056-X www.shantisadan.org.

336. Eight upaniShad-s with the Commentary of shaMkarAchArya, Volume 1, translated by swAmI gambhIrAnanda, Advaita Ashrama, 1957. ISBN 81-7505-016-0.

337. Creation Theories in Advaita Vedanta, Vidyasankar Sundaresan. Electronically available from http://www.advaita-vedanta.org/avhp/creation.html.

338. Private Email communication, Nathan Gill, Feb 2006.

339. Kiss the Sun and Swallow the Mountain, Ken Wilber, Self Enquiry, December 2000, Vol. 8 No. 3. (Quarterly Review of the Ramana Maharshi Foundation UK.). ISSN 1357 0935. Reprinted from the Foreword to Talks With Ramana Maharshi: On Realizing Abiding

Peace and Happiness, Inner Directions Foundation, 2000, ISBN 1878019007.

340. Vivekachudamani by Adi Sankaracharya, Compiled and edited by Jay Mazo, International Gita Society. Electronically available from http://www.gita-society.com/section3/VIVEKACHUDAMANI.htm.

341. dRRiShTi-sRRiShTi, Sri R. Visvanatha Sastri, translated by Professor V. Krishnamurthy. Electronically available from http://www.geocities.com/profvk/Appa/dRSTisRSTiHpage1.html.

342. Post to Advaitin Egroup, Dennis Waite, June 2005.

343. Discourse on Isavasya Upanishad, Swami Chinmayananda, Central Chinmaya Mission Trust, 1980. No ISBN.

344. Studies in the Upanishads, Govindagopal Mukhopadhyaya, Pilgrims Book Pvt. Ltd., 1999. ISBN 81-7624-068-0.

345. Consciousness and the Absolute: The final talks of Sri Nisargadatta Maharaj, Edited by Jean Dunn, The Acorn Press, 1994. ISBN 0-89386-041-7.

346. Living Reality: My Extraordinary Summer with "Sailor" Bob Adamson, James Braha, Hermetician Press, 2006. ISBN 0935895-10-8.

347. Belief and Faith, Ananda Wood, private email, February 2006.

348. Neo-Vedanta and Modernity, Bithika Mukerji, Internet Edition electronically available from http://www.anandamayi.org/books/Bithika2.htm.

349. What is Neo-Advaita?, James Swartz, Electronically available from http://www.shiningworld.com.

350. Ask the Awakened: the Negative Way, Wei Wu Wei, Sentient Publications, 2002. ISBN 0971078645.

351. Svetasvatara Upanishad, Translated by Swami Tyagisananda, Sri Ramakrishna Math, Chennai. Electronically available from http://www.celextel.org/108upanishads/svetasvatara.html.

352. pUrNamadaH pUrNamidam, Swami Dayananda, Sri Gangadhareshwar Trust, 1988. No ISBN.

353. Women of Wisdom: The Journey of the Sacred Feminine through the

Ages, Paula Marvelly, Watkins Publishing, 2005.
ISBN 1 84293 139 3.

354. Teaching Methods, Private Correspondence, James Swartz, March 2006.

355. Witness Teachings, Dr. Gregory Goode, Private Correspondence, March 2006.

356. Private Correspondence, Jan Kersschot, March 2006.

357. The Living Gita: A Commentary for Modern Readers, Sri Swami Satchidananda, Integral Yoga Publications, 1988.
ISBN 0-932040-27-6.

358. The Bhagavad Gita: A Transcreation of The Song Celestial, Alan Jacobs, O Books, 2003. ISBN 1 903816 51 3.

359. The Book: On the Taboo Against Knowing Who You Are, Alan Watts, Vintage Books, 1966. ISBN 0-679-72300-5.

360. Atma Darshan: At the Ultimate, Sri Atmananda, Advaita Publishers, 1983. ISBN 0-914793-16-0.

361. Atma Nirvriti: Freedom and Felicity in the Self, Sri Atmananda, Advaita Publishers, 1983. ISBN 0-914793-05-5.

362. The Collected Works of Ramana Maharshi, edited by Arthur Osborne, Weiser Books, 1997. ISBN 0877289077.

363. Introduction to Vedanta: Understanding the Fundamental Problem, Swami Dayananda, Vision Books, 1989. ISBN 81-7094-037-0.

364. The TM Technique: An Introduction to Transcendental Meditation and the Teaching Method of Maharishi Mahesh Yogi, Peter Russell, Routledge & Kegan Paul, 1976. ISBN 0 7100 0068 5.

365. Tat Tvam Asi (That Thou Art), Raphael, Aurea Vidya Foundation, 1977. ISBN 1-931406-02-2.

366. The Wisdom of Balsekar, Edited by Alan Jacobs, Watkins Publishing, 2004. ISBN 1 84293 079 6.

367. Simply This, Liz Jones, Simply This Publishing, 2005.
ISBN 0-9549428-0-9.

368. Private Correspondence, Tony Parsons, 1st March 2006.

369. Private Correspondence, Tony Parsons, 17th March 2006.

370. Private Correspondence, Dr. Gregory Goode, 21st March 2006.

371. Private Correspondence, Dr. Kuntimaddi Sadananda, 22nd March 2006.

372. Atmabodha (Self Knowledge), Translated and commentary by Raphael, Aurea Vidya Foundation, Inc. 2003. ISBN 1-931406-06-5.

373. The Mandukya Upanishad: An Exposition, Swami Krishnananda, The Divine Life Trust Society, 1981. ISBN 81-7052-100-9.

374. Noticing What you Already Know (And That You Already Know It), Robin Dale, Wyrd Publications, 2006. ISBN 0 7340 3610 8.

375. Private Correspondence, David Carse, 25th March 2006.

376. Post to Advaitin Egroup, July 2006, V. Subrahmanian.

377. Sri Vidyaranya Swami's Panchadasi: A Summary [Chapter by Chapter], S. N. Sastri. Electronically available at http://www.celextel.org/articles/summaryofpanchadasi.html.

378. Vedanta or The Science of Reality, K. A. Krishnaswamy Iyer, Adhyatma Prakasha Karyalaya, 1957. No ISBN.

ACKNOWLEDGEMENTS AND PERMISSIONS

The author would like to thank the following for permission to reproduce material, endorsements and general assistance and support as indicated. Every care has been taken to trace copyright holders. If anyone has been omitted, sincere apologies are offered and corrections will be made to any future edition if the author or publisher is notified. The numbers in brackets after each acknowledgement reference the related publication in the Bibliography. The listing is in alphabetical order of surnames.

Acorn Press (129); Nicole Adams of The Infinity Institute for Compassionate Living (42, 66, 79, 155) for permission to use the extracts of her husband, Robert Adams ("Don't forget the most important thing: Love, Compassion and Humility."); "Sailor" Bob Adamson (9); Advaita Ashrama (1, 12, 26, 27, 34, 35, 85, 88, 124, 191, 225, 227); The Advaita Fellowship (29, 60, 113, 133, 146, 164, 198, 235, 334); Adyashanti (208, 309); Monica Alderton (272) and for her encouragement and useful review comments); Swami Amaleshananda, Ramakrishna Math, Kalady (71); Prem Anjali, Integral Yoga Publications (11, 357); Atagrasin (307); Ramesh S. Balsekar (7, 60, 111, 145, 146, 164, 198); Manju Bazzell, The Gangagi Foundation (131); Bhaskar (325); James Braha (346) and for his kind endorsement; Sundance Burke (211); David Carse (313) and for his kind endorsement; Ram Chandran (161, 331) and for his kind endorsement; Cee (258); Chetana Pvt Ltd. (5, 7); University of Chicago Press (241); Central Chinmaya Mission Trust (6, 18, 33, 75, 81, 122, 156, 213, 230, 343); The Chiltern Yoga Trust (38); Anthony Collins, Shanti Sadan (24, 335); Robin Dale (374); Katie Davis (249) and for her kind endorsement; Tanya Davis (56); Swami Dayananda (31, 58, 90, 112, 186, 256, 264, 352, 363); Professor Eliot Deutsch (82); General Secretary, The Divine Life Society Headquarters (2, 23, 36, 67, 126, 138, 144, 214, 228, 245, 288, 373); Martha

Doherty for obtaining permission from Swami Dayananda; Durga for help during the writing; Jenell Forschler, Shambhala Publications, Inc. (311); Carlo Frua, aurea vidyA Foundation (69, 182, 372); Nathan Gill (25, 338); David Godman (17, 243); Dr. Gregory Goode (53, 57, 226, 289, 355, 370) and for his critical reviews, extensive suggestions and endorsement; Ranva Görner, advaitaMedia (206); Burt Harding (147); Steven Harrison (210, 265); Dr. Harsh K. Luthar (310); Leo Hartong (22, 239, 328); Hans Heimer (266); Chuck Hillig (320) and for his kind endorsement; Unmani Liza Hyde (301); Catherine Ingram (312); Inner Directions Foundation (157, 284); Alan Jacobs (121, 269, 358, 366) and for his kind endorsement; David Jennings (169); Judy Kennedy, A. P. Watt Ltd. on behalf of Michael B Yeats and Benares Hindu University (74); Jan Kersschot (148, 180, 236, 356); The Jean Klein Foundation (19, 64, 132); Professor V. Krishnamurthy (135, 224, 327, 332, 341); Gina Lake (203) and for her kind endorsement; Brian Lake & Naama Livni (171) and for their kind endorsement; John Lehman for his kind endorsement; Roger Linden (237); Michael Lommel, Krishnamurti Foundation of America (97); Francis Lucille (8, 59, 72, 274); Stig Lundgren (105) and for his help with the lineage of Swami Satchidanandendra; Paula Marvelly (78, 353) and for her support and encouragement throughout the writing... and for the wonderful foreword; Mark McCloskey (251); Philip Mistlberger (134) and for his kind endorsement; Professor Gummuluru Murthy (68, 329); Chittaranjan Naik (106, 188, 259, 276, 305, 314, 316, 321); Madathil Nair (318) and for his feedback on the Coda; Shawn Nevins (233); Nirmala (254) and for his kind endorsement; Tony Parsons (47, 55, 63, 238, 368, 369) and for his assistance in ensuring that the neo-Advaitin position is correctly represented in the final chapter; Swami A. Parthasarathy (16, 23, 282); Pilgrims Book Pvt. Ltd. (344); Swami Muni Narayana Prasad (101, 130, 260); Prema of Zen Satsang for help in obtaining permission from Adyashanti; Chritina Prestia, Osho International Foundation (166); Chris Quilkey for obtaining permission from Sri Ramanasramam and for his kind endorsement on behalf of Mountain Path; The Ramana Maharshi Centre for Learning (61, 246, 271); V.S. Ramanan for all of the material published by Sri Ramanasramam (17, 39, 49, 80, 95,

110, 173, 174, 178, 179, 181, 220, 231, 242, 278, 290, 362); Sri Ramakrishna Math, Chennai (43, 50, 52, 104, 193, 296, 298); The Ramakrishna Vedanta Centre, Boston (14); Carol Raphael, What Is Enlightenment? (145); Michael Reidy (330); Karl Renz (157, 284); Ramana Maharshi Foundation for material from the Self-Enquiry journal (41, 42, 59, 63, 66, 79, 115, 184, 232, 238, 252, 266, 268, 269, 339); Möller de la Rouvière (91, 303) and for his kind endorsement; Dr. Kuntimaddi Sadananda (30, 94, 100, 153, 154, 172, 222, 371), for his kind endorsement and for clarification of a number of issues discussed in the book; Ranjeet Sankar (163); S. N. Sastri (377); Nancy Saumya for help in contacting Swami Muni Narayana Prasad; Justus Kramer Schippers (279, 319) and for his kind endorsement; Kees Schreuders for permission to use material from Amigos e-journals and for obtaining permission from the relevant authors (128, 151, 194, 267, 275, 308, 315); Isaac Shapiro (197) and for his kind endorsement; Professor Arvind Sharma (326); Rupert Spira and Raj Thakur for help in obtaining permission from Francis Lucille; Subharam Trust (Regd.) (292); V. Subrahmanian (375); James Swartz (349, 354) and for his kind endorsement; Aja Thomas (93); Madhukar Thompson (185); Joan Tollifson (195); Dr. Nitin Trasi (149) and for his kind endorsement; Velury Krishna, Samata Books (28); Andrew Vernon (20); Dr. Blake Warner and the Infinity Institute for Compassionate Living for obtaining permission for the Robert Adams extracts (42, 66, 79, 155); John Wheeler (70, 270) and for his kind endorsement; Roy Whenary (207) and for his kind endorsement; Stephen Wingate (234); David Winsland for providing a reader's eye view of the material; Ananda Wood (54, 162, 170, 175, 216, 262, 263, 291, 306, 347); and for his kind endorsement. B. Zelikovsky, Ramakrishna-Vivekananda Center of New York Publications (120, 136).

GLOSSARY OF SANSKRIT TERMS

Each word is presented in the following format:

Typical English Spelling (*ITRANS representation*, Devanagari Script) – meaning.

Words appear in order of the English (Roman) alphabet, not the Sanskrit alphabet.

(This section is considerably expanded from the Dictionary contained in Ref. 114.)

a (*a*, अ) – as a prefix to another word, it changes it into the negative. E.g. vidya – knowledge, avidya – ignorance.

abhava (*abhAva*, अभाव) – non-existence, absence. See anupalabdhi.

abhyAsa (*abhyAsa*, अभ्यास) – exercise, discipline; in Raja Yoga, this refers to "the effort of the mind to remain in its unmodified condition of purity (*sattva*)." Ramana Maharshi sometimes refers to a spiritual aspirant as an *abhyAsI* – i.e. one who practices.

acharya (*AchArya*, आचार्य) – a spiritual guide or teacher. See Shankaracharya.

achintya (*achintya*, अचिन्त्य) – inconceivable or beyond thought.

adhama (*adhama*, अधम) – lowest, vilest, worst.

adhibhautika (*adhibhautika*, अधिभौतिक) – (resulting) from such things as wars, disagreements, natural disasters. *adhi* means from, from the presence; *bhautika* means anything elemental or material.

adhidaivika (*adhidaivika*, अधिदैविक) – (resulting) from the presence of divine or supernatural forces. *adhi* means from, from the presence; *daivika* is the adjective from *deva* (god) meaning coming from the gods, divine.

adhikari (*adhikArin* or *adhikArI*, अधिकारिन् or अधिकारी) – a seeker who is mentally prepared (see *chatuShTaya sampatti*) and therefore ready to receive the final teaching from the guru; literally "possessing authority, entitled to, fit for."

adhisthana (*adhiShThAna,* अधिष्ठान) – substratum; literally basis, support, that upon which something rests.

adhyaropa (*adhyAropa,* अध्यारोप) – erroneously attributing one thing to another.

(*adhyAropa-apavAda,* अध्यारोप अपवाद) – One of the principal methods of teaching Advaita, whereby an attribute is applied to brahman initially (and erroneously – hence *adhyAropa*) but is later taken back, once the point has been understood. *apavAda* means denial or contradiction. An example would be the teaching of the *kosha*-s.

adhyasa (*adhyAsa,* अध्यास) – used to refer to the "mistake" that we make when we "superimpose" a false appearance upon the reality or mix up the real and the unreal. The classical example is when we see a snake instead of a rope, which is used as a metaphor for seeing the world of objects instead of the reality of the Self. This concept is fundamental to Advaita and Shankara devotes a separate section to it at the beginning of his commentary on the Brahmasutra.

adhyaya (*adhyAya,* अध्याय) – lesson, lecture or chapter.

adhyatmika (*adhyAtmika,* अध्यात्मिक) – resulting from self, i.e. problems such as pain and mental suffering. *adhi* means from, from the presence; *Atmika* means relating to self.

Advaita (*advaita,* अद्वैत) – not (*a*) two (*dvaita*); non-dual philosophy. (Adjective – *advitIya* – unique, without a second.)

agama (*Agama,* आगम) – acquisition of knowledge, science; traditional doctrine; anything handed down and fixed by tradition.

agamin (*AgAmin,* आगामिन्) - That type of sanskara which is generated in reaction to current situations and which will not bear fruit until sometime in the future. It literally means "impending," "approaching" or "coming." Also called *kriyamANa*, which means "being done." See prarabdha, sanchita, sanskara.

agocara (*agochara,* अगोचर) – (literally) imperceptible by the senses but treated as anything that is unavailable to any *pramANa* other than *shabda* (i.e. scriptures).

aham (*aham*, अहम्) – I am.

aham vritti (*aham vRRitti*, अहम् वृत्ति) – the thought "I am" as opposed to thoughts about objects, feelings etc. – idam vritti. See vritti.

ahankara (*ahaMkAra*, अहंकार) - the making, kara (*kAra*), of the utterance "I," aham (*aham*) – this is the equivalent of what we would call the "ego" but specifically refers to the identification or attachment of our true Self with something else, usually the body or mind but can be much more specific e.g. I am a teacher, I am a woman. It is one of the "organs" of the mind in classical Advaita – see antakarana.

ahimsa (*ahiMsA*, अहिंस) – not injuring anything (one of the yama-s).

aikya (*aikya*, ऐक्य) – unity, oneness; in Advaita specifically the identity of *Atman* and *brahman*.

ajati (*ajAti*, अजाति) - *a* – no or not; *jAti* – creation; the principle that the world and everything in it, including these mind-body appearances were never created or 'brought into existence'. Most clearly stated by Gaudapada in his karika on the Mandukya Upanishad. *jAta* is the adjective, meaning born, brought into existence. The theory that there has never been any creation is called either *ajAta vAda* or *ajAti vAda*.

ajnana (*aj~nAna*, अज्ञान) – (spiritual) ignorance. See jnana. An *aj~nAnI* is one who is not enlightened, i.e. still (spiritually) ignorant.

akasha (*AkAsha*, आकाश) – space, ether or sky; one of the five elements in the Upanishads, the subtle fluid supposed to pervade the universe. Associated with sound and hearing.

akhaNDAkAra vRRitti (अखण्डाकार वृत्ति) – the mental 'occurrence' which effectively causes enlightenment. This is the vRRitti (thought) in the form of (AkAra) the formless or undivided (akhaNDa).

akshara (*akShara*, अक्षर) – imperishable, unchangeable.

alAtashAnti (*alAtashAnti*, अलातशान्ति) – the fourth topic in *gauDapAda*'s *kArikA* on the *mANDUkya upaniShad* – "On the Quenching of the firebrand." *alAta* is a firebrand or coal; *shAnti* is "peace."

alpaprana (*alpaprANa*, अल्पप्राण) – In Sanskrit, describes a consonant that is sounded without any additional expelling of air. It means "with little breath." Specifically, it is used for those consonants on the 1st and 3rd rows of the main groups, namely *k*, *ch*, *T*, *t*, *p* and *g*, *j*, *D*, *d*, *b*.

amsha (*aMsha*, अंश) – part or portion.

amurta (*amUrta*, अमूर्त) – unmanifest, formless, shapeless.

anadi (*anAdi*, अनादि) – without any beginning, often used to refer to 'ignorance'.

ananda (*Ananda*, आनन्द) – "true" happiness; usually called "bliss" to differentiate it from the transient variety that always alternates with pain or misery. It is an aspect of our true nature and is often combined with the other elements of our real nature – sat and chit – into a single word, satchidananda. See sat, chit and satchidananda.

anandamayakosha (*Anandamayakosha*, आनन्दमयकोश) – the sheath made of bliss (one of the "five Coverings" that surround our true essence).

ananta (*ananta*, अनन्त) – eternal, without end.

anatman (*anAtman*, अनात्मन्) – something other than spirit or soul (not Self or atman); perceptible world. See atman.

anichchA (*anichChA*, अनिच्छा) – without desire. See prArabdha.

anirvachaniya (*anirvachanIya*, अनिर्वचनीय) – not able to be categorized; literally: unutterable, indescribable, not to be mentioned. Used to describe nature of reality etc.

anitya (*anitya*, अनित्य) – transient. Also **anityatva** (*anityatva*, अनित्यत्व) – transient or limited existence (mortality).

Annamayakosha (*annamayakosha*, अन्नमयकोश) – the sheath made of food, *anna*. (One of the "five Coverings" that surround our true essence).

anta (*anta*, अन्त) – end, conclusion, death etc.

antakarana (*antaHkaraNa*, अन्तःकरण) – used to refer to the overall "organ" of mind; the seat of thought and feeling. It derives from *antar* – within, interior – and *karaNa*, which means "instrument" or sense-organ (an alternative for indriya). It consists of a number of separate functions – see manas, buddhi, chitta and ahankara.

antaranga (*antara~Nga*, अन्तरङ्ग) – essential to, internal, interior as opposed to *bahira~Nga*, external or worldly (in relation to spiritual displines).

antaryamin (*antaryAmin*, अन्तर्यामिन्) – the soul, "internal ruler."

antasta (*antaHsthA*, अन्तःस्था) - The Sanskrit term for the "semi-vowels": *y*, *r*, *l*, *v*. These are formed by combination of *i*, *RRi*, *LLi* and *u*, respectively with the vowel *a*. The word literally means "stand between."

anubhava (*anubhAva*, अनुभाव) – perception, understanding, experience; knowledge derived from personal observation. Intuition as (opposed to reasoning – *yukti*).

anubhuti (*anubhUti*, अनुभूति) – knowledge gained by means of the *pramANa*-s.

anugraha (*anugraha*, अनुग्रह) – grace; literally showing favor or kindness, conferring benefits.

anumana (*anumAna*, अनुमान) – inference (in logic); one of the 6 means of obtaining knowledge. See pramana.

anunasika (*anunAsika*, अनुनासिक) – in Sanskrit, sounded through the nose, nasal.

anupalabdhi (*anupalabdhi*, अनुपलब्धि) – non-perception, non-recognition; one of the 6 means of obtaining knowledge. See pramana.

anusvara (*anusvAra*, अनुस्वार) – This literally means "after sound." It is represented as *aM* but is not actually a letter and does not occur on its own. It changes the sound of a letter, causing the associated vowel to be sounded through the nose. In ITRANS, it is represented by *M* or *.n* and in Romanised transliteration by a dot, above or below the preceding consonant. The precise nature of the sound is determined by the consonant that follows. It will take on the sound of the *anunAsika* in the same group as this consonant. e.g. in *saMdhi*, the sound will be that of *n* while in *shaMkara*, it will be that of *~N*.

anvaya-vyatireka (*anvaya-vyatireka*, अन्वय व्यतिरेक) – a method in logic for determining the truth of something. For example, is the clay or the pot real? *anvaya* establishes the logical connection that "when the pot **is**, the clay **is**." *vyatireka* establishes the logical discontinuity that "when the pot **is not**, the clay **is**." Therefore the clay is *satya*, the pot is *mithyA*. *anvaya* means "connection, association"; *vyatireka* means "distinction, separateness, exclusion."

anyonya ashyraya (*anyonya Ashraya*, अन्योन्य आश्रय) – mutual dependence in a "cause-effect" situation such as the chicken and egg example.

ap (*ap*, अप्) – water – one of the five elements or *pa~nchabhUta*. Associated with taste.

apana (*apAna*, अपान) – one of the five "vital airs," relating to excretion. More generally refers to rejection of irrelevant material gained from perception etc. and to the formation of limited views.

aparigraha (*aparigraha*, अपरिग्रह) – renouncing of all possessions. One of the five *yama*-s in Raja yoga.

aparoksha (*apArokSha*, अपारोक्ष) – immediate (relating to gaining of knowledge, i.e. does not require application of reason).

aparokshanubhuti (*apArokShAnubhUti*, अपारोक्षानुभूति) – one of the works attributed to Shankara. The word means "knowledge acquired directly by one of the valid *pramANa*-s."

apaurusheya (*apauruSheya*, अपौरुषेय) - literally "not coming from men"; used to refer to the shruti – scriptural texts passed on verbatim from generation to generation since their original observation by realised sages. See shruti.

apta-vakya (*Apta vAkya*, आप्त वाक्य) – something reported by another in whom one has faith. Literally "a correct sentence." *Apta* means "respected, trustworthy"; *vAkya* means "statement, declaration."

arambha (*Arambha*, आरम्भ) – literally "beginning, commencement" but encountered in the context of a material cause in which the effect is clearly distinguishable from its cause but has not actually been transformed, e.g. cloth made from cotton as opposed to butter made from milk.

arambha vada (*Arambha vAda*, आरम्भ वाद) - the theory that the world (i.e. universe) is the result of the coming together of atoms.

arankyaka (*Aranyaka*, आरन्यक) – a class of religious or philosophical writings closely connected with the *brAhmaNa*-s and so-called because they were written or studied in the forest.

artha (*artha*, अर्थ) - acquisition of wealth. One of the four *puruShArtha*-s. See purushartha.

arthapatti (*arthApatti*, अर्थापत्ति) – inference from circumstances, presumption; one of the 6 means of obtaining knowledge. See pramana.

asana (*Asana*, आसन) – sitting in special (and peculiar) postures for long periods supposedly in order to gain spiritual benefit. One of the eight steps of Raja yoga.

asat (*asat*, असत्) - non-existent. See sat.

asatkarya vada (*asatkArya vAda*, असत्कार्य वाद) – the doctrine which denies that the effect pre-exists in the cause (usually in reference to the creation).

asha (*AshA*, आशा) – wish, desire, hope, expectation; aspiration.

ashrama (*Ashrama*, आश्रम) – generic term for one of the the four "stages" in the life of a Hindu brahmin, viz. *brahmacharya, gRRihastha, vanaprastha, saMnyAsa*.

ashtanga (*aShTA~Nga*, अष्टाङ्ग) – consisting of eight parts, as in the *aShTA~Nga* yoga of Patanjali.

asparsha (*asparsha*, अस्पर्श) – intangible, touchless; name given to the "contentless" yoga of Gaudapada in the Mandukya Upanishad.

Astavakra (*aShTAvakra*, अष्टावक्र) – the eponymous Sage of the Astavakra Gita (or Samhita). The word literally means "twisted" (*vakra*) in "eight" (*aShTan*) ways. Astavakra was so called because he was born severely deformed after being cursed in the womb by his father (because the unborn child had criticised him for making mistakes whilst reading the scriptures!). (Later in life, after he had secured his father's release through defeating the court philosopher in debate, his father blessed him and, after swimming in a sacred river, was cured.) See gita, samhita.

asteya (*asteya*, अस्तेय) – not stealing. One of the five *yama*-s in Raja yoga.

astika (*Astika*, आस्तिक) – literally "there is or exists"; used to refer to one who believes in the existence of God or, more specifically, one who defers to the authority of the Vedas. See nastika, veda.

asura (*asura*, असुर) – demon, spirit, opponent of the gods.

atah (*ataH*, अतः) – hence, therefore.

atha (*atha*, अथ) – now, then therefore; often used to express the sense of an auspicious beginning e.g. to reading a key verse of scripture.

atma (*Atma*, आत्म) – see atman.

atmabodha (*Atmabodha*, आत्मबोध) – knowledge of Self or supreme spirit; a book attributed to Shankara.

atman (*Atman*, आत्मन्) – the Self. Usually used to refer to one's true (individual) nature or consciousness but Advaita tells us that there is no such thing as an 'individual' and that this atman is the same as the universal Consciousness, Brahman. see also jiva.

atmavicara (*AtmavichAra*, आत्मविचार) – *vicAra* in this context means reflection or examination upon the *Atman*, the Self. See atman.

atmiya (*AtmIya*, आत्मीय) – subjective; literally "one's own."

Atmopanishad (*AtmopaniShad*, आत्मोपनिषद्) – one of the minor Upanishads.

avacheda-vada (*avachCheda-vAda*, अवच्छेद् वाद) – theory that the Self is limited by ignorance in the forms of *upAdhi*-s. *avachCheda* literally means "cut-off." See upadhi.

avantara (*avAntara*, अवान्तर) – intermediate.

avarana (*AvaraNa*, आवरण) – the veiling power of maya. In the rope-snake metaphor, this power prevents us from seeing the reality of the rope. See maya, vikshepa.

avastha (*avasthA*, अवस्था) – state; literally "to stay, abide, exist, remain or continue doing (anything)." In Advaita, it is most frequently encountered as avasthA traya – the three states of waking, dreaming and deep sleep.

avidya (*avidyA*, अविद्या) – ignorance (in a spiritual sense) i.e. that which prevents us from realising the Self. See also maya.

avrita (*AvRRita*, आवृत्) – covered or concealed.

avyakta (*avyakta*, अव्यक्त) – unmanifest, imperceptible, invisible; the universal spirit (paramAtman).

badha (*bAdha*, बाध) – sublation or subration. This is the process by which an accepted point of view or understanding is superseded by a totally different one when some new information is received. An example is seeing a lake in the desert and then realising that it is only a mirage. The adjective is *bAdhita*, meaning negated, contradictory, absurd, false.

bahiranga (*bahira~Nga*, बहिरङ्ग) – exterior, external, worldly as opposed to inner ग्यानतारॉन्गा), (in relation to spiritual disciplines).

bala (*bala*, बल) – strength (of mind), power.

bandha or bandhana (*bandha* or *bandhana*, बन्ध or बन्धन) – bondage, attachment to the world.

(*bhAga tyAga lakShaNa*, भाग त्याग लक्षण) – a technique used by the scriptures to point to aspects that cannot be explained directly in words. The oneness that is pointed to (*lakShaNa*) is understood by "giving up" (*tyAga*) the contradictory parts (*bhAga*). An example would be in the apparent contradiction of the *jIva* being "created" while *Ishvara* is the "creator." Both are given up in order to recognize their identity as *brahman*.

Bhagavad (*bhagavat*, भगवत्) – holy; prosperous, happy; illustrious, divine. In the context of Bhagavad Gita, it refers to the God, Krishna and Bhagavad Gita means Krishna's Song (the *t* changes to a *d* when the words join). See below.

Bhagavad Gita (*bhagavadgItA*, भगवद्गीता) – the scriptural text forming part of the Hindu epic, the Mahabarata. It is a dialogue between Krishna, the charioteer/God, representing the Self and the warrior Arjuna, representing you and me, on the battlefield of Kurukshetra prior to the commencement of battle. The scripture is regarded as smriti. See Bhagavad, smriti.

bhaj (*bhaj*, भज्) – to pursue, practice, cultivate or seek. (As in the work attributed to Shankara – *bhaja govindam*, "Practice, Govinda.")

bhakta (*bhakta*, भक्त) – one who practices bhakti yoga. See bhakti yoga.

bhakti (*bhakti*, भक्ति) **yoga** – devotion or worship as a means to enlightenment. See also karma and jnana.

bhamiti (*bhAmatI*, भामती) – literally "lustrous"; name of one of the two schools of Advaita, also called the *vAchaspati* school, after the philosopher *vAchaspati mishra*. The other school is the *vivaraNa* school.

Bhartihari (*bhartRRihari*, भर्तृहरि) – poet and grammarian in 7th century AD, composer of *vAkyapadIya*.

bhashya (*bhAShya*, भाष्य) – explanatory work, exposition or commentary on some other scriptural document. Thus Shankara, for example, has written bhashyas on a number of Upanishads, the Bhagavad Gita and the Brahmasutra.

bhasyakara (*bhASyakAra*, भाष्यकार) – various commentators (on a philosophy).

bhava (*bhAva*, भाव) – condition or state of body or mind.

bhavana (*bhAvana*, भावन) – reflection, contemplation.

bhoktri (*bhoktRRi*, भोक्तृ) – one who enjoys, an experiencer or feeler.

bhrama (*bhrama*, भ्रम) – confusion, perplexity, mistake (N.B. Not to be confused with brahma or brahman!).

Bhuma (*bhUmA*, भूमा) – the supreme reality, Brahman (used in the Chandogya Upanishad); literally the aggregate of all existing things (plural). bhUman, the singular noun, means abundance, plenty, wealth.

bodha (*bodha*, बोध) – knowing, understanding.

Brahma (*brahma*, ब्रह्म) – God as the creator of the universe in Hindu mythology (the others are Vishnu, *viShNu*, the preserver and Shiva, *shiva*, the destroyer). N.B. Not to be confused with Brahman!

brahmacharya (*brahmacharya*, ब्रह्मचर्य) – the first stage of the traditional Hindu spiritual path, in which the Brahman begins his life as an unmarried, religious and chaste student. (*charya* means 'due observance of all rites and customs'.) One of the five *yama*-s in Raja yoga. See also grihasta, sanyasa, vanaprastha.

Brahman (*brahman*, ब्रह्मन्) – the universal Self, Absolute or God. There is only Brahman. It derives from the Sanskrit root *bRRih*, meaning to grow great or strong and could be thought of as the adjective 'big' made into a noun, implying that which is greater than anything. See also atman, Brahma, jiva, jivatman, paramatman.

brahmana (*brAhmaNa*, ब्राह्मण) – an aspirant; a member of the first of the traditional four castes in India (also called Brahmin); alternatively a portion of the Vedas, containing information relating to the use of mantras and hymns in sacrifices.

brahmanishta (*brahmaniShTha*, ब्रह्मनिष्ठ) – one who is absorbed in contemplating brahman and committed only to that purpose. *niShTha* means "devoted to."

Brahma Sutra (*brahmasUtra*, ब्रह्मसूत्र) – a book (in sutra form, which is terse verse!) by Vyasa. This book is the best known of the third accepted source of knowledge (nyaya prasthana). Effectively, it attempts to summarise the Upanishads. It has been extensively commented on by the three main philosophical branches of Indian thought, dvaita, advaita and vishishtadvaita, and the proponents of each claim that it substantiates their beliefs. Shankara has commented on it and provided extensive arguments against any interpretation other than that of Advaita. See bhashya, nyaya prasthana, sruti, smriti.

brahmavidya (*brahmavidyA*, ब्रह्मविद्या) – knowledge of the one Self. (Also *brahmavitva*, with someone with this knowledge being called a *brahmavit*.) See brahman.

Brihadaranyaka (*bRRihadAraNyaka*, बृहदारण्यक) – one of the major Upanishads (and possibly the oldest). The word derives from *bRRihat* – great, large, wide, tall etc. and *Aranyaka* – produced in (or relating to) a forest. See Upanishad.

buddhi (*buddhi*, बुद्धि) – the organ of mind responsible for discrimination and judgement, perhaps nearest equated to the intellect in Western usage. See also, ahankara, antakarana, manas and chitta.

chakra (*chakra*, चक्र) – literally "circle" or "wheel"; one of the points in the spine through which energy is supposed to flow in kundalini yoga.

Chandogya (*chhAndogya*, छान्दोग्य) - one of the major Upanishads. See Upanishad.

chatushtaya sampatti (*chatuShTaya sampatti*, चतुष्टय सम्पत्ति) – the fourfold pre-requisites specified by Shankara as needed by a seeker before he can achieve Self-realisation. *chatuShTaya* means "fourfold"; *sampatti* means success or accomplishment. See sadhana, vairagya, viveka, mumukshutvam.

chetana (*chetana*, चेतन) – consciousness, intelligence etc.

chidabhasa (*chidAbhAsa*, चिदाभास) – false appearance or reflection (*AbhAsa*) of consciousness (*chit*) - i.e. the ego.

chit (*chit*, चित्) – pure thought or Consciousness. See ananda, sat, satchidananda.

chitta (*chitta,* चित्त) – the organ (part) of mind responsible for memory. See antakarana, ahankara, buddhi, manas.

chodya (*chodya,* चोद्य) – goal motivated, impelled or incited.

dama (*dama,* दम) – self-restraint but understood as control over the senses; one of the six qualities that form part of Shankara's chatushtaya sampatti. See chatushtaya sampatti, *shamAdi shhaTka sampatti.*

darshana (*darshana,* दर्शन) – audience or meeting (with a guru); viewpoint; one of the six classical Indian philosophical systems (purvamimamsa, uttaramimamsa, nyaya, vaisheshika, samkhya, yoga).

dehatmavada (*dehAtmavAda,* देहात्मवाद) – materialism.

deha (*deha,* देह) – person, individual, outward form or appearance (body).

deva (*deva,* देव) – (pl. noun) the gods; (adj.) heavenly, divine.

Devanagari (*devanAgarI,* देवनागरी) – the script used in Sanskrit representation. The word literally means "city of the Gods" (deva – gods; nAgara – belonging or relating to a town or city).

devadatta (*devadatta,* देवदत्त) – fellow, common noun for "man" used in philosophy; literally "god-given."

dharana (*dhAraNA,* धारणा) - concentration of the mind. The sixth step of Raja yoga.

dharma (*dharma,* धर्म) - customary practice, conduct, duty, justice and morality. One of the four *puruShArtha*-s. The favored meaning of most traditional teachers is, however, "nature, character, essential quality," which they often translate as "essence." Our own dharma (*svadharma*) is what we ought to do with our lives in order to dissolve our accumulation of sanskara. See sanskara, karma.

dhyana (*dhyAna,* ध्यान) – meditation, usually in the sense of the mechanical act using a mantra as opposed to *nididhyAsana.*

dipa (*dIpa,* दीप) – a lamp. In the *advaita bodha dIpaka,* it provides the "knowledge of Advaita" through its illumination.

dirgha (*dIrgha,* दीर्घ) – a long vowel in Sanskrit (sounded for 2 *mAtrA-s* or measures); literally long, high, tall.

dravya (*dravya*, द्रव्य) – substance.

drg-drsya-viveka (*dRRigdRRishya viveka*, दग्दृश्य विवेक) – "Discrimination between the Seer and the Seen" – a work attributed to Shankara. *dRRik* is the seer or perceiver and *dRRishya* that which is seen or which can be objectified.

drishtanta (*dRRiShTAnta*, दृष्टान्त) – the end or aim of what is seen, example or instance.

drishti-srishti-vada (*dRRiShTisRRiShTivAda*, दृष्टिसृष्टिवाद) – the theory that our mistaken view of the world arises from a mental image (based on memory and sense data) superimposed upon the reality. *dRRiShTi* means "seeing"; *sRRiShTi* means "creation"; *vAda* means "thesis" or "doctrine." See also adhyasa, ajati, srishti-drishti-vada.

dukha (*duHkha*, दुःख) – pain, sorrow, trouble.

dvaita (*dvaita*, द्वैत) – duality, philosophy of dualism; belief that God and the atman are separate entities. Madhva is the scholar most often associated with this philosophy.

dvesha (*dveSha*, द्वेष) – hatred, dislike.

ekagra (*ekAgra*, एकाग्र) – one-pointed, fixing one's attention on one point. *ekAgratA* – intentness in the pursuit of one object.

Gaudapada (*gauDapAda*, गौडपाद) – The author of the commentary (karika) on the Mandukya Upanishad. He is said to have been the teacher of Shankara's teacher. See karika, Mandukya, Upanishad.

gita (*gIta*, गीत) – a sacred song or poem but more usually refers to philosophical or religious doctrines in verse form (*gIta* means "sung"). The most famous are the Bhagavad Gita and Astavakra Gita. If the word is used on its own, it will be referring to the former. See Bhagavad, Astavakra.

gocara (*gochara*, गोचर) – (literally) perceptible by the senses but also regarded as seen by the mind, inferred etc.

grihasta (*gRRihastha*, गृहस्थ) - this is the second stage of the traditional Hindu spiritual path, called the period of the householder, in which the Brahman performs the duties of master of the house and father of a family. See also brahmacharya, sanyasa, vanaprastha.

guna (*guNa*, गुण) – According to classical Advaita, creation is made up of three "qualities," sattva, rajas and tamas. Everything - matter, thoughts, feelings – is "made up of" these three in varying degrees and it is the relative proportions that determine the nature of the thing in question. See sattwa, rajas and tamas for more details.

guru (*guru*, गुरु) – literally "heavy"; used to refer to one's elders or a person of reverence but more commonly in the West to indicate one's spiritual teacher.

halanta (*halanta*, हलन्त) – a consonant that is not sounded with a vowel after it. It is marked as such by the use of a *virAma*. The term derives from the *pratyAhAra "hal,"* which refers to "any consonant," and *anta*, which means "end," since such consonants normally occur at the end of a word.

hatha (*haTha*, हठ) – *haTha yoga* refers to the physical aspects of Raja yoga, i.e. *Asana*-s and *prANayAma*. It literally means "violence, force or obstinacy," "absolute necessity" and stems from the idea of "forcing the mind" to withdraw from objects. Monier-Williams has the additional words: "performed with much self-torture , such as standing on one leg , holding up the arms , inhaling smoke with the head inverted etc."

hetu (*hetu*, हेतु) – cause or reason; the logical reason or argument in a syllogism.

hrasva (*hrasva*, ह्रस्व) – a short vowel in Sanskrit; literally, short, small, dwarfish, weak etc.

iccha (*ichChA*, इच्छा) – wish, desire, inclination.

idam vritti (*idam vRRitti*, इदम् वृत्ति) – thoughts of objects, concepts, feelings etc., as opposed to aham vritti – the thought "I am." See vritti.

indriya (*indriya*, इन्द्रिय) – the number five symbolizing the five senses. The five sense organs are called j~nAnendriya-s and the five "organs" of action are the karmendriya-s.

Isha Upanishad (*IshopaniShad*, ईशोपनिषद्) – also known as the Isavasya Upanishad, because its first verse begins: OM IshA vAsyamidam{\m+} sarvaM. IshAvAsya means "pervaded by the lord."

ishta (*iShTa*, इष्ट) – wished, desired, liked, beloved.

Isvara (*Ishvara*, ईश्वर) - the Lord; creator of the phenomenal universe.

See saguna Brahman.

jada (*jaDa*, जड) – inert, lifeless.

jagat (*jagat*, जगत्) – the world (earth), mankind etc.

jagrat (*jAgrat*, जाग्रत्) – the waking state of consciousness. The "waker ego" is called visva. See also, sushupti, svapna, turiya.

janma (*janma*, जन्म) – birth.

japa (*japa*, जप) - the simple repetition of a mantra; usually associated with the initial stage of meditation. See mantra.

jati (*jAti*, जाति) – birth, the form of existence (as man, animal etc.); genus or species.

jijnasu (*jij~nAsu*, जिज्ञासु) – one who desires to know oneself; a seeker.

jiva (*jIva*, जीव) - the identification of the atman with a body and mind; sometimes spoken of as "the embodied atman." See atman.

jivanmukta (*jIvanmukta*, जीवन्मुक्त) – someone liberated (in this life) from all future births. I.e. self-realized. (*mukta* is the adjective – liberated; *mukti* is the noun – liberation)

jivatman (*jIvAtman*, जीवात्मन्) - another word for atman, to emphasise that we are referring to the atman in this embodied state, as opposed to the paramatman, the "supreme Self." See atman.

jnana (*j~nAna*, ज्ञान) **yoga** – yoga based on the acquisition of true knowledge (j~nAna means "knowledge") i.e. knowledge of the Self as opposed to mere information about the world of appearances. See also bhakti, karma.

jnana kanda (j~nAna kANDa, ज्ञान काण्ड) – those sections of the Vedas concerned with knowledge, i.e. the Upanishads.

jnanendriya (*j~nAnendriya*, ज्ञानेन्द्रिय) – an organ of perception (eye, ear, nose, tongue, skin), plural j~nAnendryAni.

jnani or **jnanin** (*j~nAnI* or *j~nAnin*, ज्ञानी or ज्ञानिन्) – one who practises jnana yoga. (*j~nAnin* is the *prAtipadika*; *j~nAnI* is the nominative singular *pada*.) See jnana yoga.

jnatri (*j~nAtRRi*, ज्ञातृ) – a knower.

jneya (*j~neya*, ज्ञेय) – something to be known.

kaivalya (*kaivalya*, कैवल्य) – absolute unity, detachment of the soul from further transmigration, leading to eternal happiness or emancipation.

kali yuga (*kali yuga*, कलि युग)– the present age (Iron age) in the cycle of creation. See kalpa.

kalpa (*kalpa*, कल्प) – one day in the life of Brahma, the Creator; equal to 994 cycles of ages and 4,320,000,000 years (if you're really interested).

kama (*kAma*, काम) – desire, longing; one of the four puruShArtha-s. Not to be confused with karma. Shankara differentiates this from *rAga*: *rAga* is attachment to something one already has whereas *kAma* is wanting something one doesn't have. See purushartha.

kanda (*kANDa*, काण्ड) – part or section, division of a work or book, especially relating to the Vedas.

karana (*karaNa*, करण) – "instrument" in the context of *karaNa kAraNa* – instrumental cause. (The first "a" is *hrasva*.)

karana (*kAraNa*, कारण) – cause (noun) as in *nimitta kAraNa* or causal (adj.) as in *kAraNa sharIra*. Literally "a cause (in philosophy i.e. that which is invariably antecedent to some product)." (The first "a" is *dIrgha*.)

karika (*kArikA*, कारिका) – (strictly speaking) a concise philosophical statement in verse. The most well known is that by Gaudapada on the Mandukya Upanishad. (Not to be confused with *karika*, which is an elephant!). See Gaudapada, Mandukya, Upanishad.

karma (*karma*, कर्म) – literally "action" but generally used to refer to the "law" whereby actions carried out now will have their lawful effects in the future (and this may be in future lives). Note that karma yoga is something different – see below. See also sanskara.

karmakanda (*karmakANDa*, कर्मकाण्ड) – that portion of the Vedas relating to ceremonial acts, the rituals we should follow, sacrificial rites and so on.

karmaphala (*karmaphala*, कर्मफल) – the fruit (*phala*) of action; i.e. the result or consequence of our actions.

karma yoga (*karma yoga*, कर्म योग) – the practice of acting in such a way as not to incur karma, by carrying out "right" actions, not "good" or "bad" ones. See bhakti, karma, jnana.

karmendriya (*karmendriya*, कर्मेन्द्रिय) – an organ of action, plural karmendriyAni. These are hand, foot, larynx, organ of generation and organ of excretion.

kartri (*kartRRi*, कर्तृ) – one who makes, does or acts; the agent of an action.

karya (*kArya*, कार्य) – effect or result.

kataka (*kataka*, कतक) – the "clearing nut" plant, used for precipitating dirt from drinking water.

Katha Upanishad (*kaThopaniShad*, कठोपनिषद्) – one of the 108+ Upanishads and one of the 10 major ones. *kaTha* was a sage and founder of a branch of the Yajur Veda. See Upanishad.

Kena Upanishad (*kenopaniShad*, केनोपनिषद्) - one of the 108+ Upanishads and another one of the 10 major ones. *kena* means "whence?" ("how?," "why?" etc.) and is the first word of this Upanishad. See Upanishad.

khalvidam (*khalvidam*, खल्विदम्) – in the statement sarvam kahlvidam brahma – all this is verily Brahman. *khalu* means "indeed, verily," *idam* is "this" (neutral pronoun).

koham (*koham*, कोहम्) – who am I? (*ka* – who?; *aham* – I am)

kosha (*kosha*, कोश) – literally "sheath" as in the scabbard of a sword; one of the five layers of identification that cover up our true nature.

krama srishti (*krama sRRiShTi*, क्रम सृष्टि) – step-by step creation of the creation myths from the Vedas.

kriya (*kriyA*, क्रिया) – *kriyA* yoga is a branch of Raja yoga (for the intermediate student); *kriyA* literally means "doing, performance."

krodha (*krodha*, क्रोध) – anger, passion.

kshatriya (*kShatriya*, क्षत्रिय) – a member of the second of the traditional four castes in India, the military caste.

kShetra (*kShetra*, क्षेत्र) – literally a "field" or "property"; used in the Bhagavad Gita to refer to the body-mind organism in which we find ourselves.

kshetrajna (*kShetraj~na*, क्षेत्रज्ञ) – that which knows the *kShetra*, i.e. the true Self.

kutastha (*kUTastha*, कूटस्थ) – the immovable, unchanging spirit (literally "standing at the top."

lakshana (*lakShaNa*, लक्षण) – pointer; indicating or expressing indirectly; accurate description or definition.

lakshya (*lakShya*, लक्ष्य) – that which is to be characterized, defined, indicated or expressed.

laukika (*laukika*, लौकिक) – worldly, belonging to or occurring in ordinary life. *laukika anumAna* is inference by scientific reasoning, based on observation.

laya (*laya*, लय) – literally "dissolution" (and the last stage in the cycle of creation, preservation and destruction of the universe). Used here to refer to the four-stage process for dissolving ignorance described in the Astavakra Gita. See Astavakra, Gita.

lila (*lIlA*, लीला) – literally "play," "amusement" or "pastime"; the idea that the apparent creation is a diversion for a creator – a means for Him to enjoy Himself. He plays all the parts in such a way that they are ignorant of their real nature and believe themselves separate.

linga (*li~Nga*, लिङ्ग) – sign, mark or badge; evidence. Sometimes used as *li~Nga sharIra* to describe the subtle body.

loka (*loka*, लोक) – world, universe, sky or heaven etc. (adjective laukika).

Madhva (*madhva*, मध्व) – founder of the school of dvaita philosophy.

madhyama (*madhyama*, मध्यम) – middle, intermediate. *madhyamA* – mediating; the third stage in the production of sound; the "medium" in which something is expressed.

mahavakyas (*mahAvAkya*, महावाक्य) – *maha* means "great"; *vAkya* means "speech, saying or statement." The four "great sayings" from the Vedas are: - "Consciousness is Brahman," "That thou art," "This Self is Brahman" and "I am Brahman."

mahaprana (*mahAprANa*, महाप्राण) – In Sanskrit, describes a consonant that is sounded with additional expelling of air. It means "with much breath." Specifically, it is used for those consonants on the 2nd and 4th rows of the main groups, namely *kh, Ch, Th, th, ph* and *gh*, *jh, Dh, dh, bh.*

mahat (*mahat*, महत्) – great, important, distinguished.

manana (*manana*, मनन) - reflecting upon what has been heard (shravana). This is the second stage of the classical spiritual path, to remove any doubts about the knowledge that has been received via shravana. See also samshaya, shravana, nididhyasana.

manomayakosha (*manomayakosha*, मनोमयकोश) – the mental sheath (one of the "five Coverings" that surround our true essence).

manas (*manas*, मनस्) – the "organ" of mind acting as intermediary between the senses and the intellect (buddhi) on the way in and the intellect and the organs of action on the way out. These are its primary functions and "thinking" ought to consist only of the processing of data on behalf of the intellect. Unfortunately, it usually tries to take on the role of the intellect itself and this is when thinking becomes a problem. See ahankara, antakarana, buddhi and chitta.

Mandukya (*mANDUkya*, माण्डूक्य) – One of the major Upanishads and possibly the single most important, when considered in conjunction with the karika written by Gaudapada. (In many versions of this Upanishad, there is no distinction made between the original and the additions made by Gaudapada and there is some argument over which is which.) See Gaudapada, karika, Upanishad.

mantra (*mantra*, मन्त्र) - a group of words (or sometimes only one or more syllables), traditionally having some mystical significance, being in many religions an actual 'name of God' or a short prayer. Often used in meditation (always in Transcendental Meditation). See japa.

marga (*mArga*, मार्ग) – path, track, way. *vichAra mArga* is translated as "Direct Path," referring to the particular method of teaching Advaita.

mata (*mata*, मत) – belief (also thought, idea, opinion, sentiment, doctrine).

math or matha (*maTha*, मठ) – (religious) college or temple.

matra (*mAtrA*, मात्रा) – a measure of any kind. In Sanskrit, the short vowel is said to be 1 *mAtrA* and the long vowel 2, i.e. sounded for twice the length.

matrika (*mAtRRikA*, मातृका) – In Sanskrit, refers to the 14 vowels, together with the *anusvAra* and *visarga*.

maya (*mAyA*, माया) – literally "magic" or "witchcraft," often personified in Hindu mythology. The "force" used to explain how it is that we come to be deceived into believing that there is a creation with separate objects and living creatures etc. See also avarana and vikshepa.

mayakara (*mAyAkAra*, मायाकार) - a maker of magic i.e. a conjurer or magician. See maya.

mimamsa (*mImAMsA*, मीमांसा) – profound thought, reflection, examination. See purvamimamsa, utteramimamsa.

mithya (*mithyA*, मिथ्या) – dependent reality; literally "incorrectly" or "improperly," used in the sense of "false, untrue." It is, however, more frequently used in the sense of "depending upon something else for its existence." It is ascribed to objects etc., meaning that these are not altogether unreal but not strictly real either i.e. they are our imposition of name and form upon the undifferentiated Self. See adhyasa.

moha (*moha*, मोह) – delusion, bewilderment, infatuation, preventing the discernment of truth; "love" in its selfish form of love of another person, where something is desired for oneself, as opposed to *prema*, "pure unselfish love."

moksha (*mokSha*, मोक्ष) – liberation, enlightenment, Self-realization; one of the four *puruShArtha*-s.

mudra (*mudrA*, मुद्रा) - particular positions or intertwinings of the fingers, commonly practiced in religious worship.

mukti (*mukti*, मुक्ति) – setting or becoming free, final liberation. (*mukta* is the adjective – liberated)

mumukshu (*mumukShu*, मुमुक्षु) – one for whom the desires to achieve enlightenment is the predominant goal in life; a seeker.

mumukshutva (*mumukShutva*, मुमुक्षुत्व) - the desire to achieve enlightenment, to the exclusion of all other desire. See sadhana, chatushtaya sampatti.

Mundaka Upanishad (*muNDakopaniShad*, मुण्डकोपनिषद्) – Another one of the 108+ Upanishads and also one of the 10 major ones – but not to be confused with the Mandukya. *muNDa* means "having a shaved head" and the Upanishad is so called because every one who comprehends its sacred doctrine is "shorn," i.e. liberated from all error. See Upanishad.

murta (*mUrta*, मूर्त) – manifest, material, embodied.

naimittika (*naimittika*, नैमित्तिक) – occasional, special. *naimittika karma* are those occasional duties that we have to perform, such as helping a neighbor who has helped one in the past.

Naiyayika (*naiyAyika*, नैयायिक) – a follower of the *nyAya* philosophy.

nama-rupa (*nAma-rUpa*, नामरूप) – name and form.

naraka (*naraka*, नरक) – hell. (Also pAtAla.)

nastika (*nAstika*, नास्तिक) – atheist, unbeliever; usually refers to one who does not recognise the authority of the Vedas.

neti (*neti*, नेति) – not this (*na* – not; *iti* – this). From the Brihadaranyaka Upanishad (2.3.6). Used by the intellect whenever it is thought that the Self might be some "thing" observed e.g. body, mind etc. The Self cannot be anything that is seen, thought or known. See Brihadaranyaka, Upanishad.

nididhyasana (*nididhyAsana*, निदिध्यासन) – meditating upon the essence of what has now been intellectually understood until there is total conviction. The third stage of the classical spiritual path. See also shravana and manana. It is to be understood as "right apprehension" (*vij~nAna*) rather than simply mechanical as *dhyAna* might be construed.

nidra (*nidrA*, निद्रा) – sleep.

nimitta (*nimitta*, निमित्त) – literally the "instrumental or efficient cause" but normally used (*nimitta kAraNa*) as meaning the latter.

nirguna (*nirguNa*, निर्गुण) – "without qualities"; usually referring to Brahman and meaning that it is beyond any description or thought. Since there is only Brahman, any word would imply limitation or duality. See Brahman, saguna, Isvara.

nirodha (*nirodha*, निरोध) – restraint.

nirupadhika (*nirupAdhika*, निरुपाधिक) – without attributes or qualities. *nirupAdhika adhyAsa* is superimposition as of the snake on the rope, as opposed to *sopAdhika adhyAsa* e.g. the sunrise, which is still seen even when the mistake is realized.

nirveda (*nirveda*, निर्वेद) - being indifferent towards or even having a loathing for worldly objects.

nirvikalpa (*nirvikalpa*, निर्विकल्प) – (referring to samadhi) 'without' doubts about one's identity with the one Self. See savikalpa, samadhi, vikalpa.

nirvishesha (*nirvisheSha*, निर्विशेष) – making or showing no difference. *nirvisheShaNa* – attributeless.

nishkama (*niShkAma*, निष्काम) – desireless, disinterested. *niShkAma karma* is so-called "right action," performed in response to the need, neither selfishly nor unselfishly – it generates no *saMskAra*.

nishtha (*niShTha*, निष्ठ) – committed or devoted to; having a basis or grounding in. *niShThA* is the noun, meaning firmness, steadiness, devotion.

nitya (*nitya*, नित्य) – eternal. It also means "ordinary, usual, necessary, obligatory." It is used in this latter sense in connection with action. *nitya karma* are those daily duties that we have to perform, such as looking after one's children.

nivritti (*nivRRitti*, निवृत्ति) – giving up, abstaining, renouncing (esp. of desires in the path to enlightenment – *nivRRitti mArga*).

niyama (*niyama*, नियम) – restraining, controlling; any fixed rule or law; necessity. There are five *niyama*-s in Raja yoga.

nyaya (*nyAya*, न्याय) – logical argument; literally, "that into which a thing goes back," a "standard" or "rule"; one of the 6 classical Indian philosophical systems, whose principal exponent was Gautama in the 3rd Century BC. So called because the system "goes into" all physical and metaphysical subjects in a very logical manner.

nyaya prasthana (*nyAya prasthAna,* न्याय प्रस्थान) - refers to logical and inferential material based upon the Vedas, of which the most well known is the Brahmasutra of Vyasa (*nyAya* can also mean method, axiom, logical argument etc.). See pramana, prasthana-traya, smriti, sruti.

Padmapada (*padmapAda*, पद्मपाद) – one of the four principal disciples of Shankara.

paksha (*pakSha*, पक्ष) – subject of the discussion, proposition to be proved.

panchabuta (*pa~nchabhUta*, पञ्चभूत) – the five elements, viz. earth - *pRRithivI*; water - *ap*; fire - *tejas*; air - *vAyu*; space or ether - *AkAsha*.

Panchadashi (*pa~nchadashI*, पञ्चदशी) – literally means "fifteen" because it has this many chapters - a book written by Vidyaranya (*vidyAraNya*), based upon the Upanishads. It discusses many Advaitic truths and uses some original metaphors to illustrate the concepts.

panchakosha (*pa~ncha kosha*, पञ्च कोश) – the five sheaths.

Panchapadika (*pa~nchapAdikA*, पञ्चपादिका) - a commentary by Padmapada on Shankara's commentary on the first part of the *brahma sUtra*.

pandita (*paNDita*, पण्डित) – literally "wise" as an adjective or "scholar, teacher, philosopher" as a noun and used in this way in the scriptures. However, it has come to mean someone who knows a lot of theory but does very little practice. We sometimes use the word "pundit" in our language - the word "sophist" would probably be a good synonym.

papa (*pApa*, पाप) – literally "bad" or "wicked" but used in the sense of the "sin" that accrues (according to the theory of karma) from performing "bad" actions, i.e. those done with a selfish motive. See also punya.

para (*parA*, परा) – the first stage in the production of sound. Also means beyond, distant, remote, highest, supreme; could be translated as "transcendent."

parama (*parama*, परम) – chief, highest, most prominent, best etc.

paramartha (noun), (*paramArtha*, परमार्थ);

paramarthika (adj.), (*pAramArthika*), पारमार्थिक) – the highest truth or reality; the noumenal as opposed to the phenomenal world of appearances (vyavaharika). See pratibhasika and vyavaharika.

paramatman (*paramAtman*, परमात्मन्) – usually translated as the "supreme Self" as opposed to the atman in the embodied state, the jivatman. Swami Dayananda insists that it actually means "limitless" in the sense of not limited by time or place and therefore changeless (Ref. 58). See atman.

parampara (*paramparA*, परम्परा) – literally "proceeding from one to another"; "guru parampara" refers to the tradition of guru – disciple passing on wisdom through the ages. See also sampradaya.

parechcha (*parechChA*, परेच्छा) – relating to the desires of others – see prArabdha.

parinama (*pariNAma*, परिणाम) – literally "change, transformation into"; encountered in the context of a material cause in which the effect is a transformation from its cause as opposed to simply distinguishable from, e.g. butter made from milk as opposed to cloth made from cotton.

parinama vada (*pariNAma vAda*, परिणाम वाद) – the doctrine of evolution as proposed by *sAMkhya* philosophy.

paroksha (*pArokSha*, पारोक्ष) – remote, mysterious, invisible, hidden (also *pArokShya*); opposite of *pratyakSha*.

pashyanti (*pashyantI*, पश्यन्ती) – seeing; the second of the four stages of sound production. Could be translated as "visualization," from the verb *pash*, meaning "to see."

patala (*pAtAla*, पाताल) – hell. (Also *naraka*.)

Patanjali (*pata~njali*, पतञ्जलि) – philosopher, writer of the "Yoga Sutras" and responsible for *aShTA~Nga* or *rAja yoga*.

phala (*phala*, फल) – fruit; often used in the context of the consequences that necessarily follow as a result of action. See *karmaphala*.

pluta (*pluta*, प्लुत) – a lengthened vowel in Sanskrit (sounded for 3 or more mAtrA-s or measures).

prajna (*praj~nA*, प्रज्ञा) – (verb) to know or understand, find out, perceive or learn; (noun) wisdom, intelligence, knowledge. Not to be confused with *prAj~na* below.

prajna (*prAj~na*, प्राज्ञ) – the "deep sleep ego" in the deep sleep state of consciousness, sushupti. Literally, "wise, clever" (adj.) or "a wise man" or "intelligence dependent on individuality." See also visva, taijasa.

prajnana (*praj~nAna*, प्रज्ञान) – consciousness.

prakarana (*prakaraNa*, प्रकरण) – subject, topic, treatise etc. but especially opening chapter or prologue.

prakarana grantha (*prakaraNa grantha*, प्रकरण ग्रन्थ) – this is the term used to refer to authoritative commentaries on the scripture but which are not part of the *prasthAna traya*. It is frequently used in respect of the works attributed to Shankara such as *upadesha sAhasrI*, *vivekachUDAmaNi* etc. The word *grantha* literally means "tying or stringing together" though can itself mean composition or treatise.

prakriti (*prakRRiti*, प्रकृति) – literally the original or natural form or condition of anything; generally used to refer to what we would call "nature."

prakriya (*prakriyA*, प्रक्रिया) – a methodology of teaching; literally a chapter (esp. the introductory chapter of a work).

pralaya (*pralaya*, प्रलय) – dissolution, destruction, annihilation, specifically relating to the universe at the end of a *kalpa*.

prama (*pramA*, प्रमा) – true knowledge, basis or foundation.

pramana (*pramANa*, प्रमाण) – valid means for acquiring knowledge. There are 6 of these in Vedanta: - perception (*pratyakSha*), inference (*anumAna*), scriptural or verbal testimony (*shabda* or *Agama shruti*), analogy (*upamAna*), presumption (*arthApatti*) and non-apprehension (*anupalabdhi*). The first three are the major ones referred to by Shankara.

pramatri (*pramAtRRi*, प्रमातृ) – the subject of knowledge obtained via a *pramANa*; authority, one who has a correct notion or idea.

prameya (*prameya*, प्रमेय) – the object of knowledge obtained via a *pramANa*; also "thing to be proven" or "topic to be discussed."

prana (*prANa*, प्राण) – literally the "breath of life"; the vital force in the body with which we identify in the "vital sheath."

pranamayakosha (*prANamayakosha*, प्राणमयकोश) - the sheath made of breath (one of the "five Coverings" that surround our true essence).

pranava (*praNava*, प्रणव) – mystical or sacred symbol (OM); OM is usually called *praNava shabda*, though either word separately can also be use with the same meaning. *praNu* means "to make a humming or droning sound."

pranayama (*prANayAma*, प्रानयाम) – usually understood to mean control of breathing in advanced yoga techniques or as a prelude to meditation. According to Swami Chinmayananda, however, it does not mean this but relates to the five "departments" of active life as described in the chapter on Spiritual Practices.

pranidhana (*praNidhAna*, प्रणिधान) - meditation on/contemplation of/devotion to Ishvara. One of the five *niyama*-s of Raja yoga.

prarabdha (*prArabdha*, प्रारब्ध) - This literally means "begun" or "undertaken." It is the fruit of all of our past action that is now having its effect. This is one of the three types of sanskara. See agamin, sanchita, sanskara. Also, there are three types of prArabdha karma - *ichChA*, *anichChA* and *parechChA* (personally desired, without desire and due to others' desire).

prasthana-traya (*prasthAna traya*, प्रस्थान त्रय) - *prasthAna* means "system" or "course" in the sense of a journey; *traya* just means "threefold." It refers to the three sources of knowledge of the Self (*shabda*), nyaya prasthana, sruti and smriti. See nyaya prasthana, shabda, sruti, smriti.

pratibhasa (noun) (*pratibhAsa*, प्रतिभासफ)

pratibhasika (adj.) (*prAtibhAsika*, प्रातिभासिक) – appearing or occurring to the mind, existing only in appearance, an illusion. See paramartha, vyavahara.

pratibimba (*pratibimba*, प्रतिबिम्ब) - a reflection. In logic, *bimba* is the object itself, with the *pratibimba* being the counterpart with which it is compared.

pratibimba-vada (*pratibimba vAda*, प्रतिबिम्ब वाद) – the theory that the jiva is a reflection of the atman, similar to the reflection of an object in a mirror.

pratijna (*pratij~nA*, प्रतिज्ञा) – (in logic) an assertion or proposition to be proved.

(*pratipAdya – pratipAdaka sambandha*, प्रतिपाद्य प्रतिपादक सम्बन्ध) – refers to that type of knowledge where the knowledge itself brings about the goal without the need for any action. *pratipAdya* means "that which is to be explained or revealed"; *pratipAdaka* means "that which reveals, explaining or demonstrating"; *sambandha* means "relationship."

pratyabhijna (*pratyabhij~nA*, प्रत्यभिज्ञा) - recognition

pratyaksha (*pratyakSha*, प्रत्यक्ष) – "present before the eyes, clear, distinct etc." but particularly "direct perception or apprehension" as a valid source of knowledge. Opposite of *pArokSha*, hidden. See pramana.

pratyagatman (*pratyagAtman*, प्रत्यगात्मन्) – the individual soul.

pratyahara (*pratyAhAra*, प्रत्याहार) – withdrawal of the senses from external objects.

pratyaya (*pratyaya*, प्रत्यय) – belief, firm conviction, certainty; basis or cause of anything.

pravritti (*pravRRitti*, प्रवृत्ति) – active life, following one's desires (*pravRRitti mArga* as opposed to the path to enlightenment – *nivRRitti mArga*).

prayojana (*prayojana*, प्रयोजन) – motive or purpose.

prema (*prema*, प्रेम) – love, in its pure, unselfish form (as opposed to *moha*).

preyas (*preyas*, प्रेयस्) – the 'pleasant' as opposed to the 'good'; more agreeable, more desired.

prithivi (*pRRithivI*, पृथिवी) – earth – one of the five elements or *pa~nchabhUta*. Associated with smell.

punya (*puNya*, पुण्य) – literally "good" or "virtuous"; used to refer to the "reward" that accrues to us (according to the theory of karma) through the performing of unselfish actions. See also papa.

purna (*pUrNa*, पूर्ण) – full, complete, satisfied, perfect.

purusha (*puruSha*, पुरुष) – person (usually male), spirit.

purushartha (*puruShArtha*, पुरुषार्थ) – The general meaning of this term is "any object of human pursuit" but it is used here in the sense of human (i.e. self) effort to overcome "fate," the fruit of one's past actions. The four classical pursuits are kAma, artha, dharma and mokSha. *puruShArtha-labha* is fulfillment of those pursuits. See karma, sanskara.

purusha-tantra (*puruSha-tantra*, पुरुषतन्त्र) – subjective.

purva (*pUrva*, पूर्व) – former, preceding.

purvapaksha (*pUrvapakSha*, पूर्वपक्ष) – the first objection to an assertion in any discussion or, more generally, the "objector" in a debate.

Purva mimamsa, (*pUrva mImAMsA*, पूर्व मीमांसा) – the philosophical system based upon the first part of the Vedas and attributed to Jaimini. Mainly concerned with enquiring into the nature of dharma or right action. See mimamsa, uttaramimamsa.

raga (*rAga*, राग) – any feeling or passion but especially vehement desire; interest in, attachment. Shankara differentiates this from *kAma: rAga* is attachment to something one already has whereas *kAma* is wanting something one doesn't have. *rAga-dveSha* is love-hatred.

raja (*rAja*, राज) – literally "king or sovereign," as in *rAja yoga* (or *aShTA~Nga yoga*) of Patanjali, where it is usually translated as "royal yoga."

rajas (*rajas*, रजस्) – the second of the three guna. Associated with animals and activity, emotions, desire, selfishness and passion. Adjective – rajassic (Eng.); *rAjasa* or *rAjasika* (Sansk.) See guna.

Ramanuja (*rAmAnuja*, रामानुज) – founder of the *vishiShTAdvaita* school of philosophy.

rishi (*RRiShi*, ऋषि) – author or singer of sacred Vedic hymns but now more generally used to refer to a saint or Sage.

rupa (*rUpa*, रूप) – form, outward appearance.

sadguru (*sadguru*, सद्गुरु) – the ultimate guru – one's own Self (*sat* = true, real). See guru.

sadhaka (*sAdhaka*, साधक) – a seeker or, more pedantically, a worshipper.

sadhana (*sAdhana*, साधन) – literally "leading straight to a goal"; refers to the spiritual disciplines followed as part of a "path" toward Self-realisation. See also chatushtaya sampatti.

sadhu (*sAdhu*, साधु) – a sage, saint, holy man; literally leading straight to the goal, hitting the mark.

sadhya (*sAdhya*, साध्य) – (that which is) to be concluded, proved or demonstrated.

saguna (*saguNa*, सगुण) - "with qualities." The term is usually used to refer to Brahman personified as the creator, Iswara, to symbolise the most spiritual aspect of the world of appearances. See Brahman, Isvara, nirguna.

sahaja sthiti (*sahaja sthiti*, सहज स्थिति) - Once Self-realisation has been attained, there is full and lasting knowledge of the Self. "*sahaja*" means "state" but this stage of samadhi is not a state – it is our true nature. It is permanent (*sthiti* meaning "steady" or "remaining"), unlike the earlier stages of samadhi. See nirvikalpa, samadhi, savikalpa, vikalpa.

sakshin (*sAkShin*, साक्षिन्) – a witness, the ego or subject as opposed to the object (also sAkshi).

sakshibhava (*sAkshibhAva*, साक्षिभाव) - being or becoming (*bhAva*) a "witness" (*sAkshin*).

sama – see shama.

samadhana (*samAdhAna*, समाधान) – contemplation, profound meditation; more usually translated as concentration; one of the "six qualities" that form part of Shankara's chatushtaya sampatti. See chatushtaya sampatti, s*hamAdi shhaTka sampatti*.

samadhi (*samAdhi*, समाधि) – the state of total peace and stillness achieved during deep meditation. Several "stages" are defined – see vikalpa, savikalpa samadhi, nirvikalpa samadhi and sahaja sthiti.

samana (*samAna*, समान) – one of the five "vital airs," concerned with the digestive system. More generally, relates to assimilation and integration of perceptions with existing knowledge.

samanya (*sAmAnya*, सामान्य) – general, universal, opposite of specific; genus as opposed to species.

samashti (*samaShTi*, समष्टि) – totality, as opposed to vyaShTi, the individual.

sambandha (*sambandha*, सम्बन्ध) – relationship, literally "union, association, conjunction."

samhita (*saMhitA*, संहिता) – a philosophical or religious text constructed according to certain rules of sound. There are many of these in the Vedas. The reference in this book is in conjunction with the Astavakra Samhita or Gita. This book is not part of the Vedas. See Astavakra, gita.

samkhya (*sAMkhya*, सांख्य) – one of the three main divisions of Hindu philosophy and one of the six darshanas; attributed to Kapila.

sampradaya (*sampradAya*, सम्प्रदाय) – the tradition or established doctrine of teaching from master to pupil through the ages. See also parampara.

samsara (*saMsAra*, संसार) – the continual cycle of death and rebirth, transmigration etc. to which we are supposedly subject in the phenomenal world until we become enlightened and escape. *saMsArin* – one who is bound to the cycle of birth and death.

samshaya (*saMshaya*, संशय) - uncertainty, irresolution, hesitation or doubt. See manana.

sanatana (*sanAtana*, सनातन) – literally "eternal" or "permanent"; in conjunction with dharma, this refers to our essential nature. The phrase "sanatana dharma" is also used to refer to the traditional (also carrying the sense of "original" and "unadulterated") Hindu practices or as a synonym for "Hinduism." See dharma.

sanchita (*saMchita*, संचित) – one of the three types of sanskara, literally meaning "collected" or "piled up." That sanskara, which has been accumulated from past action but has still not manifest. See agamin, prarabdha, sanskara.

sandhi (*saMdhi*, संधि) – A comprehensive set of rules governing the way in which sounds combine in Sanskrit when they appear next to each other. These prevent, for example, the situation where one word ends in a vowel and the next word begins with one, by merging the two. There are three "classes" of *saMdhi*, vowel, consonant and *visarga*.

sanga (*sa~Nga*, सङ्ग) – assembly, association, company. See satsanga.

sankalpa (*saMkalpa*, संकल्प) – conception, idea or notion formed in the mind (or heart); will, volition, desire, purpose, intention.

sanskara (*saMskAra*, संस्कार) – Whenever an action is performed with the desire for a specific result (whether for oneself or another), sanskara is created for that person. These accumulate and determine the situations with which we will be presented in the future and will influence the scope of future actions. There are three "types" – agamin, sanchita and prarabdha. The accumulation of sanskara (sanchita) dictates the tendencies that we have to act in a particular way (vasanas). This is all part of the mechanism of karma. See agamin, karma, prarabdha, sanchita and karma.

santosa (*saMtoSha*, संतोष) – satisfaction, contentment with one's lot. One of the five *niyama*-s in Raja yoga.

sanyasa (*saMnyAsa*, संन्यास) - the final stage of the traditional Hindu spiritual path; involves complete renunciation. The word literally means "putting or throwing down, laying aside"; i.e. becoming a professional ascetic. One who does so is called a sanyasin (*saMnyAsin*). See also brahmacharya, grihasta, vanaprastha.

(*sarva-vedAnta-siddhAnta-sArasaMgrahaH*, सर्व वेदान्त सिद्धान्त सारसंग्रहः) – book attributed to Shankara. *sarva* means "whole"; *siddhAnta* means "conclusion"; *sAra* means "epitome" or "summary"; *saMgraha* carries the sense of "complete summing-up." So, as a whole, it means something like "Everything you always wanted to know about Vedanta."

sarvajna (*sarvaj~na*, सर्वज्ञ) – all knowing (of Ishvara).

sat (*sat*, सत्) – existence, reality, truth (to mention a few). See also ananda, chit, satchitananda.

satchitananda (*sat - chit - Ananda* or *sachchidAnanda*, सच्चिदानन्द) – the oft used word to describe our true nature, in so far as this can be put into words (which it can't). It translates as being-consciousness-bliss but see the separate bits for more detail.

satkarya vada (*satkArya vAda*, सत्कार्य वाद) – the doctrine of the effect actually pre-existing in the cause (usually in reference to the creation).

satsanga (*satsa~Nga*, सत्सङ्ग) - association with the good; keeping "good company"; most commonly used now to refer to a group of people gathered together to discuss (Advaita) philosophy.

sattva (*sattva*, सत्त्व) - the highest of the three guna. Associated with stillness, peace, truth, wisdom, unselfishness and spirituality, representing the highest aspirations of man. Adjective – sattwic (Eng.); *sAttva* or *sAttvika* (Sansk.). See guna.

sattvapati (*sattvApatti*, सत्त्वापत्ति) – the (4th) stage on a spiritual path, after which there is no longer any need for effort to be made (so-called because there is now an abundance of sattva). *Apatti* means "entering into a state or condition."

satya (*satya*, सत्य) – true, real. *satyam* – truth. Also one of the *yama*-s – truthfulness, sincerity.

savikalpa (*savikalpa*, सविकल्प) – (referring to samadhi) still "with" doubts about one's identity with the one Self. See nirvikalpa, samadhi, vikalpa.

shabda (*shabda*, शब्द) - scriptural or verbal testimony. See pramana, nyaya prasthana, prasthana-traya, sruti, smRRiti

shakha-chandra-nyaya (*shAkhA-chandra-nyAya*, शाखा-चन्द्र-न्याय) – the rule of the moon on a bough. Relates to the situation where one thing (the moon) is effectively pointed out by its relationship to something else (the bough).

shakti (*shakti*, शक्ति) – power, strength (especially in connection with a deity).

shama (*shama*, शम) - literally tranquillity, absence of passion but more usually translated as mental discipline or self-control; one of the *shamAdi shhaTka sampatti* or "six qualities" that form part of Shankara's chatushtaya sampatti. See chatushtaya sampatti, *shamAdi shhaTka sampatti*.

(*shamAdi ShaTka sampatti*, शमादि षट्क सम्पत्ति) – the six qualities that form part of Shankara's chatushtaya sampatti. These are *shama, dama, uparati, titikShA, samAdhAna* and *shraddhA*.

Shankara (*shaMkara*, शंकर) – 8th Century Indian philosopher responsible for firmly establishing the principles of Advaita. Though he died at an early age (32?), he commented on a number of major Upanishads, the Bhagavad Gita and the Brahmasutras, as well as being attributed as the author of a number of famous works, such as Atmabodha, Bhaja Govindam and Vivekachudamani.

Shankaracharya (*shaMkarAchArya*, शंकराचार्य) – The title given to one of the four teachers (see acharya) following the tradition in India established by Shankara (see Shankara). He set up four positions, North, South, East and West, to be held by realized men, who would take on the role of teacher and could be consulted by anyone having problems or questions of a spiritual nature.

shanti (*shAnti*, शान्ति) - peace, tranquility.

sharira (*sharIra*, शरीर) – one's body (divided into gross, subtle and causal aspects); literally "that which is easily destroyed or dissolved."

shastra (*shAstra*, शास्त्र) – order, teaching, instruction; any sacred book or composition that has divine authority.

shastriya anumana (*shAstrIya anumAna*, शास्त्रीय अनुमान) – inference based upon the material contained in the scriptures.

saucha (*shaucha*, शौच) – purity of mind, integrity. One of the five *niyama*-s in Raja yoga.

shraddha (*shraddhA*, श्रद्धा) – faith, trust or belief (in the absence of direct personal experience); the student needs this initially in respect of what he is told by the guru or reads in the scriptures; one of the "six qualities" that form part of Shankara's chatushtaya sampatti. See chatushtaya sampatti, s*hamAdi shhaTka sampatti*.

shravana (*shravaNa*, श्रवण) - hearing the truth from a sage or reading about it in such works as the Upanishads; first of the three key stages in the classical spiritual path. See also manana, nididhyasana.

shreyas (*shreyas*, श्रेयस्) – the 'good' as opposed to the 'pleasant'; most excellent, best, auspicious.

shrotriya (*shrotriya*, श्रोत्रिय) – someone (usually a *brAhmaNa*) who is well-versed in the scriptures.

shruti (*shruti*, श्रुति) - refers to the Vedas, incorporating the Upanishads. Literally means "hearing" and refers to the belief that the books contain orally transmitted, sacred wisdom from the dawn of time. See nyaya prasthana, pramana, smriti.

shubhecha (*shubhechChA*, शुभेच्छा) - good desire; the initial impulse that start us on a spiritual search. *shubha* means "auspicious," "good (in a moral sense)" and *ichChA* means "wish," "desire."

shuddhi (*shuddhi*, शुद्धि) – cleansing, purification as in chitta-shuddhi, purification of the mind.

shudra (*shUdra*, शूद्र) – the fourth and lowest of the traditional four castes in India, their purpose said to be to serve the three higher castes.

siddhanta (*siddhAnta*, सिद्धान्त) – final end or purpose; conclusion of an argument.

sisya (*shiShya*, शिष्य) – pupil, scholar, disciple.

smriti (*smRRiti*, स्मृति) - refers to material "remembered" and subsequently written down. In practice, it refers to books of law (in the sense of guidance for living) which were written and based upon the knowledge in the Vedas, i.e. the so-called dharma-shastras - Manu,

Yajnavalkya, Parashara. In the context of nyaya prasthana, it is used to refer to just one of these books – the Bhagavad Gita. See pramana, nyaya prasthana, sruti.

sopadhika (*sopAdhika*, सोपाधिक) - *nirupAdhika adhyAsa* is superimposition as of the snake on the rope, as opposed to *sopAdhika adhyAsa* e.g. the sunrise, which is still seen even when the mistake is realized.

sri (*shrI*, श्री) – used as a title, c.f. "reverend," to signify an eminent person. May also be used in a similar manner to refer to revered objects or works of scripture, for example.

srishti (*sRRiShTi*, सृष्टि) – creation.

srishti-drishti-vada (*sRRiShTidRRiShTivAda*, सृष्टिदृष्टिवाद) – the theory that the world is separate from ourselves, having been created (by God or big-bang) and evolving independently of ourselves, i.e. the "common sense" view of things. See also adhyasa, ajati, drishti-srishti-vada.

sthitaprajna (*sthitapraj~na*, स्थितप्रज्ञ) - meaning one "standing" (*sthita*) in "wisdom" (*prajna*); a man of steadiness and calm, firm in judgement, contented. The name given by the Bhagavad Gita to one who is Self-realised.

sthula (*sthUla*, स्थूल) – large, thick, coarse, dense; the gross body (*sthUla sharIra*).

sukha (*sukha*, सुख) – comfortable, happy, prosperous etc. *sukham* – pleasure, happiness.

sukshma (*sUkShma*, सूक्ष्म) - subtle, as in the subtle body – *sUkShma sharIra*.

sushupti (*suShupti*, सुषुप्ति) – the deep-sleep state of consciousness. The "sleeper ego" is called prajna. See also, jagrat, svapna, turiya.

sva (*sva*, स्व) – one's own.

svabhava (*svabhAva*, स्वभाव) – one's natural disposition.

svadharma (*svadharma*, स्वधर्म) – one's own dharma. See dharma.

svadhyaya (*svAdhyAya*, स्वाध्याय) - self-study or more specifically studying the scriptures, literally reciting the Vedas in a low voice to oneself. One of the five *niyama*-s in Raja yoga.

svapna (*svapna*, स्वप्न) – the dream state of consciousness. The "dreamer ego" is called taijasa. See also, jagrat, sushupti, turiya.

svara (*svara*, स्वर) – Sanskrit term for a vowel, literally meaning "sound"; sounded for 1 *mAtrA* or measure.

svarga (*svarga*, स्वर्ग) – heaven.

svarupa (*svarUpa*, स्वरूप) – one's own character or nature and, e.g., *svarUpAnanda* – one's own Ananda (limitless bliss).

(*svataHprAmANyavAda*, स्वतःप्रामाण्यवाद) – the theory of the "self-validity of knowledge," i.e. accepting a given explanation, if reasonable, until something better comes along.

svatantra (*svatantra*, स्वतन्त्र) – independent, self-willed, free. (Also *svAtantrya* – following one"s own free will or choice).

svayam (*svayam*, स्वयम्) – of or by oneself.

svecha (*svechChA*, स्वेच्छा) – free will.

taijasa (*taijasa*, तैजस) – the "dreamer ego" in the dream state of consciousness, svapna. See also visva, prajna.

Taittiriya (*taittirIya*, तैत्तिरीय) – one of the principal Upanishads. (*taittirIya* was one of the schools of the Yajur Veda.)

tamas (*tamas*, तमस्) – the "lowest" of the three guna. Associated with matter and carrying characteristics such as inertia, laziness, heedlessness and death. It literally means "darkness" or "gloom." Adjective – tamasic (Eng.); *tAmasa* or *tAmasika* (Sansk.). See guna.

tantra (*tantra*, तन्त्र) – main or essential point. (Also doctrine or theory and the body of scriptures relating to attaining mystical union with the divine through meditation.)

tapas (*tapas*, तपस्) - austerity, living a simple life without comforts. One of the five *niyama*-s in Raja yoga.

tarka (*tarka*, तर्क) – reasoning, speculation, philosophical system or doctrine.

tarkika (*tArkika*, तार्किक) – logician or philosopher.

tatastha (*taTastha*, तटस्थ) - a property distinct from the nature of the body and yet that by which it is known. An example would be telling someone that the house they are referring to in the street ahead is the one with the crow on the chimney. The house is what the listener is interested in but the crow is a *taTastha lakShaNa*, i.e. that by which it is known.

tejas (*tejas*, तेजस्) – fire (or light) – one of the five elements or *pa~nchabhUta*. Associated with sight.

titiksha (*titikShA*, तितिक्षा) – forbearance or patience; one of the "six qualities" that form part of Shankara's *chatuShTaya sampatti*. See chatushtaya sampatti, s*hamAdi shhaTka sampatti*.

trikalatita (*trikAlAtIta*, त्रिकालातीत) - that which transcends past, present and future (describing the Self).

turiya (*turIya*, तुरीय) – the "fourth" state of consciousness (turiya means "fourth"). In fact, some (e.g. Sri Atmananda Krishna Menon) define it rather as the background against which the other states (waking, dream and deep sleep) take place. In this latter case, it is also our true nature. (If defined merely as the highest "state" then our true nature is called turiyatita.

tyaga (*tyAga*, त्याग) – renunciation.

udaharana (*udAharaNa*, उदाहरण) – example, instance, illustration.

udana (*udAna*, उदान) – one of the five "vital airs," associated with the throat. More generally relates to the understanding that has been gained from past experience.

upadana (*upAdAna*, उपादान) – literally "the act of taking for oneself"; used to refer to the "material cause" in logic (*upAdAna karaNa*).

upadesha (*upadesha*, उपदेश) – instruction or teaching.

upadesha sahasri (*upadesha sAhasrI*, उपदेश साहस्री) – "A Thousand Teachings" - book attributed to Shankara (with more certainty than most). *sAhasrika* means "consisting of a thousand."

upadhi (*upAdhi*, उपाधि) – Literally, this means something that is put in place of another thing; a substitute, phantom or disguise. In Vedanta, it is commonly referred to as a "limitation" or "limiting adjunct" i.e. one of the "identifications" made by *ahaMkAra* that prevents us from realizing the Self.

upamana (*upamAna*, उपमान) – comparison, resemblance, analogy.

upanishad (*upaniShad*, उपनिषद्) – one of the (108+) books forming part (usually the end) of one of the four Vedas. The parts of the word mean: to sit (*Shad*) near a master (*upa*) at his feet (*ni*), so that the idea is that we sit at the feet of a master to listen to his words. Monier-Williams (Ref. 5) states that, "according to native authorities, upanishad means "setting at rest ignorance by revealing the knowledge of the supreme spirit." See Vedanta.

uparama (*uparama*, उपरम) – see uparati.

uparati (*uparati*, उपरति) – desisting from sensual enjoyment; "revelling" in that which is "near" i.e. one's own Self; also translated as following one"s dharma or duty; one of the "six qualities" that form part of Shankara"s chatushtaya sampatti. See chatushtaya sampatti, *shamAdi shhaTka sampatti*.

upasana (*upAsana*, उपासन) – worship, homage, waiting upon; literally the act of sitting or being near to; sometimes used in the sense of "meditation."

upaya (*upAya*, उपाय) – another term for "path" (see marga) – that by which one reaches one's aim, a means or expedient, way.

ushman (*UShman*, ऊष्मन्) - The Sanskrit term for the sibilants, *sh*, *Sh* and *s*, together with *h*. The word itself literally means "heat, steam or vapour."

uttama (*uttama*, उत्तम) – uppermost, excellent, highest.

uttara mimamsa (*uttara mImAMsA*, उत्तर मीमांसा) – the Vedanta philosophy, based on the latter (uttara) part of the Vedas rather than the earlier (purva). Its founder was Badarayana, who authored the Brahmasutras. There are three main schools – dvaita, advaita and vishishtadvaita. See Brahmasutras, mimamsa, purvamimamsa, veda.

Vachaspati (*vAchaspati*, वाचस्पति) - name of one of the two schools of Advaita, after the philosopher *vAchaspati mishra*. It is also called the *bhAmati* school. The other school is the *vivaraNa* school.

vak (*vAch*, वाच्) – speech, language sound; speech personified as the Goddess, wife of *prajApati* (lord of creatures).

vada (*vAda*, वाद) – speech, proposition, discourse, argument, discussion, explanation or exposition (of scriptures etc.)

vaikhari (*vaikharI*, वैखरी) – speech; the fourth stage in the production of sound.

vairagya (*vairAgya*, वैराग्य) - detachment or dispassion; indifference to the pleasure that result from success or the disappointment that result from failure. Literally to be "deprived of" (*vai*) "passion or desire" (*rAga*). See sadhana, chatushtaya sampatti.

vaisheshika (*vaisheShika*, वैशेषिक) – one of the six classical Indian Philosophies, a later development of nyaya by the theologian, Kanada; named after the nine "essentially different substances" believed to constitute matter. See darshana, vishesha.

vaishvanara (*vaishvAnara*, वैश्वानर) – the gross physical condition, or waking state of man (more usually known as *vishva*). brahman "located in" the bodily form. Literally means "relating to or belonging to all men, universal."

vaishya (*vaishya*, वैश्य) – a working man, trader or farmer – the third of the traditional four castes in India.

Vakyapadiya (*vAkyapadIya*, वाक्यपदीय) – book on Sanskrit grammar, written by *bhartRRihari*.

valli (*vallI*, वल्ली) – relating to the sections of particular Upanishads.

vanaprastha (*vanaprastha*, वनप्रस्थ) - the third stage of the traditional Hindu spiritual path, in which the Brahman retires from life and becomes a "forest dweller," living as a hermit. Traditionally speaking, "a properly initiated *dvija* or twice-born." See also brahmacharya, grihasta, sanyasa, vanaprastha.

vasana (*vAsanA*, वासना) – literally "desiring" or "wishing" – latent behavioural tendency in one's nature brought about through past action (karma) and the sanskara that resulted from this. See karma, sanskara.

Vasishta (*vAsiShTha*, वासिष्ठ) – eponymous sage of the "Yoga Vasishta" one of the classical works of Advaita.

vastava (*vAstava*, वास्तव) – substantial, real, true.

vastu (*vastu*, वस्तु) – a thing that exists, object, subject matter. Strictly speaking, there is only one vastu – Atman. Everything else is incidental – it comes and goes. Only Consciousness is always there, intrinsic.

vastu-tantra (*vastu-tantra*, वस्तुतन्त्र) – objective, dependent on things.

vayu (*vAyu*, वयु) – air (or wind) – one of the five elements or *pa~nchabhUta*. Associated with touch.

veda (*veda*, वेद) – knowledge, but the word is normally only used to refer to one of the four Vedas (see Vedanta) and vidya is used for knowledge per se. See vidya.

Vedanta (*vedAnta*, वेदान्त) – literally "end" or "culmination" (*anta*) of knowledge (*veda*) but veda in this context refers to the four Vedas, the Hindu equivalents of the Christian bible (called Rig, *RRig* Veda; Sama, *sama* Veda; Atharva, *atharva* Veda; Yajur, *yajur* Veda). Traditionally, the last part of the vedas (i.e. "end") is devoted to the Upanishads. See upanishad.

Vedantasara (*vedAntasAra*, वेदान्तसार) – literally "essence of Vedanta"; a treatise on Vedanta by Sadananda Yogindra.

vichara (*vichAra*, विचार) – consideration, reflection, deliberation, investigation. vichAra mArga is translated as "Direct Path,"

vidya (*vidyA*, विद्या) – knowledge, science, learning, philosophy. *Atma-vidyA* or *brahma-vidyA* is knowledge of the Self.

Vidyaranya (*vidyAraNya*, विद्यारण्य) – author of the Panchadashi

vijnana (*vij~nAna*, विज्ञान) – discerning, understanding, comprehending; "right apprehension" in the case of *nididhyAsana* as opposed to *dhyAna*. vij~nAna vAda is the philosophical theory of Idealism.

vijnanamayakosha (*vij~nAnamayakosha*, विज्ञानमयकोश) – the intellectual sheath (one of the five "coverings" that surround our true essence).

vikalpa (*vikalpa*, विकल्प) - doubt, uncertainty or indecision.

vikara (*vikAra*, विकार) – transformation, modification, change of form or nature. Also *vikAratva* – the state of change; and *vikAravat* – undergoing changes.

vikarma (*vikarma*, विकर्म) – prohibited, unlawful – actions that must be avoided.

vikshepa (*vikShepa*, विक्षेप) – the "projecting" power of *mAyA*. In the rope-snake metaphor, this superimposes the image of the snake upon the rope. See avarana, maya.

vilakshana (*vilakShaNa*, विलक्षण) – not admitting of exact definition.

viparyaya (*viparyaya*, विपर्यय) – error, misapprehension, mixing up the nature of one thing with another or mistaking something to be the opposite of what it actually is (literally reversed, inverted).

virama (*virAma*, विराम) – In Sanskrit, the diagonal mark underneath a consonant to indicate that it is not to be sounded with a vowel after it. The literal meaning is "cessation, termination or end." (All consonants are sounded with *a* by default, unless indicated otherwise.) A consonant with such a mark is called a *halanta* consonant. (The term also refers to the single vertical mark to indicate the end of a sentence or single line of a verse of poetry.)

visarga (*visarga*, विसर्ग) – this literally means "sending out" or "emission." In Sanskrit, it is represented as *aH* but is not actually a letter and does not occur on its own. Its effect is to add a brief, breathing out sound after the vowel sound associated with a consonant; represented by two dots placed to the right of the associated letter.

vishaya (*viShaya*, विषय) – object of sensory perception; any subject or topic; the subject of an argument.

vishesha (*visheSha*, विशेष) – literally "distinction" or "difference between"; particular or specific. The Vaisheshika philosophy believes that the material universe is made up of nine substances, each of which is "essentially different" from any other. See Vaisheshika.

visheshana (*visheShaNa*, विशेषण) – adjective; the act of distinguishing between.

visheshya (*visheShya*, विशेष्य) – noun; that which is to be distinguished (from something else).

vishishta (*vishiShTa*, विशिष्ट) – distinguished, particular, excellent.

vishishtadvaita (*vishiShTAdvaita*, विशिष्टाद्वैत) – qualified non-dualism; belief that God and the atman are distinct but not separate. Ramanuja is the scholar most often associated with this philosophy. See advaita, dvaita.

visva (*vishva*, विश्व) – the "waker ego" in the waking state of consciousness, jagrat. Also sometimes referred to as *vaishvAnara*. See also taijasa, prajna.

vivarana (*vivaraNa*, विवरण) - literally "explanation" or "interpretation"; name of one of the two schools of Advaita. The other school is the *vAcaspati or bhAmati* school.

vivarta (*vivarta*, विवर्त) – an apparent or illusory form; unreality caused by avidya.

vivarta vada (*vivarta vAda*, विवर्त वाद) – the theory that the world is only an apparent projection of Ishvara (i.e. an illusion).

viveka (*viveka*, विवेक) – discrimination; the function of buddhi, having the ability to differentiate between the unreal and the real. See sadhana, chatushtaya sampatti.

Vivekachudamani (*vivekachUDAmaNi*, विवेकचूडामणि) – the title of a book attributed to Shankara. *chUDAmaNi* is the name given to the jewel worn on top of the head. An English version of the book is called "The Crest Jewel of Discrimination."

vritti (*vRRitti*, वृत्ति) – in the context of Vedanta, this means a mental disposition. In general, it can mean a mode of conduct or behaviour, character or disposition, business or profession etc. See aham vritti and idam vritti.

vyakta (*vyakta*, व्यक्त) – manifested, apparent, visible, perceptible to the senses as opposed to avyakta – transcendental.

vyana (*vyAna*, व्यान) – one of the five "vital airs," concerned with the circulatory system. More generally, alludes to the discriminatory faculties, evaluating and judging etc.

vyanjana (*vya~njana*, व्यञ्जन) - Sanskrit term for a consonant, meaning a "decoration" (of the basic vowel sound).

vyapti (*vyApti*, व्याप्ति) – inseparable presence of one thing in another, invariable concomitance (as in e.g. no smoke without fire).

vyashti (*vyaShTi*, व्यष्टि) – the individual or "individuality" as opposed to the totality, *samaShTi*.

vyavahara (noun) (*vyavahAra*, व्यवहार);

vyavaharika (adj.), (*vyAvahArika*, व्यावहारिक) – the "relative," "practical," or phenomenal world of appearances; the normal world in which we live and which we usually believe to be real; as opposed to *pAramArthika* (reality) and *prAtibhAsika* (illusory). See paramarthika and pratibhasika.

yama (*yama*, यम) – restraint. Literally, rein or bridle. There are five of these forming the first step of Raja yoga – *ahiMsA*, *satyam*, *brahmacharya*, *asteya* and *aparigraha*.

yoga (*yoga*, योग) – literally "joining" or "attaching" (our word "yoke" derives from this). It is used generally to refer to any system whose aim is to "join" our "individual self" back to the "universal Self." The Yoga system pedantically refers to that specified by Patanjali. See bhakti, jnana, karma.

yuga (*yuga*, युग) – one of the four ages in the cycle of creation. See kalpa, kali yuga.

yugapat-srishti (*yugapatsRRiShTi*, युगपत्सृष्टि) – instantaneous creation, i.e. simultaneous with the perception of it. *yugapad* means "together, at the same time."

yukti (*yukti*, युक्ति) – reasoning, argument, induction, deduction (as opposed to intuition – *anubhava*).

INDEX

Page numbers in **bold** indicate that this is a major reference. Note that many words, such as Atman, Self, Consciousness etc. have few references because they occur so frequently. Accordingly, only a few specific ones have been included. Sanskrit terms have not been included unless these are discussed in detail in the Glossary.